The Pattern of California History

Edward Staniford
CHABOT COLLEGE

⌗ **Canfield Press**
SAN FRANCISCO
A Department of Harper & Row, Publishers, Inc.
New York • Evanston • London

To my students for their questions
my colleagues for their expertise
my family for its forbearance

The lines quoted on p. 494 are from *The Selected Poetry of Robinson Jeffers* by Robinson Jeffers (New York: Random House, 1938, p. 168). Copyright © 1938 by Random House. Reprinted with permission.

Photo Credits Facing Page 1: Courtesy of the Director of Bancroft Library. Page 6: U.S. Forest Service. Pages 17, 20, 58, 103, 131, 156, 170, 188, 207, 242, 252, 285, 328, 334, 439: Courtesy of the Bancroft Library. Pages 68, 214, 320, 428: Title Insurance and Trust Company. Pages 116, 466: California Historical Society, San Francisco. Pages 145, 290: California State Library. Pages 364 (top), 443, 596: State Department of Transportation. Page 364 (bottom): Pan Am. Page 420: Standard Oil Company of California. Page 506: U.S. Air Force. Page 512: George L. Hersh. Page 568: State Department of Water Resources. Page 617: Judy Sidonie Tillinger. Cover: Bancroft Library, California Historical Society, State Department of Transportation, U.S. Air Force.

Text and cover design: Judy Sidonie Tillinger
Art: Larry Jansen
Editing: Ramona Michaelis

Library of Congress Cataloging in Publication Data

Staniford, Edward F.
    The pattern of California history.

    Bibliography: p.
    Includes index.
    1.   California—History.   I.   Title.
F861.S77   979.4   74-19480
ISBN 0-06-388597-2

75 76 77 10 9 8 7 6 5 4 3 2 1

Contents

Preface

The sustained and colorful drama of California's history is perhaps unmatched by that of any other state. The state's extraordinary geographical features, its unique historical background, and the people who contributed to its development produced a society with a particular brand of representative government, a capitalistic economy, and a pluralistic social order. These elements, though American in form, were influenced by an Indian, Spanish, and Mexican heritage. A century and a decade after California joined the American Union, it had become the nation's most populous and affluent state. The evolution of California's distinctive society is the theme of this book.

To catch the essence of the story, I have applied the Madisonian concept to the development of California society. In Number 10 of *The Federalist Papers*, James Madison presented his premise as follows: Society is made up of "factions" or groups of people who have common interests that differ from the interests of other groups and of the community as a whole. Such factions consist of people with and without property, creditors and debtors, farmers, merchants, manufacturers, and many other groups that have different stakes in society. The principal task of government is to balance these conflicting special interests for the general welfare.

I would hypothesize that today Madison might say that government is the regulator of the public affairs of society (any community of people). In the political sphere it serves to protect persons and property, to establish a fair system of justice, and to promote the general welfare in order to provide security for the people. In the economic sphere it seeks to promote the maximum production of goods and services and to establish a balanced system of prices and income for the people to assure their livelihood. It attempts to maintain a social order that will insure harmony and equilibrium among groups in society. Government creates and shapes institutions—the organizations, rules, and established practices (such as the courts, legal codes, and civil liberties)—that constitute arrangements for carrying out these functions.

In fashioning their societies nations have had to deal with the basic problem of liberty and authority—the freedom of individuals and groups to enjoy privileges and pursue enterprises and the responsibility of government to maintain order for the well-being of society. Nations since the beginning of time have worked out feudalistic, capitalistic, and socialistic schemes of society that would balance—or imbalance—freedom and security. California has experienced the first two of these schemes and may be approaching a form of the third, but it has not completely achieved the liberty so essential to a harmonious and viable society. However, California may have gone further than any other society in striking the balance.

These concepts will help us to map California's historical patterns and to show the evolutionary growth of society. Patterns, as I have used the term, refer to series of events related to a single topic and arranged in a meaningful sequence that reveals trends in historical development. This history follows the patterns by periods of time in order to show the basic patterns and major interrelationships of political, economic, and social developments, which generally shift by periods of time. Fundamental shifts came with the changes in national government: Spanish, Mexican, and American. Since the patterns in the American period are far more complex than in the Spanish and Mexican periods, they required extended periodical and topical treatment. I have treated only the essential features of these patterns, a profile that is neither complete nor definitive, hoping that a simplified picture will present a clear view of the patterns whose visibility is so often clouded by detailed treatment. I have learned from a decade of college teaching experience that one can comprehend complex patterns and interrelationships when presented in this fashion.

My object is to put the California story in broad perspective, to show the aspirations and actions of its leaders and major groups and the impact of their accomplishments on the land and the people. The focus will be on the prime movers—those individuals and groups of people whose thoughts and actions influenced public policies and gave direction to such various activities. In this way we can appraise past achievements and perhaps acquire a more realistic understanding of present developments and future prospects.

California may be viewed as a microcosm of a society. We can put it under an imaginary microscope and see it evolve from a simple to a complex organism. The environment, its land and its resources, comprise the field; the people are the individual cells; the special interest groups are the cell clusters; and the leaders are the activating agents which affect the mass and give shape to the society. So we see California evolve from rudimentary Indian clusters, to pioneer Spanish settlements, to growing Mexican pueblos, then to American communities which rapidly transform from frontier towns to mature rural and urban areas. Along the way we see the impact wrought by outside catalytic forces: national and international events and movements. After adjusting the microscopic lens the basic elements of our present society become clear: the myriad of its heterogeneous people, the mosaic of its multi-use land pattern, and the complicated interweaving of human and physical activity. All these diverse elements are interrelated with one another and blended into the whole entity which we know as our state. Now you may see, as I see, the marvelous interplay of human elements with physical resources—people carving out their lives and enterprises in a rich and bountiful land that has become somewhat worn and abused.

A few words about the presentation. I have attempted to keep this book to a manageable size for the use of college students and casual readers, yet serve the classroom needs of teachers and the varied wants of scholars. Hence information for its own sake is generally omitted, persons are confined to representative or transitional figures, incidents are selected for illustration, reference information is contained in parentheses, dates are used for time sequence only, and numbers (reduced to round figures for convenience) are meant to facilitate comparisons. In keeping with the purposes of the book, my story is sparing in anecdotes, descriptions, and discussion, and the presentation is informal. Readers who prefer a "short history" can read *The Setting* (or *Development* or *Analysis*) in each chapter, by-passing the other sections, without losing the basic patterns and the main line of developments. Readers preferring the topical approach can follow a title heading (*Agriculture, Journalism,* and so on) through each historical period. A summary of the period appears at the end of each part.

This account of California history owes much to the spadework done by scholars and other writers in the field. Some will recognize the influence of H. H. Bancroft and Herbert E. Bolton throughout the first third of this book. While I have undertaken to synthesize many excellent studies into this account, I have relied heavily on Robert F. Heizer for the prehistoric Indians, on Charles Chapman for the Spanish Period, on Woodrow Hansen for the Mexican Period. For the American Period, I drew valuable clues and insights from master historians, especially those of the *New American Nation Series*, and other scholars cited in the text. I drew heavily from my manuscript, *The Dynamics of California Society, 1846–1975*, for the economic and social portions of this book. Much of my story was built from information culled from innumerable documents, theses, newspapers and secondary works.

I am deeply grateful to several men whose ideas and perspectives were incorporated into this account: John D. Hicks, former professor of history, Samuel C. May, former professor of public administration—both were my mentors during student days—and Ewald T. Grether, dean emeritus of business administration at the University of California in Berkeley; A. Alan Post, the legislative analyst, and William R. Mac-Dougall, former general manager of the County Supervisors Association— my employers during a journeyman sojourn at the State Capitol; Franklin Hichborn and Herbert L. Philips, veteran journalists and perceptive reporters of the Sacramento scene; and William N. Davis Jr., chief of archives, California State Archives. Among the many authorities who read manuscript portions were C. Raymond Clar, Richard H. Dillon, George L. Hersh, Ward C. Krebs, Eugene C. Lee, David F. Myrick, Chester D. Rhoan, Henry Schacht, Philip S. Staniford, A. E. Stevens, Kevin Starr, and Charles Wollenberg. I am especially indebted to Professor Hicks, Dean Grether, and Dr. Post who reviewed major portions of the manuscript. While all parts of the book were reviewed by appropriate authorities, I, of course, assume responsibility for the content. H. R. Lewis, my friend and collaborator, lent his literary skill to the manuscript.

Writing history is a never-ending process of discovery and examination. I hope that this book stimulates comment, criticism, and further exploration. If it imparts some insights and understanding into the complex workings of California society, its aims will have been well-served.

Berkeley, California   *Edward Staniford*
February 1975

I The California Setting

Geography has ever influenced the course of history. The lives of the California Indians were entirely determined by it. Its workings once isolated the land, filled the mountains and deserts with minerals, formed fertile valleys, and created an unyielding problem—water.

1 Geography and the Indians

1 Geography and the Indians

THE SETTING

The Lay of the Land

History, so the eighteenth-century German philosopher Johann Gottfried Herder tells us, is geography in motion. California's history illustrates this maxim well. As each wave of people—Indian, Spanish, Mexican, and Anglo-American—came upon the land, their manner of living and way of doing things were affected by the unique environmental conditions that confronted them. Each group was stimulated or retarded by the influence of these geographical factors in fashioning its way of life. In time, the empty virgin land was transformed into the most affluent and populous state of a powerful nation.

A glance at a relief map of North America will show California's remote location on the Pacific side of this vast continent, far from the governing centers of Spain, of Mexico, and of the United States. The most notable geographic feature of the California area in this continental setting is the great mountain range of the Sierra Nevada that towers along its eastern border. Such natural barriers as this effectively contained the earliest Indians who migrated into the coastal region and central valley of California. They consequently developed cultures distinctly different from those of Indian groups even in neighboring regions. Later, the Spanish, Mexicans, and Americans undertook major, and often heroic, efforts to overcome great distances and physical obstacles in order to settle and to govern California. Nevertheless, because of their relative isolation from the main centers of national life, Californians throughout most of their history were left to fashion their own way of life.

California's unique geography presents an unusual combination of varied land forms, singular .climatic conditions, and abundant resources. This diversity in its physical complexion is the result of a long, dramatic geological development. In its journey through several geologic eras (see Table 1), California periodically experienced violent upheavals of its surface area—earthquakes, volcanic activity, and glaciations—all accompanied by very active erosion of soils and rocks. These cataclysms resulted primarily from its proximity to the Pacific Ocean and the Great Basin (formerly an inland sea) and its location above a major break in the earth's crust, the source of the San Andreas and other geologic faults. Such sporadic geological development produced the varied marine sediments and rock materials that account for the diversity of California's soils, and minerals such as gold, oil, quarry rock, and metallic ores.

California as we know it today constitutes a distinctive land. Nature has endowed a diverse and immense terrain, which includes the largest continuous mountain range (Sierra Nevada), the highest mountain in conterminous United States (Mount Whitney), the deepest valley (Death Valley), the tallest trees (Coast Redwoods), the largest trees (Sequoia), the biggest alpine lake (Tahoe), the highest American waterfall (Yosemite), and the nation's heaviest snowfall (average in the Sierra). The state boundary was drawn by political act: the northern boundary was set by the 1819 Treaty between Spain and the United States; the southern boundary, which marked the Spanish demarcation between Alta and Baja California, was fixed by the 1848 Treaty between Mexico and the United States; and the eastern boundary was conceived by the 1849 California Constitutional Convention, and modified by subsequent surveys. The state comprises an area of 158,693 square miles, or almost 100 million acres, making it the third largest state after Alaska and Texas, and about the size of France or Spain. Its north-south medial line spans 720 miles and its east-west spread varies between 150 and 350

TABLE 1   CALIFORNIA'S GEOLOGIC EVOLUTION*

Era	Time (Million Years)	California Developments
	(Earth's crust solidified about 4000 million years ago.)	
Precambrian	2700-600	Oldest rocks and mountains Mountain building in Southern California Land uplifts
Paleozoic	600-225	Shallow seas probably over most of California Volcanos and mountain building
Mesozoic	225-70	Building of Sierra Nevada, Klamath and Peninsular Ranges Formation of Central Valley and mountain systems
Cenozoic	70-0	Widespread coastal seas Building up of Coast and Transverse Ranges Continued faulting and mountain building
	California's land forms recognizable about 70 million years ago Evidence of Indian occupation about 12,000 years ago First settlement by Europeans 1769	

*Compiled from table in Gordon B. Oakeshott, *California's Changing Landscapes* (New York: McGraw-Hill, 1971), p. 70. Estimated time periods overlap.

miles. The state has a longitudinal slant that makes Eureka the western-most terminus of the United States and places San Diego east of Reno. California has an economic productivity that (measured by gross national product) is exceeded by only six nations in the world—United States, Russia, Japan, West Germany, Great Britain, and France.

California derives its name from an early Spanish novel, *Las Sergas de Esplandián* ("The Exploits of Esplandián"), written around 1510 by Garcí Ordóñez de Montalvo, who mentioned a mythical island named California located "very near the terrestrial paradise." In the time of Cortes (see Chapter 2), when fantasy and truth were not always separable, explorers in the California area gave the legendary name to the newly discovered land. The accomplishments of nature and people since that time have still not entirely separated fact and fiction in people's minds.

Major Areas

From its dramatic geological evolution came California's distinctive arrangement of volcanic and glacial mountains, arid and fertile valleys, desert plateaus, and extensive river systems. An examination of the relief map of California (see Figure 1), shows that these landforms are arranged into natural regions, what geologists call geomorphic provinces. They include the Central Valley, Sierra Nevada, Coast Ranges, Klamath Mountains, Cascade Range, Modoc Plateau, Transverse Ranges, Peninsula Range, Great Basin, and Mojave and Colorado Deserts.

The great Central Valley is a huge alluvial plain in the shape of an elliptical bowl which is walled in by mountain ranges on all sides. Two vast river systems—the Sacramento River and its tributaries in the north, and the San Joaquin with its tributaries in the south—form natural basins within the valley. These two basins drain the waters from the Sierras into the central delta. From here they eventually flow into San Francisco Bay and then into the Pacific through the Golden Gate, the only break in the mountain wall of the Coast Ranges where the waters of the interior can escape into the sea. The Central Valley is California's heartland. Its diverse soils and long growing season have made possible the great production of foodstuffs for national and world markets which has marked this rich, fertile valley as the state's prime agricultural area.

The mighty Sierra Nevada, which extends two-thirds of the state's length on the eastern boundary, contains mountains rising to heights above 14,000 feet. Among these is Mount Whitney (14,496 feet), the highest point in the continental United States outside of Alaska. The upward thrust of this mountain range is so great that its few passes and some forty peaks over 10,000 feet in elevation have made it a formidable physical barrier. This barrier arrests the flow of prevailing winds from the Pacific, causing the interaction of wind currents and sun rays that influences the climatic conditions and water precipitation in the Central Valley. The Sierra contained the vast deposits of gold, silver, and other minerals, as well as timber forests, that were utilized for the state's economic development.

The rolling Coast Ranges extending along California's coastline from Oregon to the Transverse Ranges comprise numerous more or less distinct mountain chains, with peaks rising over 8,000 feet in some areas. Each chain is broken into barren ridges or forested spurs which enclose narrow fertile valleys usually drained by rapidly flowing streams. The Coast Ranges also provide a mountain backdrop for several coastal basins, the largest of which is the San Francisco Bay area, a historic center of population and industry. Several of these valleys and basin areas have been particularly suited to soil cultivation and other resource-

FIGURE 1   California Relief Map

6   The California Setting

oriented activities, such as lumbering, mining, and oil production.

In the north, the glacially-formed Klamath Mountains extend from Oregon into California's northwestern area and contain a river system that drains northwesterly into the Pacific. Farther east is the Cascade Range, a series of volcanic mountains projecting from Oregon into the northcentral area. The southern portion of the Cascades is dominated by Mount Shasta (14,161 feet), a towering snowcapped mountain that produces the headwaters of the economically important Sacramento River area. In the northeast is the volcanic Modoc Plateau, which is actually a westward extension of the Great Basin. While the northern region has always been sparsely populated, the heavy timber forests of the Klamath and Cascades have been an important lumber-producing area. Even the barren Modoc Plateau supports limited agriculture.

The southwest region is marked by two complex mountain systems. These are the northerly Transverse Ranges and the southerly Peninsular Ranges. They bound the Los Angeles Plain, which comprises the coastal basin all the way to the Mexican border. Los Angeles became the largest center of population and industry in the state, while remaining a substantial agricultural area. Today it is the second largest metropolis in the nation.

The southeast comprises the vast arid plateau of low, rugged mountains and desert valleys that extend from the Great Basin. The California portion of this basin area is dominated by Death Valley, which includes the lowest point in North America (282 feet below sea level), and extensions of the Mojave and Colorado deserts, the nation's largest desert areas. Since Gold Rush days, the myth that this plateau is wasteland has been gradually dispelled by the increasing development of rich mineral deposits in desert sinks and barren mountains, by irrigated agriculture in the fertile Imperial Valley (once a desert), near the Colorado River, and by the existence of thriving desert communities.

Climate

California has many climates. Some are extremes such as Death Valley, which holds the nation's record for heat (134°), and Mount Lassen, which recorded one of the nation's coldest temperature (56° below zero). These two areas are only 300 miles apart. Historically, many of the mountain and desert regions, which constitute a considerable portion of the state's area, have been rendered unsuitable for habitation partly because of such extreme climates. Even today they are sparsely settled.

The most significant of California's many climates, however, is the temperate climate of the coastal area. So equable is the coastal climate that the average winter and summer temperatures seldom vary more than ten degrees within an area. The moderate range of temperatures between San Francisco and San Diego is considered unique, for such conditions exist on approximately 1 percent of the earth's surface. This climatic factor has been significant in encouraging the concentration of people and economic development in the Los Angeles Plain since the turn of the century.

Resources

California's unusual geological evolution has produced an abundance of minerals, forests, soils, and water. The state also has an extensive variety of marine, plant, and animal life. Perhaps no other state is so richly endowed with natural resources. Of the sixty-odd commercial minerals mined in the United States, California leads the states in producing 16 of these. The state's economic development owes much not only to the great deposits of gold, petroleum, and natural gas, but also to the variety and quantity of metals, industrial minerals, and other mineral fuels. While arable soils constitute a relatively small portion of California's total area, they include 500 different types (the next ranking state is Pennsylvania with 23 soil types), which makes these arable areas uncommonly productive for agriculture. The heavy timber forests of the north and in parts of the Sierras have yielded considerable lumber over the years, but a substantial portion of their potential yield is still in reserve. Such abundance of resources has served to meet most of California's residential, agricultural, and industrial needs, a fact of particular significance considering the state's distance from the nation's resources and industrial centers. In California's historical development, however, it has been not so much the presence of these resources that attests to their importance, but their availability for use at a given time. How different would California's history have been if the Spanish had penetrated into the interior to find gold deposits in the Sierras, or if the Americans had not found good soils for cultivation and the rich deposits of metallic ores so important for industrial development!

Of all these resources, water has probably had the greatest long-range effects on California's history. Cyclonic storms that originate in the Alaskan area move down the Pacific Coast each year, depositing great quantities of rainwater along the way before being dissipated in the Northern California area. As a consequence of this cyclonic storm pattern and other geographic factors already described, water resources are unevenly distributed throughout the state. Northern California generally receives two-thirds of the state's water supply, while Southern California experiences more or less arid conditions. Since the turn of the century, however, Southern California has undergone the greater population growth as well as economic expansion. It has great need of the water resources so readily available to its northern neighbor.

DEVELOPMENT

The First Californians

The California Indians are something of an anomaly in history. Among the Indians of North America, they are set apart by their relatively dense population, their diverse local cultures, and their varied arts of life. They were exploited ruthlessly by their Spanish, Mexican, and American rulers, who applied to the natives they encountered preconceived ideas of the aborigines as inferior people. Even today in California, the Indians suffer from indifference, ignorance, and prejudice of a kind and to a degree not experienced by any other minority group. Below is a general account of their existence before the coming of the white man.

General Characteristics

At the time of the arrival of the Spaniards, the California Indians had a way of life that was a survival of Stone Age culture. Like other peoples at this cultural level, they had no knowledge of the wheel, did not use metals, and had no system of writing. They were comparatively isolated by vast expanses of mountains and deserts, so the well-ordered scheme of their existence remained virtually undisturbed by the transforming influence of contact with other Indians. The physical facts of geography, rather than their biological traits, explain the cultural status of the California Indians at that time.

The Spaniards, Mexicans, and Americans generally regarded the California Indians as a simple people living in primitive ways. Actually these aborigines had well-developed and even complex material and social cultures. They were without peer in some activities, notably in their cult religions, their basketry designs, their stone implements, and their acorn preparation. Many of their foods, medicines, baskets, and other implements reflect their sophisticated knowledge of plants. Most impressive, though, is the extent to which the California Indians utilized natural resources with little waste and coexisted peacefully and noncompetitively with their neighbors. This was not always the case among other Indian groups. Well adapted to their environment, they lived in harmony with nature.

These characteristics of the California Indians owed much to the migratory pattern of the original immigrants and to the diverse environmental conditions they encountered. It is generally believed that they were elements of the great migration of Mongoloid peoples who infiltrated from Eastern Asia. Crossing the Ice Age land bridge at the Bering Strait into North America, they fanned out in several directions in the process of colonizing the two American continents. During several thousand years of this prehistoric period, small contingents presumably moved across the western mountain barriers into California, a marginal area difficult of access and far from the main migration routes east of the Rockies. Bands of these migrating groups crowded successively into a desirable habitat, hemmed in by mountain and desert barriers. This so-called fish-trap theory explains the presence of such great numbers of Indians, as well as the diversity of their physical types, languages, and cultures.

In supporting these large numbers, geography was kind to the California Indians. It also influenced their distribution. At the time of the Spanish arrival, they numbered over 300,000. So great was the density of Indian population that California, which constitutes about 1 percent of the North America land area north of Mexico, contained about 10 percent of the total number of Indians. The distribution of population was ultimately determined by the availability of water supply and food resources. The Indians were concentrated along rivers and other well-watered places, such as the coastal and central regions, which produced edible plants, abundant game, and fish. They were sparsely settled in the desert and mountain areas, where the supply of water, wild food, plants, and game was limited.

The Indians spoke numerous languages, which greatly hampered communication among them. There were as many as 21 separate languages comprising over 105 dialects. Such a rich variety of native languages in an area of comparable size is not to be found elsewhere in North America—and some say in the world.

The California Indians came to be labeled "Diggers," a descriptive term for the economic activity of digging edible roots for food. This word was first applied to the Indians of the Great Basin by early explorers beginning in 1830. When California was occupied by Americans, the label was transferred to the Indians here. It is not appropriate, even descriptively, and it has persisted with the derogatory implication that people who dig roots for food are stupid savages. Such labels reinforced the justification by Americans for seizing Indian lands and killing the native occupants. Manifest Destiny at its worst is exemplified in the frontiersman's attitude toward the native Californians.

Major Groups

California Indian cultures can be best described within the context of six cultural areas (see Table 2). A cultural area is one that has geographic limits within which the people share a way of life distinctively different from that shared by the people in an adjacent area. Cultural differences may be primarily, but not exclusively, the result of environmental conditions such as terrain, temperature, rainfall, and animal and plant life. The availability of foods often influences the degree of cultural development. In an area abundant in natural foods, the Indians had leisure time to engage in ceremonial rites and to produce material artifacts. In barren areas, the Indian preoccupation with food-gathering allowed limited opportunity for such activities. A description of representative tribes in each cultural area will provide a picture of the diverse Indian society—or more properly, societies.

The northwest area is part of the North Pacific culture which extends as far north as Alaska. The Yurok on the Klamath River and the Hupa on the Trinity River are fairly typical of the 14 tribes that occupy the California portion of this cultural area. The bountiful rain forest environment resulted in a way of life based on plank dwellings and dugout canoes. The Yurok lived in village groups that were essentially aggregations of individuals centered on family lines reckoned through males. They placed great emphasis on material wealth. This was apparent from their social organization, their laws, and their religion. While land in California was generally owned in common by the tribe, the Yurok also

TABLE 2   CALIFORNIA INDIANS—CHIEF CHARACTERISTICS*

	Northwest	Central Valley	Southwest	Southeast	Northeast	Great Basin
Number of Tribes	14	18	20	2	2	6
Hearth Tribes	Yurok Hupa	Pomo Patwin	Chumash Gabrieleno	Mojave Yuma	Modoc Achomawi	Paiute
Village Basis	Aggregation of individuals	Village groups	Village groups	National groups	Village groups	Villages
Dwellings	Frame houses: gable roofs plank walls	Earth houses, pole-bark leantos	Dome brush-earth houses	Willow-mud houses	Earth houses	Domed willow houses
Food Staples	Salmon, acorn	Acorns, berries, grasses, game	Fish, mollusks, acorns	Corn, beans, pumpkin	Roots, seeds game	Small game, seeds
Religious System	World renewal cult	Kuksu cult	Toloache cult	Dream song-myth cult	None	None
Group Conflicts	Kin groups over personal injury	Intertribal over village trespass	Intertribal over village trespass	National military campaigns	Intervillage feuds	Intertribal over seed areas
Tools and Weapons	Skilled: ornate tools and baskets	Simple tools, elaborate baskets	Skilled, artistic: tools and baskets	Extensive pottery, some basketry	Simple basketry	Simple basketry
Ritual Costumes	Showy dance regalia	Fancy colorful costumes	Simple and somber ceremonies	Colorful regalia	None	None
Transportation Means	Dugout canoes	Tule balsa	Plank canoes	Tule balsa	Log dugout	Tule balsa
Land Ownership	Village and individual	Village exclusively	Village exclusively	Tribal nation ownership	Village	Village
Notable Features	Precise law system (Yurok)	Intertribal trade	Maritime economy (Chumash)	Agricultural people	Simple culture, food preoccupation	Nomadic people, simplest culture

*Compiled from information in Robert F. Heizer and M.A. Whipple, *The California Indians: A Source Book* (Berkeley: University of California, 1965); and Robert F. Heizer, "The California Indians, Archaeology, Varieties of Culture, Arts of Life," *California Historical Society Quarterly* XLI (1): 1-28, March 1962.

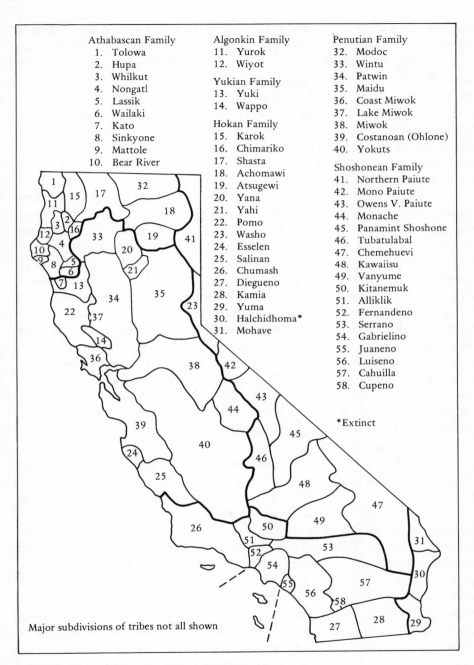

Athabascan Family
1. Tolowa
2. Hupa
3. Whilkut
4. Nongatl
5. Lassik
6. Wailaki
7. Kato
8. Sinkyone
9. Mattole
10. Bear River

Algonkin Family
11. Yurok
12. Wiyot

Yukian Family
13. Yuki
14. Wappo

Hokan Family
15. Karok
16. Chimariko
17. Shasta
18. Achomawi
19. Atsugewi
20. Yana
21. Yahi
22. Pomo
23. Washo
24. Esselen
25. Salinan
26. Chumash
27. Diegueno
28. Kamia
29. Yuma
30. Halchidhoma*
31. Mohave

Penutian Family
32. Modoc
33. Wintu
34. Patwin
35. Maidu
36. Coast Miwok
37. Lake Miwok
38. Miwok
39. Costanoan (Ohlone)
40. Yokuts

Shoshonean Family
41. Northern Paiute
42. Mono Paiute
43. Owens V. Paiute
44. Monache
45. Panamint Shoshone
46. Tubatulabal
47. Chemehuevi
48. Kawaiisu
49. Vanyume
50. Kitanemuk
51. Alliklik
52. Fernandeno
53. Serrano
54. Gabrielino
55. Juaneno
56. Luiseno
57. Cahuilla
58. Cupeno

*Extinct

Major subdivisions of tribes not all shown

FIGURE 2   California Indians—Major Groups

recognized private land ownership: an individual might have exclusive rights to the acorns in an oak grove or to the salmon in a certain pool. Their highly developed system of law contained precise procedures for compensation in material and labor for injury to persons or destruction of property. Their World Renewal Cult included complex rituals that revolved around the display in elaborate dance ceremonies of an individual's material possessions. Such ceremonies were aimed at guaranteeing the continuance of the world and what it held, to prevent earthquakes, famine, pestilence, and floods, and to insure food resources (acorns, deer, salmon) in the coming year.

The central area (Central Valley) contained 18 tribes that were among the most populous in the state. The Pomo near Clear Lake and the Patwin in the southwestern part of the Sacramento Valley are representative tribes. The environment contained a wide variety of food staples and dwellings among the tribes in this region. Tule reed rafts were commonly used for river travel. These Indians lived in village communities, or tribelets, comprising clusters of several village settlements that recognized the headship of the chief in the principal village. Their villages were actually political units, for they engaged in warfare over trespasses of village boundaries and participated in intertribal trade. These Indians practiced the Kuksu Cult, in which dancers in colorful costumes impersonated the spirits of deities. The ceremonies were held at regular times during the year; they involved elaborate feasts and dance cycles that might last several weeks, probably like combining the 4th of July, Thanksgiving, and Christmas into one big holiday period.

The southwest area comprised 20 tribes which are best represented by the Chumash and Gabrieleno in the Santa Barbara and Los Angeles region. The Chumash were a canoe-using maritime people who relied on shellfish and fish as staples and lived in large, relatively permanent villages of round-domed grass or mat-covered houses. The Gabrieleno made their home in the interior and are noted as the originators of the Toloache Cult, which was widespread throughout the southern region. This complex religious cult featured simple and somber ceremonies that centered around an all-powerful deity called Chingichnich. Young boys were initiated by drinking an infusion of the jimsonweed plant, which contains narcotic properties. After experiencing visions while under the influence of the drug, they listened to the priests deliver long moralistic sermons concerning their daily conduct. The carefully prepared Toloache drink rendered the initiated boys unconscious for 12 hours or more; it was reported that an overdose at times caused death.

The Mojave and the Yuma in the southeast differed from all other California tribes in that they were strong political entities. They possessed a political organization and a military spirit based on tribal sentiment. The village-community or tribelet organization of the rest of California was not followed, because of their sense of larger tribal unity. Their villages of mud-covered willow dwellings were little more than physical settlements since their inhabitants thought of themselves as belonging to the larger tribe. These Colorado River people were the only California tribes that depended on farming for their livelihood, their chief crops being corn, beans, and pumpkins, which were planted in the moist silt of the river bottom after the annual floodwaters had receded. They had a song—myth system in which every man found his "self" in his dreams, which he communicated to others by means of lengthy song cycles. While the dream—song system was primarily an individual matter, there were rituals in which the whole public participated.

The barren northeastern area was occupied by the Modoc and Achomawi tribes. These Indians lived on roots, seeds, and small game, which provided a meager but sufficient livelihood. Their material culture was comparatively simple and their ceremonies unelaborate.

The remaining Indians in the California area of the Great Basin are related to the nomadic tribes of the Nevada—Utah region. Theirs was the simplest of the California Indian cultures. Because of the desert environment they roamed constantly in search of food to maintain their existence. They often suffered from poverty and hunger, something that was practically unknown among the other California tribes.

ANALYSIS

Political Scheme

The village community was the basic unit of political organization, but such organization was usually of a rudimentary kind. Typically, a tribelet was a people who shared a dialect, a group name, and a territory. Some villages were merely physical settlements comprising a collection of individuals. Most were communities that usually embraced several settlements. These village communities, or tribelets, ranged in size from 3 to 30 villages and usually contained anywhere from 150 to 500 people, although some Chumash and Patwin villages had as many as 1000 inhabitants. The basis of village organization varied. In the northwest, it was based on the extended family; in the central area, on the village community; in the southeast, on the tribal nation. The Yokuts in the San Joaquin Valley were a unique exception in that each village community had characteristics of a true tribe: a group name, a separate dialect, and a tract of land.

The exact nature of village leadership is unclear. The chief was often a civil leader but his authority was limited. Other persons than the chief usually performed major community functions: one with special skills was the military leader; one with extensive supernatural knowledge, the priest; and one with the gift of personality, the shaman. The shamans were not actually officials, but medicine men whose primary function was to treat diseases. Their curative techniques were fairly uniform, although differing considerably in their dependence on supernatural powers. Shamans exercised over the people great powers based on fear and superstition. Not infrequently, they were killed for prescribing the wrong remedy or for failure to effect a cure.

Economic System

The California Indians maintained their livelihood through an economy of bountiful subsistence. They were the most omnivorous people in North America. The wide variety of their foods proved to be more significant than the abundance of individual foods. If one failed, other foods were always available. Thus, where other North American Indians depended on corn, buffalo, seal, salmon, or other staple, the California Indian used a number of foods to supplement his staple diet, be it acorn, salmon, or shellfish. Such supplementary foods might include bear, deer, rabbits, gophers, mice, snails, insects, berries, grasses, and edible roots. Even the desert area yielded nutritious foods. Some Southern California desert Indians utilized at least 60 edible plants, among which mesquite, cactus, and yucca were important. Generally men hunted and women gathered food plants and cooked the food. The abundance of plants and animals tended to inhibit agricultural development. Here there was no need for a planned food supply as in the agricultural communities.

The acorn was the most characteristic food of the California Indians, but it was not readily available to all tribes. Oak groves are confined to certain areas in the coastal and central regions and are almost entirely absent in the higher mountains and deserts. In most instances,

Indians migrated to oak grove areas, usually in autumn, to gather acorns and store them in baskets or underground granaries for future use. The acorn is nutritious food, but unlike most nuts its tannic acid content has a bitter flavor that usually makes it inedible. The Indians overcame this by first pulverizing the husked acorn in a stone or wooden mortar. They then removed the tannic acid element by either leaching the ground meal in a sandy basin or basket vessel, roasting it over a fire, mixing it with clay, or burying it in moist ground. Finally the substance was mixed with water to be boiled in watertight baskets into which fire-heated stones were dropped, baked, or roasted into acorn meal or bread in an earth oven. The successful adaption of acorn technology made it a popular staple diet and precluded the agricultural development that occurred in other areas.

The artifacts of California Indians reflect the nature of their food economy. The baskets they used as containers were their most developed art form and almost their only one. They had no equals, though, in the aesthetic design and technical construction of baskets. In the southwest, pottery fashioned from the local clays also served as containers. Many tools and other implements were fashioned out of stone, displaying a great deal of knowledge and skill. Dense textured stone was used for

Indians preparing acorns—gathering them in a basket, pounding them in a mortar, and cooking them in a watertight basket. Sketched from life near Sutter's Fort on Wilke's U.S. Exploring Expedition, 1841.

mortars and pestles, steatite (soapstone) for pipes, obsidian and flint for knives and arrowheads. Bows and arrows, which were used for hunting animals and in war, varied in detail depending on the wood and stone materials available locally. The Indians developed at least 131 mines and quarries as sources for their stone materials.

It is historically significant that these stoneworkers made no use of easily available gold for fashioning their artifacts, as had the Aztecs and Incas in other parts of the Americas—a fact that determined the nature of their subjection by the white man's civilization.

Social Order

The California Indian usually owed his primary allegiance to the family group rather than to the tribelet. He was born, and he expected to die, among his own people. His ancestral home was the land his family occupied by a stream or river, while land lying outside these family settlements was generally considered no-man's-land—or more appropriately, everyman's land.

The family group as the basic social unit was an effective one for community living. It usually traced descent in the male line and was sustained by marriage outside the immediate group. Marriage was generally by purchase, and a man could have more than one wife if he could afford them. Marital unions were based on utility to the family group rather than on moral or religious sanctions. Adultery, for instance, was treated as an economic injury to the husband, who received his claim for compensation in material goods.

The *temescal* or sweathouse was a typical community institution, although not universal among, nor exclusive to, the California Indians. Its use was usually confined to men. It was based on kinship and friendship rather than other membership requirements. The Indians worked up perspiration by exposure to direct heat from an open fire in the sweathouse structure. Then they jumped into the cold water of a nearby stream or lake.

Religion and mythology were intimately associated. Myths tell how the world and man were created and are usually set in a prehuman time when animals talked and acted like humans. Organized religious rituals referred to these myths which, while they were pure inventions, nevertheless had a reality to Indians—a concept and practice foreign to us today. Many tribes believed themselves to have descended from animal ancestors, a concept sometimes referred to as totemism. Unlike the

Indians of British Columbia, the California Indians did not have visible symbols like totem poles to distinguish his totemic groups. Kinship taboos identified with totem animals were observed in Central California, especially in regulating marriage and the eating of the flesh of certain totem animals. Ceremonial rituals were public affairs that were participated in by a few initiates. They often involved elaborate costumed dances and song chants for celebrating the crises of life, notably the initiation of adolescent boys and girls into maturity and the burials of the dead, and observing annual commemorative rituals of mourning for the dead.

SUMMARY

The Indian heritage is an important part of California history. The Indian belongs to California's natural setting as much as the mountains, valleys, and deserts. He was the first to inhabit the land. He is known to have been in California for at least 7000 years and possibly 12,000 years. His former presence is felt in over a dozen counties, the streams, mountains, and scenic spots that bear Indian names, through numerous Indian village sites and Spanish missions. The Indian was the basis of the labor system during Spanish, Mexican, and early American days. He presents today a continuing political and social problem, which has yet to be resolved.

Overleaf: Mission Santa Barbara.

II Spanish California

After Columbus discovered America for Spain, the Spanish Crown established in the western hemisphere foundations for the world's greatest empire. The Crown extended the northern borderlands of the empire, a process that eventually led to the discovery and settlement of California. Under Crown auspices, a chain of presidios, missions, and pueblos was set up in an effort to establish California as a buffer province for the defense of the northwest frontier. However, Spain failed to overcome geographical and historical obstacles in attempting to achieve the self-supporting civil society that she had envisaged for her California province.

2 The Spanish Design
3 Spanish California Society

2 The Spanish Design

THE SETTING

The Imperial Design

When Columbus staked the new lands of America for his Catholic sovereign in 1492, the Spanish Crown immediately embarked on its grand venture of building a great empire. Intrepid soldiers of fortune, or *conquistadores*, organized private military expeditions which conquered the great Indian empires with their teeming populations, cultivated lands, and vast treasures of precious metals. Later *adelantados*—an early version of our modern land developers—led expeditions of colonists into marginal areas to establish settlements. In time, these settlements were built up by waves of traders, miners, ranchers, planters, and farmers.

Into less attractive areas of strategic importance, the Crown sent teams of soldiers and *padres* ("priests"; literally "fathers") to set up presidios and missions as a preliminary step in preparing the way for civilian settlements of the Spanish type. The presidios were military posts manned by small garrisons of soldiers who explored the unoccupied areas, subdued hostile Indians, and maintained order within the missions and other settlements. Missions were field stations of the Church which served a double purpose: to convert Indians to the

Christian faith, and to train them to Spanish ways. These frontier agencies were intended to complete pacification and preparation of the land for permanent settlement within ten years. With this accomplished, they were to be reestablished on newer frontiers, leaving the newly formed *pueblos* ("towns") of Indians and Spaniards under municipal government.

The organization to accomplish effective Spanish occupation of such vast lands has no parallel in world history. To control these far-flung territories with their many different subjects and vast resources, the Crown extended its monarchical authority throughout the Americas. It imposed a highly centralized structure of government over its American "kingdoms" through its viceroys (literally "in place of the king"), whose rule of these colonies was as absolute as that of the king in Spain. The powerful Catholic Church and the military, both integral parts of the royal hierarchy, served as effective instruments of Crown authority. The Crown also imposed controls over economic activities by granting franchises or special privileges to favored individuals to engage in farming, ranching, mining, and other enterprises, and by issuing monopolistic trading privileges to great merchants who usually resided in Spain. The Crown even regulated social affairs through elaborate decrees that served to maintain a strict class system based on caste. So systematic was this effort that within a century the Spanish Crown had secured a virtual monopoly over large portions of choice lands in the two American continents. It had also achieved effective control over several hundred thousand people spread over the countryside and in some 200 cities. All of this had taken place long before the English, French, and Dutch rivals implanted any permanent colonies in America at all.

Throughout the long development of empire, the Spanish Crown revealed a remarkable adherence to the imperial design that was to be manifested in its occupation of California. From the beginning, the Crown exploited its American colonies so as to build up its national power and prestige at home. It developed a version of the mercantilist system whereby the Crown regulated the trade of the empire for the benefit of the mother country. Gold and silver bullion from the mines in New Spain and Peru, supplemented by heavy taxes on trade and almost every other colonial activity, fed the royal treasury. With this wealth, the Crown was able to finance the costly military ventures, diplomatic alliances, and dowries for the royal marriages which were required to maintain Spain's primacy in European affairs. To achieve the ends of

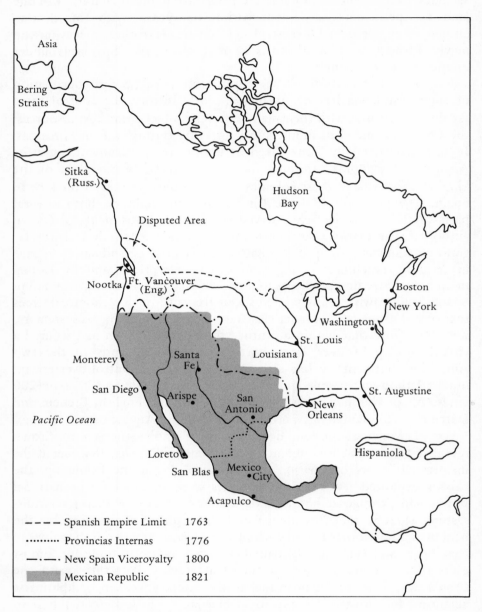

Asia

Bering
Straits

Sitka
(Russ.)

Hudson
Bay

Disputed Area

Nootka • Ft. Vancouver
(Eng.)

Boston
New York

Washington

St. Louis

Monterey

Santa
Fe

Louisiana

San Diego

Arispe

San
Antonio

St. Augustine

Pacific Ocean

New
Orleans

Loreto

Hispaniola

San Blas

Mexico
City

Acapulco

- - - - Spanish Empire Limit   1763
.... Provincias Internas   1776
—·—·— New Spain Viceroyalty   1800
Mexican Republic   1821

FIGURE 3   Hispanic North America

24   *Spanish California*

empire, the Crown freely committed its resources to a degree almost unknown in the colonial enterprises of its European rivals. Whenever the private enterprises of the conquistadores or adelantados failed, the Crown financed the endeavors of its soldiers, padres, and other royal agents. To be sure, the Crown was not always vigorous in carrying out its program, but its methods for pursuing its ends were remarkably consistent.

So successful was the policy of Spain that she retained her preeminence as a leading world power for over three centuries. She was the first to establish colonies in America and the last among European nations to lose the bulk of her empire—a fact that attests to the durability of her imperial design.

DEVELOPMENT

The Northwest Advance

Crown Strategy

Of all the Spanish colonies in the Americas, New Spain (present-day Mexico and most of Central America) was the oldest, wealthiest, and most favored by the Crown. In its periodic efforts to extend the northern limits of New Spain, the Crown encountered a new set of conditions that determined its mode of occupation. The Spanish advance into the northern borderlands constituted a four-pronged movement in the direction of what is now Florida, Texas, New Mexico, and California. California was especially important in the Spanish effort to find the Pacific end of the fabled Strait of Anian, or Northwest Passage, a shorter water route through or around North America that would facilitate trade between Europe and Asia. Conquistadores and adelantados had breached these areas in search of wealth and fame only to find themselves much too far from established population centers. They were stranded in barren lands that contained few mineral deposits, meager water resources, and hostile Indians. These factors did much to impede the normal course of settlement in the north.

At first the Crown's interest in the northern borderlands was limited to charting and mapping unknown areas, which it did with systematic and thorough zeal. Spain regarded the Pacific as a Spanish lake. As European transgressors made voyages in Pacific waters, and later undertook overland expeditions from northern bases toward the Spanish borderlands, the northern frontier of New Spain assumed strategic importance, especially considering the exposed position of the silver mines there. The Crown made persistent efforts to protect its northern provinces throughout this period. Military expeditions to eject foreign intruders were undertaken, as were colonizing expeditions under either adelantados, who founded only a few permanent settlements, or under the more successful soldier–padre teams. The discovery and occupation of California was a phase in this Spanish advance into the borderlands of the northwest.

The Explorers

The northwest advance properly begins with the preliminary explorations of Hernan Cortes. This great conquistador, who completed his conquest of Mexico in 1521, reached the Pacific in 1522 and for the next 17 years attempted to find rich lands and the Strait of Anian. Under incredible hardships, Cortes's men built several ships and undertook four expeditions between 1532 and 1540 in attempts to explore and colonize Baja or Lower California. Thereafter, Cortes returned to Spain—never to make another voyage.

A second stage marked by direct explorations under Crown auspices extended from 1540 to 1604. The first viceroy of New Spain (Antonio de Mendoza) carried on Cortes's explorations of the northwest, primarily to resolve the "northern mystery" and put an end to what he considered the wasteful efforts of the conquistadores in their search for glory and wealth. In 1540 Mendoza authorized Francisco Vazquez de Coronado, governor of a frontier province, to lead a lavishly equipped expedition to what is now the New Mexico–Kansas–Texas area in search of legendary cities of gold. The disappointed Coronado returned two years later empty handed but with considerable information about the region. In 1542 the viceroy also dispatched Juan Rodriguez Cabrillo, a skilled mariner, to the north with two ships to find the Strait of Anian and a shorter route to the Indies from New Spain. In the course of this difficult voyage, which Cabrillo did not survive, his crew explored the coast as far north as Oregon and discovered California. Carefully charting the unknown, storm-ridden area in bulky ships with crude navigational instruments, these hardy mariners gave proof of their courage and tenacity in performing their duty to the Crown.

Then followed a lull of three decades, which ended when Philip

II, the greatest of Spain's monarchs, ascended the throne in 1556. With Spain at the height of its glory, Philip II inaugurated a comprehensive program for expansion of the empire. This included land expeditions to extend the northern frontier in the direction of Florida, Nueva Vizcaya (New Biscay), and New Mexico, and a sea expedition to the Philippines. This last (the Legazpi–Urdaneta voyage, 1564–1565) opened the Manila galleon trade, an indispensable link in Spain's new route through New Spain to the Orient. In the course of this expansionist program, the Crown renewed its exploration of the California coast, having been stirred to new activity by the appearance of European transgressors in the Pacific.

The first of these foreign intruders was the English merchant–adventurer Francis Drake, who passed a month on the California coast in 1579 in the course of his famous three-year voyage around the world. While plundering Spanish ships and colonial cities, Drake was searching for the Northwest Passage on the Pacific side and laying English claim to new lands, as he did by leaving his celebrated "plate of brass" on the California shore in what is now Drake's Bay. Drake's feat alarmed the Spaniards, for they surmised incorrectly that he had found the Strait of Anian.

Stimulated by this and other foreign incursions, the Crown ordered commanders of its Manila galleons (Gali in 1584 and Cermenho in 1595) to explore the California coastline on their voyages to New Spain. Their instructions were to find a suitable harbor that would serve as a way station for the recuperation of mariners on their lengthy, dangerous journey. It was also to be an outpost for the defense of the galleons against pirates and a base for further explorations to the north to find the elusive Strait.

These explorations were capped by the voyage of Sebastian Vizcaino, a merchant–adventurer, who was granted a concession to set up a pearl-fishing venture in Baja California on condition that he chart the northern coast. In 1602 he led an expedition up the coast from Acapulco in frigates smaller and more navigable than the bulky galleons, charting the coastline as far as Cape Mendocino. He gave many of the places their present names, including the harbor he found for the way station, which he named for his viceroy, the Conde de Monterey. With Vizcaino's voyage, the Crown had completed its systematic survey of the California coast.

A third stage extending from 1604 to 1769 reflected relative neglect by the Crown of the northwest frontier. The Crown exhibited little interest in Alta or Upper California but gave some attention to the perimeter areas: Sonora and Baja California. From his base in Sonora, the great padre–explorer Eusebio Francisco Kino pushed the frontier of Jesuit missionary activity after 1687 northward to the Gila and Colorado Rivers in Arizona, continually urging the Crown to undertake settlement of Alta California. In Baja California, Vizcaino's venture stimulated other commercial expeditions to develop pearl fisheries, but these private ventures, including a government-sponsored one, failed to take hold. It remained for Jesuit missionaries, who in 1697 established a mission chain, to secure a permanent foothold in the area. Activities such as these provided steppingstones for the later occupation of Alta California.

The Imperial Crisis

Carlos III

The accession of Carlos III to the Spanish throne in 1759 was a turning point in the affairs of the empire which was to change the situation in California. When this enlightened despot mounted the throne, he found to his dismay a kingdom beset by governmental inefficiency and corruption, by the squandering of its wealth, and by the moral decay of its people. The Crown's control over the vast empire in America was deteriorating as a result of increasing foreign control of the imperial commerce, the lethargy of colonial officials, and the indifference of the colonists. Spain had been reduced to a second-rate power.

Furthermore, the king was faced with a crisis in the empire resulting from the Treaty of Paris in 1763. The treaty brought to a close the Seven Years War among the major European powers, a struggle which had established England's primacy in international affairs. In accordance with the terms of the treaty, France ceded to England both Canada and Louisiana east of the Mississippi. Spain was forced to cede Florida to England, while France ceded to Spain Louisiana west of the Mississippi to compensate her for the losses incurred as France's ally. As a result of these and other concessions, Spain lost strategically important areas, and her empire was exposed more than ever before to the predatory ambitions of her European rivals. This state of affairs was to shape Spanish Crown policy at home and abroad for the next quarter century.

Confronted with this imperial crisis, Carlos III sponsored a vast program of reforms that was to bring about the regeneration of Spain. A remarkable group of talented ministers with reforming zeal initiated a series of public works to restore economic prosperity. They sought to improve agricultural production, manufacturing industries, and internal commerce; to restore governmental efficiency by centralizing administrative controls; and to improve the lot of the people by breaking down the monopolies granted to favored groups. Attention was also given to building up the languishing army and navy. To pay for these costly projects, the Crown overhauled its entire fiscal system. In tapping the resources of the empire to support this program, it established a *visita* ("visitation, inspection") for New Spain for the double purpose of building up defenses and securing revenues from its richest colony. The occupation of Alta California was a by-product of this reform.

Galvez

The visita for New Spain was entrusted to Jose de Galvez, who was appointed in 1765 *visitador general* ("inspector general"). Born of a poor, obscure family of the lower aristocracy, Galvez had risen to prominence as a government lawyer–functionary in the all-powerful Council of Castile by currying favor with important persons in the Spanish Court, including the chief minister of state. Despite his insatiable personal ambition and petty nature, Galvez had a broad vision and an executive ability that were to mark him as Spain's greatest—and as it turned out, last—visitador general. After spending three years at Mexico City, the capital of the viceroyalty, undertaking reforms that greatly increased the royal revenues, Galvez spent the remainder of his six-year tour of duty on the northwest frontier attending to its defense.

The defense of the northern borderlands, of major concern to the Crown, had also become more complicated because of the changing character of foreign encroachments. The sporadic raids of English and other privateers on Spanish treasure galleons in the sixteenth century had given way to the more ominous, steady advance of French, English, and Russian trader–trapper groups and government scientific expeditions in the eighteenth century. English trappers were coming overland from their base in Hudson Bay toward British Columbia, while English trading ships were sailing in the Pacific. Russian traders were moving across Siberia into the Aleutians in the wake of explorations by Vitus Bering (1727–1742) and were sailing in Alaskan waters. The Treaty of Paris, while it had removed the menace of French trappers in the Mississippi basin, brought the borders of the empire even closer to the well-established Anglo-American colonies of its chief rival, England. The real dangers of these foreign threats were comparatively slight during the reign of Carlos III, but the anxiety they caused Spain was to have a dominant influence on her policies in the northwestern area.

Compounding the problem of Spanish control over the northwest territory were hostile Indians. These Indians had not only successfully withstood continuous Spanish efforts to subdue them completely, but their presence also made the area unsuitable for settlement. Spanish occupation of the northwest in the 1760's was actually in a state of decline, limited as it was to scattered presidios and missions interspersed with sparsely settled communities of miners and ranchers.

This was the situation facing Galvez when he arrived on the northwest frontier. The Crown had made clear its intent to strengthen the area by pacifying the Indians at Sonora, improving the mission settlements in Baja California, and bringing about the occupation of Alta California with the establishment of settlements in San Diego and Monterey. It remained for Galvez to carry out the Crown's desire.

To provide for effective administration of the area, Galvez conceived an ambitious plan. The keynote of this plan was the organization of the area into the *provincias internas* ("interior provinces"), known as the *comandancia general* ("commandancy general"), which would unite into a single unit the frontier provinces of Sinaloa, Sonora, Nueva Vizcaya (Chihuahua, Durango, and southern Coahuila), and the Californias. The comandancia general—a military government usually designed for a frontier province—was to be administered by a comandante general with status equal to the viceroy and reporting directly to the Crown. A major feature of the plan was to accomplish the occupation of California by planting a settlement at Monterey to checkmate similar ambitions of Spain's rivals. As Galvez explained in a report to the Crown, his plan would provide for effective control of the area against European transgressors and Indian plunderers. Tranquillity would allow for the steady growth of missions and presidios into civilian settlements. It would also make possible the exploitation of gold and silver deposits believed to exist in the area, which would in time provide additional revenues for the royal treasury. Galvez's plan clearly called for the Crown to commit its resources in developing the potential wealth of the area in order to realize greater returns in its investments.

During his sojourn in the northwest from 1768 to 1770, Galvez launched several projects for the pacification and occupation of the area as he prepared to carry out his plan. He established the port of San Blas, which was to serve as a naval and supply base primarily for the Alta California colonizing expedition. Under his supervision, a military expedition was dispatched to Sonora to subdue the hostile Seri and Pima Indians. A gold discovery on this expedition spurred the permanent settlement of Sonora in the 1770's and strengthened the Spanish belief that precious metals were to be found in the Californias. In Baja California, Galvez revitalized the withering mission system, replacing the out-of-favor Jesuits with Franciscans headed by Junípero Serra. (In 1767 the Crown had expelled the Jesuit order from the empire, believing it to have excessive power and wealth and to be plotting against the king.) The way was paved for Galvez to arrange the occupation of Alta California as part of Crown reform of the northwest frontier.

The Sacred Expedition

From Baja California, Galvez undertook the long-cherished project of the Crown for the settlement of Alta California. This plan was envisaged as a spiritual as well as a military conquest—the Sacred Expedition. He personally organized the expedition, drawing from the peninsula missions most of the foodstuffs, domestic animals, church implements, and other supplies, as well as missionary and Indian contingents. The military force consisted of 25 soldiers under Captain Fernando de Rivera and 25 troops drawn from the Sonora expedition under Lieutenant Pedro Fages. The expedition was put under the command of Captain Gaspar de Portolá, governor of Baja California, a seasoned veteran of European military campaigns. The aged Junipero Serra, *padre–presidente* ("father–president") of the Baja California missions, joined the expedition to head the missionary endeavor of the new enterprise.

Despite extensive preparation, it took remarkable endurance and perseverance for the expedition to achieve its objectives. From the embarkation point at Loreto, it proceeded in four contingents on two land and two sea routes. One overland group was composed of soldier–padre teams headed by Rivera, with some 400 horses and cattle, who broke the way for the other group of Portolá and Serra. Traversing some 400 miles of the Baja California wastelands, they completed their difficult journey in 51 and 48 days respectively. Two supporting supply ships, one carrying Fages's soldiers, completed their tedious voyages in 110 and 55 days respectively. Another supply ship was lost at sea and never heard from again. So great were the hardships of the journey that only half of the 300 men in the expedition reached the meeting place at San Diego. Of those who did not complete the journey, about one-fourth died either from starvation on land or from scurvy and other hardships at sea, while the remainder were Indians who deserted the ranks when the food ran low.

After a brief recuperation from famine at San Diego, Portolá led an overland group, supplemented by Perez's supply ship, to found a settlement at Monterey. Failing to find the harbor on the first trip (during which they slaughtered pack mules for food), they returned to San Diego. On the second attempt they succeeded in establishing the settlement at Monterey in 1770. The success of the expedition was a tribute to Portolá rather than to Serra, who is often given credit, for it was the able leadership and persistent effort of this hardy professional soldier that overcame the formidable obstacles to settlement at San Diego and Monterey.

Foundation Years, 1770—1776

A Precarious Beginning

The first seven years were precarious for Alta California. The settlements struggled in relative isolation on meager resources and their survival was periodically at issue. On Portolá's return to Baja California in 1770, Fages was left in charge as comandante and lieutenant governor under the governor at Loreto. At the outset, effective leadership of the colony was seriously hampered by continual quarreling between Fages and Serra, primarily over their respective responsibilities in carrying out the Crown program. The governor's emphasis on political and military matters and the padre–presidente's concern for the religious conversion of the Indians both served the Crown's ultimate objective, which was to secure the California province for the strategic defense of New Spain. The conflict between Fages and Serra was manifested in disputes over the priorities given to the presidios as against those given the missions, and the vaguely defined authority given to each in setting up the missions. Serra also made an issue of the fact that Spanish soldiers consorted with Indian women, which aroused Indian hostility and complicated the padres' missionary work. Compounding the situation were the clashing personalities of the two men and rival ambitions of

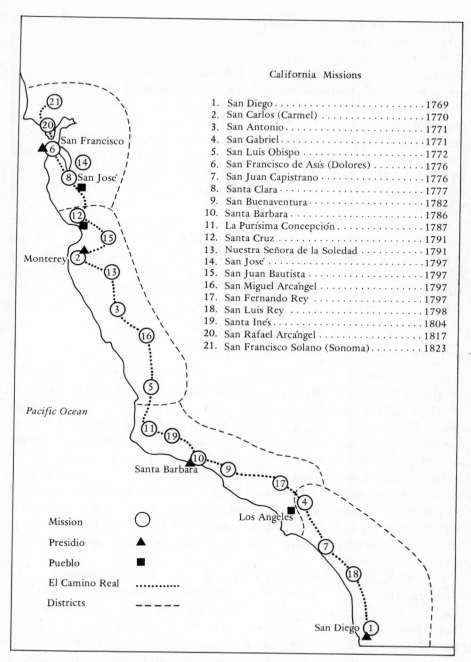

California Missions

1. San Diego...........................1769
2. San Carlos (Carmel).................1770
3. San Antonio........................1771
4. San Gabriel........................1771
5. San Luis Obispo....................1772
6. San Francisco de Asís (Dolores)........1776
7. San Juan Capistrano.................1776
8. Santa Clara........................1777
9. San Buenaventura...................1782
10. Santa Barbara......................1786
11. La Purísima Concepción..............1787
12. Santa Cruz.........................1791
13. Nuestra Señora de la Soledad.........1791
14. San José...........................1797
15. San Juan Bautista...................1797
16. San Miguel Arcángel.................1797
17. San Fernando Rey...................1797
18. San Luis Rey.......................1798
19. Santa Inés.........................1804
20. San Rafael Arcángel.................1817
21. San Francisco Solano (Sonoma)........1823

Pacific Ocean

Mission   ○
Presidio   ▲
Pueblo   ■
El Camino Real ....
Districts   - - - - -

FIGURE 4   Spanish California

other men, like the sulky Rivera who envied Fages's appointment to the Alta California command.

The food supply, vital to the survival of the colony, was also a serious problem. The colonists faced starvation because they did not know how to farm the needed crops, and because of the delays of the supply ships from San Blas. Since so many of the domestic animals had died on the journey to Alta California, those remaining were too precious to be killed as they were needed for breeding purposes. When famine hit the colony for the second time in 1772, Fages averted disaster by providing the needed food supply through what the historian Charles Chapman has called the "most celebrated bear hunt in the history of Alta California."

In the face of these and other difficulties, the progress of the settlements proceeded at an excruciatingly slow pace. Serra and his colleagues were able by painstaking labor to build crude foundations for five missions. Difficulties also dogged the construction of the presidios at Monterey and San Diego. Convinced that his accomplishments were not sufficient, Serra in 1773 journeyed to Mexico City to seek further aid from the Crown for the missionary effort.

Bucareli

At this critical juncture, California affairs received the personal attention of the viceroy, Antonio Maria de Bucareli. A patrician of broad vision and great ability who was completely dedicated to the service of his king, Bucareli is regarded as the greatest of Spain's viceroys in the Americas. He was never completely in sympathy with Galvez's grandiose scheme, believing that the danger of foreign transgressors was too remote to justify the Crown's heavy financial commitment to the California project. Nevertheless, on receiving reports of English and Russian activity in the north and Serra's description of the desperate plight of the Alta California settlements, he made a determined effort to save the colony. To this end, he implemented a series of far-reaching measures that were to insure its survival.

In a preliminary step taken in 1772 Bucareli authorized the division of missionary effort in the two Californias between the Dominicans, assigned to Baja California, and the Franciscans, who henceforth devoted their full attention to Alta California. In 1773 he issued the *reglamento provisional* ("provisional regulation") for the internal management of the two Californias and the San Blas Department, giving special attention to Alta California. Bucareli's *reglamento* and the supplementary instructions he issued to the governors (Rivera in 1773 and Neve in 1776) did much to clarify the responsibilities of the lieutenant governor, who was given control over the settlers as well as the soldiers and was assigned full leadership over the northern province independent of the governor at Loreto. Thus separation of the two Californias was virtually assured. In the absence of subsequent Crown action, these documents in effect served as the code of laws by which California was governed until the end of the Spanish rule.

In these documents Bucareli had spelled out the details for implementing the Spanish design for California. The attention given to Alta California made clear that San Blas was to function as a permanent naval base and supply port for the northern province and that Baja California was of secondary importance. Missions were to be set up carefully, for their sites would eventually become "great cities." Indians were brought to the missions so they might be "civilized"—that is, be made to think and act like Spaniards. To encourage emigration, Spanish settlers would be given free passage, paid sailors' wages for two years, and provided food rations for five years until they could subsist by their own efforts as farmers. In response to Serra's complaint about mistreatment of Indian women by bachelor soldiers, soldier–families were to be recruited for service in Alta California. It was made clear that the Alta California settlements were to advance the spiritual conquest as well as the expanding Crown control over its northern borderlands. The reglamento also improved upon the means for financing the great costs of the California settlements (see Chapter 3).

Bucareli next undertook immediate steps to prevent further food shortages in the Alta California settlements. He organized the operations of the San Blas Department so that ships sailed regularly with adequate supplies for the northern province. The timeliness of this step was apparent in 1774 when the province, in the midst of its third and worst famine, was saved by the extra supply ship thoughtfully provided by the viceroy.

In attending to the foreign danger, the viceroy undertook to extend Spanish claims to the perimeter areas in the north and to establish a settlement at the great bay of San Francisco as a northern outpost. Exploratory expeditions were dispatched north in 1773 and in 1775. These expeditions fully achieved their objective of carefully exploring the coast, including San Francisco Bay and northward to present-day British Columbia. They came none too soon, for in 1776 Captain James Cook, the great English navigator and explorer, appeared in California waters on his third scientific voyage.

Bucareli recognized that the key to prosperity in Alta California lay in a practical overland route that would permit an easy flow of colonists and trade to the northern province. On the viceroy's orders, Rivera, while on his way to replace Fages at Monterey, recruited a mixed company of 55 colonists in Sinaloa for the overland journey up Baja California in 1774, bringing the first settler families to the northern province. The hardships of the Baja California land and sea routes were so apparent that the viceroy finally approved the request of Anza to open an overland route farther east in the Sonora–California region.

Anza

Juan Bautista de Anza was a simple, hardy man of unblemished character and unusual abilities. A third-generation frontier soldier and veteran Indian fighter, he was captain of a presidio on the Sonora frontier. He organized two expeditions to carry out the project, the first in 1774 with a small group to explore the route, and the second in 1775 to bring colonizing families and domestic animals to the northern province. In this second expedition, Anza safely guided a group of soldier–colonists and civilian settlers, together with a large herd of stock, across arid wastelands inhabited by hostile Indians. Of the 240 in the party, only one was lost (a woman in childbirth), with eight babies born on the way, so that the expedition actually ended with a larger number! Considering the many hazards, this was an extraordinary feat. The group arrived in San Diego and then moved on to Monterey. From here Anza went on to San Francisco to lay out the missions and presidio. These were settled in 1776, soon after Anza's departure. The Anza expedition proved to be a momentous event for California. It brought the only large group of colonists and opened up the overland route that was intended to be the lifeline for the northern province.

Reorganization and Crisis, 1776–1781

The years from 1776 to 1781 were in a sense the climax of this critical period. Galvez became Minister of the Indies in 1776, and immediately carried out his original reform plan. The new *comandancia general* included the five northwestern provinces (Sinaloa, Sonora, Nueva Vizcaya, and the two Californias) with headquarters centrally located at

Arispe in Sonora. Galvez transferred Alta California from the viceroyalty to the comandancia general in an order which barely mentioned the other provinces. He also ordered the governor to reside in Monterey and the lieutenant governor in Loreto. Thus the importance of Alta California was reaffirmed in the imperial design.

Croix

The important post of comandante general went to Teodoro de Croix, nephew of the Viceroy de Croix who had cooperated closely with Galvez during his visita the decade before. A vain but able soldier, Croix was apparently more interested in conducting military campaigns against the Indians than in administering the government of the frontier provinces. He spent most of his early term in office pressing the campaign against the Apaches in the northeast, withdrawing troops from Sonora to do so. This considerably weakened the Spanish presence in the northwest. Control of the Indians on the Sonora–California border and effective development of the Alta California area suffered accordingly.

Neve and Serra

Croix's neglect of Alta California settlement in these years was compensated to some extent by the determined and sometimes heroic efforts of the governor, Felipe de Neve (1775–1782). A resourceful and arbitrary official, Neve was unquestionably the best of the Spanish governors in California. With conscientious and persistent effort, he carried out Bucareli's measures for developing the California province, something his predecessor, Rivera, had failed to do. In line with the viceroy's instructions of 1776, Neve transferred the provincial government from Loreto to Monterey to permit effective administration of California affairs. He developed a code of laws for the colony and promulgated a reglamento (1779) which elaborated upon Bucareli's reglamento of 1773. He supervised the establishment of two pueblos: San Jose, settled in 1777, which drew upon married soldiers from the Monterey and San Francisco presidios; and Los Angeles, settled in 1781, which drew on the Sinaloa settlers brought overland on the Anza road by Rivera's ill-fated expedition of that year. The governor also extended occupation of the central region by establishing a mission and presidio at Santa Barbara (1782). It is a mark of Neve's accomplishments that he set up the last presidio and the most durable civilian settlements of Spanish rule.

By this time Alta California was enjoying a degree of prosperity and stability. To Neve's fruitful accomplishments were added the growing successes of Serra's missionary endeavors. The governor attempted to assimilate mission Indians into secular communities in accordance with Crown policy but Serra resisted Neve's moves with delaying tactics in his determination to keep the Indians under mission control. The California settlements increased in this period through the addition of two missions and the presidios at San Francisco and Santa Barbara.

Although Alta California was no longer under his jurisdiction, the viceroy continued his careful attention to the external affairs of the colony. He saw to the regular sailings of the San Blas supply ships, which were vital to the survival of the northern province. In the wake of Cook's voyage, he sent another expedition in 1779 (the Artega–Bodega voyage) to search out foreign intruders as far north as Alaska. Shortly afterward, however, the Crown discontinued these expensive expeditions, thereby indicating its unwillingness or inability to maintain the seaward defense of its northern province.

The Yuma Massacre

Meanwhile on the California–Sonora border, trouble was brewing among the Indians. After a lengthy delay, Croix in 1780 finally established two consolidated mission–presidio–pueblo stations for control of the Gila–Colorado areas. These meager posts were hardly adequate for conducting missionary work among the restless Indians or for protecting the strategic junction where the Anza road crossed the Colorado River. In 1781 Rivera's expedition of 42 soldiers (30 with families and livestock) arrived at the Colorado crossing en route to California. After the soldier-colonists and their escort had moved on to California, hostile Yuma Indians attacked the settlements, killing about 45 Spaniards, including Rivera and the rear contingent of his expedition. The Yuma uprising wiped out the Spanish presence in this area.

The Yuma Massacre, as it was called, was one of the worst disasters suffered by the Spanish in the Americas. Its long-range effects were incalculable, for it marked the end of the promising beginnings of the Sonora–California overland route that was meant to be the lifeline to the northernmost province. Although subsequent efforts were made, the Crown failed to reestablish the route, leaving Alta California to subsist thereafter on its own resources. It is ironical that Galvez had so carefully planned the comandancia general to take care of such situations, only to have his plan undone by Croix, the man he had appointed to carry it out.

Alta California reached a turning point in its development with the change in Crown leadership in the 1780's. With Croix's elevation to the viceroyalty of Peru in 1783, Neve was promoted to comandante general, and Fages appointed to the California governorship. The great Bucareli had died in 1779, and both Serra and Neve in 1784. The death of Carlos III in 1788 brought an end to the imperial reforms which had provided the impulse for the Crown's development of the Alta California province. Alta California had emerged from the intense activity of the critical decade with its settlements well established and its institutions very much shaped by these men. With their passing, California entered a new era.

The Pastoral Years, 1781—1821

California Isolated

From the 1780's on, the Crown's increasing preoccupation with troubles at home lessened interest in her colonies. Spain was drawn into another round of struggles with other European powers which involved her in the American Revolution, the French Revolution, and, after 1800, the Napoleonic campaigns. Warfare abroad eventually brought to a virtual standstill the imperial reforms that had figured so importantly in California's early development. Under the dull-witted Carlos IV and his group of mediocre ministers, Crown communications with the overseas colonies broke down, leaving affairs in the hands of colonial officials of limited abilities and resources.

As a result, California now entered into a period of relative tranquillity and isolation which may be best described as the pastoral years. The forty years remaining to Spanish rule witnessed the slow and steady growth of the settlements within a structure of society that underwent little change. Historians often depict these pastoral years as a romantic time of simple pleasures and rustic calm. Actually these were troubled years, especially in the last decade of Spanish rule. The missions managed to thrive, but the presidios and pueblos struggled to subsist without the benefit of active Crown support and deteriorated in the process.

The Governors

In the absence of strong Crown controls, the California governors exercised their own judgment in administering the affairs of the province. The six governors whose rule spanned the next four decades were able administrators who managed provincial matters well enough under the circumstances, considering that they were continually handicapped by lack of support from the ruling comandante general or viceroy. For the most part, they were preoccupied with routine administration and social amenities.

The political pattern of these years is reflected in the governorships of Fages (1782–1791) and Borica (1794–1800). The temperamental but likable Pedro Fages was already an experienced veteran of California affairs when he ruled the province for the second time. He took steps to encourage civilian settlements by beginning the distribution of lands to retired soldiers for ranchos (see below). He attempted to resolve the issue of conflicting authority between the governor and the padres as Neve had done, but he had little support from indecisive Crown officials. His expedient ways did much to stabilize the development of the presidios, missions, and pueblos during this transitional decade.

The administration of the jovial and urbane Diego Borica was marked by active measures for building up the settlements. He encouraged the pueblos and missions to develop industries, notably sheep raising, hemp and flax manufacture, and artisan crafts. He advanced irrigation works for extended agriculture. He personally supervised the political and economic affairs of the motley settlers in the San Jose and Los Angeles pueblos, even censoring their morals in an attempt to put the settlements on a sounder basis. After extensive preparation, in 1797 he launched near Santa Cruz the pueblo of Branciforte. This was to be a new type of pueblo colonized by retired veterans whose discipline would lend the settlement strength and stiffen defense of the area. It soon languished, however, because of few recruits and inadequate finances. In response to the imminent foreign danger, he strengthened the presidios and coordinated military operations. He worked closely with the padre–presidente, Fermin de Lasuen, in constructing five new missions. But even the energetic activity of an enlightened governor like Borica—a lone representative of this type among the governors—was not sufficient to overcome the inertia which had come to permeate the Spanish system.

The Padres–Presidentes

By the time of Borica's administration, the missions had assumed primacy over the presidios and pueblos as the principal centers of settlements. That the padres accomplished as much as they did in developing the missions, which was indeed considerable under the extremely difficult circumstances of the California situation, owes much to the work of Serra and Lasuen. Their terms as Padres–Presidentes spanned 34 of the 52 years of Spanish rule, and each built nine of the 20 missions. Both men were similar in their unselfish devotion, tireless energy, and intense zeal for the mission idea. But they differed completely in character: Serra temperamental, irritable, and blunt; Lasuen urbane, gentle, and tactful. Much controversy has raged over the comparative contributions of these two men, but it is quite evident that the California mission system would never have reached the high point of its development without the combined contributions of both.

Visitors and Traders

Foreign activity in California increased in tempo during this period. In 1786 the great French scientist–navigator, Comte Jean de La Pérouse, had landed in California for a cordial visit, the first non-Spaniard to land there since Drake. Cook's well-publicized reports of trade possibilities in the Pacific area led to an increasing number of European and American ships in California waters from this time onward. The Spanish Crown responded to the growing foreign menace by bolstering its claim in the North Pacific area. It dispatched an expedition in 1788 to establish a post at Nootka Sound (a bay on Vancouver Island), only to find English and American ships already there trading with the Indians. The altercation that followed brought on a diplomatic crisis (the Nootka Sound Controversy, 1789–1794) between England and Spain which resulted in Spain's humiliation and ended her control of this area.

Thereafter, European traders arrived with greater frequency in California waters. George Vancouver, the English commander who had been sent to Nootka to represent British interests, made reports of his voyages (including three visits to California, 1792–1794) which attracted more English traders into the area. Ebenezer Dorr, a Boston trader on a world voyage, appeared in California in 1796 to signal the arrival of the Yankee traders. The Russian American Fur Company established its base in 1799 at Sitka near the Aleutians and shortly afterwards made an appearance in California. These traders primarily hunted sea otter in the North Pacific, utilizing their furs in the profitable China trade. Some traders extended their operations south to California waters, where they made occasional landfalls for needed food, supplies, or repairs, in spite of the apprehensions of local Spanish officials.

Meanwhile, in Europe, Napoleon had invaded the Iberian Peninsula in 1808 to extend his control over the continent, thereby abruptly bringing on a decade of revolutionary activity in Spain and in her American colonies. After 1810, during the low ebb of Spanish power, supply ships from San Blas to California stopped altogether. Thereafter, foreign traders pursued their activities with increasing boldness. The Russian American Fur Company in 1812 established an outpost above San Francisco at Fort Ross (American corruption of "Fort Russia"). The Russian settlement served primarily to raise foodstuffs for their trading posts in the barren Aleutians, but it also traded otter skins for needed grains and other provisions from the Spanish settlements. Up to a dozen foreign vessels a year, mostly Yankee, visited the California coast to engage in trade activity in these last years of Spanish rule.

The Spanish governors attempted to enforce Crown prohibitions against foreign trade, seizing the contraband cargo of such ships when they were able to capture them. The foreign traders, however, were able to conduct successful smuggling operations, using isolated coastal areas to exchange needed goods with padres and other classes of people. Often this was done with the connivance of the presidial commanders at Santa Barbara and San Francisco and sometimes with the knowledge of the governor. As Governor Jose Arguello (1814–1815) so aptly rationalized the situation: "Necessity makes licit what the law makes illicit." The Spanish Crown had by now clearly defaulted its northern province to the alien poachers, having defended the area with excessive zeal only a generation earlier when the foreign danger was remote.

The Closing Years

The steady deterioration of Spanish rule through the long and relatively uneventful period of pastoral existence was readily apparent in the administration of Pablo Sola, the last of the Spanish governors (1815–1822). Unlike his predecessors, who rose through the ranks of presidio service on the frontier, Sola was from a wealthy aristocratic Spanish family. He obtained his appointment through influential officials. A conscientious administrator with limited military experience, Sola undertook measures to check the declining state of affairs on the California province. He allowed foreign ships to trade at designated ports to stimulate commerce and imposed a tariff on their imports to secure adequate revenue for the neglected provincial government. The chief beneficiaries of this trade continued to be the missions, for only they had the surplus goods to exchange, much to the resentment of the pueblos and presidios which were struggling merely to subsist. On Sola's suggestion, the padres in 1817 established a mission above San Francisco at San Rafael (the first since 1804 and the last under Spanish rule), ostensibly to extend the faith to the Indians in the area but more likely to be closer to the market at Fort Ross. He sought to relieve the presidio population by increasing their food allotments from the mission, over the padres' objections to assuming this responsibility. Sola issued land grants to military veterans—including the extensive one to Peralta in the Berkeley–Oakland–Alameda area—as rewards for Crown service, rather than to promote rancho development. He ordered a "grand expedition" in 1816 and other expeditions to round up mission Indian runaways and other Indian renegades who made periodic raids on the outlying settlements. Sola's rule reflects the holding actions of a capable governor dealing with Crown neglect of its distant province.

The Californians were subject to only one test of their loyalty during this period, but their response was more a defense of their homes and lives than a sign of their allegiance to the Crown. In 1818, a renegade revolutionary expedition, sailing under the Argentine flag and led by a Frenchman, Hippolyte de Bouchard, marauded several California settlements in a week-long raid, apparently less for sheer piracy than to strike a blow for Spanish American independence. The Bouchard incident was mute testimony to the helplessness of the Californians. Belatedly the viceroy responded to Sola's plight by sending 200 troops, but half of these were *cholos* (low-class persons) equipped with antiquated weapons and meager supplies. The Californians were well insulated from the revolutionary activity in the south. Their ignorance of such movements resulted from lack of communication with Mexico and the protective custody in which they were held by the military and the padres who owed their positions to the Crown. While the War for Independence raged in Mexico, the Californians continued their struggling existence in ignorant bliss to the end of Spanish rule.

3 Spanish California Society

THE SETTING

To the Spanish mind, a society governed by the Crown and the Church was the realization of God's kingdom on earth. The Crown considered itself the heir of the Roman state and the Roman Catholic Church. The king, God's right arm, ruled his realm with absolute authority. His decrees were carried out through a single line of authority from top to bottom of a rigid hierarchy accepted as the divine order of society. He was head of the Spanish Church and was its ardent champion in propagating the Catholic faith. He governed the people and was their symbol of social justice. The Spanish code was based on tradition and order. It emphasized the virtues of simplicity, uniformity, and obedience to the authority of the king, whose representatives were public officials, churchmen, and family patriarchs.

Spanish California was a frontier version of Spanish society. The Crown's intent had been to establish a prosperous province based on thriving pueblos peopled by converted Indians and immigrant Spanish settlers. The province, however, evolved as a feudalistic society run by the clergy, in which missions dominated the presidios and pueblos. The governor and padre–presidente were partners in sustaining Spanish tradition and order through authoritarian rule and conservative princi-ples. The people lived an austere life marked by strict moral standards in a society where the religious spirit permeated secular life.

ANALYSIS

Political Scheme

Spain's rule of empire was the ultimate expression of monarchical government. The Crown administered the affairs of empire through a highly centralized bureaucracy which implemented the king's authority in far-off provinces like California. It governed through reglamentos and other royal decrees based on the Roman Code, a codification of written law. (Anglo-Saxon and American common law also treat unwritten customs and usages as fundamental law.) Viceroy Bucareli's reglamento of 1773 provided the basic framework of government, but it was provisional in that it constituted temporary instructions to remedy immediate problems. Governor Neve's 1779 reglamento (issued by the Crown in 1780) was of a permanent nature. It provided detail to Bucareli's measure and brought California more in line with Spain's prevailing system. The reglamentos and supplementary Crown instruc-tions constituted the basis of California's political "constitution." They also provided a framework for economic and social development. This was to insure that the frontier province would evolve into a fully developed, self-supporting member of the empire in accordance with the imperial design.

The Crown hierarchy extended throughout the California prov-ince. The viceroy and the comandante general alternated, according to the Crown's whim, in supervising California affairs. Since the coman-dante general and later viceroys were little disposed to be deeply involved, the governor ruled the province with virtually a free hand. He was chief executive with civil and military power for implementing his authority. He administered provincial affairs through the comandantes of the four presidios. Each comandante supervised district affairs and even saw to it that the settlers' behavior conformed to detailed Crown instructions regarding their work, religious duties, and moral obligations. Public records reveal that the governors and comandantes, authoritarian as they were, generally displayed a conscientious regard for the need of their charges.

The military performed the basic functions of political control.

They patrolled the settlements and coastal areas and constituted the expeditions which explored the interior and pursued Indian fugitives. They were severely handicapped in their task of maintaining Spanish control of the province. The four presidios were too few and insufficiently supplied to defend the lengthy 400-mile line of settlements. The military garrisons were never adequately staffed or equipped to carry out their assigned tasks. Toward the end of Spanish rule, the number of active soldiers on duty at the presidios ranged from 80 at Monterey to 55 at San Diego, although technically they were augmented by reserves or local militias comprising all able-bodied men between 16 and 60 years of age and sick and retired military. The weakness of the military was amply demonstrated by its inability to prevent illegal trade by foreign ships and to check the destructive raids of marauding Indians. On one occasion the comandante at the San Francisco presidio had to borrow gunpowder from a visiting Russian ship to fire the customary salute. Despite these shortcomings, the presidios accomplished their primary purpose of policing settlements and deterring foreign occupation of the province.

Administration of Justice

As the military arm of the provincial government, the presidios also functioned to preserve law and order within the province. Military contingents stationed in missions and pueblos were agencies for policing the settlements. In the missions the padres had full charge in handling their straying converts. In the pueblos the *alcalde* served as the civil magistrate, or justice of the peace, in adjudicating civil and criminal matters. His decisions were sometimes appealed to, and always reviewed by, the comandante and the governor, whose word was final. The governor's authority in such matters provoked a contemporary to remark he "might carry the entire legal code about in his mouth." In punishing offenders, military authorities made greater use of public flogging or confinement to a public stock (a wood frame for shackling hands and feet) than execution or jail, presumably as a warning to the settlers. Military justice was harsh and stern, but probably no more so than elsewhere in the empire.

Fiscal Administration

The Crown kept a tight rein on imperial finances in keeping with its policy that the colonies be paying propositions. For the California venture the Crown drew funds from the royal treasury to support the presidios and pueblos, and from the Pious Fund to finance the missions and special projects, such as the 1769 Sacred Expedition and the 1775 Anza expedition. (The Pious Fund, created in 1697, had been built up from private contributions in churches throughout the empire for missionary activity in the Californias.) The Crown paid original settlers two-year wages, granted them five-year tax exemptions, and sold government supplies at cost to both settlers and soldiers. The Crown's benevolence, however, had its limits. It collected from settlers each year a unit of wheat (a *fanegas* or about 1½ bushels) as tribute. It deducted from soldiers' salaries about 50 percent for freight and other supply charges, and it collected interest on loans made to the padres. A paymaster dispensed funds, kept accounts, and also served as postmaster in each presidial district.

The revenue picture is a telling comment on the Crown's design for California. Settlers and soldiers paid a church tax (the ecclesiastical tithes) and a sales tax. Taxes could be paid in grain or livestock which the Crown then sold. The missions were exempt from taxes, presumably because the padres were Crown agents in charge of the Indians. The Crown also derived revenues from papal indulgences (an individual's payment to redeem his sins), cattle sales from royal ranchos, postal revenues, and revenues from the government sale of tobacco, playing cards, gunpowder, salt, and later trade revenues (see below). The Crown derived most of its revenue not from taxes and trade, as befitted the imperial scheme, but from its tobacco sales—a government monopoly. It received little revenue return on its original investment and spent heavily for the California project.

Economic System

Spain sought to perpetuate a self-sustaining empire based on productive colonies and a trade monopoly which would produce wealth for the Crown. The Crown spelled out in the Bucareli and Neve reglamentos a plan for the economic development of its California province. The Crown's scheme for frontier provinces comprised two stages: establishment of nucleus settlements, and development of substantial communities which would exchange goods for the imperial trade and contribute tax revenues for the royal treasury. It relied on the missions and presidios to accomplish the first stage. They would lay foundations and prepare the way for the Indians and Spanish settlers to occupy and develop pueblos. In time the pueblos would evolve from self-supporting settlements into active trading communities that would be the economic centers of the province.

The Crown's scheme was not to be, for by 1800 the missions had emerged as the main centers of economic activity. During Serra's presidency (1769—1784), the missions were able to produce enough livestock and crops for their subsistence, although they depended heavily on government ships from San Blas for additional foodstuffs and manufactured articles. Lasuen in his long rule (1785—1803) expanded the economic base of the missions to make them independent of the irregular supply ships. He utilized skilled artisans sent from New Spain at Crown expense to teach Indians to be carpenters, blacksmiths, and masons. Before long the missions were producing surplus grain and cattle products (hides, tallow, and beef) which were used not only to supply the presidios but also to trade with passing ships against needed manufactured articles. Several factors favored mission development: the missions had unlimited land at their disposal; their Indian converts constituted an abundant labor force; and their padres were talented managers who enjoyed Crown priority in obtaining seeds, plants, implements, and other supplies. Furthermore, they exceeded the pueblos and presidios in numbers. By the end of Spanish rule, the missions were substantial food-producing centers, attending to the needs of the province as well as their own.

The pueblos failed to develop into the thriving, self-supporting agricultural communities based on individual land ownership which had been envisaged by the Crown. For one thing, the Crown recruited settlers from a destitute class of people on the Sinaloa and Sonora frontier. These people lacked the skills, the drive, the substantial means, and the social acceptance to develop into independent farmers. For another thing, the Crown so regulated settler affairs that it stifled much of their initiative in managing their own enterprises. Only a small proportion of settlers developed into enterprising farmers owning their own lands. Many of them relied on the Indians, who farmed their fields for a one-third or one-half share of the produce. Contrary to the imperial design, the Crown further undercut pueblo development by giving the missions priority in supplying foodstuffs to the presidios. The pueblo settlers were simply too handicapped by circumstances to improve their status. Like the presidios, the pueblos went into economic eclipse after 1800.

Land

The Crown showed great care in distributing its California lands. It claimed absolute title to all the territory. It recognized the Indians as owners of the land they used for subsistence, but exercised its prerogative in disposing of the remaining land for Spanish-type settlements. The Crown took possession only of the presidio sites and the adjoining lands set aside for the royal ranchos which supplied horses, other livestock, and crops for the military. It assigned to the missions lands which the padres were to hold in trust for the Indians until they could take them over as individual citizens. When the mission and presidio were converted to pueblos, or when pueblos were formed outright, Indian and Spanish settlers, as pueblo citizens, were assigned lots as follows: each settler received a house lot in the pueblo proper and four field lots in the outlying areas. Other areas became the plaza, common lands for the use of all settlers, reserve lands for Crown use, and open lands for new lots and fields. The settlers received formal title to their lots only after they had cultivated crops and met other prescribed conditions. This was the nearest approach the Crown took toward private land ownership in California.

The Crown's land scheme was implemented only to a limited extent. The padres and comandantes, although they had the authority to do so, rarely granted lands to Indians and settlers in anticipation of mission and presidio conversion to pueblos. In the pueblos themselves only a few settlers fulfilled Crown requirements for formal land title. Many settlers who abandoned or failed to cultivate and to fulfill other requirements forfeited their land claims to the Crown. In Los Angeles, the largest pueblo, a small portion of settlers—perhaps no more than two dozen—owned outright title to their farm lots, while the remainder farmed on the commons, rented their land, or worked for others as tenants. Provincial authorities strictly followed formal procedures in assigning lands but were lax in observing land boundaries, so that the mission, presidios, and pueblos often extended their boundaries well beyond the limits of their original grants. Most missions had sizable landholdings. Mission San Fernando had 50 square leagues (206,500 acres or 350 square miles), and Mission San Juan Capistrano was even larger. The missions had a virtual monopoly of the land, especially in proportion to the presidio and pueblo settlements.

Since pueblo growth was the keystone in royal economic policy, the Crown took a dim view of making large land grants to individual settlers who wished to develop ranchos beyond pueblo areas. It regarded rancho grants as detrimental on several counts: such isolated ranchos would be difficult to defend from Indian attacks; they would invite potential quarrels between rancheros and neighboring mission padres over land and cattle rights; and the Crown could expect little productive enterprise from the ranchos—all of which later proved true. Nevertheless, the Crown succumbed to pressure and made such land grants, usually to retired soldiers for their subsistence as rewards for long military service, rather than to enterprising settlers for profit-making enterprises. It issued these lands as provisional grants, conveying temporary possessory title, not title of permanent ownership. Actually these grants were little more than grazing permits intended for the use of the grantee during his lifetime, although in a few instances they passed on to his heirs. During Spanish rule no more than 30 grants were issued to California settlers, and many of these reverted to Crown control after the grantee's death. The rancho lands were located mostly outside the mission, presidio, and pueblo areas. At least half of them were in the Los Angeles vicinity.

The Crown, then, defeated its intent by its own actions in distributing the vast royal domain. It allocated lots to pueblo settlers in a fashion so restricted that it retarded their private enterprises. It made more grants to retired soldiers than to young and ambitious settlers whose private enterprises could have contributed far more to the economic development of the province. In assigning such large grants to the missions, it laid the foundations for the missions' primacy in the provincial economy.

Agriculture

Livestock was the most conspicuous feature of agricultural development. Cattle and horses brought from New Spain with the early expeditions (Portolá in 1769 and Anza in 1775) were allocated among the missions and pueblos, where they multiplied with such rapidity that great herds roamed wild on the interior ranges. After 1800 several thousands were killed annually to prevent the ruin of range forage by overgrazing—an early version of Spanish conservation. A large mission had as many as 10,000 cattle and horses and 12,000 sheep grazing on outlying open ranges and managed by Indian men and boys. Indians were particularly skilled as *vaqueros* ("cowboys"). Cattle were rounded up twice annually for the *rodeo* ("roundup") where they were branded for identification. Cattle slaughters to satisfy the insatiable Indian demand for meat were weekly affairs. One padre reported an Indian consumed 16 pounds of meat daily—probably an exaggerated figure but indicative of the Indian's heavy meat diet. Horses and mules were used as saddle, pack, and work animals.

The missions raised varied crops from imported seeds and plants. The padres developed orchards for oranges and other fruits; gardens of beans, corn, peas, and other vegetables; and vineyards for table and wine grapes—the imported European grape (presumably Spanish) of unknown species became the famous Mission grape. They planted extensive fields of grain, notably wheat and barley, as staples for the Indian converts. In later decades they produced limited amounts of cotton, flax, hemp, and silk fibers to supplement shorn wool for cloth and blanket manufacture. Meanwhile they suffered occasional setbacks from droughts, poisonous plants which killed livestock, and locusts which ravaged crops. Governor Sola wrote in 1816 of the extensive damage done to orchard and field crops by grasshoppers and squirrels.

The raising of grain illustrates the crude methods used for crop production. In planting, the Indians used a plow made from a crooked tree limb, sometimes with an iron plate attached, and pulled by men or animals. Seed was then sown in the plowed furrows and covered by dragging tree branches over it. In the harvest, Indian women plucked the ripened grains from the stalks and deposited them in wicker baskets carried on their backs. Grain was threshed by dumping it into an acre-wide circular flat area, where it was beaten by the hooves of 75 to 100 horses driven over it by vaqueros. The threshed grain was then stacked on one side and thrown into the air with wooden shovels so that the breeze could blow off the chaff and stalk, allowing only the grain kernels to fall onto the cleared ground. Some missions ground grain to flour by using a draft animal which hauled a rolling stone over grain scattered on a flat surface. San Fernando mission and one or two others built crude water-powered mills for grinding grain. Inefficient as these methods may seem, the mission had abundant Indian labor to produce substantial amounts of grain for their needs and for those of the presidio.

Agricultural activities figured importantly in "civilizing" the Indian converts. The padres used food to attract such Indians into the missions, and the daily three square meals to keep them there. They were disconcerted by the Indian subsistence on "all kinds of unclean things," like plant roots, insects, lizards, rats, and other small game. They were determined to replace the native diet with the more civilized one of beef, cereals, and other cultivated foods. The padres were also assigned the task of training Indians to be independent farmers. As it turned out, these farmer–Indians helped perpetuate the mission's existence long after its intended demise.

Manufacturing and Mining

Manufacturing was confined mostly to processing raw materials into finished goods for local consumption. The first artisans were among the presidial soldiers—the armorers, blacksmiths, and carpenters—and the talented padres. In the 1770's the Crown began recruiting sailors to teach Indians handicrafts; when the sailors proved inadequate, it sent skilled artisans in the 1790's to train the Indians. Before long, Indian artisans, operating out of mission shops, engaged in blacksmithing, carpentry, masonry, and other trades. They made brick for construction, tile for making fire-proof roofs of missions and other buildings, and pottery for vessels and kitchenware. They tanned cattle hides for making botas (wine bags), shoes, saddles, and other leather products, and boiled cattle fats in big pots into tallow for candles. On crude looms they spun and wove coarse blankets and cloth. They pressed grapes for wines, utilizing cement cisterns for fermentation, and dried grapes for the raisins used in cooking. San Fernando mission produced plowshares, beartraps for protecting livestock herds, hammers and nails for construction, and other ironware. The missions were virtually the only manufacturing centers of the province. Presidial and pueblo settlers engaged in a few home manufactures to serve the needs of family and neighbors only.

Mining was practically nonexistent, although precious minerals were found. The padres reported the presence of mercury in 1769, of silver and gold later. A presidio soldier (Ignacio Ortega) actually mined silver near Gavilan Peak after 1800. Though Spain produced at this time most of the world's gold, silver, and mercury (the chemical catalyst for processing both), the Crown failed to develop California's vast mineral wealth. The reasons are not hard to find, though the Spanish miner had no equal in ferreting out precious metals. The military land explorations did not penetrate the Sierra, which contained great gold deposits. The padres, who collected some gold for mission coffers, had little desire to publicize mineral discoveries which would invite rampant settler exploitation and disrupt their missionary endeavor. Historians have speculated that a Spanish gold rush would have secured the Crown's control of California. The prospect, however, was unlikely, for the Crown in these declining years of empire had little capacity for further developing her northernmost province.

Trade

Trade in the province never developed much beyond its narrow frontier limits. Spanish mercantilist policy called for the exchange of the colonies' raw materials for home or foreign-made manufactures from Spain, which would produce royal revenues, protect home industries, and perpetuate the Crown's trade monopoly. California suffered from Crown policy in several ways. The Crown's program for subsidizing the initial trade of the province came to a virtual halt when government ships carrying needed foodstuffs and manufactures from San Blas to the northern province arrived only at long irregular intervals, leaving the northern province to fend for itself. California would likely have benefited from the great reforms of Carlos III for stimulating the imperial economy (free trade for Spanish America and tariff duties on foreign traders), but New Spain and the northern province were specifically excluded from these. The Crown prohibited the California province from dealing with foreign traders, presumably to tie California into New Spain's trade orbit and to minimize the risk of foreign seizure of this remote province. The province did not produce enough surplus raw materials to share in the benefits of the Crown's trade protection. What products it did produce competed with New Spain, which enjoyed a special priority in the imperial trade. California was clearly an orphan in the imperial trade scheme.

The sea otter trade illustrates well the workings of the Spanish mercantilist system. This highly lucrative trade, first developed by the Russians around 1750, centered in the North Pacific. Here trade ships acquired the animal skins from the Aleut Indian hunters at their Alaskan bases and went on to China, where otter skins were exchanged for silks, spices, and other luxury goods for sale in Europe. (The Chinese mandarins prized the soft, lustrous, warm furs for headwear and garment decoration.) The Spanish discovered this trade opportunity through their Pacific Coast expeditions in the 1770's (see Chapter 2), and the Crown granted a monopolistic concession to a Spanish merchant to develop the triangular trade between New Spain, California, and China via the Philippines. In California, furs were acquired by settlers, soldiers, and padres through their Indian workers, the padres serving as royal agents under the governor's supervision. The trade flourished in the early 1790's—Governor Fages collected around 2000 skins annually—until the merchant–sponsor ceased operations.

The arrival of Yankee and English merchant–traders shortly afterwards opened new trade outlets for the Californians. By this time the quest for the sea otter extended from Alaskan waters to the California coast. Some foreign traders made landfalls on the California offshore islands and in isolated mainland coves, primarily to escape detection by Spanish authorities while processing otter skins and obtaining needed supplies and repairs. For a decade after 1803 a group of Yankee ship captains and Russian fur traders engaged in a highly profitable joint venture, using Aleut Indians from the Alaskan area to exploit the abundant sea otter field off the California coast. When the Russian American Fur Company established its base at Fort Ross above San Francisco (1812), it took the trade from the Americans. Several padres, soldiers, and settlers cooperated with these foreign traders, giving rise to a thriving contraband trade in which otter skins were exchanged for foodstuffs and manufactures. Governor Sola levied duties on the trade carried on by the missions with foreign traders to replenish provincial revenues unpaid by the Crown in the declining years of Spanish rule. Apart from that, California failed to gain substantial benefits.

Thus, the Crown, in these various ways, denied Californians opportunities to develop the private enterprises and trade outlets so important for the economic development of the province.

Social Order

The People

By the end of Spanish rule, California comprised two distinct societies: Spanish and Indian. Spanish California contained a population of approximately 3000 souls. The Spanish referred to their people as the *gente de razón* ("people of reason"), their way of classifying people as civilized or barbaric. They included *peninsulares* ("men of the peninsula"–Spain itself), *crillos* (American-born whites), *mestizos* (Spanish–Indian unions), and converted Indians. Such class distinctions were loose, especially in frontier areas like California, since crillos and mestizos had some fusion of Negro blood and many crillos also had Indian blood. Economic status was more important, although some settlers maintained class pretensions. Foreigners numbered 13, most of them American sailors who had jumped ship and were allowed to live in the province. Of the full-blooded Indians living in the area of the Spanish settlements, some 20,000 were neophytes (converts) living within or near the 20 missions, and another 50,000 were gentiles (pagans) living in the Indian villages of the so-called mission strip.

California's population grew from the natural increase of the first settlers, primarily those in the Portolá, Rivera, and Anza expeditions in the first decade of the 1770's, and the small groups of settlers and convicts who immigrated there in the 1790's. Civilian emigration to California practically ceased after 1800, while military personnel were sent sporadically to the end of Spanish rule. Spanish California, thus, had a homogeneous Hispanic population and the mark of a closed society.

Indian society—or more appropriately, societies—consisted of the remaining Indian population, those gentiles living beyond the Spanish settlements. Little is known about them owing to the absence of records. They probably numbered around 250,000 in 1821, and they presumably continued to live as did their ancestors. Their numbers are mute testimony to the failure of the Crown to convert the vast majority of California Indians into Spanish subjects according to the imperial design.

Missions

The missions were the principal settlements of Spanish California. By the end of Spanish rule there were 20 of them. They were located roughly a daylong horseback ride from each other and linked by a winding dirt road (El Camino Real—"the royal highway") in a 400-mile chain stretching from Santa Rosa to San Diego. Each mission contained a large open plaza enclosed by a tier of buildings: the chapel, shops for various crafts, and living quarters for the padres, military guard, guests, and sometimes Indian neophytes. Outside the mission compound were dormitory or hut dwellings for the neophytes. Beyond were extensive lands, which were divided into cultivated areas for garden and field crops and into pasturage for livestock.

The mission was essentially a theocratic community structured along the lines of a feudal institution. It had usually one to three padres and a military guard of five to ten soldiers. The padres ruled their mission domain much like the lord of a medieval manor, ministering to their Indian converts who ranged in number from about a hundred in the smaller missions to around 1,500 in the larger missions. Indians were first

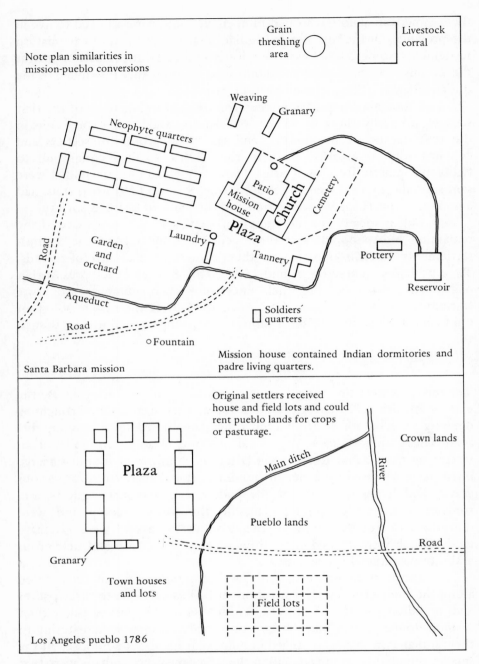

FIGURE 5 Basic Plan of California Missions and Pueblos

lured into the missions by gifts of food and trinkets, and later by military roundups in distant rancherias.

Once in the mission the Indians rarely could leave it, and the padres were their absolute masters. They were forced to give up their native ways for the austere life, communal ways, and disciplined rule of the padres. Families lived in guarded thatched huts, while unmarried boys and girls—and in some missions, married men and women also—slept in locked segregated dormitories. They ate the Spanish diet of cultivated foods (primarily beef and grain staples), although at times, especially during famines, they were allowed to seek native foods, such as acorns and small game, outside the missions. They were put to work farming crops, raising livestock, manufacturing articles, and performing other menial tasks for support of the mission. The padres selected a talented Indian neophyte to serve as *mayor domo* ("foreman") for work projects and as *alcalde* ("mayor") for governing Indian affairs, but in a way that would sustain their control over the Indians rather than promote Indian self-support or self-rule. The mission was a self-supporting agrarian community.

The padres ruled their Indian subjects with strict paternalism. They played the role of father as well as spiritual patriarch, teaching their Indian "children" Spanish ways and supervising their domestic affairs. When not at work, the Indians were at school learning the Catholic catechism or in the chapel praying. This busy daily routine was broken only by the weekly Sabbath, which was devoted to religious service and rest, and occasional holidays for celebrating the feast days and birthdays of the saints. Indians were punished for violations of rules, often by confinement in the stocks or flogging for minor infractions. Such penalties were considered harsh even by standards of the day. Though the Indians were generally docile, there was always a group of deviants, renegades, and deserters who caused constant trouble. The rigid rule of the padres was tempered by allowing the Indians to indulge in gambling games or gathering acorns outside the mission.

In the light of the imperial objective, the California mission was only a qualified success. The padres under the dedicated, talented leadership of Serra and Lasuen overcame great obstacles in establishing and maintaining thriving missions, which still survive as cherished monuments. These missions accomplished their frontier role of occupying the land and converting a portion, though only a small one, of the Indian population to Spanish ways. Most of the gentile Indians, however, were neither converted nor organized into productive pueblos. Furthermore, the presence of so many missions long after the ten years during which they were supposed to have completed their task is stark evidence of their failure to achieve the Crown's long-range goal. Instead, the padres made their Indian converts dependent on the mission. This preserved the mission as it was, but blocked its intended transformation into a pueblo of Indian citizens.

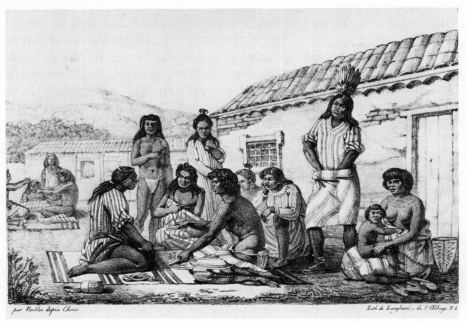

Indian neophytes playing traditional gambling games at the San Francisco mission. The padres disapproved of such games, but allowed neophytes to indulge in their "pagan pleasures." The striped wool cloth was woven at the mission. Drawn from life during the Rezanov Russian Expedition, 1806.

Presidios

The presidios were the political and military centers of the province. The four presidios (San Francisco, Monterey, Santa Barbara, and San Diego) were located at strategic points along the California coast, forming a sort of backbone for the California settlements. The presidio was originally established as a military post comprising soldiers and their families. Later it was augmented with Spanish and Indian settlers to take on the character of a pueblo. The Crown encouraged this trend by providing all presidios with municipal government by 1794, thereby elevating them to the status of presidio pueblos. By 1821 the presidio pueblos numbered 700 in population. The military continued to be the chief agency for governing the settlements and defending the province.

While the presidio pueblos eventually assumed the form of civilian settlements, they continued to retain their military character. Compared to the other settlements, the presidio population had a greater proportion of white settlers to native Indians, for the military tended to be largely crillos and mestizos. Life in the presidios was characterized as "one continuous round of hospitality and social amenities," punctuated by frequent social affairs, sporting events, and religious festivities. Both civilian and military settlers lived off their lands raising livestock and crops. They relied extensively on Indians to do the field work, either as tenant farmers or *vaqueros* ("cowboys"), or on convict laborers from the local jail. The military garrison depended on food allotments contributed primarily by the missions, which were paid in military warrants that were rarely honored by the Crown—an obligation the padres did not always accept without protest. The Crown's neglect of California affairs after 1800 worked a hardship on the presidio settlers, who were reduced to a destitute and impoverished lot by the end of Spanish rule.

Pueblos

The pueblos were regarded as the least important of the Spanish settlements, although they contained the greatest number of settlers. The three pueblos totaled by 1821 approximately 930 people (Los Angeles 615, San Jose 240, and Branciforte 75). The pueblos—at least the two larger ones—had a central plaza or public square that served as a marketplace and as a center for religious and social celebrations. Fronting the plaza were the church, public buildings for housing the municipal government and the military garrison, and several homes of settlers. The pueblo jurisdiction extended over four square leagues, which were divided into house lots and farm lots for individual settlers. The remaining public lands were shared by settlers for pasturage, rented for municipal revenue, reserved for Crown use, or maintained as vacant suburbs. The pueblo land pattern clearly reflected the Crown's desire to develop pueblos as self-supporting agrarian communities.

The pueblo, which came into existence so promisingly under

protection of the Crown, developed slowly on its own meager resources. The settlers were generally drawn from a poverty-stricken class of mestizos in the Sonora and Sinaloa frontier areas. Besides their house and farm lots they received the necessary implements for raising crops and livestock, as well as wages and rations for two years. By 1800 the pueblos appear to have reached their peak, the Los Angeles pueblo ranking behind only the San Gabriel mission in the production of crops and livestock. However, the trade activity so vital to the development of such agricultural communities was limited because of the missions, which produced more and therefore dominated what commerce existed. This restricted the natural growth of the pueblos. As a consequence, the pueblos failed to develop into the thriving communities based on individual land ownership which had been planned by the Crown.

Ranchos

The ranchos, which were destined to be an important feature in California society, were less significant in Spanish California. A formidable institution in other parts of the Spanish empire, the rancho in California was only a simple cattle ranch, which sometimes had, in addition to herds of cattle and horses, cultivated fields and a substantial ranch house. The rancho developed from land grants issued to retired soldiers for the use of the grantee during his lifetime (see above). Only a few of the 30 grants issued during Spanish rule developed into substantial cattle ranchos. They were mostly on lands outside the missions, pueblos, and presidios, and at least half of them were in the Los Angeles vicinity. Among the surviving ranchos were those of the original 1784 grantees: Dominguez (74,000 acres), Nieto (150,000 acres), and Verdugo (36,000 acres) around Los Angeles. Other ranchos were those of Pico near San Diego (1795), Yorba near Santa Ana (1810), and Peralta around Oakland (1820). These few grantees developed the basis of the private rancho, utilizing Indian labor to work the cattle, horses, and crops for its subsistence.

Rancherias

The Spanish called Indian villages *rancherias*, a term which has survived to this day. We know little about them, yet they were the most numerous settlements in the province. A rancheria numbered from about 50 to several thousand people. It generally comprised a collection of hut dwellings with a roundhouse or its equivalent for public affairs, and perhaps other community buildings. The gentiles living in the rancherias generally followed the native ways of their ancestors. Community affairs were run by the *cacique* (Spanish for "chief"), priest, and shaman. Their native ways were altered to the extent of their contacts with the white invaders. As was customary throughout the empire, the governor and military authorities dealt with the caciques of rancherias within reach of Crown authority.

The Indians

Spain in bringing civilization to the Indians and saving their souls saw itself as the Indians' saviour and protector. Crown policy focused on mission conversion of Indians and teaching them enough to become pueblo citizens. It even stipulated Indian rights of land ownership, fair wages for private employment, and other privileges—a far more benevolent policy than that of other nations. We have seen Crown policy implemented in the missions, presidios, and pueblos to fulfill the imperial design. Let us consider the impact of the Spanish occupation upon the Indians. Anthropologist Sherburne Cook gives us the following picture based on careful calculations.

The most profound impact came from the mission system. The number of mission Indian residents generally increased until 1800 and then diminished, usually averaging about 20,000. The continuing conversion of gentiles masks the picture, for Indian converts actually suffered from a declining birth rate and excessive deaths. In the early years well over half the Indians died in epidemics of smallpox and other diseases, although succeeding generations became more immune to these dreaded scourges. The padres tended to attribute such epidemics to God's will or His "strange ways," rather than to unsanitary conditions in the crowded mission compounds. Neophytes also suffered from the effects of mission confinement, homesickness, diet, labor, punishment, and sexual restraints, which combined to sap their strength. Many fled from the missions, but they did not find former ways adaptable. Nor did they always receive a friendly reception in the rancherias—gentiles on a number of occasions cut them to pieces. In an 1807 incident only 30 of over 100 mission escapees survived a slaughter at the hands of gentiles. Indian fugitives increased in the final years of Spanish rule—over 4000 in 1817. The mission toll of Indian lives was high; the negative effect on living Indians was lasting.

The Indians fell victim to Spanish occupation outside the missions, as well. In the presidios, pueblos, and ranchos, they worked as domestic servants and field laborers for soldiers and settlers, and as gang labor for constructing roads, bridges, and other public projects. Crown policy of wage payments was soon ignored. The Indians were consigned to a forced labor system that amounted to slavery. In rancherias of the mission strip, Indians were prey to padres in quest of converts, and to soldiers and settlers seeking women and barter trade. Neophyte fugitives and military expeditions searching for fugitives and captives also severely disrupted community life. More deadly was exposure to venereal disease, especially syphilis, transmitted by soldiers and settlers, which was often fatal to the Indians. Indians in the distant rancherias also suffered heavily from diseases carried by fugitives. Military expeditions claimed relatively few lives (240 gentiles killed in 11 of 29 expeditions during Spanish rule) as they often found deserted rancherias in the course of their advance. The gentiles of the interior thus did well to keep apart from the Spanish and preserve their native ways.

From the Indian standpoint, then, the Spanish impact was devastating. Before the Spanish arrival the Indians were well adapted to their natural environment and lived in relative harmony with their neighbors—perhaps more so than any other Indians or white group. The Spanish substituted alien ways to which the Indian was simply unable to adapt—no more so than white men could adapt to Indian ways. The Spanish reduced the Indians to bondage, decimated their numbers, demoralized their spirit, and thus undermined their life style. In utilizing neophytes in missionary and military expeditions to secure converts, fugitives, and captives, the Spanish provoked for the first time violent warfare among the Indian tribes, thus breaking down their ancient system of intertribal adjustment. The padres, however well meaning their missionary efforts, failed to carry out the Crown's long-range policy of training converts to become pueblo settlers. The governor and the military failed to protect Indians as prescribed by Crown policy. Yet the Spanish authorities displayed a humanitarian attitude (attributed to their religious conviction) toward their Indian subjects which was conspicuously absent in their Mexican and American successors. Certainly they showed little of the systematic abusive exploitation of the Indians for reasons of self-interest and personal gain which was characteristic of the Mexicans, and even more so of the early Americans.

The Family

The family concept was essential to Spain's ideal of God's kingdom on earth. It was expressed through the fatherhood theme in the sacred hierarchy of Spanish society. The King at the top and the family patriarch at the bottom each managed his "family flock" in God's name. It was perpetuated by Crown decrees that embodied in secular law church doctrines dealing with family affairs and marriage relations. Spanish law held the father to be lord and master of his family. His wife and children were beholden to his authority, as he was accountable to Crown and Church. People's lives were governed by the prevailing code of tradition and order, which emphasized conventional and respectable ways—at least outwardly. Personal happiness focused on fulfilling one's obligations to family and society for God's glory.

The family institution in Spanish California was a frontier version of Spain's model. The governor, padres, and family patriarch performed their roles in maintaining the family institution. The governor or his agents (presidio comandantes and pueblo comissionados) kept surveillance over settler families, sometimes personally inspecting their homes to praise or blame their conduct. The padres served as family counselors and father confessors. They usually exerted strong influence in family affairs, especially in the upbringing of children and in approving marriages. As family patriarch, the father commanded the household. The mother bore the burdens of homemaking and child-raising, and the children remained in the parents' custody even in early adult years.

Family relations were close and disciplined. The military families were representative. From meager records we draw a picture of duty-minded men, devout wives, and chaste daughters, and of their sedate dress and sober manners. Juan Alvarado and Mariano Vallejo, sons of military families, told of their disciplined upbringing and the strong family bonds created by filial obedience and devotion. Daily life was marked by morning mass, assigned work, siestas (afternoon naps), and family meals with prayers. People lived by simple and conventional rules. They accorded respect to the elderly and to their superiors, such as personal salutations to churchmen and public officials. Their humdrum existence was enlivened by family fiestas or by numerous public festivities (usually in town plazas) in celebration of religious events and birthdays of church saints.

Culture

Education

Illiteracy was widespread in the province. Except for the governor, military officers, and padres, only a few settlers could read and write. The personal interest of the governors (notably Borica and Sola) resulted in the establishment in some pueblos and presidios of primary schools for teaching children reading, writing, arithmetic, and Catholic dogma. Bancroft describes the classroom scene: Children took their seat after kissing the soldier–teacher's hand and receiving his bellowed permission to sit. Each child read or recited his lessons aloud on his feet. Sometimes they were rewarded with sweetmeats, other times they were punished by rod blows on the hand or iron-pointed whip lashes on the bare back for simple infractions like laughing, spilling ink, or not knowing the Catholic doctrine. The enlightened Governor Sola presented Spanish law books (including the liberal 1812 Spanish Constitution) and copies of *Don Quixote* to favored boys (Alvarado, Castro, Pico, and Vallejo among them), but such rewards were exceptions in the frontier province.

Literature

Literature was meager. Two representative literary works were among the few circulating in the frontier province: Miguel Cervantes's *Don Quixote* (1605 and 1615) and Francisco Palou's *Life of Serra* (Mexico, 1787). Cervantes's imcomparable classic (as Chapman tells us) caught the "epic spirit of idealism" reminiscent of Homer's *Odyssey*. It provides insight into the Spanish mentality and makes for delightful reading even today. Palou's biography praises his beloved padre–presidente's noble character and great achievements, passing over his complaining temperament and giving him credit for accomplishments more appropriately due Portolá and others. The governors and padres might possess law and church tomes and a few other books; otherwise, libraries were nonexistent.

Foreign visitors who wrote accounts of their voyages constituted an important part of California literature. Notable were the journals of the French scientist–navigator Comte de La Pérouse (Paris, 1797), the English naval commander George Vancouver (London, 1798), and the American China trader William Shaler (Philadelphia, 1808). Their journals stimulated the interest of their countrymen in the distant Spanish California province, as James Cook's earlier journal (1784) had attracted American and European interest to the North Pacific and the China trade. They add considerably to our knowledge of Spanish California.

Religion

Catholicism was a religious affair of state. Catholic doctrine was based on the seven sacraments: baptism, confirmation, extreme unction, matrimony, penance, holy orders, and the Eucharist or Lord's Supper—religious ceremonies ordained by Jesus Christ and recognized by the Roman Catholic and Eastern Orthodox churches. The Spanish Catholic ethic emphasized pious conduct and loyalty to King, Church, and Family. The governor and the padres were partners in preserving Catholicism against the inroads of Protestant and heretical beliefs. They made public examples of serious crimes, especially of the seven deadly sins (adultery, anger, gluttony, lust, sloth, pride, and usury). Governor Sola ordered a widow involved in an illicit love affair "corrected for her reform and as a public example"; her hair was cut, one eyebrow shaved, and after a public display at mass she was assigned to a family of good reputation. A boy convicted of sodomy with a mule was hanged and the bodies of both were burned before public assembly as a purification rite. Vallejo recalled that a lazy beggar could never settle down at any of the presidios, for the military and church officials kept after the slothful and corrupt. Soldiers, settlers, and Indian converts were obliged to attend church masses on Sundays and on the birthdays of church saints in the parish churches or chapels of the pueblos and presidios. The combined efforts of church and state undoubtedly helped sustain religious feeling and strict morality in the frontier province.

Despite its restrictions on daily life and personal conduct, religion offered settlers a secure feeling about God and solace in a troubled world. For example, Concepción Arguello, the daughter of the San Francisco presidio comandante, was involved in a celebrated courtship with Count Nikolai Rezanov, a visiting agent of the Russian American Fur Company (1806), who apparently intended to combine matrimony with business to realize his dream of a Russian California. Though she was Roman Catholic and he was Eastern Orthodox, the couple secured the blessings of her parents and of the padres for their marriage, pending approval of the Russian Czar and of the Pope in Rome. Rezanov died on his return trip to Russia. The 16-year-old Concepción, not hearing from her lover, retired to a convent where she came to be known for her gentle kindness and charitable works. She did not learn of her lover's fate until decades later. Her tragic love affair is considered the most poignant romance to come out of Hispanic California.

SUMMARY

Spain implemented in her California territory an extension of her imperial design. The Crown undertook the California project to extend its control in the northwest area of its great empire in America, originally to establish title by discovery and later to secure the region by occupation. In occupying the area, the Crown sought to establish a Spanish province that would achieve the two-fold objective of defense for the northwest borderlands and of revenues for the royal treasury. After 52 years of rule, the Crown transformed the barren outlying areas into a frontier province with a line of well-established settlements. It developed these settlements in the 1770's with considerable investment of men, money, and supplies, but dissipated this effort after 1800 by neglecting to provide for adequate maintenance of the settlements. Consequently the settlements deteriorated instead of developing into thriving communities. In fine, the Crown realized its primary end of defense but fell short of its secondary aim of revenue.

The California that Spain developed was essentially an authoritarian society based on feudal institutions. Herein lies the key to judging the extent to which Spain achieved her design for the northwest province. The Crown was able to overcome formidable obstacles to discovery and occupation through paternalistic policies and arbitrary rule by talented leaders like Galvez, Bucareli, Portolá, Neve, Serra, Lasuen, and others. It was able to achieve settlements through the effective performance of its two frontier agencies, the mission and the presidio, under the forceful rule of the padres and military.

The same elements that account for the Crown's successes also contributed to the failings of the imperial design. Absorbed by possessory instincts, the Crown continued to pursue outdated mercantilist policies whereby only Spanish merchants could conduct the commerce of the empire. However, only her European and American rivals were capable of conducting the sort of trade that was so vital to the natural growth of the California settlements.

Within the province the military and the padres continued to pursue their authoritarian rule. Consequently they perpetuated the frontier-oriented presidio and missions and did little to advance the development of free enterprise in self-supporting pueblos, as was their assigned task. Crown policies failed to bring about the emigration of Spanish settlers and the conversion of Indians into Spanish citizens, both so important to the development of the pueblos. When the Crown became preoccupied with European affairs after 1800, it deprived the California province of its paternal benevolence. Contrary to the imperial design, the missions thrived in this isolation, while the presidios and pueblos declined. The paternalistic Crown policies that had served well in establishing the settlements proved, eventually, to be restrictive, and even repressive, of their natural growth.

The real significance of the imperial design lies in the heritage Spain left for her Mexican and American successors. The Spaniard passed on to them his tradition of custom and law, a land pattern of large acreage under the control of a few, a perplexing Indian problem, and a large number of Spanish–Indian people. All of these elements were to be interwoven into the fabric of California society under Mexican and, later, American rule. California's first contact with western civilization was thus of a Latin, rather than an Anglo-Saxon, character.

Overleaf: Rodeo scene on a California rancho, from a painting by Vischer.

III   Mexican California

After Spanish rule in New Spain was overthrown in a violent revolution, the newly established Mexican Republic experienced a continuing struggle over the order of the new society. For the next half-century, conservative groups sought to establish a centralist society along Spanish lines, in bitter opposition to liberal groups that attempted to set up a federalist society patterned after the United States. California's development under Mexican rule accurately reflected the changing status of these conflicting conservative and liberal groups. The decline of the padres and the rise of the rancheros and merchants were evidence of the profound changes that marked the transition from the Spanish order to that introduced by the newly arriving Americans, who were eventually to conquer the land.

4 The Mexican Transformation
5 Mexican California Society

4 The Mexican Transformation

THE SETTING

The Republican Plan

When the call for Mexican Independence was issued in 1810, New Spain became embroiled in violent revolutionary struggle that extended over the next decade. The outcome of this bitter conflict was the tenuous establishment of the Mexican Republic in 1821. With the removal of the viceroy, the entire royal hierarchy collapsed. With it went the complicated system of loyalties which had joined together classes of people and distant provinces under the control of the small ruling Spanish minority. The long drawn-out struggle left the Mexican people badly divided into opposing groups. Various factions of the upper, middle, and lower class were pitted against each other. The provinces were isolated more than ever from control of the central government in the national capital. For the next half-century, the Mexican people experienced the throes of conflict between rival groups for control of the new society.

These many-sided conflicts centered primarily on the struggles between conservative and liberal groups to establish an order of society which would best protect their respective interests. The conservatives generally comprised the great landowners, who possessed haciendas (large agrarian estates) and extensive livestock ranchos; the wealthy merchants, who held monopolistic trade franchises; and high officials of the Church. These people were generally crillos residing on great landed estates in rural areas or in mansions in Mexico City. They had inherited the ancient privileges and aristocratic status of the Spanish ruling minority and they sought to conserve many of the Spanish feudal institutions in modified form. They envisaged a strong central government, even along monarchist lines, that would protect their property and capital and preserve their privileged status. These conservatives strove to retain an authoritarian structure in order to maintain the orderly society that they had known under Spain.

The liberals included a wide assortment of small landowners and small merchants in scattered communities of the provinces, along with the professional men, shopkeepers, artisans, and mechanics in the cities, as well as many of the lower clergy in the Church. They were generally crillos or mestizos. They were often opposed to each other, but were united in their opposition to the conservative elite. They cooperated in efforts to remove the special privileges and oppressive remains of Spanish institutions that for so long had restricted the opportunities to improve their economic position and social status. The liberals favored a federal or decentralized government in which the distribution of power between the national and state governments would more effectively represent their interests. They sought to establish a competitive capitalistic economy that would provide greater opportunities for developing their enterprises. Such a system based on a democratic structure would promote the sort of free economic society they admired in the United States.

Involved with both groups were the Indians and the military. The Indian population comprised the peons or servile class, including domestic servants and the labor force of the haciendas, ranchos, mines, and, in frontier areas, neophytes in the missions. They were, for the most part, landless and illiterate people who were extensively exploited and easily led by their *patron*, or landlord, whether of conservative or liberal leanings. They were the unfortunate pawns in the seesaw struggles between the conservatives and the liberals.

The military played a special role in the new Mexican society.

They had emerged from the revolutionary struggles as scattered army groups led by *caudillos* ("military chieftains" or "strong men"), who maintained leadership with the support of a tight group of followers. In a society where citizens lived with a tradition of obedience to authority and were untrained and inexperienced at self-rule, powerful caudillos were able to impose their authority. Such men asserted political leadership by the force of their personalities, backed by military support from their own troops and those of other caudillos. The leading caudillos were the brokers in the contests between the conservatives and the liberals, cooperating with whichever group best served their personal interests.

In the course of the nation after independence, conservative and liberal groups played politics within the constitutional framework and through their political parties and governmental system. When circumstances made it feasible, however, they would readily do away with such legal processes and resort to the *pronunciamiento*, or proclamation, of a favored caudillo in order to protect their interests and achieve their aims. The proclamation was a plan which declared the aims and principles of a leader in a rebellion. It constituted his justification for seizing the government by force and it usually included a program of action for the new government. While the proclamation was always issued by a caudillo, it embodied either a conservative or liberal program for the purpose of winning popular support. As Leslie Simpson points out, the proclamation may be regarded as the fundamental constitution of Mexico, for every government since independence has been established by military force and justified by a proclamation. In a real sense, then, the proclamation became the focal point in the contests for control of the government.

In the first half-century after independence, conservatives and liberals, through their caudillo champions, were to engage in a long, uncompromising struggle over their respective plans for developing a republican order of society. As they lacked experience in political self-rule and were suffering from a failing economy beset by an ancient feudal system, their struggle was predictably to be a painful one. Adding to the problem were the antics of Santa Anna, the formidable caudillo who dominated this era. During this period of Mexican rule, California was to be a faithful mirror of the fateful struggle taking place in the national capital.

DEVELOPMENT

Transition to the New Order, 1821—1824

Iturbide

On the eve of independence in 1820, a royalist officer, Colonel Agustín de Iturbide, persuaded insurgent leaders to join forces with him and break the deadlock to bring an end to the decade-long revolutionary struggle. The war-weary people quickly rallied behind a proclamation issued by Iturbide which called for the Three Guarantees: independence from Spain, supremacy of the Catholic Church, and equality for all Mexicans. Upon assuming leadership of the new nation, the ambitious Iturbide soon revealed his true colors. He dismantled the revolutionary army and transformed his constitutional monarchy into an empire, with himself installed as emperor. Shortly afterward, General Antonio de Santa Anna raised the standard of rebellion to rally insurgent generals behind his plan which proclaimed abolition of the empire, banishment of Iturbide, and establishment of a federal republic under a constitution. Iturbide was forced into exile in Europe. He later returned to Mexico to lead a counterrevolution, only to be recaptured and executed in 1824.

Governmental Affairs

In California the shift from Spanish to Mexican rule was a relatively routine affair. In 1822 Agustín Fernandez, the pompous canon of the cathedral church at Durango who was then serving as an emissary for Iturbide's government, arrived in California to effect the changeover to the new government. The eagle-crested banner of the Republic was raised in place of the royal standard of Spain. On the governor's call, each of the four presidial districts and Los Angeles pueblo selected an elector to meet in Monterey, where Governor Sola was elected as the California representative to the national congress. On Fernandez's instructions, they set up a *diputación* ("legislature"; literally "body of deputies") for the California province and elected themselves as its members! They chose Luis Arguello (Jose's son), a native Californian and the popular comandante of the San Francisco presidio, as governor. They made the *ayuntamientos*, or town councils, in Los Angeles and San Jose pueblos into more self-governing bodies by removing the governor's commissioner and adding a secretary–treasurer and legal counsel. With the establishment of the republican form of government, Fernandez departed for Mexico, advising the Californians that they would learn the art of self-government by practice.

The new governor and the diputación displayed considerable energy in establishing the foundations of the republican order in the California territory. Under the guidance of the able Arguello, a five-point program to achieve that end soon emerged. It provided for civil government, mission secularization, land grants, Indian emancipation, and trade development. With this program the new leaders set the course of California's development during Mexican rule. They envisaged a republican order based on representative government and a capitalistic economy. They were, however, to encounter persistent difficulties in reconciling their desire for a republican society with their attachment to imperialistic traditions.

The task of establishing a civil government presented the problem of reconciling royalist tradition with the new republican ideas. At Arguello's behest, the diputación drafted a plan of government by which the governor was to exercise both civil and military powers (republicanism called for separating them), and the diputación was constituted as an advisory body, rather than a policy-making legislature. The constitutional document, issued in 1824, indicated that the Californians still had to learn the real meaning of republican ideas of the Mexican Revolution's liberal groups, who wished to convert the military–religious system into a genuine civil society. The California scheme never went into effect, for in far-off Mexico City the liberal-minded federalists had ousted Iturbide and taken over the national government.

Secularization

Mission secularization, a basic tenet of the Mexican Revolution, proved to be a thorny problem for the new republic. At the time of independence, the Catholic Church owned over half the lands in Mexico which farmers, ranchers, miners, and others wanted for their individual enterprises. In California, mission secularization was inextricably interwoven with land grants and Indian emancipation. Secularizing the missions—transferring the control of the missions from the Church to the government—was closely related to the government's plan for distributing such mission properties to settlers as large land grants, and to the Indians as small land lots. Arguello issued nine land grants of extensive lands lying between the missions to influential men for developing cattle and horse ranchos. His plan for allocating mission lands to Indians was arrested by a serious Indian revolt (1824). Convinced the Indians were not ready for emancipation, the governor worked out a compromise agreement with the padres: the government would not press its secularization plan if the padres would submit to taxation and give "loans" in the form of supplies from their well-stocked warehouses. The expedient arrangement proved successful enough to help retard secularization by a decade.

Trade

The new Mexican policy of opening trade served the double purpose of producing revenues for the government and encouraging agricultural production for enhancing the nation's wealth. The governor designated Monterey and San Diego as ports of entry for all ships and imposed duties on goods to secure revenues for support of the territorial government. Foreign traders quickly appeared on the scene, led by William Gale, agent for a Boston firm, William Hartnell, Lima-based agent for a British firm, and John Cooper, a Boston sea captain. Gale and Hartnell pioneered the trade by which assorted American and European merchandise was exchanged for California cattle hides to be used for shoe and other leather manufacture and tallow for candles. Hartnell and Cooper were the first of the resident merchants, who became the middlemen in conducting the California trading ventures. They set a style of living for later foreign traders: they became Mexican citizens (which involved embracing Catholicism and promising to obey Mexican laws), married into prominent local families, and acquired ranchos to become respected adopted sons. California's trade with the outside world had gotten off to a rousing start.

The Federalist Era, 1824–1836

The Liberal Program

By 1824 the Federalists had assumed power, elected an insurgent general as first President of Mexico, and issued a liberal constitution for the nation. The Mexican constitution, patterned after the United States model, applied the federalist principle of distributing sovereign powers between the national government and the 19 states and 3 territories. It also divided governmental powers between the executive and legislative branches at the national and state levels. The Federalists eventually

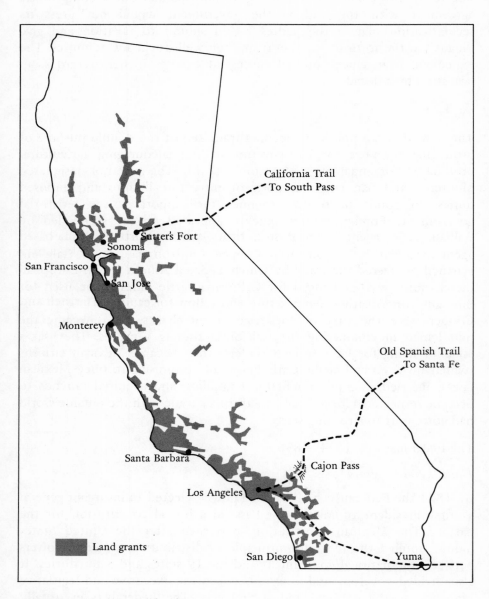

FIGURE 6 Mexican California

carried out their liberal program of confiscating Church lands for distribution among settlers and emancipated Indians, and opening foreign trade to stimulate economic development. The conservative and liberal forces were to engage in a bitter struggle over this program.

The New Elite

In California, a group of native sons filled with libertarian republican ideas gained increasing strength in California affairs. Prominent among these were: Mariano Vallejo of Sonoma, Jose Castro of San Jose, Juan Alvarado of Monterey, Jose de la Guerra of Santa Barbara, Jose Carrillo of Los Angeles, Juan Bandini and Pio Pico of San Diego. Sons of presidio officers, occupied in agrarian or mercantile enterprises, they shared an intense pride in their Spanish Californian heritage, an active interest in local and territorial politics, and a strong desire to acquire their own ranchos. Steeped in the authoritarian military tradition of their fathers, these young Californians had little understanding of Mexican revolutionary ideas until they were captivated by a fiery advocate of liberal republican ideas, Jose Padres. While serving a tour of duty in 1830 as an army inspector, the charming Padres "educated" his young disciples to the real import of the liberal republican program: secularize the missions so that their land could be allocated to the newly emancipated Indians and to prospective rancheros such as themselves. The diputación, their representative body, was the very agency to promote this program. These young Californios came to assume leadership in California's political economy.

Allied with these ranchero–politicos were the newly arrived Anglo-American merchants, who had come by sea and settled in the pueblos to become important local figures. Included in this group were: Henry Fitch in San Diego, Abel Stearns in Los Angeles, William Dana and Alfred Robinson in Santa Barbara, Cooper, Hartnell, and Thomas Larkin in Monterey, and Nathan Spear in San Francisco—men who established their niche as pioneer businessmen in their respective communities. These men, except for the British-born Hartnell, all came from Massachusetts, that center of maritime commerce whose capital city, Boston, was known at that time as the "Hub of the Universe." The merchants, except for Larkin, merged with the rancheros by acting as their business agents, marrying their daughters, becoming naturalized citizens, and acquiring ranchos which, in some instances, were more substantial than those of the Californios. By sharing common ties of friendship, marriage, and business, the resident merchants became part of the ruling elite.

Governmental Affairs

California, having less than the required 40,000 population for statehood, was set up as a territory under the rule of the national congress—like United States territories. The governors sent to California had almost a free hand in administering national programs, for there was no direct supervision from the distant national government. The governors held army rank (usually colonel or general) and served as both political chief and military comandante, thus exercising virtually dictatorial powers. During the interim between gubernatorial appointments, which became more frequent, the senior member of the diputación served as political chief, and the ranking military officer served as comandante—an important factor in California's political development. In the absence of effective constitutional checks, the governors left an imprint of personal rule upon the territory.

The first Mexican governors did not reckon with the growing influence of the ranchero-dominated diputación. Governor Jose Echeandia (1825—1831), an easy-going administrator swayed by personal whims, pressed for Indian emancipation at the expense of padre and ranchero interest. To counter padre opposition, he was forced to end his delaying tactics with the diputación in a move to enlist its support for his secularization plan. When the governor convened the long-delayed body (1830), the diputación approved his program. It then pressed its own measures for confirming land grants to rancheros and for establishing ayuntamientos or town councils, for the Monterey and Santa Barbara presidial pueblos to replace military rule with civil government.

Governor Manuel Victoria (1831), appointed during a conservative interlude in the national government, was described as a "foe of republicanism and a friend of the padres." The reactionary Victoria suspended Echeandia's plan for emancipating the Indians. He exiled prominent liberals like Padres and Carrillo, refused to convene the diputación, and recommended that the national government abolish the ayuntamientos and restore military rule. Within a short time, rebelling ranchero—politicos, led by Bandini, Carrillo, and Pico, issued a proclamation calling for Victoria's overthrow, justifying their action by his abuse of the liberal system and their "natural rights" to oust him. In the military showdown between Victoria's forces and the rebel group at Cahuenga Pass, the governor opened fire and scattered the rebels. Suddenly a daredevil rebel charged alone into Victoria's camp. In the ensuing fight, the governor was wounded, the rebel and another man were killed. This misadventure reversed the tide of battle. Victoria lost his desire to continue, retired in defeat from the field, and returned to Mexico. In the aftermath, the diputación assumed control of territorial affairs until arrival of the new governor, thereby enhancing its growing prestige.

Here was the first of California's "comic opera" revolutions, where rebel groups challenged the ruling group for control of the government in a military showdown. Eventually in these colorful affairs, uniformed soldiers engaged in spirited marches, loud shouting, the firing of guns and flashing of swords—with reasonable care that no one got hurt. The leaders of both sides held occasional conferences until they were able to compose their differences in an agreement for ending the conflict. In a society that lacked strong republican traditions and a workable elective system for a peaceful transfer of governmental powers from one group to another, the Californians developed their version of a military showdown to achieve the same end—the mock battle where issues were resolved by the display, rather than the use, of force. In contrast to Mexico, California settled such encounters through force of words, rather than of arms.

Figueroa

The governorship of Jose Figueroa (1833—1835) was a turning point in California affairs. The liberal-minded Figueroa was a veteran administrator, who proved to be the best of the Mexican governors sent to California. Upon arriving in California, he found the territory near anarchy, the people divided and "gripped by insidious grudges." Rallying all groups, he outlined a series of reforms designed to bring about constitutional government, and liberal programs for converting California's military—religious system into a civil republican society. He worked closely with the diputación, seeking its approval for all his measures before putting them into effect. He instituted ayuntamientos (1835) for the remaining presidial pueblos at San Diego and San Francisco. He ordered Vallejo to establish the new pueblo of Sonoma for improving military defense of the northern frontier. He began the long-delayed breakup of the missions, secularizing almost half of them.

Recognizing the need for gradual and flexible emancipation, he allocated lands on mission sites and established four pueblos for Indians who desired self-government (similar to Echeandia's plan). Loosely interpreting the colonization acts, he generously granted lands between missions, thus accelerating the rancho movement. He opened up California ports, especially to stimulate foreign trade and to secure increased import duties and promote economic development, intending to replace trade for the missions as the chief source of revenues for the government. Freed of dependence on the padres, he was now in a better position to secularize the missions. It is a tribute to Figueroa's rule that he accomplished the program envisaged by Arguello for bringing about California's transition from a military–clerical society to a civil republican order.

Secularization

The national program for mission secularization was slow in taking form. The Colonization Acts of 1824 and 1828 authorized the territorial governors, with approval of the diputación, to grant vacant lands (for example, nonmission lands) not only to Mexican settlers, but also to naturalized foreign settlers who applied for them. Apparently only two land grants were issued under these acts during the Echeandia and Victoria administrations. The remainder were mostly reaffirmations of earlier land grants lying between the missions. During the first decade of Mexican rule, the national congress and territorial government were hardly inclined to act boldly on either land grants or Indian emancipation which might provoke church reaction.

The push for mission secularization came in the 1830's from an unexpected source. In Mexico City, Jose Padres, by now an influential liberal politician, organized a colonization project for California, involving Jose Hijar, a wealthy Mexican land-owner who put up the money, and Juan Bandini, who lent his influence as California's deputy to the national congress. At their behest, the congress in 1833 adopted the Secularization Act, which provided for the immediate breakup of the missions and transfer of mission lands to settlers and Indians. A presidential executive order authorized the Padres–Hijar project, appointing Hijar as governor and Padres as military comandante of the California territory, and approving their scheme for bringing a colony of settlers to the province. On receiving word of the 1833 Act in California, Governor Figueroa, with the help of the diputación, drafted a plan for secularizing 10 of the 21 missions, to be administered by commissioners appointed among the Californios. In the autumn of 1834, shortly before the arrival of the Padres–Hijar colony, Figueroa received from President Santa Anna, who had just assumed power, orders which countermanded the new appointments. Figueroa was instructed to retain the governorship. Padres's plan was not only thwarted by the President, an archenemy, but also by California leaders of the diputación. The latter had become thoroughly disenchanted with their former teacher on learning that among the settlers were 21 Mexican commissioners who were intended to administer the secularized missions! In the end, the governor deported Padres and Hijar and allowed colonists to return to Mexico or stay in California, according to their desire.

American Traders and Trappers

In the wake of Gale, Hartnell, and Cooper came a stream of traders and trappers. They were predominantly American and they came to California in such growing numbers (240 by 1835) that by Figueroa's time they had become a significant factor in the territory's economic development. In one group were the previously mentioned traders who came by sea and settled in coastal pueblos as resident merchants engaging in the maritime trade. The other group consisted of the traders and trappers who opened the overland trade routes.

Pioneer traders and trappers came to California on the overland trails in the course of extending their fur-hunting activities in the Rocky Mountain area. The Rocky Mountains in the 1820's and 1830's were the scene of the bustling and highly competitive activities of the fur-hunters—that unique breed of remarkable "mountain men," as they liked to call themselves. They operated from three jumping-off places: Taos, in the Mexican province of New Mexico; Fort Vancouver, headquarters of the Hudson Bay Company of England in the jointly occupied American–British Oregon country; and St. Louis, Missouri, the American supply base for fur traders. In the late 1820's their vanguard was moving into the California area.

The overland trails to California were first opened by the extraordinary explorations of the intrepid Jedediah Smith. In 1823 Smith led the first expedition through the Central Rockies to find South Pass (in present-day Wyoming), which later was to be the main pathway for the immigrant trains of American pioneers to the Pacific. While seeking new trapping fields and a Pacific outlet for his newly formed fur company, Smith undertook two other expeditions between 1826 and 1828 during which he discovered a way from the Great Salt Lake to California through Cajon Pass in the Southwest. He explored the Central Valley of California and from there found a way through the Sierras, becoming the first man to cross that formidable mountain barrier (traveling eastward through Ebbetts Pass). He went on to open the way through Oregon to Fort Vancouver in the Northwest on his return to the Great Salt Lake region.

Other notable trappers and traders improved upon these routes and developed the overland trade. In 1828–1829 the Patties, a father–son trapper team, found a Santa Fe–San Diego route during their Southwest explorations. In 1829–1830, Antonio Armijo led a Mexican trading party from Santa Fe to Los Angeles to pioneer the Old Spanish Trail for the Mexican, and later American, caravan trade. Anglo–American trappers from the Hudson Bay Company posts and other rendezvous points roamed the Central Valley, and occasionally the coastal areas, in quest of beaver, otter, and other fur-bearing animals. Some traders and trappers took residence in the pueblos, such as Isaac Graham and his group of hunters, who settled outside of Monterey, and Benjamin Wilson and William Wolfskill, who became prominent Mexican citizens in the Los Angeles area. Some of them continued their endless wandering through the California interior and the West. With few exceptions, they were a rough lot of undisciplined men, but the Californios respected them for their expertise with a rifle and admired their ingenuity of enterprise, so important to economic development.

Home Rule, 1836–1842

The Conservative Program

At this time, Mexico underwent a major political upheaval that transformed the national government and set the stage for California politics during the remainder of Mexican rule. Conservatives, reacting to liberal reforms, rallied around Santa Anna to regain control of the *cortes* (congress) and, in the fall of 1835, abolished the 1824 Federal Constitution. Shortly afterward, the Texas province proclaimed its independence of Mexico and defeated Santa Anna's army in a showdown battle. The conservative coalition of military and clerical groups, however, retained control and, in the fall of 1836, issued a new centralist constitution. In the new constitutional order, the national government assumed sovereign powers. Departments were set up as administrative units in place of the abolished states, ruled by governors appointed by the central government. At each governmental level, the executive took precedence over the legislative: the president, aided by an advisory cortes, and the governor, assisted by a departmental *junta* or council, which replaced the diputación. Several national laws in 1837 further implemented the conservative program for restoring order. One law set up prefects as administrative units under the governor to supervise the alcaldes and ayuntamientos. Another instituted a system of courts to provide effective administration of the law. Under the 1836 setup, Mexico was ruled by the military dictatorship of Santa Anna.

The Gubernatorial Pendulum

California's political structure took a peculiar turn from the national pattern in these years. The territory experienced a round of political–military maneuvering between rival contenders for the governorship. In the game of musical chairs that took place between members of the diputación (Alvarado and Castro) and Mexican-appointed officials (Mariano Chico and Nicolas Gutierrez), the governorship within one year passed from Castro to Gutierrez to Chico, back to Gutierrez, and then settled upon Alvarado. The national government did so little to impose its will upon the California Department that this period (1836–1842) may be called the Home Rule Years.

Chico's gubernatorial appointment was an omen of the conservative program for California. Described as the "daring champion of that party," Chico convened the diputación only to make clear his intentions to have his way and to denounce as a "false idol" the 1824 Constitution that the Californios had come to revere. He announced that he would attempt to save the remaining missions and would prohibit foreign commerce in an effort to reserve trade for the Mexicans. To preserve order, suspected criminals would be tried under military rather than civil jurisdiction. During his brief three-month tenure, Chico's high-handed acts soon led Alvarado, Castro, and others to plot the governor's expulsion.

Chico, however, laid the ground for his own downfall by committing a breach of protocol in Monterey society. The alcalde there had arrested for adultery a captain and his mistress, who happened to be a friend of Chico's niece (known to be Chico's mistress). When Chico, at his niece's request, permitted the captain's mistress to leave her prison to attend the theater, the alcalde arranged for the imprisoned captain to sit across from her in the theater, where they openly greeted each other. Angered by the alcalde's boldness, Chico afterward invaded his home to arrest him, thus arousing the enmity of Monterey citizens. After a showdown with the diputación over the affair, the governor left for Mexico, vowing to come back with new forces. He never returned to California. The Californians thus achieved the governor's withdrawal, as Woodrow Hansen puts it, "by appeal to Venus rather than Mars."

On his departure, Chico designated Nicolas Gutierrez, the ranking military officer, as his successor. Gutierrez, in the absence of a legal governor, refused to deliver the office of political chief to the leading member of the diputación (Castro), as required by law. He further insulted the diputación by refusing to convene it, declaring that he had "no need of deputies of pen and voice when he had plenty of deputies of sword and gun." The diputación through its president, Alvarado, responded by a proclamation in the autumn of 1836. In this *Plan de Independencia*, California protested the abolition of the social compact between California and Mexico embodied in the 1824 Constitution, and declared that, until the Constitution was restored, California would be a "free and sovereign state." The diputación chose Alvarado as governor, appointed Vallejo as comandante general, formulated a constitution to legitimize the new government, removed the recent restrictions on foreign trade, and reaffirmed Catholicism as the state religion.

Alvarado proceeded next to win the necessary public support and legal recognition of the new California government. After a series of quick political and military maneuvers, Alvarado, with his native and foreign supporters, was able to overcome the opposition of forces in the south led by Bandini, Carrillo, and others. In the summer of 1837, a commission arrived from Mexico to receive the oaths of support for the new national government established under the 1836 conservative constitution. At this critical point, Alvarado delivered a masterful stroke of political statecraft. In an agreement later confirmed by the national government, he and Vallejo led other California officials in taking the oath of allegiance to the new constitution, and in return were allowed to retain their offices. Alvarado had, in effect, abandoned his federalist principles, but had entrenched himself in the governorship and undercut further opposition by his Southern California rivals.

Thus Californians, for the first time, secured control of their own affairs, and Mexico acquiesced. Preoccupied with her own troubles at home, she was hardly in a position to do otherwise.

Governmental Affairs

Once assured of his position as the first native Californian to be constitutional governor (Arguello was only provisional governor), Alvarado acted with energy and dispatch to carry out his program for home rule. He sought to put the republican government on a firm basis by cooperating closely with the diputación, separating the civil and military powers of the governorship, and setting up an adequate administration of justice in civil and criminal cases, as befitted the liberal ideal. He pressed for economic development by completing mission secularization, distributing mission and other lands to Indians and prospective rancheros, and promoting foreign trade. His program rounded off what Arguello had begun some 15 years earlier.

Alvarado succeeded in carrying out much of his plan for a genuine republican government. He worked closely at all times with the diputación (now renamed the *Junta Departamento*, or Department Council). This continued to be an active policy-making body because of Alvarado's self-restraint in using the extensive gubernatorial powers available to him. Alvarado also established the first judiciary in Mexican California, a three-tier court system for handling criminal and civil cases. The court system was especially important to merchants as a means of enforcing business contracts, but this ambitious plan for a working judiciary was blocked by inherent difficulties. It might have fared better in more stable times.

The governor set up the prefecture system required by law. The California department was divided into two districts headed by prefects (chief administrative officers), and into *partidos*, or sections, headed by sub-prefects, who supervised the alcaldes, ayuntamientos, and justices of the peace. To assure adequate finances for the department and to downgrade the military, Alvarado decreased funds for maintaining the militia, thus arousing Vallejo's anger and leading to a break between nephew and uncle. On hearing of a plot against him by Vallejo, Carrillo, and Pico, Alvarado supplied the prefects with the necessary arms for protection.

Despite such difficulties, the centralized system of government with Alvarado's modifications—centralized responsibility with local autonomy—proved to be admirably suited to the California situation.

Secularization

Alvarado also modified his program for mission secularization and Indian emancipation. He pressed for secularization of the remaining missions, appointing his ranchero and pueblo friends to dispose of mission property and supervise the Indians, which they did with a freedom that often led to rampant exploitation. Indian neophytes had received from the governor their lands, stock, and equipment, but they proved incapable of developing their property into profitable enterprises. Practically all of it passed into the hands of rancheros and others. The Indians either sold their property (usually to buy liquor), gambled it away, or simply left it. The governor attempted to prevent abuse of the Indians by appointing the able and conscientious Hartnell as inspector, but this effort was successfully resisted by Vallejo, Pico, and other rancheros. Of the 18,000 Indian neophytes in the 21 missions in 1831, less than a thousand remained around the former missions in 1841. Many had gone to enjoy the "freedom" of economic bondage as servants in pueblos or as workers on ranches. The remainder spurned the white man's way by returning to their tribes or becoming outlaws.

The governor displayed a generous spirit in issuing land grants to native and naturalized foreigners who showed ambition for enterprise. Vacant lands from Sonora to San Diego, including former mission lands, passed into private ownership, with much of the land in the Napa and Sacramento valleys falling into the hands of foreigners. John Sutter's enormous grant at this time was large even by California standards, but not untypical of grants made to foreigners.

Alvarado also sought to stimulate trading enterprises in order to develop a diversified economy. Trade reached a high point of development in these years. New England firms and other merchant groups, through their Californian and Hawaiian agents, expanded their trade lists from horses, cattle hides, tallow, and beef to include various agricultural products, lumber, beaver, and other furs, as well as products from the whaling operations conducted from California bases. With mission secularization in full swing, Alvarado, like Figueroa, came to rely on the expanded trade as the principal source of revenue for the government and to increase the wealth of the province. To this end, he lowered import duties which, with the expanded commerce, more than tripled annual trade revenues, despite sizable losses of potential revenue through smuggling.

An impending dark cloud not readily apparent at this time was the fact that foreigners were acquiring disproportionately large shares of the new wealth created by the expanding economic development. As the governor pointed out, however, the foreigners were instilling in the native sons a "love for ambitious enterprise" which would enable them to realize their dreams for a thriving republican society.

American Farmers

In 1841 California reached the peak of its development as an independent republic under Alvarado's home rule. The cloud on the horizon now took an ominous form with the arrival of the first group of American emigrant farmers seeking to establish homesteads in California. In the fall of the year nearly 200 Americans had come overland—two groups out of Missouri: the Bidwell Party, which crossed the Sierras at Walker Pass, and the Rowland Workman Wilson Party, which came over the Sante Fe and Old Spanish trails; and a group of discouraged Oregon settlers who accompanied a United States naval expedition (see below). These alien settlers, the vanguard of coming waves of American farmer groups, received lands for homesteads from the governor and from Sutter, whose trading post-fort (1839) was the terminus of their trip.

With the coming of these American pioneer farmers, the friendly attitude of the native sons soon turned to suspicion. Before long, Alvarado and Vallejo sent to the national government dispatches expressing concern and requesting aid to stem the American tide. The national government, already sensitive about the growing American immigration into California, responded by sending troops under a newly appointed governor. Thus it was that the Californians under Alvarado, having gained control of their affairs by clever maneuvers in 1836, lost it in 1842 by hesitating to exercise their powers independently. The Californios simply could not sustain their dream of independence in the face of changing conditions they felt unable to control.

Chaotic Years, 1842—1846

Reactionary Politics

Mexico, meanwhile, experienced another round of political disorders. The conservative-dominated national government revised the Constitution (1843) to strengthen its centralized rule by broadening the president's powers. It was, however, hardly able to maintain control over the country, and several provinces were on the verge of seceding. The continuing problems of Texas further complicated the situation. Since Texas had won its independence in 1836, Texan and American groups sought to incorporate the area into the American Union. Mexico, however, served notice that it intended to recover the province and regarded annexation to the United States as an act of war. Mexican leaders already expressed concern that the "Texas game" might be played in their California province.

Micheltorena

To regain control in California, the national government put its hope in the new governor. Manuel Micheltorena was a political conservative and a somewhat inactive administrator who attempted to accommodate his program to the California situation. His most pressing problem was his cholo troops, a pitiful lot of 300 convicts and vagrants recruited in Mexico to supplement his 200 regular troops. These unpaid soldiers became such an intolerable nuisance by their constant marauding raids on the homesteads of citizens, that the governor, throughout his administration, devoted an excessive amount of time to securing revenues for their support. He acquired loans from rancheros in return for generous grants of land, exceeding even Alvarado in granting land to the arriving American immigrants whose flow he was supposed to halt. He enforced trade regulations to secure additional revenues from import duties, forcing Boston traders to withdraw from the risky California trade. He reduced government expenditures by cutting salaries of officials and abolishing the prefect, which seriously weakened his centralized administrative control. He restored to the padres management of several missions on the condition that they contribute a portion of their annual produce to the departmental treasury—a measure to provide government revenues, not to reestablish the mission system, as commonly believed. Micheltorena's policies eventually proved to be his undoing. After two military showdowns with rebelling groups led by Alvarado and others in the name of the *Asamblea* ("Assembly"—the reconstituted Junta), Micheltorena in 1845 was deported with his troublesome cholo troops.

The Californios once again took control of their government, this time with approval of the national government. Pio Pico as leader of the *Asamblea* took over the governorship, while Jose Castro took over as comandante general, and Alvarado as California's deputy to the national cortes. Pico, California's last constitutional governor under Mexican rule, was a man of limited education and little apparent ability who surprised almost everyone with his statesmanship as governor. During his brief tenure in office (1845–1846), he attempted to restore political order, revive economic development, and renew California home rule as developed by Alvarado under the 1837 laws, but he was hampered by running feuds with Castro and other leaders. Even worse was the pending crisis developing between Mexico and the United States over Texas.

The American Takeover

Prelude

American interest in California had developed along two lines. One line consisted of those groups of enterprising Americans who, over the past half-century had made their way by sea and land routes in search of economic opportunity: the Yankee sea hunters and traders, the Massachusetts-born resident merchants, the Missouri-based traders and trappers, and the pioneer settlers from the western frontier of the United States. Spurred by reports of Larkin and John Marsh in California, and guided by maps drawn by Fremont's army's exploratory expeditions and by ambitious promoters like Lansford Hastings, these pioneer settlers came overland in greater numbers, over 250 in 1845 and over twice that in 1846. The perils of the journey were illustrated by the Donner Party tragedy in 1846, when a party of 87 persons made an unwise attempt to cross the Sierra summit in the dead of winter. Forty perished, and some survived by resorting to cannibalism.

The other line of American interest in California was the United States government, which attempted to acquire the California province by diplomatic and other means. President Andrew Jackson tried in 1835 and 1837 to purchase California, along with Texas, but both attempts failed. Jackson sought to acquire California, with its fine bay at San Francisco, as a base for American commerce in the Pacific and to placate the North for the annexation of Texas as the slave state strongly desired by the South. In 1842 Daniel Webster, then Secretary of State, attempted a similar plan. It was nullified by an American blunder in which a United States naval squadron under Commodore Thomas ap Catesby Jones sailed into Monterey harbor in the mistaken belief that the United States and Mexico were at war, seized the town, and withdrew after a one-day occupation with profound apologies to the governor. U.S. government interest was also manifested in scientific expeditions. A naval expedition on a world voyage, commanded by Charles Wilkes, anchored on the Columbia River, and overland and seaward parties were dispatched to San Francisco Bay for scientific explorations. Army expeditions led by John Fremont explored practical overland routes to California: one expedition in 1842 went to South Pass, and the other in 1843—1844 came to California via Oregon, traveled the length of the Central Valley, passing Sutter's Fort, and returned on the Old Spanish Trail. Fremont's reports were "best sellers." They helped publicize the Far West and enhanced the popularity of the young, ambitious soldier–explorer. By 1845 American interest had grown into a nation-wide clamor for the acquisition of California along with Oregon and Texas. A crusading slogan—Manifest Destiny—expressed what Americans believed to be their right to acquire contiguous territory extending to the Pacific, their natural western frontier.

Growing United States interest came to a climax in the administration of James Polk, who had won the presidency on the issue of American expansion. Upon assuming office in 1845, Polk clarified his campaign pledge as including annexation of Texas, full title to Oregon, and the acquisition of California. He sought to acquire California either by outright purchase; by annexation, should the Californios declare their independence and request it (the so-called Texas Game); or by conquest, should the United States and Mexico go to war over the Texas issue. Mexico had made it clear since Texas won its independence that United States annexation of its former province would mean war between the two nations. Nevertheless, Polk went ahead with his plan. He sent a special emissary to negotiate the purchase of Alta California and New Mexico. He instructed Thomas Larkin, the American consul and secret confidential agent, to encourage Californians to declare their independence and request annexation to the United States. He sent secret orders to John Sloat, commander of the naval squadron in the Pacific, to undertake the occupation of California in the event of war with Mexico. Then the President went before Congress urging support. The Senate responded by ratifying the treaty for annexing Texas into the American Union. As historian Glyndon Van Deusen summed up the year's events, Polk was determined to acquire California "in one way or another, sooner or later."

By 1846 the die was cast for war. Public opinion was inflamed by the chauvinistic sentiment and warlike statements of national leaders, the Americans calling for their "manifest destiny," and the Mexicans urging the recapture of Texas by force. The spark which set off open hostilities came in the winter of 1846 when American troops under General Zachary Taylor faced Mexican troops on the Rio Grande River. Following a border skirmish between patrols of the two armies, Polk led Congress into declaring war on Mexico.

Meanwhile, in California, events early in 1846 were moving toward a local outbreak of hostilities. Pico's administration had reached the low point of its deterioration. It had no public funds for operating the departmental government, no military force for defending the territory, and no direction from the national government for dealing with the impending crisis. Californians, whether native, naturalized, or foreign, were deeply divided in their sentiments on the outcome of the crisis. Mexico, racked by internal dissensions at home, was clearly unable to administer and defend the province. During the winter, Fremont appeared in California with an armed force not authorized by the United States government. Ostensibly he was on an exploring expedition, but actually he roamed about the province awaiting an opportunity to participate in the anticipated conquest. Emboldened by Fremont's return, dissident American settlers around Sonoma set off the Bear Flag Revolt in which they raided the town, imprisoned Vallejo, and proclaimed their "republic" with a battalion of volunteers organized by Fremont. The much romanticized revolt, perpetuated for many years in a distorted account in California history books, was little more than a raid undertaken by an assorted lot of rough frontiersman. The abortive affair was ended two weeks later when United States naval forces under Sloat entered Monterey harbor to announce the news of war and to take American possession of California.

Military Showdown

The American conquest of California was a messy affair punctuated by singular heroic achievements. It was from the beginning a by-product of the war over Texas, fought mainly in the north of Mexico. United States military strategy in California fluctuated between the soft-line concilia-tory approach of Sloat, which won over apprehensive Californios to American rule, and the hard-line conquest tactics of Stockton, who succeeded him shortly afterward and absorbed Fremont's California battalion into his command. Stockton's arbitrary rule antagonized the

Californios and provoked the Angelenos under Jose Carrillo to stage a successful local showdown (Battle of the Old Woman's Gun) which prolonged resistance by the Californios. A United States cavalry unit of Taylor's army under General Stephen Kearny arrived in May after completing one of the longest and most difficult marches in United States military history. His worn-out forces fought well-mounted rebels under Andres Pico (Pio's brother) to an indecisive outcome (Battle of San Pascual). Shortly afterward, a joint force under Kearny and Stockton recaptured Los Angeles. Hostilities ended in January 1847 when the rebel forces, persuaded by their hopeless situation and on promise of clemency, surrendered to Fremont, who extended full pardon to all rebels. The so-called American conquest of California was more of a peaceful takeover. Mexico had, for all practical purposes, abdicated the territory. Only a handful of Californios resisted, and they more out of local pride and a confusing situation than of anticipated victory against the Americans.

The surrender ended organized resistance among the Californios. It also marked the end of Mexican rule and the beginning of American rule in the California province, although this change was not formally brought about until the adoption of the Treaty of Guadalupe Hidalgo between the United States and Mexico a year later. The story of that year, when California was in limbo between the two nations, belongs properly to the American period.

5 Mexican California Society

THE SETTING

The Mexican idea of society emerged in 1821 from the "Three Guarantees," which called for political independence, racial equality, and the primacy of the Catholic Church. As conservative and liberal forces fought for control in the early decades of nationhood, Mexico emerged with a hybrid republican society that combined its Spanish legacy and American customs. Its liberalism was reflected in representative government and a private enterprise stimulated by secularization and open trade. Its conservatism was manifested in the authoritarian rule of caudillos and the dominance of feudalistic estates (haciendas and ranchos). Roman Catholicism did continue to be the state religion, but the Indian people, who were a majority, achieved only a small measure of the promised equality. The disruption of the old order left people struggling for a secure existence in a turbulent society.

Mexican California was a battleground for conservative and liberal forces seeking control of the frontier province. Spanish traditions persisted for a while, but Mexican liberalism "kept filtering into the province despite a pall of conservatism." The rising ranchero–merchant class eventually overwhelmed clerical and military forces. They did away with the missions and built up ranchos and pueblos to establish the basis of a libertarian republican society. Imbued with a secular outlook, the new elite was absorbed in social diversions, though some yearned for educational and cultural benefits. The liberal-minded *hijos de país* ("sons of the land") retained their pride in their Spanish ancestry and acquired a dislike of things Mexican—so much so that they came to identify themselves as Californios. They struggled to fashion a republican order, but personal inexperience and extenuating circumstances led to disorderly conditions that bordered on anarchy. Historian Leonard Pitt says they took pride in their way of life whatever its failings: they had land, wealth, regal fun, family pride, a stake in government, and a sense of aristocratic refinement rare in other frontier provinces of Latin America. It was an easygoing society for them, but a painful experience for less fortunate people like the Indians.

ANALYSIS

Political Scheme

After independence from Spain, Mexico established a republican order focused on representative government, a two-party system, and the Spanish legal system based on the Roman Code. The national government, during its rule of California, swung from Iturbide's dictatorship (1821) to the liberal constitution (1824) to the conservative constitution (1836) to "dead center" government after 1845. Mexico underwent the full swing from the rigid centralism of Spanish authoritarianism to the libertarian federalism of the United States to her version of conservative centralism, imposing upon California three different constitutional plans within the brief quarter-century of Mexican rule. Mexico, however, was so engulfed in the conservative–liberal struggle for control of the national government that the distant California province was relatively free to work out its own political destiny.

California developed her version of republicanism, a territorial government where the governor shared powers with the diputación and autonomous local government. It found ultimate expression in the home rule years of Alvarado's governorship. The governor was the prime mover in political affairs. He was the chief executive and, whether Mexican or Californio, he ruled with little interference from the national capital. His position was tempered, however, by his reliance on the support of local groups, since the 1824 constitution provided no organization for the territorial government and the 1836 constitution assigned military powers to the department comandante. The colonization acts (see Chapter 4) and other specific measures provided that the governor and the diputación share powers—finances, trade regulations, and land grants. Furthermore, the ranchero class, which emerged in the 1830's as the ruling elite, was able to utilize the diputación as their vehicle to depose unpopular governors and even to name their own, as they did in the cases of Alvarado and Pico. Thus, the Californios perpetuated their form of home rule, despite setbacks imposed by the 1836 constitution and by the factional conflicts among the ranchero elite.

The pueblos, centers of local government, became the political mainstay of the province. Mexico established municipal government in all its pueblos, replacing the military rule with alcalde–ayuntamiento government in Monterey and Santa Barbara in 1822, and in San Francisco and San Diego in 1835. (This form of government already prevailed in Los Angeles and San Jose.) Mexico also abolished the governor's commissioner on the ayuntamiento (see Chapter 4) and added a legal counselor and a secretary, which strengthened the traditional body of alcalde and *rigidores* ("councilmen"). As the pueblo grew, town officials were assigned fiscal, police, and other municipal functions. As ranchos formed and the cattle industry developed in surrounding areas, a *juez de plano* ("justice of the plains"), who might be an alcalde, was appointed by the ayuntamiento to administer rules and settle disputes among rancheros and their men at the rodeos and *matanzas* (see below). The pueblos were more than centers of local politics; they were the arenas where ranchero factions and Mexican officials fought the game of territorial politics.

The alcalde emerged as a strong figure, something akin to a village patriarch. Since his office encompassed executive, legislative, and judicial powers, he exercised immense authority, far more than his counterpart in Mexico or the United States. He was primarily a civil magistrate, for his most significant powers were judicial. (The American mayor thrives on his political powers.) As presiding officer of the ayuntamiento, he was usually able to run his own show, especially since that body functioned more as a forum for local leaders than as a genuine local legislature. When the conservative plan of prefects replaced the alcalde–ayuntamiento system between 1839 and 1844, the alcalde role was actually strengthened, for the newly appointed *juez de paz* ("justice of the peace") was simply the alcalde in another form. This type of local home rule was to continue in the American period.

Administration of Justice

A grave deficiency in the workings of California's republican order was the lack of a judiciary as a third branch of government. Courts play a vital role not only in maintaining law and order, but also in arbitrating differences between the executive and legislative branches, in protecting individual rights and the public interest, and in upholding the sanctity of business contracts and property rights. Mexico failed to set up a court system at the territorial or departmental level. Thus, disputes between the governor and the diputación were resolved more by force of personalities than by court of law, and appeals from the alcalde's decisions in civil and criminal cases could be forwarded only to the national court in far-off Mexico City. Alvarado's attempt to set up a departmental supreme court (see Chapter 4) was a failure. Some appointees refused to serve, and the remainder accomplished little during its brief existence (1839–1843, 1845–1846).

The alcalde court was the backbone of the court system, even though its jurisdiction was limited to criminal and civil cases involving amounts up to $100. In civil cases, the alcalde court was designed to *prevent* litigation: the alcalde or justice of the peace sought to conciliate contesting parties, settling their differences by concessions on each side rather than by strict rule of law. As a result, merchants were sometimes unable to collect claims on their contracts. However, Alfred Robinson, a resident merchant representing a Boston firm, tells us that the rancheros were particularly conscientious in paying their debts. In criminal cases, the fact that death sentences imposed by the alcalde court had to be approved by Mexico City, contributed to the disenchantment with the public authorities' ability to check local crime. In 1837 an irate citizen group in Los Angeles seized from the local jail a woman and her lover who had killed her husband, and shot them to insure their desired execution—the first recorded vigilante activity in California. Despite occasional waves of crime and violence, California generally enjoyed law and order since the population was sparse and scattered, and the citizens had a submissive attitude born of their authoritarian Spanish tradition.

Fiscal Administration

Provincial finances throughout Mexican rule were in a state of chronic deficiency. Mexico continued Spain's antiquated fiscal administration with little change. The national government made many promises of funds but, aside from initial subsidies (1822 and 1825), remitted so little money for support of the province that the territorial government had to provide for itself. At first the territory relied principally on mission taxes resulting from Governor Arguello's compromise with the padres (see Chapter 4). As the missions deteriorated in the 1830's, import duties, mostly from the foreign trade, became the chief source of revenue.

The governor resorted to expedient devices to secure funds during emergency periods and for special projects. He exacted forced payments in the guise of voluntary contributions, public charges, and loans (rarely repaid) from merchants and rancheros for public works, and from foreign traders for port improvements. He even took salary deductions from government employees and occasionally persuaded higher officials to pay their own expenses—Vallejo as military comandante sometimes paid troops out of his own pocket. Pueblos relied primarily on licenses, fees, and fines for local governmental expenses, and they too made forced impositions. In addition, settlers were saddled with sales taxes on purchased goods and services: as much as 25 percent on flour, butter, and salmon, and up to 100 percent on liquors. As a result, a thriving contraband trade developed. Governor Alvarado's earnest efforts at fiscal reforms (he appointed Hartnell to supervise district and port finances) stabilized and simplified provincial finances. Such efforts came to naught in the long run because of inherent defects in the workings of Mexico's economic system.

Economic System

The Mexican government conceived an ambitious scheme for making the northern province an important part of the national economy, a plan outlined in the *Fomento de las Californias* (Development of the Californias, 1827). Monterey would be the great maritime–commercial center of the Pacific, where Mexico hoped to share, if not dominate, the lucrative China trade. Secularization of the missions would lead to the emergence of the ranchos as major producers of livestock and crops, and of the pueblos as the manufacturing and trading centers for the new market economy. California would share in the government-sponsored company (it would own stock in the Asiatico–Mexicana Compañía), which would be the instrument for implementing a national trade monopoly on the Pacific. Californios and Mexican leaders decried the national government's failure to implement the *Fomento—*

Alvarado commented later that it had "died without being born." Actually the *Fomento* contained basic ideas actually being carried out by government leaders and national measures, so that it may be regarded as Mexico's public economic policy for California.

While Mexico's grandiose scheme never came to pass, the cortes enacted measures for transforming California's economy from a feudal to a capitalistic system. The overall plans for mission secularization, land distribution, Indian emancipation, Mexican and foreign immigration, and open trade were enacted into national law (as recommended in the *Fomento*), but it took time and circumstances to implement them. It remained for the conscientious Governor Figueroa to put into effect the liberal-sponsored laws, and for the California-born Governor Alvarado, his successor, to complete the legal framework for getting the process fully under way. Thus, Mexican California in the first decade continued under the dominance of the Spanish mission system. Not until the mid-1830's did the pueblos and ranchos supersede the missions, and not until the 1840's did the process toward a capitalistic economy begin in earnest.

Though the provincial economy was in a constant state of transition through the entire period of Mexican rule, the pueblos and ranchos, by their steadily growing importance, came to be the dominant economic institutions in Mexican California. The ranchos became the chief producing centers. The pueblos emerged as the marketplaces for the expanding trade that developed from the growth of neighboring ranchos and local commercial activity. Trade focused at first on the rancho-produced cattle hides and tallow, and later on horses, crops, lumber, and other products which were exchanged for imported manufactured articles and luxury goods. The trade was conducted mostly under the auspices of the naturalized American and Mexican merchants, although some rancheros operated stores and maintained warehouses in the pueblos. While many townspeople raised crops and stock on their pueblo lots, their products were primarily for local consumption rather than for the profitable foreign trade. Thus California's native and adopted sons took the initiative in the economic development of the province.

Land

Unlike Spain, Mexico adopted a liberal policy of distributing land freely, for the dual purposes of encouraging settlement and stimulating agricultural development as the basis for a stable economy. It sought in particular to break up the huge land holdings of the Church, allocating small tracts to Indians and large grants to other settlers for farms and ranchos. The Colonization Acts of 1824 and 1828 provided the legal framework, but it was not until passage of the Secularization Act of 1833 and the sympathetic administrations of Governor Figueroa and his successor, Alvarado, that the national policy was effectively administered in California (see Chapter 4).

Once the national land policy was fully implemented, the rancho movement accelerated at a rapid pace. In the half-century between the early Spanish land grants (1784) and mission secularization (1834), only about 50 land grants had been issued for prospective ranchos. In the 13 years between mission secularization and the end of Mexican rule, at least 750 grants were issued. They ranged in size from 1 to 11 leagues (the Spanish league equaling 4,439 acres, or about four-fifths of a mile). At least a dozen exceeded the legal 11-league limit, and some were of immense size. Even more astonishing were the multi-holdings of individual grantees, like de la Guerra's four ranchos totaling over 200,000 acres, and Vallejo's two ranchos amounting to 156,000 acres. The family holdings were likewise huge, such as the Vallejo family with 296,000 acres, the de la Guerra family with 415,000 acres, and the Pico family whose 700,000 acres were the largest of such holdings. Such grants were large even by Mexican standards, but they were not uncommon in isolated frontier provinces of Northern Mexico like Texas, New Mexico, and California. Here land was abundant and low in value, settlers were few in numbers and fewer yet in enterprising ability. Here the national government was particularly generous in administering its land policy.

The distribution of these lands set the pattern for the rancho movement. The governor issued grants rather generously on petition of a prospective ranchero, who was expected to build his home, acquire stock, and cultivate crops. Local officials were casual in surveying locations and running the boundaries. Most of the grantees were retired or semi-retired military personnel, enterprising settlers, or their descendents. Politicians, who were or had been active in the territorial diputación, the pueblo *ayuntamientos,* or other government posts, were able to secure sizable grants for themselves and their families. A number of grants were issued to naturalized citizens, including American traders, trappers, resident merchants, and later pioneer farmers. A few grants were given to Indians, notably chiefs of rancherias within Mexican settlements, and individuals who had "crossed the line" to become substantial citizens.

The distribution of mission lands for Indians, however, was a practical failure. Governor Figueroa's experimental Indian pueblos (San Juan Capistrano, Las Flores, and San Antonio), built up from nearby missions in Southern California, apparently languished to near extinction. Administrators charged with disposing mission lands, including commissioners who allocated the lands and *mayor domos* who managed the remaining mission property, were often local rancheros who frequently assigned large land tracts, complete with Indians and facilities, to themselves, to relatives, and to friends. They ignored the entreaties of padres and rebuffed conscientious government efforts to stop them. When Alvarado sent Hartnell to check out the faithful performance of Figueroa's secularization orders, Vallejo actually arrested him to prevent interference. Governor Pico's policy of renting and leasing the remaining mission estates after 1845 resulted in the final disposition of these lands, mostly to American pioneers. The small number of Indians who received lands from the few honest administrators rarely succeeded in retaining and farming their lots. Most of these mission lands, then, were absorbed into the neighboring property of the rancheros. The land grant scheme, as historian Theodore Hittell puts it, was a "grand Mexican homestead act." It applied, however, to favored white settlers and not to the vast Indian majority of the population.

Agriculture

The rancho economy was an adaptation of the mission's agrarian-based economy. Livestock, enhanced by favorable conditions, became the dominant industry. With the advent of secularization, men easily acquired land, Indian labor, cattle, horses, and other livestock from the broken-up mission to set up their private ranchos. The ranchos varied in size and scope. Vallejo had up to 15,000 heads of cattle, 8,000 horses, and 3,000 sheep grazing on his Sonoma rancho. A few, like Stearns and Yorba, had a lot more, but many others had considerably less. Raising stock required less attention than raising crops. The ranchero usually relied on a trusted *mayor domo* who, as his resident manager, ran operations with a crew of 10 to 20 Indian vaqueros. With trade growing, the ranchos flourished, although they suffered occasional setbacks from drought, poisonous plants, and forage overgrazing by wild horses and cattle, which greatly reduced the herds. Jedediah Smith reported wild horses corralled into pens where they died from starvation, to save range grasses for tame horse herds. In the extreme drought between 1828 and 1830, an estimated 40,000 horses and cattle perished. At one mission (La Purismo Concepción) a herd of horses were driven over a cliff into the sea to save forage for cattle and sheep.

Livestock was important to the way of life, as well as a thriving industry for the rancho. The periodic roundups of cattle (*rodeos*) and horses (*recogidas*) were major highlights of rancho life. The rodeos were held twice a year, one in late summer for counting and branding cattle and the other in late spring for the slaughterings (matanzas). Cattle were butchered, stripped of hides and meat to be salted and sun-dried, their fat boiled into tallow, and their carcasses left to be devoured by predatory birds. The annual recogidas involved corralling and breaking wild horses for use on the ranchos as saddle or work animals. These roundups were colorful affairs. Rancheros and their entourages gathered on the plains for the rendezvous presided over by the juez de plano, and punctuated by lively riding, roping, and other contests between vaqueros, considered to be among the world's best horsemen and unmatched in the use of the lariat.

Cattle products were basic to rancho subsistence. Hides were used as carpets or mats, tallow for soap and candles, bones for implements, and meat as a staple food—*the carne de seca*, or dried beef, was cooked in various dishes for poor and rich alike. The treated rawhide was an all-purpose item. It was used for door latches and hinges, shoelaces, chair seats, window panes, bucket handles, lariat rope, and in many other ways.

The rancho adapted the mission system for raising crops which were grown primarily for subsistence. Vallejo's rancho was probably typical of the larger ones: he cultivated 500 of his 145,000 acre rancho in field crops like wheat and corn, vegetable gardens, orchards, and vineyards, using Indian laborers to farm them. The incoming immigrants added improvements. The Jean Vignes (uncle and nephew) pioneered in grape cultivation for winemaking, and William Wolfskill experimented with oranges. They were apparently the first to build up vineyard and orchard operations for commercial production. Grain and other crop production improved little from the primitive mission ways. American farmers settling in the Sacramento Valley in the 1840's introduced better implements, but relied for the most part on California methods in raising their crops. Their use of Indians for field labor helped perpetuate the feudalistic agrarian economy.

Mining and Manufacturing

Mining activity made modest beginnings in this period. Gold was discovered in mission lands near Carmel in 1825 and at San Isidro near San Diego in 1828, but evidently the padres kept their discoveries secret. The gold discovery in 1841 at Placerita Canyon near Los Angeles by a ranchero (Francisco Lopez) spurred a local rush for gold which enjoyed limited circulation in the province. (Abel Stearns had the first gold pieces processed at the United States mint in Philadelphia in 1845). Mercury was discovered near San Jose and developed by a Mexican army captain (Andres Castanares) at the New Almaden mine in 1845. Alvarado and other Californios pressed the national government for help in developing mineral resources but received no response from Mexico.

The rancho and pueblo engaged in only limited manufacturing activities compared to the earlier missions. After secularization, some Indian artisans in the missions went to work on the ranchos and in the pueblos, but many others returned to native ways in the rancherias. Some rancheros manufactured goods for their needs: Yorba had four wool combers, two tanners, a carpenter, a plasterer, a winemaker, and a dairyman. Some Mexican and American settlers started lumber enterprises, felling trees and hewing lumber, first with hand tools and later by whipsaw (a narrow pit saw), for sale to rancheros, pueblos, and trading ships. Improvements came with John Cooper's pioneer sawmill in 1833, and in 1845 when Stephen Smith, at Bodega, introduced the first steam engine used to saw timber and grind corn. Pueblo artisans produced assorted manufactured goods, like textiles, distilled liquors, and tools and other ironwares for local consumption. Rancheros and other settlers found compensation for their deficient home manufactures in the growing foreign trade.

Trade

Trade was the most significant activity in the economic development of Mexican California. Mexico's trade policies both retarded and stimulated the California economy. The cortes, or national congress, declared a free trade policy, especially with foreign merchants, to stimulate the national economy. Despite this, it enacted a restrictive tariff system reminiscent of Spain's mercantilist system for producing revenues and for protecting Mexican home manufactures. Where the *Fomento* called for open trade to develop California's commerce, the cortes imposed duties on California, even for the coastal trade with Mexico! Mexico's short-sighted policies reduced California to colonial status. Rancheros and merchants were thus handicapped in finding trade outlets, for the remote province relied almost exclusively on the sea for its commerce. Monterey was the chief port for trade.

Foreign traders from the outset dominated the California trade. With the Bostonians Gale and Cooper and the Britisher Hartnell paving the way for sea traders, California, within a decade, had several active trade outlets. The Boston-based Bryant, Sturgis, and Company, through their California agent (Alfred Robinson), led others in carrying cattle hides and tallow to New England via Cape Horn. Another Boston firm (Marshall and Wildes) spearheaded the China trade via Hawaii, carrying horses and, later, grain and lumber to the Islands and otter skins for China. Mexican and other Latin American nationals on the Pacific carried otter skins, cattle tallow, and other items for the Pacific Coast

Monterey, the capital of Spanish and Mexican California, was also the chief port for trade. Sketch by J.W. Revere, grandson of the American Revolution hero, during a U.S. Navy cruise, 1846.

trade. New England whalers operating in the North Pacific developed California bases for processing whales for the homeward journey. They developed a profitable sideline in local trade with ranchos and pueblos. New Mexican traders, first led by the Armijo party (see Chapter 4), opened a lucrative overland caravan trade between Santa Fe and Los Angeles, exchanging blankets and textiles for Chinese merchandise, and California mules and horses. All these traders brought in assorted manufactured articles that Californios could not provide for themselves: fine liquors, finished textiles, fancy merchandise, tools, utensils, and other metalwares. Hartnell and Cooper also paced the pioneer merchant–residents who established wholesale–retail trade outlets in the major pueblos from San Francisco to San Diego.

The Californios found the new trade a mixed blessing. Rancheros disposed of their products for tidy profits, but paid the foreign traders exorbitant prices for desired manufactured articles. The governor and the diputación collected considerable amounts in import duties, but they lost much potential revenue through irregular trading activity. Traders of all nationalities engaged in contraband trade to circumvent government regulation, and Mexico provided no naval vessels for enforcing its policies. The *contrabandistas*, like the modern bootlegger, used various methods to smuggle their goods. They entered closed ports under the pretext of obtaining water and provisions, disposing of their cargoes under cover of night through bribed military guards, and they landed at isolated coastal points where they hid or transshipped their cargoes. Even Californios connived with smugglers. Vallejo reported that in the mid-1830's rancheros, merchants, and others, except high government officials, were involved. Mexican nationals in the coastal trade took advantage of legal loopholes for evading customs to sell foreign goods at lower prices—a practice which so undercut reputable Boston merchants who dutifully paid import duties that they dropped out of the California trade after 1840. Such developments deprived the California government of potential revenue.

The Californios were also frustrated in their own maritime enterprises. Governor Arguello commissioned Cooper's ship for several voyages in the 1820's to carry otter skins for the China trade, but such California ventures could hardly sustain competition with the experienced Boston traders. When Mexico failed to deliver promised ships for the Pacific Coast trade, Californios sponsored at least two schooners (the *Rosalia*, backed by the Vallejos, and the *California*) which operated as government traders between 1838 and the mid-1840's, when the national government took them out of operation.

The Californios benefited from trade, but never realized the full potential of open trade so important for their economic development. They demonstrated a capacity for undertaking the maritime enterprises so necessary for controlling their commercial affairs, but were denied such prospects. Their opportunities had been thwarted by discriminatory national policies and greedy Mexican and foreign traders who exploited the Californios for their own narrow advantage. Jessie Francis, in her careful study of the Mexican California economy, believes that with more time and better opportunities the ambitious Californios would have achieved what they believed to be their economic destiny.

Social Order

The People

Mexican California, like Spanish California, contained two distinct societies: Mexican and Indian. Mexican society was made up of approximately 7000 *gente de razón* ("educated people"—whites, as opposed to Indians) in 1845, the year before the American invasion substantially altered its character. The foreigners numbered around 700, of which 680 were Americans, most of them naturalized citizens of Mexico living in the Los Angeles, Monterey, and San Jose areas. The Indian neophytes during Mexican rule declined in numbers as the mission system deteriorated. Of the approximately 6,600 ex-neophyte Indians in 1846, half were estimated to be living in the pueblos, on the ranchos, and in the rancherias located on or near former mission sites. The remainder lived among the rancherias of gentile Indians located in the area of the Mexican settlements.

Mexican California owed its population growth chiefly to natural increase. Population increase through group migrations was limited, although greater than in the Spanish period. Group migrations from Mexico were confined to the three groups of almost 200 exiled convicts sent between 1825 and 1830, and less than half of the 250 colonists from the Padres–Hijar 1833 expedition remained in California. Group migrations from the United States comprised five parties totaling 635 settlers between 1841 and 1845. Practically all these pioneer farmers lived on ranchos or in small Americanized settlements on tributaries of the Sacramento and San Joaquin, notably P.B. Reading near Shasta,

Peter Lassen near the volcanic peak named after him, John Bidwell on Chico Creek, and the German–American Charles Weber on French Camp Creek on the San Joaquin. Unlike the pioneer merchants, they rarely assimilated the ways of Mexican society. Numerical comparison of the Mexican and American immigrants reflect Mexico's failure to attract her own substantial citizens to the far-off province.

The other society in California—the 100,000 or so Indian gentiles living in scattered rancherias within and beyond the areas of the Mexican and American settlements is discussed below.

Missions

The missions continued to be the chief settlements throughout the first half of Mexican rule. The twenty-first mission was set up in 1823, when the mission at Solano was added to the chain to consolidate mission activity and strengthen the defense of this northern frontier area. The missions retained a substantial amount of land and stock. They performed the important role of raising surplus goods for the pueblos and presidios, and providing cattle hides and tallow for the trade. The padres were able to continue their ministration to the Indians during the first decade after Mexican Independence, but, despite this continuing activity, the missions underwent steady deterioration before their secularization.

Pueblos

With secularization, the pueblos and ranchos emerged as the dominant institutions of California society. There were six pueblos of Spanish origin—Los Angeles, San Jose, and the presidial pueblos of San Diego, Santa Barbara, Monterey, and San Francisco. With the further decline of military rule in the Mexican period, the presidial pueblos came to be substantial rural communities like the original pueblos. The remaining pueblos continued to exist as struggling settlements, rather than as thriving communities. They included the hamlet of Branciforte and the four Indian pueblos (San Juan Capistrano, San Diegueto, Los Flores, and San Pascual) which had taken form during the Figueroa administration. In addition, there were communities of American families in the Sacramento and Napa valleys.

In physical appearance, the pueblo was built on a central rectangular plaza. The broad dirt streets were lined with flat-roofed, mostly single-storied adobe buildings. These included the few small shops, the numerous small dwellings of Mexican and Indian townspeople, and the larger patio-enclosing homes of the wealthier merchants and rancheros. Pueblo life centered on an open parklike plaza bordered by civic buildings, the parish church (often the former mission chapel), and business establishments. Contemporary observers remark on the lack of public improvements: the streets were unpaved, the sewers were open, and water for domestic and agricultural purposes ran in open canals.

The pueblos were also the social center, for their plazas often were the scene of public celebrations of the feast days and birthdays of the Catholic saints. Society reflected the life styles of three dominant classes: the ranchero–merchant elite, the storekeepers and artisans, and the Indian laborers. The leading merchants and rancheros had substantial homes and indulged in a social life that was notable for its continuing round of gay fiestas and intense gambling activity. The other townspeople, for the most part, eked out a meager existence as small landowners, tenants, and laborers. But this did not prevent them from indulging in much the same amusements.

Ranchos

Important as the pueblos were, the ranchos were actually the most conspicuous development in Mexican California society. The rancho was basically a large, self-contained feudal estate. It centered on the large adobe *casa* ("house") that was the domicile of the ranchero and his numerous relatives. Nearby were clusters of buildings comprising the work shops, storage for equipment and supplies, and dwellings for Indian workers. Some ranchos even contained Indian rancherias whose inhabitants might also be workers on the ranchos. Beyond were the vast open lands allocated for pasturage of livestock and cultivation of grains and garden crops. These ranchos were working estates—that is, they produced the necessary food and handmade articles required for the support of their inhabitants.

The rancho proved to be the controlling factor that gave form and shape to California society. It constituted the economic base and mainstay of the foreign trade which contributed so greatly to the development of the province. It produced a stratified society with a ranchero–merchant elite at the top, a small middle class of artisans and storekeepers who lived in the pueblos, and a large lower class of Indian workers in both the rancho and pueblo. While the ranchero–merchant elite had no special legal status, they were the prime movers in the political and economic affairs of the province. They were elected with monotonous regularity to the *diputación* or *ayuntamiento*, and they enjoyed monopolistic privileges in the profitable foreign trade. Of greater significance, the rancho movement considerably extended a land pattern that took the form of large acreages under the ownership of a few.

Rancherias

The rancherias apparently changed little in basic form in that the cacique and the shaman continued to be the leading figures. They were still the most numerous settlements, but undoubtedly declined in number owing to the decimation of the Indian population, according to travelers who reported finding deserted Indian villages. As the Mexican settlement areas extended from the coast to the interior, notably into the Central Valley, a large number of rancherias were drawn into the Hispanic orbit. This exposed them to widespread contacts with white men, which contributed further to the deterioration of native life in these communities. Gentiles (pagans), in rancherias beyond the pale remained relatively free to pursue their native ways.

The Indians

Mexico in proclaiming independence from Spain declared the emancipation of the Indians. That they had been granted citizenship with equal political and legal rights was announced in California by Commissioner Fernandez in 1822 and confirmed by the 1824 Federal Constitution. On learning of their liberties and rights, the Indians became increasingly troublesome, less controllable, and even rebellious. The older Spanish padres, their energies spent with age and their spirit demoralized by the policies of the national government, passed away with the years. The padres sent from Mexico as their replacements were fewer in number and, as the historian Hubert Bancroft observed, had less missionary zeal and concern for the welfare of their Indian subjects. Indian neophyte population increased over a few years and then declined steadily before secularization (about 21,500 in 1825 to 14,900 in 1834), owing to escapes, deaths, and a declining baptism rate.

If the mission decline demoralized the Indian neophyte, secularization in 1834 was devastating. The government-appointed administrators who replaced the padres showed little of their humanitarian ideals. They revealed an excessive zeal in pursuing their own interests and a callous disregard for their Indian subjects, as when they successfully resisted Governor Alvarado's efforts to protect Indian rights (see Chapter 4). Within five years most of the missions were broken up, and the ex-neophytes were released from mission bondage with little preparation or training for their new life of freedom.

The rancho system was highly dependent on Indian labor. A typical rancho might have around a hundred of such Indian workers serving as domestic servants, vaqueros, and field laborers. Vallejo had at least 300 and Sutter had some 600 with their families, but most rancheros had less. The workers might be mission-trained neophytes or gentiles living on the rancho proper or in the nearby rancheria, or they might be captive gentiles rounded up in government or ranchero expeditions against distant villages. The Indians performed the hard work of the rancho and in return received food, clothing, and shelter. Rancho life left a deep imprint on them: a visiting Hudson Bay Company official described Vallejo's Indian workers as "well grown, yet every face bears the impress of poverty and wretchedness"—a commentary reiterated by other contemporary diarists. These Indians lived in economic bondage much like mission neophytes in Spanish times and like the peon in Mexico at that time.

In sharp contrast were the ex-neophytes and gentile Indians in the pueblos and rancherias. In the pueblos, Indians went to work as domestic servants and common laborers. Many who could not find work formed a new class of vagrants who subsisted by beggary and thievery, and sank into a life of vice and destitution. In the rancherias, Indians who could not adapt to settled native ways became outlaws, raiding ranchos for cattle, grain, and other foods. Before long, a vicious cycle developed in which rancheros undertook punitive expeditions against defenseless rancherias, seeking retribution by killing natives, and the Indians retaliated by killing and by looting ranchos. Even the enlightened Vallejo, who carefully cultivated Indian alliances based on mutual respect, was capable of stern retribution, such as the 1841 Clear Lake massacre of 150 defenseless Indians. Vallejo, however, punished Christian Indians for kidnapping gentile Indian children for rancheros. Rancheros in these and other expeditions, often with Indian auxiliaries, seized captive gentiles to work on the ranchos, especially for the harvest. By the 1840's Indian raids had become so numerous and destructive that the government sent larger expeditions to subdue them. These succeeded in killing many natives but failed to stem Indian plunder, which reached its peak in 1845. Gentile Indians in several areas of the state became adept at guerrilla tactics to avoid subjugation and to preserve their way of life.

In the end the Indians suffered appallingly from the ways of the Californios. Sherburne Cook estimated 1,200 were killed in Northern California expeditions between 1830 and 1848, including the barbarous 1837 massacre of 200 by two ruffians, and butcheries by American settlers after 1841. Even more devastating was the high toll from disease (an estimated 18,500) and starvation. A malaria epidemic in 1833, apparently touched off by Hudson Bay fur-trading expeditions coming to California from Astoria on the Columbia River, claimed 4,500 gentile lives in the Sacramento Valley alone, wiping out entire tribelets. Indians in the pueblos, ranchos, and rancherias also suffered from syphilis and other diseases, a factor which certainly contributed to their widespread apathetic condition. In 1846 Indian population stood at about 100,000, less than half of what it had been in Spanish times. Thus, the Indians were reduced in number by homicide, disease, and starvation, and to destitution by bondage and vagrancy—an ironic commentary on the opportunities envisioned for them in the Mexican Plan.

The Family

The family institution was strengthened during the Mexican era. California families, whether ranchero, merchant, or Indian, were generally large: Segundino Robles had 29 children, Hartnell sired 19 progeny, and Tomas Sanchez, who married the 13-year-old Maria Sepulveda, had 21 children and was survived by more than 100 descendants. Women dominated their numbers—only one-seventh of the Mexican Californians were adult male.

Ranchero families came to be the most important type in Mexican California. They emerged when secularization brought about the conversion of mission lands into rancho estates. Paced by the military, the new class of rancheros built up self-supporting estates based on huge land grants and cattle enterprises as the mainstay for their large, growing families. Typically, the ranchero's household provided a home for a family that included his many children, a host of poor relatives, and a large staff of domestic servants, as well as for passing friends and travelers.

The ranchero ruled the household like a feudal lord of a medieval manor. He perpetuated this pretension by assuming the Spanish title *don* ("gentleman"), which, of course, did not represent the aristocratic birth and lordly status of the Spanish noble whom he sought to emulate. He was the patriarch of his extended family, patron to the numerous Indian workers living on his estate, and genial host to visitors. They all owed him unfailing obedience. Some rancheros lived in regal spendor: Bernardo Yorba had 26 servants to maintain his 50-room house and a labor force of skilled artisans and field workers. Most rancheros, however, lived a comfortable, leisurely existence that was abundant in basic necessities but sparing in luxury. Despite their austere habits, they were noted for their addiction to fancy dress, their boundless hospitality, and their intense preoccupation with gambling and sports. Life on these isolated ranchos was enlivened by fiestas, colorful open-house affairs for celebrating family events and Church and national holidays.

Family life blended Spanish tradition and new ways. Rancheros and their sons lived a disciplined existence ruled by a strict personal code of morals. They rose early and spent much of the day on horseback at work or play. Their women were industrious helpmates who, when not supervising servants or preparing for fiestas, kept busy embroidering, sewing, and entertaining. Domestic relations were marked by family pride, filial piety, and religious devoutness. In the de la Guerra household in Santa Barbara, family members attended morning mass, family and servants took siesta after the noonday dinner, children kneeled and kissed papa's hand before dashing off to bed at night, and even adult sons asked father's permission before smoking in his presence. Vallejo tells us that in the breast of the Californios "love of family was stronger than selfish and vile interest."

Marriages were elaborate gala affairs. Typically, suitors formally asked parents and the padre for permission to marry, and the nuptial pair were lavishly entertained at colorful fiestas before and after the wedding ceremony. Foreigners had to secure the governor's permission to marry native daughters. In a celebrated courtship, Henry Fitch eloped with his beloved Josefa Carrillo (Don Carlos's daughter) with the blessings of parents and priest. They were married at sea but on their return they were separated, and remarried after Fitch had fulfilled the requirements. William Dana chafed at the two-year delay in complying with requirements of baptism and citizenship before he could marry another Josefa Carrillo (Don Joaquin's daughter). Once in the family, they were treated as warmly as other family members.

Women

Women apparently had greater freedom of movement compared to Spanish times. They were less bound to formal codes of dress and manner, and often rode and hunted with their menfolk. In speaking of the ranchero women, the puritanical Richard Henry Dana (William's nephew) charged that their excessive fondness for dress was their ruin. But Alfred Robinson (who married a de la Guerra) praised their charm, chastity, deportment, and physical grace. Edwin Bryant (one of Fremont's men) claimed "there are no women in the world for whose manners nature has done so much, and for whom art and education . . . have done so little . . . . In their deportment toward strangers they are queens." American *gringos* imbued with Protestant rectitude often mistook the charming flirtations of ranchero daughters, usually under the watchful eyes of elderly chaperones, as sexual advances (so Kevin Starr tells us), and often lumped them together with the lower-class women of loose ways.

Culture

Education

Illiteracy continued to be widespread in Mexican California. Rancheros, who rarely could read or write themselves, sometimes hired tutors to educate their children, and a few even sent them to Mexico, the United States, or Europe for their education. Primary schools were few apparently because of lack of funds, teachers, and public interest. Hartnell operated a school for his many children and probably for children of neighboring rancheros.

Literature

The Californios had a sparse literary tradition. The absence of newspapers, the small number of private libraries, and the scarce writings of the *hijos de país* reflect the undeveloped state of literature. What little literary production there was we owe to visiting Americans like Pattie, Dana, and Robinson, whose well-written personal accounts were widely read. James Pattie's *Personal Narrative* (1831) is a journal of a bawdy border-state frontiersman, an epic of mountain men and fur trappers in the Southwest and California in the 1820's. Richard Henry Dana, Jr., in his book *Two Years Before the Mast* (1840), provides a probing account of the seaman's life and the California hide and tallow trade in the

1830's, as seen through the eyes of a cultivated New England Puritan. Alfred Robinson's *Life in California* (1842) gives us an intimate glimpse of the ranchero life of which he was a part as an adopted son of the country and as agent for Bryant, Sturgis, and Company. (He was Gale's assistant and later successor as the company's California agent.) The open-minded and sympathetic Robinson balances Dana's somewhat derogatory picture of the rancheros.

Foreign journals that contributed valuable information about Mexican California included that of Alexander Forbes, British merchant and consul in Mexico (1839); that of Sir George Simpson, a top official of the Hudson Bay Company, on his world voyage; and that of Duflot de Mofras, a French diplomat on a government mission to report on resources of the California–Oregon area (both 1841–1842). The three writers suggested that their governments take over California before the Americans did. Their works were significant in arousing the interest of Americans and Europeans in the far-off Mexican California province.

Religion

Church organization underwent a transformation. Under the 1833 Secularization Act, the mission system operated by the Franciscan clerical order was converted into a parish system ruled by the regular Church. The mission chapel became a parish church. Mission padres were allowed to retire to their college or convent in Mexico, but many accepted appointments as parish padres serving the faithful in pueblos or former mission areas. The padre–presidente ruled the missions and the parishes (local units of a bishop's diocese), serving in the latter capacity as vicar (deputy) under the Bishop of Sonoma until 1840, when California was formed into a separate diocese with its own bishop. Control of the Pious Fund (see above) passed from the Franciscan order to the bishop, and in 1842 was absorbed into the national treasury in a move by President Santa Anna to plunder mission estates and revenues for his own ends.

Catholicism remained the state religion. The faithful attended the regular masses held in parish churches to hear the curates. As ranchos developed, the patron sometimes invited padres from nearby mission sites to conduct family services. Political liberalism, however, eventually undercut religious sentiment and church obligation. Alvarado apparently lost little status when he was excommunicated from the Church for reading a banned book. Vallejo was a nominal Catholic and gave financial support to the local parish church. However, in keeping with his liberal ideas of church–state separation, he refused to pay the ecclesiastical tithes. Many Santa Barbara rancheros, like de la Guerra, regularly paid such church taxes. Toward the end of Mexican rule, church congregations came to comprise mostly women and Indian neophytes. The dismantling of the mission system and spread of libertarian secular ideas contributed to the steady deterioration of church affairs in the province.

SUMMARY

Mexico after its revolt from Spain in 1821 sought to extend to California its new republican order. The national government initiated a program to transform the Spanish monarchical system into a republican society that would give greater voice in government to the people, including the vast Indian population, and wider opportunity for them to become enterprising, self-supporting citizens. It evidently thought that appropriate laws, implemented by the appointed governors, would be sufficient to bring about this change in California.

The Mexican nation, though, was racked by internal disruptions, later intensified by external troubles, which hindered the realization of her plan for California. The national government was torn by such intense conflicts at home that it gave little attention to California affairs. What action was taken was too often inadequate and contradictory. The national government did not reckon on the ambitions of the California ranchero–merchant elite, who eventually took matters into their own hands. Neither did it reckon with the covetous ambitions of its aggressive neighbor to the north, who eventually took over the province.

In California the native sons of the military, together with the immigrating New England traders, emerged to form the new ranchero–merchant elite. They gradually established their version of a republican society centering on diputación rule, a rancho–pueblo economy based on foreign markets, and a social elite comprising themselves. The ruling elite demonstrated a capacity for undertaking capitalistic enterprises, but they showed exclusivist tendencies in clinging to their newly won privileges. The great majority of pueblo settlers, denied opportunities to participate in the market economy, simply sank into a life of meager subsistence. The great Indian majority, always the victim in the system, had the choice of submitting to peon status on the ranchos, becoming part of the destitute labor force in the pueblos, or subjecting themselves to the uncertain ways of Indian rancheria life.

California emerged in the Mexican period as a society in transition. It was an authoritarian society, but it had begun to develop libertarian traditions. Attracted as they were to American ideas, the Californios were unable to break completely from their attachment to native Spanish authoritarian tradition and restrictions of the Mexican government. The ranchero professed liberal ideas and tolerant attitudes toward the immigrants and open trade, which contributed much to the development of the provinces. Yet these rancheros, in their family life and public ways, were as authoritarian as their missionary predecessors. The sea traders, Mexican and American, revealed a zeal to exploit commercial advantages for selfish gain that left little in the way of mutual benefits for the Californios, and helped thwart development of their province into a thriving self-supporting political economy. By the end of Mexican rule there had developed a hybrid society, one that blended Spanish authoritarian and American libertarian traditions in a feudal–capitalistic system. With the arrival of the Americans, California completed its transition to a republican capitalistic system of the American type.

Mexico had begun the process of change that was to transform California into a genuine republican order. This undoubtedly made it easier for the Californians to adjust to the new order that was to come about in the shift from Mexican to American rule. The Mexicans also set the pattern of strong local home rule, land distribution, Indian labor, cattle industry, and other Hispanic traditions that were to be adopted by the Americans.

Historians have perpetuated a popular view of the Californios as a decadent people in an undeveloped society. When compared with their Spanish predecessors or with their American successors, the Californios had a commendable record of achievement. Significantly, Hispanic people did not have the inherent advantages of tradition and experience that the Americans had for developing a republican society. They made progress toward home rule and demonstrated a capacity for undertaking private enterprises essential to a self-supporting economy. They certainly did not lack ambition or ability (as so often charged) to carry out their scheme for a republican society. As Jessie Francis aptly surmises, their *mañana* was not putting things off until tomorrow—or indefinitely; their *mañana* was *waiting* until tomorrow when things would be done. Given favorable circumstances of time and opportunity—which were not to be—ambitious Californios might well have worked out their salvation.

IV American California

SCENE ON A BRANCH OF THE SACRAMENTO.

After the American conquest, California entered a frenetic period characterized by sporadic upheaval, spectacular development, and remarkable achievement. Dazzled by the lure of gold, people from all walks of life and ethnic origins flowed into the state in great numbers seeking opportunities in mining, agriculture, commerce, and other enterprises. Amidst these chaotic conditions, the dominant Americans transformed the existing society. By the end of this interregnum (1847–1850), California entered the Union with her version of the American order, one which rested upon representative government, a capitalistic economy, and a pluralistic society.

6 The American Interregnum
7 American California Society

6 The American Interregnum

THE SETTING

The Democratic Scheme

At the time of the California conquest, the United States had already existed for 60 years. In 1789 the American people established a constitutional republic based on a federal system in which sovereign powers were distributed between the national and state governments. In practice, however, the republic was controlled by the nation's elite. By the time of Andrew Jackson's administration, popular control had supplanted the elite, and a democratic republic came into being. The steady flow of immigrants from Europe was making the United States a populous nation of growing cities and an expanding frontier. Throughout a half-century of such growth and expansion, the Americans, through purchase, conquest, and diplomacy, had pushed their boundaries from the Mississippi River to the Pacific Coast. By the time of California's admission into the Union, the United States consisted of 30 states and 4 territories. The young republic had evolved into a relatively stable society that was continually expanding through the activities of a restless and energetic people.

The Americans developed a distinctive republican government

based on a balance of powers and the representation of the people. In the colonial period, they had acquired a liking for individual enterprise and a dislike of arbitrary government. In the early national period, they developed in their institutions ways to protect the individual's freedom of action, yet maintain an orderly society. They built into their republican government features designed to serve these ends. The executive, legislative, and judicial branches of government were sharply separated by a division of powers, so that no single group of people might control the public business. The national and state legislative bodies represented the sovereign power of the people, and were based on a system of representation that gave a vote to most adult white males and a voice to every district, state, and territory in the country. The Constitution contained a Bill of Rights and other provisions to insure that government would not restrict basic individual freedoms cherished by the people.

The Americans also evolved a type of capital economy based on a free market system. They emerged from the colonial period with a strong tradition of private enterprise that made them the most capitalistic-minded people in the world at that time. They wrote into their Constitution special protection for property (an essential feature of private enterprise) in the provision that no person shall be deprived of life, liberty, or property without due process of law. Congress was delegated broad powers to regulate commerce, which were subject to judicial review by the Supreme Court in case of conflicts between private enterprise and the public interest. In the early national period, the Americans developed a framework of government regulations that allowed a wide interplay of private enterprise in a relatively free market economy. The government occasionally lent assistance to enterprises but hardly regulated them, in keeping with the prevailing attitude that government should not interfere in economic affairs. By Jackson's time, a chief task of government was to preserve the competition of many entrepreneurs and to combat monopoly by a few, in order to sustain a viable market economy. Yet the social order that evolved out of this political–economic system resulted in an imbalanced society. It was a white and largely Protestant society, one that gave little, if any, voice or opportunity to nonwhite races and others (paupers and women); these were simply left out of the scheme.

Within the republican framework, competing groups of Americans found in political parties an effective medium for promoting their interests in the government. In the early days of the republic, these groups were organized into two political parties based on the opposing ideas of Alexander Hamilton and Thomas Jefferson. By Jackson's time, party leaders and bosses had worked out effective ways of organizing public support through political organizations on behalf of their constituent groups.

Our present-day parties still pay homage to their Hamiltonian and Jeffersonian antecedents. The party of Hamilton—the Federalists, later the Whigs and Republicans—consisted primarily of conservatives. It comprised the men of great wealth and large property owners, including merchants, traders, bankers, manufacturers, large farmers and planters, and later the industrialists. The party stronghold was in the North, but centers were found also on the seaboard of the South and in the thriving cities of the West. The primary concerns of these men were business enterprises. They favored a strong national government which they believed would maintain the orderly development of society. They sought to concentrate economic power through monopolistic privileges and corporate enterprises. They constituted an elite of position and power in the business and social communities. The conservatives of Hamilton's and Henry Clay's time envisioned a society based on the benevolence of a centralized government and a balanced economy of agrarian and commercial interests under the control of the rich and well-born.

The Jeffersonians—the Democrat–Republicans, later the Democrats—embodied the liberal tradition. They embraced the small property owners (farmers and planters), the small merchants, the artisans, and the laborers. The party drew its strength primarily from the rural areas of the South and the West, and from the cities of the North. It was less concerned with property rights than with individual rights, which would insure the freedom of action needed to pursue modest enterprises. The Jeffersonians emphasized the role of state and local government because it was closer to the people and, they felt, would be more protective of their enterprises. They sought to maintain an agrarian society based on the competition of many individuals, thus spreading economic wealth more evenly. They constituted the large middle class that formed the backbone of American society. The liberals of the Jefferson and Jackson eras favored a decentralized government where "the government which governs least governs best"—and an agrarian-dominated economy which they believed would spread benefits among people.

These competing groups were able to promote their interests and resolve their conflicts tolerably well through the game of politics. They accepted the rules of the game as set forth in their national and state constitutions, holding to the basic tenets of majority rule and minority rights. They agreed on fundamental political principles, but were divided on specific issues that affected their vested interests. They relied, however, on the art of compromise to settle in a peaceful manner their differences over such issues.

The professional politicians—whether party leaders or public officials—played a vital role in this political process. They were the brokers who reconciled the varied interests of the conservative and liberal groups within each party. They fought their political battles primarily in two arenas: the party conventions and the legislative bodies at the national, state, and local levels. In party conventions, they sought to nominate their candidates to public office and to commit the party to their position. In the Congress, as in the state legislature and in local governments, they sought to influence public policies which affected the vested economic interests of their constituent groups. Thus government became highly responsive to the needs of varied groups.

These groups feared government action that would impede individual action, but did not hesitate to enlist government aid for their private enterprises. So it was that farmers, planters, merchants, industrialists, and others effectively applied the appropriate political pressure to acquire the government's help. State and local governments since colonial times—and later the national government—had developed a legal framework and administrative practices for aiding private enterprises. They gave tax exemptions to lessen their financial burdens. They granted subsidies or loans to provide necessary capital for financing costly projects, notably roads, canals, and railroads. They provided uniform standards and public inspection to insure against inferior goods and the unfair practices of unscrupulous enterprises. They collected and disseminated information that was required for planning and building certain enterprises. They even undertook public ownership of enterprises requiring great amounts of capital for expensive large-scale projects when private enterprise could not finance them. To be sure, government occasionally overextended its favors to certain groups at the expense of others. On the whole, however, the Americans had worked out an effective formula of government aid to private enterprises which contributed greatly to their economic development.

The democratic system developed in the United States, then, consisted of intimate interactions between government and political parties, and close relationships between governmental operations and the activities of private enterprises. Through such a system, the United States had, by 1850, emerged as one of the leading agricultural and commercial nations in the world, and was on the threshold of even greater industrial expansion.

California was to adapt this system after the American conquest, grafting it onto persistent features of its Spanish and Mexican traditions. It was to be further modified by the dynamic forces already transforming the new territory.

DEVELOPMENT

The National Scene

At the time of California's appearance on the American scene in the 1840's, the United States was entering a period of transition. Jacksonian Democracy was still in vogue but was in its twilight years. Merchant capitalists—the same sort who had been active in Mexican California—were giving way to rising industrialists as the dominant force in the nation's economy. For the moment, however, the prevailing tone of American society was still set by small merchants, farmers, planters, and artisan laborers, whose middle-class ways constituted the national norm. National politics were also in a state of flux. The Democratic and Whig parties were both in disarray. They had abandoned the cherished principles of their earlier years and now engaged in a politics of expediency that practically obliterated the differences between them. The Mexican War (1846–1848) revived animosities between the North and South over the status of slavery in the newly acquired territories. In the two years following the war, Congress was engulfed in a bitter debate over how this perplexing issue might be resolved.

The national crisis over slavery inadvertently set the stage in California for what might be called the *interregnum* ("between reigns"), which covers the years from 1847 to 1850. This interregnum, over-lapping both Mexican and American sovereignties, is American in the sense that the Americans dominated it. It was a period of great confusion and disorder. Congress, which had sole authority, failed to establish regular governments for any of the new territories, even after the

Mexican War. The military government, therefore, continued to administer California affairs throughout these years. Three major events—The Treaty of Guadalupe Hidalgo, the Gold Rush, and the Constitutional Convention—took place during this brief three-year span. While each of these events contributed to California's long-range development in a distinctive way, they also set in motion forces which greatly complicated the affairs of California at the time. Out of these forces were to emerge the basic elements of California society as we know it today.

The Military Government

General Kearny's arrival in California for the military conquest signaled the official beginning of military government. By January 1847 Kearny had set up a temporary civil government authorized by the United States government. Kearny and his successor, Colonel Richard Mason (May 1847—April 1849) established the basis of civil government that was to prevail during the interregnum. Here the governor was in a difficult position. On the one hand was the increasing flow into the territory of various sorts of Americans: military personnel, enterprising farmers, merchants, and other adventurous immigrants in search of opportunities. On the other hand were the apprehensive Mexican and American settlers and the restless Indians who viewed with growing concern the changes which were disturbing their secure existence. Compounding the governor's situation was the lack of adequate military forces for policing the territory. To cap his difficulties, the governor had to contend with California's vague status, a result of the fluctuating policies of the United States and congressional inaction (see Chapter 7).

In light of such circumstances, the military governor simply made expedient uses of available resources. As chief executive officer, he assumed the initiative in directing California affairs but confined himself to issuing instructions to the alcaldes and proclamations to the people. He was ably assisted by his staff of two West Pointers (later to be prominent Civil War generals): Henry Halleck, his Secretary of State, who handled civil matters; and William Sherman, his adjutant, who dealt with military matters. He relied heavily on the existing alcalde system, appointing or having elected prominent Californios or Americans to this position. Since he established no territorial legislature or effective judiciary, local government gained ascendancy and strength.

The governor dealt with other pressing problems in the same expeditious manner. He generally upheld land titles as they were at the time of the conquest, which favored existing owners of Mexican-granted lands and aroused the ire of aggressive American newcomers who coveted these lands for their enterprises. He reduced trade restrictions to insure the flow of much-needed goods into the province but insisted duties be paid in cash instead of goods. This antagonized merchants but served the purpose of providing revenues for support of the military government. He appointed experienced agents to oversee Indian affairs (Vallejo and Sutter in the north, a Mormon Battalion captain for the south), but they were unable to cope effectively with the perplexing problem. In managing public affairs, the governors showed a tendency to uphold the status quo as far as the demands of a situation allowed.

New elements were added to the cast of characters in California public affairs during the interregnum; the Mormons and the New York Volunteers. The Mormons, who had already suffered a decade of public attacks in the East for their religious beliefs, were in the process of leaving the "wicked nation" to find refuge in the Far West. In the autumn of 1846, two Mormon contingents came to California, one the Mormon Battalion who came overland with Kearny's army, and the other a settler group led by Samuel Brannan who came by sea from New York to San Francisco. The New York Volunteers arrived in the spring of 1847. After completing military service, generally garrison duty in the pueblos, these soldiers of the Mormon Battalion and the New York regiment took up civilian pursuits as artisans, business and professional men, and aspiring politicians. They not only contributed their talents to the development of the province, but some became important figures in California's emerging political economy.

The Treaty of Guadalupe Hidalgo

Meanwhile peace negotiations got under way as the war between the United States and Mexico drew to a close. After completing negotiations, representatives of both nations signed the treaty in February 1848 at Guadalupe Hidalgo, a village suburb outside Mexico City, and submitted it to their respective nations for ratification. Public sentiment in both nations was sharply divided over the treaty. The Americans argued whether the United States should acquire all, part, or none of Mexico. The demoralized Mexicans talked of "war to the death" and "peace at all costs," and many were even willing to be annexed to the United States. The treaty was finally consummated in May 1848. Thus California was incorporated into the American Union at a time of great stress for both participating nations.

The treaty brought an official end to the war and laid down conditions for the peace. It defined the new boundary, which was drawn substantially along its present limits. The United States acquired from Mexico the northern provinces of Alta California and New Mexico, and Mexico received compensation of fifteen million dollars for the loss. Mexican citizens residing in these transferred lands were given the choice of returning to Mexico or becoming American citizens. Contrary to popular belief, the treaty as finally adopted did *not* recognize the validity of land grants issued by the Mexican government (this was the original draft's Article X which was stricken by the United States Senate); but it stipulated that the rights of Mexicans would be respected. The treaty confirmed the transfer of territory (the combined California and New Mexico provinces) in which Mexico lost over one-half of her domain and the United States gained an additional one-fifth of hers.

The significance of the treaty is that it ended the war and established the peace. As for the California phase, the outcome was inevitable. Herbert Priestley puts it simply when he says: "two races met and clashed on a coveted frontier and the battle went to the strong."

Once California was in the Union it was to have a continuing effect—more so perhaps than any other single state outside of New York—upon the modern development of the United States. For the moment, however, one event was to overshadow all else. While treaty negotiations were being concluded in Mexico City in the winter of 1848, a new excitement was developing in California. It was to change the destiny of the province and affect the development of its new parent nation.

The Gold Rush

Gold! That treasure that has gripped men's imagination since ancient times was found in the Sierra foothills of California. James Marshall, an eccentric carpenter and millwright, discovered it in January 1848 while constructing a sawmill for John Sutter at Coloma on the American River. News of the strike traveled slowly in the beginning because of poor communications and public skepticism. California's only two newspapers, both in San Francisco, published the first reports in March. In May the news took, and the stampede to the Sierras was under way. Thus began the greatest gold rush of modern times. It was to transform completely California society and have a profound effect on national and world developments.

The Gold Rush during the interregnum underwent two phases, covering 1848 and 1849. The first phase may be characterized as a local affair. While Marshall's discovery attracted only people in the vicinity of Sutter's Fort, it was the antics of Sam Brannan which touched off the stampede from San Francisco and other areas. On hearing of the gold strike, Brannan thoughtfully stocked his stores in San Francisco and Coloma with mining implements and food supplies. Then, one day in May, he went through the streets of San Francisco, with hat and bottle of gold in hand, shouting, "Gold, gold, gold from the American River."

Brannan's caper had an electrifying effect, for it set off a chain reaction of public response. By June three-fourths of San Francisco was depopulated. During the summer, people flowed from all parts of the province to the mines, leaving practically deserted communities in their wake. By the end of summer, gold seekers were arriving from the outside, notably Oregon, Sonora in Northern Mexico, Peru, and Chile (the last three being mining areas), and even from Hawaii and far-off Australia. Before the year was out, California's population soared to an estimated 20,000, of which 7000 were Californians, 6000 to 8000 Americans, several thousand Latin Americans, and the remainder from the Pacific Islands.

The search for gold took place in scattered areas on the western slope of the Sierra foothills. Ranchers and farmers, soldiers and sailors, merchants and hunters of varied national and ethnic origins were quickly transformed into miners. They took off from two junction points: Sacramento, for the tributaries of the Sacramento River (the northern mines), or Stockton, for the tributaries of the San Joaquin River (the southern mines). They searched out gold particles and chunks on the banks of flowing rivers or the bottoms of streams dried out by the long hot summer. They worked from sunup to sundown, swinging a pick, shovel, or crowbar in the hot sun; digging dirt, gravel, and sand (usually down to four feet); slogging in cold, muddy water; bending constantly to pry with a knife, to swish the pan, or to rock the cradle (see Chapter 7). By the end of the year, some 5000 miners at work in the diggings had taken out an estimated $245,000 worth of gold.

The forty-eighters found gold mining to be an exciting adventure, but it was also hard, backbreaking work. They existed in a carnivallike atmosphere, living in temporary dwellings of flimsy tents, lean-tos, and shacks, often leaving in the open their belongings, including bags or bottles of gold which were left undisturbed. Some struck it big, but the average miner made only modest profits for prices were fantastically high. Storekeepers provided food supplies, mining implements, and other merchandise at prices governed by severe shortages, transportation costs, and the careless spending habits of the miners. Yet when compared to their successors, the forty-eighters were a relatively prosperous lot.

1849

The year 1849, the second phase of the Gold Rush, was an international affair. News of the gold strike was first published outside of California in August 1848 in the *New York Herald*, but the incident was treated as a freak. Public skepticism was firmly dispelled in December 1848 when President Polk, in his annual message to Congress, confirmed the gold discovery. His endorsement touched off a gold mania that was to attract immigrants from major continents of the world.

The international rush to the gold fields of California was a world-wide movement. Events in 1848 set in motion an immigrant tide in 1849. Americans were on the rebound from the controversial war with Mexico and the hard-fought national election. Military veterans, politicians, and others sought new opportunity in the Far West. The famine in Ireland and revolutionary upheavals in Europe and China (Taiping Revolt) prompted discontented farmers, merchants, and others to leave for better things in America. The American and European gold seekers found their way to the new El Dorado ("the gilded place") by way of three major routes: the combined sea–land route from New York to San Francisco over the Isthmus of Panama, the all-sea route from New York to San Francisco via Cape Horn, and by overland trail from river towns on the Mississippi and the Missouri (Independence, St. Louis, and St. Joseph were popular jumping-off places) over the Sierra into California's Central Valley. Whichever of these major routes and secondary byways they took, the argonauts suffered diseases and other hardships that left scars on mind and body. Travel to California was such that only the hardy and enterprising survived. The journey was as formidable an experience as the gold venture itself. By the end of 1849, these argonauts—adventurers in search of gold—had swelled California's population to 100,000 people, of which one-half to two-thirds were Americans, one-fourth foreign born, and the rest Californians, exclusive of Indians. Most argonauts apparently intended to return home once they were rich.

The forty-niners continued the main search for placer deposits in the same general area of the Sierra foothills. Restless elements moved from crowded diggings to prospect virgin areas, opening new diggings below the Tuolumne in the south, in the more remote regions of the northwest, and on the eastern slopes of the Sierra. As the placers along the river areas were played out, the miners developed new ways to find gold. They diverted streams to get at the gold lying on river bottoms (river mining), extended ditches for carrying water away from streams to feed cradle operations in distant diggings, and dug tunnels as much as 100 feet deep to reach underground gold-embedded rock strata (quartz mining). Some 40,000 miners took an estimated ten million dollars from the gold fields that year.

The forty-niners, more than the forty-eighters, regarded mining as a serious venture that required hard work and much optimism. They were a more orderly and pragmatic lot, their ways were more systematic. They built durable cabins that would accommodate them over the winter months. Notwithstanding improved mining techniques, they had to work harder to acquire a profitable yield of gold. Despite these efforts, the forty-niners realized less profit than their predecessors. The prices of goods soared to their greatest peak in the entire Gold Rush period, supplies costing 100 to 400 percent more than in San Francisco. The situation undoubtedly contributed to the forty-niner's intense preoccupation with his work, even at a time when a movement was underway to establish a new government for the province. Contemporaries are practically unanimous in describing the forty-niners as a plain, hard-working, and straightforward lot, fair and honest in their dealings.

The Struggle for Order

Governmental Crisis

Meanwhile the Gold Rush was spurring rapid developments in other parts of Northern California. The emigrants who did not go to the Sierra diggings to search for gold flowed into the northern communities of San Francisco, San Jose, Sonoma, Sacramento, and Stockton to pursue opportunities in agriculture, manufacturing, and trade. Each of these communities experienced the painful throes of sudden population growth, hectic commercial development, and the increasing inability of local government to cope with problems resulting from both. A new concern arose with the threat to life that resulted from the sudden increase in robberies, assaults, murders, and other violence, and the lack of an effective police system. There was mounting criticism of the military government's inability to deal with the increasingly chaotic situation.

San Francisco, in particular, underwent a drastic transformation. Owing to its strategic position as the chief port of entry for people and cargo heading for the Sierra mines, the sparse community burgeoned overnight into a bustling commercial center. The population jumped from around 800 in the winter of 1848, to 2000 a year later, to 6000 by the summer of 1849. Town lots were rapidly disposed of at prices as high as $10,000, including land underwater for prospective wharves. A self-appointed group called the Regulators constituted a volunteer police force to check the growing number of crimes. They proved to be such a disorderly band of ruffians that they were soon brought to bay by a counter-organization which included Sam Brannan among its leaders—the first vigilante activity in the city's history. Local governmental affairs were hopelessly confused; at one point, two city councils were actually conducting public affairs at the same time.

By the winter of 1849, public exasperation with this chaotic state of affairs evolved into a movement for a provisional civilian government. The spark for public action was the news that Congress had adjourned the previous autumn still without having established a territorial government for California. Public meetings calling for pro-visional government were held for the next three months at San Jose, San Francisco, Sacramento, Sonoma, and Monterey. In San Francisco, political affairs reached such an impasse that in February local citizens set up a Legislative Assembly, a representative body with a code of laws and a judicial system, which quickly replaced the two rival city councils. San Francisco citizens, in effect, had established in this municipal government a form of self-government which preempted the authority of the military government in that city. In March delegates from several communities met to call for a convention in August to draft a constitution.

The men who took the initiative in this movement for establishing a civil government, surprisingly enough, were the newcomers. They included mostly former New York Volunteers, such as the printer Edward Gilbert in San Francisco, and other military or naval men turned civilian, such as the lawyer Charles Botts of Monterey. Others who were active were recently arrived settlers, like Brannan and Peter Burnett, a lawyer–farmer who had served on the supreme court of the Oregon Territory before emigrating to California, and older settlers, like Bidwell and Sutter—all active in Sacramento affairs. As Woodrow Hansen suggests, these men could enjoy the "frenzy of capitalistic enterprise in security" only—that is, only if based on the underpinnings of a well-established government.

The military government at this point was at a critical stage. When General Bennett Riley took over as governor in April, he at first sustained Mason's policies and perpetutated the military government, but circumstances forced him to change his mind. The arrival of forty-niners in great numbers, and the continued desertions of military personnel to the mines, compounded his difficulties in administering the affairs of the territory. When Sacramento in that month followed the example of San Francisco in setting up a Legislative Assembly, he faced the prospect of other communities following suit to challenge his authority. On receiving news in May that Congress had adjourned once again without acting on the California situation, the governor made his move. He issued a call for delegates to meet in convention at Monterey in September for the purpose of organizing a territorial government or drawing up a state constitution for submission to Congress for approval. Immediately San Jose and Monterey concurred in Riley's action, followed by San Francisco and other communities. This, of course, undermined the legislative assembly in San Francisco and aborted the August convention proposed by the civilian leaders. Riley by this move had taken extra-legal action to meet the crisis of growing anarchy by arranging for the establishment of a civil government, and had helped restore public confidence in the military government.

The Constitutional Convention

The constitutional convention which met at Monterey in September 1849 was as remarkable a body as ever met in the annals of political conventions. Governor Riley's call resulted in the selection of 73 delegates from ten geographical districts, but only 48 showed up at the convention, the mining districts having sent only half of their apportioned delegates. Of the 48 delegates, six were born in California, seven were foreign born, and the remainder were American born from 15 different states (half of the states then in the Union), of which 22 were northern and 13 southern. In age, they ranged from 25 to 53 years, 36 years being the median age. By occupation, 16 were farmers or ranchers, 14 were lawyers, 9 were merchants; the rest comprised other professions and one who professed "elegant leisure." The convention was unusual for its mix of nationality, age, occupation, religion, and social status. The body was representative of diverse groups, although it consisted predominantly of young American Protestants, middle-class entrepreneurs, and professional men—the sort of men who had a conscious stake in the future of the society for which they were framing a constitutional government.

Colton Hall, Monterey. Built by Walter Colton, U.S. naval chaplain and Monterey alcalde. It was used as a government building and a schoolhouse, then as the site for the 1849 Constitutional Convention.

The convention was especially outstanding in that all the major groups of California society had a voice, save the Indians. Furthermore, each group had talented leaders to speak for its interests, as tempered by the individuality of their strong personalities. The Californios included members of the leading ranchero elite who were well represented by

Carrillo, Pablo de la Guerra (Jose's son), and Vallejo. The older Yankee merchants had their spokesmen in Larkin and Stearns. The American pioneer farmers who had immigrated overland before the conquest were represented by Robert Semple. The military had Halleck, who by now was probably the man most versed in California affairs. The San Francisco politicians included former New York Volunteers like Gilbert, and William Gwin, a physician turned politician and a former congressman now seeking to become the first United States Senator from California. A good number of these delegates, like Botts and Sutter, had been active in the local movement for civil government. Among the distinguished visitors at the convention were other aspiring politicians, like Fremont and Thomas Butler King, the pro-slavery Whig from Georgia who was also a personal emissary of President Zachary Taylor.

The delegates in choosing the presiding officer selected Robert Semple, a man who was, in a sense, most representative of that body. The giant Kentuckian was a transitional figure, for here was an older settler who had been active around Sutter's Fort, in the Bear Flag Revolt, and in the local movement for civil government. As a nonpracticing dentist, he had been successful as a farmer (Sacramento Valley), a printer (Monterey), a land speculator (San Francisco), a ferryman (Carquinez Straits), and town developer (Benicia). He was a Southerner who showed a Northerner's love of enterprise and who had, as a contemporary, Elisha Crosby, pointed out, "a great high head full of brains and practical common sense . . . a good judge of Bourbon and honest as he was tall."

The convention delegates performed their tasks with considerable dispatch and harmony. They shared a basic understanding of republican ideals and fundamental issues. Even the Californios were well grounded in a liberal tradition of their own, one which stemmed from the Mexican Constitution of 1824. The debates were lengthy but of high quality and, for the most part, free from acrimony. The convention completed its deliberations in the remarkably short time of six weeks.

The delegates were practically of one mind on the matter of California's political structure. They voted overwhelmingly in favor of state government. The Californio delegates opposed it in favor of a territorial government, for they believed (correctly, as it turned out), that as large landholders they would assume the burden of taxation under a state government. The delegates established the customary form of state government, with the three separate departments—the executive, legislative, and judicial—carefully circumscribing the powers and functions of each in order to insure the proper workings of checks and balances. In organizing their governmental system, they retained a strong flavor of Jacksonian Democracy which suited a frontier society.

When the delegates took up the matter of the suffrage, they faced the controversial problem of who were to be acceptable as voting citizens of the new state. The delegates were in complete agreement in granting the suffrage to all adult white males over 21 years of age, but they were sharply divided over giving the same right to nonwhites—the Indians and the Negroes. With regard to the Indians, the issue focused on those full and part-blood Indians who had rights of suffrage under the Mexican Constitution—a delicate matter, since many Californios were of mixed blood. In the end, the delegates provided that white male citizens of the United States and Mexico were entitled to vote, and that the legislature, in special cases, could grant the vote to Indians by a two-thirds vote. For Negroes, the issue involved both slave and free blacks. The delegates were unanimous in prohibiting slavery, but the admission of free Negroes into the state was something else again. The fear of free Negro immigration was strong, for these black people might successfully compete with Caucasians in pursuing opportunities. In the end, the delegates rejected the proposed provision barring immigration of free Negroes, evidently on the grounds that such a provision might jeopardize the acceptance of California's constitution by the Congress, still deadlocked over the slavery issue in the new territories.

An important matter related to suffrage was legislative apportionment, or the allocation of assemblymen and senators among the voters of the state. This vital matter of distributing the power in the legislature evoked sharp controversy over whether representation should be based solely on population, or partly on consideration of property interests. Here the delegates from the populous North, notably the mining districts, were pitted against the South, where a few rancheros owned most of the land. The delegates eventually adopted a plan which apportioned both the Assembly and the Senate according to population, in a manner that gave two mining districts (Sacramento and San Joaquin) half the representatives in both houses.

Another vital issue before the convention was the status of corporations, especially banks, that affect the development of property and enterprises. The question before them was the kind of capitalistic economy they desired—one that would allow skillful and industrious men, with the aid of bank credit, to acquire vast amounts of wealth, or one that would insure most men modest wealth based on hard money transactions and their accumulated savings. The delegates were sharply divided on this issue. Larkin wanted banks in order to obtain additional capital for developing his ambitious projects. Gwin bitterly opposed banks, for he had borrowed, speculated, and lost all in the Panic of 1837—as had several delegates. The convention was involved here in the usual American struggle between merchants and industrialists on the one hand, and agrarians and artisans on the other. At the time, banks were the dominant form of corporation, so the issue also touched on whether corporate enterprise or individual enterprise should be favored in the use of California's wealth for economic development. The majority of the delegates, by agreeing on severe restrictions on corporations in general and banks in particular, showed their bias in favor of individual enterprise.

Establishing a constitutional basis for state finances was a difficult task for the convention, especially in a society like California whose economy was at an embryonic stage of development. The delegates dealt with the matter of expenditures by setting the limit of debt to be incurred by the legislature ($300,000), with provision for a higher limit with voters' approval. Finding revenues for supporting the new government was an intricate matter. Historically, the chief source of revenue among the states had been primarily the tax on real property, based on the premise that those who enjoyed the protection of property by the government should contribute to its support. If applied to California, it was apparent the ranchers would assume the greater burden of the tax. They presumably received proportionally less income from the cattle on their large landholdings than did the transient miner, who used but did not own or rent his land, or the merchants and other owners of town lots in the wealthier populous communities. Eventually the delegates, in a compromising spirit, adopted a provision by which taxation was made equal and uniform throughout the state. All property was to be taxed in proportion to its value as determined by assessors elected by the voters of the district, county, or town where the property was located. Collectors of the tax would be similarly elected. In this way, local citizens, rather than a state-appointed agent, would select the officials, who would presumably administer the tax in a more sympathetic fashion.

California's boundary was a vexatious issue which, in provoking the lengthiest debates and greatest controversy, at one point almost broke up the convention. The question was where, between the Sierra and the Rocky Mountains, California's eastern boundary should be established. This issue became entangled with the related issues of slavery in the extended territory, people unrepresented at the convention (notably some 30,000 Mormons in the Utah colony), usable land beyond the Sierra, the desires of the Californians, and the views of the President of the United States and Congress. The delegates finally voted for a compromise line which marks the present boundary and included the California communities at that time.

The delegates, in disposing of other assorted items, dealt with social values that provide further insight into their kind of society. The legislature was instructed to provide for public schools and a university, implementing the precept held dear by Americans that education—the key to democracy—would train youth to better opportunities. Married women were entitled to own property separately, a special dispensation to women that was already incorporated in the civil law of Mexico and intended as bait to lure them to this predominantly male province. Dueling was prohibited, at least on paper, the humanitarian impulse prevailing over the romantic (and to some, barbaric) tradition which glorified the field of honor. Such provisions reflected the predominance of democratic sentiments and liberal attitudes of a society in ferment.

The constitution as adopted by the convention reflects the heterogeneous character but common aims of its authors. It was a compilation of provisions from the constitutions of the nation and of other states (mostly Iowa and New York), rather than an original document. In drafting the constitution, the delegates did not act as political representatives of special interest groups, nor were they political theorists drawing up the ideal society. As the debates clearly reveal, they regarded themselves as representatives of the constituent communities from which they were selected to attend the convention. The delegates were pragmatic men seeking workable solutions to real problems, including the ones imported from out of state, such as slavery and the bank issues. They showed a marked disposition to lay aside sectional and partisan prejudices and to resolve their differences by practical compromises. They were young men with an ambitious eye for prospective opportunities that would bring them wealth and status. The constitution they drew up was conceived in this spirit.

When the convention completed its work in October, Governor

Riley called for an election in November to ratify the proposed constitution and to select officials for the new state government. Local groups in numerous communities gathered in open meetings to hear spokesmen argue the provisions or to hear candidates campaign for office. Election day was rainy, which probably explains the low voter turnout. The substantial margin of the vote, however, made the election results conclusive—the constitution was ratified by a vote of 12,064 to 811. The winning candidates included Peter Burnett of Sacramento for governor, John McDougal of Sacramento for lieutenant governor, Edward Gilbert and George Wright, both of San Francisco, for the lower house of the Congress. At last the Californians had a civil government of their own making.

The New State Government

Governor Riley announced by proclamation in December 1849 that the constitution for the new state government was now in effect. The legislature convened shortly afterwards; the houses proceeded to organize themselves and to elect jointly two senators for the United States Congress. Among the prominent senatorial aspirants were Fremont, Gwin, Halleck, Thomas Butler King, and Semple. After a round of politicking and drinking at the open houses of these candidates, the legislators voted for the popular Fremont and the much respected Gwin. When Burnett was installed as governor, Governor Riley turned over his office, thus phasing out the military government in favor of the new state government that now came into operation.

The governor in his inaugural message outlined the work to be done. The legislature, however, made clear from the start that it intended to formulate public policy itself. It completed the organization of the state government, setting up the constitutional and statutory officers to round off the executive branch, and establishing the judiciary. It provided a firm basis for local government, dividing the state into 28 counties, enacting municipal incorporations for the major cities, and adopting a general law for incorporating towns and other cities. It granted county and municipal governments considerable self-government on grounds that the state capital was geographically and politically too far removed to give adequate attention to local problems, which could be better handled by locally elected officials. By this provision, the legislature established the basis of home rule for county and municipal government which was to become a California trademark in the nation's governmental system.

Of greater importance was the system of law that would serve as the basis for the administration of justice. The issue was whether California should adopt a code on the Roman model, based on statute, or whether it should adopt the common law of England, which grew from precedent and experience. The former operated in Spanish and Mexican California; the latter had been adopted in most American states. Governor Burnett recommended a combination of the two to incorporate the best features of both. The legislature, however, decided to adopt the English common law exclusively, insofar as it did not conflict with the constitutions of California and the United States. As the legislative committee pointed out, the Roman code, with its strict control over men, preserved the antiquated order of the past, whereas common law looked to the future and treated men as free agents capable of making contracts and pursuing enterprises. This legal system, which still prevails today in basic form, is the foundation of our civil and criminal laws.

Entry into the Union

When the California delegation (the two new senators and two congressmen-elect) made its appearance in the United States Congress in January 1850, it presented a resolution requesting admission of the state into the Union. The Congress at this point was reaching a climax in resolving the bitter two-year debate over the status of slaves in the territory newly acquired from Mexico. The congressional debate entered a crucial stage, dominated by that venerable trio in the Senate: Clay of the West, Webster of the North, and the dying Calhoun of the South. Clay drafted a compromise of bills which included the admission of California as a free state. Webster supported Clay, making a dramatic plea for California's admission. Calhoun opposed it, taking the Californians to task for their defiance on the grounds that they had acted without instructions from Congress and should first go through the territorial stage. President Taylor favored California's admission but opposed Clay's compromise, which he derisively labeled the "Omnibus Bill." The highly emotional and drawn-out debate became so bitter that Clay, for the first time in his life, felt the Union was in jeopardy. Southerners actually met in a convention to discuss whether to secede from the Union. Several developments helped turn the tide in this complicated situation, including the influence of the popular Fremont and the respected Gwin (a close friend of Calhoun). Clay's compromise, as modified, was finally enacted in October and passed into history as the Great Compromise of 1850.

Back home, the Californians, whose confidence of quick acceptance into the Union had turned to dismay over the congressional deadlock, now rejoiced in public celebration—a full year after they had completed their constitutional document. California, after so difficult a trial, was firmly established—the thirty-first star in the Union. As Joseph Ellison put it with poetic relish, "California sprang full panoplied into the sisterhood of sovereign states without tarrying in territorial purgatory."

7 American California Society

THE SETTING

The essence of American society was—and still is—its particular democratic scheme. Democracy embodies the twin concepts of freedom and equality. The Americans held to a concept of freedom in which political liberty was based on economic freedom, and both were tied to social rights and religious independence. It derived from their English heritage in the colonial period, as modified by their experience in nationhood. The American concept of equality was born of the frontier experience—"a man is a man for what he is" irrespective of class or status. This meant equal political rights, economic opportunities, and social privileges. The Americans were slow, inconsistent, and irregular in developing these concepts—they have never implemented them fully. Nevertheless, these ideas remain the pillars of their democratic structure.

California society during the interregnum was in a critical stage of development. The United States had secured California by military conquest and intended to set up a territorial government as prelude to statehood. Congress, however, deadlocked over the slavery issue, failed to set up the standard governmental apparatus, thus leaving Californians to work out their destiny under a weak military rule. In this situation, the Americans in California revealed a natural capacity for self-organization. They established forms of government for managing public affairs with due regard for law and order based on individual rights. They developed various forms of individual and group enterprises in order to realize greater profits from cooperative efforts. They set up churches, schools, and printing presses for implanting their Protestant tradition. The newcomers were making a conscious effort to "Americanize" the new territory.

ANALYSIS

Political Scheme

California's status during the interregnum was vague. Until the signing of the 1848 treaty, California was under international law by which the ruling American military governor was obligated to uphold local customs and enforce the prevailing laws pending the peace settlement. (The United States was technically still at war with Mexico.) The military governor, of course, could suspend such laws and impose martial law whenever he felt United States interests were threatened by hostile acts. The governor's problem, however, was not with the Californios as much as it was with his own government and Americans in California. United States policy had run the gamut from California self-government to United States annexation to American conquest. California had gone through five governors in ten months (Sloat, Stockton, Fremont, Kearny, and Mason), which left inhabitants wondering what they had gained in the shift from Mexican to American rule. The treaty, by confirming United States title, clarified California's legal status. The territory was now subject to United States national law—that is, the law of Congress. However, Congress failed to establish a governmental apparatus for the territory, thus leaving California in political limbo. In this unstable setting, Californians began the pattern of political innovation and governmental experimentation still characteristic of the state.

The military governor in California bore the brunt of responsibility in establishing the basis of his authority. When General Kearny arrived in California, he had to contest with Stockton and Fremont over who had the authority to act as governor of the province. In the outcome, Kearny was reaffirmed as governor. Fremont was arrested, recalled to Washington, and convicted by a court martial of insubordination, but was allowed to resign from the army. Backed by his superiors in

Washington, Kearny assumed the initiative and set up a civil government, upholding local customs and enforcing Mexican laws when they were not in conflict with the United States Constitution. The governor operated under military code until after the 1848 treaty, when he governed the civilian population according to civil laws. Since he had all along been acting through the established local officials, there was little change, if any, in military rule for the remainder of the interregnum.

California was a proving ground for several kinds of local governments. Since the governor lacked effective authority and adequate troops, local officials exercised considerable discretion in managing public affairs. Alcaldes prevailed in most of the communities. They were either appointed by the governor or elected by citizens, depending on local circumstances. They were for the most part Americans who showed considerable talent for adapting Anglo-American features to the existing Mexican system. In the mining areas, Americans usually took the initiative in setting up the local apparatus for governing themselves. They would establish a mining district, embracing one or several mining communities; then they would organize a government in one of three ways: a body of miners in general meeting; a committee, council, or court of selected representatives; or an alcalde or justice of peace. Later, when alcalde governments of San Francisco and other communities suffered deterioration from the malfeasance of corrupt officials and conflicting factions, aroused citizens organized a legislative assembly as an autonomous local government, though it undercut the governor's authority. These spontaneous forms of self-government proved to be effective devices for social control in the absence of remedial action by the military governments and by the Congress.

Considering the neglect by the national government and the difficulties of the times, the record of the military government is a commendable one. The governors proved to be conscientious and efficient professional soldiers who administered civil affairs with a great deal of fairness, tact, and common sense. They bore mounting criticism (mostly from Americans) of their arbitrary rule, but what few charges had validity could be defended on grounds of wise expediency. They established the conditions which allowed local governments to do the job they were ill equipped to do. Historian Theodore Grivas sums up the measure of their achievement by pointing out: "The province was held, lawlessness and disorders were kept to a minimum; and self-supporting government was organized and maintained."

Administration of Justice

The American newcomers wasted no time or opportunity in implementing their brand of law and justice, expecially in jury trials. As alcaldes they applied effectively the ready-made judicial functions of the office when performing as American-style justices of the peace. Walter Colton, a naval chaplain who became the prominent alcalde of Monterey, impaneled the first jury (August 1846). Before long most of the northern communities had a jury system, with a sheriff acting as executive officer of the court as well as of the local peace office. Judicial affairs, however, were sometimes irregular. Sam Brannan was the defendant in the first jury trial in San Francisco (about the same time as Monterey's first trial) and soon played both judge and prosecutor in a jury trial in Sacramento.

San Francisco experienced a wave of lawlessness which culminated in a reign of terror by mid-1849. Former members of the New York Volunteers regiment had formed into the Regulators, ostensibly for maintaining public order. They soon were called Hounds for the way they intimidated the populace, parading down streets in drunken bands, extorting tribute from merchants, and looting foreign settlements at night. After a brutal attack on the Chilean settlement in which some of them murdered a mother and raped her daughter, a counterorganization was created by Sam Brannan and others as the Law and Order Party. This vigilante group jailed 19 of the Hounds, and after a summary trial 9 were banished, thus restoring some semblance of temporary order to the community.

In dealing with criminals, the miners preserved many of the legal forms they were familiar with but devised their own list of penalties. They held public trials, with mass or select juries, legal counsel for both sides, and a presiding judge. The accused, whether camp thief, sluice robber, horse thief, or murderer, might be whipped, banished, or hanged. Sentence was usually carried out immediately, since there were rarely jails for incarcerating convicted men. Wrongdoers, real or alleged, were swiftly tried, convicted, and punished by irregular procedures before emotionally charged audiences—all in the name of popular justice, which too often resembled group vengeance. As historian Rodman Paul points out, such simple forms of popular justice were little more than lynch law (punishment for crimes without due process of law) "dressed in the full trappings of judge–and–jury trials." While harsh, this vigilante justice did preserve during the interregnum a semblance of order in the absence of other law in the mining communities.

Economic System

California's economy during the interregnum was a wide-open affair. In the absence of public economic policy, the military governor confined his attention to basic requirements for support of the territory, such as land titles and trade development. The Conquest started the flow of American settlers, the Gold Rush accelerated it and spurred private enterprises. People could freely exploit opportunities without the restrictions of the government regulations that had existed in Spanish and Mexican California. The newcomers found a fertile field for varied enterprises. They developed them with imaginative schemes, limited funds, hard work, and personal courage in the face of miscalculations and catastrophes. Many did not survive the hardships of the times, but those who did had complete freedom hampered only by individual constraints and by community consensus.

Land

Land titles were a vexatious matter for the military government. The military governor had no authority to distribute lands or even to compensate public services with land grants, as was customary elsewhere, but he did so. In the case of San Francisco, General Kearny granted the municipal government title to its beach and waterfront land, so that wharves and other public facilities could be built to accommodate the growing immigration and commerce. The governor's policy of upholding land titles as they were at the time of the conquest did not endear him to aggressive Americans, who were eager to acquire such readily accessible lands. They wasted little time. As land in the pueblos and ranchos rose in value, American pioneer settlers and recent immigrants showed a strong inclination for buying and selling land for speculative profits. San Francisco, then rapidly growing into a busy commercial center, was the scene of intense lot sales, first promoted by American alcaldes and carried on by local merchants like Brannan and outsiders like Larkin and Sutter.

Mining

Gold mining, which suddenly became the center of economic life, focused in the Mother Lode country in the Sierra. The Mother Lode (mother vein) refers to a gold-bearing area about 120 miles long and from a few hundred feet to two miles in width, from just above Coloma, and south to the neighborhood of Fremont's estate in Mariposa. In the course of geologic history, earthquakes, volcanic activity, and erosion produced from the admixture of earth elements a gold-embedded underground rock strata. Where the vein had been exposed on the surface, gold fragments had broken away from the attached rock, drifted down flowing streams and rivers, and settled on their banks and bottoms in the form of either flakes intermixed with sand or dirt or nuggets lodged between gravels and stones. The miners adopted the Spanish term *placer* ("sandbank") for this gold found on riverbanks and bottoms, to distinguish it from underground quartz or vein gold. Similar gold deposits were to be found in other parts of California.

Fortunately for these amateur gold seekers of 1848 they had among them veteran miners from the American South, Mexico, Peru, and Chile, who taught them the rudiments of mining. The first of these was Isaac Humphrey, a former gold miner from Georgia working at Sutter's Fort at the time of Marshall's discovery, who showed the miners at Coloma the way to extract gold by pan and by cradle. Since gold outweighs its equivalent volume in dirt and rock, the miners were able to sort out the heavier gold particles from the lighter substances by these two methods. By using a metal pan or wooden bowl, a single person could wash gold particles from dirt or sand with water from a nearby stream. By working a cradle, or rocker, one to five men could shovel dirt and bail water into this oblong box mounted on rockers (much like a baby's crib), then shake the contraption to separate the gold. The miners also made extensive use of their knives to scrape gold from crevices and holes. These primitive methods were not overly efficient, but they permitted untrained men to acquire the precious mineral by the simplest method, with the least amount of capital and minimum delay. Here in the making was the most fundamental form of individual enterprise: the direct acquisition of what was considered basic wealth, gold itself!

The increasing population in the mining areas in 1849 made the placers less accessible, and inventive miners developed other ways to extract gold. One was river mining, where they dammed up a stream or diverted its water into an artificial channel in order to get at placer deposits in the potholes and cracks of the riverbed. Another was quartz mining, in which they dug tunnels or sank shafts to chip quartz chunks from the underground vein, hauled out the chunks, and pulverized them by such devices as the stamp mill (a heavy pounding machine) or the *arrastre* (a mule-drawn stone wheel rolled over a flat rock surface). Still another improvement was the use of mercury (quicksilver) to sift gold from the sand and dirt mixture left over from the workings of the pan and cradle, or from the crushed quartz chunks pulverized by the stamp mill and the arrastre. Mercury is a volatile metal which, when added to such earth mixtures, coalesces with gold; when the resulting amalgam is heated in a vessel, the mercury evaporates, leaving pure gold. Some miners went so far as to dig tunnels into hillsides, branching out with side tunnels in an operation known as coyoting, to get at the gold-mixed gravels deposited by ancient underground rivers buried by centuries of earth erosion.

Mining methods were improved early in 1850 with the development of the long tom and the sluice. The long tom was a larger adaptation of the cradle or rocker, operated by three to six men. A continuous stream of water fed directly into this boxlike contraption, where it first sifted gold from dirt or sand and then poured into an open trough which caught the remaining particles in the cleats of its riffled, or rippled, bottom. The open trough of the long tom was later extended to become a sluice (a long inclined wooden trough for catching more gold particles from the dirt–water flow) operated by five to twenty men.

The Miners at Work. From left to right: washing with a cradle or rocker, washing with a pan, tunnel mining, mining through a shaft, washing with a long tom, washing with sluices, a water company aqueduct. Woodcut around 1851–1852.

Mercury was added to the mixture in the trough or sluice of the long tom, as in the cradle, to help catch the finer particles of gold. Through such improvements the miners were able to continue producing gold long after the more accessible placer deposits were played out.

These improvements—river and tunnel mining for placer, quartz, and gravel deposits, and the use of mercury—together caused a revolution in mining operations. It was now profitable to work lower-yield areas in large-scale operations. Such operations required the organized effort of several men. Joint stock associations of working miners as early as 1849 were engaged in river and tunnel mining enterprises on the American River. Beginning in 1850, they were constructing ditches and wooden flumes for conveying water short distances to long tom and sluice operations. In a few instances, individuals or partners formed companies supported by local merchants subscribing stock and by miners purchasing water.

So it was that the forty-niners began to organize working partnerships and associations which enabled them to realize greater profits. Such organizations at this time retained traits of individual enterprise, since they required their members to share the work, as well as the profits, from their cooperative efforts. Here was the forerunner of the pattern that was to be a conspicuous feature of California's economic development: individual enterprises which evolved into partnerships and associations, and eventually into corporations of stockholders.

Agriculture, Manufacturing, and Commerce

American pioneer settlers and early argonauts paved the way for the production and distribution of goods and services needed in the rapidly growing territory. They brought varied implements and supplies on their overland and sea journeys, and established their enterprises. Brannan's Mormon colony carried in its ship supplies for outfitting several hundred men, including tools, materials for farming (plows, rakes, and scythes), blacksmithing, carpentry, printing, sawmills and grain mills. Their agricultural colony (New Hope, on the Stanislaus River) operated in the middle months of 1847, but broke up when several Mormons left to join the main colony at Salt Lake and the remainder went to work at Sutter's Fort. In the winter of 1848, Sutter employed James Marshall and several Mormon workers to build a sawmill near Coloma, with materials supplied by Brannan, to provide lumber for the growing settlements. When argonauts flowed into the Sierra after 1848, rancheros and homesteaders in the San Francisco Bay Area, along the Sacramento, and in southern California found bonanza markets for their surplus livestock, grains, and other foodstuffs.

San Francisco, strategically located at the sea–land junction for the argonaut flow to the mines, emerged as the leading port and manufacturing and commercial center. Brannan established several nucleus enterprises, including a printing shop, a general store, a real estate office, and two flour mills. He organized with other merchants a wharf, business buildings, and public projects for civic improvements. Argonauts who did not go to the mines stayed to build up manufacturing enterprises. Peter Donahue and his brothers in 1849 set up an iron foundry for producing mining and farming implements. Henry Meiggs, a Maine lumberman, early in 1850 set up a planing mill for processing lumber. At first, resident merchants, like Brannan, handled commercial and banking transactions. Then, in 1849, Henry Naglee, a former New York Volunteer, established his Miner's Bank. George Wright, newly arrived from Massachusetts, and other merchants also set up banking operations. Manufacturing and commercial enterprises in San Francisco and in river port towns like Benicia and Sacramento were marked by intense competition and irregular practices, and by spectacular successes and failures.

Communications and Transportation

Sea and land routes linking the United States and the far-off California province were developed early and rapidly. Private express service for delivering mail and passengers was begun early in 1847: locally between San Francisco and Sacramento, and overland between California and Missouri—the latter was another enterprise pioneered by Brannan. Congress, in the spring of 1847, granted franchises to two New York-based steamship companies, one on the Atlantic and the other on the Pacific side, to carry mail and passengers to Pacific Coast settlements. Pacific Mail Steamship Company, which received the West Coast franchise, opened regular service early in 1849, when the international rush to the gold fields got under way. The deficient postal sea deliveries prompted the prominent Adams and Company and other Eastern-based express companies to introduce improved overland mail deliveries in the same year. Local express services, too, were established on a regular basis when James Birch set up an effective delivery system between Sacramento and the mining communities. By then, travel routes were well developed.

American and foreign sailing ships deposited passengers and cargoes in San Francisco. Some went even farther to Benicia and Sacramento. Immigrants and cargoes were transported to the mines and other settlements by means of makeshift boats, ferries, wagons, horseback and mule train, and by foot.

Social Order

The People

California's population grew enormously during the interregnum, jumping from about 7000 in 1847 to around 100,000 in 1850. Ninety percent of the people were located in San Francisco and between that city and the Sierra. The Americans dominated, making up from one-half to two-thirds of the people, while Californios were one-tenth, and the remainder, foreigners. Indians numbered around 100,000. For the first time, the Caucasians outnumbered the Indians, and newcomers outnumbered the native born. The Californios and the Indians were from then on minority people.

The argonaut immigrants imparted a heterogeneous character to California's population. The influx of foreign-born included Northern and Southern Europeans, Moors and Blacks from Africa, Hindus, Orientals, Polynesians, and a mixture of all of these. It was a predominantly male population with women constituting less than eight percent of the total (as low as two percent in mining communities). It was also a young population with "scarcely a gray head to be seen." Bancroft gives us this picture of the people: "the trader . . . the toiling farmer, whose mortgage loomed above the growing family, the briefless lawyer, the starving student, the quack, the idler, the harlot, the gambler, the hen-pecked husband, the disgraced; with many earnest, enterprising, honest men and devoted women."

Communities

California communities coalesced into four regions: San Francisco, Northern California, Southern California, and the Sierra. San Francisco, in a brief two-year span, became the largest city, chief port, and commercial center of the new state. Bancroft describes its 20,000 to 25,000 population as a "Babylonian confusion of tongues and a medley of races and nationalities." The city was a scene of tents and flimsy buildings with identifiable areas for the city hall, business establishments, vice dens, and residences for various groups, notably Little Chile for the Latin Americans and Sydney Town for the Australian criminals (China Town for the Orientals came later). The town was in a state of continual construction, expanding commerce, wild speculation, factional politics, and rampant crime. It also suffered the first of those disastrous fires which periodically ravaged the city, but failed to slow its vitality.

The other regions stood out in sharp contrast. The Northern California area, outside of San Francisco, included the established pueblos (Monterey, San Jose, and Sonoma) and fledgling river port towns (Benicia, Sacramento, Marysville, and Stockton). These were the established commercial centers for surrounding farms and ranchos, which produced food for the growing mining population, and junction points for argonauts heading for the Sierras. The Sierra was a beehive of mining communities scattered as far north as Shasta and as far south as Mariposa. Placerville and Sonora were regional trading centers for the northern and southern mines respectively, serving straggling irregular camps and few substantial towns. The Southern California pueblos and ranchos remained virtually undisturbed by events transpiring in the north. Indian rancherias throughout the state were, for the most part, in varying degrees of deterioration in the wake of the argonaut invasion. Only in remote mountain, desert, and valley areas were Indians relatively free from the trespass of intruders, and there rancherias continued to exist as before.

Ethnic Groups

The presence of minority ethnic groups—especially Indians, Latins, Negroes, and Asians—engendered serious social conflicts which left an indelible mark on California society. Ethnic groups refer to groups of people who have distinct physical traits and social customs. Americans had a long tradition of discriminating against racial minorities and other aliens who did not fit in their mold. In California, Americans had difficulty in reconciling their idealistic notions of social equality with their actual desire to exploit, or exclude these minority groups. This was apparent when Americans in the 1849 Constitutional Convention debated over the status of Latins, Negroes, and Indians in California society.

California, inheriting much of this American nativism, was confronted with an even more complex situation, especially with the already vexatious Indian problem. Americans had a more hostile attitude toward Indians than toward other ethnic groups, an accumulated hostility derived from two centuries of frontier warfare. Americans coming into California failed to distinguish between the peaceful California Indians and the more warlike Indian tribes they had known in the East.

As American and foreign newcomers moved into Indian-occupied areas after 1847, Indian troubles mounted. The military governor, unable to cope with the situation through his Indian agents, followed the traditional frontier policy of supplying settlers with guns and ammunition to defend themselves where the military was not able to do so. The effects were readily apparent. Americans trespassing on Indian lands showed a callous disregard for the native occupants, ignoring their customs, raping their women, and disrupting their food-gathering habits. Indians deprived of their natural food sources resorted to stealing cattle in order to feed their families. This intensified the deadly cycle of miner and farmer raids on rancherias for massive punishment, and Indian attacks on isolated farmers, miners, and travelers for revenge. As clashes between the two races increased, regular troops or volunteer groups of miners, farmers, and ranchers pursued Indian renegades and occasionally attacked Indian rancherias, killing men, women, and children, and using survivors for captive labor. In the Sierra and Northern California, settlers pressed Indians to work for them, took Indian women as concubines or in prostitution, and accelerated the spread of venereal and other diseases, further disrupting Indian labor and reproductive patterns. The American horde was rapidly destroying the remaining traces of gentile Indian society in ways that set the pattern of American–Indian relations for the next quarter-century.

American nativism was manifested against other ethnic groups as well. The argonaut flow brought to the mines great numbers of different alien groups. Yankees as early as April 1849 posted signs prohibiting Latins, Negroes, and Indians (Chinese came later), harassing and ejecting them from mining communities. Latin Californians, who had participated in the 1848 Gold Rush, generally heeded these disturbing signs and discreetly stayed away from the mines. Latins from Mexico, Peru, and Chile congregated among their own kind in Sonora and other communities in the southern mines. Eventually they were run out by invading American groups on grounds that they had no right to occupy United States lands. Free Negroes searched for gold mostly in remote mining areas. Many mining communities by 1850 were driving out these ethnic groups, concentrating especially on master–slave combinations, whether Southerners with Negro slaves, Latin patrons with peons, or, later, Chinese merchants with indentured labor. Thomas Green, a prominent Texas politician, worked his claim with several Negro slaves, only to be ejected by Yankees who resented this unfair competition. Latin Americans, being the most numerous, suffered greatly from these violent altercations. They were assaulted (beatings, whippings, and ear croppings), banished en masse from the diggings, their property sold at public auctions, and some lost their lives. The mines, as Leonard Pitt observes, became the "rehearsal place for broad scale assault on the Spanish speaking" and, one might add, on Negroes, Chinese, and Indians.

Culture

California society underwent a sudden dramatic cultural transformation. The immigrating Americans were imbued with a strong sense of Anglo-Saxon superiority, Protestant faith, and patriotic pride, and revealed a taste for implanting their cultural tradition in the frontier province. During the interregnum, ministers, educators, and journalists set up churches, schools, and newspapers in major communities of the San Francisco Bay Area and the Sierra. Some came with the idea of bringing civilization to tame the wild frontier. Others, including those who suffered misadventures in the gold fields, simply hoped to make a living this way. Despite the hardships of the times, these pioneers established the beginnings of cultural institutions that played an important role in the "Americanization" of California society.

Religion

The Americans had a rich diversity of religious traditions. They were predominantly Protestant, comprising Congregationalists, Methodists, Presbyterians, and several other religious denominations, but they were also Catholics and Jews. Protestantism emphasizes individual salvation with God through personal experience, whereas in Catholicism the individual reaches God through the intermediary of the Church. The American Protestant tradition spoke of God's kingdom that was to arrive in the new land—America was the Lord's heaven on earth. It stressed church–state separation, multiple denominations, and religious toleration. It included the Puritan ethnic which called for intense piety, strict morality, and hard work. Prior to the California Gold Rush, the nation was gripped in a great wave of religious revivalism as churchmen participated in a broad movement to "Christianize the nation." In a "great awakening" (initiated by the great New England prelate Lyman Beecher), churchmen expanded missionary activities to bring civilization to frontier areas. They developed schools and colleges to promote salvation of the soul through education of the mind, and pressed for moral and social reforms like temperance and the abolition of slavery. Some groups, such as the Mormons, broke away from conventional Protestantism. Each group had its version of individual salvation and God's kingdom on earth. The nation was caught up in a religious ferment hardly remembered today.

With the Gold Rush, Americans brought this Protestant tradition to California in many ways. In San Francisco, Sam Brannan, as leader of the Mormon Colony, conducted worship services and performed the first Protestant marriage ceremony held there. Among the argonauts in 1849 were clergymen and lay preachers of different faiths who immediately turned to ministerial and missionary work. They held services in makeshift facilities, including public buildings in towns, saloons in mining communities, or under a tree by a roadside. Samuel Willey, a Congregationalist minister sent by the American Mission Society, settled in Monterey where he spearheaded church, charitable, and educational activities. William Taylor, a colorful Methodist evangelist, rode a scheduled circuit to deliver his message to groups gathered on San Francisco streets, at rural crossroads, and in mining communities. By 1850 San Francisco had a dozen churches. Sacramento and other communities were already erecting simple churches as vehicles for bringing religion to their frontier communities.

Education

American educational tradition evolved from several historical developments. It stemmed from the English Protestant idea of common schools to train children in church dogma and in citizenship. It borrowed from the European intellectual tradition of a classical education and scientific scholarship for producing educated men. After the nation was formed, the states developed varied educational systems comprising primary and secondary schools, colleges, and universities, under public, private, and church auspices. Educational ideas were shaped by Jeffersonian ideals of a classical education for training the talented few, and Jacksonian ideals of practical education for the masses and popularization of science and technology. By mid-nineteenth century, the schools were systematized, but reformers like Horace Mann, Massachusetts's celebrated school superintendent, were calling for educational improvements to promote citizenship training and individual self-improvement. The school movement was strong in frontier areas.

The American taste for education manifested itself during the interregnum. In Monterey, Alcalde Walter Colton persuaded a teacher immigrant (Olive Mann Isobell) to conduct an elementary school in 1847, and Samuel Willey established another school two years later. In San Francisco, a local group led by Sam Brannan established an elementary school supported by private donations in 1848, then, in the following year, established a public school with minicipal funds. The Constitutional Convention made a strong commitment in providing for a state school system, supporting Robert Semple's eloquent argument that education was the foundation of republican institutions and the school system "suits the genius and spirit of our form of government." The school system begun under the precarious circumstances of the Gold Rush managed to take hold, reflecting the ardent desire of Americans to bring education to the California frontier.

Journalism

Americans have developed a strong tradition of aggressive independent and partisan journalism. From Ben Franklin's famous newspaper in colonial times and Tom Paine's crusading pamphlets on behalf of the Revolution, it evolved into the great party organs of Hamilton and Jefferson. By Jackson's time, journalism was being transformed by large-scale newspaper production for the public masses and by powerful independent editors. Legendary figures in this shift from party to personal journalism were the cynical James Bennett of the *New York Herald* (1835), reform-minded Horace Greeley of the *New York Tribune* (1841), and the practical Henry Raymond of the *New York Times* (1851). All were gifted, egocentric, and innovative personalities. Greeley is remembered for his outstanding gifted staff (Karl Marx was his man in London and Bayard Taylor was his reporter on the California Gold Rush) and for his advice to footloose youth: Go west and grow up with the country. Frontier journalism was steeped in American folklore. It was characterized by the traveling printer using a makeshift press to produce a crude newspaper for news-hungry settlers.

California journalism was a product of frontier journalism. In Monterey during the American military occupation, Walter Colton found an old press (the Zamorano press used since 1834 to print public pronouncements) and, with Robert Semple, produced the first newspaper, *The Californian*, in August 1846. In San Francisco, Brannan set up his printing press and employed fellow Mormons, including the youthful Edward Kemble, to print the *California Star* after January 1847. Kemble left later to join the Gold Rush, and he and other proprietor-printers were putting out newspapers in various mining towns by 1850. Editors and printers with their presses were conspicuous in the argonaut invasion (some were former employees of Bennett and Greeley), and soon established foundations for California journalism.

SUMMARY

California society during the interregnum was in a critical stage of development. The United States had secured its title to California by military conquest and confirmed it by treaty. The national government had intended to set up in California a territorial government, as it usually did when incorporating new areas into the Federal Union. Territorial status was the normal preparation for statehood. The Congress, however, deadlocked on the slavery issue in lands acquired from Mexico and failed to set up the standard governmental apparatus for California. Consequently, the military government continued throughout the interregnum, leaving California in political limbo.

So it was that the American system in California was not instituted by a national government, as Spain and Mexico had implemented their systems. It was established primarily by ambitious Americans already there—the merchants, farmers, and others who had come during the Mexican rule, and the motley horde who came after the American occupation. The gold strike brought about a drastic economic and social transformation which increased the difficulties of the military government in coping with conditions that were rapidly approaching anarchy.

In this situation, the Americans revealed a natural capacity for self-organization. They developed various forms of individual and group enterprises, notably partnerships and joint stock associations, in order to realize greater profits from cooperative efforts. They established forms of government for managing public affairs with due regard to law and order based on individual rights. In the course of the interregnum, they modified alcalde government in the pueblos, established new local governments in San Francisco and mining towns, and initiated on their own a state government. This capacity for self-organization had its negative features. When they so chose, less enlightened men formed vigilante organizations to apply to wrongdoers their own brand of justice.

By the end of the interregnum, these Americans in California had established a constitutional framework for a new state based on their collective experience. The new society was a California version of the American system—so unlike its Mexican predecessor and its American successor, yet a genuine blend of both. That society was democratic with a note of racial discrimination. It favored individual enterprise over corporate enterprise, and professed liberal sentiments while including conservative restraints. The coming decades would show how well this scheme would be realized in practice.

California society in the interregnum may be considered the product of a crucible in which gold was mixed with diverse people, traditions, and circumstances. By the end of the period, the crucible was still hot, but the amalgam was formed and would remain the basis of California society from that time forward.

Overleaf: The clipper *Flying Cloud*, built by the famous Donald McKay, was the largest and one of the fastest ships afloat. Its record 89-day run between New York and San Francisco set the pace for California clippers during their heyday in the 1850's.

V   Frontier Ferment

1850-1870

CLIPPER SHIP "FLYING CLOUD"

*When California was admitted into the Union in 1850, its people had
already established the foundation for an Americanized society. The
argonaut horde poured through San Francisco and Sacramento, outposts
of the principal gateway to the Sierra mines, extending main lines of
settlement between the Bay Area and the Delta, and from there up
and down the Central Valley and the Sierra. In the hectic growth of
frontier cities, towns, and country, settlers scrambled for quick
riches. Eventually they found their niches in government and professional services or in farming, ranching, manufacturing, and other
enterprises. Experimental public policies, extraordinary economic
growth, and intense social ferment brought on a round of frenzied
speculation, widespread extravagance, corruption, and violence. It
took another two decades to develop a workable, if rambunctious, system
of representative government and a capitalistic economy. California
entered the period as a turbulent frontier society based primarily on
mining and agriculture. It emerged 20 years later as a stable, but
expanding, society. Having begun as a self-governing dominion relatively
isolated from the national mainstream, it became a full-fledged
state well integrated into the national union.*

8 Rambunctious Politics
9 An Explosive Economy
10 A Restless Society

8 Rambunctious Politics

THE SETTING

Party System

The American political system took definite form in California after the 1850 legislature provided for an election system. In that year, Democrats and Whigs in San Francisco and San Jose formed party organizations for local and state elections. Both parties set up state conventions for coordinating local party units behind statewide party tickets, to include nominations to public office. Local party organizations reflected the political style of the dominant elements in the community. In San Francisco, David Broderick, a former New York politician, organized a local Democratic Tammany-type machine to become the city's first political boss. (Tammany Hall in New York City has been the epitome of a party machine in municipal politics.) In Los Angeles, two Southern lawyer–politicians, Joseph Brent and Benjamin Hayes, joined with Tomas Sanchez, a prominent ranchero and local politico, to develop a Democratic machine based on the "boss-patron" system. It rested on the close friendship of Yankee *gringos* (Spanish "foreigners, Anglo-Saxons") and Californio dons, backed by the latter's numerous relatives and workers. In Santa Barbara, the leading rancher–politicians, like Antonio and Pablo de la Guerra (Jose's sons), sustained the *cacique* ("chief") system and extensive family connections to maintain dominance over local politics. In the mining communities, local groups at election time generally revived the convention apparatus to formulate their party tickets. Henceforth, rival groups within each party vied for control of the party mechanism in order to influence local and state party and public policies affecting their community interests.

Public patronage held together party leaders and their supporters. The Jacksonian ideal that any citizen, irrespective of his skills, could serve in public office meant, in practice, that the party in power distributed public offices to its more favored members. Party leaders and their candidates, once elected to office, enjoyed lucrative salaries (often supplemented by the fees of their office) and had the patronage (administrative and clerical jobs) with which to reward their supporters. These officials often received from their employees "kickbacks," or a portion of their salaries, to finance party activities. Democratic party leaders in the 1850's, for instance, assessed the incomes of officeholders 10 percent and their subordinates 5 percent. Kickbacks in some instances were as much as 50 percent of the incumbent's salary.

Public offices of particular interest to party leaders were those which commanded considerable patronage or yielded public favors in the form of administrative policies and regulations affecting special interest groups. The highly prized "political plums" in municipal government were the positions of city attorney, police and fire officials; in county government, district attorney and sheriff; in state government, department and bureau chiefs; and at all levels, the offices of judges, tax officials, and members of boards and commissions. Federal patronage in California, which was distributed by the President (usually through the United States Senators and Congressmen of his party) included the important posts of judge, district attorney, tax agent, postmaster, and port official, including the customs collector for San Francisco port. The intense competition among professional politicians for these lucrative positions occasionally led to secret bargains and unscrupulous schemes. Party treachery infected local and state governments to a point where corrupt officials indulged in excessive favoritism, bribery, embezzlement, and other scandals.

Party politics had a provincial character not untypical of a frontier state. Political parties were considered quasi-public organizations operating by group consensus without state regulation. Politicians and voters frequently changed their party affiliations. Local party leaders closely followed the lead of state party leaders, so that local organizations were more like state appendages than strong local units. In the 1850's, at least 11 different parties made their appearance in state elections. Some were national parties, like the Democrats (and their sometimes autonomous factions), Whigs, and Republicans, while others were locally oriented like the Settlers and Miners Party. Party conventions were occasionally dull affairs long on rhetoric, but often they were noisy rough-and-tumble showdowns, punctuated by temperamental outbursts, physical assaults, vote bribery, and rigged elections. Party platforms had little meaning beyond serving as a rallying point for party supporters at election time. Some party leaders even tampered with public elections by buying votes (the going price then was usually a dollar a vote), stuffing ballot boxes, and other corrupt practices. Such party abuses, in the absence of state regulation, were to some extent tempered by the outraged cries of newspapers, of defeated candidates, and occasionally of the public.

Governmental System

State government operated in this setting of party politics. Professional politicians, joined by politically ambitious lawyers, merchants, miners, farmers, and ranchers—Americans and a few Californios—formed a special class of party regulars and public office seekers. The governors lacked the personal traits and political power to be effective leaders, especially since they had to share their administrative responsibilities and patronage appointments with other state executives (see below). The legislature assumed leadership, and became the prime mover in formulating public policies. Special interest groups operating in the legislature sought to exert influence on public policies by backing the election campaigns of legislators, and hiring lobbyists to further influence them. Legislators connived with lobbyists to engineer measures promoting their schemes, notably individual projects, town developments, and transportation enterprises. San Francisco, at the outset, attained a conspicuous influence in state affairs by virtue of its talented politicians, its well-developed party organizations, its large voting electorate, its considerable public patronage, and its sizable voting bloc in the legislature.

Public policies were shaped by the interaction of many elements: the desires of the leaders, the political bargains and vote trades of legislators, and the pressure of special interest and community groups. This continues to be the basic manner of operation of California's party and governmental system.

DEVELOPMENT

The Tempestuous Fifties

The 1850's were turbulent years throughout the United States. The North and West underwent a rapid transformation brought on by growing manufacturing industries, increasingly mechanized agriculture, and expanded railroad lines that tied the two sections closer together. The South, under its plantation system, lagged behind in economic development, yet it still retained a commanding influence on national affairs. Party politics became more bitter as the deteriorating Whig and Democratic parties were challenged by the new antislavery parties: the Free Soilers in 1848 and 1852, and the Republicans in 1856. The presidential elections were good barometers of the decade. The people chose in 1852 Franklin Pierce and in 1856 James Buchanan, both Northern Democrats with Southern sympathies, and in 1860 Abraham Lincoln, the Republican standard-bearer who opposed the expansion of slavery. The slavery issue clouded all other issues during the decade. It affected even a nonslave state like California.

California was experiencing the hectic changes of a frontier state caught in a gold-induced mania. Men in the grip of great expectations and speculative fever plunged into get-rich-quick schemes that infected every phase of state life. Ambitious enterprises brought about remarkable, but sporadic, developments in mining, agriculture, transportation, and other areas, bringing much wealth to a few and great disappointment to many. Party and public affairs rumbled with political turbulence. In such precarious times, mixed concentrations of people produced unstable and unrestrained communities. The California cauldron was boiling with the elements of both lowly and heroic achievement.

Personality Politics

State politics in the 1850's operated in an atmosphere of self-interest, provincialism, lax morality, and unrestrained exuberance. Public officials often were described as a mediocre lot, but many talented men—former and future governors, senators, and congressmen of other states— occupied key posts. They indulged in personal feuds and public charges that not infrequently led to physical assaults and duels. In one such episode, Edward Gilbert, former congressman and senior editor of the *Alta California*, was killed in a duel with Secretary of State James Denver over offensive remarks. (Denver was nevertheless reappointed, later ran for the California governorship, and still later became wartime governor of Kansas and gave Colorado's capital city its name.)

California in the 1850's was a citadel of Democratic politics dominated mostly by politicians with Southern sympathies. The Democrats won virtually every state election. Democratic politics polarized around two remarkable men: William Gwin, leader of the Southern Chivalry Wing, which held Jeffersonian ideas and proslavery sentiments; and David Broderick, leader of the Tammany wing, which supported the cause of the working-man and held antislavery sentiments. Gwin, as United States Senator, had created as early as 1851 a statewide organization based on his control of federal patronage in San Francisco and other parts of the state. Broderick relied on his local machine in San Francisco, through which he was able to control considerable state patronage. Both men were seasoned politicians and talented leaders who shared a consuming ambition to be California's United States Senator, but the similarity ends there. Where Gwin was gracious, dignified, and a master of the old-style platform politics, Broderick was temperamental, arrogant, and a master of behind-the-scene politics. The fight of the two men for the senatorial prize dominated state politics for most of the decade.

The Gwin–Broderick feud between 1851 and 1857 centered on Broderick's efforts to secure legislative election to the United States Senate. The legislature in 1851 failed to agree on a successor to John Fremont. Thomas Butler King led a field of some 18 contenders, including Fremont, Broderick, and John Weller, a pro-Southern Democrat from Ohio. In the state election that autumn, Broderick (then acting lieutenant governor) backed John Bigler's successful bid for governor and, as part of the bargain, got control of state patronage to help his Senate bid. When the 1852 legislature elected the Gwin-supported Weller over Broderick for United States Senator, the angry Democratic boss thereafter pursued the prize with unrelenting vehemence. In the 1854 legislature, he lost by a one-vote margin his unprecedented scheme to win Gwin's seat a full year before it expired. Shortly afterward, at the Democratic state convention, Broderick attempted to stack the convention and win party support. His scheme, however, resulted in a tense confrontation between gun-wielding delegates, which ended only when the chairmen of the factions walked out together arm in arm. Gwin's Southern Democrats won over Broderick's Northern Democrats and Whigs in the ensuing three-way 1854 election. The 1855 legislature, after another bitter Democratic showdown, deadlocked again over Gwin's election, thus leaving his seat vacant.

Public reaction to Democratic shenanigans and widespread corruption in party and government affairs paved the way for the American Party (Know-Nothings) takeover. The Know-Nothings were reactionaries who answered questions of their beliefs with "I don't know"—Californios slyly translated the name as "Ignorantes." They organized as a third party composed of dissident Whigs and some Democrats, which publicly professed government reforms but privately drew support because of its antiforeign and anti-Catholic sentiments. In the 1855 state election, the Democrats' split and the Whig demise enabled the Know-Nothings to win every state office, including ex-Whig J. Neely Johnson for governor and ex-Democrat David Terry for Supreme Court Justice. Gwin's seat, meanwhile, remained vacant. The Know-Nothings, outmaneuvered by an alliance of Gwin–Broderick forces, failed in their 1856 legislature to secure the senatorial prize.

State politics reached a turning point in 1857. When the legislature met, this time to elect two United States Senators, Broderick and Gwin closed ranks. Each man won a seat. Broderick won his prize over fierce opposition and through incredible chicanery: he edged Weller out of his seat, then played Milton Latham (former congressman and San Francisco Customs collector) off against Gwin to secure, through a secret bargain, control of the federal patronage. Gwin, to win his seat, sacrificed his political integrity, as well as his party base.

The state elections that autumn revealed the new alignment of the parties. The Democrats regained control, with Weller winning the governorship (he had received the party nomination as a consolation prize). The Republican Party, organized the year before by a small merchant group (Cornelius Cole, Edwin and Charles Crocker, Mark Hopkins, Collis Huntington, and Leland Stanford), was absorbing Northern Whigs and other antislavery elements. The American Party, or Know-Nothings, fell from power as fast as it had risen. The Know-Nothing movement was a significant bridge between the old and the new politics: the old oriented to state issues, and the new oriented to the national issue of slavery, which now became entwined with state politics.

The Gwin–Broderick feud between 1857 and 1859 became enmeshed with national politics over the slavery issue. Congress in 1858 deadlocked again over the bitter slavery issue, this time over the admission of Kansas with its proslavery Lecompton Constitution. In the emotionally charged Senate debate, Gwin sided with Buchanan's administration forces in seeking Kansas's admission, while the controversial Broderick worked as Senator Stephen Douglas's chief lieutenant in opposing the Kansas admission. President Buchanan, for other reasons, also denied Broderick the federal patronage on which the latter hoped to rebuild his political base (he had, meantime, lost control of his city and state patronage). Gwin stuck to his secret bargain but still benefited from the President's political support and patronage appointments.

Gwin and Broderick, on their return to California in 1859, were caught in a fateful sequence of events. In the hard-fought 1859 state elections, Gwin's Lecompton Democrats won the entire state ticket from Broderick's anti-Lecompton Democrats and the Republicans. In the governorship race, Latham beat out Weller and James Denver to be the Lecompton Democrat candidate, then went on to win over the anti-Lecompton and Republican (Stanford) candidates. Shortly after the election, the dispirited Broderick was killed in a duel by Chief Justice David Terry, who had resigned from office to seek satisfaction for the Senator's earlier disparaging remarks. The 1860 legislature, completely controlled by Lecompton Democrats, elected Governor Latham to Broderick's vacant seat in the United States Senate.

The national elections in 1860 brought on a political showdown between the major parties, now realigned on the slavery issue. In the four-way presidential race, California gave Republican Abraham Lincoln a narrow victory over Senator Stephen Douglas (leader of the anti-Lecompton Democrats). The two together polled two-thirds of the total vote over Vice President Breckenridge (leader of the Lecompton Democrats) and the Constitutional Union Party (a Whig–Know-Nothing combination). Lincoln's victory meant the die was cast on the slavery issue which had engulfed the nation over the past decade. It also meant the end of the Gwin machine, which had staked its future hopes on Breckenridge's victory. Gwin, as California's leading senator, had over the years rendered his adopted state great service, but was henceforth doomed to political oblivion.

So ended the first decade of California's turbulent politics. The political contest between Gwin and Broderick, who dominated it, was without parallel in state history. It twice deadlocked the legislature and state Democratic conventions, resulting in unmatched chicanery and bribery. It affected the public careers of four governors (Bigler, Johnson, Weller, and Latham) and a host of other public officials. It engendered intense loyalties and hatreds between men and principles which led to several duels (Gwin and Broderick each fought at least one). California, for half the decade, had only one of its two allocated solons sitting in the United States Senate, partly because of this feud. The state felt political consequences from this contest well into the next decade.

The Expansive Sixties

The United States during the 1860's experienced the greatest upheaval of its national life. The long-smoldering conflict between the North and South broke into the mortal combat of the Civil War. The fratricidal showdown left in its wake an appalling loss of life, a terrible destruction of the land, an enormous waste of human and physical resources, and—ironically—great technological and industrial progress. The triumphant North, which had emerged from the war with an expanding industrial economy and an entrenched Republican Party, now dominated the national leadership. The defeated South, slowly and painfully reconstituted its plantation economy and adjusted its political system. The West, which had been a tributary to the mainstream of the war, was developing, with the help of Northern capital, into a rapidly expanding agrarian economy, as miners, ranchers, and farmers opened new frontier areas. The federal government, under Northern Republican leadership, during and after the war gave increasing attention to the West, particularly in drawing new states and territories close into national life. California, with its strategic location and vast wealth, was the chief beneficiary of this new national orientation to the Far West.

Union Politics

With the advent of the Civil War, state politics underwent realignment. Lincoln's election in November 1860 evoked intense public debate over California's course in the anticipated North–South split. Douglas Democrats and Republicans stood firmly by Lincoln for the Union. Breckenridge Democrats, while not daring to advocate openly California's support of Southern secession, urged that the state remain neutral, or even reorganize into an independent Pacific Republic (see below). Then came the shelling of Fort Sumter. Shaken by the advent of the war, Governor Downey, the legislature, and the congressional delegation abandoned their earlier pro-Breckenridge sentiments and professed their loyalty to the Union. The 1861 legislature, now controlled by Douglas Democrats, selected for Gwin's seat in the United States Senate, James MacDougall, a Douglas Democrat and a strong Unionist. In the state elections of November 1861, the Republicans swept all state offices, with Leland Stanford winning the governorship over John Conness, a Union Democrat and a merchant–politician from El Dorado, a mining county.

Growing public sentiment for the Union cause during the war years gave a strong impetus for party unity. Republicans and Union Democrats (formerly Broderick–Douglas Democrats) in 1862 fused into the Union Party to gain ascendancy in state affairs during the middle years. Union Party leadership was assumed by John Conness, who, by organizing Union leagues (local patriotic clubs), was able to win party control and secure election in 1863 to Latham's seat in the United States Senate. As California's leading senator (1863–1867), Conness, a staunch Lincoln supporter, effectively wielded federal patronage to control state politics and help Frederick Low (former congressman and San Francisco customs collector) in 1863 to win his bid over Stanford for the governorship. The Breckenridge Democrats (formerly Gwin–Lecompton Democrats) became by 1863 the regular Democratic Party under the leadership of a group which included four ex-governors (McDougal, Bigler, Weller, and Downey). An opposition newspaper designated these men the "four johns" to describe the "aromatic condition" of the party.

After the war, the Union Party was badly split by factional discords which again shifted party lines. Conness in 1865 sponsored Governor Low's bid for MacDougall's seat in the United States Senate. But the bitter hatreds aroused in the party primaries by the roughhouse tactics of the pro-Low "short hair" and the anti-Low "long-hair" factions caused Low to withdraw in favor of another merchant and Unionist, Cornelius Cole, who won the legislative election. When Conness forces in 1867 won the Union Party gubernatorial nomination of George Gorham, the party split was complete. The 1867 legislature elected a Democrat, Eugene Casserly, a wealthy San Francisco lawyer, to Conness's seat in the Senate. In the 1867 state elections, the Democrat Henry Haight won the three-way contest for governor by capitalizing on the Union Party division and appealing to the growing anti-Negro and anti-Chinese sentiment (see Chapter 10). With the passing of the Union party, state politics was henceforth conducted along Republican and Democratic party lines, placing California more in formal alignment with the national party system.

ANALYSIS

The State Capital

One of the first issues in the new state was the question of a permanent site for the state capital. Competition for this prize was intense. Promoters indulged in high-pressure lobbying and suspected bribery. San Jose, Vallejo, and Benicia, through aggressive efforts and extravagant offers of land and money, outdid the logical contenders—Monterey, the old capital, and San Francisco, the leading city. Mariano Vallejo was front man for a promoter group which offered 156 acres in the town of his name and $350,000 for the state capital and other buildings. San Jose countered by offering 960 acres of land, and Sacramento promised a one million dollar donation raised by public subscription. The legislature, within the first five years, moved the state capital from San Jose to Vallejo to San Jose to Vallejo to Sacramento to Vallejo to Benicia and finally, in 1854, to Sacramento. There the state government resided in leased quarters pending completion of the capitol building, which was constructed between 1860 and 1874 at a cost of $1.2 million. The state capital issue is a reflection of California politics: the shabby spectacle of political jobbery that nevertheless results in an impressive achievement—in this case, the imposing structure that is the state capitol today.

Administration of Justice

The new state's machinery for administering the law emerged only after several years of legislative trial and error. Congress in 1851 extended the national judiciary, establishing for Northern and Southern California federal district courts with their grand jury and district attorney complements. The legislature in 1851 adopted the civil and criminal codes drafted by Assemblyman Stephen Field from the New York codes—the target of the code reform movement pioneered by his famous brother David. The same legislature also provided for the triad of county sheriff, city police, and town constable for maintaining the public peace in local areas, supplemented by the state militia in the event of local breakdown in law enforcement. By mid-decade the state was divided into judicial districts, and a court hierarchy took definite form: municipal and justice courts in cities and towns, county and district courts, and the supreme court for hearing final appeals and arbitrating constitutional and intragovernmental questions. The court system at the local level was complemented by the county and municipal grand juries for conducting investigations and bringing indictments, the district attorney and city attorney for prosecuting cases, and other personnel for maintaining court order and peace.

In the early years of statehood the court system experienced tribulations of trial and error. Judges were elected officials, as were prosecuting attorneys and sheriffs. Some even had criminal records. Many were often ignorant of established legal procedures and administered the law in irregular ways which often reflected their personal dislikes and prejudices. Grand juries showed a relaxed attitude toward homicides and harsh views toward property thefts. A Tuolumne grand jury on one occasion brought murder indictments against several persons for "improper use of deadly weapons"—reflecting a frontier attitude more concerned with the manner than the results of the crime. Criminal prosecutions were handicapped by low-paid, inexperienced prosecutors pitted against high-paid, skilled, and often unscrupulous defense attorneys, and by juries frequently composed of riff-raff "courthouse hangers-on." The counties were slow in voting funds for local jails—many counties had no jail facilities for the first half-decade. The shortage of jails prompted the 1851 statute, put into practice several times before its repeal in 1856, which made grand larceny and theft punishable by death. The "wheels of justice" turned erratically and unpredictably.

The rough character of the court system can be seen in the men who sat on the bench and practiced before the bar. The career of Stephen Field is a case in point. As a Marysville lawyer in the Gold Rush, he was involved in a vindictive feud with a hot-tempered district judge; as an assemblyman, he spearheaded an unsuccessful attempt to impeach that judge. He was elected to the state supreme court in 1857 and ended up on the United States Supreme Court in 1863, rising from practicing lawyer to justice on the nation's highest tribunal within 15 years. On the state's high court sat such men as: the talented S. C. Hastings, the first chief justice, who had served as Iowa's chief justice; the much absent Hugh Murray, who, at 29, was the youngest chief justice; the impetuous David Terry, a Southerner with a "reputation carved by his bowie knife," who resigned to duel Broderick; and the energetic Edwin

Crocker, Central Pacific Railroad's chief attorney, who wrote over 200 opinions—some still law school case studies—in the half-year before his untimely death. Eminent jurists made significant contributions to law development, notably Field in the legal codes and mining law, and Ogden Hoffman, the federal district judge for Northern California, in the controversial land title cases. Principled lawyers like Henry Halleck, Benjamin Hayes, and Hall McAllister, pioneer leader of the state bar association, helped sustain the integrity of the courts. Such men more than compensated for unscrupulous and incompetent judges and lawyers whose actions occasionally resulted in miscarriages of justice.

The state experienced a severe breakdown in law enforcement in the first decade. In these years it was swept by a wave of highway robberies and cattle rustling carried out by American outlaws, Mexican bandits, Indian half-breeds, Sydney ducks (British convicts from the Australian penal colony), and other outcasts, who often killed their victims to destroy evidence. Outlawry reached its peak between 1852 and 1853 in the real and alleged exploits of Joaquin Murietta, a famous bandit whose escapades made him a legendary figure. The "Joaquin Scare" aroused an unprecedented state-wide hysteria. The 1853 legislature authorized a special ranger company which, after a three-month search, claimed to have captured the desperado and to have preserved his head in a pickle jar in order to obtain the handsome reward. The rampant lawlessness and lax law enforcement resulted in an estimated 4,200 murders between 1849 and 1854, with few convictions and rarely an execution. As Governor Burnett remarked some years later, this demoralizing situation led impatient men to form vigilante committees and fill "the courts of Judge Lynch."

Vigilantism

Vigilantes (Spanish "watchmen; guards") are a self-appointed group of citizens who administer their brand of law and order. Vigilantism is a form of mob action which usually results in a summary trial, flogging, exile, or execution by hanging. Vigilantism has an age-old tradition in Latin and Anglo-Saxon institutions and elsewhere. In California it was born primarily of local circumstances. The first recorded instance of vigilante activity occurred in 1836 in Los Angeles, but the movement really took root during the Gold Rush and reached its height in the 1850's. The gold strike attracted a heterogeneous horde of enterprising men, including criminals and other parasites, who lived by different

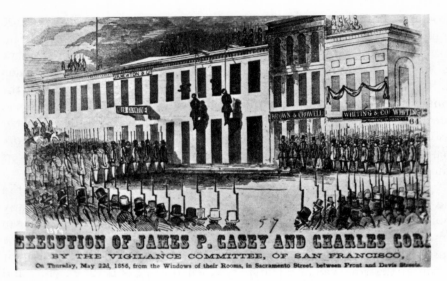

EXECUTION OF JAMES P. CASEY AND CHARLES COR...
BY THE VIGILANCE COMMITTEE, OF SAN FRANCISCO,
On Thursday, May 22d, 1856, from the Windows of their Rooms, in Sacramento Street, between Front and Davis Streets.

The San Francisco vigilantes of 1856. A vigilante version of the hanging of a convicted pair outside Committee headquarters (Fort Gunnybags) after conviction, as shown on a contemporary print sheet.

codes of personal conduct. Notable among the diverse elements were New York toughs, Southern firebrands, and Sydney ducks, who sought a better life in California. Some reformed, but many unrepentant criminals organized in quasi-fraternal gangs. The gold strike also inoculated men with such a craze for sudden riches that many who became embittered by their unfilled ambitions turned to the easier ways of crime. In settling their differences with other men, many made use of the knife or the gun.

San Francisco was the main scene of the revival of vigilantism (see below). The Law and Order organization had brought the Hounds to bay in 1849, but crimes increased steadily until 1851, when irate citizens took action. A vigilante committee comprising over 700 members and headed by former Law and Order men (including Sam Brannan) conducted quasi-formal proceedings for dealing with suspected wrongdoers. When the committee disbanded four months later, it had made nearly 90 arrests, had hanged four men, whipped one, deported 28, released 41—and remanded 15 to regular authorities for trial. The committee was criticized by the mayor, condemned by the grand jury, and warned by the governor—all to no avail.

Other communities following San Francisco's example manifested local variations in their vigilante activity. In the larger towns of

Northern California, such as Marysville, Sacramento, Stockton, and Sonora, vigilantes organized standing associations of local citizens. In the mining communities and smaller towns, vigilante committees were organized only for special occasions. Miner vigilantism was particularly notable for severe prosecutions (horse stealing and gold theft often called forth death penalties, while murderers were usually let off), an excessive number of Latin American victims, and harsh punishment (banishment, flogging, cheek branding, ear cropping, and hanging). In Los Angeles, the town council established a vigilante committee that made legal executions difficult to distinguish from lynchings. El Monte, a town heavily populated by Texan immigrants, spawned a self-constituted group of mounted rangers who carried their brand of justice on wide-ranging expeditions extending as far as Los Angeles. Vigilantism was frequent and violent in Southern California, still a raw frontier. In the 1850–1870 period, Los Angeles had 35 hangings, while San Francisco had only eight.

Vigilantism reached a climax in San Francisco in 1856. After two sensational killings, a vigilante committee with over 2500 members headed by William Coleman, a leading San Francisco merchant, formed a military organization complete with a fortified headquarters called Fort Gunnysacks. They seized from jail the two men involved in the killings and hanged them in an elaborate public cememony. They intercepted a San Francisco-bound ship carrying United States arms for the state militia. They jailed David Terry of the state supreme court who had stabbed a vigilante policeman in a fracas over vigilante piracy. They successfully resisted countermoves by the mayor, the sheriff, and a militia force under William Sherman. When they disbanded after three-months' operation, they had hanged three men (a fourth committed suicide in his cell) and deported thirty. Thereafter, vigilantism appeared only in isolated incidents.

From its beginning, the vigilante movement has provoked intense debate. It was praised by admirers as a popular tribunal applying justice, and denounced by critics as a mob seeking vengeance. From a historical view, this much is evident: where vigilantism during the interregnum was the symbol of law where none existed, it was after 1850 a parody of the established courts and law enforcement machinery. Vigilante activity was conducted by respectable middle-class citizens with an obsessive zeal for order, as well as by dissolute men obsessed by passions of the moment. Interestingly enough, no lawyers served on vigilante committees. Field, McAllister, and other prominent members of the legal profession were outspoken opponents of vigilantism. The vigilantes contributed to some measure of safety, but by tactics of terror and intimidation rather than by respectable legal methods. They failed to achieve the intended reform of the courts and of the political process. Nevertheless, the vigilante precedent was established in tradition as a perverted reform movement. It was to recur periodically in later years.

Fiscal Administration

California's financial position during this transitory period was precarious. The state was handicapped from the start: there was no sound currency in circulation and no money in the state treasury. Coins were produced from gold dust by entrepreneurs, Broderick among them. Money speculators and foreign bankers reaped lucrative profits, buying gold dust from miners at $16 an ounce and selling it in the East and Europe for $18 an ounce or more. The federal government, after constant prodding by California's congressional delegation, finally established in San Francisco a branch mint (1854) for producing United States coins, thus putting the coinage system on a more stable basis.

Still at the peak of the Gold Rush, the state encountered great difficulties in resolving its finances. The first legislature set up the basic scheme for financing the state government. It established a general tax on real and personal property as the chief source of revenue. It also imposed a poll tax to tap the state's floating population (like miners), a military commutation tax on evaders of militia service, and license taxes on entertainers, foreign miners, merchants, and other groups doing business in the state. Confronted with an empty treasury, the 1850 legislature resorted to the expensive expedient of authorizing bonds to pay its current expenses and accumulated debts.

The legislature in the first decade indulged in an orgy of fiscal irregularities. It voted generous sums for salaries of public officials and expenses of state institutions. It granted exemptions to politically powerful groups—an 1854 measure exempted from state taxes gold claims of miners and growing crops of farmers. Instead of apportioning property taxes, it set the tax rate *before* determining governmental costs so that any matching of revenues with expenditures was strictly coincidental. To avoid levying high taxes, the legislature resorted to "living off" borrowed money, by authorizing bonds. It adopted funding acts to pay off the principal and enormously swollen interest from the bond issue—$700,000 in 1851, $600,000 in 1852, $700,000 in 1855,

$1.5 million in 1856! When the state supreme court finally ruled unconstitutional the funding and other bonds since they exceeded the constitutional $300,000 limit, the legislature authorized two huge bond issues (1858 and 1860) to pay all its debts.

Legislative irregularities were an invitation to administrative malpractice. County officials, out of dishonesty or ignorance, exercised their wide discretionary powers in various irregular practices. A common practice was to underassess properties in their respective counties to enable property owners to pay a smaller share of the state tax, thus leading to a destructive system of "competitive undervaluation" among the counties. State officials spent legislative appropriations in careless ways, sometimes absconding with public monies. The bankers entrusted with state bonds (Palmer, Cook, and Company) speculated with them for their profit and, after bankruptcy in 1855, the directors defaulted sizable sums. One state treasurer left office under a cloud of suspicion, and his successor went to jail for unexplained losses amounting to $127,000—both men were involved with the bankers' schemes. These financial misappropriations prompted the legislature to establish a state board of examiners, comprising the governor, secretary of state, and attorney general, to approve claims and examine accounts. This reform achieved little more than perfunctory fiscal control.

Even more serious was the political revolt by Southern Californians. The revenue system based on the property tax allowed moneymaking miners to escape paying taxes, and placed the growing tax burden on merchants, aliens, and transients. The burden was heaviest on the large landowning ranchers, most of whom lived in Southern California. The governor, as early as 1851, described the inequities of tax policies by pointing out that Southern California's six "cow counties" with over 6000 population paid $24,000 in state taxes, while 22 mining counties with 120,000 population paid only $21,000. Southern California leaders, notably Assemblyman Andres Pico (Pio's brother) in almost every legislative session pressed for reforms to remedy gross disparities and outright discrimination resulting primarily from tax inequities and unequal representation. Finally, in 1859, the legislature adopted Pico's measure for forming the six southern counties (San Luis Obispo, Santa Barbara, Los Angeles, San Bernardino, San Diego, and Tulare) into a separate territory as a prelude to independent statehood. But the United States Congress in 1860 was so engrossed with the pending sectional showdown over slavery that it failed to consider passage of Pico's measure. Thus ended the decade-long effort of Southern Californians to rectify their situation by partitioning the state.

During the Civil War, the state became embroiled with the national government over its currency policy. Congress, to produce money for paying off war expenses, in 1862 authorized greenbacks, or paper money, as legal tender acceptable for payment of taxes and debts. Californians long accustomed to gold and silver currency reacted strongly to federal policy. The 1863 legislature, under merchant pressure, enacted a measure requiring the courts to uphold any contract which specified gold or silver payments. The issue provoked bitter conflict between federal and state authorities. It was not resolved until they settled on a compromise by which national gold banks were authorized by Congress (1870) for redeeming paper money with specie or coin. California benefited by adhering steadfastly to its specie policy. The state's specie currency contributed to economic stability and headed off the ruinous effects of inflationary paper money which gripped other states.

Fiscal administration was not much improved in the 1860's. The legislature, under merchant pressure, required miners to pay state taxes on their claims (1861) but still exempted farmers growing crops—perhaps because farmers were customers of merchants who distributed their crops. It did little to curb extravagances in expenditure or the malpractices of state and county officials in collecting and disbursing state moneys. The state debt, which reached a high in mid-decade, was met by generous but expensive funding acts after the war. The long anticipated tax reform finally came about when the 1870 legislature created a state board of equalization to adjust assessments among the counties in order to insure more uniform tax administration. After two decades of fiscal tribulations, the state was moving toward stability in its financial affairs.

Political Organization

Americans have a long tradition of reform movements designed to correct deficiencies in society, stemming from Jeffersonianism in the Revolutionary period and Jacksonianism in the middle years of the nineteenth century. Reform movements represent the efforts of discontented groups to change existing conditions for a new and improved setup, whether in the political, economic, or social sphere. A prevailing idea of the time was that reforms of the political apparatus would result in desired governmental, economic, and social changes, an idea which captivated disenchanted Californians.

California party and government organizations evolved in the traditional manner of American frontier states and retained this frontier character without much change in this period. As we have seen, these institutions operated in irregular fashion and were often corrupt. Aroused groups attempted reform for greater economy and efficiency and the correction of inequities. Dissident Whigs, as early as 1852, decried the extravagant expenditures and heavy tax burdens of the Democratic administration, and tried unsuccessfully to engineer a legislative call for a constitutional convention to remedy the situation. In San Francisco, the business-minded vigilantes who forcefully did away with criminal elements to restore public order in 1856 went on to overthrow boss rule. This inaugurated a decade of sound, though tightfisted, municipal administration, the earliest example of effective local reform. Federal and state agencies made some effort to clean up corruption with little success. J. Ross Browne, a United States confidential agent in the mid-1850's, reported to federal agencies on the misconduct of their field agents in California. A contemporary described him as a "hard nose Diogenes who could smell out fraud and sloth as a ferret can detect rats," but his exposés apparently resulted in only minor changes. Southern Californians sought to remedy tax inequities and unequal representation by partitioning the state.

The patriotic fervor of the Civil War provided the reform impulse for eliminating long-resented abuses and corruption in state government. Constitutional amendments adopted in 1862 extended the governor's term from two to four years and converted the legislature from annual to biennial sessions, and reiterated the prohibition against special legislation in a major effort to improve the governmental process. It also established special elections for judges and state superintendent of public instruction to remove them from partisan politics. The 1865 legislature adopted a direct primary law, the nation's first, to permit citizens to select local candidates in open elections, but the optional feature practically nullified the law's intent. These government and party reforms fell far short of their goals, but they established California's long tradition of political reform.

9 An Explosive Economy

THE SETTING

The Entrepreneurs

The Gold Rush opened the door to unlimited opportunity for enterprising men. The argonaut horde created heavy demands for food, clothing, shelter, tools, and other goods. Ranchers, lumbermen, merchants, manufacturers, and other entrepreneurs scrambled to supply them. They were soon joined by disappointed gold seekers who had abandoned the diggings to take up former occupations, and by ambitious immigrants from everywhere lured by the prospect of quick riches. The merchants—storekeepers, wholesalers, and shippers—played the middleman role in the growing market economy. They were also the financiers who supplied funds for development of the early mining, agricultural, manufacturing, and transportation enterprises in the rapidly growing frontier state.

These entrepreneurs were a remarkable breed of self-made men. They were mostly of middle-class origins with at least enough means to pay the long way to California. Relatively few came from either humble or wealthy circumstances. They were generally men of ambition, energy, imagination, and fortitude eager to improve their status. They were inclined to undertake risky ventures and to discard unworkable methods and experiment with new ones to find effective solutions to their problems—something their eastern colleagues did not always do. For some it meant greater profits, for others it was simply a matter of survival. Many managed to make a comfortable livelihood; some barely subsisted; some did not make it at all. They were predominantly small entrepreneurs who laid the foundations of the state's agricultural, manufacturing, and other enterprises.

Out of the competition among these many entrepreneurs arose a few who not only made it big but assumed a commanding position in California's economy. They were mostly merchant–financiers, located primarily but not exclusively in San Francisco. They had the shrewdness and persistency to cope with unpredictable conditions. Most of them came to California as argonauts in modest circumstances, amassed a fortune and gained a dominant position in one area, then invested their profits in other areas to gain even greater wealth and power. They were a diverse lot—some principled and some unscrupulous, some concerned with material and social progress, but others obsessed with power and wealth—who generally played a ruthless game of business competition. They pioneered a trend in high finance by occasionally combining their resources to form syndicates for accomplishing costly, large-scale, but highly profitable projects.

These merchant–financiers and other big entrepreneurs were largely responsible for bringing about California's fantastic economic development. Representative of the group were Sam Brannan, whose far-flung enterprises made him California's foremost merchant in the 1850's and reputedly its first millionaire, and William Ralston, who made generous loans and investments of his and other people's money to become the leading financier of the 1860's. Both men had a hand in every major type of enterprise. It was characteristic of the times that both later went bankrupt.

Business Organization

Entrepreneurs used a wide variety of organizations for conducting their enterprises. Most of them formed proprietorships, partnerships, and joint stock associations, relying on their individual and collective resources. The associations usually comprised working partners who could raise considerable funds but faced greater risks in managing their ventures. Some merchant groups resorted to the relatively new corporation device—still confined to banks and insurance and transportation enterprises in the East. The corporate organization proved to be an effective device for securing additional capital to finance costly large-scale enterprises, especially in mining and railroads where people were eager to invest their savings in shares of corporation stocks. These early corporations had simple structures: a president and a few officers who personally handled legal matters, finance, supplies, and sales; and a general superintendent or manager who supervised the working force or field operations. Several groups consolidated their enterprises by merging their companies into a larger corporation. Other groups experimented with cooperative organizations, such as agricultural colonies, workers' manufacturing firms, business associations, and other self-supporting communities, such as Brannan's ill-fated Mormon colony.

DEVELOPMENT

The market economy gradually evolved out of the efforts of merchant middlemen who developed various mechanisms for marketing goods and services. Struggling through the early hectic years of the Gold Rush, they operated in makeshift facilities under haphazard conditions. In San Francisco, the state's chief commercial center, central trading operations were established in the Merchants Exchange (set up in 1850 and reorganized in 1863) and the Produce Exchange (organized in 1857) to facilitate the buying and selling of goods. San Francisco merchants led the way for other communities in organizing a local chamber of commerce (1850) as a means of promoting and protecting business enterprises. When the Comstock silver bonanza precipitated a mania of public stock speculation after the first decade, a group of merchant brokers organized the San Francisco Stock Exchange (1864) on the New York model to facilitate transactions of mining stock and later other corporation securities. Though these market facilities were risky and unstable institutions often racked by wild speculation, sporadic growth, and unscrupulous operations, they nevertheless constituted an effective market structure that served the basic needs of numerous growing enterprises in the rapidly expanding state.

In those days, the state played a more important role than the federal government in determining public economic policy. Private enterprises were primarily small-scale operations focused on localized markets; only a few types of enterprises were regional or statewide in scope. Congress confined its actions to public lands and to a few existing interstate enterprises like some banks and transportation facilities.

In California the 1849 Constitution had already stipulated that associations and corporations could be formed under certain conditions prescribed by law. The legislatures of the 1850's extended government privileges for incorporating various enterprises but wrote rigid safeguards into the laws to prevent monopolistic tendencies. So few corporations were organized under this restrictive law that the 1853 legislature enacted a special incorporation act that required similar restraints but granted wider powers to specific types of corporations, including mining, manufacturing, commerce, and transportation. Legislators liked the American idea of free individual enterprise, but they had the Jacksonian fear of corporate enterprises whose large-scale operations could hurt small entrepreneurs.

During the 1860's the legislature was more responsive to merchant groups who sought laws favorable to corporations. The merchants gained greater influence in public affairs through their alliance with party bosses and gained public support from later American immigrants, who understood better the importance of corporations, especially in building the indispensable railroad, water, and other public facilities. Furthermore, the Comstock silver boom prompted miners, merchants, farmers, clerks, and laborers to invest their earnings in mining stocks in anticipation of huge profits. The desire for profits overcame earlier fears of monopolies. The legislature responded in kind: it authorized wide powers for the banks (see below) and showed greater leniency in granting to corporations special charters with broad powers. The usefulness of corporate enterprises was clearly recognized by public economic policy.

Out of the frontier environment emerged what were to be characteristic features of California's market economy. The mainstay was the large class of entrepreneurs, a heterogeneous lot of small and big operators who spearheaded the state's economic development. If they could not carry on individually or with partners, they formed cooperatives and corporations to pool their money and efforts. If they could not afford Caucasian labor, they sought cheap alien labor, devised improved processes, and invented machines to do the work. They organized into various types of associations to coordinate their efforts, to regulate operations (mining districts and rodeos), to promote the production and distribution of their goods (trade associations), or to protect their group interests (homestead and settler associations). The merchant financiers, joined by rising manufacturers, assumed a commanding role. They made greater use of the corporate device which enabled them to conduct large-scale operations for greater profits—bigger size meant lower costs, and lower costs meant bigger profits. All of them pressed for public policies and for governmental assistance which would benefit their enterprises. Although they often professed sentiments of rugged individualism and free enterprise, they did not hesitate to impose group controls or to seek government aid.

ANALYSIS

Land

Land was a major focus of attention. Speculators—Americans and some Californios—acquired rancho tracts, pueblo lots, or public lands to plot towns, subdivide property, or simply to hold and sell later. Merchants, ranchers, and farmers sought lots and tracts for developing their respective enterprises. American settlers sometimes purchased and rented these lands, but more often—in tune with their frontier tradition—squatted on them, staking out homesteads and farms.

Private Lands

American efforts to secure title to their lands resulted in long, complicated, and intense struggles with each other and with government authorities. Congress was confronted with the immediate task of confirming Mexican land grants—that is, reaffirming titles to private lands granted by Mexico conditioned by the treaty stipulation that property rights of Mexicans, like those of United States citizens, be "inviolably respected." A power struggle developed between Senator Gwin, who championed the squatters' cause, and Senator Benton, who took up the grantees' rights (a view probably conditioned by the fact that Fremont and another son-in-law possessed sizable Mexican land grant claims). Congress, after a lengthy debate, set up a three-man federal commission to adjudicate each claim with either party having the right of court appeal.

The legal disposition of these Mexican land grants was incredibly time-consuming, controversial, and complex. The land commission, during its tenure between 1852 and 1856, handled 813 claims totaling over 12 million acres (the combined area of Massachusetts, New Hampshire, and Maine), but practically all these claims were appealed to the district courts and 99 eventually went to the United States Supreme Court. The courts got into intricate points of law which resulted in retroactive and contradictory decisions. Federal land agencies were slow, and occasionally unscrupulous, in surveying boundaries and completing official titles—field agents were often accused of direct connivance with landowners and of other malpractices. The commission and the courts eventually confirmed 604 claims involving 8.7 million acres. By 1870 only half of the approved claims (322) had completed titles, 17 years being the average length of time between submitting the claim and receiving a patent (certificate of title). Some fraudulent claims were approved, apparently some legitimate claims were not. Several valuable claims were particularly notorious for their fraudulent schemes, legal high jinks, and high-level politics, including Fremont's claim to the ten-league Las Mariposas rancho grant in the Mother Lode region. Towns of Spanish origin and the Catholic Church acquired title to pueblo lands and mission-based church sites. The Indians, however, unaware of American ways, failed to submit claims for their pueblos and town lots, thus losing a rare opportunity for securing their lands.

Land disputes over the Mexican grants broke out in almost every community in the state. In Sacramento, merchants and speculators (Brannan among them) who had acquired lots from Sutter clashed with a squatter group in two violent showdowns in which the mayor, the sheriff, and several others were killed. In San Francisco, squatters formed armed bands and set up barricades to defend their claims; some used shotguns to resist the sheriff's orders to eject them. Some 50 squatters along the Russian River in Sonoma County were thwarted in burning down Healdsburg by local citizens defending the town. Harassed rancheros fought to defend their land, stock, crops, and homes—a few even lost their lives in the process. The Berryessa clan, once powerful in the Napa and San Jose areas, suffered tragically: three were lynched, three went insane, and some 70 others, victimized by litigation, fraud, and violence, became completely landless and virtually penniless. Conniving lawyers and swindlers divested rancheros and settlers of their lands by legal trickery and exorbitant legal fees (reputable lawyers like Halleck, Larkin, and Hayes often took only token fees). In the Central Valley and in Southern California, rancheros fared well by the commission and court decisions and experienced comparatively little trouble with squatters. Most of them lost their lands later because of economic setbacks.

Public Lands

The Congress in disposing the public lands precipitated another round of troubles. The conflicts this time were between the federal and state governments and, in turn, between speculators and settlers. Congress made a series of public land grants for the two-fold purpose of encouraging actual settlement and for promoting community development, particularly education, internal improvements (public works), and economic development. California, however, ignored careful federal stipulations for disposing of these lands, because of pressure of speculators and settlers desiring a free hand in pursuing their various schemes. Congress in 1850 allocated 500,000 acres for the state to sell settlers lots on surveyed lands and to use the revenues for public works. The 1852 legislature, however, enacted a measure which enabled persons to acquire these lands on easy terms *before* the federal surveys. Congress, by another 1850 act, granted some two million acres of swamplands (in this case overflow lands along major rivers) for reclamation purposes, but the state failed to certify the swampy character of this land with the result that many persons acquired valuable fertile land as swamplands. Congress in 1853 granted 5.5 million acres for public schools, and extended federal preemption policy to surveyed lands by which settlers could occupy up to 160 acres and secure title later. These two measures were also subject to state abuses and to the schemes of unscrupulous speculators and settlers. Government administration of these public lands was haphazard and marked by clashes between federal and state land agencies.

Congress in the 1860's enacted four landmark measures of great consequence to the state. The Pacific Railroad Act (1862) granted the Central Pacific and Union Pacific a right-of-way and additional lands in the public domain as enticement for constructing the transcontinental railroad. The College Land Grant Act (1862) gave public lands to each state to endow institutions of higher learning. The Homestead Act (1862) offered 160 acres to a settler who would obtain title after five years' continued residence and improvements. Congress in 1866 finally resolved the long-standing state–federal disputes over conflicting land titles. It confirmed state titles to disputed lands, and for good measure gave titles to claimants of mineral lands in the public domain! These federal land policies began an era of public land distribution which profoundly affected California's development over the next half-century.

Public land administration, like the settlement of Mexican grant titles, underwent great turmoil. Speculators, settlers, and public officials were involved in legal manipulations, lengthy litigation, malpractice, fraud, and violence. Speculators with ready cash, familiar with the law, clearly outdid settlers in taking advantage of legal loopholes and other complicated features of federal and state laws. They employed such devices as "dummies," in which they paid a person to sign forged land applications, or "stealing in lieu" in which they stole applications and completed title before the original applicant did. Such speculators easily bribed the low-salaried government land agents, and some even worked in the state land agency to further their villainous schemes. Settlers were handicapped by cumbersome procedures, contradictory policies, and irregular practices. Most of them had little choice but to purchase desired lands at the speculator's high price (usually from $2.50 to $10 per acre), rather than at the government's standard price of $1.25 per acre. By 1870 almost half of California's vast public domain of eight million acres had passed into private ownership.

California's experience after two decades resulted in a distinct but complex land pattern. A few men came to control a large portion of California lands. In 1870 there were 22 owners of 70,000 acres or more apiece who together occupied as much land as 23,000 owners with 500 acres or less. William Chapman acquired, through the use of dummies and through connections with government land agents, over a million acres of land to become one of the nation's largest landowners. Chapman was an extraordinary speculator. He pioneered in crop experimentation, irrigation projects, and immigrant colonies to develop agrarian communities, setting an example for others. These large landowners used their lands in various ways: some for pure speculation, and others for diverse farming, ranching, lumbering, mining, or real estate enterprises. The varied forms of land tenure that emerged in this period created the pattern of land use and development that has survived to our own day.

Agriculture

The farmers and ranchers who sought their opportunities in agricultural enterprises encountered a formidable situation. They recognized the state's tremendous assets: its favorable terrain, mild climate, and productive soils. They were beset, however, by unpredictable weather conditions, uncertain land titles, inadequate transportation facilities, distant markets, and the speculative nature of their enterprises. Considerable imagination, talent, and daring were shown in overcoming such obstacles. They experimented with local and imported species, with individual, cooperative and corporate organizations, with small- and large-scale operations, and with new methods for producing goods. One important ally was the merchant who developed the facilities for marketing their products. Also important to the farmer and rancher were the agricultural specialists, such as nurserymen, purebred stock breeders, and manufacturers of farm machinery, who supplied imported seeds, plants, stock, and implements. Agricultural journalists assisted by publicizing farming methods, available supplies, and other basic information. James Warren, a merchant-journalist, was especially influential; he spearheaded the state agricultural fair (1852) and published the *California Farmer* for disseminating crop and livestock among settlers. Mining fathered many of these early enterprises by providing a ready market for agricultural products at high prices and attractive profits.

In public policy on agriculture, the ranchers at the onset clearly outdid the farmers. The 1850 legislature enacted the rancher-sponsored fencing law which required farmers to fence their property or be liable for injury to wandering livestock, thus assuring ranchers of open land for grazing and for their cattle drives. The 1851 legislature authorized rancher-appointed judges of the plains (see Chapter 4) to settle disputes among ranchers and to supervise the annual rodeos for branding cattle. This measure gave to ranchers what miners had in their mining codes: local control of their cattle enterprises. The farmers also obtained several important measures. The legislature in 1854 incorporated the state agricultural society and granted annual appropriations for state and county fairs. In 1862 it enacted a general bounty measure for subsidizing experimental crops. The farmers began to get the upper hand after 1864 when they obtained piecemeal fencing laws making cattlemen bear the costly burden of maintaining fences. The agricultural fairs were immensely important in the early development of agriculture: they gave information on techniques, demonstrated machinery, and awarded prizes for the finest stock and crops.

Livestock

The ranchers enjoyed a spectacular boom in supplying livestock for the mines and Northern California towns during the Gold Rush. At first

Southern California rancheros were the chief suppliers, sending drovers with large cattle herds up the coastal and valley routes to San Francisco and the Sierra. American ranchers soon appeared from the Mississippi Valley and the Southwest, driving large herds of cattle and horses, flocks of sheep, and hogs. Slaughterhouses for processing the animals became thriving enterprises in major towns. Philip Armour, a Placerville butcher for several years, went back to the Midwest, where he eventually built up his meat-packing empire.

The booming cattle industry went into a steady decline after 1856 until it approached extinction by the mid-1860's. Cattlemen suffered from the ravages of ruinous competition, an oversupplied meat market, and overgrazed forage. They were hard hit by devastating diseases (notably Texas cattle fever) and severe droughts and floods between 1861 and 1864. Southern California rancheros were also hit by exorbitant loans to pay heavy debts from high living and property taxes. Many, like Bandini and Pio Pico, lost their cattle through mortgages foreclosed to American entrepreneurs. The cattle industry declined from its peak of three million head in 1862 to around 460,000 head in 1870.

Sheep raising grew rapidly into a large-scale industry. Sheepmen fared well in the 1850's, selling mutton in the mines and wool in San Francisco. They benefited greatly from the expanded woolen industry during the Civil War; California's wool helped replace the South's wool in Northern textile mills. The state then developed its own woolen mills, notably the famous Pioneer Mills and Mission Mills (a Ralston enterprise). By 1870 California had 2.3 million sheep and ranked second among the wool-producing states. Sheep raising had clearly superseded cattle ranching.

The California ranchero with his colorful tradition faded into oblivion. His place was taken by enterprising American entrepreneurs like Henry Miller and James Irvine. Miller was a German immigrant who built up the largest of the cattle empires. He acquired contiguous ranchos and public lands strategically located on the San Joaquin, carefully managed his herds by improving his cattle breeds and irrigating his forage lands, and developed (with a partner, Charles Lux) a slaughterhouse in San Francisco to secure his market outlet. James Irvine, an Irish immigrant who became a wealthy San Francisco merchant, went into partnership with three pioneer Monterey-based sheepmen, the Flint brothers (Benjamin and Thomas) and their cousin Alexander Bixby. In the mid-1860's the partners purchased ranchos from the indebted

Stearns, Sepulveda, and Yorba, substituted sheep for cattle, and increased their flocks with purebred, building up one of the state's largest sheep enterprises.

Grain

Grain rapidly superseded livestock as the state's leading agricultural product. Cereal grains were easily cultivated on northern rancho lands to meet the heavy demands for flour and animal feed. Farmers, unlike ranchers, required little capital and only modest equipment to begin operations: usually a simple plow, scythe, pitchfork, horserake, and (with luck) local Indians or Chinese for harvest labor. Soon they graduated to horse-drawn mechanical seeders, reapers, and threshers. Some experimented with combines and steam-operated machines.

Spurred by bonanza crops, the Comstock boom and Civil War demands, farmers in the 1860's developed improved seeds and farm machinery for large-scale production. Central Valley farmers developed superior seeds, the world-renowned gang plow in which three to five plows were bolted on a single beam to turn over wide amounts of soil, and a header–thresher harvester combine (1868). Farmers used up to eight-horse or -mule teams to haul their combines and heavy wagons. Some experimented with steam engines with traction wheels (1868). Grain production was phenomenal. California ranked first in barley after 1852, and fifth among the nation's 35 wheat-producing states in the 1860's.

Marketing was an equally spectacular development. By 1854 water- and steam-powered mills were grinding wheat for special uses—bread, cereal, beverages, and animal feed—in such abundance that the state was exporting its flour and grains. Prominent millers in this development were Isaac Friedlander in San Francisco, James Lick in San Jose, Austin Sperry in Stockton, and A. D. Starr in Vallejo. Before long, wheat merchants and shippers suffered badly from intense speculation and market miscalculations due to inadequate trade information. Friedlander mastered the situation by plotting a unique trade pattern that earned him the nickname of the Grain King. He calculated from information acquired from a network of agents at home and abroad the market for California wheat in the Liverpool exchange, then purchased wholesale lots from Central Valley farmers and chartered a fleet of sailing ships to deliver the wheat via Cape Horn to England. England was the chief customer for American wheat, and its millers favored the superior California variety and bulk deliveries. By 1870 California stood high among the states in flour production.

Fruits

Fruit also emerged as an important crop in this period. Pioneer growers like Luis Vignes in San Diego, William Wolfskill in Los Angeles, and Mariano Vallejo in Sonoma had already laid foundations for an extensive fruit industry, upon which the incoming Americans expanded. The professional nurserymen played an important role, experimenting with local and imported species and making available seeds, cuts, and plants for the rapidly developing orchards and vineyards. Fruit processors appeared on the scene early. Daniel Prevost began preserving jellies in San Francisco in 1856, then graduated to canning fruit.

Some entrepreneurs broke new ground with their innovations. Charles Kohler and John Frohling, German immigrants and musicians-turned-vintners, established their winery in San Francisco in 1854. They helped set up a cooperative of 50 German immigrants who built up the famous vineyards of the Anaheim Colony (Los Angeles Vineyard Society, 1857). The two men were soon operating the state's largest commercial wine firm, producing and marketing high-quality wines for world wide markets. Agoston Haraszthy, a Hungarian immigrant and versatile vintner, built up his famous Buena Vista estate at Sonoma (1857) with 200,000 vine cuts and roots of over 1,400 varieties which he collected on a European trip (1861). Later he converted his estate into a large corporation, with help from Ralston and other San Francisco financiers, in a move to dominate the state's grape and wine industry. Within two decades, viniculture was transformed from a pioneer enterprise to a highly organized and integrated industry, setting a pattern that was to develop in other segments of agriculture and in other industries of both the state and the nation.

Mineral Resources

Gold

Gold miners through most of this period were the chief beneficiaries of public economic policies. Miners had the political cards so well stacked in their favor—talented leaders, effective organizations, and a large voting bloc in the legislature—that they were able to enact measures protecting their interests. They were notably successful in taxing foreign miners, exempting miners from state taxes, and securing government sanction of their mining codes. Congress debated intensely over the lease, sale, or free use of public mining lands in California. It finally adopted a laissez faire, or hands-off, policy, evidently for reasons of political expediency. The 1851 legislature enacted a measure drafted by assemblyman Stephen Field which instructed the state courts to enforce mining codes. When the matter of federal mining policy came up again in the 1860's, Congress enacted the landmark 1866 law, drafted by Field (then sitting on the United States Supreme Court), which instructed federal courts to follow local mining laws, thus giving federal sanction to the miners' codes. California's chief justice described the miners' code as a "few, plain, simple, and well-understood" rules based on universal acceptance (English common law)—unlike detailed and restrictive state statutes.

Hydraulic Mining in the Malakoff diggings. Monitors trained water streams under high pressure on hillsides to wash soil into iron sluices below, where gold was separated from debris, leaving devastated land behind.

Meanwhile gold mining was undergoing marked changes in the 1850's as a result of bold experimentation, large-scale operations, wild speculation, and unstable times. Sluice mining came into its own as an independent device when the open trough was separated from the long tom (see Chapter 6). It called for bringing water by ditch or flume to wooden sluices (board sluicing), and later to hillside ditches (ground sluicing), into which miners shoveled dirt material to be washed free of gold particles. Hydraulic mining got under way in the early 1850's when Anthony Chabot and Edward Matteson developed devices utilizing water pressure in sluice mining. In this process water supplied by ditches and flumes was compressed in nozzled canvas hoses to wash dirt down hillsides into large wooden sluices below. Here the gold was sifted from the debris, which then flowed into nearby rivers. Quartz mining was greatly enhanced by improved drills, hoisting devices, and stamp mills, as well as by available capital—some 20 companies were registered on the London stock market in 1853. River mining diverted literally miles of streams over great wooden flumes for exploiting the natural riverbeds. It was the most common form of large-scale operation until mid-decade, when it was superseded by quartz and hydraulic mining. The mining industry was racked by speculative companies unwisely managed by inexperienced managers, and by unstable times induced by droughts and floods, and by other mineral discoveries. Miners departing for rushes to the California Kern (1855), British Columbia (1858), and the Nevada Comstock (1859) left in their wake many completely or partially deserted mining towns.

Gold mining in the 1860's developed into a more stable industry. Quartz and hydraulic companies, by applying scientific methods and engineering techniques to develop the deep veins and gravels, hit real pay dirt. Soon they dominated gold production. Among their innovations were new devices, like the diamond-tipped drill for tunneling; the substitution of dynamite for black powder in blasting and of iron pipes for wooden flumes in transporting water; and the chemical process of chlorination for isolating gold particles. Alvinza Hayward, one of the few working miners who made it big in company mining, overcame initial failures by innovation, persistence, and luck to hit a bonanza in one mine, after which he launched several successful hydraulic and quartz companies. By the end of the decade, the larger companies with heavily capitalized machinery and labor produced the most gold. Many working miners became wage earners employed by these corporations. Gold production, which had peaked at $81 million in 1862, was yielding a relatively stable $17 million annually by 1870. Gold mining had fallen in importance to agriculture in the state's economy, but it was still a highly productive industry producing 45 percent of the world's gold supply.

The impact of California's gold industry was far-reaching and manifold. It profoundly affected the state's economic development. It provided a medium of money exchange. It made considerable capital readily available for the development of many other industries. It attracted ever greater numbers of people and capital investments. California gold not only uplifted the nation's economy when it was at a low ebb, but also helped make the nation a leading world trader. Gold mining, as it turned out, contributed to the development of many trends, including a strong local government, large-scale corporate enterprises, and lawless social behavior.

Other Minerals

California's wandering gold prospectors discovered silver deposits which spurred other mining strikes, the most famous being the Comstock Lode in Nevada. Miners stampeded to Virginia City, which boomed after 1859 as a mining center for the Comstock operations on Mount Davidson. One of the first arrivals was George Hearst; he had uneven success in the California mines but struck his fortune in the Comstock. Promoters organized mining companies which undertook construction of long tunnels and underground caverns to get at the elusive veins in the mountains. When hard times hit Comstock mining in the mid-1860's, these companies sought loans from the newly formed Bank of California, which soon foreclosed on many troubled companies to gain control of the Comstock. William Sharon, the bank's manager at Virginia City, with the collaboration of several bank officers (William Ralston, D. O. Mills, Alvinza Hayward, and John P. Jones) formed a company to operate the bank-owned mills and soon forced miners and mining companies to process their ores through his mills. By 1870 he was hailed as King of the Comstock. The Comstock's first boom contributed significantly to California's development. It was financed and peopled by Californians, primarily San Francisco capitalists and Sierra miners. It opened the way for silver strikes in California, notably Cerro Gordo east of the Sierra but extending as far south as San Bernardino. It also led to major dislocations in the state.

Pioneer oilmen in the 1850's were already using rudimentary

methods to procure crude petroleum from meager local deposits and distill it for illumination and lubrication. Commercial development did not make headway, however, until Edwin Drake's inventive drilling method in 1859 opened the Pennsylvania oil fields and spurred exploitation in California and other fields. When Benjamin Silliman, Jr., prominent Yale mineralogist, came to California in 1863 to investigate oil prospects and issued an optimistic report of the state's oil resources, the rush for oil was on. An estimated 75 companies were organized to tap oil, mostly in present-day Humboldt County, but also in Santa Clara, Ventura, and Los Angeles. They drilled wells, sank shafts, and dug tunnels, but produced limited amounts of crude oil for San Francisco and other refineries. In San Francisco, Stanford's three brothers competed with Lloyd Tevis's firm for marketing kerosene products, which were shipped to far-off New York, Peru, and Australia. The oil boom fizzled out after 1868, largely because of disappointing yields from drilling and the resumption of imports of finer grade oil from the eastern United States after the Civil War. Yet the first oil boom was significant in that oil developers established the pattern for working the petroleum fields, establishing mining districts and self-governing codes, much like the gold miners.

California miners also uncovered and exploited other mineral deposits. Mercury production in Santa Clara County increased to keep up with the expanding California and Nevada mines. Copper mining, centering mostly in Calaveras County, precipitated a brief boom in the 1860's when the county was the chief producer of copper for eastern smelters during the Civil War. Coal was found near Mount Diablo in Contra Costa County and was mined commercially after 1859 when several companies shipped profitable yields via Pittsburgh to San Francisco for iron foundries and railroad operations. These mineral enterprises, like gold, silver, and oil, were launched by bonanza strikes and spurred by speculative crazes which resulted in sudden successes and failures. Nevertheless, they laid the foundation of the state's broadly based mineral industry and contributed to its diversified industrial economy.

Timber Resources

Lumbering, being a basic industry, kept pace with the state's rapid growth. Argonauts, notably former New England lumbermen, developed logging and milling operations near populous Northern California towns. These early lumbermen relied on traditional methods: felling timber with ax and saw; moving logs with block, tackle, and hemp-rope devices; rafting logs down rivers and hauling them by ox or horse teams to the sawmills. The first sawmills were crude affairs, utilizing vertical saws— and, after 1860, circular saws—to cut logs into lumber. Millowners emerged as the key men in the industry. They organized logging crews to cut trees, and set up lumber yards for distributing the lumber. Lumber was delivered by boat or wagon—and later by rail—to San Francisco and Sacramento. From there it was transshipped direct or processed into various refined lumber products by local planing mills for local and regional markets. Henry Meiggs, former Maine lumberman and prominent San Francisco lumber merchant, headed a company which set up a sawmill on the Mendocino coast in 1852 to supply redwood lumber for his planing mill in San Francisco, thus pioneering a trend in the industry. Lumbering was a risky enterprise because of hazardous operations, limited capital, and speculative markets.

By 1860 the lumber industry acquired its characteristic regional pattern. The northwest coast was already the state's leading producer. Lumbermen invented new tools to mill the giant redwoods along the coast for delivery by boat to San Francisco, Australia, and China. In the San Francisco Bay Area, lumbermen soon depleted the redwood forests above Oakland and steadily worked the redwood stands in the Santa Cruz mountains through lumber ports at Redwood City and near Santa Cruz. The Lake Tahoe area, spurred by railroad construction and the Comstock boom, emerged as another major lumber producer. Pioneer lumbermen also developed operations in the Sierra, and in Southern California's San Gabriel and San Bernardino mountains.

Public policy was such that lumbermen enjoyed considerable freedom from government regulation. State policy was confined primarily to fire hazards: the basic 1850 law assigned to counties the responsibility for enforcing fire laws. Public attention was called to the majestic beauty of Yosemite Valley, rediscovered in 1851, and, in 1859, to the incomparable prehistoric giant redwood trees at Sequoia. Prominent visitors like Horace Greeley (1859) and Frederick Olmsted (1863) drew national attention to these wonders of nature. In response to growing public demand to end abusive practices of lumbermen in these and other areas, the 1864 legislature prohibited timber cutting on state lands—but a provision apparently added by lumber interests, excepted timber cut for manufactured products! At the behest of prominent leaders, Congress in 1864 transferred Yosemite Valley to the state for a public park—the first of its kind in the nation—and the 1866 legislature set up a state commission, which included Olmsted and Josiah Whitney, the state geologist, to oversee its preservation. The federal transfer undoubtedly saved the magnificent valley from the incursions of lumbermen, homesteaders, and other settlers.

Water Resources

Without doubt water was—and still is—the most important single factor in the state's economic development. Almost all major groups required water: miners for placer and hydraulic operations, ranchers for their livestock, farmers for their crops, lumbermen for transporting their logs and lumber, manufacturers as a power source for their mills and factories, and communities for household, firefighting, sewage disposal, and other domestic purposes. The peculiar seasonal and regional variations in the state's water supply (see Chapter 1) presented complex problems. Californians from the beginning devised practical, if not well thought-out, laws and conceived imaginative ways for developing existing water resources.

Water Rights

The principal problem at the outset was the water rights of major users. At issue were two conflicting doctrines: riparian law and prior appropriation. Riparian law (from Latin *ripa* "riverbank"), expressed in English common law and applied to well-watered areas, recognized the rights of owners of riverbanks or lands bordering a stream. Prior appropriation had its origin in Spanish law and was applied to arid areas. It gave precedence to the rights of first users who diverted or appropriated water from streams. The miners had already acted on this matter before statehood. Their mining codes regulated the use of water for mining operations, stipulating that the first users of the water had a possessory right to it—a basic principle in irrigation law today.

The state, in the absence of clear-cut congressional policy on water rights, took the initiative to resolve the conflict. When the legislature, under pressure from miner, farmer, and rancher groups, passed contradictory laws, the state supreme court straddled the issue in an 1855 decision which upheld both doctrines. Congress in its 1866 law confirming state title to conflicting public land titles (see Chapter 8) in effect sanctioned the state's dual water rights system. Since economic development in this period was concentrated in Northern California where water was abundant, water users were involved in no serious conflicts over their rights—but the stage was set for a bitter showdown later.

Water Users

Water users—miners, farmers, and ranchers—in the beginning generally located near rivers and streams to be assured of adequate supply. Some experimented with different ways of conveying water to their operations in distant areas. They dug ditches or canals and constructed wooden flumes, using crude brush dams for headgates on nearby streams. They built rudimentary reservoirs for storing and distributing surface water runoffs of annual rainfalls. They drilled artesian wells, using steam or horse-driven pumps or windmills to tap the underground water. These early water projects were simple affairs developed by individuals, partnerships, or joint stock associations. Before long, water companies were formed for building dams, canals, and flumes to sell water to miners and later to farmers and ranchers. The 1862 legislature, at the behest of canal builders, enacted a general incorporation law for water companies, granting them (like railroads) rights of way on state lands for their projects. By this time, water companies had taken over many cooperative projects of farmer and miner groups to become the principal developers of water systems.

Water projects were imaginative but risky business affairs. Beginning with the Mormon colony in 1851, irrigation projects sprang up in Southern California, the Central Valley, and the Sierra. Several projects in the Sierra were expensive as well as big and daring. The South Yuba Company, which had Alvinza Hayward as a chief stockholder, in 1854 consolidated three miners' ditch companies and built up a vast one million dollar system which, in a decade, comprised several dams, 20 storage reservoirs, timber flumes over 100 feet high crossing deep canyons, iron pipes for carrying water up hillsides, a half-mile tunnel, and 450 miles of canals. Such water companies turned from local merchants and miners to financiers in San Francisco, the East, and Europe for capital to construct even bigger projects to meet the insatiable demands of hydraulic mining companies. When mining company operations declined, many companies were able to ride out the hard times by selling water to an increasing number of farmers who were growing orchards and crops in the Sierra foothills.

Reclamation

Reclamation proved to be a formidable undertaking. Ranchers and farmers in the Central Valley attempted to reclaim those agricultural lands made temporarily useless by annual winter overflows of the Sacramento and San Joaquin, particularly in the Delta region where the two rivers meet. Individuals built dams across sloughs and erected levees (three to four feet high) along streams with rudimentary horse-drawn equipment, to protect their lands from overflows. Henry Miller built extensive canals to drain his flooded lands on the San Joaquin, insuring pasturage for his cattle.

Such projects were the focus of government attention. Congress by the 1850 Swampland Act (see above) not only opened such lands to settlers at lower prices, but stipulated that revenues from these land sales pay for reclamation projects. The legislature established a state board (1861) but later gave responsibility to the counties (1866) to supervise such projects. One of the few completed projects was Cache Slough in the Delta, an 11-mile drainage canal for drawing off the winter overflow in the Yolo Basin. Another was Grand Island in the Delta, which was reclaimed by 6-foot levees. These individual, county, and state projects laid foundations for extensive reclamation later.

Municipal Supply

From the beginning, towns and cities relied on private and public systems to provide their water supply. Older communities depended on the publicly owned *zanja* ("ditch, gully") water system established by their Mexican predecessors, by which municipal authorities tended the water works. Newer communities relied on privately owned water supplies developed by enterprising individuals or companies. These early water projects generally tapped nearby streams with open canals and numerous ditches, or drew underground water from local wells for domestic supply, irrigation, and sewerage. A pioneer in establishing local water systems was Anthony Chabot who, after leaving the mines in the mid-1850's, built water supplies for San Francisco, San Jose, Vallejo, and Oakland. In San Francisco, Chabot's enterprise was taken over by the Spring Valley Water Company (1865). In Los Angeles, municipal authorities granted a franchise to a private water company (1868) to supplement its public zanja system. In Oakland, Chabot extended his original system; he organized a water company to provide area-wide facilities and tie his water projects to land development—San Leandro was his special domain. These three communities reflect the pattern of pioneer municipal water supply that has prevailed to the present day.

Fuel and Power

Californians showed remarkable facility in adapting both traditional and innovative ways under difficult circumstances to produce mechanical power required for their various enterprises. They built waterwheels of all sizes and descriptions for harnessing the flowing water of nearby streams and rivers, the water being conveyed by sluice or pipe to turn the bladed waterwheels. They also used various steam engines with their boilers to convert water into steam pressure for piston–valve components. When necessary, they used horses, mules, and even oxen as work animals. Windmills were used widely in some localities—Stockton was called the City of Windmills—to provide power as well as to draw underground water. A Stockton company tapped underground natural gas to provide lighting for the courthouse area (1865)—three-quarters of a century before natural gas was widely used.

Manufactures

Manufacturing enterprises developed as suppliers to other industries, especially in producing basic goods required for local mining, agriculture, and transportation. Manufacturers faced sharply contrasting conditions. On the one hand, they were favored by big demand and high prices for their products, and by long delays in importing goods. Furthermore, local markets often called for specialized implements and machines that the East could not readily supply. On the other hand, manufacturers were handicapped by high interest on loans for capitalizing their ventures, high wages for labor (reputed to be the world's highest), and the undependable supply of the materials they required. Public policy seems to have had no effect in promoting manufacturing industries.

Among the leading industries, ironwork gained rapid prominence, for manufactured implements were needed immediately. Iron foundries fashioned imported bar, plate, and pig iron for manufacture into tools, pipe, wire, and machinery that could meet the specialized needs in agriculture, mining, and transportation. In San Francisco, Peter Donahue's Union Iron Works led the way. In the 1860's it produced light and heavy implements, including mining machinery for the Comstock and locomotives for the rising railroads. Benicia Agricultural Works took the lead in manufacturing specialized farm implements and machinery. Pacific Rolling Mills was organized (1868) by San Francisco financiers (notably Ralston and Hayward). Several foundries and blacksmiths were well established in scattered communities throughout the state. By 1870 the state had a well-rounded, thriving iron industry.

The manufacture of vehicles—carriages and wagons, boats, ships, and locomotives—received a strong impetus from transportation demands. Phineas Banning's Wilmington shop (1852) produced an improved Concord stagecoach which took his name. John Studebaker (a future automaker who in 1853 worked in a Placerville shop) remodeled wagons so that they could withstand rough mountain travel. George Kimball established an Oakland factory (1868) which produced large numbers of the big heavy wagons used in western freighting. Shipbuilding was a similar story. As early as 1850, San Francisco paced river and coastal towns in establishing dry-dock facilities for boat repair and construction. Union Iron Works built the first ocean steamer by 1864 and a dozen locomotives for the rising railroads between 1865 and 1870. Major river and coastal ports had dry docks, and just about every major town had a wagon repair shop and staging yards for horses and mules, pointing the way to our modern-day garages and gas stations.

Explosives, used extensively in mining operations and railroad construction, were imported from the East until the Civil War ended such shipments and inspired another home industry. California Powder Works (1863) was organized by Ralston, Tevis, and other San Francisco financiers to pioneer black-powder production. When Alfred Nobel, the Swedish inventor–manufacturer, developed dynamite for high explosives, his San Francisco agents immediately formed the Giant Powder Company (1865) to produce it for the California mines—the first time dynamite was used in the nation. California Powder Works, not to be outdone, produced its own version of a high explosive when its chemist invented Hercules powder. By now the company included among its stockholders the Du Ponts of Delaware, the nation's largest and oldest manufacturer of explosives. The presence of the Du Pont and Nobel interests was to have great future significance for California's explosives industry.

California's local manufacturers within two decades were producing a variety of products that was nothing short of phenomenal. Domenico Ghirardelli set up a chocolate factory (1852) to launch confectionary manufacture. A.S. Hallidie established a wire-manu-facturing firm (1854) which produced his inventive cable buckets and wire-rope implements for mining and other operations. The Civil War, in reducing trade imports, spurred entrepreneurs in other fields. Winemaker Charles Kohler joined others in forming a glass works (1863) to make bottles for their products. Banker William Ralston helped expand a pioneer textile mill (1864) to manufacture local wool into the famous mission blanket and other products. Merchants William Coleman and Claus Spreckels set up sugar-refining firms (1863) for processing sugar cane imported primarily from the Orient. Spreckels actually pioneered the sugar industry, for he invented improved processes and built the state's largest refinery plant (1867) to serve lucrative local markets. Californians by 1870 had developed a substantial basis for a thriving local manufacturing industry.

Transportation

California badly needed a transportation system that would overcome land and water barriers and facilitate the flow of people and trade so important for economic development. Counties and towns, spurred by merchants, sought connecting links to the main overland and waterway thoroughfares which they believed necessary for their survival. Entrepreneurs who developed stage, wagon, boat, and railroad facilities competed intensely with each other and vied for state and federal funds. Generous aid from the legislature and Congress enabled California to surmount the obstacles to developing an effective transportation system.

Roads

The 1850 legislature provided the basic framework for roads, bridges, and ferries. It assigned to the counties major responsibility for public facilities and authorized private companies to operate toll, or pay, facilities. The 1854 legislature, prodded by San Francisco citizens, provided for state construction of a wagon road from Placerville to the Nevada border (along present-day Highway 50) to connect up with the overland road, but actual construction was blocked by opposition from the rival steamship and railroad companies. Congress in 1857 finally authorized the transcontinental road. It was built shortly afterward from Missouri to the Nevada border—just in time for the inauguration of the overland stage service.

California's road system failed to produce good roads. No matter how poor, however, most roads were well traveled by pack trains, freight wagons, and stagecoaches. These vehicles delivered groceries, merchandise, heavy goods, and sometimes mail between towns within the state and throughout the West. The heavy stage and wagon traffic on some Sierra thoroughfares during the rush to the Mother Lode, and later to the Comstock, was similar to our modern bumper-to-bumper auto and truck traffic.

Stagecoach line development pointed to a characteristic California pattern in transportation. Stage lines usually operated with sturdy Concord and Banning coaches carrying passengers and mail, drawn by two-to-four-horse teams under hardy "Knights of the Lash" known for their chivalry toward the ladies. The pioneer lines of James Birch in Sacramento, Crandall and Smith in San Francisco in 1850, and Phineas Banning in Los Angeles in 1852 were followed by numerous competing local firms throughout the state. The California Stage Company, organized under Birch in 1854, consolidated five-sixths of the local lines and in the 1860's was reputed to be the second largest in the nation.

Waterways

River and ocean transportation also underwent rapid development. On the inland waterways, river routes were the commercial lifelines, particularly for the Sacramento and Feather Rivers, before the coming of the railroad. Steamers quickly outdid sailing brigs and frigates in carrying passengers and cargo from San Francisco up the Sacramento as far as Red Bluff and down the San Joaquin above Fresno. Their captain–owners competed ruthlessly by cutting rates and racing with overloads that led to frequent collisions and explosions, injuries, and deaths. They ended their ruinous competition in 1854 by organizing into the California Steam Navigation Company which comprised three-fourths of the river steamers. This near-monopoly regularized schedules, lowering the accident rate, but raised prices to exorbitant levels. Their colorful horn-tooting side-wheelers, sometimes hauling barges, enjoyed a golden age in California rivers comparable to that of the picturesque Mississippi river boats.

Ocean liners in the early days enjoyed a preeminence over land traffic. Local and foreign lines of sailing ships and steamships plied the coast out of San Francisco, exchanging passengers and cargoes at coastal points between Eureka and San Diego and with world-wide ports. The

California clipper ships enjoyed a heyday as the fastest afloat. Their long sleek hulls under high masts of billowy sails carried passengers and cargo until they were eclipsed by workaday ocean steamers working in conjunction with the Panama railroad upon completion of its rail line across the Isthmus (1855). The Pacific Mail Steamship Company, the pioneering New York-based corporation, controlled the Isthmus route about the same time, and a decade later extended its operations to the Orient to become undisputed leader in the Pacific. By 1870 it had the largest United States steamer fleet and the world's biggest line of steam-auxiliary ships.

Railroads

Railroads, still in their infancy in the East, were generally recognized to be the ultimate solution to California's transportation problem. Government became a partner of private enterprise in developing certain railroad lines. The legislature in the 1850's eased requirements for forming railroad corporations, and granted them rights of way on state lands. It authorized counties to purchase stocks of railroad companies (1859) and provided state aid for bonds (1864). Due to exigencies of the Civil War, Congress lent backing for a transcontinental railroad. It provided federal bonds and land grants for the overland railroad over a central route (Pacific Railway Acts of 1862 and 1864), stipulating that the California-based Central Pacific build the western part and the Union Pacific build the eastern part. Congress in 1866 authorized another transcontinental railroad over a southerly route, granting lands but not bonds to the California-incorporated Southern Pacific Company for the western route and to the Atlantic and Pacific for the eastern portion. These public investments by Congress and the state, supplemented by contributions from affected counties and cities and by the sale of company bonds and stocks, provided the major funds for railroad construction.

Railroad construction was a formidable enterprise. Railroad builders in the 1850's were so handicapped by various obstacles that, by the end of the decade, several local railroads had been organized but only one was operating: the Sacramento–Folsom 23-mile line built by Theodore Judah. In the 1860's attention focused on the transcontinental railroad. The chief impetus was provided by Judah, a brilliant railroad engineer–promoter who developed the idea for the overland line, planned the western route through the formidable Sierra barrier, and lobbied Congress and the state legislature for support. In seeking financial backers, he first appealed to San Francisco financiers without success (they thought his scheme too visionary), then won over a group of Sacramento merchants. Judah and four of these merchants—Leland Stanford, Collis Huntington, Mark Hopkins, and Charles Crocker (hereafter the Big Four)—in 1861 formed the nucleus group which incorporated the Central Pacific Railroad Company for building the transcontinental line.

After Judah's untimely death (1863), the Big Four took on the formidable task of constructing the Central Pacific line. In building the railroad line, they formed a dummy construction company through which they were able to manipulate funds for gaining enormous profits. In laying the rails through the tremendous physical barrier of the Sierra, they utilized cheap Chinese labor to perform amazing engineering feats. Eventually they finished construction of the railroad between Sacramento and Promontory in Utah, where in 1869 it was linked with the Union Pacific to complete the nation's first transcontinental rail line.

The Big Four during this time also did battle with rivals who threatened their supremacy. The most formidable of these was Lloyd Tevis. In a series of business intrigues, Tevis, with several partners, maneuvered to gain control of the Southern Pacific and the San Francisco–San Jose line of Peter Donahue's group, then turned them over to the Big Four in return for important concessions. Tevis, with Carpentier and Stanford, formed the Oakland Waterfront Company to control the city's waterfront and provide the Central Pacific with an East Bay terminus. The Big Four had better luck in outmaneuvering Sam Brannan, Peter Donahue, and Milton Latham to secure their regional lines between Sacramento and San Francisco. In the process the Big Four eliminated rival lines, controlled strategic terminus points in Oakland and San Francisco, and acquired California Steam Navigation. By 1870 they had secured strategic control over transportation in and out of the state. The Big Four by daring courage and ruthless methods overcame the formidable obstacles of a risky enterprise to complete the railroad that was to figure so importantly in California's development.

Communications

Postal Service

The express company—a sort of private post office or mail forwarder whose swift regular service outdid the slow irregular operations of the United States Post Office—made great headway in establishing effective communication lines. Numerous local and national express companies utilized ponies, stages, and steamers for carrying their letter, money, and parcel shipments. Adams Express beat eastern rivals to the California field, but Wells Fargo, a New York firm, set up operations in 1852 and gained ascendancy after 1855, when Adams went bankrupt. Wells Fargo expanded its California operations by absorbing small independent express firms and hooking up with the California Stage Company and other local stage lines. By the end of the decade, it had branch offices in almost every major California town.

The United States Post Office gave stimulus to the overland express and stage lines in 1857 when it shifted its mail deliveries from Pacific Mail's ocean route to a transcontinental route. Congress in 1857 granted the franchise to a company formed by John Butterfield and his associates, which included eastern giants like American Express and Wells Fargo, to carry the United States mail on a southerly route from St. Louis to San Francisco via El Paso. Then followed the "battle of the giants" for control of the overland mail and stage over contesting northern, central, and southern routes. By 1867 Wells Fargo beat out its rivals by absorbing the Butterfield stages, Russell Majors and Waddell Company who had pioneered the spectacular but short-lived transcontinental pony express (1861), and Ben Holladay's (the Stage Napoleon) vast trans-Mississippi system. Its far-flung and highly efficient system was reputed to be the nation's largest transportation system. The founders of Wells Fargo were soon outdone by a California entrepreneur. Lloyd Tevis obtained from the Central Pacific the franchise for handling the overland mail for his small express company. He then pulled off a brilliant business coup against the mighty Wells Fargo leaders, who had expected to get the mail franchise so important for their survival. He became chief stockholder and later president (1872) of Wells Fargo.

The Telegraph

The telegraph system, patented by Samuel Morse in 1837, was soon introduced into Northern California. The San Francisco Merchants Exchange in 1853 replaced its mechanical signal on Telegraph Hill with a telegraph line for announcing the arrival of incoming vessels. Over the next decade, numerous companies attempted to establish local lines under risky conditions, including hilly terrain, high costs, and business fluctuations. California State Telegraph, holder of the Morse patent, was started by a New York group (1852) but was taken over by a California group which completed the pioneer San Francisco–Sacramento line in 1853. Local companies were spurred by the great demand for rapidly available information for commercial transactions and stock speculations.

Competition for a transcontinental telegraph got under way by 1858. Back East, Western Union, another holder of the Morse patent, outmaneuvered its rivals to get the federal franchise. It lobbied Congress to enact the Pacific Telegraph Act (1860), which granted land right of way and funds to the companies building the eastern and western portions of the line from Missouri west and from San Francisco east to Salt Lake City as the common terminus. Holding the franchise for the eastern portion, Western Union sent to California a representative to effect a merger of rival companies vying for the western portion. In the course of delicate negotiations. Lloyd Tevis was instrumental in helping Horace Carpentier's California State Telegraph absorb its local rivals and join Western Union to form the Overland Telegraph, which constructed the western line to link up with Western Union's eastern line at Salt Lake in 1861. (Tevis apparently pulled off a coup on Western Union, as well: from them he got $200,000 with little or no cash collateral as his original investment!) Shortly afterward, California State Telegraph absorbed Overland Telegraph, and in 1866 Western Union absorbed the California company to control the world's longest telegraph system.

Labor

As the argonauts tended to seek quick riches, there was a shortage of men willing to work for wages in the early years. The legislature attempted to formulate a public labor policy that would foster a working force. It enacted in 1850 a mechanics lien law which protected the wages of workingmen upon the bankruptcy or death of their employers (like creditors, they could claim wages owed them), and it adopted in 1853 a ten-hour day for laborers on public works. It also, however, adopted measures that paved the way for the use of Indians, Mexicans, Chinese, and convicts as cheap labor. The legislature, in short, provided the basis of a dual labor system: it sustained working standards for white workers and sanctioned the use of minority ethnic groups and other disadvantaged groups for cheap labor.

A class of wage earners soon evolved in San Francisco and other major towns. They fared well under high wages prompted by labor shortages. As San Francisco developed into the principal industrial center, skilled workers soon organized into trade unions to improve their conditions further. The printers led the way: they formed the first local union in 1850 and obtained the first national charter three years later. Before the end of the decade, skilled workers had organized unions in almost every trade. They succeeded in striking for higher wages to keep up with rising living costs and for shorter hours to be on a par with laborers on public works. The notable absence of government interference in their strikes, even when violent and destructive, was undoubtedly due to Broderick's local Democratic machine. It wooed the labor vote and relied heavily on workingmen to carry out its party activities.

During the prosperous years of the 1860's, San Francisco union leaders spearheaded notable gains for labor. When employers sought to meet high wartime costs by reducing wages, workers strengthened their union organization. Labor leaders, led by the astute Alexander Kenaday of the printers union, organized in 1863 the first city-wide central labor body in the state, and later, under the talented A. M. Winn, formed a state body along craft lines. These leaders campaigned hard for better conditions and secured from the 1868 legislature two landmark laws: the eight-hour day and an improved mechanics lien law. Despite these successes, pioneer unions experienced difficult times. Except for the printers, riggers, and stevedores, they were short-lived organizations lasting usually a few months to a year, and their legislative gains were undercut by unsympathetic courts. Nevertheless, this organized labor activity in Northern California laid permanent foundations for union organization.

Meanwhile, employers attempted in several ways to remedy their labor problem. Farmers and ranchers relied sometimes on Indians, but generally on Chinese and transients—unemployables and tramps, rather than migrant workers as in more recent times. Mining companies usually hired Caucasians for skilled jobs but used Chinese and Mexicans as workers. Employers also attempted by individual and collective efforts to recruit field and factory workers in eastern cities. They even formed local employer associations to combat organized labor but achieved little success. The times were hardly favorable for anti-union activities. Labor shortages were a real problem for entrepreneurs and an asset for the workingman.

Banking

Banking institutions experienced steady but haphazard growth in the early years. San Francisco bankers dominated the field. They were a mixed lot that included the adventurous Sam Brannan, the cautious and respected William Sherman, and the unscrupulous J. C. Palmer. In other communities there were Sacramento's D. O. Mills, a trained banker, and Marysville's Frederick Low, a merchant-turned-banker. Some bankers were agents for eastern and international establishments like the famous Rothschilds of London. Most of the early banking was carried on by the express companies, notably Adams and Company and Wells Fargo, which received deposits and delivered bullion among the scattered mining and agricultural towns. The absence of regulatory laws in banking and the presence of adventurous entrepreneurs eager for quick riches led to embezzlement, fraud, and corruption, bringing a wave of scandal. The politically oriented Palmer, Cook and Company, which marketed the state bonds, defaulted over $800,000 in state funds. The directors of the reputable Adams and Company juggled accounts, bilking their California customers of over $200,000. The bankruptcy of a major bank (Page, Bacon and Company) brought on a panic that ruined many banks and business firms and depressed the state's economic development for several years.

Banking institutions developed rapidly in the 1860's as a result of a change in public attitude. Several factors combined to restore public confidence in organized banking. There was a new influx of immigrants demanding banks for their accumulated savings. Mining, railroad, and other enterprises were desperately seeking funds to expand. There were dazzling opportunities for profitable investment with the opening of the Comstock mines. The legislature, under strong pressure from bankers like Brannan, enacted the 1862 law authorizing savings banks to incorporate and make loans secured by property. In 1864 another law allowed commercial banks to incorporate and make loans without any collateral at all. The state court sanctioned the measures, choosing to rationalize away the constitutional prohibitions against such bank activities.

Thereafter, banking developed rapidly. The Bank of California, the first to organize under the 1864 act, was also the largest. Under the adroit management of William Ralston, a shipping clerk-turned-banker, it became the undisputed leader in California banking, acting as chief promoter of the Comstock and a generous patron of enterprises, small or large. Los Angeles got its first banking institutions in 1868 when Isaiah Hellman, a German merchant–immigrant, and John Downey each formed local banks. San Francisco by 1870 rounded off its financial institutions when James Phelan and Peter Donahue organized the first national bank for redeeming paper money with gold. Thus there were several commercial and savings banks performing the important function of providing the capital so vital to agricultural, manufacturing, transportation, and mercantile enterprises.

Trade

Trading underwent fluctuations arising primarily from the haphazard conditions of the Gold Rush and later the Comstock boom and the Civil War. San Francisco, from the beginning, sustained its primacy as the trading center and principal port for California and the Far West. The merchants, by reason of their strategic position in the port city, outdid competitors based in the East, in Europe, or in other California towns.

The wholesale traders were particularly powerful. They often were able to manipulate the exchange of goods, sometimes cornering the market—that is, they held back their goods by mutual agreement so they could sell at enormous profits later. Some merchants who exported California products beat out their rivals by developing their own trade outlets, as Isaac Friedlander did in wheat and Charles Kohler in wine. Those importing outside goods were no less innovative. William Coleman combined a merchandise and shipping operation that made him San Francisco's leading trade merchant. His firm (organized 1852) eventually included branch agencies in New York, London, and Paris, a fleet of fast clipper ships, and a wholesale–retail outlet in San Francisco for distributing goods, including the still existing Coleman's Cough Drops. Levi Strauss, was another imaginative merchant–importer. Heeding the advice of miners and later cowboys, he restyled his denim overalls with copper-riveted pockets and tapered pants legs to meet their particular needs. His popular Levis became standard apparel in the mines, on the ranches, and elsewhere.

In the retail distribution of goods, the city teemed with general merchandise or dry goods stores, like Felix Verdier's City of Paris (1850), and a host of specialty stores. San Francisco's wholesale merchants were the chief suppliers for the numerous general stores scattered throughout the state, including those of prominent pioneer merchants like Newton Booth in Sacramento and Harris Newmark in Los

Angeles. Merchants in the busy river ports and Sierra mining towns competed intensely for the local retail trade. One who did not survive it was R. H. Macy of Marysville—he returned to New York City and opened his famous department store there in 1858.

Despite market fluctuations, California trade underwent remarkable progress. Governor Bigler in 1856 reported California to be practically self-supporting. The severe reduction of imports and acceleration of exports resulting from the Civil War gave California a highly favorable balance of trade. The completion of the transcontinental railroad in 1869 affected the trade pattern in an unexpected way. It produced only a temporary, rather than the anticipated permanent, setback in the ocean trade. San Francisco was gaining greater importance as the chief terminus for the expanding Pacific trade, including Alaska (purchased by the United States from Russia in 1867), Hawaii, Australia, and the Orient. California's trade by 1870 was big and diverse. Since that time, it has deviated little from this basic pattern.

The forest of masts—ships from all over the world gathered in San Francisco harbor during the Gold Rush. Taken in 1850, this is the earliest photograph of the city.

10 A Restless Society

A. SOCIETY
THE SETTING

California in this period was an expanding state marked by turbulent development. Its growth was sudden, more varied and explosive than that of any other frontier region in American history. At the outset, it lured men seeking quick riches in the Gold Rush, but it also attracted men with families looking for a better life. Its people were of diverse origins, coming from just about every race, state, and continent. It was a youthful society dominated by men. The state had been predominantly rural with an urban metropolis in San Francisco. The outsiders took over and transformed it.

The immigrant left an indelible imprint on the state. The foreign element, especially the Irish and Chinese, was conspicuous in the development of the political economy. Despite the heavy foreign influx, however, California was decidedly more American than it had been in 1850. While the Americans had assimilated European elements, they had segregated the nonwhite elements into town ghettos and isolated communities. Even in Southern California, where they were out-numbered by the Californios, the Americans controlled the centers of government and commerce. The various groups retained many of their cultural traits, giving California a distinctly cosmopolitan diversity, but American institutions were so entrenched that the political economy was like that of any other American state.

ANALYSIS

The People

The population over the first two decades increased over threefold, from approximately 166,500 in 1850 to 560,000 in 1870. Most of the Americans came from the eastern states and the northern tier of midwestern states. In the grouping of related states, 64 percent came from the North, 26 percent from the South, and the remainder from the Pacific Coast—a fact that has bearing on the state's political and cultural base. The foreign-born were led by the British, of whom the Irish constituted three-fourths, followed by the Chinese, Germans, Canadians, and Mexicans. During this period, the native-born constituted half the population, with the remaining half born in other states or in other nations.

The distribution and composition of the state's population was unbalanced. Well over three-fourths of the people resided in the central region extending from San Francisco Bay to the Delta and the Sierra mines. Over four-fifths of the people lived in rural areas. The young had an overwhelming preponderance over the old, and men outnumbered women 12 to 1. Of the nonwhite population, the Chinese represented 7 percent, more than double the number of Indians, and Negroes were few (less than 1 percent). The state, then, had a diverse and predominantly young population—a volatile and enterprising people.

Communities

Counties

The counties differed widely in their stage of development from frontier settlements to established communities. A bird's-eye view of a typical county would show isolated towns with neighboring homestead tracts, strung together by long dirt roads traveled by horsemen, stages, and wagons, or sometimes alongside ribbonlike rivers carrying boat traffic and surrounded by a broad and empty land. In the central area of the state, one might see water ditches and flumes and newly laid rail lines.

The counties took form through legislative implementation of the constitutional mandate. The 1850 legislature established 27 counties—some formed of entire mining districts—and out of historical sentiment gave all but three (Butte, Sutter, and Trinity) Indian and Spanish names. By 1852 the legislature had completed the county governmental machinery. Each county had an elective board of supervisors as its governing body, and executive and judicial officers—the basis of the present-day legal framework.

The counties experienced such constant shifts in area development and settler movement that the legislature was called upon to make adjustments. It carved new counties from older ones and frequently adjusted county lines. Local groups, usually farmers versus miners or ranchers, fought each other for the county seat and boundary changes that would enhance their influence in county affairs. They carried their battles to the legislative arena, which occasionally became the scene of bitter conflicts. In one instance, the legislature actually took steps to create a county *outside* of the state. At the behest of miners in the Truckee–Carson area, then in Utah Territory, it set up the county of Pautah in 1852, but the effort failed because of legal technicalities, thus ending California's display of manifest destiny. By 1870 an additional 22 counties brought the total to 49.

Towns and Cities

The emergence of many thriving towns in this period was testimony to the popular American pastime of building towns and cities. Communities took form when settlers began congregating in an area, usually on a favorable site. First came the pioneer settlers, who set up camps and homesteads on developed farms, ranches, and mining enterprises. Then came the tradesmen and craftsmen—storekeepers, saloonkeepers, hotel-keepers, and blacksmiths—whose establishments formed the nucleus of the town. Stability was lent by the arrival of the banker, merchant, printer, and other tradesmen, and the construction of the town hall, churches, schools, public utilities, and transportation facilities such as stagecoach and railroad stations. With the influx of more people and industries, towns evolved into cities.

Community development was more than just a product of this settlement process. It involved land speculation and town promotion, a form of private enterprise at which Americans excelled. Promoters acting as individuals and in groups plotted communities on acquired ranchos, public land tracts, or nucleus settlements, often in competition with each other or with nearby established communities. As towns grew into cities, real estate promoters undertook projects for developing commercial, residential, and industrial areas within the community. Community development was a continuing process throughout the state, though it occurred in spurts. Its most conspicuous signs were occasional booms when real estate speculation of several years' duration reached epidemic proportions and produced a spate of new towns and expanded city areas.

The First Boom

California's first town boom came in the flush of the Gold Rush. It began with the argonaut arrivals in 1849 and petered out with the economic decline after 1854. It centered in Northern California, where paper towns sprouted around the Bay and along the Sacramento River as adjunct communities serving San Francisco and the Sierra mines. These prospective communities went through an orgy of speculation, particularly in residential, manufacturing, and waterfront areas. In the Bay Area, Redwood City was set up as a lumber port, and San Rafael was plotted as a residential community. In the Carquinez Straits, Benicia was challenged by Antioch, a produce-shipping port founded by a church group, and Vallejo, which failed to become the state capital, but took hold as a regional center. Another town, New York of the Pacific, set up by Jonathan Stevenson (former colonel of the New York Volunteers) and plotted by William Sherman, failed as a speculative venture but developed into the coal-shipping port of Pittsburg. In the Sacramento Valley, new towns competed to become the navigation head for the river trade: Sacramento edged out Sutterville as the chief junction and trade center. A host of other prospective towns declined into oblivion, but still others became firmly established along rivers and rail lines and survived the collapse of the boom.

Town promoters were a varied lot, but none perhaps matched the unscrupulousness of Horace Carpentier, who laid the foundations of Oakland. This cunning lawyer–politician with two partners ingeniously swindled the Peralta family by staking out sections on their land and hoodwinking the family patriarch with religious guile and legal trickery to obtain title. As an assemblyman, he played on his friendship with Broderick to secure from the 1852 legislature the incorporation of Oakland. As the town's first mayor, he obtained from the council (of which he and his two associates formed the majority) the title deed to the valuable Oakland waterfront. For years municipal affairs were

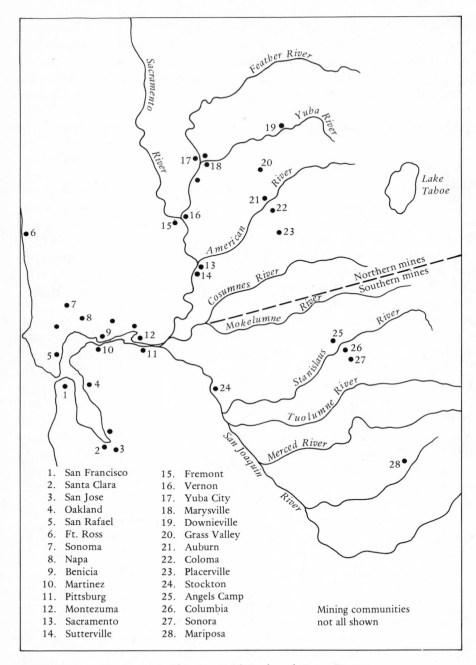

1. San Francisco
2. Santa Clara
3. San Jose
4. Oakland
5. San Rafael
6. Ft. Ross
7. Sonoma
8. Napa
9. Benicia
10. Martinez
11. Pittsburg
12. Montezuma
13. Sacramento
14. Sutterville
15. Fremont
16. Vernon
17. Yuba City
18. Marysville
19. Downieville
20. Grass Valley
21. Auburn
22. Coloma
23. Placerville
24. Stockton
25. Angels Camp
26. Columbia
27. Sonora
28. Mariposa

Mining communities
not all shown

FIGURE 7   Northern California—Gold Rush and Town Boom

entangled with the machinations of Carpentier and his associates. Oakland, as scholar Mel Scott puts it, was "conceived in iniquity and nurtured on corruption."

Communities also sprouted up elsewhere in the state, fashioned from squatter, cooperative, and corporate ventures. A colony of Texas squatters in 1851 poached on rancho lands and set up El Monte, the first American-type town in the Southland. In the same year, a group of 400 Mormons purchased San Bernardino ranchos and built up an agricultural colony as a supply station for the Mormons en route from San Diego port to their "promised land" in Utah. (Later they were called back to the Mormon mother colony.) In 1857 San Francisco entrepreneurs set up in Anaheim an agricultural colony of 50 German-American immigrants to produce grapes for the Bay City winery (see Chapter 9), and Phineas Banning laid out Wilmington near San Pedro harbor for his stage line and other enterprises. In the San Joaquin, agricultural colonies were established in 1868 by Irish immigrants in Tulare County and by Southern planters and former Confederate officers near Madera (Alabama Colony) on land purchased from Chapman and Friedlander. In the far North, settlers on the public domain took advantage of federal law (the 1844 Township Act) to acquire tracts for building up towns, including Eureka and Red Bluff in the 1850's and at least a dozen others in the 1860's. These American townbuilders pioneered a tradition which has survived to this day.

Community Development

The early towns and cities developed in a haphazard way. Most of them suffered catastrophic floods, fires, earthquakes, epidemics (chiefly cholera and smallpox). They experienced rampant disorders resulting from civic corruption, vigilante activity, squatter troubles, economic fluctuations, and unplanned growth. Pioneer surveyors, notably Jaspar O'Farrell who plotted the towns of San Francisco, Benicia, and Sonoma, established the trend of laying out communities in gridiron fashion. They replaced the meandering roads with orderly rectangular streets, frequently disregarding terrain irregularities. During his California sojourn in the 1860's Frederick Law Olmsted, pioneer landscape architect, town planner, and designer of New York's Central Park, aroused public interest in community planning. In Berkeley, community leaders ignored his far-sighted "neighborhood plan" for the new townsite in favor of a rigid rectangular scheme that was then considered a mark of urban progress.

In San Francisco, the city fathers met his vision for a "pleasure ground second to none in the world" by establishing the huge, lovely Golden Gate Park, but they rejected his imaginative street plan. They extended the streets of the older areas, imposing upon the city a gridiron pattern that has survived to this day and served as a model for other populous communities.

By 1870 the surviving towns (98 scattered among 37 counties) had established firm foundations. Four of the incorporated cities (San Francisco, Oakland, Sacramento, and Stockton) were thriving American communities, while Los Angeles and San Jose were essentially sparsely settled Hispanic–American communities in transition. As a result of early hardships, towns acquired a strong sense of community tradition. Their inhabitants, filled with the pride of accomplishment and a strong spirit of community independence, continued to push toward further development in the name of progress.

Los Angeles around 1853. The pueblo's plaza is the nucleus for the church, stores, and residences in the expansive plain.

Social Classes

American society, like all others, has tended to class stratification. Generally people have been divided into upper, middle, and lower classes according to birth, wealth, or sometimes personal character, public service (government leadership and military rank), and cultural and intellectual attainments. In the American class system, conditioned by growing cities and an expanding frontier, class lines were fluid. The ambitious climbed the social ladder by acquiring wealth, whether in land or money. The aristocracy of the colonial period—Southern cavalier planter and Northern merchant elite—was hard hit by the leveling effects of the American Revolution. A new elite of landed gentry and moneyed capitalists emerged from entrepreneurs who had acquired great wealth. Every generation thereafter witnessed the rise of the new rich. They sought the social trappings that befitted their upper-class status. They learned etiquette from guidebooks (notably *Godey's Lady's Book*), built imposing homes, and partook of culture, philanthropy, and sports in their leisure. Dixon Wecter tells us their social pretensions were sustained by imitators and followers who aspired to upper-class status, but were condemned by intellectuals and frontiersmen. The western frontier, where the "rifle and the ax made all men equally tall," changed from its posture of disdain for the eastern aristocrat strongholds (Boston, New York, and Washington) when it too matured into a settled society and produced its version of a class system based on acquired wealth. The nation's society, as Dixon Wecter points out, began as "a democracy of opportunity which created an aristocracy of achievement." By mid-nineteenth century, high society was a cult in "worship of the Golden Calf."

California's class system after 1850 evolved according to the American pattern, but conditioned by a greater diversity of people, a quicker pace, and a more healthful climate. The provincial aristocracy of California rancheros under Mexico was undermined by the leveling effects of the Gold Rush and the American invasion. During the peak of the Gold Rush in the early 1850's, San Francisco and the mines experienced social democracy. People from all walks of life—clerks, lawyers, and generals—intermingled freely. Typical of the classless spirit is the story of the newcomer just off the boat who offered a boy 50 cents to carry his bag only to get the retort, "Here's a dollar, carry it yourself." People formed groups based on fraternal (Odd Fellows), national (French and German), regional (New Englanders and South-erners), occupational, religious, or racial ties. Prominent people, notably lawyer–politicians, military officers, and new-rich elements, enjoyed their recognized status as social leaders. Among them were the William Gwins, John Fremonts, and Henry Hallecks (his wife descended from Alexander Hamilton).

Toward the middle of the decade, class lines took form as the rich and poor fell into place in the social scale. Wives and daughters of the emerging elite pressured their menfolk to take on fashionable dress, manners, and homes—guided by the *Hesperian* (see below), a social arbiter modeled after *Godey's Lady's Book*. Leading families established summer homes on huge gardenlike estates "down the Peninsula." Class lines were further sharpened by the expanding middle class of artisans, managers, and shopkeepers, and the downward drift of people into the lower class of clerks, laborers, and unemployables. Within a decade, San Francisco's "gay but nebulous and anonymous mass" evolved into a three-tier class system which remained essentially unchanged down to the turn of the century.

Elsewhere in California the American class system took root. In older Hispanic communities, American newcomers emulated pioneer compatriots by marrying into California ranchero families, thus producing a new elite that merged Mexican and American elements (represented by John Downey who married into the Los Angeles Dominguez family). Some Americans (James Irvine for one) moved from the Bay Area to Southern California where they established "baronial estates" in the manner of pioneer settlers like Benjamin Wilson to become a new type of landed gentry. The new-rich commercial elements and the big rancher–farmers formed the basis of the California community's upper class. At the same time, California's class system was characterized by an unusual degree of social mobility which has continued to this day.

Extremist Groups

Extremist groups, as a social movement, have a special place in our story. The American version of democratic society did not work well for extremist groups. Generally, conservative and liberal groups were able to compromise their differences through the regular party and governmental apparatus in resolving public issues. Dissident groups, frustrated with the workings of consensus politics, organized social movements to achieve their ends through extremist actions. Reactionaries, who felt a loss of status from changes in society, sought to recapture familiar customs and traditions of earlier times. Radicals, thwarted by the slow progress in achieving cherished ideals, sought to accelerate reforms that would bring about the ideal society. Though the two groups occupied opposite positions on the political spectrum—the reactionaries on the right and the radicals on the left—they shared common attributes as extremist groups in that they embraced an ideology and an authoritarian structure. They usually exhibited antidemocratic behavior and what Richard Hofstadter calls a paranoid style. They sought changes by reform, usually as a third-party, in a trade union, or by revolution of society itself. The extremist movements were usually short-lived, but they often had pervasive influences on current developments and sometimes left a lasting impact. They have been vital forces in shaping American society.

California was the recipient of early American extremist movements. The United States had experienced right-wing extremists (The Illuminati, 1790's; Anti-Masons, 1820's) seeking to preserve Protestant orthodoxy and American tradition against pervasive freethinkers and foreign immigrants. The American Party, or Know-Nothings, in the 1840's and 1850's was another phase of the same movement; it was developed by eastern-based nativist groups against foreign immigrants in general and Catholics in particular. In California, the Know-Nothings made a brief appearance in state politics in the mid-1850's. During the transition between Whig demise and Republican emergence, opportunistic politicians filled the vacuum by campaigning for state office on the Know-Nothing ticket, playing down nativist prejudices and focusing on state government corruption. In Southern California, however, they ran heated campaigns for local offices, winning handily in nativist strongholds, but losing overwhelmingly in Hispanic towns like Los Angeles and Santa Barbara. These early manifestations of extremism were of little consequence in the fluid frontier environment, but they marked the beginnings of an extremist tradition which persists to this day.

Ethnic Groups

American nativism took on a broader context in California as ethnic groups became conspicuous elements. Americans have been imbued with a belief in the innate superiority of Anglo-Saxon people, the Protestant ethic (hard work and puritanic morals and piety), and their democratic capitalistic institutions. They have long discriminated in various ways against people of other races, religions, and institutions, usually on grounds that the cheap labor and lax morals of these "inferior people" might corrupt American ways. Yet these Americans divided sharply over dealing with aliens. There were the politicians who coveted their votes; planters and manufacturers who would utilize their cheap labor for field and factory work; small farmers, artisans, and laborers who feared their competition, and priests and ministers who would save their souls.

California as a new state faced an increasingly complex situation over the ethnic groups within its borders. The argonaut influx during the Gold Rush added great numbers of aliens. Those of Anglo-Saxon stock, Protestant or not, were readily assimilated into the dominant American order, helped by the tolerant attitudes usually found in western frontier areas and by wide opportunities for all. In time, each of the alien groups showed tendencies toward certain occupations. There were many Irish Catholic politicians like Broderick and Gwin, and Jewish merchants like Hellman and Strauss. Each group contributed native traits that enriched the frontier culture. They represented California's version of immigrant assimilation in national life—the stereotyped American melting pot.

People of nonwhite and non-European stock were in an entirely different situation. The ruling Californians, with their inherited American nativism, implemented public policy that reduced the political and legal status of certain groups—Latins, Chinese, Negroes, and Indians—who they believed threatened their image of society. The state constitution had granted the suffrage to Latin-descended Californios without Indian blood, and left to legislative mandate the voting privileges of Indians and free Negroes. The legislature, by not exercising its constitutional option, failed to extend the suffrage to these two groups. It further provided that Indians and free Negroes could not testify against a white man. The state supreme court in 1854 restricted Chinese from testifying in court on grounds that being Mongolian people they were classified as Indians! These basic measures in effect denied these people representation in the legislature and a legal procedure for redressing their grievances. The legislature also enacted class legislation barring them from such basic privileges as the right to own land and to practice native traditions. The way was paved for subjecting them to personal indignities, such as theft, assault, and murder, and for group exploitation of their cheap labor. Being reduced to the status of second-class citizens, they were denied government protection of their lives and property, and deprived of equal opportunity for the economic livelihood granted to other citizens and to alien Anglo-Saxon residents.

The Latinos

The Latins, among the ethnic groups, experienced the most varied treatment, ranging from assimilation to exploitation to exclusion. They comprised in the main the Californios and Latin American nationals. The Latin American nationals were the most numerous. They were predominantly from Sonora and other northern provinces of Mexico, but there were also Chileans and Peruvians. In a major purge of their kind between 1850 and 1853, great numbers headed back home never to return, while the remainder were scattered in San Francisco and in rural and mining communities where they became primarily laborers.

The California natives—the *hijos de país*—fared comparatively better. The ranchero elite were able to retain considerable power, primarily because of strong leaders, large landholdings, social prestige, and their close association with sympathetic Yankee gringos in business and political affairs. They controlled local politics in Southern California where they had a numerical majority and effective organizations, like the Brent–Sanchez machine in Los Angeles. In the state legislature, they had prominent representatives, among them Pablo de la Guerra and Andres Pico. They did not entirely escape class legislation and other forms of discrimination. The 1855 legislature enacted a series of laws that restricted their social customs, citizenship, and employment. One anti-vagrancy measure was frankly labeled the "Greaser Act"—the offensive label was written out by another law the next year. Los Angeles, in particular, suffered violent showdowns between Californios and their American friends on one side, and firebrand American elements on the other, over a rash of wanton and avenged killings and irregular law enforcement that had strong racial overtones. While Californios suffered personal indignities, their declining influence in public affairs should not be attributed to such legal and social discriminations, but rather to their economic setbacks.

Chinese

The Latins were replaced by the Chinese as the largest alien minority in the state. These Asian immigrants were mostly poverty-stricken farmers fleeing a southeast China ravaged by the long Taiping Rebellion after 1848. They made the journey to California's "Golden Hills" by entering into contracts with Chinese merchants who paid their ship passage. They were either indentured persons, who arrived here on a credit-ticket system whereby they sold their labor for a period of years to pay off their passage and other debts, or coolies (hired laborers) working directly for Chinese entrepreneurs. They lived in segregated Chinatowns where they eked out a meager existence by working in labor gangs for farmers, manufacturers, and mining, highway, and railroad companies. The Chinese lived and moved within an elaborate structure sustained by hierarchical organizations which emerged in the 1860's as the Chinese Six Districts. At the top of each district were powerful Chinese merchants who controlled the passenger traffic and trade from China, governed Chinese establishments like banks, hotels, restaurants, stores, and vice dens, and handled labor contracts of indebted workers. The Chinese merchants operated through a veritable army of employees, including the infamous "hatchetmen" or enforcers, to maintain tight control.

The Chinese enjoyed considerable immunity from American interference with their internal affairs. State and local officials generally did not interfere with such extra-legal or even illegal activities of the Chinese primarily because of Chinese tax revenues and various pay-off schemes. In San Francisco the Six Districts kept city police on the Chinatown detail on their own payrolls, and retained American lawyers to defend their cases in the courts. Employers were happy to have cheap Chinese laborers, whom they regarded also as dependable and hard workers. Occasionally Chinese suffered from the violence of irate mobs who burned their shops and subjected them to such personal indignities as the cutting off of their long pigtails—incidents which served further to isolate them from the white community.

Negroes

Black people, although relatively few in number, were a conspicuous minority that attracted considerable public attention. By the terms of California's admission into the Union, Negroes were presumed to be free. Yet former slaves had their status jeopardized by pro-slavery elements in the state. The 1852 legislature enacted a fugitive slave law, based on the national model, which provided for returning former slaves to their masters who were leaving the state. Although the measure was inoperative after 1855, the state supreme court ruled, in a widely ridiculed decision, that Archy Lee, a former slave, while technically free, be returned to his ailing master who needed his services. (Lee was freed shortly afterward by a United States marshal.) Former slaves working in the mines accumulated money enough to purchase freedom not only for themselves but for their relatives. In one bizarre case, Alvin Coffey, with profits from gold mining, bought freedom for himself and his relatives, and went home to Missouri. Upon learning there that he had been sold to another master, he returned to the gold fields where he earned enough gold to buy his freedom a second time!

Meanwhile, free Negroes, chafing under legal restrictions and social discrimination, campaigned to obtain their civil rights. In the mid-1850's they organized the Franchise League to secure the vote and to eliminate the prohibition on giving legal testimony. Success, however, did not come until after the Civil War, with the change in public sentiment. The 1866 legislature in the wake of the Federal Civil Rights Act, which spelled out the Negro's legal and political rights, removed the testimony prohibition for Negroes in the state. The 1868 legislature, under the combined leadership of Jeremiah Sanderson, a prominent Negro educator, and John Swett, the state school superintendent, provided public (but separate) education for black children. These postwar gains, however, were nullified by the 1869 legislature. In response to anti-Negro sentiment and the governor's recommendation, it refused to ratify the Fourteenth Amendment to the United States Constitution which guaranteed legal due process and citizenship rights for the Negro. Although the Fourteenth Amendment became the law of the land, symbolic state sanction was not given until a century later.

Indians

The Indians, reduced by 1850 to a large but helpless minority, were caught in a maelstrom of contradictory public policies and confrontations with white men. Violent clashes reached a high point by 1850. They were the inevitable result of rapid and widespread incursions by miners, farmers, and ranchers on ancestral Indian lands in the Sierra and other parts of Northern California. When Governor Burnett called for a war to exterminate the Indians "until that race was extinct," the legislature, beginning in 1850, voted large appropriations for suppressing them. Then, evidently not content with citizenship restriction and military suppression, it adopted in 1851 a comprehensive measure euphemistically entitled the "Government and Protection of the Indians." The measure provided means by which white persons could use Indian men, women, and children, or Indian vagrants and convicts, through indentures and labor contracts. At no other time in California history did the legislature enact such a comprehensive measure for channeling people into a system of outright exploitation.

Congress meantime attempted to improve the situation for its legal wards. It extended the national Indian removal policy of 1832 to

California by creating a commission to arrange with Indians their removal to lands far from white settlers. The three-man commission signed with 118 Indian tribelets 35 treaties (1852—1853) by which Indians would supposedly cede 75 million acres and move into ten reservations comprising 7.5 million acres, where they would benefit from federal aid and protection. In response to angry Californians who denounced the generous granting of valuable mining and farm lands to Indians, the United States Senate refused to ratify the treaties. Nevertheless, federal authorities went ahead and removed Indians to reservations without treaty arrangements, thus depriving California Indians of the legal process the government had carefully followed in other parts of the country—a situation Congress was to make amends for a century later (see Chapter 19). Anthropologist Robert Heizer characterized the treaty process "a farce from the beginning to the end."

State and federal policies had an appalling effect upon the Indian population. Federal and state officials at the outset clashed on basic approaches: the former charged white settlers with cruelty, and the latter complained of Indian depredations on the settlers. The United States Army and state militia expeditions in pursuit of Indian renegades led to indiscriminate attacks on Indian rancherias, resulting in wholesale killings of men, women, and children. Military commanders reported (some with embarrassment) finding no Indian weapons or meeting no Indian resistance. One described the attack on Indians hiding on an island in Clear Lake as a "perfect slaughter pen." Volunteer forces of local farmers and ranchers conducted similar raids. White renegades indulged in savage acts of scalping (introduced into California by white men) and senseless killings. One made a blanket of Indian scalps, and another bragged he shot Indians to "see them fall." Perhaps worse for the Indians was the systematic way they were exploited under the 1851 law. Farmers and ranchers acquired, through questionable and outright illegal procedures, Indian children, vagrants, and others for domestic and field work. The Indian population declined sharply (from 90,000 in 1850 to 29,000 in 1870). The survivors, reduced by apathy to a life of idleness and beggary, often died at an early age from disease or malnutrition.

The Family

American family tradition was shaped largely by religious, political, and economic experience. In colonial times, Puritans and other dissenters from England's state church replaced church control with government regulation of family affairs. Marriage as a church sacrament gave way to the civil contract, though it was still considered a sacred covenant. State family laws, based on the English legal precept that a strong, secure family required a single leader, held the man to be its head. The man as the husband was lord and master of the family. The woman as wife and mother was mistress to the master, her personality submerged to his, her legal rights suspended in marriage, and her political rights nonexistent. The man had control of his wife's property, but was obliged to discharge his wife's debts from before and after marriage. He could be imprisoned for her liabilities and frauds, and was held responsible for her well-being and that of their children. Although women found ways to get around their husbands' authority and assert their independence, family life was governed by the male.

Frontier conditions reenforced the family as a socio-economic institution. Man and wife were economic partners in providing shelter, food, clothing, and other necessities for family subsistence. The pioneer homestead on the frontier and the established farms in rural communities were built on this foundation. The family institution worked well in the capitalistic scheme, for it formed the basis of an economic enterprise—whether farm, ranch, or store—producing surplus goods or providing services for the marketplace. The prevailing notion around 1850 held the family to be a sacred institution under God's divine plan, and a social institution under state supervision which served society as well as the needs of family members.

In frontier California the family was a relatively weak institution. The family institution remained the same under American rule as under Mexican. It existed to serve the basic function of regulating sex relations and producing children for the propagation of society. The legislature continued the patriarchal tradition by designating the husband as head of the family and the wife subject to him. The Gold Rush, however, profoundly altered the character of family life. Its impact retarded family development in California. It brought a horde of men who preferred quick riches to a settled life, creating a predominantly male society. It had unsettling effects on the family life of the Californios, American pioneer settlers, and recent immigrants to rural communities. Bachelorhood, separation, and divorce were commonplace—San Francisco had more bachelors and a lower birth rate then any other of the nation's cities down to the twentieth century. Men gratified sexual appetites by keeping mistresses, visiting brothels, or taking Indian concubines. In time, however, the family institution overcame these obstacles and took firm root throughout the state.

Many families, filled with "wanderlust," rarely ceased traveling. The Pikes were an example. They were originally poverty-stricken families from Pike County in Missouri—historically a depressed area of hardy people—but later included the large number of destitute Southern whites who were dispossessed of their homes and wandered out West after the Civil War. Their travels brought them to California, where many settled as farmers in frontier towns like El Monte, but others continued their gypsylike wanderings as a way of life. Clarence King described a Pike County family he came across on a Sierra trip in the mid-1860's as part of the "dreary brotherhood . . . cursed with permanent discontent . . . [a] most depressing spectacle." In California's transition from a frontier to an agrarian—commercial life, established communities helped stabilize family life, but such mobile elements persisted from this time forward.

Women

Women in California enjoyed considerable rights and freedom, partially a result of the state's Hispanic tradition. Early leaders sought to attract women to the far-off state by incorporating into the 1849 constitution the Spanish law of community property by which a married woman could retain full possession of her property, and by providing liberal rights for married women, including easy divorces—rights denied women back East. Women in California, as in the East, were denied the right to vote and were held subservient to men in family laws.

The lot of women in frontier California was varied. The Gold Rush lured young girls of different classes and nationalities. They came by wagon overland from the East and by boat from all over the world. San Francisco offered dazzling prospects for them. Most were prostitutes seeking quick riches—a reporter in 1850 described a shipload of girls from Paris as a "host of fallen angels who go to purify themselves in a bath of gold." Occasionally ships from Boston and New York brought wives and daughters joining their menfolk, and girls seeking husbands. The latter were organized primarily by church groups to bring civilization to the frontier.

Talented girls found their niches as actresses, dancers, and singers in the theaters and entertainment halls which abounded in the city. Some found the limelight they craved, like the exotic Lola Montez who won international notoriety for her affairs with the great personages and, even in her decline, still thrilled San Francisco audiences with her famous spider dance. Respectable women also found opportunity for their talents, some as poets and writers for the city's many periodicals, as partners, managers, or clerks of small shops, as teachers, church helpers, and social workers. As everywhere in the West, women enjoyed a privileged status and excessive attention. In surviving frontier hardships, they acquired an independence and self-reliance that won them much respect.

Several women who left their mark reflect the diverse character of San Francisco society, a microcosm of the larger California society. "Countess" Irene McCready pioneered the city's glittering bordello tradition. The respectable Phoebe Apperson Hearst (George's wife) won public attention for organizing charity drives, launching a long career in philanthropic activities. Lillie Hitchcock Coit, an irrepressible daughter of high society and the belle of Firehouse Number 5, won public attention for her unconventional behavior (she was memorialized by the landmark tower on Telegraph Hill named after her). Sarah Pellett, a physician and suffragette, made her memorable pitch for women's rights (1854) when the national movement was in its infancy, only to be subdued by newspaper ridicule. The excesses that came with the freedom of the city's social life became a part of the colorful San Francisco legend.

Elsewhere in California, women's lives were no less varied. Representative of the indomitable pioneer women are Nancy Kelsey, who spent a hardy lifetime following her wandering husband, and family-minded women, like Sarah Royce, who were preoccupied with burdensome homemaking activities and usually devoted leisure time to religious and charitable works. History has not accorded such women the attention they deserve.

B. CULTURE
THE SETTING

California's frontier society was the stage for the development of a unique culture. Cultural development took place primarily in the rising towns and cities—the traditional centers of intellectual life. San

Francisco, by virtue of its concentrated population, preponderance of literate people, and ready wealth, quickly established itself as the cultural capital of California, and later of the Far West. Other towns soon had ministers, editors, teachers, housewives, and others who, as self-appointed cultural custodians, fought vigorously for the "souls and minds" of men. These pioneers confronted overwhelming obstacles, notably the hectic toil of making a living (as one preacher elsewhere put it: men must have bread before books) and the anti-intellectual attitude of semi-literate "plain folks" who disdained the "highbrow" learning of educated people. They were hindered also by distance from cultural centers and inadequate facilities. However, they found ready allies among people seeking self-improvement, educated persons yearning for intellectual activities, and many others who craved spiritual solace.

California's cultural growth was conditioned by other factors as well. The polyglot argonauts of different national and racial groups contributed alien traits to the cultural mainstream. Foreign immigrants, imbued with their cultural heritage, pursued clannish ways and ethnically oriented activities, and even published their own newspapers. The influx of American-born and British-born immigrants gave preponderance to English as the spoken language and to Anglo-Saxon tradition and customs. These English-speaking immigrants clearly intended to "Americanize" California in thought as well as deed, subordinating if not driving out Latin and other alien influences. Some who were deeply attached to the religious ideals and strict morality of New England Puritanism provided much of the impulse for religious and educational development. Others were proud freethinkers, self-taught through experiences in frontier life and distant travels. These often contributed intellectual stimulation and tolerance for deviant thought and behavior. Most immigrants had a strong belief in the idea of progress, the thought that material advances and cultural attainments would transform the environment into their image of society—the American dream.

The argonauts also included a high proportion of the literate and well-educated, who provided the impetus for cultural activities. Many immigrants from the eastern seaboard and midwestern areas were familiar with the classics: they could quote from the Bible and Shakespeare and the memorable oratory of statesmen like Clay, Calhoun, and Webster. Franklin Walker tells us they had cultural roots in the British Isles and the Mediterranean; they knew Shakespeare better than Emerson, they preferred Milton over Poe, they admired Greek philosphy and Roman law, and they revered Palestine as the birthplace of Adam and Jesus. They made generous references to such topics in conversation, speeches, books, and newspapers.

California acquired early foundations for high culture and diverse public entertainment. Sacramento had its first theater in 1849 and by the 1860's a prominent art gallery (Edwin Crocker's venture). San Franciscans heard the first music concert in 1849, the first opera in 1851, and a symphony orchestra by 1864. Thomas Maguire, a gambler–saloonkeeper and local impresario, paced the city's fare in plays and opera production until eclipsed by Ralston's elegant California Theatre (1869). The Bella Union, which featured burlesque, minstrel, and variety shows, was a popular showplace. Itinerant actors, dancers, and music groups performed on traveling circuits through mining and other towns; Shakespeare's plays and Hispanic dances were especially popular. The saloon and gambling halls, however, were the landmarks of public entertainment. These heterogeneous elements imparted a cosmopolitan flavor to California's emerging culture.

ANALYSIS

Education

California was quick to adopt American educational traditions, though it was slow to build a public school and university system. The 1849 Constitution established an elected state superintendent of public instruction, and provided for a state fund derived from the sale of anticipated federal land grants to support primary schools and a state university. Congress in 1853 granted the lands, stipulating that two sections in each township (the famous sections 16 and 32) be set aside for primary schools, and two townships in the state for colleges. In 1862 Congress enacted the landmark Morrill Act which provided land grants to states for agricultural and mechanical arts colleges. It remained for the legislature to work out the details.

Primary and Secondary Schools

The legislature, during the first hectic decade, built up in piecemeal fashion a rudimentary school system. By 1855 it had laid down the basic structure, including an elected local board to build schools and hire teachers and a state board of education for overseeing both. The elective state superintendent and county superintendents administered the school system. San Francisco paced the state with the first school district, and Sacramento with the first public high school (1856). The few existing school districts operated by irregular procedures on meager funds collected from public subscription and school tuition, as well as from public land revenues and state and local taxes. Hardly one-fourth of the eligible children were attending public schools at the end of the first decade.

The dramatic change in public school education came in the 1860's. Vigorous leadership came from the state superintendents, notably John Swett (1863—1867), a Yankee schoolteacher who was the first professional educator to be superintendent and whose accomplishments marked him as California's Horace Mann. The legislature approved Swett's proposals for building up a uniform school system, most of which were embodied in the landmark 1866 school law. Distinctive features of the new setup were the state board's authority to adopt uniform textbooks for all schools (1863), establishment of two-year state normal schools for training teachers, annual state teachers' institutes for upgrading professional standards, free though separate schools for Indian and Negro children, and an education code for consolidating the school laws. By the end of the decade, the state had primary schools educating over three-fourths of the eligible school children, nine public high schools, and a state normal school (San Jose). California's public school system under centralized state control put it in the front rank of frontier states.

Private and parochial or denominational schools established by pioneer educators or ministers played an important role in supplementing the public school system. These schools had a precarious existence, but they helped create an interest in education and often formed the first school district in a region.

Colleges and Universities

The same missionary impulse of educators and ministers that led to private and parochial schools also led to non-public colleges and universities. Among the survivors of the many early colleges and universities are the University of Santa Clara (1851), University of San Francisco (1855), and St. Mary's College (1863)—Catholic; the University of the Pacific (1851)—Methodist; and the College of California (1855)—Congregationalist—all originally in the Bay Area. The College of California in Oakland owed its success in surmounting formidable obstacles to the business management of Samuel Willey and to the academic leadership of its pioneer president, Henry Durant, a Yankee schoolmaster who came to California with "college on his brain."

The long-delayed movement to establish a state university bore fruit in the 1860's. The legislature had wasted 15 years on such diverse schemes as a mining college, a military institute modeled on West Point, a polytechnic college, and a Harvard or Yale of the Pacific. The end product was the result of two chance circumstances: the College of California was burdened with heavy debts and a limited student body, and the Agricultural and Mechanical Arts College had been authorized but not yet set up by terms of the 1862 Morrill Act. Under prodding from Governor Low, the 1866 legislature enacted the university measure, drafted by Durant, Willey, and Assemblyman John Dwinelle. This created the University of California, comprising the agricultural, mechanical arts, and liberal arts colleges (the latter incorporating the College of California facilities). When the University of California opened its doors in 1869, it became the capstone of the state's public education system.

Journalism

Newspapers abounded in cities and towns—San Francisco alone had at least a dozen newspapers in 1850. These pioneer journals varied greatly in quality and, good or bad, their mortality was high—less than a dozen of some 150 survived the hectic 1850's. They were characteristically small enterprises operated by proprietors or partnerships, and the turnover of ownership and staff was high. The newspapers suffered badly from inferior presses, unreliable news accounts, and fluctuating business conditions, so that only a few were profitable. They were geared to particular audiences rather than to mass appeal—some to personal crusades, some to propagating religious and political propaganda, and some to French, German, and other ethnic groups. Rural newspapers, like their city counterparts, often served as the community's conscience and as a force for local order and for civic improvements such as churches, libraries, and schools.

The pioneer journalists cut a wide swath in early California society. They enjoyed a freedom of action perhaps unsurpassed since, with the inevitable extreme results. Editors engaged in first-rate reporting, crusading reforms, and personal quarrels at a time when hurling "journalistic stink pots" was in vogue. In the process they confronted vengeful readers, tyrannical printers, and angered mobs. Several journalists stood out in the hurly-burly 1850's. The first editors of the pioneer *Alta California* were renowned: the boyish Edward Kemble, a respected veteran among his colleagues, and his senior, Edward Gilbert, former congressman and apparently the first editor killed in a duel (see Chapter 8). The impetuous James King of William, a banker-turned-editor, used his *San Francisco Bulletin* for vicious attacks on municipal corruption: his assassination by a corrupt county supervisor awoke the city's conscience and sparked the rabid Vigilante Committee. The fearless *San Francisco Herald*, the city's leading paper at mid-decade, was operated by John Nugent, a former Bennett employee. It decried the Vigilantes and was soon forced to quit after merchants switched their advertising patronage to the *Alta California*.

The newspaper pattern began to crystallize in the 1860's. The *Alta California* under John Hittell's editorship became chief spokesman for the business community. The *Bulletin*, which became the biggest paper, lost its crusading zeal with prosperity. In 1865 appeared the *San Francisco Examiner*, which was established on the ruins of a pro-Southern paper wrecked by a mob avenging Lincoln's assassination, and the *San Francisco Chronicle*, which the youthful de Young brothers built from a theater housebill to a substantial general newspaper within a few years. John Nugent's reestablished *Herald* and James McClatchy's *Times*, edited by Henry George, a printer-turned-editor, were short-lived attempts at independent liberalism. The newspaper debates between George and Hittell over pressing issues like corporate monopolies, Chinese labor, and land reform represent the high tide of quality journalism in this period. A trend in the making was newspaper consolidation, when in 1869 the *Alta* absorbed the *Times,* and the *Bulletin* absorbed another paper.

Elsewhere in the state, journalism followed the familiar patterns. Sacramento newspapers established a long independent tradition with the *Union* (1850), and the *Bee* (1859), the latter set up by James McClatchy on the model of Greeley's *Tribune* for which he had worked, and the *Reporter*, a Democratic organ edited briefly by Henry George. In the Southland, pioneer newspapers were represented by the bilingual *Los Angeles Star* and the crusading *El Clamor Publico*, which spoke out for the Californios. Andres Pico's short-lived paper (the *Southern Californian*, 1856—1858) won dubious fame for running a graphic account of a lynching two hours before it happened! Frontier newspapers were an important medium of communication for communities scattered throughout the state.

Literary journals, usually published weekly or monthly, played a distinctive role in frontier life. The *Golden Age* was the most ambitious of these many journals. Its chatty, informal style and wide coverage of news, poetry, and fiction enjoyed wide popularity in San Francisco and the mines. Rollin Daggett, its colorful coeditor and a literary light himself, encouraged aspiring writers, notably Bret Harte and Mark Twain. The *Hesperian*, under the editorship of Madam F. H. Day, advertised a literary fare of subjects ranging from "sublime thoughts of Milton to the best method of making muffins." California journals reached their high point with the *Overland Monthly* (1868), published by Anton Roman and edited by Bret Harte. It concentrated on talented authors or original writings on wide-ranging subjects and was the literary sensation of the day. These journals proved to be valuable vehicles for budding writers.

Literature

American literary tradition took shape as a native form in the early nineteenth century. Edgar Allan Poe pioneered literary forms for the short story and created the detective story, greatly influencing American and European writers. Essays and poetry reached a high point in the writings of Ralph Waldo Emerson and Walt Whitman. The novel took root with James Fenimore Cooper's romantic adventures after 1820, and matured with Herman Melville's epic *Moby Dick* (1851), the story of a sea captain's relentless pursuit of a white whale representing the forces of good and evil. Though the theater was steeped in the Shakespeare vogue, plays were shaped for popular entertainment rather than literary form: dramatists wrote classical farces and romantic melodramas for thrill-seeking audiences. American writers veered toward the personal expressionism of Emerson and Whitman rather than toward Poe's esthetic standards. The reading public leaned to sentimental authors like Harriet Beecher Stowe (Lyman Beecher's daughter), whose vivid antislavery book *Uncle Tom's Cabin* (1852) pioneered the propaganda novel. At midcentury, romanticism was still a strong literary force: it glorified nationalism, democracy, individualism, and frontier life. In California, in particular, talented writers of the local-color school of writing were exploiting regional manners and subjects.

Creative writers in California found a congenial atmosphere. San Francisco, literary capital of California and the Far West, abounded with willing publishers, encouraging editors, numerous presses, and an avid reading public, all of which produced a favorable climate for aspiring writers. Book publishers competed for promising writers. The 1860's witnessed a hot rivalry between Anton Roman, patron–publisher of aspiring writers like Harte and Hittell, and Hubert Howe Bancroft, who applied business methods to literature to become the biggest publisher west of Chicago.

Several among the numerous writers who came to California made important contributions to the state's literary tradition during the first decade. J. Ross Browne, an inveterate traveler who served in various government posts, authored writings that anticipated Melville's *Moby Dick* and Twain's famous travel book *Innocents Abroad*. His humorous sketches are among the best vignettes of California's open and varied frontier life. Louise Clappe, wife of a physician in a mining town, wrote in the *Shirley Letters* (1856) vivid descriptions of mining life that are literary gems. John Rolling Ridge, half-Indian, wrote a powerful, imaginative story on Joaquin Murietta, which immortalized the famous bandit in California's most original legend. George Derby, a West Pointer stationed in San Diego, wrote hilarious sketches which set a vogue for realism in humor. They established Derby as the first of our Far Western humorists, and for a while the nation's favorite. An incurable practical joker, he was once left in temporary charge of a friend's newspaper and, in his absence, proceeded merrily to burlesque the news and switch the paper's political support from Democratic to Whig in a time when men took their politics seriously.

Anomg the early writers to achieve national fame in the 1860's were Bret Harte and Mark Twain. Harte's short stories are masterful studies of assorted characters struggling against fateful events. "The Luck of Roaring Camp" centers on the death of the camp's prostitute in childbirth and the miners who adopt her child. "The Outcasts of Poker Flat" tells of a gambler and a prostitute sacrificing their lives to save their companions in a snowstorm. Twain's pungent humor exposes human frailties in delightful homespun yarns. His tale about the celebrated jumping frog of Calaveras County who was humiliatingly deprived of his sure victory (someone before the contest weighted him with birdshot) won him national fame. As Twain relates of the frog's reputation:

> "Why, I've seen him set Dan'l Webster down here on this floor . . . and quicker'n you could wink he'd spring straight up and snake a fly off'n the counter there, and flop down on the floor ag'in as solid as a gob of mud, and fall to scratching the side of his head with his hind foot . . . You never see a frog so modest and straightfor'ard as he was, for all he was so gifted."

Harte and Twain drew inspiration from their California predecessors. Harte's stories are sometimes based on actual incidents described in Clappe's letters, and Twain's humor reminds us of Derby.

These luminaries were part of a circle of gifted writers in San Francisco's turbulent cosmopolitan life of the 1860's. As described by Franklin Walker, they were a remarkable group of colorful personalities who led eventful lives marked by personal tragedies, and who shared congenial friendships that proved important in their personal literary development. Ina Coolbrith, a niece of Joseph Smith, the Mormon prophet, escaped from an unhappy marriage and divorce in Los Angeles to San Francisco. There she perfected her genteel, ladylike poetry while teaching school, and played sweetheart to Harte and Twain and mother to other promising writers. Joaquin Miller (original name Cincinnatus Heine Miller), an eccentric itinerant who borrowed his first name from the famous California bandit, parlayed his versatile abilities into an eccentric personality act that startled people everywhere and into flowing verses that won him recognition as Poet of the Sierra. Ambrose Bierce, an ill-humored wit and misanthrope, tried his hand at poetry and prose until he found his forte as a newspaper gossip columnist in a city that gave license to his talents for fierce satire and insult. Clarence King, a sometime member of the circle, was noted for his polished narratives of Sierra mountaineering. None of these writers was California born, but all were indebted to the frontier state for their formative literary development.

By 1870 California's golden age of literature was approaching a close. The transcontinental railroad for opening California to the world was as symbolic for literature as it was for the state's political economy. Over the next few years, all these writers (except Coolbrith, who almost went) took the return train to make pilgrimages or search for new laurels in the East and Europe. Bierce, Hittell, and Miller were among the few who returned to take residence in California. Of greater significance was the merging of California's local-color school into the fabric of American literature.

Religion

Religious institutions were quickly set up, especially in the San Francisco Bay Area. Pioneer churchmen were particularly noted for their organizing talents and energetic efforts, notably the Congregationalist Samuel Willey, the Catholic Joseph Alemany (California's first archbishop), and later the Unitarian Thomas Starr King. San Francisco had a branch of the Young Men's Christian Association in 1853, two years after the first American branch in Boston; it was a London-based form of urban revivalism for encouraging Christian living among youth. The city by 1855 already boasted 32 churches, though membership was apparently low. Makeshift facilities gave way to substantial edifices, spurred by both religious dedication and competition among church leaders. Strong financial support came from mission societies in the East. Pioneer Protestant churchmen worked together in cooperative church, charitable, and educational activities, usually under Willey's persistent leadership. Among their cooperative accomplishments were the establishment of the College of California (see above) and the Pacific Theological Seminary (1868) for training Protestant ministers. By 1870 the state had over 1000 churches, with the Methodists leading the Protestant denominations, and the Catholics running strong, plus Negro churches, Jewish synagogues, and Chinese temples.

The men of the cloth constituted a strong social as well as religious force. Many were eager, as historian Louis Wright puts it, to meet the "challenges of iniquity and prosperity of the Gold Rush (to do) battle with minions of the devil." They established schools and sometimes doubled as teachers—education to them was as useful for the salvation of the soul as it was for the enlightenment of the mind. They joined the Temperance Party's effort to get rid of the "drinking curse" and supported Vigilante efforts supposedly intended to replace anarchic conditions with order and "Christian decency." They also lobbied for state and local "Sunday laws" which prohibited gambling and other boisterous entertainment that "profaned the Sabbath"—an oblique attack on the Latin Catholic minority whose dancing, gambling, and cockfights were part of their Sunday fiestas. Their penchant for humanitarian and patriotic causes prompted William Hanchett to suggest that they were more significant as a social force than a religious one in taming California's frontier.

The church movement suffered severe trials on the rambunctious frontier. A church historian (W. W. Sweet) attributes religious corruption in frontier areas to the migration process: people in moving westward lost close ties to the conventional religion of established home churches and adapted church doctrines and practices to the new environment to produce hybrid faiths. The Gold Rush compounded the situation. Preachers complained constantly of difficulties with men stirred not by God but by greed and lust, not by making homes but by quick riches. Yet their influence was evident. A Downieville preacher arranged a funeral for a man shot by a gambler, only to learn that his audience of gamblers intended to make *him* the burial victim; he continued to defame them, nonetheless. Even the intense Mormons could not persuade all their Saints to leave California for the Promised Land in Salt Lake (see Chapter 7). Religious cults were organized by eccentric individuals who modified Christian tenets through metaphysical and emotional excursions. The first sect was apparently founded by William Money, a Scots quack doctor in Los Angeles who preached a "reformed Testament"—he claimed to have been born with four teeth and the "likeness of a rainbow in his eye." San Francisco was the center for the flourishing cults of the Far West in these years.

Science and Technology

Science and technology are major catalytic forces in the development of society. Science, the systematic acquisition of positive knowledge, involves accumulating facts from observation and experience in order to deduce scientific hypotheses (the generalizations of pure science) or for practical application (applied science). The Englishman Isaac Newton (1642–1727) established the basis of modern science: he propounded the idea of the world as a universe operating mechanically according to natural laws perceived by scientific study. He wielded a powerful influence on the American mind. Technology is a form of applied science—the so-called mechanical arts—characteristically, inventions and specialized techniques utilized in agriculture and manufacturing. Historically, science developed as a branch of philosophy; technology, which developed apart from science, was closely related to economic progress. James Watt, for instance, was not a scientist, but a mechanic who utilized scientific knowledge to invent the steam engine as a source of power for operating machinery.

In early nineteenth-century America, science and technology developed along several lines. Mechanics devised numerous ingenious inventions and machinery, such as McCormick's reaper, Singer's sewing machine and Morse's telegraph, which were transforming agriculture, manufacturing, and commerce. Scientists were building up an independent profession and bridging the gap between pure and applied science, as did Yale's Benjamin Silliman, Jr., for instance, who pioneered in agricultural chemistry and applied geology (see Chapter 9). The federal government became directly involved in scientific–technological endeavors. Prominent scientists entered government service, like Alexander Bache (Ben Franklin's grandson), who headed the coastal survey, and Joseph Henry, who headed the Smithsonian Institution, a national agency to promote science. The Bache–Henry dream for consolidating government–science activities reached fulfillment in the prestigious National Academy of Science (1863).

California was a direct beneficiary of American science and technology. In the 1840's federal expeditions for amassing scientific information reached California, notably the Wilkes naval expedition (1838–1842) for Pacific explorations and the Fremont military expeditions (1842–1845) for exploring overland routes in the trans-Mississippi West. In the 1850's Bache's Coast Survey—the symbol of government science—thoroughly mapped the Pacific Coast, plotting California harbors and lighthouse sites for commerce, while the Army's topographical engineers mapped transcontinental routes for wagon roads and railroads. In the 1860's soldier–civilian teams under Army auspices collected data and specimens for the Smithsonian while mapping the railroad to California. On another front, talented American immigrants to California—blacksmiths, mechanics, and farmers—invented machines and mechanical devices that contributed heavily to the state's economic development. Mention has been made of the gang plow for wheat farming, hydraulic mining, and other innovations. John Hittell was not untypical of the many who devoted spare time to tinkering with contraptions, and even patented inventions. The establishment of the University of California's agricultural, mining, and mechanical colleges under federal auspices provided new impetus for technical–vocational education.

California's biggest scientific endeavor was the state geological survey. Following the failure of Congress to do the job, and inspired by the example of other states, the California legislature sponsored scientific surveys to provide accurate information about undeveloped regions, a prerequisite to the exploitation of natural resources by private enterprise. The amateurish efforts of state geologists in the 1850's underscored the need for serious scientific investigation. The initiative was taken by Stephen Field, then state supreme court justice, who drafted the unusual 1860 law which not only stipulated a state survey for scientific rather than utilitarian purpose, but also *named* its director— Josiah Whitney, Yale's distinguished geologist. Whitney assembled a remarkable group of talented scientists and carried out a systematic investigation of the unexplored Sierra region. The nation's leading scientific journal called it the most auspicious of state efforts. The survey's outstanding crew went on to fashion prominent national careers: William Brewer as Yale's great agricultural expert, Charles Hoffman as the father of American cartography, and Clarence King as the first chief of the United States Geological Survey. All left their names in the Sierra and contributed important commentaries on California. The work of the survey was never completed, but it contributed valuable data on California's unique geology, especially on the analysis of earthquakes.

Philosophical Views

The Gold Rush attracted a good share of thoughtful men who examined life around them and offered their critiques. While men were generally preoccupied with the pursuit of gold and other get-rich-quick schemes, the philosophers and theologians among them sought a rationale for the frontier society which would square human conduct with ideals, and give meaning to men's existence. San Francisco was a prominent haven for freethinkers, including French and German liberal refugees who had fled the conservative reaction after the 1848 European revolutions. Protestant churchmen were quick to challenge freethinkers and other nonbelievers. When John Hittell, a leading freethinker, wrote his *Evidences Against Christianity* (1855), an amusing polemic and California's first intellectual work, his "red flag" provoked a raging reaction from Samuel Willey's Congregational journal and James King's crusading *Bulletin*. The public was treated to several first-rate intellectual battles between the forces of religion and science.

The two men whose thought perhaps best reflects the frontier mind in California are John Hittell and Josiah Royce (Sarah's son), who wrote about this period at a later time. Hittell was a self-taught linguist, a lawyer by training and a newspaperman and professional writer. His writings reveal him to have been a strong proponent of industrial capitalism and government laissez faire, and a strong critic of Christianity because it hindered progress. In extending the concepts of Hamiltonian industrialism and Jeffersonian agrarianism, he denounced the wasteful, self-centered "vagrant individual miner" and applauded the mining capitalist who used machinery and Chinese labor to exploit effectively resources that contributed to the material prosperity of people. Hittell's philosophy assigned moral value to the industrialist as the savior of modern society.

Josiah Royce was born in 1855 in Grass Valley, a California mining town. He received his education at the University of California, at Johns Hopkins University, and in Europe, and became a renowned professor of philosophy at Harvard. Nourished by his California experience and by German idealist philosophers, he became a leading proponent of philosophical idealism and developed a philosophy which based human community on loyalty rather than on material production. In his classic study *California*, he traces the state's historical development from the American conquest to the 1856 San Francisco Vigilante Committee, stressing the moral struggle of men torn between the forces of anarchy and order in their effort to establish a stable society. He saw the necessity of miner's justice, but denounced its lynch law. He laid the cause of San Francisco vigilantism to the "civil irresponsibility of good men." As historian Robert Clelland aptly points out, Royce's analysis of the community spirit is timely today, as then, in aiding our understanding of the American character and the basic problems of our cities.

The two men caught the common sentiment and opposing ideas which permeated the minds of California's heterogeneous populace. Both saw California as being in the mainstream of American development, the one as a talented writer applying American ideas in California's development, the other as an original thinker explaining the new state to Americans so they could better understand themselves. Both had faith in California's future, but where Hittell believed in material progress, Royce believed in the primacy of community. Where both men saw the efficacy of businessmen (the ruling class to Hittell), Hittell saw the infinite good where Royce saw "moral elasticity." Hittell was moved once to remark that the inventor James Watt, who discovered the uses of steam power, was worth more than a score of poets like Robert Burns. Royce, in contrast, saw poetry as "man's greatest spiritual food." One was an adopted son and the other an expatriate native, but both were products of the California experience.

SUMMARY

The United States incorporated California into the Union in 1850 as a fullfledged state. National affairs were so dominated by the North–South conflicts over slavery in the 1850's, and the Civil War and Reconstruction in the 1860's, that the federal government attended only to the basic matters of its distant province, though it was ever sensitive to California's vast gold riches. When the new state raised issue over important matters (for example, currency standard and public land distribution), the federal government generally compromised or deferred to it. Congress was hardly in a position to do otherwise, considering the circumstances of the time.

California, left much on its own, contended with the rough-and-tumble experience of frontier development. It struggled from the near anarchy of the Gold Rush and established a constitutional base for an orderly society by the end of the interregnum. The struggle for order continued through the first two decades of statehood. The Gold Rush had set off a chain of events that brought into the state a heterogeneous horde of people and stimulated diverse enterprises. Men caught in the scramble for quick riches exploited land and resources with enterprises of all kinds, overcoming formidable obstacles with drive and ingenuity. The dominant Americans rode roughshod over native Californios and alien groups who were in their way. They fought relentless battles among each other for control of state and local governments to promote their interests. The miners, who had the upper hand in state affairs in the 1850's, gave way to merchant control in the 1860's. In agriculture, ranchers were losing out to farmers in their group conflicts. In the first period of American rule, the newcomers had transformed the turbulent frontier into a fairly stabilized rural society in which agricultural and commercial activities replaced mining. The mixture of people contributed to a rich cultural diversity and a colorful variety of social customs and practices. Eventually, merchants in alliance with party bosses emerged as the dominant group in the state's political economy.

California emerged from these two decades of trial and tribulation with a well-defined version of American society. The 1849 constitution established the basis of a democratic capitalistic society—one that would promote representative government, the competition of small enterprises, and a plural social order. It augmented the American concepts of the distribution of power between the national and state governments (federalism) by stipulating that state and local governments share the governmental authority, and the granting of equal rights to all (democracy) by including a bill of rights to guarantee personal liberties. The founding fathers' vision of a California society in the Jacksonian mold did not quite develop that way. The machinations of party bosses and merchant–financiers eventually produced a society conspicuous for its machine politics, large-scale enterprises of few entrepreneurs, and great social disparities. Free enterprise produced in the state a grossly unequal distribution of wealth which hurt many people and retarded progress in other ways.

In establishing their version of authority and liberty in society, the American Californians replaced the Hispanic model, which they detested, with one steeped in American tradition. Spain had implemented governmental authority through personal rule of Crown officials. Mexico had established a constitutional setup which operated too often at the whim of ruling elements. The Americans, on the other hand, sanctified their constitution as the basis of authority and liberty in society. The constitution was a sacred document which spelled out the "rules of the game" to be observed by government in managing public affairs, and by men enjoying personal liberties and profiting from private enterprises. However, the rise of dominant special-interest groups, who subverted the letter and spirit of the constitution to their own ends, resulted in a form of elite rule that was less narrowly stratified and rigid than Hispanic predecessors. The American Californians, then, replaced the Hispanic model with another kind of authoritarian order.

The frontier period was a highly significant phase of California's overall development. California completed its transition from the Spanish–Mexican setup into a thoroughly American capitalistic political economy. The Gold Rush, as a powerful catalytic force, shaped the character of institutional development which has continued in basic form to this day. It perpetuated Hispanic ways, notably the large land pattern and social customs. It produced a California version of American ways, marked by strong local government and self-governing associations, private enterprises with experimental cooperative and corporate models, and a distinctive social order that was more a mosaic than a melting pot of diverse people. These characteristic features which evolved out of the frontier period continued in basic form over the next half-century. Some have even persisted to the present day.

Overleaf: The *C. P. Huntington*. Pioneer of the California rails, the *Huntington* was shipped around the Horn for service in California until its retirement in 1900. This wood-burning locomotive with its big driving wheels, diamond stack, oil lantern, brass bell, and cowcatcher (actually to nudge cattle and clear debris off tracks) were familiar train features of the period.

VI   The Corporate Sway

1870-1910

With the completion of the transcontinental railroad, California after 1870 entered a new era of greater growth and expansion. The railroad and other corporate enterprises overcame formidable obstacles and spurred major economic and social developments. People poured into the state in unprecedented numbers to pursue the dazzling prospects advertised by land promoters. They opened settlements in Southern California and the San Joaquin Valley, building up rural communities as the mainstay of society and developing diversified resources that greatly broadened the state's economic base. The sudden transformation, however, was accompanied by sharp economic fluctuations which badly hurt farmers, laborers, small merchants, and other groups. These groups battled with corporations for control of government and public policies in a continuing effort to remedy their grievances. However, the Southern Pacific and its corporate allies held sway in politics to sustain its economic primacy. After the turn of the century, California, still troubled by unresolved maladjustments, was undergoing a transition brought on by national urban industrial development. By then it became apparent that California affairs had become inextricably interwoven with those of the nation.

11 Machine Politics
12 The Heyday of Private Enterprise
13 The Plutocratic Society

11 Machine Politics

THE SETTING

The dictum that he who controls the party, controls the government, found ultimate expression in California politics in this period. The alliance between party bosses and corporation leaders, which had taken seed in the previous decade, now took firm root. Where party bosses had earlier played the dominant role, corporation executives now exerted the stronger influence. The Big Four of the Central Pacific after 1870 came to outdo them all in manipulating party politics and governmental affairs to assert primacy in the political economy.

The Party System

Party organization was now more refined, regular, and settled in its ways, but no less susceptible to corruption. The county organizations formed the backbone of the state party machinery. These ranged from skeletal party frameworks, which were revived at election time, to elaborate, self-perpetuating political machines run by the county boss and his gang. The county boss achieved control of the party organization by securing at primary elections or conventions a bloc of faithful delegates to the county convention. These delegates voted for his hand-picked candidates to the central committee, which in turn selected the executive committee, the governing apparatus by which he was able to control convention proceedings. The boss drew financial contributions from professional politicians aspiring to public office, from public officials for kickbacks or assessments, and from business leaders and vice elements (gambling, liquor, and prostitution) for assorted payoffs. He relied on machine-controlled public officials to deliver on patronage jobs or graft from public works or franchises and other governmental favors which he used to reward his supporters or deliver to his clients. To sustain his power base he had to retain a majority of the county board of supervisors and a hold over other officials.

The party machine at the municipal and state level operated similarly with variations. The city bosses were especially important in delivering large blocs of votes in regional and statewide conventions and elections. San Francisco, with its sizable voting bloc, alone accounted for 20 of the 120 assemblymen and 10 of the 40 senators in the state legislature; hence the interest shown by the Southern Pacific and other big bosses in the machine politics of the metropolis. The district and state conventions were actually political arenas where the county and other bosses or leaders bargained and traded votes on their candidates to congressional and state offices.

The patronage so important for the sustenance of the party organization evolved into an elaborate system. Patronage lists, greatly expanded by the state legislature and local governing bodies, included just about every appointive public office, ranging from the top administrators to janitors. The federal patronage distributed by the United States senators or congressmen was particularly important to party leaders: the mint superintendent and the collectors of the port or internal revenue especially had many subordinate positions to fill; the postmasterships went to city and rural party leaders, and the prestigious diplomatic posts went to former governors or other prominent politicians. Leaders of the Federal Brigade (incumbents of United States public offices in California) wielded considerable influence in state and local politics.

This party system derived much strength from the strong loyalties of the party rank and file. For some, the party perpetuated the principles of its revered leaders: Jefferson and Jackson for the Democrats, and Lincoln for the Republicans. For others, the party was an institution, whether for social affairs like party clubs and picnics, for welfare services like jobs and handouts, or for political displays like campaign parades and election celebrations. For still others, the party was the path to political advancement or business advantage. Party bosses effectively exploited these binding ties to sustain strong spirit among their followers, punishing those who strayed from the reservation and rewarding those who accepted their dictates. Party leaders generally took their allegiance seriously, and their adherence to party principles often outweighed their distaste for the party bosses who perverted their cause.

The Governmental System

State governmental operations continued much along traditional lines of laissez faire, local primacy, and party loyalty. The laissez faire spirit limited state government to minimal action. People still took seriously the idea that the least government was the best government, and generally held a dim view of government regulation. The primacy of local government continued to give county government preeminence over the state government in managing public affairs. People still held to the idea that government closest to them was the best. The doctrine of party loyalty permeated governmental as well as party affairs: the party in control of county and state government took full advantage of patronage and other benefits from public office. These Jeffersonian–Jacksonian political ideas reflected the state's expansive agrarian economy and predominantly rural society.

The party system helped undermine the political processes of local and state government. Local government, whether at the county, city, or town level, was thoroughly permeated with patronage politics, which seriously compromised its capacity to govern. At the state level, the governor, legislature, and even the supreme court were susceptible to the influences of boss pressure and machine politics. State and county institutions were often riddled with patronage, politics, and graft. Railroads were the weathervane issue for the parties and government throughout the period, although occasionally other issues assumed greater importance. The state reached a peak in political corruption that probably has not been equaled since.

Governors still played a secondary role to the legislature in state affairs and public policy matters. They were by the standards of the times basically honest, if of limited ability, men who either played along or fought fruitlessly against the system. Exceptions to the mediocre level of governors include the talented James Budd (1895–1899) and the inept Henry Gage (1899–1903). Only when he had a segment of strong public support could a governor make headway with progressive measures against the dead weight of the system as did George Pardee (1903–1907).

The legislature as the state arena for public affairs resembled more a marketplace for vote-trading than a forum for debating issues. Contending political factions and special interests fought long, hard battles over public policies and other measures affecting their interests. Party bosses and their legislative leaders were the prime movers in organizing blocs of legislators, trading votes, and striking bargains. Corporation lobbies were also active, their able agents and well-financed activities giving them greater influence than farmers, labor, and other less well-organized groups. Unscrupulous legislators engaged in political blackmail and other shenanigans. Conscientious legislators could and did play the game honestly and squarely: they sometimes got their way by adroit maneuvering. C. C. Wright, a freshman assemblyman in the 1887 legislature, pushed his landmark irrigation district bill (see Chapter 12) through the lower house, as one newspaper reporter put it, "while the big boys were away fishing." Nor could powerful bosses control situations where major groups fought over vital issues, as in the farmers' showdown with the miners over hydraulic mining operations. Nevertheless, machine politics of the day left its indelible mark on the legislature, which lived up to its reputation for corruption and venality throughout the years.

The Southern Pacific was the most successful practitioner of the prevailing system. Its political machine exerted the most enduring and powerful single influence in party and governmental affairs in the state. It operated mainly at the state level, particularly in party conventions and the legislature, but its influence was felt at the local level through deals with party bosses and public officials, and extended to the federal level in Washington.

Out of these developments emerged major trends toward voluntary associations and state agencies, which were well underway by the 1890's. Farmers, merchants, civic and other groups improved upon voluntary associations as cooperative devices to strengthen their enterprises and to secure favorable public policies. They also helped create state agencies to extend governmental assistance and beneficial regulation, thus leading to numerous state boards for implementing these public policies and government programs. As government functions became specialized, state boards added departments which were subdivided into divisions and bureaus. Before long, these bureaus acquired professional administrators and technical personnel to gather information, conduct research, and administer specialized programs serving client interest groups, thus giving rise to the bureaucratic movement. These bureaus enlisted their staff from experts in the field—whether self-educated, university trained, or government experienced—and they worked closely with related local and federal agencies, the state university, and voluntary associations. Reform-minded politicians and public officials, in building these bureaus, attempted to replace patronage appointments with appointments based on merit in an effort to establish a permanent staff, sound principles, and uniform rules to insure administrative continuity and efficiency. The state agencies in this period went through a formative stage of developing workable procedures by trial-and-error process, and resolving conflicts among entrepreneur, association, university, and government groups. The state bureaucracy established foundations for its advance later under the Progressive aegis.

The Southern Pacific, along with corporate and party boss allies, was also a catalyst in evoking varied reform movements. Discontented groups attempted in various ways to redress deficiencies in the existing society that would adjust their balance with such "predatory groups." They became part of larger reform movements of the times: the agrarian-oriented Grangers in the 1870's and the Populists in the 1890's, and the urban revolts in the 1890's which evolved into the Progressive movement after 1900. The urban revolt, which focused on San Francisco and Los Angeles, was spearheaded by civic-minded groups, primarily business and professional men, who attempted to eliminate machine politics from municipal government. When municipal reform suffered setbacks, these urban groups united forces with like-minded rural groups to launch the movement for state political reform. In 1910 antimachine forces captured the state government to end the era of machine politics.

DEVELOPMENT

The Terrible Seventies

In the 1870's the United States hit a new low in national life. The railroads were spearheading a remarkable expansion of agricultural, commercial, manufacturing, and transportation enterprises which also produced widespread speculation in railroad stocks and contributed in some regions to severe economic dislocations. Industrial tycoons united with national party leaders in an unsavory alliance to play a commanding role in public affairs, leading to unprecedented plunder of public offices and swindles in major business corporations. The hard times intensified the distress of merchants, farmers, and laborers. The reckoning came with two major developments of the decade: the rise of the farmer-oriented, reform-minded Granger movement (see below) and the Panic of 1873 with the subsequent long depression.

California during the 1870's reflected these national trends. When the decade opened, the state was already experiencing economic distress. The decline of gold mining saddled Sierra and Northwest counties with burdensome public debts and only sporadic employment for miners. The rapid development of wheat production in the Central Valley subjected farmers to the unpredictable whims of nature, the sharp and often unscrupulous business practices of the San Francisco grain merchants, and the Central Pacific Railroad. The completion of the transcontinental railroad, which accelerated the flow of people and goods into the state, did not bring the anticipated prosperity. It brought instead oversupplied markets, which led to falling prices that badly hurt merchants and manufacturers in San Francisco and other major cities. The railroads, once constructed, laid off some 10,000 Chinese construction workers and proceeded to bring in increasing numbers of immigrants. This contributed to an excessive labor force, accompanied by a reduction of wages and growing unemployment. The renewed boom of the Comstock mines after 1871 only aggravated the situation, for it induced merchants, clerks, farmers, laborers, and others to gamble their dwindling savings on risky speculations. The widespread economic distress prompted Gertrude Atherton to describe her times as the Terrible Seventies.

The Politics of Discontent

These economic adversities forced California's political parties to shift their attention from national issues to state problems. Discontented groups, while not fully understanding the complex underlying causes, easily found visible scapegoats for their troubles. Farmers and merchants blamed the railroad, water companies, and land speculators for mono-polizing land and water. Laborers saw in the Chinese the cause of their unemployment, and denounced the steamships and railroads for im-porting Chinese and exploiting their cheap labor.

Elections during the decade brought on showdowns over the grievances of these discontented groups. In 1871 both parties responded by adopting antimonopoly positions. The Republicans swept into office with their gubernatorial candidate, Newton Booth, a prominent Sacra-mento merchant who had switched from an earlier pro-railroad to an anti-railroad position. The 1872 legislature, however, gave little consid-eration to railroad measures. In the 1873 midterm election, assorted farmers (now organized into the State Grange) and miner, merchant, and labor groups formed the People's Independent Party, which embraced a comprehensive reform program, embodying tax equalization, corpora-tion regulation, and other Granger proposals. The 1874 legislature enacted some Granger-oriented measures, but failed to implement the Granger's call for a constitutional convention. The legislature's limited reform effort is attributed to the railroad's countermoves and the governor's preoccupation with his senatorial aspirations. (One of Huntington's letters written about this time implied that the governor was "safe" for the railroad.)

In the 1875 elections, both parties felt the heavy hand of railroad "programmers," who succeeded in undercutting anti-railroad planks. The Democrats won the election with the help of the Independents, who cut deeply into the Republican vote, but William Irwin, the new governor, proved to be a conservative who equivocated on the pressing railroad issue. The 1876 legislature, however, adopted the merchant-sponsored measure establishing a railroad commission to regulate rates, instead of the farmer's measure which would have established direct rate regulation. The merchants were no less antagonistic than the farmers to the railroads, but they were more conservative in their approach to remedial measures.

The deepening economic depression finally evoked a violent showdown of unemployed workers. Severe droughts in 1876 and 1877 greatly reduced mining and agricultural production, so that unemployed workers drifted to San Francisco and other hard-pressed towns to augment other unemployed groups clamoring for public aid. That summer, violence broke out in San Francisco. In August, a workers' mass meeting, called to express sympathy for eastern railroad workers then on strike, degenerated into raids by hoodlum groups on Chinese establishments. A Committee of Safety was immediately set up under William Coleman, the city's leading merchant. It quickly organized some 6000 volunteers into a vigilante-style "merchants militia," which dispersed the workers and disbanded within several days. In September, agitating labor leaders in city sandlot meetings organized their followers into a local Workingmen's Party under Denis Kearney. The politically ambitious Kearney was a drayman, or teamster, who had just served in Coleman's pickhandle brigade. Now he harangued workers with incendiary speeches, calling for an armed "workers militia" and some judicious hangings of corrupt officials, oppressive capitalists, and "heathen Chinese." Although his inflammatory speeches frightened city authorities and businessmen, Kearney was actually only seeking political action to implement reform measures, along with an end to business frauds and land monopolies. The workers' movement spread rapidly to other cities and by January 1878 culminated in the statewide Workingmen's Party.

The mounting protests of assorted groups reached a climax in 1878. In response to intense pressure, the legislature adopted by an overwhelming vote the call for a constitutional convention. In the hotly contested election campaign that summer, conservative businessmen called for the elimination of Kearney's "communist scourge," and radical workers urged an end to capitalistic monopolies. Some farmers, ranging from large landholders to small tenants, lined up with conservatives or workingmen, but most of them aligned with the independent, nonpartisan group seeking a middle ground that would accomplish something of both ends. Republicans and Democrats united behind a nonpartisan ticket in the statewide election, but many party regulars refused to go along and elected party tickets in local elections. The election was an overwhelming victory for farmer and labor delegates.

The convention (see below), which met between September 1878 and March 1879, drafted a new constitution which was ratified in the general election of November 1879. Angry farmers and workingmen, who went to the convention to redress their grievances, found their positions modified by astute corporation representatives who were able to win important concessions. The convention incorporated into the new constitution state agencies to equalize taxes and to regulate railroad rates, and other provisions which modified governmental procedures. The 1879 Constitution was described as a "bundle of compromises" which made little change in the basic structure of government.

The state capitol. Constructed between 1860 and 1874, it contained the legislature and most of the executive offices throughout this period. It also served as the site of the second Constitutional Convention, 1878-1879.

The Expansive Eighties

In the 1880's the American nation was again on the upswing with the return of prosperous times. The railroads renewed construction, accelerating immigration and agricultural development in open areas of the West, and stimulating heavy industries in the urban centers of the East. Industrial leaders, like Rockefeller in oil and Carnegie in steel, set the pace for consolidating corporations into monolithic trusts which contributed to immense industrial production, expanded markets, and an improved standard of living. They also produced a greater maldistribution of wealth, accentuating class differences between a few wealthy industrialists and hard-pressed merchants, farmer entrepreneurs, and an increasingly proletarian labor force. Industrial tycoons and party bosses continued their incredibly corrupt schemes in business and politics. Dissident groups, however, secured congressional measures for regulating the railroad (Interstate Commerce Commission, 1887) and business monopolies (Sherman Anti-Trust Act, 1890) only to have them undermined by conservative courts. Organized labor rebuilt national unions (Knights of Labor and American Federation of Labor) and waged industrial warfare (Haymarket Riot, Chicago, 1886). The good times, then, were deceptive. The plutocrats fared well, but merchant, farmer, and labor groups continued to struggle with limited success for a fair stake in the growing industrial order.

This situation prevailed in California, as well. Economic activity accelerated as extended railroad lines stimulated agricultural and commercial enterprises. Waves of immigrants flowing into the state populated older areas, but more dramatically created numerous new settlements in the lower San Joaquin and Southern California. With expansion came social maladjustments which accentuated the distress of merchant, farmer, and labor groups. But people seemed preoccupied with exciting economic opportunities, which probably accounts for the listless behavior of the electorate in this decade. Even the newspaper exposé of railroad shenanigans in the Colton Letters after 1882, and the United States Pacific Railroad Commission investigation in 1887, caused only ripples on the political waters. Prosperity evidently had a tempering effect on politics. The railroad loosened its grip and reformers softened their agitation. No one wanted to be accused of "rocking the boat" in good times.

The Politics of Bossism

In the aftermath of the constitutional convention, both parties went through a brief transition. Party factions regrouped into new align-ments—the Workingmen's Party and a reform-oriented Constitutional Party—but the two organizations quickly sank into political oblivion. Party loyalty proved so strong that the Republicans and Democrats soon recaptured earlier bolters to regain their former strength. The Southern Pacific's manager, W. W. Stow, intensified the company's activities, especially to keep the newly created state railroad commission and state equalization board from enacting measures harmful to railroad interests. He had important allies among other corporation representatives, but he faced increasing opposition from rival railroads, large business entre-preneurs, merchants, and farmers. More dangerous to the Southern Pacific was the emergence on the state scene of Christopher Buckley, San Francisco's powerful and corrupt Democratic boss, who played the role of railroad programmer or reformer, whichever served to his advantage.

Party bosses in this decade enjoyed their heyday in managing party and governmental affairs. The Republicans in an election sweep in 1879 took over the state government, headed by George Perkins, a shipping magnate and party regular, and Secretary of State Daniel Burns, Republican boss from San Francisco. The legislature, under such conservative and boss influences, effectively emasculated the railroad commission and other constitution-induced reforms. In the 1882 election, George Stoneman, a former Civil War general with an anti-railroad record, won the Democratic nomination from George Hearst, the mining magnate, who was backed by the Buckley machine. Stoneman then beat out the Republican candidate. The conscientious governor attempted to implement railroad regulation only to be blocked by the legislature.

The legislative contest for United States Senator dominated state politics at mid-decade. It was a bizarre round-robin affair unmatched in state history. The Southern Pacific's Stow, on Huntington's orders, lined up machine forces (including Buckley) in the 1885 session to elect as United States Senator Aaron Sargent, the congressman who had served the railroad so faithfully. Much to the public's surprise and to Huntington's chagrin, Leland Stanford stepped into the race at the last moment and won the senatorial prize. Stanford's secret campaign was accomplished with payoffs to legislators estimated at over one million dollars. In 1886, when the other incumbent senator (John Miller) died, Governor Stoneman appointed Hearst, but when the Republican-dominated legislature met in special session that summer it elected a party member (A. P. Williams) to the senatorial post instead. The Democratic legislature that convened in 1887 turned the tables and elected Hearst to the vacant seat. The senatorial flip-flop ended with Hearst and Stanford safely lodged in the United States Senate through machine maneuvers.

Boss politics reached a low around 1890. Democrat Hearst and Republican Stanford apparently agreed to trade support for their reelection. The legislature in the 1891 session reelected Stanford, who had help from the Hearst-Buckley forces. Hearst died the same year and was succeeded by a Republican (C. N. Felton). Stanford paid a heavy price for his senatorial politicking. The disenchanted Huntington had ousted him from the railroad company's presidency (1890) in such a cruel way that it was said to have hastened Stanford's death in 1893. Thus the selection of the people's representatives had been reduced to a game of personal politics among leading party bosses and politically ambitious business tycoons.

The Restless Nineties

The Nineties were dominated by a grim depression in the middle years of the decade. Industries increased greatly, even through the depression years, and became more concentrated. The consolidation movement took on a new dimension as railroads, which represented the greatest concentration of wealth, came under the control of J. P. Morgan and other financiers who had superseded industrialist capitalists. Industrial progress, however, was offset by fluctuating business conditions, a declining agriculture, depressed labor, and cities saddled with poverty, slums, and crime. The victims of these maladjustments rose in protest: the farmers by organizing the Populist Party, which fragmented both major parties; and the laborers by striking against Homestead Steel (1892) and the Pullman railroad car company (1894), which revived industrial warfare. Political battles were waged with greater involvement of the electorate and with greater intensity over issues. The political stage was dominated by principled leaders like William Jennings Bryan, the Populist leader, and Mark Hanna, the millionaire businessman-politician; they superseded the patronage bosses. It was a restless decade, says historian Harold Faulkner, when people were pressing for remedies to assuage their disillusionment and discontent.

California was in close touch with these developments. The state sank into severe depression. Distress was widespread. Discontented merchant, farmer, and labor groups focused their anger on the corrupt machine bosses and the Southern Pacific business monopoly, to which they attributed most of their troubles. Leading newspapers of the state gave increasing publicity to Southern Pacific misdeeds, playing up the Huntington-Stanford feud which broke out into the open after 1890. They published the anonymous "Dear Pard" letters which Stanford's vengeful assistant J. M. Bassett wrote after 1892 to expose Huntington's activities, and, after 1894, the hard-hitting weekly letters of Arthur McEwen, crusading editor of several journals. Public disenchantment evolved into a growing chorus of protest.

These discontented groups experimented initially with various schemes but soon resorted to political action. In San Francisco, Buckley was indicted by the 1891 grand jury and fled the state to avoid prosecution. The city merchants moved in the early 1890's to break the Southern Pacific transportation monopoly by forming a traffic association which organized a competing shipping line and a rival railroad to the San Joaquin (see Chapter 9). Reform politicians elected as mayor the Populist Adolph Sutro (1893–1897), a popular mining magnate, and Democrat James Phelan (1897–1901) a respected, liberal-minded financier. In Los Angeles, assorted groups attempted to free municipal government from machine politics, notably the business-oriented Citizens League (1893) and the Direct Legislation League (1895). Municipal authorities, backed by powerful local merchants, labor unions, and major newspapers, fought a bitter decade-long battle to checkmate the Southern Pacific's brazen attempts to monopolize the city's harbor facilities (see Chapter 9). Both cities were beset by running battles between business elements and labor unions which complicated the cause of local reform. The activities of these urban groups set the tone for public affairs through the decade.

Meanwhile, the Southern Pacific had shifted gears. When Stow retired from long and faithful service in 1893, Huntington appointed William Herrin, a brilliant young corporation lawyer, as chief of the company's law department in charge of legal and political activities. Herrin put the machine operations on a businesslike basis and forged Southern Pacific alliances into a powerful combination, extending the railroad's influence throughout the state.

Populist Politics

The farmers revolt, which culminated in the Populist movement, overshadowed these anti-railroad groups. California's Populism was an extension of the national movement and an outgrowth of the Granger and other earlier farmers' protest organizations. It evolved from three successive organizations between 1890 and 1892: the National Party, a utopian socialist group which enjoyed astonishing but brief success (California had more members than any other state); the Farmers Alliance, an agrarian movement to unite farmers and labor behind candidates supporting a broad reform program; and the People's Party, an independent third party comprising farmer and labor groups which pressed for a comprehensive agrarian-oriented program emphasizing currency reform. The People's or Populist Party, which by 1892 had absorbed the other two organizations, became the catalyst of state politics for the remainder of the decade. The farmer's failure to win labor's support reduced the party to a farmer-oriented third-party movement. It suffered internal dissensions caused by rival leaders supporting opposing strategies: Thomas Cator, who rose with the Nationalists and favored party independence to preserve their principles; and Marion Cannon, who helped organize the Farmers Alliance and favored fusion with the Democrats to insure election victories. What the Populists lacked in numbers they made up in crusading fervor and militant adherence to principle. They divided Republicans and Democrats and forced both parties to abandon expediency and take a stand on the issues.

The Populists were a stormy petrel in state politics. In the 1892 elections, they made their debut by undercutting the Republicans to give the Democrats control of the legislature. In the legislative contest for United States Senator, they were badly split between Cator's uncompromising Populist stand and the Democratic-Populist fusion of Stephen White, Los Angeles Democratic leader. The bitter contest ended when Bryan interceded for the Los Angeles Democrat, and Cannon led some Populist leaders in contributing the vote to White's victory. Shortly after, Cannon was excommunicated from the party. In the 1894 state election, the Populists split with the Democrats to give the Republicans a near sweep of state offices—the one exception was the popular James Budd's gubernatorial victory.

In the crucial 1896 national election, the public faced a big-party showdown over major issues of the day. Bryan led his Populists into the Democratic fold to win the presidential nomination, while McKinley captured the Republican nomination. The national leaders turned the tables completely on California's two parties. The state Democrats and Republicans were forced to abandon independent positions on major issues and support their national party stand. The independent-minded Populists unhappily followed Bryan's dictates to coalesce with the Democrats. The election results reveal the extent of party deterioration. California Republicans won the state for McKinley by a narrow vote. The Populist demise was complete two years later when the party fused again with the Democrats, and their popular leader, the disillusioned Cator, quit politics. Thus ended the excruciating politics of a troubled state hit by the hard times of the decade.

The Revolutionary Decade

The new century witnessed startling changes which affected just about all aspects of society. The United States, after the Spanish-American War (1898–1899), acquired a colonial empire to begin its career as a world power, accelerating American expansion into Latin America and the Pacific, especially the Far East. Finance capitalists replaced industrial capitalists as the prime movers in the national economy. They consolidated their power by setting up holding companies, the "combination of all combinations." Morgan formed United States Steel Corporation (hereafter US Steel), the first billion dollar corporation, and backed the epic Northern Securities Company, which combined major railroad lines into the first true holding company. Prosperity came with industrial progress—but while it improved the conditions of labor and farmers, it hardly changed their status. Labor still suffered oppressive working conditions, and farmers still struggled under heavy debts.

The advent of Theodore Roosevelt to the presidency in 1901 inaugurated a new era in politics. He was the first president since Jackson to be the popular hero of the people, articulating their resentment of the status quo and their demand for change. He was the first since Lincoln to boldly assert presidential power, shifting the center of national power from the financier's capital on New York's Wall Street to the government capital in Washington. He became the energetic spokesman for the rising Progressive movement, where assorted groups at the local, state, and national levels spearheaded broad-scale reforms to remedy gross maladjustments arising from poverty amidst prosperity. These difficult transitional times were filled with intense controversies, violent showdowns, uncertain experimentation, and drastic change. They were, as historian George Mowry observes, revolutionary years. The United States emerged as a transformed society in which basic relationships were reestablished between government and the economy, between capital, labor, and agriculture, and between the nation and the world.

California, in the wake of these national trends, was in an economic upswing. Industries were expanding and people came in greater numbers than before. The Southern Pacific was at the peak of its economic primacy and political control, but all was not well in the land of Zion. Challenges came from discontented groups and rising special interests, especially among the newcomers in the state. They demanded adjustments in the status quo and a place in the changing order. The ground swell of earlier protest was gathering momentum and would soon break into open rebellion.

Politics in Equilibrium

Public opposition to the Southern Pacific and its allies accelerated. Discontented farmers and workingmen now had experienced leaders and effective organizations. Antimachine newspapers intensified their propaganda campaign to whip up public sentiment. Rival railroads, notably the Santa Fe and Western Pacific, joined by new industrialists and other entrepreneurs whose interests conflicted with those of the Southern Pacific, lent support to antimachine forces seeking to break its grip. Organized labor, which earlier had suffered heavy setbacks, rebounded by reviving union activity and taking part in politics. The leadership for the renewed attack on the railroad machine, however, came from none of these groups but from professional groups in the urban centers of the state. The rising cities foisted on municipal governments new types of urban problems which overwhelmed the old-style boss rule and machine politics. These new forces offset machine control in party and government affairs, putting state politics in equilibrium throughout the decade.

The first sign of a significant break in machine control came at the turn of the century. In a move to foil growing antimachine sentiment in the Southland, the Southern Pacific's Herrin sought to make Dan Burns, San Francisco's unsavory boss, United States Senator. The long drawn-out senatorial contest was filled with bitterness, corruption, and scandal. In the 1899 legislature, Burns and U. S. Grant, Jr. (son of the former President) led the field through 104 ballots to a deadlock. Grant, a wealthy San Diego businessman, was one of several candidates backed by archfoes of the Southern Pacific. The candidates were openly charged with wholesale bribery of the legislators. Eventually, the Assembly speaker was convicted for accepting bribes from at least two of the candidates. The newspapers unmercifully lampooned the lawmakers, who retaliated with recriminatory measures. One bill made the shooting of editors justifiable homicide, and another bill required editors to sign articles so that, as one editor surmised, the legislators would know whom to go gunning for! When the legislature convened in 1900, the antimachine forces united to elect Thomas Bard, a wealthy Ventura oilman, respected conservative and an antimachine leader. Bard's election represented a serious breach in the Southern Pacific's power.

State politics in the first half-decade reflected the widening gap between the Southern Pacific and antimachine forces. Governor Henry Gage (1899–1903) proved to be so inept and subservient to machine interests that an unkind critic remarked that Gage was not "broad-gauged nor even narrow-gauged. He is just a slot in the cable track." In the 1902 election campaign, the Southern Pacific sought to reelect Gage, but the effective challenge of a militant antimachine candidate caused Herrin to support the more compromising George Pardee, Oakland physician and a former mayor with an antimachine record. Pardee went on to win over Franklin Lane, a reform-minded Democratic candidate supported by the

San Francisco Phelan machine. Pardee was a competent chief executive who initiated some measures which were precursors to later Progressive reforms. As a politician, he was a middle-roader whose compromises antagonized both machine and antimachine elements and cost him the antimachine support he so ardently sought.

Factional cleavages badly split both parties in the 1906 election campaign. In the Republican state convention, the Southern Pacific wielded a heavy club in lining up safe candidates, including James Gillett, congressman from Eureka, for governor. Even then it secured its slate only after paying Abe Ruef, San Francisco's wily boss, $14,000 for alleged campaign expenses. In the Democratic state convention, anti-machine forces won control but were badly split: Theodore Bell, congressman from Napa and a militant reformer backed by the McNab—Phelan and Ruef factions, was nominated over William Langdon, San Francisco's reform-minded district attorney backed by Hearst. Hearst severed his relations with the Democratic Party and formed the Independence League to sponsor Langdon's nomination on a prolabor and anitmachine platform. Gillett, with solid Republican support, won the governorship in a narrow victory made possible by Langdon's cut into Bell's vote.

Governor Gillett (1907–1911) ably directed state administrative affairs, but his middle-road style in political matters made him appear subservient to machine interests, compromising his integrity. The Southern Pacific, with a tight grip, pushed through pro-railroad measures and ruthlessly battered down railroad regulatory and other reform bills. One state senator remarked later that there was hardly a vote taken that "did not reflect Southern Pacific ownership, petty vengeance, or legislative blackmail."

The machine's rough performance proved to be its undoing. Two aroused newspaper editors reporting on the legislative session, Edward Dickson of the *Los Angeles Express* and Chester Rowell of the *Fresno Republican*, initiated a statewide reform movement which led to the formation, by the summer of 1908, of the League of Lincoln—Roosevelt Republican Clubs. The League was formed by assorted antimachine leaders to free the Republican Party from machine domination. It emphasized the party principles articulated so well by Lincoln, and supported Roosevelt's enlightened policies. By adroit tactics in the midterm elections it secured a bloc of lawmakers in the 1909 legislature for another reform effort. The outnumbered antimachine forces had their measures emasculated by machine forces, but they secured compromise railroad regulation and direct primary measures. As it turned out, the direct primary was a decisive factor in the next election.

The 1910 state election marked the final showdown between machine and antimachine forces. The new primary election law enabled reformers to bypass party boss devices in selecting delegates to party conventions and candidates for public office. In the Republican race, Hiram Johnson, the League candidate and a San Francisco lawyer who had won fame in the city's Graft Prosecution (see below), canvassed the entire state in his "Red Devil" automobile, pledging his crusading slogan: "Kick the Southern Pacific out of politics." The Southern Pacific, already befuddled by several strong candidates who could hardly be denied machine support, was unable to deal with the League's onslaught. The Democrats, dominated by reformers, nominated Bell, who now had Hearst's backing. In the general election, Johnson beat out Bell by a narrow margin, and the Republicans swept up state offices and the legislature. The Southern Pacific was not entirely undone in the final outcome, for there is evidence that Herrin delivered "a political kiss of death" to Bell by throwing him machine support so that Johnson might win over the more militant reformer.

ANALYSIS

Constitutional Convention

The constitutional convention that met at Sacramento in September 1878 was the second and last effort to redraft the state constitution. The legislature, in preparing the enabling measure, stipulated that three delegates be elected from each of the 40 senatorial districts, but conservative elements seeking to counter the apparent dominance of farmer and labor groups amended the original measure by adding 32 delegates elected at large (four from each of the eight congressional districts). Of the 152 delegates, 78 were elected as Non-Partisans, 51 as Workingmen, 11 Republicans, 10 Democrats, and 2 Independents. By occupation, 57 were lawyers, 39 farmers, 20 mechanics or laborers, 13 merchants, and the remainder scattered among other occupations. Most of the delegates were born in other states, predominantly the Northeast. Twenty were foreign born and only three California born. It was not a fully representative convention for the Latinos, Indians, and Negroes were absent. The convention represented a wide cross-section of the majority American-born white population.

Convention politics was dominated by the interplay of farmer, labor, and corporate groups. At the outset, it appeared that the farmers would be the dominant group and, together with the workingmen, would outnumber the corporate interests. Actually the farmers constituted the majority of delegates elected from local districts, but the addition of the 32 at-large delegates, of whom 22 were lawyers, gave the attorneys the numerical majority. The lawyers, mostly conservative, were well distributed among the organized groups. The farmer-oriented Non-Partisans, the largest group, actually comprised considerably more lawyers (38) than farmers (23) of the 76 delegates. The 51 Workingmen were mostly from San Francisco (30), and a bare majority were mechanics (27), but the remainder were sprinkled with sympathetic lawyers, merchants, farmers, and other supporters. Even the party tickets had an edge of lawyers over farmers and others. The occupational status of the delegates had an important bearing on their votes on the issues.

The 1878–1879 convention, unlike its 1849 counterpart, was notably lacking in outstanding leadership. Historian Carl Swisher gives us this picture of the situation: The lawyers were better at political manipulation and debating than at persuasive leadership. The Non-Partisan lawyers included the shrewdest party politicians and ablest corporation lawyers in the state—Joseph Hoge, the Democratic state chairman since 1869, and S. M. Wilson, Hoge's former law partner, an outstanding speaker and prominent attorney for the Central Pacific, Bank of California, and other corporations. The farmers, independent entrepreneurs inexperienced in politics, were unable to unite behind any leader. They were represented by such diverse types as the Non-Partisan delegates, like W. J. Tinnin, a merchant–miner politician from Trinity, and James Shafter, a lawyer-turned-dairyman from San Francisco; the Workingmen delegates, like Henry Larkin, a farmer politician and respected newspaper editor; and the Democratic delegate, H. C. Wilson, a big farmer from Tehama. The Workingmen's Party failed to elect men of political or intellectual ability, like Denis Kearney, James McClatchy, and Henry George, the latter two men prominent editors of prolabor newspapers. Their chief spokesmen were two San Francisco lawyers, men of abrasive manner and limited ability.

The convention first took up its organization. The leading contenders for president were Hoge, the choice of the Non-Partisan caucus, Larkin for the Workingmen, and Tinnin for a farmer group. After several ballots, Hoge by one vote beat out Tinnin, who had the combined farmer–workingman vote. President Hoge, in naming the 30 committees, gave most of the chairmanships to Non-Partisans loyal to the caucus, thus securing the convention from radical elements.

During the convention, the farmer, workingman, and corporation groups formed various combinations on specific issues. Farmers and workingmen, angered at tax inequities and corporation monopolies, combined on measures designed to curb corporation abuses. Since farmers and corporate groups have vested interests in property (land or stock securities), they united against measures of the workingmen which would have radically changed the existing order. Some groups broke from their caucus and joined other groups to work out compromises on controversial issues. Generally, anti-workingmen coalitions or the conservative-minded corporations and farmers were more cohesive combinations than the radical workingmen, who were too labor oriented to command wide support, and the farmers alone, who rarely voted as a single group. These temporary coalitions were the modus operandi in resolving basic issues and in drafting the new state constitution.

The basic issues of greatest concern to the convention delegates dealt with tax inequities, corporation abuses, land monopolies, government malpractices, and the Chinese. The tax issue was the most perplexing problem. The convention adopted numerous sections (18 compared to the one section in the 1848 constitution) related to taxes but directing special attention to two aspects: relieving farmers from double taxation in paying property taxes, and establishing a state board of equalization which would ensure that railroads and other corporations paid their share of the tax burden. The corporation issue focused primarily on railroad abuses. The convention enacted extensive restrictions (21 sections), including one establishing a railroad commission to regulate railroad rates. The land issue aroused strong sentiment but resulted in little action beyond expressing public policy in favor of small landholdings. Many delegates believed that the tax equalization provisions would take care of this matter, which later proved not to be the case. The Chinese issue called forth the lengthiest debate and produced the vaguest provision, leaving unclear the convention's position. The convention made little change in the basic governmental structure, but it adopted important modifications of the existing system. It prohibited the legislature from enacting special legislation, and expanded the state supreme court so it could better handle its workload.

The convention produced a constitution that was very much a

product of the times. Where the 1849 convention had focused on fundamental principles and a grand design for a future society, the 1878–1879 convention was preoccupied with remedying, in piecemeal fashion, persistent defects of the existing society. Where the founding fathers had confined their efforts to formulating organic law, the 1878–1879 delegates supplemented organic law with detailed provisions that resembled a code of laws rather than a constitution. The delegates in working out remedies to complex problems—the product of compromising conflicting group interests—produced an extremely lengthy and complicated constitution. Where the 1849 delegates had formed a society of whole cloth, the 1878–1879 delegates attempted to clean the soiled spots from the existing society.

Administration of Justice

The state judiciary underwent evolutionary changes in adapting to the growing state. The code commission, led by the talented Creed Haymond, completed its work in 1872, making California the first state to codify its laws. It consolidated constitutional and statutory laws into compact political, civil, and criminal codes, eliminating redundancies and making clarifications. The constitutional convention of 1878–1879 took up judicial reforms in response to public criticism. It expanded the state supreme court from four to six justices, replaced district and county courts with superior courts, and required justices to submit written decisions, thereby improving court procedures and remedying court abuses. These structural developments constitute the basis of our present judiciary system.

Legislative enactments and local practices further shaped the judicial system. The district attorney, already established as an agent of the state attorney general, developed as an agent of county government and the courts, as well. He was made legal counsel to the county board of supervisors (1872) so that the county could better handle increasingly complicated problems, and was made public prosecutor of cases before the superior court (1880). The grand jury became more conspicuous for its watchdog function than for its indictments. Its chief targets were governmental matters like county jails, indigent inmates, local expenditures, and taxes. Later it gave more attention to government corruption and vice.

The judicial process was tempered somewhat by the performance of judges, the mainstay of the court system. Judges were still nominated for election through the vote trading and boss manipulations of the party conventions. This often compromised their integrity and demeaned the office. They came under heavy criticism for the extreme inconsistency of sentences in criminal cases. An 1881 Assembly committee revealed that persons convicted for robbery had been sentenced to terms ranging from one year to life, while murderers were sometimes freed on legal technicalities and by virtue of their influence. Judges were also criticized for personal bias in civil cases. They were often charged with excessive favoritism toward corporate interests at the expense of less powerful farmer, small business, and labor groups. In constitutional and political matters, judges displayed a rigid conservatism in protecting the status quo. They showed a marked tendency to invalidate reform-oriented measures of the legislature and local governing bodies. The courts, of course, had a number of eminent jurists who served with great distinction, notably Stephen Field on the United States Supreme Court, Ogden Hoffman on the federal district court (these served down to the 1890's), and other luminaries in the state court system.

The Southern Pacific's influence was very much in evidence in the judicial process. It retained the most talented lawyers of the day to handle its affairs, as in the 1880's when it hired Creed Haymond as its chief attorney. It sometimes acted through machine bosses in selecting judges and juries. San Jose's county boss, James Rea, described how he supplied Herrin with lists of prospective jurors to enable the Southern Pacific attorneys to impanel sympathetic trial juries on railroad cases. Herrin, on at least one occasion, received advice from members of the state supreme court on presenting arguments before the lower courts in a case which might eventually be appealed to the high court. Although some justices sitting on the state's highest tribunal were known as outright railroad men, other justices were outstanding for their independence from railroad influence. Both groups of justices included men of mediocrity and men of talent.

Law enforcement reflected the unsettled ways of agrarian California in the period. The sheriff, city police, and town constables, though nonprofessional men and political appointees, apparently did tolerably well in maintaining the public peace in local areas. Their activities were supplemented by privately employed special police serving as peace officers, notably on downtown patrols for merchant groups and on railroads and steamship lines. Some public figures retained personal bodyguards. Justice Field's personal bodyguard killed David Terry in an 1877 confrontation between these bitter enemies.

Public lynchings and other mob violence were confined to occasional incidents of impromptu hangings, usually for heinous crimes and mostly in isolated communities. The worst of these outbursts was in 1871 in Los Angeles—then a frontier town—when hoodlum elements pillaged the Chinese quarter near the downtown plaza and killed eight Chinese. Vigilantism appeared in San Francisco in 1877 when that perennial vigilante chieftain, William Coleman, organized a committee of safety with a merchant militia to suppress labor rioters destroying Chinese establishments (see above). Vigilantism also appeared in Los Angeles in 1898 when a merchant group organized a committee of safety to tackle unsolved crimes, but disbanded when advised that they would be legally liable for false arrest. Of the 54 persons lynched in 38 recorded incidents between 1880 and 1910, well over three-fourths were murderers. Vigilantism slowly gave way to the orderly law processes of an increasingly stable agrarian society.

Fiscal Administration

The state fiscal system, completely revamped by the 1872 Political Code, had an auspicious start. The 1872 legislature enacted an entire new revenue law which strengthened the state board of equalization. The state board worked zealously with county boards of equalization to produce dramatic results: the state in 1872 produced its greatest amount of revenue to date from its lowest tax rate! Bankers, disenchanted with tax provisions, led a revolt which soon undid the promising reform. The state supreme court in 1873 found the state board usurping constitutional powers of the elective county boards and invalidated its actions.

Fiscal affairs soon reverted to their former state. Tax figures increased all along the line. State expenditures were at an all-time high. The state debt was hardly reduced and county debts again were on the rise. More glaring were the gross inequities in tax administration. Farmers paid double taxes on the full value of cultivated lands (they were taxed on real property and on the mortgage), whereas railroads and land speculators holding immense acreage of uncultivated land paid proportionally lower taxes, on the basis that unimproved land had little value. The *San Francisco Chronicle* complained that railroad land grants worth at least $100 million were practically exempt from taxation, while holders of six to eight million acres of cultivated land paid nine-tenths of the taxes. Actually, the Southern Pacific, then the state's chief taxpayer, paid few taxes on large amounts of its land because much of it comprised desert area. The indebted farmers suffered acute distress in these hard times.

The constitutional convention in 1878–1879 grappled with the perplexing tax problem. The outcome was a hodgepodge compromise. The farmers got out of paying the mortgage tax, which was to be paid by the lender, but they failed to obtain a usury provision which would prevent lenders from raising the interest above the going rate to cover such a tax. The railroads had to pay on their land and on mortgaged bonds secured by land, thus subject to double taxation. The Southern Pacific's support of this provision raised the suspicion that since it could not get its way, it connived at establishing a basis for securing court nullification later—as proved to be the case. Land speculators and other landholders now had to pay taxes by a provision that taxed cultivated and uncultivated land on an equal basis. The new constitution also established a state board of equalization to insure uniform administration of property taxes between state and county boards, but by such vague provisions as to require later court interpretation. The convention delegates failed to establish a fiscal system based on fundamental principles. Instead they wrote into the constitution expedient compromises which reflected their fiscal ignorance and their desire to shift the tax burden from constituent groups. The legislature and the courts, for years afterwards, had plenty of work "divining the intent" of the constitution makers when they wrote the elaborate fiscal provisions.

The hope that the constitution would settle the taxation issue was dashed by subsequent developments. The Southern Pacific, from the outset, successfully evaded or scuttled tax payments by delaying tactics or legal maneuvers. The delinquent railroad taxes (over one million dollars in 1882) seriously deranged county and state finances and caused much public concern. When the state supreme court in 1882 knocked down the Southern Pacific's claim of double taxation, the United States circuit court, represented by Justice Stephen Field, held the constitution void for assessing the railroad by a different method. Public outrage at the Southern Pacific's tax evasions prompted Governor Stoneman in 1884 to call a special session to act on the railroad matter, but the legislature adjourned without action. After 1890 favorable court decisions and renewed public agitation spurred by the Populists prompted Governor Budd and the legislature in 1893 to enact a reassessment measure by which the Southern Pacific was to pay back taxes from 1879. The railroad by 1896 had paid $2.5 million to complete payment, but it had enjoyed practically free use of such money and paid back a reduced amount in the end.

Public attention turned again to fiscal reform after the turn of the century. Governor Pardee launched a broad attack on the existing system, calling attention to the depleted state general fund and gross tax inequities. The 1903 legislature set up a commission with Professor Carl Plehn, the University of California's fiscal expert, which submitted the most comprehensive study of state finances to date. The commission's report (1905) roundly denounced the entire system. It pointed out that farmers paid 10 percent equivalent taxes while manufacturers paid 2 percent and banks practically none as a result of the distorted general property tax and unequal personal tax. It indicted the fiscal system as a "school of perjury" which worked a "special severity upon the poor and the greatest severity upon the honest."

After four more years of steady push over legal and political obstacles, the commission's recommendations were finally implemented into law by 1910. Under the new law, state and local taxes were separated. The state received its revenues from taxes imposed on corporations such as railroads, banks, and insurance and utility companies. Counties, cities, and towns collected taxes imposed on real and personal property (except banks). A foreboding note was the warning of some reformers who voiced their suspicions of the measure because of the strong campaigning by corporate groups in favor of it. The landmark tax reform, the first comprehensive revision since 1879, brought an end to a fiscal era.

This measure also represents a radical change of the basic concepts on which state finances had been based. Theoretically, a property tax paid by all groups on equal terms had been thought of as the mainstay of the entire fiscal system, at least in a democratic society. In practice, this had not worked. Now the property tax became the base of local revenues only, and was imposed in varying degree according to the needs of a particular municipality or county. The state, meanwhile, moved to entirely different sources. In essence, the simple, all-embracing rationale of an earlier day had been discarded.

Political Organizations

In this heyday of party politics, political machines held the power. These extra-legal bodies had inherent advantages of disciplined organization and ruthless methods with which ruling bosses could influence regular party and governmental affairs. Machine bosses were prime movers in local and state politics. Corrupt bosses had the added advantage of unscrupulous ways that often outdid principled party leaders and honest bosses who played the game of politics according to party rules. These unsavory bosses manipulated conventions and rigged elections by means of strong-arm tactics, vote buying, ballot-box stuffing, and other dishonest devices. They often outdid each other in trickery and underhanded tactics to beat out rivals and ward off reformers. Several factors conspired with corrupt bosses: the absence of state regulation of party activities, the preoccupation of men with economic opportunities, and the general apathy of people in political affairs. The wide prevalence of inefficiency, fraud, and scandal in governmental affairs was the inevitable result.

Local Machines

Party bosses of county and municipal machines generally set the tone of local politics. Perhaps no boss matched the corrupt machinations of San Francisco's Christopher Buckley. Buckley was the powerful Democratic boss, the first important citywide boss since Broderick's time, who dominated the politics of San Francisco during the 1880's. A colorful personality and a masterful organizer, he welded rival Democratic clubs into a tight personal machine manned by a spirited army of party workers and public officials known as Buckley's Lambs.

The Blind Boss (actually he was partially blind), with great finesse, used force and fraudulent methods to manipulate party primaries, local elections, and municipal government. He systematically plundered municipal offices of kickbacks, contracts, franchises, graft, and other emoluments with such effectiveness that he virtually escaped retaliation from rival bosses and city authorities. His graft and patronage extended to the courts and the schools, to federal and state civil service, and to just about every major business in the city. Some companies paid him legal fees and gave him inside tips on the stock market just to keep him honest (that is, faithful to their bargains). As a political broker, the Blind Boss was more a professional than a party boss, for he delivered the goods, whether votes or favors, to the highest bidder. From his power base in San Francisco, he gained a dominating influence in Democratic state councils and in the state government, and on occasion he was able to beat Southern Pacific bosses at their own game. San Francisco historian John Young described this autocratic boss as the "cunningest and most corrupt politician the West ever produced."

Many corporations expanding their enterprises after 1870 played a direct role in politics in order to promote and protect their business interests. As towns, cities, and counties grew, entrepreneurs of transportation, utilities, and other public-oriented enterprises became more generous in support of local bosses who would secure measures favorable to their business profits. In the legislature, corporation leaders with large financial resources were outdoing other groups in lobbying for public benefits. These corporate leaders sought franchises, direct subsidies, tax benefits, and other favorable measures. They also fought against government supervision of their activities, especially in regulating customer rates for their services.

The Southern Pacific was the biggest of these corporations. Indeed, it was just about the only statewide corporation just before the turn of the century. Its political machine enjoyed advantages of size, power, and wealth over local machines and other organized groups in influencing party and governmental affairs. Journalist Chester Rowell once described the Southern Pacific machine as "a business organization, paid by a business corporation, to do business with politics."

Political affairs of the railroad were generally masterminded by Collis Huntington of the Bit Four. After 1870 Huntington lived in the East where he could handle matters in Congress and direct California affairs through political aides. He conducted activities through an informal hierarchy of personal contacts. His chief lieutenants were talented lawyers and politicians, like W. W. Stow, Stephen Gage, and S. M. Wilson. Stow was the chief liaison with county bosses and other professional politicians who served as railroad programmers or campaign managers in county, district, and state party conventions, and with public officials in local and state government. Gage (Stanford's alter ego in company affairs) supervised legislative affairs in both California and Nevada. Wilson, a much respected corporation lawyer prominent in party and governmental councils, apparently handled special assignments. Huntington also relied on the company's field employees, notably land agents, district superintendents, and station masters, who were in a strategic position to oversee and even participate in local politics. Gage once remarked that the Southern Pacific "employed everyone who could pull a pound."

Huntington's chief efforts were directed at securing federal, state, and local franchises and subsidies for extending the Central Pacific lines and for constructing the Southern Pacific transcontinental system. He fought running battles in Congress to defeat both federal aid to rival railroads and funding bills designed to make the company pay back its federal loans. In the state legislature, he sought to elect favorable United States senators and to head off regulatory measures in an attempt to checkmate rival railroads and other challenges to his company's transportation monopoly. To achieve these ends Huntington relied on several methods. He lobbied for special measures, using direct bribery and personal pressure which ranged from polite persuasion to outright intimidation. He used prominent politicians (like ex-senator Gwin) and influenced important persons by putting them on the company payroll, paying legal fees, or giving them free railroad passes. He subsidized newspapers to advertise the company's position and educate the public—and sometimes to buy off newspaper opposition. These methods called for considerable financial outlay. The railroad between 1876 and 1884 paid out at least $500,000 annually for activities that were vaguely listed in the company's books as general and legal expenses. Huntington and his aides conducted their activities so secretly that it was years before the public had an adequate understanding of railroad operations.

In the 1890's Southern Pacific's political operations underwent a major change. Following Stow's retirement in 1893, Huntington appointed William Herrin, a brilliant young corporation lawyer to be the chief of the company's law department in charge of legal and political activities. Herrin centralized machine operations, so that his office was referred to as the political bureau. He replaced the personal approach and irregular methods of the Huntington–Stow regime with systematic arrangements, and refined the use of legal fees, business patronage, and railroad passes. Where Stow had concentrated railroad politics primarily on populous Northern California counties, Herrin extended Southern Pacific influence to local party and governmental bodies throughout the state. He forged the Southern Pacific alliances into a uniquely powerful combination—what Arthur McEwen called the "Associated Villainies." It comprised business allies to lend political and financial support, local machines and affiliated vice interests to contribute valuable grass-roots support, and professional politicians and company employees to do yeoman work. In putting the machine on a businesslike basis, Herrin wielded enormous power in the party apparatus and governmental system at the state level. The Southern Pacific machine under Herrin's leadership reached a peak of efficiency and durability unmatched by any other in the state—and by few, if any, in the country.

12 The Heyday of Private Enterprise

THE SETTING

The Entrepreneurs

California's entrepreneurs were a diverse group—Americans and foreigners, native born and immigrants—attracted to the open opportunities of the state. They were mostly of the middle class, but included an increasing number of well-to-do and wealthy men eager to develop new enterprises. They improved techniques of producing and distributing goods and services, making notable contributions in industry technology, business management, and marketing methods. They showed a ready disposition to organize collectively to coordinate their activities and secure government action. Finding California a fertile field for their talents, real and imagined, they exploited opportunities to the limit—of success or bankruptcy.

Small entrepreneurs were still the mainstay of the state's market economy, particularly in the rural areas where most people lived. Economic activity revolved mostly around local markets served by nearby entrepreneurs, though certain regional and national markets figured importantly. Rural communities were still self-contained economic entities. However, they showed increasing reliance on big entrepreneurs, who contributed considerably to community growth and stability.

The big entrepreneurs who assumed a commanding position in certain segments of the state's market economy were characteristically ambitious, aggressive, self-made men. What captains of industry, like Carnegie in steel and Rockefeller in petroleum, were doing at the national level, master entrepreneurs attempted to do in California. The Big Four owed their dominant position to their broad-based political machine and their virtual monopoly of the railroad at a time when railroads were preeminent in the nation's economic development. Although Huntington was the only man of outstanding ability among the Big Four, a group unity rare among the nation's tycoons lent them extraordinary strength. For individual achievement each was at least equaled by a half-dozen men, including the short-lived Ralston, Hayward in mining, Miller in cattle, Kohler in wine making, Donahue in iron manufacturing, and Hellman in banking. These men, based in San Francisco, made notable contributions in other fields as well as their own.

In overall achievement Lloyd Tevis exceeded them all. Long-time president of Wells Fargo, he made notable contributions in several areas and held his own against encroachments of eastern giants like Rockefeller. He even extended his operations outside of California, joining Haggin and Hearst to develop Montana's famous Anaconda copper mine and South Dakota's Homestake as the world's largest gold mine. Though a relatively unobstrusive person, he was an industrial capitalist probably unexcelled in the Far West.

Conspicuous in the state's economic development were the eastern giants. Among those invading the California field were Armour in meat packing, Du Pont in explosives, Rockefeller in petroleum, and Schwab in steel. These outsiders gained important toeholds in the California market, but seldom dominated the state's economic development.

Business Organization

Entrepreneurs in California, as elsewhere, continued to employ the variety of organizational devices for producing goods and services which they had begun to explore in the period prior to 1870. California growers, processors, and distributors of foodstuffs pioneered cooperative devices for surviving intense business competition. They and others formed into associations not only to launch their enterprises or to unite colleagues for controlling prices and other market conditions. They utilized such forms to eliminate merchant wholesalers and other middlemen who they thought were undercutting their hard-earned profits.

Industrial capitalists relied on the corporate device which was already being effectively used in banking, mining, and railroad enterprises. Corporations could amass large funds with which to acquire land, raw materials, a labor force, facilities and machines, and patents for inventions and techniques. The boss generally managed his enterprise personally, relying on superintendents to supervise territorial operations or functional units and foremen to direct actual operations. As corporations grew bigger, professional managers were hired to head the large staff of each operating division. Banking institutions were especially important in the development of these mammoth corporations. They not only supplied the enormous funds required for their expansion, but also often took an active part in their management, as well. Although outnumbered by proprietorships and partnerships, the corporation became, in the economist Thorstein Veblen's words, the "master institution."

As competition became intense, corporate groups sought ways to minimize ruinous conflicts or to attain monopolistic power. Some merged their operations by absorbing rival products or services of the same kind (horizontal merger), as the Big Four did in railroads. Others combined production, processing, and distribution functions (vertical merger), as Kohler did in California's grape and wine industry. At the national level, corporations developed new devices for monopolizing market areas. They became so powerful that they emerged as prime movers in the market economy.

DEVELOPMENT

These corporations did not go unchallenged. Aggrieved farmers, manufacturers, merchants, and allied groups fought them, aided by newspapers whose exposes of their malpractices whipped up public hostility. These discontented groups waged their battle against the railroads and other large corporations along several fronts in politics and in the economy at the national and state levels.

The 1870's

National attention focused on the expanding railroads and their battle with the farmer-oriented Granger movement. Railroad companies paced other corporations in the use of pools, or informal gentlemen's agreements, for cutting prices, dividing territories, or splitting profits. They pursued hard-line and discriminatory practices which antagonized various groups, such as charging merchant and farmer clients "all the traffic could bear," favoring big shippers with rebates at the expense of small farmers and other shippers, and keeping workers' wages at the lowest possible levels. The farmers hit back by developing the Grange (1867), a national organization which served as a vehicle for remedying their grievances. Under Granger guidance, local farmers formed cooperative facilities to provide services that would bypass middleman merchants as well as railroads. They also pressured state legislatures into imposing state regulation of railroad abuses. The railroads fought back, but the United States Supreme Court upheld the so-called Granger laws (Munn vs. Illinois, 1877), thus reaffirming state regulation of railroads. The courts ruled that pool agreements were not legally binding, so maverick rivals proceeded to break them. This contributed to intense battles among major railroad tycoons, including California's Big Four.

In California, farmers had running battles with the monopolistic practices of land speculators and water companies, but particularly with San Francisco merchants and the Southern Pacific over grain-shipping practices. Farmers began in 1870 to form local clubs which by 1872 merged with the State Grange, affiliated with the national organization. Local granges (64 by 1874) organized cooperative banks, storages, and produce and stock exchanges. They waged a bitter two-year war against Isaac Friedlander and other grain brokers by contracting with a New York shipping firm to carry their grain to the Liverpool market, but the firm's bankruptcy and Friedlander's countermoves brought their venture to a dismal end. They also entered politics (see below) where they secured a railroad commission for regulating freight rates and a state equalization board for making the Southern Pacific and other big landowners pay just shares of property taxes. The farmers revolt was the most conspicuous, but labor and merchant groups also reacted to depression conditions aggravated by corporation malpractices.

The 1880's

Railroads and other corporate groups rode high during the decade. The trust, pioneered by Rockefeller, emerged as a popular device for corporate control: Stockholders exchanged their shares (that is, their votes) for trust certificates so tycoons could control market operations. Public agitation increased against persistent railroad malpractices and the rapidly growing trusts. State railroad and trust regulation proved ineffective. When the United States Supreme Court reversed its position by invalidating state laws regulating railroads (Wabash case, 1886), Congress created the Interstate Commerce Commission (1887, hereafter ICC) to regulate railroad rates and prevent malpractices. It also adopted the Sherman Anti-Trust Act (1890), which prohibited conspiracies like trusts from monopolizing trade. These landmark measures inaugurated federal policy for regulating corporate enterprises but, as it turned out, they were not immediately effective.

California of the 1880's witnessed busy entrepreneurs pursuing opportunities opened by accelerated state expansion, especially into Southern California and the San Joaquin, and the return of prosperity. Public attention focused on two showdowns of the decade, both in the Central Valley. Farmers won their long war with hydraulic miners when the state supreme court outlawed the latter's operations which were desecrating Sacramento Valley farmlands. Henry Miller won his celebrated court case against James Haggin in the long legal battle over waters of the Kern in the San Joaquin, an important step in resolving the state's vital water rights problem. The Southern Pacific maneuvered its way out of congressional efforts to collect its railroad loan (the funding bill) and state attempts to collect railroad back taxes, despite embarrassing exposés of railroad malpractices. Like other corporations, it was enjoying a heyday of expansion.

The 1890's

The grim depression plunged the nation into a sharp economic decline that had serious repercussions. A wave of business bankruptcies and cutbacks was followed by farmer, labor, and merchant clashes with the railroads and other corporations. The farmers turned to politics, organizing the Populist Party as their vehicle to press the silver standard and other reforms. Labor unions resorted primarily to economic action, launching strikes against major corporations like Homestead Steel (1892) and Pullman railroad cars (1894). Corporate expansion continued unabated. Corporations utilized liberal state laws, pioneered by New Jersey, to form a holding company by which the parent company could acquire stock control of subordinate or subsidiary companies. The first great wave of corporation consolidations (1879–1893) came to a practical halt with the depression, but another wave started up again on an even bigger scale with the return of prosperity.

California's depression was no less excruciating, marked as it was by a statewide economic upheaval and major conflicts. Agrarian groups formed a state Populist Party to supplement the national movement for political reforms. Some turned to economic action, forming cooperative marketing organizations, notably the fruit growers and canners. Labor groups fought employer cutbacks in disorganized, sporadic local actions. Some tied their efforts to national labor movements under way in 1894. Unemployed workers formed a state contingent which joined Jacob Coxey's celebrated industrial march on Washington for federal help. Railroad workers struck the Southern Pacific to complement the midwestern railway union strike against Pullman railroad cars.

Merchant groups in the state's leading port cities waged a decade-long battle against the Southern Pacific's monopolistic grip. In San Francisco, the city merchants formed the Traffic Association (1891) to reduce Southern Pacific's high freight charges. They contracted with an independent steamship company to open a competing water route to eastern markets, and organized a railroad which completed an alternate line to the San Joaquin (1898). Both ventures brought only temporary relief and ended in failure. In Los Angeles, the local chamber of commerce spearheaded the attack to prevent the Southern Pacific from diverting congressional harbor improvement funds from Los Angeles' San Pedro port to the railroad-owned Santa Monica port. Congress resolved the conflict in 1896 when it designated an army engineering arbitration board; it decided for San Pedro. This turmoil did not deter corporate expansion, but it did lead to the rise of agrarian cooperatives and better-organized merchant associations as countervailing forces to corporate domination.

The 1900's

By the turn of the century the nation experienced general prosperity. Public attention focused on the growing giant holding companies that were dominating segments of the nation's economy, especially United States Steel (.1901), the first billion-dollar corporation, and Northern Securities (1901) a transportation combine that amalgamated two great western railroad empires—both companies backed by Morgan banking interests. President Roosevelt launched his celebrated trust-busting campaign, carefully distinguishing between good trusts which traded fairly and passed their economies on to consumers, and bad trusts which selfishly monopolized their wealth. The United States Supreme Court revitalized the Sherman Anti-Trust Act in support of federal prosecutions of Northern Securities (1904), Du Pont, Standard Oil, Southern Pacific, and over 40 other trusts. Congress followed up by enacting landmark measures for extending federal controls to check corporate malpractices.

California after 1900 experienced startling changes as a result of accelerating urbanism, maturing industries, and increasing government intervention. Oakland, Sacramento, Fresno, and San Diego were emerging as important manufacturing centers. All became inextricably involved with intensified area-wide industrial disputes between labor-management groups in Los Angeles and San Francisco. California enterprises, some with eastern financing, evolved into such giant organizations as the cooperative California Fruit Growers Exchange, the corporate Pacific Gas and Electric, and Union Oil. Competing seriously for the state's resources and markets were such eastern corporations as Bethlehem steel, Du Pont explosives, Standard Oil, and Western Pacific Railroad. The public reacted with mixed feelings: it marveled at the remarkable achievements of the big enterprises but was alarmed at their malpractices. The ICC's California investigation (1904) exposed Southern Pacific rebates to Miller and other big shippers. The San Francisco graft prosecution following the city's devastating earthquake (1906) revealed the evil alliance of party bosses and business tycoons. The legislature responded by enacting the 1907 Cartwright Act, the state's own anti-trust measure, which prohibited combinations and conspiracies in restraint of trade. It was modified by the important 1909 amendment which exempted from the act farmers' cooperative associations. The state's market economy was undergoing a basic shift, becoming evermore intricately enmeshed as a regional entity in the nation's market economy.

ANALYSIS

Land

Public Lands

Congress, in order to accelerate settlement of the public domain, enacted in the 1870's several measures for encouraging homesteads on marginal lands. The Timber Culture Act (1873), designed to encourage timber growth on prairie lands, gave each person who maintained 40 acres of trees free title to 160 acres. The Desert Land Act (1877), aimed at settling arid lands, gave each person 640 acres at a low price if he conducted water to it for reclamation. The Timber and Stone Act (1878) offered a settler at minimum prices 160 acres valuable for timber or stone but unfit for cultivation. Congress also set up a public land commissioner to strengthen administrative machinery but ignored pleas of federal land officials for additional authority, staff, and funds to administer these laws effectively.

The administration of federal laws, already subject to widespread abuses, now became blatantly bad. Individuals and corporations took full advantage of defective laws, inept or corrupt land officials, and easy opportunities to appropriate large amounts of public lands. Speculators took out entries and held them for long periods for profitable sale later, thus removing such lands for entry by actual settlers. Cattlemen, lumbermen, and oilmen used dummies to make homestead entries to acquire valuable pasture, timber, and petroleum deposits on designated agricultural lands in the public domain. They often made entry for title, used the grasses, cut the timber, drilled the oil, and then gave the despoiled lands back to the government instead of completing their titles. Within a week after passage of the Desert Land Act, claim for 50,000 acres of fertile arid land in Kern County was filed by 76 persons, all friends connected through business association with Senator Aaron Sargent, one of the bill's authors. The United States Land Commissioner in 1885 reported that only 5 percent of the land issued under the Timber Culture and Desert Land Acts actually went to bona fide settlers.

The mounting public protest against government land abuses built to a climax by 1890. A reform movement, spearheaded by assorted professional and civic groups, culminated in the General Land Revision Act adopted by Congress in 1891. This measure repealed the Timber

Culture Act, modified the Homestead Act (1862) and the Desert Land Act to eliminate loopholes, and authorized the president to withdraw forest lands from the public domain for preserving natural resources. Successive presidents withdrew large portions of forest lands. Congress, however, pressured by special interests, enacted compromise measures which often provided opportunities for speculators and others to acquire these lands by legal loopholes and outright fraud.

After 1900 Congress enacted other laws for distributing agricultural lands to help small settlers earn their livelihood. The Federal Reclamation Act (1902) provided settlers with 160 acres of arid public lands if they contributed payments to publicly financed water projects for irrigating their arid lands. The Enlarged Homestead Act (1909) allowed settlers to acquire larger tracts (320 acres with an additional 160 acres for homestead) in submarginal areas not well suited for farming. These land reforms checkmated some evils in land distribution, but they did not eradicate persistent frauds and other abuses which served to perpetuate the predominant pattern of large land acquisitions.

State lands, like federal lands, were also subject to gross mismanagement. The legislature was a battleground where speculators and entrepreneurs generally outdid the settlers on land laws. Speculators continued to work closely with land-office agents, using dummies and other corrupt schemes to acquire school lands and swamps. A United States land agent doubling as a state registrar acquired in Inyo County 137,000 acres of alleged swampland which, a legislative committee in 1874 reported, was so dry that it required irrigation for farm crops. The same committee found that for $400 someone had purchased 320 acres of land which contained a mine valued at over one million dollars. Several state surveyor generals were involved in major land scandals.

Private Lands

Public resentment of large private landholdings was widespread. Newspaper editors carried running campaigns against them, notably Henry George and James McClatchy, who used his *Sacramento Bee* to condemn the "giant evil of land monopoly." Aroused farmers in the reform-oriented Granger movement spearheaded antimonopoly planks in party platforms. The legislature conducted investigations and considered antimonopoly bills, but little came of them. At the constitutional convention, delegates argued long and loud over ways to curb large landholdings, but antimonopolists succeeded only in securing a mild expression of public policy. Then in 1879 Henry George published his popular classic *Progress and Poverty*, a searing indictment of big landowners who prospered at the expense of small, impoverished landowners. He popularized the single tax idea, by which a single tax on unimproved lands only would end speculation and unearned wealth. This highly controversial idea helped keep alive public sentiment against land monopolies in California.

Land disputes continued unabated. On the range, big and small landowners clashed in numerous confrontations over land titles and water rights, resulting in lengthy court litigation. Violence occasionally flared when cattlemen, sheepmen, and farmers resolved their differences by shootouts. In the celebrated Mussel Slough incident in Tulare County, settlers lured by glowing railroad advertisements (land as low as $2.60 an acre) took land with uncleared title and developed farms with irrigation works in the 1870's. When the railroad secured its title in 1878, it offered the land for higher prices ($17 to $40 an acre) and, on the settlers' angry refusal, sold it to two outsiders for $25 an acre. When the new owners, accompanied by the United States marshal, attempted to eject settlers one day in 1880, the "Battle of Mussel Slough" erupted, resulting in the deaths of the two owners and five settlers. Public indignation and rage persisted for years over this incident—apparently an isolated one—of overzealous railroad promotion, and over other large land acquisitions by speculators and developers.

The pattern of land distribution was complicated because of the diverse schemes for land development. Large landowners—individual or corporate—leased, rented, or sold their lands outright. They developed ranches, farms, and lumber, oil, and other enterprises directly, or subdivided their property for tract and town development. For example, the Irvines (father and son) leased lands to small and big tenants, augmented livestock with different field and orchard crops, sold tracts to town promoters (Laguna Beach and Newport Beach), and built their community of Irvine. Over a 15-year period Tevis and his partners (Haggin and W. B. Carr) systematically acquired public lands (swampland, desert land tracts), private lands (homesteads and ranchos), and railroad lands in the lower San Joaquin. They organized the Kern County Land Company (1890) for managing their enormous land empire—the largest and most sophisticated multi-land development of its day. Some of these large landowners made enormous profits, but a number of them—including William Chapman, the biggest of them all—went into debt or became insolvent. The benign Chapman eloquently defended the much-maligned land speculators, pointing out that they were important middlemen who converted the land to manageable sizes for entrepreneurs to buy and develop, as the government was not able to do. Such enlightened speculators and developers, however, were outnumbered by unscrupulous ones who ruthlessly exploited their lands for more narrow aims. Large landowners were prime movers in determining the form and shape of land development.

The much-ignored small farmers were another major element in land development. They were practical-minded men with an inherent love of land who accommodated their talents and traits to their adopted land. Confronted with high land prices and costly farming (irrigation, machinery, and transportation), they organized into cooperative groups to pool their resources and establish land colonies which eventually evolved into thriving rural communities. The land booms attracted a great number of "dirt farmers" who actively worked their lands, as well as the much publicized well-off "capitalist farmers" who invested in costly self-sustaining orchard tracts of modest sizes. The latter were concentrated mostly in Southern California where their land colonies evolved into substantial towns like Azusa, Glendale, and Pasadena. The San Joaquin attracted a wide variety of foreign settlers: Armenians, Italians, Germans, Scandinavians, Swiss, Syrians, and Japanese. Some had religious ties (Lutheran, Methodist, Mennonite); others had social ties (Lodi Temperance and Kaweah communist colonies). Individual settlers less inclined to join organized settlements and unable to buy land first rented land or worked as farm laborers, then acquired their own lands which they built into sizable holdings. The small settler contributed significantly to California's private-land pattern.

The small and large individual and cooperative ventures made for a more complex land pattern that revealed a remarkable capacity to adapt to changing conditions and local circumstances. Farmlands, which constituted 11.5 percent of total land acreage in 1870, rose to 28 percent in 1910. While the numbers of farms increased threefold, large landholdings still dominated, particularly in the Central Valley and Southern California. Unimproved lands, held mostly for speculative purposes, also increased, from six million acres in 1870 to eleven million acres in 1910. The varied ways in which entrepreneurs acquired public and private lands and their multiple uses for development provided the basis of the exceedingly complex land pattern that exists today.

Agriculture

Agriculture, the primary sector of the state's economy, was transformed by phenomenal growth and the intensive cultivation of many products. Factors contributing to this development were: population inflow and growing communities, which expanded local markets; improved techniques for producing, processing, and marketing products; widespread irrigation which permitted intensive crop production; and expanded railroad and shipping lines that opened up national and world markets. Ranchers and farmers concentrated on cash crops and diversified their operations by producing various combinations of livestock and crops. As the state agricultural society, with its affiliate state and county fairs, became less effective in dealing with new problems, ranchers and farmers formed product-oriented associations to deal with obstacles to the production and marketing of specialized products. They called upon the University of California and state and federal agencies for practical and technical help in crop production. They also received valuable information from farm journals like the *California Farmer* and *Pacific Rural Press*.

Livestock

The cattle industry underwent revival and transformation after 1870. Fencing laws, which made ranchers instead of farmers assume the costly burden of fence building, forced ranchers to alter livestock operations. Some enclosed their lands with the inexpensive barbed wire (patented 1872) and irrigated them for pasturage and forage crops. Others moved to unsettled areas to utilize the open ranges, taking their cattle to Sierra plateaus for summer feed. Henry Miller, still the state's leading cattleman, pastured his 100,000 head of cattle on a million acres of land in 11 California counties, Nevada, and Oregon. Tevis's Kern County Land Company, which ranked second, developed extensive operations, including breeding calves in Arizona and New Mexico and fattening the cattle in California for slaughterhouses in Los Angeles and Chicago. Chicago packers gained ascendancy by integrating California cattle and meat markets into their nationwide system. Led by Philip Armour and Gustavus Swift, they shipped California and other western cattle to their Chicago stockyard and meat-packing plants to serve the expanding eastern market. On the cattle range, the cowboys enjoyed their heyday made familiar to us in motion pictures and on television: the hardy cowmen distinguished by their Stetson hats, Levis with leather chaps, holstered Colts, world-renowned Visalia saddles, and famous western stock horses.

Other livestock industries experienced significant developments. The booming sheep industry reached its peak in 1876, then was nearly wiped out by droughts during the next two years. Many sheepman, like Irvine, sold out and turned to other enterprises, while big sheepmen like the Flints increased their flocks to enormous sizes, producing mutton for San Francisco and Chicago meat packers and wool for California and eastern textile mills. A thriving dairy industry was built up by immigrant Danish, Swedish, and Swiss dairymen in the Bay and Delta areas. Horse raising developed into a specialized industry, including huge mules developed for heavy field work and freight transportation, and race-horses bred for wealthy sportsmen like Haggin and Stanford. Poultry emerged as a thriving industry after 1900, centering around Petaluma ("the world's egg basket") and Sacramento.

Grain

Wheat, the state's chief crop through most of this period, was stimulated by the pressing demands of European markets. Local farmers and manufacturers, particularly in the San Joaquin Valley, designed and produced field machines to accelerate production of bonanza crops. Huge mechanical combines included gang plows attached to seeders for cultivating the soil and harvesters for reaping, threshing, and sacking grain in a single operation. Steam engines with cleated iron wheels were hauling gang plows and wagons after 1870—a contemporary described one of these smoke-belching road locomotives as a "steamboat hunting for water." Benjamin Holt of Stockton and Daniel Best of San Leandro contributed important farm-machine innovations; the former invented the caterpillar tractor (1904). Most farmers still used horse-drawn combines even after the amazing steam-powered machines came into popular use after the mid-1880's—ironically at a time when wheat was in a decline. These California inventions spearheaded a revolution in farm machinery and agricultural technology.

Wheat growers soon developed highly productive, large-scale field operations. Hugh Glenn, known as the "wheat king of the world," worked his 55,000-acre Colusa ranch with a 750-man force. Plowing was done by many eight-mule teams pulling gang plows in formation so they could cut 100-foot swaths during a continuing one-day trip around a large field. Harvesting was carried out by numerous combines which fed

Steam harvester combine operating on wheat ranch circa 1906.

monstrous, movable steam-threshing machines. In 1880 Glenn chartered 20 ships to deliver his crop to the Liverpool market.

Wheat was produced for both the California and Liverpool markets. San Francisco and Oakland were the chief ports until the 1880's, when the Bay ports were surpassed by ports on the Carquinez Straits where A. D. Starr, a Vallejo mill owner, built Wheatport (now Crockett) in 1884 as the world's largest granary operation. He was outdone several years later by George McNear, a San Francisco grain merchant who developed Port Costa as another enormous combined warehouse–mill operation. By 1890 California's wheat trade was already in decline. Wheat growers sold their lands or converted them to irrigated fruits and other profitable ventures. McNear absorbed Starr and competed with Austin Sperry, Stockton flour maker, in merging other granary operators until 1910, when Sperry Flour absorbed McNear. Wheat, the state's great pioneer cash crop, had lost its primacy to the fruit industry.

Fruits

The fruit industry grew steadily after 1870, until by the mid-1880's it was gaining on wheat in importance. Fruit growers experimented with seeds and plants to find the ones which grew well in local soils. They greatly benefited from allied groups. The pioneer Riverside colony set up in 1870 demonstrated the success of the cooperative community for raising fruits, and paved the way for many such communities, especially in Southern California. A member of the colony secured from the United States Department of Agriculture the orange tree species from Brazil (Washington navel) that was the basis of the state's citrus industry. Technical assistance was provided by commercial nurserymen, like Luther Burbank of Santa Rosa who was world renowned for plant experimentation, by University of California professor Eugene Hilgard, a prominent soil expert, and by governmental agencies. When growers suffered devastating damage from dreaded plant diseases, they pressured the state legislature into establishing state and county agencies to set up quarantine programs for exterminating infected plants. Only after years of dealing with technical and other difficulties and with group conflicts were fruit growers able to develop a workable system of cooperative effort to achieve successful productive enterprises.

Fruit processors and shippers, too, encountered nagging problems which were overcome by persistent effort. The canners made important technological breakthroughs, like the steam pressure cooker (1874). Mark Fontana, a leading canner, conceived the idea of labeling fruits (Del Monte Brand) to pioneer a trend. E.T. Earl, who emerged as the biggest shipper, pioneered rail shipments of fresh fruits to eastern markets (1876) and produced an improved refrigerator car (1891) to prevent fruit spoilage. Such innovative men assumed leadership in the field.

The fruit industry did not become stabilized until after a long complicated trade war involving California growers, canners, and shippers with invading eastern giants like Armour and Swift. Armour teamed with Southern Pacific to form Fruit Growers Express (1895), and it took over Earl Fruit Company (1901). The Santa Fe provided an outlet for shunned independent grower–processor groups. Fontana with allies formed the California Fruit Canners Association (1899), which consolidated major canners to control much of the processing of canned and dried fruits. Citrus growers broke new ground by forming a regional federation of local growers association (1895) for producing and packing fruit. This evolved into the statewide California Fruit Growers Exchange (1905, hereafter CFGE). As the nation's largest cooperative, CFGE became famous for its innovative campaign for selling its trademarked Sunkist oranges. Other grower groups which followed suit included the deciduous fruit growers, who organized the California Fruit Exchange (1901). Fruits, led by grapes, were the state's top crop in 1910, while fruit canning ranked third among the state's manufactures. The basic pattern—large-scale organization of small and big operators—established in this period remains much the same today.

Mineral Resources

Gold

Gold mining continued to be a thriving industry, although it declined in relation to agriculture and other expanding industries. Quartz mining, located mostly in the Central Sierra, was a risky business. Out of the 500-odd quartz companies operating in 1880, Hittell estimated that fewer than 80 were making a profit. Among the larger companies dominating production was that of Alvinza Hayward.

Hydraulic mining, centered in the High Sierra, was the big boomer of the period, but it became victim to its own spectacular success. Mine operations washed great volumes of dirt—gravel—sand debris down mountain streams into the Sacramento River where it raised river bottoms, impeding navigation, and laid deposits on farmlands, ruining fertile soil for cultivation. Angry farmers and merchants fought a long battle with miners in the newspapers, the legislature, and the courts. The state supreme court in 1884 resolved the conflict by prohibiting hydraulic operations in a remarkable action which, in effect, outlawed a major industry because it was injurious to the public interest.

Dredge mining, after years of sporadic attempts, finally came into its own near the turn of the century. It started up in 1898 after a San Francisco firm developed a practical dredge consisting of a long boom with buckets which scooped river-bottom debris onto barges where the gold was separated out for mill processing. Dredging companies, operating mostly on the Sacramento River tributaries, were highly profitable ventures. They illustrate the innovative ways of California entrepreneurs.

Silver

The Nevada Comstock, the world's greatest silver strike at that time, continued to be essentially a California venture. The Comstock underwent another boom in the 1870's marked by a series of bonanza strikes, remarkable engineering feats, and company manipulations which milked numerous small investors and made enormous fortunes for the few owners. The Bank Crowd, which controlled the Comstock, split in 1871 when Alvinza Hayward and J. P. Jones, in a high level double-cross, undermined the Ralston–Sharon leadership. Before the end of the decade, both were outdone by the Irish Four (James Fair, James Flood, John Mackay, and William O'Brien), a remarkable quartet of San Francisco brokers and Comstock superintendents. Others who amassed great fortunes in the Comstock were George Hearst, William Stewart, and Adolph Sutro—all of whom became prominent California financiers. Sutro's famous three-mile tunnel into Mt. Davidson to drain water and ship out silver was an engineering marvel. The Comstock profoundly affected California's economy. It greatly stimulated economic development but also contributed to the unstable conditions of the 1870's.

Petroleum

Petroleum developed from slow, steady growth to emerge later as the state's ranking industry. In the 1870's and 1880's, professional oilmen and skilled promoters, backed by local entrepreneurs and San Francisco financiers, competed and cooperated in developing oil prospects. Drillers made slow headway in producing oil, concentrating mostly in Ventura's Santa Clara Valley ("cradle of the state's oil industry") and later in Los Angeles's Pico Canyon and the lower San Joaquin. Refiners distilled liquid petroleum mostly into kerosene for illumination and into lubricating oils. Out of these pioneer decades emerged two leaders. Pacific Coast Oil (1879), a Tevis enterprise, integrated oil production with its large refinery in Alameda, near Oakland. Union Oil (1890), involving Ventura landowner Thomas Bard and former Pennsylvania oilman Lyman Stewart, produced oil for its Santa Paula refinery.

Then followed two decades of startling oil discoveries that led to vigorous competition and rapid expansion of the industry. Chemists were developing gasoline and oil fuels for automobiles, steamships, and railroad engines, and for heating plants and industrial machinery. In Los Angeles, Edward Doheny, a lawyer-turned-prospector, and his partner produced oil from La Brea tar pits (1892), touching off the first of California's fabulous oil booms. Oil wells were dug so close, so a story goes, that tools lost in one well were fished out from another. Shortly afterwards, the San Joaquin burst out as another bonanza oil field which replaced Los Angeles as the state's leading producing area.

Then came the battle for the California fields. Rockefeller's Standard Oil by 1895 entered California to monopolize national production as it had refining and distribution. It absorbed Pacific Coast Oil (1900) and built refineries at Point Richmond and El Segundo to process oil from the San Joaquin and Los Angeles fields. Union Oil, headquartered in Los Angeles, set up a rival system with refineries at Oleum and San Pedro. In Los Angeles and the San Joaquin, Doheny and other independent operators organized their own systems. The Southern Pacific and Santa Fe railroads, which had become heavy oil users and carriers, now leased their properties to oilmen and soon produced their own oil. The big companies played the oil game hard and rough, riding roughshod over weaker rivals. The California companies, big and small, stymied whatever intention Standard Oil had to dominate completely the state's oil industry.

Other Minerals

There was a remarkable, but uneven, development of other minerals. Coal, still a major fuel for steam engines, heating, and cooking, inspired local entrepreneurs to develop deposits at Mt. Diablo, shipping out of Pittsburg to counteract the high costs of imported coal until the 1893 Depression. A coal discovery in Fresno County in the 1890's led the Southern Pacific to establish a rail line and coaling station, later named Coalinga. Borax, discovered in 1881 near Death Valley, proved useful for iron welding, meat preservation, and soap. It passed from the control of William Coleman, the San Francisco merchant prince, to Francis "Borax" Smith, a Nevada prospector whose legendary 20-mule teams hauled the mineral across the Mojave, and eventually to a British syndicate. By 1910 California was producing 40 kinds of construction, industrial, and precious minerals, making it the nations's chief mineral producer.

Timber Resources

Pioneer lumbermen developed important innovations that paved the way for greater development of the industry. Among the improvements that revolutionized the industry were John Dolbeer's versatile donkey steam engine (1881) for hauling logs out of mountainous areas to the mills. San Francisco financiers and, after 1880, midwestern lumber barons who faced depleting timber stands at home entered the field to compete in

Donkey engine in the Redwoods, Mendocino County, 1894. The powerful upright steam boiler-engine was used to haul logs piled on slope onto railroad flatcar to right of men in foreground.

the growing industry. They developed elaborate systems comprising complex machinery, manufacturing plants, huge lumberyards, and extensive transportation facilities. Some invested heavily to develop large-scale organizations for integrating logging, lumbering, and marketing operations to overcome the unstable conditions and fluctuating prices of the expanding industry.

Lumbering continued to retain its distinctive regional character, conditioned by the type of timber and local entrepreneurs. In the upper Sacramento Valley, a San Francisco group headed by Alvinza Hayward absorbed a local company and built an enormous system by which pine timber was cut and moved over 150 miles of flumes and 23 miles of tramway to its ten sawmills, and then shipped out to Sacramento and San Francisco market centers. The Connecticut-based Diamond Match Company took over the operation (1907) to supplement its nationwide system. Diamond Match earned a reputation for enlightened forest management and lumbering practices. In the San Joaquin, a San Francisco entrepreneur acquired giant sequoia timber through shady deals, and cut these great redwoods for his large Sanger mill, reducing the famous Converse Basin to tree stumps—a must-see for Sierra hikers today. Ironically the company went broke and was taken over by Hume Bennett, a big Michigan company.

The Northwest maintained its leadership in the state lumber industry. Pioneer lumbermen, like Dolbeer, ruled supreme in their local bailiwicks, exploiting their unique redwood product which resisted decay, fire, and shrinkage. Midwestern lumbermen appeared after 1880 and soon set up large-scale operations, notably Union Lumber at Fort Bragg, Pacific Lumber at Scotia, and A. B. Hammond. These three companies paced surviving family enterprises, like Dolbeer, by forming a joint marketing firm (1896) to secure a virtual monopoly of the Northwest redwood industry. The Southern Pacific in 1907 acquired a pioneer mill to produce its own railroad track ties, another example of vertical integration.

By 1910 lumbering was the state's leading industry. California ranked fifteenth among the 48 lumber-producing states, but it ranked first in redwood and high in pine and fir. The state also had the highest concentration of timberland ownership in the nation: ten companies owned 2.4 million acres, led by Southern Pacific, Hammond, Union, and Hume Bennett. The expanding industry was on the threshold of even greater expansion.

Forest Conservation

Intense logging operations, wasteful lumbering practices, and destructive fires led to rapid depletion of timberlands, evoking rising public protest. Prominent leaders—such as John Muir at Yosemite—called attention to beautiful areas threatened by despoliation. Their efforts led to California's brief experiment with a state forestry board (1885–1893), the nation's first. Forest conservation took root in 1890 when Congress assigned over a million acres in Yosemite and Sequoia areas as a park or forest reserve and authorized the President to set aside other public lands with timber stands for federal reserves (see above). The President, by the end of the decade, had set aside over 8.5 million acres in California alone.

There followed an intense battle over the public timberlands. Conservationists fought lumbermen, cattlemen, sheepmen, and speculators over the free use of public forest lands for timber, grazing, and other purposes. Even the conservationists were divided between those led by John Muir, who urged forest preservation, and those headed by Gifford Pinchot, the brilliant government forestry expert who urged scientific forest management for use as well as for preservation. Out of the battle came several landmark measures. Congress in 1897 set up what became the United States Forest Service, headed by Pinchot to manage the forest reserves. It enacted the Forest Homestead Act (1906) which allowed settlers to acquire 160 acres of agricultural lands in the forest reserves for homesteads. The United States Forest Service after a hard political and legal battle successfully implemented the new concept of conservation in administering the immense federal forest reserves in California and elsewhere.

California conservation was closely linked with the national movement. Extensive campaigning was carried on by local groups like the Sierra Club (organized by Muir in 1892) and the California Water and Forest Association (1899), a statewide amalgamation of local chambers of commerce, major newspapers, and prominent business, government, and university leaders. The conservation-minded Governor Pardee spurred the legislature, which in 1905 set up a state forestry board and state forester (a Pinchot man) to administer a program for fire prevention in the state's forest and park areas. The counties, which still had primary responsibility for forest areas, pioneered in intercounty efforts at firefighting and in replanting cut timber and fire-burned areas for watershed protection (1907). Such conservation efforts were beset by serious problems, notably the inexperience of government agencies, flagging support of the legislature, resistance of many lumber companies, and persistent frauds resulting in occasional scandals. Nevertheless, California conservation had achieved an impressive record by 1910 as state and federal programs were speeding the transition from free exploitation to careful use and scientific management, ushering in a new era in the state's lumber industry.

Water Resources

Water Rights

The rapid development of the Central Valley and Southern California after 1870 brought to the fore problems of irrigation, reclamation, and city water supplies—all inextricably interwoven with each other and with water rights. The dual system of water rights based on the riparian and appropriation doctrines (see Chapter 9) was the focus of bitter group conflicts. Miners, farmers, ranchers, and lumbermen, along with land and water companies, battled among and against each other for their share of water so important to their enterprises. A major showdown came in the long legal battle between rancher Henry Miller's riparian rights and land developer James Haggin's appropriation rights to waters of the Kern

River. The state supreme court in its longest decision ever (1886) upheld Miller, thus affirming riparian rights over appropriation rights.

The court decision only provoked further action. Aroused farmers prevailed on the legislature to enact the Wright Act (1887) which authorized farmers to form a public irrigation district through which they could exercise appropriation rights over riparian rights to secure water (using the power of eminent domain). The two parties in the Kern River controversy reconciled their differences in the Miller-Haggin Agreement (1888) involving 31 companies and 58 individuals, by which they shared use of the river water—an agreement still in effect today. Shortly afterward, Kern County Land Company was operating a vast canal network for farmer and rancher groups. While riparian rights remained the governing rule for resolving water conflicts, different groups worked out various accommodations to secure needed water, demonstrating a capacity for innovation and compromise.

Irrigation

Landowners and water companies, big and small, developed various types of irrigation projects, tapping mountain watersheds, river tributaries, and underground water tables. Each region developed distinct patterns. In the Central Valley, the San Joaquin and Kings River Canal Company (1874) was the most pretentious of large-scale projects in the area. It erected a dam for irrigating 100,000 acres of arid lands on the west side of the San Joaquin, a project costing over one million dollars which was taken over by Miller. In the Sierra, the South Yuba Canal and other water companies hard hit by the demise of hydraulic mining in the mid-1880's, adapted their systems to supply irrigation water for foothill farmers.

Southern California experienced imaginative, varied projects which rapidly transformed its arid lands into fertile agricultural areas. George Chaffee, a self-taught engineering genius, developed the idea of mutual water companies (landowners had equal shares of land and water) and built his model communities at Etiwanda (1882) and Ontario (1882), setting a trend for many farmer-sponsored irrigation districts. He also developed a plan carried out by a private canal company for tapping the Colorado below Yuma to bring water to settlers moving into the Imperial Valley's desert basin. (The Colorado, in an unprecedented flood rampage in 1904, broke through the company's flimsy headgate, poured into the valley, and converted the dry Salton Sink into the Salton Sea!)

Irrigators relied heavily on artesian wells, the source for two-thirds of irrigated lands around 1900. Even the legendary rainmakers were sometimes called into service, usually in severe drought years. The most celebrated of these water magicians was the eccentric Charles Hatfield, whose contraption on a Los Angeles farm in 1905 produced an inch of rain over a five-day period! Such freak efforts are burlesqued by modern-day writers but, as author Remi Nadeau points out, they reflect the deadly serious business of water development which could make or break men and communities.

After years of public agitation, government projects were forthcoming after the turn of the century. The United States Department of Agriculture, through Elwood Mead, an eminent irrigation authority, completed the most comprehensive investigation of the state's irrigation (1901). Congress in 1902 enacted the Federal Reclamation Act, dubbed the grand charter for public reclamation in the arid West. This act provided federally financed projects to control floods and to irrigate small tracts up to 160 acres—to be paid for by public land sales and water charges to consuming farmers. The Yuma project, sponsored by Senator Thomas Bard and completed in 1909, was the first federal venture for irrigating California lands. It was the model for western reclamation projects.

Reclamation

Destructive rampages of the Sacramento River aroused public attention after 1870. The river's periodic overflow flooded large areas, ruining town property, submerging agricultural lands, and raising river bottoms with silt debris which obstructed river navigation. Individual landowners and private companies built up dams and levees (then five to seven feet high) to drain water, reclaim land, and prevent future flooding. The legislature occasionally authorized local reclamation projects, and Congress in 1878 began appropriating funds to improve the river's flow and navigation. These piecemeal efforts, public and private, were hardly effective. Periodic floods continued to wreak devastating damage.

Eventually, growing public pressure led to government remedial action after 1890. The California Debris Commission, a state–federal agency, was set up by 1894 to improve river control. At first the commission was restricted to piecemeal projects because of the legislative wrangling of special-interest groups. After a decade of terrible floods and more public agitation, the commission in 1910 sponsored an imaginative plan for constructing a levee-flanked canal to carry flood waters around Sacramento (the present-day bychannel), and other extensive projects for improving the river flow. Haphazard, piecemeal projects were giving way to more promising achievement by government efforts.

Municipal Supply

Growing towns and cities encountered problems of water supply to serve their increasing population, expanded utilities (such as firefighting and sewerage), new industries, and surrounding agriculture. Private companies continued to build and expand local water systems, utilizing river and underground sources for supply, dams and reservoirs for storage, and flumes, ditches, and pipes for distribution. Company officers were frequently in cahoots with public officials and party bosses who got them their franchises and favorable water rates.

By the turn of the century, the larger cities had to deal with the fact that private water systems did not adequately meet their growing needs. In San Francisco, local leaders for years attempted to implement plans to expand water supplies, but the Spring Valley Water Company defeated any such plans which threatened its monopoly. When the city's new charter in 1900 authorized a municipally owned water system, Mayor James Phelan spearheaded the move to convert Hetch Hetchy Valley in Yosemite National Forest into a reservoir to supply the city. Federal officials delayed taking action as public outcry came from John Muir and other conservationists who protested the drowning of the beautiful valley. With backing from President Roosevelt and Gifford Pinchot, the city in 1908 finally secured federal approval for the Hetch Hetchy project, only to be held up the next year when the project became entangled in national politics (the celebrated Pinchot–Ballinger controversy). It took over two decades for the city to complete its much-needed municipal water system.

Los Angeles, down to the turn of the century, was served by a private water company. When the company's lease expired in 1898, the city, after a four-year legal battle, took over the company operation and converted it into the municipal water company, headed by William Mulholland, former company superintendent, When the city faced a severe water shortage caused by burgeoning population and several years of drought, the aggressive Mulholland launched a public campaign (1905) to supplement the water supply by carrying water from the Owens Valley in the Sierra to Los Angeles by aqueduct. Then followed an intense decade of bitter public controversies. One focused on a syndicate (including E. T. Earl, H. G. Otis, and Moses Sherman) which acted on inside information to obtain adjoining San Fernando Valley land that stood to gain enormous water advantages. The other controversy focused on Owens Valley settlers who fought against diversion of their valley water. After a bitter battle involving high-level chicanery by some Los Angeles leaders and federal officials, the Mulholland group, with cooperation from the Roosevelt–Pinchot group and the city's business elements, carried the project. Mulholland began construction of the remarkable 233-mile aqueduct (completed in 1913) and was already laying foundations for a municipal system that would supply public hydroelectric power as well.

Public water policy and programs by 1910 were in transition. Water projects shifted from haphazard development of individual projects to comprehensive planning of coordinated projects for multiuse and development. The classic showdowns between public and private interests, and between urban and rural interests, had profound consequences for the state for years afterward.

Fuel and Power

Gas, electric, and water-power facilities underwent phenomenal expansion all over the nation. Inventors and scientists paved the way with new devices and improved models, notably Thaddeus Lowe's process for gaslight fuel (1873), Charles Brush's electric-arc lighting system (1877), and Thomas Edison's electric incandescent lamp (1879–1881), followed a decade later by George Westinghouse's electric motors and the coil transformer that made possible high-tension electricity. Californians also made significant contributions, among them Henry Pelton, who devised the double-bucket water wheel (1880) for producing water or electric power for mining machinery, town lighting, and the like, and George Chaffee, who built the West's first hydroelectric plant (Etiwanda, 1882). Entrepreneurs teamed up with inventors and engineers in building up the utility companies which manufactured gas fuel and electric power for heat, lighting, and operating machinery.

In California, fuel and power sources urgently needed for growing cities and expanding industries were developed in a short time. Cut-throat competition among the early companies worked hardships on communities, who soon demanded and got government regulation: the

1879 Constitution provided for municipal regulation of public utilities. Gas utilities enjoyed steady, unchallenged growth in the 1870's, but felt growing competition from electric utilities after 1880. Eastern companies representing the Lowe, Brush, Edison, and Westinghouse interests invaded the California field after 1880. From the mid-1880's these local and outside companies were cooperating and competing for local, and then regional, markets, combining gas and electric systems and striving to secure monopolistic control which they considered vital to their survival. San Francisco illustrates a common pattern. George Roe, who pioneered electric companies in the Bay City and Northern California towns, joined forces with New York Edison (predecessor of present-day General Electric) to form a new company in 1891. It soon combined with Donahue's pioneer gas company to form San Francisco Gas and Electric (1896). C. O. G. Miller, after job experiences with the Lowe and Siemen patents, organized Pacific Lighting (1886) as one of the earliest holding companies; it acquired gas and electric companies mostly in the south. In the Sierra, John Martin and Eugene de Sabla pioneered large-scale hydroelectric development with financial backing from a New Yorker (John Colgate, the toothpaste manufacturer). They built powerhouses on the Yuba forks (1896–1899) which carried high-voltage electricity 147 miles to Oakland—the world's longest transmission line at the time. The remarkable feats of these promoter–engineer–financier partnerships owed much to nature's own contribution—local water and the Sierra's snow-capped peaks.

The decade after 1900 witnessed the consolidation of these local groups into the great present-day regional gas and electric companies. In Northern California, the Martin–de Sabla group, backed by New York bankers, consolidated Sierra facilities and city systems, including San Francisco Gas and Electric, into Pacific Gas and Electric (1905, hereafter PGE). PGE was a holding company operating a vast utility system comprising 19 plants serving 22 counties—then the world's largest hydroelectric system. E. T. Earl and his brother organized a company (1902) to bring hydroelectric power from the Feather River to Oakland; it became Great Western Power (1906), member of a New Jersey holding company, to become a powerful rival to PGE. In the south, the San Francisco-based Pacific Lighting consolidated many small companies into Southern California Gas and Southern Counties Gas, while another group organized local electric companies into Southern California Edison (1909). By 1910 California had a matured, highly developed utility system—the basis of its present setup—meeting the state's basic fuel and power needs.

Manufactures

The manufacturing industry experienced slow, steady growth. It continued to serve agriculture, mineral, lumber, petroleum, and transportation enterprises, supplying tools and machinery for producing goods and processing raw materials into finished products for markets at home and abroad. When eastern and British manufacturers increasingly entered the California field, local manufacturers had either to convert their plants to new products, consolidate with rivals, or abandon their plants. San Francisco continued to be the chief manufacturing center, although industrial dispersion was already under way by 1880 when iron, explosives, and other manufacturers located or relocated on East Bay waterfront sites from Oakland to the Carquinez Straits. Important regional manufacturing centers developed in Oakland, San Jose, Sacramento, Stockton, Fresno, Los Angeles and San Diego.

Ironwork was the barometer that reflected changing conditions in the manufacturing industries. As mining declined, ironmakers concentrated on products for agriculture, lumber, petroleum, transportation, and other expanding industries. The new trends were reflected by A. S. Hallidie, who expanded his wireworks in the 1870's to supply his cable-car enterprise and other street railways, and by Southern Pacific, which built a rolling mill (1881) in its Sacramento railroad shops to produce as well as repair locomotives and other rolling stock. Union Iron received a business boost in the 1880's when Congress expanded the United States Navy shipbuilding program and the company built cruisers (including Admiral Dewey's flagship at Manila in the Spanish–American War), the battleship Oregon, and after 1901, submarines. Eastern firms soon made their appearance. Charles Schwab, a Carnegie protégé, absorbed Union Iron (1905) into his growing Bethlehem Steel empire.

The explosives industry experienced great expansion and intense competition resulting in large-scale consolidations. Major companies produced different grades of explosives for mining operations, and railroad, highway, and other construction. The Du Pont-backed California Powder Works held off eastern competition through a pool agreement (Gunpowder Trade Association compact, 1875) which gave the company a Pacific Coast monopoly of black powder. Nobel's Giant

Powder retained its hold on the high-explosives market. In the 1890's Giant took on California Powder in a deadly rivalry which resulted in a ruinous rate war. Du Pont undermined the careful arrangements of eastern and European rivals in the American market when it consolidated (1902) 30 companies, including California Powder, to control over two-thirds of the nation's explosives firms. High explosives was still a dangerous business marked by occasional devastating blasts. Giant's great 1902 blast wiped out its plant, sending shock waves as far as Sacramento, 70 miles away. The company was forced to reorganize in order to rebuild the entire plant.

The sugar industry's remarkable development continued to focus on the ventures of Claus Spreckels, whose San Francisco refinery outdistanced rivals in processing imported sugar cane from the Far East. When Congress enacted the 1876 Tariff, which allowed duty-free imports of sugar from Hawaii, Spreckels got the jump on rivals. He built up a vast family-operated sugar empire, with Hawaiian plantations supplying cane sugar delivered on its ships to the rebuilt San Francisco refinery, then the nation's largest. Later in the decade, a holding company of eastern firms (the so-called Sugar Trust) invaded San Francisco and took on the sugar king in a ruinous trade war (1887–1892). Spreckels carried the war to the enemy camp in Philadelphia, where he built the world's largest refinery, forcing his rival to a costly settlement which included $5 million for the Philadelphia plant that cost him $1 million. Spreckels finally met his match in his sons: after a family battle, two sons (C. A. and Rudolph— John stood by his father) took control of the family enterprise, only to lose it shortly to a Hawaiian-based American group. He built a beet-sugar refinery (Watsonville, 1887) and, after the New York-based Oxnard brothers built their plant (1892) in Ventura County, he outdid them by building the nation's largest sugar-beet plant in the Salinas Valley (1898, at present-day Spreckels). By 1910 California was the nation's leading producer, raising sugar beets in central coast counties and the Sacramento Valley and processing beet and cane sugar in Bay Area and other refineries.

Census figures for 1870 and 1910 reveal remarkable trends in the state's manufacturing sector. Firms almost doubled in number, capital funds increased three times, the labor force increased four times, and the value of products over seven times. Large firms dominated production: 71 companies, constituting less than 1 percent of all companies, employed over four-fifths of the labor force and produced almost two-fifths of total valued goods. San Francisco's industrial development was retarded by the earthquake catastrophe; nevertheless it produced four-fifths of total manufactures. Los Angeles increased its manufactures 350 percent from 1900 to 1910, ranking ahead of Oakland and Sacramento. Manufactures had ranked tenth among California's industries in 1870. They ranked fourth in 1910, and the state was on the threshold of even greater industrial growth.

Transportation

Railroads

The great story of railroad development in this period was so dominated by the Big Four that the railroad story is virtually their story. Upon completing their Central Pacific east–west transcontinental line in 1869, they inaugurated another era of expansion. In the 1870's and 1880's they completed their Central Pacific system, building a line up the Sacramento Valley to the Oregon border, and extended the Southern Pacific system, building a line down the San Joaquin into Southern California (Los Angeles by 1876) and on to New Orleans (1883) for other transcontinental links. In 1884 the Big Four incorporated the Southern Pacific Company under Kentucky law which allowed them, as economic historian Stuart Daggett puts it, "to do most things in the world provided it did not operate in Kentucky."

The Big Four battled incessantly and hard to build up their systems. They cajoled cities and counties for funds, land, and other concessions, including valuable tidelands in San Francisco for a bay terminus and a local railroad in Los Angeles for controlling the ocean outlet at San Pedro. They successfully held off state attempts to regulate their rates and federal efforts to collect their debt. They manipulated railroad rivals with finesse, occasionally indulging in ruthless tactics, scandalous briberies, and fraudulent methods—as did some of their rivals. Huntington, the driving force of the Big Four—some say its only member with talent—skillfully fought powerful eastern tycoons attempting to extend their railroads into California, notably Tom Scott's Texas and Pacific, Jay Gould's Union Pacific, and the Santa Fe. Huntington, touted as the nation's leading railroad builder, did so well invading the eastern field that by 1884 he had achieved the unique distinction of being the only man ever able to ride in a railroad car from the Atlantic to the Pacific on tracks he owned or partly controlled.

The Southern Pacific underwent a change of character after 1883. Rival railroads gradually breached its transportation monopoly, forcing concessions from the Big Four (without Hopkins, who died in 1878). The Santa Fe, which gained entry into California at Needles, reached Los Angeles (1885) and completed a direct line to San Francisco (1905). Upon the death in 1900 of Collis Huntington, last of the Big Four, control passed to Edward Harriman, the New York railroad financier, who merged the Southern Pacific into his Union Pacific system. Under Harriman, the Southern Pacific completed its San Francisco–Los Angeles coastal route (1902), the Union Pacific built its Salt Lake–Los Angeles line (1905), and major improvements were made in California's rail facilities before his death (1910). George Gould (Jay's son) built the Western Pacific, which connected Oakland to Salt Lake and Denver (1909), to complete the present-day transcontinental systems. With corporate expansion, Big Four personalized leadership was superseded by the businesslike administration of company managers, like William Herrin, and financiers, like Harriman.

In 1910 the Southern Pacific, among the nation's largest corporations, operated one of the nation's longest transportation systems. The giant holding company owned some 35 railroad companies operating rail lines that extended from Portland via San Francisco and Los Angeles to New Orleans and along Mexico's west coast, with east–west lines running from San Francisco to Ogden. It also held whole or part ownership of such diverse corporations as Pacific Mail Steamship and Wells Fargo, as well as municipal railways, lumber, oil, water, land development, and urban real estate enterprises.

For Californians the Southern Pacific was a powerful force in their lives. It represented the greatest concentration of wealth in a single company. It was practically the only statewide corporation for many years, the biggest landowner and largest employer in the state. Although not understood, the stigma attached to the Big Four's ruthless methods—exceeded in notoriety by eastern tycoons like Jay Gould—has obscured the railroads' contribution in recruiting immigrant settlers and providing efficient transportation services so important to the state's phenomenal expansion. The railroad was the chief mode of public transportation for companies shipping goods, for tycoons who rode in their own cars, for commuting businessmen, for vacationing tourists, for family excursions, and for tramps who "rode the rods." For better or worse, the Southern Pacific was a vital force in the personal lives of people and in the economic development of the state in an age when the railroad was king.

Waterways

Water transportation was still important despite railroad dominance. All kinds of sailing and steam vessels were used to carry passengers and cargo on the inland and coastal waterways. On the Sacramento and the San Joaquin, the Southern Pacific river steamers (acquired by its takeover of California Steam Navigation in 1871) carried most of the trade although independent companies, too, carried considerable freight. The puffing, whistle-tooting steamers made stops at several hundred waterfront landings for fruit, grain, and merchandise deliveries. Numerous ferries plied river and bay crossings in an age when long-span bridges were practically non-existent. San Francisco Bay's extensive waterways were a bustling hive of assorted vessels moving among the major railroad–harbor ports of San Francisco, Oakland, Vallejo, Benicia, and Port Costa. The coastal waterways were dominated by large steamship companies operated by local entrepreneurs, like George Perkins (also governor and senator) and outsiders.

California's ocean shipping was greatly stimulated by the state's expanding economy. In the Pacific, California shippers managed to develop monopolistic shipping lines. When the New York-based Pacific Mail Steamship abrogated with the Big Four their rate agreement for neutralizing sea and rail competition between California and the Atlantic seaboard, the Big Four crowd (now including Tevis) retaliated by forming their own shipping line (1874). Pacific Mail was soon forced to divide its Pacific traffic with the Big Four and Spreckels, and by 1890 came under Huntington's control. Among other self-made shipping entrepreneurs cutting out their niches were Robert Dollar, a local lumberman, and William Matson, a Spreckels ship captain, who established foundations of their world-famous shipping lines.

Highways and Roads

State highways and local roads were important for local transportation and as connecting or feeder lines to the railroad network. The chief users of these thoroughfares were horse-drawn vehicles: passenger stages, freight wagons, and lightweight carriages. The bicycle came into popular use as it developed from freak contraptions like the unicycle to the two-wheel "safety bike" (1885), becoming an important vehicle for sports and social activities. The automobile went through a long experimental stage as inventors developed "horseless carriages" operating on steam, gasoline, oil, electric, and alcohol power. It did not come of age until Henry Ford, the Detroit pioneer, produced his relatively inexpensive automobile, the famous Model T, in 1908. The bicycle and automobile brought a revolution in personal transportation that paved the way for modern highway and road development.

California was a national leader in modern highway and road development. Originally such thoroughfares, which were the primary responsibilities of the counties, suffered the tribulations of an outmoded system operating under patronage politics, official neglect, and public apathy. Public dissatisfaction with bad road conditions was expressed by local groups, but it remained for statewide agitation in the 1890's to produce action. The 1895 legislature established two important precedents: it provided for the first state takeover of a local road and it established a state highway bureau, laying the foundations of a state highway system. After a long "good roads" campaign by bikers, automobilists, and allied groups, the 1909 legislature authorized bonds for state highway construction. Spurred by the growing popularity of automobiles, California became a pioneer in the state highway movement.

Municipal Transit

As cities and towns grew, street railways gained greater importance. A technological revolution was in the making as horse-drawn rail cars were replaced by steam-powered cars in the 1870's and electric-powered cars (the famous trolley cars operating from overhead lines) in the 1880's. A. S. Hallidie, the San Francisco wire-rope manufacturer, invented the first cable car (1873), which was pulled along by a moving underground cable powered by a stationary steam engine at the end of the line. Local transit entrepreneurs pioneered community systems which were taken over by well-established capitalists who built up vast regional systems, combining local lines with steam and hydroelectric power companies and sometimes with real estate ventures.

In California, municipal transit development focused on the state's three largest communities, each following a pattern as dictated by local circumstances. Los Angeles took the lead: assorted steam, electric, and cable lines were consolidated in the 1890's by Moses Sherman and taken over by Henry Huntington (with help from Uncle Collis and his banker, Isaiah Hellman), who built up his great Pacific Electric system. In San Francisco, Patrick Calhoun, grandson of the famous southern statesman and a New York corporation lawyer, bought out local transit magnates (including Henry Huntington) to form United Railroads (1902), which consolidated the city's rail lines. He became embroiled with the Ruef machine and became a chief target of the Graft Prosecution. Oakland's pioneers had ambitious schemes. James Fair, the mining magnate, attempted to consolidate horse and steam cars in the 1880's. Francis "Borax" Smith, who developed a vast rapid interurban electric system in the 1890's, attempted to extend his famous East Bay Key System to San Francisco and San Jose to tie together Bay Area communities. Southern Pacific maneuvers prevented both from completing their systems. The Bay Area was prevented by local politics and business competition from achieving the efficient, integrated regional transit system of the Southland.

Aircraft

Aeronautics went through a noteworthy experimental phase that laid later foundations for the aircraft industry. Since Thaddeus Lowe's pioneer balloon ascents during the Civil War, American inventors had devised airships with steam and gas engines and other flying machines, occasionally losing their lives in experiments. In California, John Montgomery, a Santa Clara University professor and an unsung aeronautics pioneer, flew the first glider (1884) and built several birdlike contraptions over the next decade. The breakthrough for practical flying machines came with the Wright Brothers' gas-engine airplane (1903). Californians were among the pioneers building aircraft, notably Glenn Martin (1909) and Allen Lockheed (1910). The international air meet in Los Angeles in 1910, the nation's first, featured assorted aircraft and gave promise of growth for the aircraft industry.

Communications

Telegraph and Telephone

The communications industry underwent rapid development amidst constant turmoil resulting from technological advances and business warfare. Bell's invention of the telephone (1876) spread rapidly to California. By 1878 San Francisco had a telephone switchboard (the world's third) and telephonic communications with Sacramento, followed shortly by Oakland and other towns. In the Sierra, lumber, mining, and water companies converted from telegraph to telephone systems for servicing their field, underground, and flume operations; a mining company (North Bloomfield) is credited with the first long-distance telephone system. Larger companies soon absorbed smaller ones into citywide and regional exchange systems, connected by pole lines and other improved facilities.

California's wire communications were rounded out after 1900. After battles among rival tycoons, the Boston-based Bell group acquired the telephone monopoly. Jay Gould controlled Western Union and competed with John Mackay, the California mining magnate, who organized Postal Telegraph with submarine cables across the Atlantic, to Hawaii (1902) and the Philippines (1904). The Bell interests reorganized their West Coast operations by incorporating California and nearby states into a regional subsidiary, Pacific Telephone and Telegraph (1906). Back east, Morgan acquired the Bell interests, secured Gould's Western Union, and organized American Telephone and Telegraph (1907) as the parent holding company, beating out Mackay and other rival groups for control of the nation's wire communications. By 1910 California was served by a mixed system of independent and subsidiary companies dominated by the New York-based AT&T giant and its chief contender, Mackay's Postal Telegraph.

Radio

The invention of wireless communication by Italy's Marconi in 1892 opened an exciting new field that immediately attracted Americans. In California, Bay Area youths eagerly pressed their experiments, notably a San Francisco group's first ship-to-shore wireless (1899), Cy Elswell's wireless radio set (1905) which competed with Western Union's wire system, Ralph Heintz's first air-to-ground wireless, and Charles Herrold's pioneer radio broadcast (1909). The real breakthrough in tapping air-borne electric waves for practical use came when Lee deForest of Chicago invented the three-part vacuum tube (1908)—the basic device for receiving, transmitting, and generating electric waves for radio telephone, the precursor of radio broadcasting. Marconi was so pre-occupied with far-flung wireless enterprises and the Morgan-controlled AT&T was so busily establishing its wire communications monopoly that the Californians were able to make the most of their opportunity in establishing a niche in the emerging radio field.

Motion Pictures

Motion pictures developed from an experimental stage into a fledgling industry in a remarkably short time. Among the early experimenters was Eadweard Muybridge, a San Francisco photographer. Commissioned by Leland Stanford, Muybridge devised a serial camera arrangement to produce photographs showing a galloping horse with all four feet off the ground at once (1877), thus helping Stanford win a $25,000 wager with another wealthy sportsman, as well as making a landmark contribution to motion picture development. The real breakthrough came by 1889 when George Eastman developed photographic impressions on flexible celluloid film, and an Edison assistant, William Dickson, devised a camera and projector for taking and showing motion pictures. The combined camera—projector machine was invented for screen projection in 1895, by 1900 vaudeville houses then movie theatres were showing motion pictures as exciting entertainment, especially for the masses. Motion picture companies soon discovered California to be an attractive place for film production, as its favorable climate facilitated inexpensive outdoor operations. By 1910 several major and independent companies had located studios in the San Francisco Bay Area and Los Angeles, laying permanent foundations for the rapidly growing industry.

Labor

Workers were a generally disorganized lot. They worked under varied conditions and acted in different ways according to their circumstances. Skilled workers fared best for they enjoyed high wages because of the abundant jobs for their small numbers. Furthermore, they were trained craftsmen who had a capacity for organized action; they thought of themselves as the aristocrats of labor. Semi-skilled and unskilled workers, on the other hand, worked longer hours for lower wages. They had to bear competition from transients, drifters, and recent immigrants, and from the hard-working Asians. They frequently endured oppressive conditions, rarely able to resist malpractices of abusive employers. They were rarely compensated for industrial accidents—injuries and fatalities were appallingly frequent in the latter part of the nineteenth century. Labor usually suffered the worst of any group from the business cycles, for it had fewer resources to ride through periods of unemployment and made slow gains when prosperity returned. Where farmers, merchants, and industrialists were able to organize to obtain government assistance, workers had few laws supporting their actions and even fewer protecting them.

Agricultural Labor

Agricultural labor expanded upon the foundations laid in the earlier period. As grain ranches and later fruit orchards increased in size and number, demand rose for farm labor, especially cheap labor that would prevent operating costs from exceeding profit margins. Family members of both sexes and of all ages (children as young as ten years), unemployed city and town workers, gypsylike drifters, recently arrived immigrants—all were recruited for planting and harvesting the crops.

Big growers relied heavily on Oriental gang labor, who worked long, hard, and steadily in the fields. After 1870 they recruited mostly Chinese workers, usually from Chinese contractors. By the 1880's deaths and restricted immigration (see Chapter 13), caused a reduction in the number of Chinese workers but other sources opened up with the arrival of Japanese immigrants and unemployed nonagricultural workers made available by the depression. When prosperity returned after 1900, the Japanese came to dominate farm employment, primarily by organizing into gangs under "Jap bosses" to underbid rival workers. The "Jap boss" was a camp boss, labor scout, and foreman rolled into one, who devised inventive tactics like work stoppages during the harvest for obtaining better wages from employers. Unlike the docile Chinese worker, the Japanese was aggressive and independent, striving to improve his status from laborer to sharecropper to land renter and owner to entrepreneur. The self-assertion of these Japanese laborers aroused farmer antagonism that foreboded trouble.

The movement of labor unions to organize industrial workers experienced gradual progress despite setbacks. The unions attempted to organize collectively to improve working conditions, but they were constantly handicapped by internal dissensions and external factors. Their leaders varied widely in ability and vision, swinging between conservative and radical approaches, peaceful and violent methods, and differing in the use of pickets, boycotts, and strike weapons. They differed on whether to organize all workers into a single union, or skilled workers into craft unions. They disagreed on whether to form autonomous locals for independent action or for greater strength to affiliate with citywide, state, or national organizations. Some wanted to stress political action to secure laws regulating working conditions. Others wanted to concentrate on economic action and bargain directly with employers for bread-and-butter objectives, like shorter hours and better wages. They constantly battled each other over strategy and tactics in dealing with employers. When they did get together, they encountered the hostile attitudes of employers who resorted to hard tactics like the "yellow dog" contracts (in which workers agreed not to join a union), blacklists, and lockouts. In these labor-management showdowns, the public attitude veered from apathy, to sympathy with isolated peaceful demonstrations, to outright hostility toward labor where mass demonstrations or violent incidents were involved.

The 1870's were a bleak decade for labor. The massive unemployment resulting from the mid-decade depression gave rise to Kearney's Workingmen's Party, which played a conspicuous role in the Constitutional Convention. San Francisco union leaders, disenchanted with Kearney's demagogic leadership and his disregard of trade unions, formed a citywide federation of local unions (1878) which helped sustain local unions during the dark transitional years.

The return of prosperity in the 1880's was followed by a wave of unionism. At the national level, the Knights of Labor united all workers into a single union, while the fledgling American Federation of Labor (formed 1881) federated craft unions of skilled workers, nationalizing the trade federation idea pioneered earlier by San Francisco unions. Both organizations carried their intense rivalry to California. In industrialized San Francisco, trade unions were revived under local federations headed by Frank Roney, a talented Irish-born labor leader, while Burnette

Haskell, a brilliant California-trained lawyer, formed his socialist-oriented organization which branched out into Northern California towns.

The 1890's were a decade of crises for organized labor. In San Francisco a Manufacturers and Employers Association organized (1891) an all-out campaign to eliminate unions, but rival citywide unions reconciled their differences to unite their forces into the San Francisco Labor Council (1892). In Los Angeles, the labor union movement was rejuvenated by the printer's strike against major newspapers led by Otis's *Times.* Out of the prolonged battle emerged a citywide federation which revitalized unions and affiliated them with the San Francisco and national unions. The mid-decade depression left a devastating wake of business failures and massive unemployment followed by widespread destitution. Mention has been made of California's participation in Eugene Debs's railway union strike against Pullman and of Coxey's "Industrial Army" of unemployed workers who marched to Washington for federal relief (see above). California for the first time was being drawn directly into the mainstream of the national labor movement.

After 1900 came climactic showdowns between labor unions and employer associations which profoundly affected their future relations. With business revival came union expansion. The San Francisco city federations split again and spearheaded the formation in 1901 of the State Federation of Labor and the State Building Trades Council. At the same time the National Association of Manufacturers (NAM) launched its militant campaigns in major cities to drive out unions, and the national AFL became directly involved in boosting local unions. Both organizations made California a target area. The decade was rife with industrial warfare, mostly in cities, accentuated by criss-crossing labor–management battles among national, state, and local forces.

Industrial warfare centered on the state's two leading cities, and the outcome was different in each. In San Francisco, employers in 1901 formed an association to break the union stranglehold, bringing on the terrible general strike that was broken by Mayor Phelan's police intervention. Angry dissidents initiated the Union Labor Party. Quickly taken over by Abe Ruef as his vehicle for becoming the city's political boss, the party captured the municipal government in the next election and launched its long prolabor administration. When the Union Labor Party was discredited by the Graft Prosecution toward the end of the decade, P. H. McCarthy of the State Building Trades stepped into Ruef's place and won the 1909 municipal elections to become the city's mayor.

Los Angeles's labor–management warfare was made more bitter by the extensive involvement of outsiders. When the citywide labor council accelerated its drive to form unions after 1901, the city's Merchants and Manufacturers Association abandoned its hitherto neutral position and joined Otis's militant employers association in an all-out counterattack. As the NAM joined the fray with its big war chest, the AFL redoubled its efforts, concentrating for the first time on a single city. The situation was further complicated by the entry of the anarchistic Industrial Workers of the World (formed in Chicago 1905, hereafter IWW) and Job Harriman's Socialists. By 1910 the outcome was clear: the unions had been broken by several crushing defeats, and the employers had just about won their open-shop campaign. Then came the climax with the bombing of the Los Angeles Times Building, which resulted in the deaths of 15 persons and evoked a wave of public revulsion, mostly against organized labor. The decade ended with a state embroiled in industrial warfare and a people much divided by labor–management controversy.

Banking

Banking institutions grew rapidly in step with the state's economic growth. They were generally centrally located in leading communities, performing basic banking functions of deposits, savings, and loans. Some banks played conspicuous roles in supplying funds to groups of entrepreneurs for areawide economic development. The list of banks reflects diverse types of financial organization. Ralston's Bank of California continued to be the undisputed leader in Northern California and the Nevada Comstock. The Irish Four of the Comstock formed their own Bank of Nevada (1875) to be free of Ralston's influence. Lloyd Tevis, who moved his Wells Fargo from New York to San Francisco headquarters, separated its express and banking functions into separate institutions (1876). In Los Angeles, Isaiah Hellman formed his pioneer Farmers and Merchants Bank, which figured conspicuously in the city's development during the land boom then under way. British capitalists had bank outlets managed by two ex-governors: Latham's London and San Francisco Bank and Low's Anglo-California Bank.

The depression in the mid-1870's brought on a major shakeup of the banks. They had enjoyed considerable freedom of action, which had led inevitably to uneven practices ranging from sound to risky investments in speculative enterprises, and recurring frauds and embezzlements by trusted bank officers. When Ralston was unable to recoup his overinvestments, he closed down the great Bank of California (August 1875) and on the same day was found dead, presumably a suicide. The bank's downfall touched off numerous failures of hard-pressed banks and businesses, which intensified the economic distress of the depression. San Francisco's leading bankers launched efforts to stabilize the situation. They formed a clearing-house to regularize transactions (1876) and persuaded the legislature to set up a state bank commission (1878) to oversee the banks. The state agency contributed some stability but was too limited in scope, staff, and funds to be entirely successful.

Nevertheless, the banks experienced steady constructive growth, performing more specialized functions. They combined savings, commercial, and trust functions for the various types of investments requried for financing diverse enterprises. Charles Crocker formed a bank (1883), later headed by his son William, to provide the Southern Pacific with another source for its investments. In Los Angeles, Joseph Sartori got a helping hand from Hellman in forming his highly successful bank (1889). The depression of the 1890's hit the financial community hard, but substantial banks like those of Crocker and Hellman recovered quickly to help expanding hydroelectric and other industrial enterprises.

Banking institutions experienced two significant developments in the decade after 1900. Following the return of prosperity and even greater expansion, bankers met competition by expanding investments and merging with other banks. Hellman, who had taken over the troubled Bank of Nevada (1890), headed its merger with Wells Fargo (1905). Bank of California merged with the London and San Francisco Bank (1905), while Low's Anglo-California Bank merged with the London, Paris National Bank (1909) headed by the Fleishhacker brothers. Amadeo Giannini, a local merchant, formed his Bank of Italy (1904) to serve his neglected Italian compatriots. Following the failure of a respected bank whose irregularities and frauds shocked the banking fraternity and the public, state banking policy underwent another major revision to correct prevailing deficiencies. The 1909 legislature, with help from the bankers, enacted the landmark banking act which replaced the bank commission with a state banking superintendent to provide rigid supervision of banks.

Now in the vanguard of states having modern banking laws, California entered a new era of regulated banking institutions.

Trade

Domestic Commerce

Marketing activities kept pace with the state's expanding economy. Merchants developed extensive facilities for exporting and importing goods on river, coastal, and ocean routes, and on local and overland highways and railroads. San Francisco sustained its commanding role in the state's commerce, but Los Angeles, San Diego, and Eureka were slowly developing as important ports for the coastal trade, while Stockton gained on Sacramento as a leading river port for the interior trade. Regional trading exchanges took shape when central exchanges on the San Francisco model were established in Los Angeles (1876) and Oakland (1904). The San Francisco chamber of commerce was for years spokesman for all merchants before the public and the legislature, until local merchants in other areas organized their own chambers. The Los Angeles chamber, organized (1887) in the midst of the land boom, played an important role in that city's development.

In the local distribution of goods, the wholesale merchants continued to rule the roost. They performed the vitally important middleman functions not always understood by their farmer–manufacturer–retailer clients, who resented "the hated Shylocks" for their chicanery, suspected and real, and excessive charges that cut deep into their profit margins. As some producers, such as citrus growers and fruit canners, developed cooperative and corporate organizations to market their products, so retailers pioneered ways to bypass wholesalers by assuming or extending their functions. Harris Newmark sent traveling salesmen throughout Southern California and the San Joaquin to sell merchandise from his Los Angeles store. The Chicago-based Montgomery Ward and Sears, Roebuck pioneered the mail-order houses and extended their services to California by the 1880's. The annual arrival of catalogues from "Monkey Ward's" and Sears thrilled a generation of Californians and other Americans imbued with the idea of ordering by mail inexpensive ready-made clothes and numerous goods. (The catalogues also became an indispensable item for many family "outhouses" in rural areas.) The chain stores, like Atlantic and Pacific for general groceries and Woolworth's for small variety goods, did not make significant entry into California in this period.

Meanwhile, the department store, pioneered by R. H. Macy in New York in the 1850's, made its appearance. As cities grew, some merchants built larger stores with special services organized as distinct departments in one building to lure customers away from small stores and firms producing ready-made apparel. Pioneering these central department stores were the Davies brothers in San Francisco, whose original store (1871) became the Emporium (1896), Harris Weinstock and his half-brother David Lubin in Sacramento (1874), Marshall Hale in San Jose (1876), and J. W. Robinson in Los Angeles (1883). Weinstock and Lubin and Hale's sons went further to establish branch stores in San Francisco and Hale Brothers also in Sacramento. Other pioneers who established great merchandising empires were Isaac and Mary Magnin with their fashionable department store in San Francisco (1888), Arthur Letts's huge Broadway Department Store in Los Angeles (1896), and Arthur Bullock's (a Letts' employee) fashionable store (1906).

Retail grocers also sought ways to improve their marketing situation through innovations. San Francisco retail grocers pioneered a trend of forming into wholesale cooperatives to buy directly from food manufacturers, notably San Francisco Grocery (1901) and United Grocers (1906). Retailers and wholesalers formed the Pacific's Grocers Association (1907) in a move to further reduce price-cutting competition. While such counterattacks by retailers and other clients cut into his business, the wholesale merchant was still the dominant figure in the distribution of goods, though he had a proportionately smaller share of the market by 1910.

Foreign Commerce

California's position in international trade grew better with improved lines to the eastern seaboard, Europe, Latin America, the Orient, and the Pacific. It was an important stopover link in the British triangular trade route which carried California wheat and other products, Australian coal, and British manufactures. San Francisco was third (after New York and Boston) among the nation's leading ports. Its strategic position as the nation's chief outlet for the Pacific trade took on added significance with the growing trade in the Far East, especially after the Spanish–American

War (1898). The nation owed much to California's gold shipments in making possible a historic shift from an unfavorable to a favorable balance of trade between 1875 and 1895.

13 The Plutocratic Society

A. SOCIETY

THE SETTING

California between 1870 and 1910 was well populated by people of diverse origins. Most people lived in rural communities, but many were settling in the growing cities. The preponderance of the young and middle-aged contributed ambitious men aggressively capitalizing on opportunities in the increasingly industrialized state. In time there emerged a group of new-rich men who acquired the status of an elite. They were the plutocrats who had begun as middle-class entrepreneurs and accumulated enormous wealth and power to attain commanding positions of leadership in society.

California was still immigrant country. The heavy influx of immigration during the land booms brought two conspicuous groups. From the Midwest came people steeped in provincial small-town tradition, characterized by an agrarian outlook, middle-class customs, religious orthodoxy, and strict morality. They claimed origin from "Ioway, Nebrasky, and Missoura." From the Northeast came those with city ways, who believed in industrial progress, upper-class leadership, religious sectarianism, and a more flexible moral code. These settlers were lured to the state by other attractions than the get-rich-quick schemes that so preoccupied the argonauts. The expanding economy offered greater promise for business investments and job opportunities than at home, especially for adventurous youth and enterprising adults seeking to improve their status. The favorable climate, especially in Southern California, offered relief for those suffering poor health, and escape from severe winters in the East for vacationing tourists and permanent settlers. They came seeking a better life, and in time sought to implant their traditions in their adopted land. Foreign immigrants who settled in California also implanted their native traditions, but these were generally less conspicuous.

ANALYSIS

The People

Population jumped from 560,000 in 1870 to 1.4 million in 1910, doubling every two decades. The American-born had widened their lead considerably over the foreign-born. Up to 1910 most Californians had been born in other states, but in that year the California-born (38 percent) outnumbered those born in other states (37 percent) for the first time. The American immigrants came from all regions, as before, except that most came from the northern tier of midwestern states. People from northern states widened their lead over those from southern states, which enhanced California's regional orientation to the North. The British led the foreign-born, the Irish constituting less than half as many, followed by the Germans, Italians, Canadians, and Japanese.

The population became better balanced. The Southern California booms shifted population concentrations so that the Southland had 40 percent of the state's population by 1910. San Francisco Bay still led with one-third of the state's population. Urban population gained rapidly, but did not yet exceed that of the rural areas. The age groups were more evenly distributed. The bulk of population was in the middle groups (20 to 40 age bracket) and the children matched the aged in number. Nonwhites were led by the Japanese, followed by the Chinese, Indians, and Negroes, each around 1 percent. The young, American-born whites held sway.

Communities

Counties

California's county complexion was rounded out by 1910. The spread of people and industry in established areas and settlement in remote areas combined with geography to shape each county. A balloonist hovering over a typical county might see a city and scattered towns, interconnected by trains chugging along rail lines, stages and wagons traveling along dirt roads, and sometimes barges moving down the great, broad rivers. In the countryside, he might see large cultivated tracts and ranchlands surrounded by empty lands broken only by rail, road, and water lines.

County alterations reflected regional developments and state growth. The 1872 Code Revision (see Chapter 11) modified county lines in the central area so that a straight line across the state separated northern counties from southern. The legislature continued to be the battleground of local groups seeking advantage by creating new counties, shifting the county seat, and altering county boundaries. Klamath suffered so greatly from economic decline that it was abolished (1874) and its territory absorbed by neighboring counties—the only county ever consigned to oblivion. Los Angeles lost a 20-year battle with dissident elements who formed into Orange County (1889), thus reducing the southern leader to its present size. Public reaction to legislative tinkering resulted in the constitutional amendment (1894) which deprived the legislature of the right to create counties by special act. So tight were the laws for forming new counties (1907) and for altering county boundaries (1910), that only one county has been formed (Imperial, 1907) to round off the present total of 58 counties.

Towns and Cities

Town and city development kept pace with the burgeoning economic expansion. San Francisco paced expanding larger cities in commercial and industrial growth, developing as a focus of satellite cities and towns to take the form of an urbanized metropolitan area. Los Angeles, which rose rapidly after 1900 to become the second-ranking city a decade later, set a trend for growing cities by expanding over outlying areas. Beyond the established areas, settlement advanced into remote regions as new towns grew up in impromptu or planned fashion, usually oriented to agricultural, lumber, mining, or railroad enterprises in the area. Some lumber and mining companies, to insure an adequate labor supply for distant field operations, built company towns in which the corporation operated the store and other facilities for the workers' families. In some instances, utopian groups organized communities based on socio-economic ideals (see below). California was a fertile field for varied types of community building—a continuous process punctuated by occasional town booms. And nowhere was the community building process more dramatic than in Southern California.

The Southern California Booms

Southern California underwent three major booms. They were products of the same factors, modified by the times: aggressive boosters or land promoters who advertised the area heavily; the railroad, which greatly facilitated transcontinental travel to the remote area; and a steady flow of immigrants lured by dazzling prospects in agriculture and other enterprises, and by the pleasant environment. Each boom played a distinctive part in settling the land and broadening the economic base. Together they brought about a drastic alteration of the Southern California country.

The first of these booms, initiated by Northern Californians, took form after 1868 and climaxed in 1876. Land companies provided the chief impetus for the breakup of ranches into towns and farms. A San Francisco group organized to dispose of Stearn rancho lands, advertising widely in California towns, the East, and Europe. A prominent Tennessee politician and veteran midwestern town developer, Judge John North, bought Lugo rancho lands to form a small farmer colony at Riverside (1870). A group of Indiana farmers organized a land colony (1873); its agents purchased the San Pascual rancho of Benjamin Wilson and his partner, organized an orange growers association, and laid out the town of Pasadena. Local promoters were also active. Wilson and ex-governor John Downey developed their lands, being the first to plan, advertise, and sell whole towns—Alhambra and Downey (1873). The boom set the pattern for land development in the Southland. It changed the region from a semifrontier to a settled rural area, laid foundations for a diversified economic base, and prepared the way for an even greater boom in the 1880's.

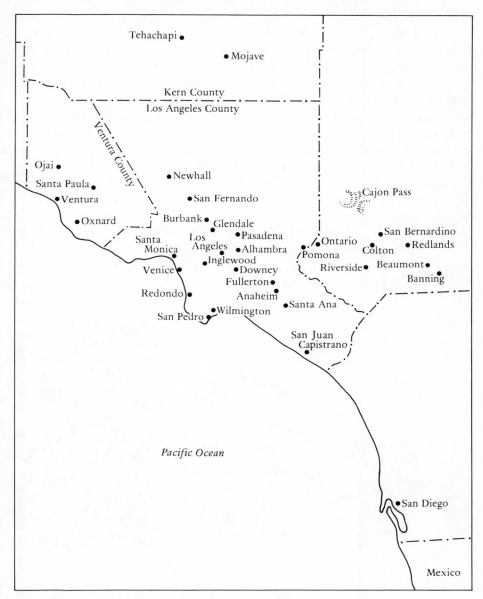

FIGURE 8   Southern California—Land and Town Boom, 1887.

That boom was the most spectacular of all. It reached a climax when the Santa Fe line reached Los Angeles in 1885 and engaged the Southern Pacific in intense competition. The two railroads undercut each other's transcontinental rates until the fare from Mississippi Valley points to Southern California went from $125 to $24 and for a brief period to $1. The effect was seen in the new towns built along the railroad lines: 8 on the Southern Pacific, 25 on the Santa Fe. Boosters, now joined by the railroads and professional town boomers from the Midwest, undertook a fantastic campaign for land promotion. They concocted imaginative schemes ranging from the visionary to outright humbug. They promoted land by flamboyant advertising—such as auction sales with brass bands, free lunches, and circus entertainment, and sheer fakery, as when a Joshua Tree desert tract near Palm Springs had cactus plants "salted" with oranges to pass as an orange grove. Over an 18-month period (1888–1889), 60 new towns were plotted to accommodate an estimated two million people. Most became defunct. Manchester, for example, had 2,300 lots, including sites for a city hall, schools, and hotels—but no inhabitants. Surviving towns which became major cities include Burbank, Fullerton, Glendale, Hollywood, Inglewood, Long Beach, and Pomona. The communities were of all types:

Immigrants and tourists. Arrival of a Southern Pacific passenger train in the heyday of the Southern California boom.

Ontario was a model farm community (Chaffee's project); Redlands, a tourist attraction with its landscape of worldwide plants developed by the wealthy Smiley Twins; and Whittier, a small Quaker farm community. The boom just about wiped out any visible remnants of the Spanish and Mexican eras.

Southern California's revived growth in the 1890's accelerated into another boom after the turn of the century. The Los Angeles Chamber of Commerce led off with innovative schemes and systematic large-scale operations for publicizing the city's assets which helped make Los Angeles the nation's best advertised city. Boosters shifted their publicity emphasis. They talked less about agricultural and business opportunities and more about the pleasant environment for good living: work, play, and retire in the sunny clime within beach and moutain areas; live in the country and work in the city. Immigrants and tourists poured into Southern California to join other settlers in searching out new homes and quick riches from property speculation and oil prospects. Promoters carefully planned suburban subdivisions. Venice was developed by Abbott Kinney as a replica of the Italian canal city and as a center for the arts and intellectual activity. Beverly Hills was designed for wealthy residents. Huntington's Pacific Electric railway and real estate development paralleled each other. Subdividers followed the track-layers along the projected rail lines where Huntington had already acquired huge tracts for resale, notably in the San Gabriel and later the San

---

The immigrant's lure: Land! Advertisement from back cover of Charles Lummis's *Land of Sunshine*, Spring 1896.

Fernando Valleys. By 1910 Los Angeles was an area fairly well saturated with well-established and partially developed towns and cities.

Community Development

Towns and cities continued to be distinctive communities, with strong traditions of community independence and local home rule. Town life focused on the main street containing the chief business establishments. City life centered on the central business district with adjoining residential and manufacturing areas. While towns and cities shared common community attributes, each had a distinctive character marked by the lay of the land, type of people, character of its leaders, and nature of its political economy. Many communities built up a distinctive socio-economic base, specializing as health, recreational, religious, bedroom, or manufacturing communities. The San Francisco Bay Area and the Los Angeles basin illustrate the contrasting ways of community development conditioned by these elements.

In the San Francisco area, community development was conditioned by the geographic limitations of the bay, well-established cities and towns, and a mixed native and foreign population that lent a cosmopolitan flavor to the scenic region. San Francisco, a compact city located on the strategic but confining tip of the southern peninsula, had little choice but to grow upward. Multiple-story dwellings appeared in the mid-1880's; these apartment buildings proved so profitable for property owners that single-family dwellings declined. High-rise buildings, which rose in New York and Chicago after 1870, made their San Francisco debut with de Young's ten-story Chronicle Building (1888), designed by the Chicago architect Daniel Burnham. By the turn of the century, San Francisco was considered the nation's most congested city. Prominent business leaders, like Phelan, launched a campaign to remake San Francisco into a beautiful and efficient city. They sponsored Burnham's imaginative, far-sighted plan for city redevelopment, including an imposing civic center, a circulatory traffic system with one-way streets, and other modern features that captivated public imagination, especially after the 1906 earthquake and fire left the city's historic center a blackened wasteland. The city, bogged down by machine politics, the *Chronicle's* opposition, business conservatism, and public complacency, was unable to match its vision with deeds.

Elsewhere in the Bay Area, cities and towns manifested an aggressive spirit of community development in spite of being restricted to the narrow bay coastline area by the mountain backdrop. Oakland converted from a village to a "city of homes" with expanding manufacturing industries. Berkeley expanded as a residential town with the state university's growth after 1900 and the migration of San Francisco residents after the 1906 quake. Richmond, benefiting from its harbor and Santa Fe rail terminus (1902), expanded as an industrial center with explosives, ironworks, oil refineries, and several manufacturing plants as its nucleus. San Jose enjoyed a boom in the 1890's when easterners disenchanted by the Southern California booms came north, where they helped convert Santa Clara Valley into a highly productive farm area and San Jose into a major trading center. San Mateo around 1900 experienced the breakup of big ranches and large estates into suburban subdivisions to take the form of a bedroom community to San Francisco. South San Francisco slowly emerged as an industrial community. The Peninsula and Marin County still remained farmlands and open area with slowly developing communities.

In the Los Angeles area, community development experienced unparalleled freedom for experiment and innovation. It was conditioned by a broad central plain with distant ocean and mountain borders, and an all-year moderate climate punctuated by sea breezes and mountain air which enticed people of both enterprise and leisure. The central plain and adjoining valleys offered open opportunity for growing communities and expanding agricultural, commercial, industrial, and recreational enterprises. Boosters at first appealed to wealthy easterners and midwesterners, but by the 1880's reoriented their pitch to attract middle-income groups, emphasizing diverse opportunities for business investment, recreation, travel, and retirement. Before long, the area acquired an overwhelming native American white population, with few of the foreign elements so conspicuous in the nation's urban centers. This unique population accentuated Los Angeles's provincial Protestant outlook. Having aggressive leaders who tackled pressing problems with zest and imagination, Los Angeles emerged as the leading community in the Southland. It beat out San Diego and rival neighboring communities to assert leadership. When real estate developers rapidly converted nearby farmlands into residential areas with little attention to community facilities, such as parks, a civic-minded developer donated a huge tract for what turned out to be the nation's largest municipal park,

Griffith Park (1891). The burgeoning city reached out to acquire adjoining areas for consolidating the community. Between 1895 and 1900 it absorbed neighboring districts (like Boyle Heights and East Los Angeles), increasing the city's territory by 50 percent and acquiring ample room for future expansion. It fought a long battle for port facilities, eventually annexing the shoestring strip between the city and the port (1906) and consolidating with the port towns of San Pedro and Wilmington (1909) to secure the ocean harbor so vital for future development. The boom-ridden area experienced such rapid growth that it emerged in 1910 as the state's second-ranking city.

Communities in the Los Angeles basin paralleled the early development of the mother city. The outlying towns showed a tendency toward community specialization that set them apart from Los Angeles's urbanism. The boom of the 1870's set the pattern: a port town (San Pedro), a Methodist teetotaler community (Compton), a midwestern farm colony (Pasadena), a seaside resort (Santa Monica), and a health resort (Sierra Madre). The boom of the 1880's added communities for New Englanders (Claremont), German Lutherans (Palmdale), gambling elements (Seabright), and war veteran families (Sawtelle). The boom after 1900 rounded out community diversification with communities for industry (Vernon) and a picturesque resort (Venice). Communities changed their character in the course of growth and development. Pasadena converted from a struggling colony of orange producers in the 1880's to become a flourishing winter resort for wealthy easterners. After 1900 Pasadena emerged as a city, a lovely, staid, conservative community with elegant hotels and palatial mansions, active cultural and educational activities, and attractions like the annual Tournament of Roses, Mt. Lowe's alpine hotel and cable railway (Thaddeus Lowe enterprises), and Mt. Wilson observatory. Pasadena was a star in the community constellation of the Southland.

Utopian Colonies

A utopian colony, as historian Robert Hine tells us, is a group of people who attempt to establish a community based on their vision of the ideal society. They comprise an assorted lot of disenchanted people from all walks of life who establish their ideal community as a model for others. Such communities are cooperative ventures in communal living which emphasize community ownership of property, reliance on man's moral character, and a belief in his natural goodness. They differ from cooperatives like the self-help profit-sharing or nonprofit ventures of farmers, laborers, manufacturers, and consumers discussed elsewhere, in that they attempt to establish a new social pattern, while the latter groups attempt to reform the existing order *within* society. Utopian colonies represent a rejection of competitive capitalistic society and a firm commitment to a cooperative way. They have deep roots in America's past, having reached a peak in New England and the Middle West during the early nineteeth century. California's experiences in the latter half of the nineteenth century represents a latent phase in the movement.

California was a fertile field for experiments in social living like utopian colonies. In the 1850–1870 period appeared the first one, the religiously based Mormon community in San Bernardino (1851–1854), but it had greater significance as part of the Mormon stronghold in Utah than as a California venture. The heyday of the California colonies was in the 1870–1910 period when ten colonies were established, far more than in any other state. They were a varied lot. Fountain Grove (1875–1900), near Santa Rosa, was built up by a transplanted New York "brotherhood" as a theological–socialist community featuring platonic marriages and communal living. Modjeska's Farm (1875–1877), modeled on the famous Brook Farm, was set up at Anaheim by aristocratic Polish émigrés, including Helena Modjeska, a celebrated actress, but their inexperience at farming spelled doom for the colony. Kaweah colony (1885—1892) in the Sierra above Visalia was set up by Burnette Haskell, the San Francisco labor leader (see Chapter 12), as a "socialist haven" in a capitalistic world to persuade the proletariat to its cause. It was plagued by internal dissensions and land litigation which led to its dissolution. At Point Loma, near San Diego, Katherine Tingley, the Theosophical Society leader (see below) established a colony as international headquarters for her universal brotherhood. Eventually all of these sects broke up but each left its mark upon neighboring communities and on California's history.

Social Classes

California society after 1870 achieved both a more stratified class system and a greater social mobility than elsewhere in the nation. It reflected the state's heterogeneous people, their varied occupations, the expanding political economy, and the ever-fluctuating conditions of the growing society. People often experienced quick changes in their status from sudden fortunes or misfortunes. They varied widely in their social aspirations, whether retaining their old ways or, if they were rising on the social scale, acquiring the style of the next upper class. Some simply fashioned a personal life style irrespective of class status, rich or poor. They were part of the Victorian Age (after Britain's dowager queen), which extended from the Civil War to the turn of the century and was steeped in the WASP idea. As historian—sociologist E. D. Baltzell explains, American concern with the growing foreign immigration of the period caused middle- and upper-class groups to reiterate traditional values (organizing into ancestral and patriotic societies) and to preserve their belief in the superiority of White Anglo Saxon Protestant (WASP) culture.

California's upper class took on a well-defined character, which exhibited much talent, wealth, and prestige. San Francisco continued to be the home of high society. The entry of the Big Four railroad kings and of the Irish Four silver kings into the upper ranks after 1870 broadened the basis of the ruling elite, the so-called Establishment. Members of the older commercial aristocracy represented by Coleman, Hayward, Phelan, and Ralston, and of the newer industrial aristocracy represented by the Crockers, the Fairs, the Floods, and the Stanfords, occupied key positions in the political economy. They reflected the ideas and values of the WASP Establishment in the East which constituted the nation's elite (as represented by Bostonian Henry Adams and New Yorker Theodore Roosevelt). The San Franciscans, however, manifested less rigid adherence to the prevailing WASP Establishment idea of an open upper class which assimilated hyphenated Americans (Irish-Catholics, Polish-Jews) of ability and ambition and the closed caste which excluded them from the inner circle.

These upper-class families vied with each other for the mantle of social leadership. They built huge mansions on city hills, notably Nob Hill, and frequented exclusive centers like the showcase Palace Hotel, the patrician Pacific Union Club (a two-club merger, 1884), and the casual Bohemian Club. They assumed fastidious dress and manners, taking their cue from social guidebooks, and they threw elegant banquets and lavish parties. They gave munificently to charity and philanthropy. Phoebe Hearst contributed heavily to University of California projects and sponsored the first settlement house for destitute immigrants. Jane

Stanford gave generously to Stanford University and to homes for orphans and the elderly. The women competed for leadership in fashion, parties, and other exclusive socials. As a British visitor observed, perhaps with bias, San Francisco had a "terribly fast so-called society set, engrossed by the emptiest and most trivial pleasures." The proliferation of high society into different groups—old guard and new rich, the older and younger sets—contributed to a more stratified upper class. Mark Twain in surveying the spectacular era of elegant living and lavish display dubbed the times the "Gilded Age."

This increased stratification was more evident in the lower and upper classes than in the middle class. The predominant middle-class backbone of California—and American—society, had a tradition of democratic sentiments and a Protestant ethic that provided the basis for social equality and the conventional morality shared by the bulk of middle-class elements.

The lower class of unskilled workers, destitute unemployables, and vagrants expanded with large numbers of needy immigrants, unlucky entrepreneurs who had lost their businesses and homes, itinerant laborers, and racial minorities. They were usually located in ghettos or segregated sections near the downtown and factory areas in cities and "across the tracks" in towns—ironically the iron rail was a symbolic social barrier. These people suffered high incidences of crime, disease, and malnutrition because of unhealthy living conditions. A notable feature of the lower class was the caste system of migratory vagrants—the hoboes of the road—in the "jungle" and on the job. Their social scale from the top down consisted of: the tramps, who were professional wanderers traveling alone or with a servant; the road kids, usually between 7 and 14 years old, traveling in gangs under a boy leader; the "bindle stiffs," hard workers of migratory habits; bums, who included the disabled and diseased, emotional misfits, and shiftless persons; and gay cats, not necessarily homosexuals, who were morally criminal types, feared and loathed by the others. The hobo element lived a life of wandering; they walked the highways, rode the rails, and lived on the land by begging and stealing. They were significant as a cheap labor force—the so-called fruit tramps—during the orchard and field harvests.

The Plutocrats

The emerging group of new-rich men, who acquired the status of an elite after 1870, deserves special commentary. In the American manner of successful men, they rose from humble or modest circumstances to become commanding leaders of society by virtue of their enormous wealth and power. In the state's political economy they manifested their will primarily through party bosses who secured benefits and privileges for promoting the interests of wealth. They also had subservient government officials, businessmen, and others to do their bidding. The Big Four, with their monopolistic railroad company and well-oiled political machine, were the most conspicuous, but they were certainly not the only ones nor necessarily the most wealthy or successful. An 1872 newspaper article listed Hayward, Mills, Miller, Ralston, Tevis, and others among their match. While San Francisco was the home for the biggest plutocrats, each city and town had its local nabobs in residence, the wealthy businessmen who enjoyed the recognition and privileges of their class. A notable feature of the new plutocrats was the diversity of their social aspirations. They were a mixed lot who differed widely in

Homes of the plutocrats—the mansions of Hopkins and Stanford on Nob Hill circa 1890.

ambition, attitudes, and behavior, ranging from simple men who retained their middle-class ways, like J. P. Jones and Sutro, to ostentatious ones, like Mills, who acquired new haughtiness, and Ralston and Sharon, who developed a flair for display. As a social class they outdid rivals in showiness.

California's plutocrats, like the nation's, failed to maintain their aristocratic pretensions. Their eclipse after 1900 was brought on by the loss of their worshippers, by their outdated mannerisms in an increasingly industrialized society, and by the introduction of the federal income tax (1913). Despite the absurdities of their social aspirations, the plutocrats contributed to an economic productivity that raised the nation's standard of living in an era when they were the ruling force.

Extremist Groups

In the heyday of business tycoons and party bosses, dissident elements worked mostly through established institutions for reforms that would remedy their grievances—notably, small farmers and merchant allies through the Populist and Granger parties, workers through labor unions, and, later, urban small businessmen through local and state party groups. Their ire centered on changes wrought by the growing industrialism. But their failure enhanced the rise of left- and right-wing extremist groups, who sought more drastic remedies.

The Left Wing

Left-wing extremism took root with the socialist movement. The concept of socialism is as old as Plato. Its nineteenth-century version rested on the theory that capitalism, with its class system and an economy "privately administered for personal profit," would mature either by evolution or revolution into a classless socialistic society, the ultimate of true democracy. The early attempts to found utopian socialist communities, inspired by the Englishman Robert Owen and the Frenchman Charles Fourier, attracted intellectuals like Emerson as well as middle-class adherents. In the later nineteenth century, orthodox scientific socialists, led by the German and Russian émigrés Karl Marx and Mikhail Bakunin, attempted through political third parties and trade unions to win over industrial workers. Landmark events were the formation of Marx's International Workingmen's Association (IWA, 1864), which evolved into the Socialist Labor Party (SLP, 1877); the reorganization of the American Federation of Labor under the conservative Samuel Gompers, who steered the labor movement away from socialism to independent trade unionism; the SLP's swing from orthodox to scientific socialism under revolutionist Daniel De Leon (after 1891); and the formation of the Socialist Party (1898–1901) by orthodox socialists led by reformists Eugene Debs and California's Job Harriman. After 1900 the Socialist Party enjoyed prominence in national politics as a reform third party allied to the Progressive movement. These developments set the course of American socialism as we know it today.

California came to be an important arena for socialist activities. German émigrés in San Francisco formed an IWA chapter (1869), one of the nation's first, which evolved into a local SLP (1877). The SLP was eclipsed by the nonsocialist Workingmen's Party organized by Kearney as a reform third party (see Chapter 11); later its members concentrated on pressing socialism within trade unions. Trade union activities in the 1880's involved labor leaders who were avowed socialists, notably Frank Roney and Burnette Haskell, who were active in the San Francisco labor movement (see Chapter 12). Labor's reaction to socialist influences is reflected in Haskell's experiences. He formed the International Workmen's Association (1882), whose members later quit to join trade unions; he attempted unsuccessfully to take over and "socialize" the Knights of Labor; he organized the Coast Seamen's Union only to lose leadership to a confirmed trade unionist (Andrew Furuseth); and he helped found Kaweah as a socialist colony but alienated many of its members.

California socialism hit its stride after 1890. The Nationalist Club movement, inspired by Bellamy's ideal cooperative society, apparently had a greater impact on American socialism than Marx. Bellamy's homespun version of a socialist society gave impetus to Christian Socialism among the clergy, spurred cooperative communities, and educated millions to socialism. In California it attracted disparate elements like Haskell, Job Harriman, a labor lawyer, and Gaylord Wilshire, a wealthy businessman. In the politics of the 1890's the nationalist clubs gave way to the Populist Party, and in turn, those members who did not join the Democrats, joined the Socialist Party, often involving the same radical elements (Haskell turned Populist in 1894). After 1900 the Socialist Party, under Harriman's inspiring leadership and emphasis on social democracy, superseded the SLP and emerged as a strong reform third party to enjoy a golden age in state politics.

The socialist movement was a radical response to "oppressive capitalism" which perverted democratic ideals. Its appeal, says sociologist Daniel Bell, was the "moral indignation at poverty and the evangelical promise of a better world." After four decades of initial development, it failed to win over "exploited" workers or angry farmers, who might have been valuable allies. The trade unions under Gomper's leadership became institutionalized within the American capitalist system. Agrarian radicals like Grangers and Populists swung from radicalism to conservatism "in tune with the business cycle." The Socialists greatly stimulated utopian colonies and gained respectability as a political party committed to the "bright and unbounded cause of social justice." However, they were constantly beset by internal conflicts over doctrine, strategy, and programs. Socialism became a barometer for radicalism, avoiding violent and revolutionary actions but pressuring the Republican and Democratic parties into implementing reforms.

The Right Wing

Right-wing extremists included mostly lower- and middle-class elements, laborers and small entrepreneurs, fearful of the foreign "immigrant horde" which threatened their status and was undermining American traditions of Anglo-Saxon capitalism and Puritan orthodoxy. The Workingmen's Party (1877–1880) was centered in San Francisco. It attacked the Chinese employed by the Southern Pacific and by other industries, blaming them for low wages and unemployment. The California-based American Party (1886–1891), organized by the Southern Pacific attorney and politician Peter Wiggington, was successful in its anti-Catholic campaign in local elections but failed as a national movement. The Midwest-based American Protective Association (1886–1895), which disguised anti-Catholic sentiment in a patriotic cloak, served as an umbrella for numerous affiliates, including ancestral and nationalist organizations (for example, the Sons and Daughters of the American Revolution). It entered California in 1893 where it worked through Republican and Populist tickets to elect supporters to legislative and congressional seats. San Francisco after 1900 was still a stronghold of nativist sentiment sustained by local journals (notably Pixley's *Argonaut*) and labor unions. This was apparently in reaction to the rise of Irish Catholics in community life and their assimilation into the business and professional class, which aroused old fears of the papacy in America.

Ethnic Groups

The pattern of ethnic groups of the earlier period was further refined after 1870. The 1872 Political Code carried over political and legal restrictions against racial minorities; state laws down to 1910 only modified them. Public attention focused primarily on the Asians: the Chinese between 1870 and 1890, and the Japanese thereafter. Each group—Asian, Indian, Latin, and Negro—confronted the discriminatory practices of the majority whites in different ways. Some attempted to assimilate, as Europeans were able to do. Most groups formed co-operative associations, corporate enterprises, and state societies for mutual interest and protection. They also developed subcultures based on native traditions in the segregated areas where they were forced to live, whether town or city ghettos. Their success in achieving expectations depended on their political and legal status, their visibility and closeness to antagonistic white groups, and their leadership and programs. California's open environment and expanded economy afforded ethnic groups wide opportunity to establish their niche, perhaps with less stress than elsewhere in the nation.

The Latins

As the old Hispanic order declined to near oblivion, the Californios continued to adapt to the new American order. Former leaders, like Alvarado, Pio Pico, and Vallejo, lived their remaining years in modest circumstances; most were gone by 1890. The widows and children of the older dons often intermarried with American newcomers, blending the need of the one for financial security with that of the other for social status and community roots. Arcadia, Abel Stearn's widow, married a wealthy New England immigrant Robert Baker who became a prominent Southern California businessman. Some had successful but temporary flings in politics, notably Romualdo Pacheco as governor and congressman, Reginaldo del Valle in the legislature, and Ignacio Sepulveda on the bench. Californios of all classes took up varied occupations in the Americanized order: farmer, lawyer, small businessman, and laborer.

Some became bandits—notably Tiburco Vasquez—and vagrants. Sometimes women of even the old landed gentry went to work as domestics, seamstresses, and prostitutes. Practically all suffered reduced status. The Spanish community retained considerable durability through political leaders like del Valle and descendants of old dons, like the Carrillos, Sepulvedas, and Yorbas, in business and the professions.

The decline of the Californio was most conspicuous in the deterioration of the rancho stronghold in Southern California. In the 1870's and 1880's the great ranchos were broken up into farm tracts and town subdivisions. The older dons sold land parcels to acquire funds for paying off debts, taxes, and home improvements, ending up with greatly reduced estates or none at all. The Verdugos lost all their rancho lands (Burbank–Glendale–La Canada area), while the Dominguez family managed to retain most of their large estate. The del Valles had their Rancho Camulos in the Tehachapi Mountains greatly reduced and the remainder mortgaged to their neighbor, Newhall, who graciously never pressed the debt. The old rancho, the setting for Helen Hunt Jackson's famous novel *Ramona*, was among the few showplaces that perpetuated customary ways, notably colorful fiestas and public celebrations. With the spread of new towns and the arrival of Mexican immigrant laborers, the Californios were gradually absorbed either into the majority white or the Mexican–American community, although a few families clung stubbornly to their older traditions. By the turn of the century, the old Hispanic order was dying out.

The Asians

The Chinese were a major focus of public attention after 1870. When the Central Pacific east–west line was complete, Chinese laborers went on to construct the Southern Pacific north–south line. Many others scattered throughout the state to work in the farm harvest, manufacturing enterprises, and construction projects like irrigation, reclamation, and roads, constituting an important supply of cheap labor. With the onset of the depression of the 1870's, the visible presence of industrious Chinese made them the target of unemployed workers and other hard-pressed groups who blamed them for the hard times. Anti-Chinese sentiment evolved from bigotry and resentment to violence, notably in Los Angeles and San Francisco. In San Francisco, the city enacted discriminatory laws, such as requiring that hair in queues (symbols of clan allegiance) of jailed Chinese be cut, laws that were nullified by the federal courts. When the Constitutional Convention failed to restrict the Chinese, anti-Chinese forces pressured Congress into enacting the 1882 law limiting Chinese immigration.

Chinese exclusion had unpredictable results. It had little immediate effect for the Chinese continued to work as before in city and country although without replacements from China their numbers gradually declined. A rash of anti-Chinese riots in the mid-1880's drove numerous Chinese from the towns into the big cities, further crowding the Chinatown ghettos. By the 1890's the long-range effects became apparent and even disastrous. In San Francisco's Chinatown, the nation's largest Oriental enclave, the orderly rule of the Six Companies was reduced to near anarchy following the defeat of the merchant group by the tongs. The tongs had originated in China as secret patriotic societies

Street scene in Chinatown, San Francisco, 1898.

that had fought Manchu invaders centuries earlier, and evolved into fraternal associations of family clans or into the fighting tongs, groups of disreputable elements without family ties. The latter warred with each other for control of extortion and other criminal activities, much like the Mafia who had immigrated from Sicily to New York and Chicago. The tongs ruled by fear and violence, assassinating rivals in their battles for control of the opium, slave-girl, and other profitable rackets. Municipal officials abetted tong dominance by their "hands off" policy; the police took payoffs not to interfere. "Little Pete," a powerful tong boss who skillfully blended Oriental and American ways to become "King of Chinatown," hired talented lawyers like Hall McAllister to beat murder and other raps. The tong reign came to an end when the 1906 earthquake and fire demolished their dens and rookeries, and police crackdowns helped prevent their return to power. The merchant group regained control of the Six Companies and built up a "chamber of commerce image" to develop Chinatown into a popular tourist attraction.

As the Chinese declined in numbers, the Japanese rose to take their place. Japanese immigration to California got under way after the mid-1880's when the Japanese imperial government allowed its subjects to leave the homeland. Immigrants were mostly middle-class farmers reduced to poverty. They quickly adapted to their new homeland. Japanese labor contractors, often "just off the boat," themselves, served as middlemen in providing newly arrived compatriots with lodgings and jobs, usually as contract laborers for farmers producing fruits. Ambitious Japanese, eager to improve their status, worked for a time as contract laborers; then, as sharecroppers, they rented and later purchased land and expanded their holdings to become independent farmers, concentrating on fruit, flower, and vegetable production. George Shima rose from contract laborer to labor contractor and by 1910 had became a wealthy farmer known as the Potato King. About half the Japanese eventually settled in cities, primarily in San Francisco, concentrating in ghetto areas called Little Tokyos.

By 1900 anti-Japanese sentiment appeared. Japan's startling victory in the Russo-Japanese War (1904–1905) provoked public fear of the new "Yellow Peril" and heightened agitation against local Japanese. The city school board's action in 1905 requiring that Orientals be segregated in separate schools brought on a diplomatic confrontation between the United States and the Japanese imperial government. The crisis was resolved in a Gentleman's Agreement (1907–1908) by which both nations agreed to restrict immigration. The San Francisco school board rescinded its order separating Japanese, but not Chinese, school children. Anti-Japanese sentiment still smoldered. When George Shima moved to Berkeley in 1909, he met neighbors' protests by putting a high fence around his yard to separate his children from others. Following their Bay Area experiences, many Japanese moved to Los Angeles, which by 1910 had the state's largest concentration. Roger Daniels, the historian, suggests that the informal Gentleman's Agreement was a far better solution than Chinese exclusion in resolving American–Oriental differences. The former made possible Japanese accommodations that delayed confrontation—at least until the next round of open hostilities.

Negroes

Negroes were less numerous than other minorities but seemed more aggressive in asserting their rights and exploiting opportunities. Public policy on Negro discrimination fluctuated, as illustrated by educational policies. The state court in 1874 upheld a San Francisco principal who barred a Negro child from a white public school presumably because separate facilities were available. Negro parents, however, won law suits to get their children admitted into white public schools whether or not separate facilities were available. The federal court backed discriminatory policies of hotels and theaters; one of the famous 1883 Civil Rights cases dealt with a San Francisco situation. The state court later allowed whites to marry Negroes.

Most Negroes found their niches as small entrepreneurs, clerks, and laborers in isolated towns or city "Nigger towns," especially as workers on construction and railroad jobs. Some were prominent. Mammy Pleasant, a wealthy San Francisco widow, counted Coleman, Sharon, Tevis, and other prominent men among her friends. Biddie Mason, a Los Angeles nurse, was noted for her charity work. Allen Allensworth, a retired army chaplain, set up a Negro cooperative community near Visalia. Negroes fared well in developing their own institutions, churches, newspapers, businesses, fraternal orders (Masons), and professional associations. When unemployed Negroes during the 1890's depression came to California looking for jobs and land, they bypassed San Francisco for Los Angeles, which harbored the largest black community by the turn of the century. Watts, a black enclave in the city, emerged from rancho land to become Mudtown, a transplanted Southern community tempered with Anglo and Mexican elements. Negro observers commented that while they suffered discrimination and prejudice it was far less than elsewhere, and at least they were able to own their own homes.

Indians

The Indians experienced erratic relations with governmental authorities and American settlers. The state government generally sidestepped Indian problems, which were considered a federal matter. It acted under pressure to promote Indian rights, such as permitting Indians to testify in court (1873) and providing public school education. Federal policy still focused on placing Indians on reservations—by military force, if necessary. In the Modoc War (1873), a band of 250 discontented Modocs fled the Oregon reservation for their ancestral home in the California north-east, to precipitate the nation's most protracted military show-down of the decade. It took 1000 federal troops over six months to reduce 70 to 80 warriors in their lava-bed stronghold to a punitive surrender in what was apparently California's only genuine Indian war. Congress in 1887 adopted the landmark Dawes Act which called for gradually breaking up the reservation system; it gave land lots to Indians for developing self-supporting farms. However, this and other federal programs simply did not work out in California. Federal officials were so oriented to tribal problems of the Plains and Southeast Indians that they were rarely able to comprehend clearly, much less administer effectively the unique situation of the California Indian, notably the numerous diversified rancherias and reservations of Indian tribelets. The rediscovery in 1905 of the 1851 treaties confirming Indian land titles prompted federal and state legislation (1906–1910) by which the government purchased small tracts for landless Indians to establish the basis of the present rancheria system.

The Indian plight continued unabated. In an unprovoked 1871 incident, four Americans surrounded a sleeping Yahi village and killed its 30 inhabitants. One shot surviving babies with a revolver because his heavy rifle would have "tore them up too bad." Settlers still encroached upon Indian lands. Generally, Indians retreated before the settlers' advance to isolated communities, making personal adjustments to local circumstances. They eked out a meager subsistence upon farming lands not well suited to agriculture, occasionally taking on seasonal jobs in nearby agricultural or lumbering enterprises, or selling homemade products to townsmen and tourists. The social disintegration that resulted from degradation and poverty took its toll in the widespread disease, malnutrition, and mortality, which reduced the California Indian population to its lowest ebb (17,000 in 1890, down from 27,000 in 1870). Talented Indians, like the Paiute Sarah Winnemucca, and influential Americans, like novelist Helen Hunt Jackson, did much to call public attention to the pitiable conditions of California Indians. By 1910 public sentiment had swung strongly toward sympathy with the Indians.

The Family

The California family gained stature and strength after 1870. The family institution in the eyes of the law still centered on male sovereignty, though sympathetic courts increasingly granted women rights over abusive husbands in the guardianship of their children. The immigrant flow brought in greater numbers of established families, especially from the rural Midwest and from Europe, where family ties were strong. The growth of agricultural communities was accompanied by a corresponding spread of families. The cohesive family partnership in farm, ranch, and store enterprises was the mainstay of community life. Family customs in these rural communities were effectively buttressed by community institutions like the church, which promoted family-oriented religious and social activities, and the newspaper, which extolled family life. In San Francisco and other growing cities, family ties were looser because of the men's absence from home on bread-winning jobs, the greater independence of women who sometimes worked to supplement the family income, and the relative freedom of children. They had more ambition to accumulate money and to climb the social ladder, or at least live up to class norms by "keeping up with the Joneses." Family ties, though never so strong as in the East, were weakening as young men and women broke away from the family early to strike out on their own in both rural and urban areas.

The middle-class rural family continued to be the majority. It was usually oriented to the extended family or kinship group (grandparents, uncles, aunts, cousins). The family was generally self-supporting. Family members, including "living-in" relatives and hired persons, had tasks to perform for maintaining the household and operating the family enterprise, whether farm, ranch, or store. The relative isolation of farm and ranch families increased their dependency on each other for economic survival and for home entertainment, contributing to strong family unity. Social activities included neighborhood visits and church or community "socials." Family beliefs corresponded closely with rural customs. Both reflected a Protestant Puritanism reenforced by prevailing Victorian morality. Town morality was safeguarded less by the local church or policeman than, as historian Arthur Schlesinger puts it, by the "intimate knowledge which everyone had of everyone else's affairs." Middle-class family life in the larger towns and cities was less provincial. Family members had relative freedom to enjoy wider social diversions with less community restraint.

The widening gap between California's upper and lower classes resulted in sharply contrasting family ways. The ambitious middle-class entrepreneurs who emerged as the new-rich upper class adapted to the different family ways represented by the plutocrats. The lower-class families—unskilled laborers, domestic servants, and drifters—handicapped by poverty, depressed conditions, and social antipathy, were more insecure and unstable, sometimes living in common-law marriages and always on the move. For some families the migratory habit became a way of life. The writer Charles Nordhoff tells of a Pike family who were migrating from California back to Texas for the fourth time "to please the old lady." California's lower-class family ways, because of the particularly large and mobile group of assorted transients, were distinctive in degree if not in kind from American family norms.

Women

The movement for women's rights was a long, evolutionary process. By the mid-nineteenth century, feminist leaders like Susan Anthony, Lucretia Mott, and Elizabeth Cady Stanton, were gradually achieving greater recognition. They railed at the arrogance and tyranny of men, demanding reforms like woman suffrage, equal education, and property rights. Some preached free love, easy divorce, and "statutory holidays" from wedlock. They made little real progress in achieving their goals.

The new dawn for the women's movement came in the decades after 1870. Their cause was enhanced by the rising industrialism which produced favorable socio-economic changes, especially in breaking down conventional ways and opening new vistas for the female sex. Women gained stature on several fronts, boldly asserting their independence and demonstrating their abilities in higher education, the professions, business, and other occupations. One sign of the times was the rapid rise of local womens clubs, pioneered by Catherine Severance in Boston, which amalgamated into a national organization (the General Federation of Womens Clubs, 1889). Women in these gatherings outside the home engaged in varied activities like community service, literary studies, political campaigns, card playing, and gossip.

These developments added great strength to the accelerating national campaign for women's rights. Conservative leaders like Anthony, Mott, and Stanton concentrated on woman suffrage, which they believed to be the key to eliminating sex discrimination. They initiated woman suffrage bills in Congress (the pioneer 1878 measure was sponsored by Anthony's friend, California's Aaron Sargent) and in several states, but scored only a few state victories. Radical leaders not only pressed for suffrage but also attacked the family institution—women were "legal prostitutes satisfying men's lusts"—and advocated free love and birth control. Charlotte Perkins (Lyman Beecher's great-granddaughter and a Californian after 1890), a powerful and widely read writer, pointed new directions for female freedom. She denounced the mother role in the family as demeaning to women (home cooking, she said, was economic slavery) and stressed their natural rights to self-fulfillment. Other feminist leaders concentrated on social reforms, such as temperance or better working conditions for women and children.

American women, after a half-century of such developments, experienced major changes in their status. They won limited victories when some states granted them property rights and the suffrage (Idaho and Wyoming), but they still suffered civil liabilities as second-class citizens. Their legal status was reflected in the adultery trials of Henry Ward Beecher (Lyman's son and a prominent prelate), in which he was acquitted, but the lady was convicted. This incensed women's rights leaders, who made issue of the case. Women were generally held in low esteem on jobs, working for lower pay than men at the same jobs. In society, they were still objects of veneration. As one observer declared, men made money with terrible dedication while women were sacrificed on the "altar of graces" or as symbols of their men's wealth, reflected in their fine dress and jewels. Feminist pioneers like Charlotte Perkins, by the turn of the century, were attacking this image, stressing woman's "inner spirit and psychology."

California reflected just about all of these manifestations of the women's movement after 1870. In Southern California, eastern women migrating to the state during the booms were especially active in launching women's organizations and activities. The local club was pioneered in Los Angeles by Catherine Severance, the mother of clubs. The pacesetter was Pasadena with its high preponderance of women and feminist leaders, notably Charlotte Perkins and her friend Grace Channing, and their diversified interests, including Shakespeare, temperance, and civic improvement. California was the target of national suffragists who supported the local campaign in the 1896 legislature for a women's vote bill. The bill was defeated, apparently by the San Francisco saloon interests backed by the Southern Pacific machine.

The lot of California women evoked mixed reactions. Contemporary observers commented on the comparative freedom of girls and women in the family, on the job, in social affairs, and in community activities, compared to the sisterhood elsewhere. The sharpest critic was probably Henry Sienkiewicz, a Polish journalist who had joined the Modjeska Colony and later became a prominent author (*Quo Vadis?*). He commented on the San Francisco women who were elaborately attired, even better than in Paris, and the town and country ladies who dressed like fashion plates at a French circus. While her John Chinaman (servant) works as a nurse, cook, and gardener, he observed, she "sits in her rocking chair, receives guests, decks herself in finery and pampers her baby—they lead a life of external superficialities, like so many frolicsome kittens." He made much of the California law which stipulated that when a man beats his wife he shall receive 21 lashes with a rawhide whip. Fortunately for him, the Polish émigré did not remain to face the feminist reaction.

Public Entertainment

Public entertainment—cultural and recreational activities—took root before 1870 in San Francisco for particular groups and evolved by the 1890's for public groups, especially in Southern California. Elements which were involved in this development were imaginative promoters, philanthropic sponsors, a leisured upper class, and later recreation-minded middle-class workers who served as clientele. (The Saturday half-day off and summer two-week vacation became fairly standard.) A big impetus came after 1880 with the increasing flow of tourists. Popular pastimes included roller skating and after 1890 bicycle trips and excursions to scenic spots like Yosemite in the Sierra. Also popular were playlands like the Southern California beaches and showplace communities like Pasadena. Horse racing and later bike and auto racing, as well as professional baseball and college football, became prominent spectator sports.

Cultural activities moved in new directions. San Francisco set the pace for public halls and theatres featuring speakers, art exhibitions, musical performances, and vaudeville and other shows. San Francisco expanded with the Hopkins Art Institute (1874, later the California School of Fine Arts), the California Theatre (rebuilt 1888), and the de Young Museum (1895). Its famous opera tradition was perpetuated by an elegant opera house (1876) and by the Tivoli, which evolved from a public beer–music garden (1875) into an opera theatre for mass audiences. Among talented natives who "made the big time" were impresario David Belasco, actress Maude Adams, and dancer Isadora Duncan. Los Angeles began with the Merced Theatre (by 1870), but did not develop extensively until the Great Boom with its music conservatory (1883), opera house (1884), and Hazard Pavillion (1887), which featured "grand opera, prize fights, flower festivals and citrus shows." By the turn of the century L. C. Behymer began his long, illustrious career as local impresario. Other communities were also favored by local philanthropists, notably Sacramento's Crocker Art Gallery (1884) and Stockton's Haggin Galleries (1887). California's climate inspired amphitheatres for outdoor performances which developed after the turn of the century at Carmel, San Francisco (Bohemian Club), and Berkeley (UC's Greek Theatre, 1903). Thus the foundations were laid for broadly based public entertainment for a heterogeneous population.

B. CULTURE

THE SETTING

California's cultural base was broadened by the blending of local traditions with outside influences. The state soon emerged with two major cultural regions. In Northern California, American midwestern and eastern cultural influences intermingled with a well-established cultural tradition that had emerged with the Americanized frontier of the Gold Rush period. It centered on cosmopolitan San Francisco and embraced scattered agricultural, mining, and lumber communities which felt the influences of the Bay City. In Southern California, the same outside cultural influences were implanted in relatively virgin land just being opened to settlement, thus leaving a direct imprint on the region's emerging culture. It focused on Los Angeles, which was then experiencing a transition from frontier town to agrarian and commercial center for farm towns scattered throughout the Southland. A rural–urban cultural division was in the making.

The rise of Southern California as a distinct cultural region came at about this time. As literary historian Franklin Walker tells us, various writers and town developers joined with other enthusiastic promoters in putting down cultural roots, a process he describes as "cultural hydroponics," an allusion to the agricultural science of growing vegetables in water and mineral salts without soil. The American newcomers, upon arriving in sparsely settled cow country, found little cultural tradition, so they proceeded to fashion one. They were inspired by the subtropical environment which reminded them of the Mediterranean, where the classic Greek and Roman civilization took root, and of Italy, whose terrain and climate resembled those of California. Grace Channing, who knew Italy well, was captivated by the analogy of California with Italy. She compared the San Francisco and Sacramento areas to the commercial Piedmont; the Central Valley to the fertile Lombard Plain; the Central Coast to gardenlike Tuscany, San Diego, and Naples, with their bays; and Santa Catalina to the Isle of Capri—and she topped it all by likening Los Angeles to Rome because both had rivers to the sea. People of growing communities were swayed by the pseudoscientific explanations of prominent physicians who claimed that the favorable climate and terrain attracted superior immigrants who would create an exceptional society. Stanford University's President David Jordan even suggested that California's environment called for ingenious pioneers, and that the processes of natural selection "have favored the survival of the ingenious" through heredity.

With this foundation, promoters and writers had little difficulty incorporating the native Spanish tradition into new settings. This could be seen in older towns like Los Angeles, Santa Barbara, and San Diego, which enjoyed rebirth, and was perpetuated in boom towns like Arcadia, Naples, and Venice. Helen Hunt Jackson's immensely popular novel *Ramona* helped crystallize California's version of a Spanish tradition. Before long, the writers produced a synthetic picture by overlaying a romantic version of the past upon historical and contemporary realities. For example, they endowed Spanish California leaders with Castilian blood (Spain's "pure" blood), ignoring the fact that the Californios and Mexican-born consigned to the "Sonoratowns" of their communities were actually mixed-bloods. Pasadena and Santa Barbara inaugurated annual flower festivals in the manner of Mediterranean towns. Entrepreneurs mixed cultural enthusiasm with business to develop flamboyant showplaces, like Abbott Kinney's Venice and Frank Miller's Mission Inn at Riverside (1902), the latter inspired by Spain's great Alhambra Palace. Later, Southern Californians would be ridiculed for their contrived culture, but as Walker reminds us, they were merely following a well-established American tendency to create from their romantic past a regional cultural tradition. As New Englanders manufactured legends of the Pilgrim fathers, and Southerners conceived a chivalrous tradition of cavalier forebears, so had Southern Californians fashioned a Hispanic tradition.

ANALYSIS

Education

Primary and Secondary Schools

The widespread discontent of the "Terrible Seventies" had an effect on public education. The Granger-dominated 1874 legislature enacted one of the earliest compulsory primary education measures, even though dissident groups voiced complaints about the school system and demanded reforms. The Grangers complained about burdensome taxes; the trade unions were for free textbooks and more vocational training; and the California Teachers Association (organized 1875) deplored inadequate state support and the slow progress in developing schools. These groups carried their fight to the Constitutional Convention, which made some concessions but in essence reestablished the existing system. The long-standing conflict over state-adopted textbooks, which focused on eastern publishers charging exorbitant prices that saddled local school districts with a costly burden, led to a famous textbook scandal. An 1880 constitutional amendment resolved the issue by authorizing the state printing office to print state-adopted textbooks from the publisher's plates. (Commercial publishers are still battling today to change this policy.)

School reform, which had been making steady headway since midcentury, accelerated after 1880. Reformers were redirecting attention from uniform treatment for all children to the individual development of each child. The impulse came from European educators, like Johann Heinrich Pestalozzi, who developed the concepts, Johann Herbart who worked out the methods, and Friedrich Froebel, founder of the kindergarten, who developed practical ways. These men virtually revolutionized educational approaches and class instruction. Francis Parker, a Chicago normal-school superintendent, became the leading American advocate of these ideas and father of the movement which came to be known as progressive education.

California was caught in this reform wave, which took several directions. Emma Marwedel, a Froebel-trained teacher from Germany who became an American kindergarten pioneer, arrived in California in 1876 and, over the next 15 years, propagated the kindergarten systems in Los Angeles, Oakland, Berkeley, and San Francisco. When Francis Parker delivered his popular talks on school reform during his California visit in 1886, he found enthusiastic audiences among school officials and teachers. In cities and towns, primary schools placed increasing stress on domestic and manual arts (a Froebel innovation), while secondary schools went further with applied sciences, social sciences, and vocational training.

The lagging public high school movement was revitalized by state university efforts to increase declining student enrollment. University of California officials joined civic groups in pressuring the 1891 legislature to enact landmark measures making it easier to establish public high schools. A result of this was the phasing out of private academies and seminaries, which hitherto had filled the educational gap between primary school and higher education. University reformers, notably the University of California Professor Alexis Lange and Stanford's president, David Jordan, cooperated to reshape the educational system on a more rational basis. Their effort culminated in the 1907 legislature's enactment of the nation's first law setting up the junior college. It was to consist of the 13th and 14th grades and serve as a post-graduate high school preparing for university upper division. Fresno in 1910 was the first to establish such a *public* junior college (though not the nation's first junior college, as often alleged). On another front, local leaders were seeking ways to help pupils make the transition from elementary to high school, and also to resolve school financing problems. Berkeley in 1910 found its remedy in setting up the nation's first junior high schools, comprising the 7th, 8th, and 9th grades. California's experimentation in developing these intermediate schools affected school systems throughout the nation.

Colleges and Universities

The University of California (hereafter UC), which had just opened its doors, had yet to map out its direction. When Daniel Coit Gilman, Yale's distinguished scientist–educator, became president in 1872, he accomplished that purpose. In his inaugural, he set forth for the university its vision: a foundation for the promotion and diffusion of knowledge, a group of agencies to advance the arts and sciences and to train men for all the intellectual callings of life to meet the requirements of society. During his brief two-year term, Gilman laid the groundwork for fulfilling the idea, establishing many precedents of present-day developments. These included private endowments, professional chairs, professional schools, an art gallery, an observatory (which James Lick presented with the world's largest telescope), and a library. Time was to prove Gilman the chief architect of UC's development as a comprehensive institution.

After Gilman, the University of California, down to the turn of the century, underwent erratic development. Inadequate financing by a stingy legislature was compensated for by generous private philanthropies. University leadership was compromised by the clique-ridden regents and by powerless presidents. The low-paid professors concentrated on instruction, though some, like Joseph Le Conte, the geologist, and Eugene Hilgard in agriculture, made outstanding contributions to research and public service. Student life was characterized by long commutes, part-time work, strong class spirit, fraternities vs. independents for student government control (organized 1887), sports like football (1892 was the first UC–Stanford Big Game), and occasional wild larks and drinking bouts. Women were admitted from the beginning, though one woman had to win a court case to gain admission to the law school. Many UC graduates, by the turn of the century, were already assuming prominent positions in the state's governmental, business, and professional life.

With the advent of President Benjamin Wheeler (1899), UC went through a major transformation. Wheeler infused the university with new vigor, lofty ideals, and ambitious schemes which infected regents, faculty, and students alike, and won the university scholarly prestige and immense popularity. He presided over the development of a handsome campus (the imposing Italian Renaissance buildings had been endowed by Phoebe Hearst), consolidated sprawling colleges, hired talented professors nationwide, strengthened student self-government, lobbied the legislature effectively, and expanded research and public service programs at home and abroad. By 1910 UC ranked among the nation's top dozen universities and was on the threshold of even greater growth and prestige.

Higher education was rounded out by several other developments. Commensurate with state growth and demands for teachers, five state normal schools were added for training teachers. Southern California's rapid growth made the area a fertile field for denominational institutions, especially since state facilities were located in the north. Among the new colleges were the University of Southern California (1880, Methodist), Pomona College (1887, Congregational), Occidental College (1887, Presbyterian), Whittier College (1901, Quaker), Pasadena College (1902, Nazarene) and the University of Redlands (1907, Baptist). Many were originally set up primarily for training clergy in the faith but soon broadened to become liberal arts colleges with open admission. The University of Southern California's interdenominational character was reflected in its original endowers, among whom were a Catholic (John Downey), a Jew (Isaiah Hellman), and a Protestant. In the north, the Leland Stanfords endowed Stanford University in Palo Alto with a $30 million grant (1885) as a memorial to their only son, who died in his youth (1884). Representing the wave of the future in the new sciences and technology were the privately endowed Throop Polytechnic Institute (1891, later the California Institute of Technology) in Pasadena, and the state-sponsored California State Polytechnic College (1901) near San Luis Obispo.

By 1910 California's educational system had come of age. It owned much to outstanding leaders and to the contributions of private and public institutions. It achieved a remarkable balance of primary, secondary, college, and university segments. The reform wave in national education that swept California was still rising in 1910. By then it was labeled progressive education: it hailed Francis Parker as its father and

John Dewey as its chief propagator. It aimed to use schools and colleges for better preparing youth for an increasingly complex society. It was in educator Lawrence Crenin's words "part and parcel of that broader program of social and political reform called the Progressive movement." Educational institutions emerged in a real sense as mirrors of the society they served.

Journalism

American journalism underwent a great transformation in this period. The second-generation publishers of the big pioneer New York newspapers set the pace—for example, James Gorden Bennett, Jr., of the *New York Herald*, who matched his father's eccentricity and enterprise in sensational news, and Whitelaw Reid of the *New York Tribune* and Adolph Ochs of the *New York Times*, who continued the high principles of their founders. Similar trends developed out West. The vituperative Joseph Medill ran his *Chicago Tribune* much like Bennett, though with a provincial outlook. The fabled Wilbur Story achieved distinction for "raw meat" journalism: his *Chicago Times* headlined the hanging execution of four repentant murderers with "Jerked to Jesus." Such publishers were matched by their opposite numbers in the likes of Victor Lawson of the *Chicago Daily News*, who pioneered the trend toward responsible, civic-minded journalism, E. W. Scripps of the *Cincinnati Post,* and Joseph Pulitzer of the *St. Louis Post-Dispatch*. Personal journalism reached its peak in the giant publishers of the day.

California newspapers mirrored midwestern journalism. In the 1870's journalism was an aggressive, competitive, and occasionally dangerous business. Editors were generally preoccupied with local issues: McClatchy's *Sacramento Bee* crusaded for land reforms, while the *Alta California*, under Hittell's sometime editorship, praised corporate entrepreneurs and castigated reformers. Henry George developed his *San Francisco Post* (1871), the first penny newspaper on the Pacific Coast, into the leading spokesman for the workingman. The *San Francisco Chronicle*, which gained ascendancy over rivals in the Bay City, was developed as an independent Republican paper in the Lawson reform tradition. During the stormy municipal administration of the Workingmen's Party in 1879, Charles de Young shot and wounded the mayor, only to be assassinated by the mayor's son, who was acquitted of the crime.

By the 1880's journalism felt the heavy hand of business influences. The Big Four, who had consolidated two papers in the state capital to set up the *Sacramento Record–Union*, extended their journalistic influence statewide by paying monthly subsidies to many city and country papers to circulate their views and presumably curb unfavorable railroad publicity. Industrial tycoons who utilized newspapers as personal vehicles include James Fair, who bought the *Alta California*, J. P. Jones, who took over the *San Francisco Post* (Henry George left soon after), and George Hearst, who bought the *San Francisco Examiner*. Rural communities generally had newspapers whose editors served as the community's conscience and as business promoters—for example, Harrison Gray Otis and his *Los Angeles Times* and the Chester Rowells (uncle and nephew) and their *Fresno Republican* (1884). Many rural publishers were products of midwestern journalism with its penchant for editorial independence and community interest.

Meanwhile, the nation was experiencing rising national trends toward yellow journalism and chain newpapers. The pioneer of yellow journalism was Joseph Pulitzer, who had taken New York by storm in the 1880's. Taking over the *New York World*, he carried forward the Bennett tradition of sensationalism by playing up corruption, crime, sex, and scandal to attract a mass audience. Edward Scripps was the first to develop the chain newspaper on a large scale, building up his midwestern newspaper empire and then retiring, while still young, to California. From his San Diego ranch, he began anew to extend his empire nationwide, buying up small, grubby newspapers and turning them over to talented young editors who transformed them into major papers. Pulitzer and Scripps inaugurated trends that became trademarks of modern journalism.

California had its champion of these trends in William Randolph Hearst (George's son). After a Harvard education and a reporter's stint on Pulitzer's *New York World*, Hearst set out to build a newspaper empire. Taking over the *San Francisco Examiner* in the late 1880's, Hearst hired a top-flight staff, including ace reporters like Arthur McEwen, and developed his formula for mass newspaper circulation. He built up large-scale newspaper production with big machinery and technical innovations, and perfected techniques for sensationalizing the news: big scare headlines, lavish pictures, misleading accounts, fake interviews, and other fraudulent methods that became earmarks of yellow journalism. While developing his methods in San Francisco,

Hearst moved on to New York where he bought the *Journal* (1896) and took on Pulitzer's *World*, the city's largest newspaper, and other newspaper giants for metropolitan leadership. The deadly battle between Hearst and Pulitzer raged for years; it brought yellow journalism to the peak of rabid sensationalism. Pulitzer, shaken by the experience, did a complete turnabout. He converted his *World* to a responsible paper and established the famous annual literary prizes. Hearst, emboldened by his success, challenged Scripps, acquiring after 1904 newspapers between Boston and Los Angeles to build his newspaper chain. He also entered politics in New York and California. A disciple of Pulitzer and Scripps, Hearst clearly outdid both masters.

By the turn of the century, major developments were reshaping journalism in California. The battle for mass circulation started by Hearst shook up the industry. Other newspaper giants, however they deplored Hearst's methods, either followed his example or fought to outdo him. Michael de Young faced the threat to his leadership in San Francisco by fighting Hearst on all fronts. Another shift was the changing guard in newspaper ownership which brought new faces. In San Francisco, the *Call* was acquired by John Spreckels (Claus's son). and the *Bulletin* came under the editorship of Fremont Older, a remarkable, crusading reformer. In Los Angeles, E. T. Earl acquired the *Express*, hiring the talented young Edward Dickson as editor to oppose Otis's *Times*. Earl and Otis were dominant influences in metropolitan affairs; they were personally friendly and next-door neighbors, cooperating and competing in business deals, but bitter newpaper rivals. In the Central Valley, leadership was asserted by McClatchy's *Sacramento Bee* (which passed in 1878 to James's sons) and the Rowells' *Fresno Republican*. The Southern Pacific fought agents of the Western Pacific in the north and the Santa Fe in the south for railroad influence over city and rural newspapers. Rivalry encouraged California newspapers to try new ideas. By 1910 they had already acquired the format of big headlines, sensational accounts, special features, cartoons, and photographs characteristic of their modern appearance.

Literature

America's literary trends after 1870 had a strongly regional and realistic flavor. Writers exploited the distinctive character of the people and the land from which they came, whether New England, the South, the "Middle Border," or the Far West. They were realistic in showing life as it actually was, though some manifested streaks of romanticism which dominated in other writers. Taking their cues from European predecessors, Americans gave realism a vivid, native expression, as pioneered in the novels of William Dean Howells, high priest of the movement, and in the poetry of Walt Whitman. California's David Belasco, in pioneering the modern New York theater, encouraged the realistic movement in play productions. The short story was paced by Henry James, the nation's most prolific writer, and Mark Twain, whose stories reflected his rugged honesty.

Coincident with the realist movement was the rise of social criticism of the emerging industrial order. Realistic novelists led the literary onslaught, hitting at the destructive plutocracy and reasserting older democratic values. The urbane Howells told straightforward, commonplace stories of middle-class America. The bawdy Mark Twain portrayed the Midwest with boisterous humor and devastating satire—his *Gilded Age* (1871), embodying a California plot, sloganized the era. The romantics had a representative in Edward Bellamy, whose *Looking Backward* (1888) compared predatory capitalism of the mid-1880's with utopian socialism of the year 2000; his novel was America's biggest seller since *Uncle Tom's Cabin*. Social criticism evolved from a literary technique of the Howells group in the 1870's and 1880's to a social philosophy conveying a subjective realism pioneered by California's Frank Norris in the 1890's and labeled naturalism. As intellectual historian Vernon Parrington explains, naturalism is pessimistic realism, showing how man is victimized in a mechanical world. Naturalism and the novel became an essential part of the Progressive movement.

California developed a two-part regional literature emanating from literary trends in the north and the south. San Francisco as the state's literary capital widened its orientation to the Bay region. Its cosmopolitan tradition from colorful pioneer days was tempered by a newly acquired staid urbanity. The Bohemian Club as the center of letters and arts pointed to a trend: formed in 1872 by leading writers and artists, it later acquired social exclusiveness when it accepted members known for their wealth rather than their literary talent. A central figure was Ina Coolbrith, librarian of Oakland's public library and later of the Bohemian Club. She continued to write genteel poetry, keep ties with her old circle, and nourish aspiring writers like Mary Austin and Jack London. After their return from distant travels, other pioneer writers, notably Ambrose Bierce and Joaquin Miller, picked up where they had left off. A new crop of writers also made their mark, like

Gertrude Atherton, member of a wealthy and prominent family, who wrote charming stories with local and foreign settings. Famous British writers visiting the Bay Area were inspired to compose literary gems: Rudyard Kipling of his San Francisco visit, and Robert Louis Stevenson of his Monterey and Napa sojourns, which provided settings for his *Treasure Island* and other famous stories. Together these writers contributed substance to the area's cosmopolitan literary tradition.

In the Southland, Los Angeles was the focus of another brand of literature. It was characterized by a regional provincialism shaped by the desert environment, Hispanic tradition, and eastern émigrés. A leading representative was Charles Lummis, a versatile writer and editor of the Southland's leading journal, *Land of Sunshine*. Lummis was a theatrical figure who often wore affected garb, usually Spanish and Indian, to portray the role he played in promoting varied civic projects and tourist attractions. He served literary Southern California as Coolbrith did the San Francisco area, sustaining a circle of gifted writers and acting as literary critic to aspiring writers. Among the many prominent figures and established writers who lent their names and talents to promote the Southern California local-color school were Jesse Fremont (John's widow), acknowedged dean of the school, Grace Ellery Channing, member of a pioneer Unitarian family, and Charlotte Perkins. a literary light as well as a militant feminist crusader. They helped to lay foundations for the Southland's emerging literary tradition.

Outstanding local writers did not appear until the turn of the century when Frank Norris, Jack London, and Mary Austin entered the literary scene. Norris (1870–1902) grew up in San Francisco of wealthy parents, attended UC and Harvard, and enjoyed a brilliant but short writing career. Norris sought to exceed Howells's objective realism, which he thought too optimistic. He portrayed the epic relations of man and nature, showing the interplay of basic human drives and powerful natural forces. His *McTeague* (1899) is a personal epic, "an odyssey of the soul," about a brutish San Francisco dentist who is driven to destitution by his "civilized" wife's greed for money, until he beats her to death and flees to a bizarre end, appropriately in Death Valley. *The Octopus* (1901) is a social epic which uses a Central Valley locale to show the railroad's tentacles crushing farmers who struggle against it. He writes the thoughts of a ruined farmer:

> He had been merely the object of a colossal trick, a sordid injustice, a victim of the insatiate greed of the monster, caught

and choked by one of those millions of tentacles suddenly reaching up from below . . . coiling around his throat, throttling him, strangling him, sucking his blood . . . Ah, the rage of helplessness, the fury of impotence!

Norris's intention to complete his grand wheat trilogy, of which *The Octopus* was the first volume, was cut short by his untimely death from appendicitis. His *Octopus* compares with *Uncle Tom's Cabin* as a great propaganda novel, which impressed men's minds and spurred reform efforts. This timely account of the famed Mussel Slough incident conditioned the minds of people to the Progressive reform crusade after 1910.

Jack London (1876–1916) stands for distinctive individualism, the epitome of virile manhood. He led a spectacular life, from his illegitimate birth in San Francisco through an adventurous youth that included stints with Coxey's Army, at UC, and in the Alaska Gold Rush (1898). He enjoyed sudden fame as a writer in his mid-20's and was dead by his own hand at 40. London's novels tell of man fighting for survival in nature as in society. His famous *Call of the Wild* (1903) tells of a kidnapped domesticated California dog turned loose in Alaska where he turns wild with a wolf pack. London gave extensive treatment to Marxist and other philosophical ideas in his plots. Critics still argue his status as a great writer, but none can doubt the popularity of his writings (all but a few of 50 titles have been translated into foreign languages and made into movies). The scholar Eugene Burdick suggests that his appeal to our present urban generation is his ability to make the lost, savage world of nature live again.

Mary Austin epitomizes communion with nature, as reflected in her love for the desert environment. A young, midwestern girl when she emigrated to California, she experienced the lonely homestead life with her family near the Tehachapis and with her husband in Owens Valley. She had a keen ability to express deep perceptions of her spiritual feeling for the desert, not unlike Emerson's transcendental feeling for God and nature. To her the desert's secret charm was the "secret of life triumphant." Her *Land of Little Rain* (1903) and other stories captured the many moods of the desert and a love of the Indians, the sheep, their herders, and other dwellers. Her love of the desert environment affected others as well.

Historical literature took root with a group of nonprofessional but competent historians. The most outstanding was Hubert Howe

Bancroft, a San Francisco book publisher, who produced a seven-volume epic chronicle of California history (1886). He employed a large staff who systematically collected historical materials and wrote a careful, comprehensive chronicle. Bancroft was criticized for not naming the major staff writers (the talented Henry Oak wrote at least five of the seven volumes), but the business-minded publisher did not feel it necessary. As the publisher who conceived and organized this remarkable work, Bancroft is without peer. The work has stood the test of time so well that it has been republished recently, and serious students still use it.

Californians revealed talents in promotional and muckraking literature. Town promoters in booming real estate ventures enticed prospective buyers with enchanting verses. A Los Angeles town advertisement began with "Sweet La Ballona's a great old town / Prices will rise when the tracks are down. . . ." Even stage robbers were bitten by the poetry bug, such as the famous Black Bart, who left behind creditable verses like:

> So here I've stood while wind and rain
> Have set the trees to sobbing
> And risked my life for that damned stage
> That was not worth the robbing
>
> Black Bart, the PO 8

Muckraking, the literature of exposure, derives its name from a seventeenth-century classic (John Bunyan's *Pilgrim's Progress*) in which a character is so busy raking muck he cannot perceive the heavenly crown held above him. Preceded by early examples like Twain's *Gilded Age*, California's Lincoln Steffens pioneered the national muckraking movement with his classic *Shame of the Cities* (1904), exposing machine politics. The movement produced the crusading journalists and novelists who were important forerunners of the Progressive movement.

California's literary output, then, was prodigious. By 1910 it had a richly diverse literary tradition that was inseparable from the literature of the nation.

Religion

Religion in the half-century after the Civil War underwent startling development. The rise of scientific thought (see below) fostered an intellectual climate that turned people from religion to the new sciences. The arrival of more immigrants from Southern Europe (hitherto most had come from Northern Europe) brought proportionately greater numbers of Catholics, Jews, and Eastern Orthodox, primarily Greek and Russian, unsettling established religious ways. The crass materialism, lax morality, and widespread corruption engendered by rapid economic expansion forced religious leaders to devote more attention to worldly affairs. Established churches backed by funds from local businessmen built large edifices and systematized their activities, extending their missionary work to eastern cities and to the West. Religious groups concentrated on blighted conditions in rising industrial cities, notably church mission societies, the YMCA, and the newly founded Salvation Army (1877) with its militaristic brass and tambourine bands—each had its way of helping the new immigrant and other underprivileged people. Out of the YMCA movement arose Dwight Moody, the great Chicago-based evangelist preacher: he was the first professional promoter to organize evangelical work on a businesslike basis, and he was unmatched among his generation in the mass conversion of people to the faith. Disaffected Protestants formed new churches and sects, notably the Theosophical Society (1875), the Christian Scientists (1876), the holiness movement, and spiritualists. Religious fever was everywhere, most conspicuously in the cities.

These developments profoundly affected church theology. Protestant liberals, led by Henry Ward Beecher (Lyman's son), departed from the old theology to stress the practical application of Jesus' teachings toward reforming the social environment, while Protestant conservatives fought to reenforce Biblical authority and church doctrine. Catholics and Jews, who scored impressive gains in membership, each had their conservative-liberal confrontations.

Public attention was drawn to the new gospels of faith. The "gospel of wealth" as expounded by Andrew Carnegie (1889), preached the sacred system of capitalistic competition which insured "survival of the fittest." This view was staple fare for Protestant as well as Catholic church sermons and moral teachings, and it inspired businessmen. The social gospel adapted ethical ideas and moral principles to the new industrial order, applying the Golden Rule and the Law of Love to all transactions in society. It influenced intellectual and civic leaders, aroused farmers, workingmen, and immigrants, and led to practical ways (the so-called applied Christianity) in remedying the ills of society, such as municipal government reform and social work. Social gospel conditioned the minds of leaders in the Progressive movement, who came into their own after 1910 in California and the nation at large.

California was an integral part of these national religious movements. Its church movement was strong and essentially conventional. Its theological mood was conservative, though it manifested its distinctive sense of freedom in the variety of cults and sects. The state was fertile ground for new religious movements. It was the foremost center for religious utopian colonies, notably the Harrises' Sect at Fountain Grove in the 1870's and the Theosophists at Point Loma in the 1890's. Dwight Moody and Henry Ward Beecher attracted large crowds to their occasional appearances. Moody's version of the three R's caught the public fancy: Ruin by sin, Redemption by Christ, and Regeneration by the Holy Ghost. In Los Angeles, charismatic leaders pioneered the holiness revival; notable among these were Phineas Bresee, a disenchanted Methodist leader whose mission (1895) evolved into the Church of the Nazarene, and William Seymour, a Negro minister whose black mission (1906) was the springboard for twentieth-century Pentecostalism. Several church denominations established seminaries for training ministers, and the Pacific Theological Seminary (relocated from Oakland to Berkeley, 1901) broadened into the famous Pacific School of Religion.

Some disciples of eastern religions made their appearance in the San Francisco Area, including Zen Buddhist priests (1898) and Vivekananda, the St. Paul of Sri Ramakrishna (the saintly Hindu mystic), who established the Vedanta Society in California around 1900. Church activities on behalf of education and temperance were widespread and especially successful in Southern California, a tradition which persisted to World War II.

Science and Technology

American science and technology made enormous strides after 1870. Technology entered its "heroic age." Basic inventions like the electric dynamo and the internal-combustion engine led to many other inventions, such as the telephone, the electric light, and the automobile, which revolutionized economic and social life. Technology was evolving from a craft of self-educated inventors to a profession of college-trained specialists—the craftsman or mechanic was becoming a professional specialist. Science made great discoveries that led to the new fields of physical chemistry, radioactivity (X-rays), and thermodynamics, and to theories of biological evolution, mathematical infinity (1883), and atomic energy (1901). Scientists became professionals, specializing in fields like biology, botany, geology, physics and zoology, and even in subfields like astrophysics, entomology, and paleontology. Science blended to such an extent with technology that the line between them blurred: Edison relied on the electrodynamic discoveries of Michael Faraday and Joseph Henry in inventing the electric light. The Carnegie Foundation (organized 1902) began making generous bequests which would greatly help accelerate the advancement of science. American science and technology, by the turn of the century, had come into their own, clearly independent of religion and philosophy and firmly established with the full support of industry, government, and the public.

Government and science cemented their alliance, primarily through service to industry. The prestigious National Academy of Science, with its elite corps of government scientists (like Henry, Powell, and Pinchot), and other science-oriented organizations spearheaded research efforts in wide-ranging fields like aeronautics, astrophysics, conservation of land and marine resources, medical science, and practical farming. The United States Department of Agriculture evolved into the largest federal department, comprising science-oriented bureaus that applied professional expertise to insect, plant, and livestock problems of farming, lumbering, and ranching enterprises. John Powell, the great explorer of the Colorado, and King's successor in the United States Geological Survey, came to personify the government scientist. Regarded as the principal government scientist since Bache, Powell fought the threat of laissez faire in the sciences to cinch the government commitment to science: he laid the foundations for scientific classification of land, water rights, and natural resources (so important to Californians). Federal ties with the states were strengthened, especially with the landmark 1887 Hatch Act, which established agricultural experiment stations in California and other states. In addition, the universities trained scientists for federal agencies. By 1910 the foundation of the federal scientific establishment was nearing completion.

California was in the vanguard of these technological and scientific developments. Inventors made important contributions to the state's economic development, among them Dolbeer's donkey engine in lumbering, Pelton's water wheel. Chaffee's hydroelectric plant, Hallidie's cable streetcar, and Holt's and Best's tractors in farming. Engineers applied ingenious technology to vast, intricate projects in mining, irrigation, hydroelectricity, manufacturing, and other areas. Industry warmed to the new technology and science. Farmers and manufacturers worked closely with scientists and technicians in resolving field and factory problems. Some corporations, especially in explosives, mining, and petroleum industries, built laboratories for their chemists and other technicians. Scientists were attracted by California's ideal climate for their experimental work, notably Josiah Whitney, whose Sierra observations helped in understanding the nature of earthquakes, and Luther Burbank, whose half-century of experimentation in his famous Santa Rosa botanical garden (established 1886) produced numerous species of improved fruit, vegetable, and flower plants for the state's expanding commercial agriculture. The adventurous experimentation of imaginative native and adopted Californians (see Chapter 12) was to have great implications for the aircraft, electronics, and other new industries.

Government, industry, and the university, at the state and national levels, developed the intricate, cooperative relationships for the advancement of science and technology that figured so importantly in the state's progress. Symbolic of California's tie with the nation's science was Clarence King's landmark survey of the 40th Parallel (1868–1872), connecting California with completed federal surveys in the Midwest and providing a geologic link as the railroad had provided an economic link. The state legislature, responding to local pressure, established science-oriented bureaus in health, forestry, horticulture, viticulture (grape growing), livestock, mining, and other areas. The state also benefited from federal contributions, such as when a United States Agriculture Department agency provided the Riverside Colony with the Washington naval orange plant, resulting in a major state industry. The state did not hesitate to draw help from prominent scientists, as in the case of Harvard's Asa Gray, father of American botany, who carried out the complex plant classification for the state geological survey.

The University of California was intricately involved with these developments. Philosophical, though practical-minded, scientists like the Le Conte brothers gave way to professional specialists like Eugene Hilgard, the soil expert and father of the state's scientific agriculture, and the science group recruited during Wheeler's presidency. Through James Lick's generous bequest, the university built the Mt. Hamilton Observatory below San Jose: prominent astronomers utilizing its 36-inch telescope, then the world's largest, made significant discoveries for international science. It was matched after 1900 by the Mt. Wilson Observatory near Pasadena; George Hale set up its 100-inch telescope with funds from the Carnegie Foundation. The university's scientific and technological contributions in mining and other industries have been noted elsewhere.

These developments were not without their trials and tribulations. Whitney quit the state geological survey after a decade of frustrating battle with a penny-pinching and unsympathetic legislature—the old battle of pure vs. applied science. Hilgard fought running battles with self-educated farmer entomologists; their conflicts led to the abolition of the first viticulture board. The self-educated Matthew Cooke, chief of the first horticultural board and father of the state's pioneer plant quarantine system, fought long and hard against narrow-minded farmers in establishing disease eradication methods for saving their crops. Amos Throop's bequest to the state for a scientific school (like those of Harvard and Yale) resulted in a deadlock of special-interest groups that caused him to set up a privately endowed independent institution (Throop Polytechnic Institute, 1891), which later evolved into California Institute of Technology. These conflicts, however, hardly slowed the state's pronounced progress in scientific and technological endeavors.

Philosophical Views

American intellectual development in the last half of the nineteenth century was dominated by the battles of philosophers. The idealism so conspicuous earlier became blurred under the impact of the rising social sciences (the professional fields of history, political science, economics, sociology, and psychology) and the physical and biological sciences, especially in the matter of Darwin's theories on evolution. After 1870—the year the pragmatists appeared—philosophy emerged as the special province of the universities, where professors were developing full-blown native systems and philosophy was a major course for students. Among the leaders who helped bring order out of the apparent chaos, establishing the basis of modern American philosophy, were two Harvard professors: the pragmatist William James and the idealist Josiah Royce.

William James, a lineal descendent of John Locke's empiricism, was the father of modern psychology. He shifted emphasis from the mind and body as separate substances to the mind and body as a single organism engaged in activity (mind) and behavior (body), thus over-throwing the traditional dualism of mind and body. To James, man is governed by ideas emanating from experience—the "stream of conscious-ness" which derives from his mind-and-body responses to his environ-ment. The truth of ideas must be verified by experience; the test of truth is usefulness or practical application in society. Many truths remain untested—beliefs or notions which constitute the "truths we live by." James's pragmatism is practicalism. As John Dewey points out, it was a "new name for an old way of thinking." Pragmatism had important consequences and applications in education through Dewey, in legal theory through Oliver Wendell Holmes, Jr., and in the social sciences.

Josiah Royce, James's close friend, was a lineal descendent of George Berkeley, Jonathan Edwards, and Ralph Waldo Emerson. He became the most articulate and influential spokesman of modern idealism. Royce formulated a comprehensive system based on analysis and logic that would embrace all realms of knowledge (he was well versed in many of them) and that would rhyme faith and reason in an all-comprehending philosophy. At the heart of his system was the concept of the absolute idea—the Self-Conscious Knower—who is the ultimate fulfillment of truth and reality. Where other idealists spoke of God as the Absolute Person or the Absolute Being, Royce spoke of God as the Absolute Spirit, replacing the conventional single God with a God that was the Spirit-of-the-Community. By so doing he "socialized God." Royce developed a scheme of community based on individual will, an ethical ideal of loyalty, and a moral code based on the Golden Rule. By helping their neighbors and performing service to the community, men of different loyalties would be united by a larger loyalty to community that would bring harmony and happiness in human affairs. Royce's abstract community underlies real communities; it is best, but not completely, expressed in the church community. It includes the science community with its quest of truth, but the ordinary political-economic community does not conform for it breeds self-centered individualism. The true individual must be a loyal member of God's community. Royce's community, then, was a complete one. He defined the nature of the individual in society, clarified the roles of ethics, religion, and science, and envisaged the practical application of God's community in this world. Royce's idealism had important implications for the social gospel movement and the Progressive ideal. It has as much relevance for our times as it did for his.

Royce has special relevance for those in California. Like Berkeley, he was a charming personality with great powers of persuasion. He was a man of noble character and giant intellect whose "moral passion swayed the entire audience and much of the world outside." As a colleague described him, he was "one of the glories of three universities (California, Johns Hopkins, and Harvard) ... a picturesque figure, a prodigious scholar, a stimulating teacher, and a playful and widely loved friend." His life touched many facets of California life: his birth in a mining camp (1855), his youth in San Francisco, his career as a University of California student and teacher and occasional lecturer in later years. His prolific writings—articles, essays, novels, and scholarly books—drawn from his California experiences as much as from observations of the American scene helped Americans understand themselves. Better than any other man of his time he explained the underlying forces and fundamental issues of society, presenting a comprehensive philosophy that welded religion and the sciences into a single system (much as Berkeley had done in his day). His cosmopolitan view fitted California's—and the nation's—heterogeneous society. His self-made career and his faith in human nature inspired many. If California has a philosophical godfather, he is surely Josiah Royce.

SUMMARY

California was still a marginal province in the nation's political economy. Congress, the chief focus of the national government, was preoccupied with nationally oriented issues like the currency and tariff; its actions affected California only in specific areas like Chinese exclusion. The transcontinental railroad opened California to the nation's markets, which greatly stimulated the state's economic development. Tycoons who dominated the growing industries in the East made excursions into the state to exploit opportunities but they were at first thwarted by the Big Four and other entrepreneurs. Not until the turn of the century did eastern tycoons breach the California stronghold, usually in collaboration with Californians. The Californians intent on running their own show did fairly well in controlling developments in their bailiwicks.

Californians were preoccupied in pursuing opportunities opened by the expanding agricultural and commercial economy. The focus was on ambitious entrepreneurs who systematically developed the land and its varied resources, which led to a heyday for private enterprise. The railroad was the catalytic force. It accelerated the flow of people, stimulated private enterprise, and expanded markets to spur the state's economic development. The Southern Pacific and its allies retained the upper hand in the state's political economy by virtue of its political machine and transportation monopoly. In each sector of industry, a few powerful elements attained dominant positions. These leading elements constituted the plutocrats who ruled the state's political economy. By the turn of the century, when the state was being transformed from rural agrarian to an urban industrial society, these industrial capitalists were already taking over strategic positions in the new order.

After four decades of rampant private enterprise, Californians developed the basis of their present-day society. The 1879 constitution, in revising the state's fundamental laws, tuned the governmental apparatus better to the agrarian and commercial order, but it did not change basic relationships among major competing groups. Business tycoons allied with party bosses ruled the state's political economy through the medium of machine politics and corporate enterprise. They were aided by prevailing public sentiment for party loyalty and laissez faire economics. Dissident merchant, farmer, and labor groups attempted to curb abusive practices of railroads and other corporations by organizing mercantile associations, agricultural cooperatives, and labor unions. They also sought laws for imposing government regulation of corporations and securing government aid for their enterprises. But it took several decades of experiment and experience to develop workable voluntary associations and effective governmental apparatus. When dissident groups failed to obtain relief from corporate abuses through self-help endeavors or legislative action, they resorted to constitutional reform, only to be outmaneuvered by corporate elements who secured strategic compromises. Later, farmers attempted a third-party movement and labor unions resorted to militant union activity, but both failed to achieve lasting success, until enlightened businessmen and anti-machine politicians made common cause with them to rid the state of predatory corporate giants and party bosses. By the turn of the century, local reformers were taking over municipal governments, and a decade later they had united their forces to capture the state government.

In historical perspective, the 1870–1910 era was the formative period of California's present-day society. The interplay of contending groups led to the development of private enterprises and the governmental apparatus for regulating them, which has survived to this day. Entrepreneurs developed the cooperative and corporate forms for carrying out their enterprises. They also worked out the forms of voluntary association by which they solved their problems through direct action or by securing government aid. They established the basis of the state bureaucracy to implement government assistance for promoting their enterprises, or to impose government regulation in order to check abusive groups. The telling proof of this can be seen in the major elements that rose to prominence in this period and still occupy important positions of industry leadership: notably, the Southern Pacific Railroad, Crocker Bank, Spreckels Sugar, Standard Oil of California, the California Fruit Growers Exchange, and Pacific Gas and Electric. Basic social relationships were worked out between the white majority and ethnic minority groups, and cultural trends started at this time continue today. If the frontier period was the incubator, this period represents the adolescent years of basic formation.

Overleaf: Transportation models, 1929. This Model A Ford, with its convertible top, side-opening hood, and spoke wheels, had a 75 mph top speed, compared to its Model T predecessor whose top speed was 40 mph. The tri-motor propeller plane, which succeeded the small single-engine plane, carried passengers in daytime flights only at 110 mph speeds. A clipper flying boat is passing by the near-completed Golden Gate Bridge (1937) on a trans-Pacific flight.

VII Adjustment and Expansion

1910-1945

After 1910 California underwent a basic transformation. An accelerating flow of immigrants settled mostly in San Francisco, Los Angeles, and neighboring cities. Urban areas more and more replaced rural communities as the centers of state life. The rise of manufacturing, coupled with ever-expanding agriculture, commerce, and transportation, contributed to an increasingly complex economy marked by highly interrelated industries. This development gave preeminence to new classes of people: college-trained professional men, technicians, specialists, and clerical employees— the so-called white-collar workers. Farmers, businessmen, and laborers were stratified further into distinct subgroups, each with its own special interest. They competed and cooperated with one another in dealing with devastating problems emanating from two world wars and the Great Depression, seeking workable solutions through scientific techniques, specialized and often large-scale operations, and collective actions. Government was called upon with greater frequency to provide services and regulate conflicts among these diverse contending groups. The traditional philosophy of individual laissez faire in business and government affairs gave way to a new concept of society emphasizing collective action and government regulation and the public interest. All these developments ushered in an era of difficult transition and remarkable achievement. They were made more complicated as California developed intricate interrelationships with other states, with different regions, and with the nation itself.

14 Reform Politics
15 The Regulated Economy
16 The Plebeian Society

14 Reform Politics

THE SETTING

Between 1910 and 1945 the nation was seething with socio-economic change wrought by industrial forces. Discontented groups—farmers, labor, business, and others—buttressed the movement toward reform. Some hoped to accomplish that aim by going back to older ways, others by finding new ones. Attention focused on the political arena, where reformers after 1910 captured state and national houses and proceeded to remake society. Reactionaries and radicals took rigid positions and their stances changed little over the next decades. Both extremes considered man primarily as an economic being. Conservatives and liberals in the middle range of the political spectrum were so profoundly affected by the new trends that they altered their ideas and shifted positions drastically—as many were to do periodically thereafter. They generally thought of man as a moral being in an ethically oriented society aimed at economic and social justice. They sought changes in the existing order that would achieve these ends. Thinking people, of course, blended these ideas in different ways. Reform was a catalyst for their convictions and behavior. In California it was a conspicuous feature in the politics of the period.

Party System

The sudden demise of the old-time machine politics in 1910 coincided with the emergence of government as a vital force. Progressive reformers, with public concurrence, effectively revamped the old political order. Their immediate objective was to demolish, or at least restore to popular control, the party system by which machine bosses had perpetuated their power. Antimachine forces secured the adoption in 1909 of the direct primary election reform measure which replaced the convention system for nominating candidates to public office. The Progressive-dominated legislature over the next half-decade enacted measures which for the first time regulated party activities. These measures failed to eliminate the party system but virtually sabotaged its effectiveness. Political scientists Winston Crouch and Dean McHenry tell us that both parties became "very nearly hollow shells without true foundations in the electorate."

Organized special-interest groups filled the political vacuum left by the weakened party system. The decade after 1910 was a transitional stage in this development. During the decade, the Progressive administration with its political apparatus attempted to serve as custodian of the public interest. Its effort proved unrealistic, for it became apparent that special-interest groups differed so much in composition, aims, and programs that a single organizing force could hardly reconcile them in its program. By the 1920's, business, labor, farmer, and governmental groups had formed new associations and coalitions for collective action and developed direct ways to influence public policies and government programs affecting their special interests. Corporate and cooperative enterprises built up professional staffs for handling public matters. In the 1930's, these groups perfected their methods and new minority groups formed more militant organizations for special programs, ranging from "reactionary" farmers combatting farm labor unions to "radical-minded" elderly citizen groups pressing old-age pension plans.

The political revolution in 1910, then, was followed by three decades of evolutionary development of the new style of politics: pressure politics by organized special-interest groups. State politics no longer centered on party machinations. It focused on the complicated interplay of diverse, organized special-interest groups. Contrary to general impression, these groups did not replace the existing party or government structure with a new system. What actually happened was that the Progressives and other reformers reallocated the *functions* of party and government organizations and of special-interest groups. They participated in party activities to endorse candidates and secure planks in the party platform. They lobbied the legislative bodies and administrative agencies to influence public policies and governmental programs. Some groups did all of these things, while others did only a few of them. Each group developed its own style and mode of operations to fit the circumstances. The lobbyist of the special-interest group replaced the party boss as the indispensable broker in public affairs. What the Progressives had sown, these groups reaped with added innovations and changes.

Partisan conflicts took new form with the Democratic Party's eclipse and Republican ascendancy. California was virtually a one-party state, the electorate generally voting Republican in state elections though voting Democratic in the national elections of the 1930's. Party conflicts were still strong in state politics: the deeply divided Progressive and reactionary factions of the Republican Party carried their battles over reform programs into the state governmental arena for over two decades. Each party continued to have its own conservative–liberal showdowns over party policy and government programs, usually over Progressive and, later, New Deal reforms.

Government System

Progressive reformers set out to revitalize the government apparatus. Their comprehensive reforms converted the government apparatus from a deadly routine to an energetic operation. The most far-reaching measures were those which implemented direct government: the initiative and referendum, which allowed citizens to draft and vote directly on proposed laws; and the recall, which provided a way to remove undesirable incumbents from public office. Progressives strove to make the revitalized government more honest, efficient, and economical, and to put it under popular control. They set into motion new trends in government reform: a regulated election system for selecting responsible public officials; the budget process for planning finances; civil service reforms for hiring employees according to merit; and governmental reorganizations for creating new agencies and regrouping them in a rational, centralized order. These continuing governmental reforms rendered political parties still more impotent. They deprived machine bosses and other party leaders of patronage and other devices for influencing the legislative processes. State and local government—and later, federal influences—became active forces in managing traditional political—economic issues and in dealing with social problems arising from the new industrialism and urbanization.

As the area of politics shifted from party convention to the governmental arena, state and local government became the chief focus in the new political order. At the state level, the governor replaced the legislature as the prime mover in governmental affairs. He asserted his powers in more positive fashion and, thanks to Progressive reforms, he was better equipped with budget and personnel controls with which to implement his policies and programs. The legislature found its status undercut not only by the rising preeminence of the governor, but also by special-interest and citizen groups utilizing pressure politics and direct legislation (the initiative and referendum) to make laws.

At the local level, large cities and urban counties, like Los Angeles, were also developed into more active and efficient governing bodies. They employed professional administrators to manage routine operations, instituted budget and civil service reforms, and reorganized local agencies. They pioneered in developing areawide special districts for handling problems beyond the capacity of the traditional government. Smaller cities and rural communities generally lagged behind these trends. Although beset by trials in developing workable methods and by the conflicts of rival interest groups, the state won national laurels for outstanding performances in governmental operations and programs.

California became inextricably involved in national developments meanwhile. With the ascendancy of the Progressive reform movement after 1910, state leaders worked closely with national leaders in consolidating party gains, synchronizing governmental programs, and advancing personal political ambitions. The advent of World War I extended state and federal activities in mobilizing manpower and resources and production for the war in Europe, establishing precedents for government regulation of society. The reform crusade was slowed down in the 1920's, more at the national level than in California, where Progressive forces were better able to temper the reaction of conservative groups.

The Great Depression of the 1930's upset the national equilibrium, producing political realignments, reducing the economy to semiparalysis, and causing widespread social distress. The New Deal program aimed at relief, recovery, and reform measures designed to restore the nation's balance and set it on the road to prosperity. It established the primacy of the federal government in public affairs and accelerated existing trends in federal–state cooperative relationships.

The developments of these three decades were accompanied by major changes in public attitudes and group relationships. The electorate showed more concern with socio-economic interests. Traditional party loyalty had given way to group allegiances and independent voting habits. Special-interest groups altered their positions within and outside both parties and realigned their forces in constant adjustment to changing conditions. Class conflicts became more pronounced as farmers, business, labor, and other groups stratified into subgroups of big and small enterprises and of major and minor or independent associations. Corporations no longer held such complete sway over public affairs as in the previous era: agricultural, labor, professional, governmental, and citizen groups now shared the political spotlight. Corporations, however, were still the most powerful force in major political spheres. Having such superior organization, group discipline, adequate finances, and managerial talent, they usually got their way over competing groups. Nevertheless, they could be and were effectively checked on occasion by organized coalitions and forceful governmental action.

These class and group conflicts became interwoven with crisscrossing sectional conflicts. The north–south conflict was revived as Los Angeles exceeded San Francisco in population in 1920, precipitating the long, intense struggle between the two sections over adjusting legislative representation (the reapportionment issue) for political control of the state. Closely intertwined with this controversy was the urban–rural conflict, which gained prominence as the urbanization trend widened the gap between manufacturing-oriented cities and agricultural communities. (Alameda, Los Angeles, and San Francisco in 1910 contained almost half the state population.) The Madisonian concept of group conflicts was taking on a new dimension with the emergence of modern society.

World War II brought further profound changes in American society. The federal government secured its position as the directing force in public affairs as it used its enormous powers to mobilize the nation for an all-out effort to win the global war. California was a major focus of federal defense and military programs, resulting in a transformation of society that marked the end of an era.

DEVELOPMENT

The Reforming Decade

The decade after 1910 was marked by a burst of reform. The reform buildup after 1900 climaxed in the great crusade to democratize the nation and later to "save the world for democracy," coupled with an ardent humanitarian impulse to implement economic and social justice at home. Under President Woodrow Wilson's forceful leadership after 1913, Congress revised the nation's banking system, tariff and trust policies, and enacted a host of other reforms, following in the wake of progressive states like Wisconsin, New York, and California, but also setting new directions for other states. These reforms went far in adapting domestic and foreign policies to the realities of the dominant urban–industrial order, adapting the ideals and values of the older agrarian order to the new setup. America's entry into World War I shifted the nation's reform zeal to an international setting as the United States joined European allies in a crusade to "restore world peace and democracy." The spirit of the decade was symbolized by Theodore Roosevelt's New Nationalism and Wilson's New Freedom. These programs resulted in expanded roles for the federal government at home and the United States as a world power abroad. The two leaders of national progressivism carried the long-evolving reform movement to ultimate fruition.

While the public spotlight focused on national politics, the nation's economy was expanding. Prosperity was widespread. Agriculture, manufacturing, and other sectors enjoyed the fruits of expanded production, improved distribution, and extended markets; they reaped their greatest harvests in the war years. Finance capitalists were still in the saddle, providing vital services and talents for promoting industrial growth, especially for the war effort. (President Wilson and Congress had been careful to solicit big business cooperation in carrying out wartime defense and military programs.) Neglected groups, like children, women, and the indigent, benefited from extensive but sporadic socio-economic reforms. Reform and its consequences had resolved some basic grievances of discontented groups, but this had been accomplished only by difficult compromises between sharply divided groups and resulted in conservative–liberal confrontations that sometimes erupted into violent showdowns.

In California the insurgent Republican takeover of state government under Governor Hiram Johnson in 1911 signaled the arrival of Progressivism. Reform was in the air. Everyone looked to the state house for anticipated changes that were bound to affect their interests: farmers, business, labor, and other discontented groups, with hope; major corporations and other privileged groups, with concern. Progressive leaders—mostly Lincoln–Roosevelt Republican Leaguers—entertained assorted reform ideas but they were generally united on their steward-ship of the public interest. They saw themselves as agents of the people who, taking custody of state government, would implement changes for the general welfare of the whole society.

When Republican Progressives took the reins of state government in 1911, Governor Johnson made clear that he was master of the house. Little known outside of Sacramento where he had been a practicing attorney, he rose rapidly to prominence as the pinch-hitting prosecutor in the San Francisco Graft Prosecution and as gubernatorial stan-dard-bearer for the Lincoln–Roosevelt Republican League. Though a novice in government, he quickly learned the ropes. As the party's chief spokesman, he voiced its convictions: government must rest on the absolute sovereignty of the people; the vested privileges of machine bosses, big corporations, and organized labor must be held in check; and the rights of underprivileged groups—laborers, women, and chil-dren—must be protected by the government. As chief executive, he transformed the governorship into a powerful instrument to carry out his program and instituted the honesty and efficiency in government that won him laurels as one of the nation's outstanding governors.

The Progressives, with crusading fervor, organized both houses of the legislature and quickly enacted a comprehensive reform program. The 1911 legislature enacted a record volume of important measures in a short time—the most prodigious legislative accomplishment in the annals of state government. (La Follette's Wisconsin accomplished as much, but over a longer period.) The electorate, too, performed spectacularly in a special election by approving all but one (railroad passes) of 23 constitutional amendments. What the legislature left undone in 1911 was just about complete by 1913. Among the long list of reforms were the nonpartisan direct primary, popular election of United States senators, the short ballot, city and county home rule, a revitalized railroad commission, public-utility regulation, corporate securities regulation, and workmen's compensation measures. Several measures which failed passage would have set minimum wages and maximum hours for children and women, regulated injunction powers of the courts, and imposed state arbitration of industrial disputes—Progressives were sharply divided over such class measures.

With their party platform translated into law, they fought over the next decade to retain control of state government and to perpetuate their reforms. They fought each other and they fought reactionaries and radicals of both parties. They battled over reform programs, Hiram Johnson's political aspirations, and national progressivism. The 1912 presidential election crystallized the party factionalism which plagued the Johnson administration. After one of the bitterest convention fights in United States history, Taft conservatives beat out Roosevelt Progressives for control of the national Republican Party, prompting Progressives to form a third party which featured Roosevelt with Johnson as his running mate. The national victory of Wilson and the Democrats deepened the split among the California Republicans. Some Lincoln–Roosevelt Leaguers refused to follow the Roosevelt–Johnson group out of the party, and standpatters like de Young and Otis denounced Johnson's "party treachery." A year later Johnson led his forces from the Republican organization to form the state Progressive Party. The 1914 midterm elections revealed the consequences of Progressive factionalism: Johnson won reelection, the first governor to do so since 1856, but James Phelan, the Democratic candidate, won the United States Senate seat, and candidates of five parties (Republican, Democratic, Progressive, Prohibitionist, and Socialist) won legislative seats to break Progressive domination. Much to Johnson's dismay, conservative standpatters captured the Republican organization.

The Progressive decline set in during Johnson's second administration. It became apparent in the 1915 legislature that the Progressives had not gone forward—the hard fact was that Progressive leaders had just about run out of ideas, and reactionary elements were organizing strong opposition. In the 1916 national campaign, Roosevelt led his Progressives back to the Republican fold. Johnson, who sought the presidential nomination (which he lost to Hughes), even lost the vice-presidential spot. Contrary to popular impression, Hughes's California defeat, which cost him a presidential victory, was not due to Johnson's widely publicized slight of Hughes when both men appeared separately in Long

Beach. It was due to Hughes's blunders and Wilson's successful reelection appeal for the peace, labor, and women's votes. Johnson's successful election bid for the United States Senate seat was tempered by the sudden death of John Eshleman, the popular lieutenant governor and heir apparent. Johnson, under pressure of Southern California Progressives (the Dickson–Earl group), appointed William Stephens, a highly regarded congressman and former Los Angeles mayor, rather than naming his own choice, in order to insure southern support for his senatorial bid. United States entry into World War I in March 1917 halted whatever remained of the Progressive movement and shifted attention to Wilson's great international crusade.

Thereafter, California followed in the national footsteps through the war and postwar years. Wilson guided the nation to military victory and toward his proposed League of Nations to enforce the peace. When peace came, the nation was soon torn by such diverse conflicts as the United States Senate battle over ratification of the League; Attorney General A. Mitchell Palmer's repressive "Red Scare" campaign, aimed ostensibly against Communists but also against labor agitators; the militant campaign for prohibition; and violent industrial disputes arising from a severe economic depression. In the 1920 national elections, the conservative-dominated Republican Party, with Senator Warren Harding as its standard-bearer, won the national elections. Hiram Johnson (along with another Californian, Herbert Hoover) lost his bid for the presidency and brusquely refused Harding's offer of the vice-presidency. Had Johnson accepted he would have been president, because Harding later died in office!

California reached the political crossroads by a similar route. The state was severely racked by postwar economic dislocations. The people were sharply divided over the League of Nations, prohibition, employer–labor showdowns, and radical agitation. The 1918 elections, according to the journalist Franklin Hichborn, were a nightmare: the prohibition issue threw Republicans and Democrats into disarray, and cross-filing so fouled up the gubernatorial and legislative races that Stephens won reelection without a real contest. The sad demise of Progressive harmony was reflected in Johnson's actions. The senator undercut the governor from the start, made friends with old conservative foes, and broke with remaining Progressive leaders. The real blow came in the 1920 election when Johnson campaigned vigorously for Samuel

Shortridge, a staunch conservative and, like Johnson, an opponent of the League of Nations, who won Phelan's senate seat.

Meanwhile, the Stephens Administration (1917–1923) rounded out the remarkable decade of Progressive reform. The governor, with hard-core Progressive leaders, ably held the legislative line against increasing conservative onslaughts against established reform programs. It was only a matter of time before California, like the nation, would be engulfed by the conservative tide.

The Reactionary Twenties

The conservative reaction that set in against Wilsonian reform crusades became the pervading spirit of the 1920's. The Republican administrations of Harding (1921–1923), Coolidge (1923–1929), and Hoover (1929–1933) implemented the general withdrawal of federal regulation of domestic affairs and United States international commitments. Republican ascendancy meant a retreat to nineteenth-century conservatism which believed in minimum government, but government aid to business—an expedient blend of Jeffersonian and Hamiltonian ideas, though Hamilton was still the party's patron saint. Each President practiced his brand of conservatism. The genial Harding harkened to McKinley platitudes and appealed for the "return to normalcy" which the Republicans adopted as their party slogan. The austere Coolidge felt, as he said, that "the business of government is business" and appointed businessmen rather than politicians to manage party and governmental affairs. The very able Hoover spoke of rugged individualism, so well personified by his own career as a self-made engineer and businessman and as a high government official. Where historians speak of the previous decades in positive terms, they see the 1920's as a negative decade—some say the most negative in a half-century.

Actually the 1920's were an important decade of adjustment, of transition, and of a strong faith in business stewardship of the nation's affairs. People were disenchanted with unfulfilled reform promises, unstable conditions, and uncertain times. They ardently desired a stable existence and better times. The Republican conservatives responded by operating government in a businesslike if pro-corporate manner, and by suppressing troublesome groups like labor unions and radical leftists—but not repressive corporations or reactionary groups like the Ku Klux Klan (which enjoyed its biggest membership in these years). In Congress, business groups generally had their way with Congress but met formidable opposition from the Farm Bloc and minority Progressive elements, who exposed the villainous schemes of oil, public utilities, and other special interests and won singular victories that bridged the gap between Progressive and New Deal reforms. The major parties experienced voter shifts, notably of urban voters from their traditional Republicanism to the Democratic ranks.

Republican ascendancy owed much to the prevailing visible prosperity of the decade. Industrial expansion advanced the nation's standard of living to the world's highest. Business prosperity, however, did not extend to farmers, who were trapped in a continuous agricultural depression, or to laborers, who suffered from unemployment, bad working conditions, and repressive union activities. Yet, as historian John Hicks points out, many Americans could tolerate such negative aspects of American life and "ride complacently on the prevailing tide of prosperity."

See-Saw Politics

In California, the conservative swing in the postwar years was accompanied by major changes in political modes and alignments. Representatives of organized special-interest groups flocked in great numbers to the state capital seeking governmental favors. The old-style lobbyists (company officials and part-time lobbyists) were overshadowed by a new breed of full-time professionals engaged in a wider scope of activities, including refined pressure on legislators, direct contact with the governor and administrative agencies, ballot propositions in election campaigns, and direct appeals for public support—that in effect bypassed party channels. Aroused business groups determined to reverse Progressive anti-corporation policies were conspicuous with their enlarged staffs conducting well-financed activities. However, numerous other special interests—agriculture, labor, professional, government, and community groups—also appeared with new organizations and expanded operations.

The weakened party system had diminished partisanship, but not factionalism. The dominant Republicans were divided over progressive and reactionary programs, and the fading Democrats fought over the rival aspirations of party leaders (Phelan and McAdoo). Politics were complicated by controversial issues like liquor prohibition and the control of utilities. The politics of the decade was like a seesaw: progressive and reactionary forces, along with allied interest groups, rode the up-and-down trends, in state politics, each group taking its turn at the top of state government.

The see-saw continued. When the decade opened, the Stephens administration was still in control, but reactionary forces had begun their all-out drive to negate Progressive reforms. In the 1921 legislature, conservative groups were lined up with the Better California Federation and the California Taxpayers Association (Cal Tax), both heavily backed by the state's largest corporations, primarily to defeat corporation tax and state water and power measures. They called for a reorganization of state government to effect economy and efficiency for reducing rising costs. This was also an oblique effort to reduce state service and regulatory agencies implementing Progressive programs seeking social and economic justice. Governor Stephens in a shrewd move sponsored a state reorganization aimed at more economic and efficient management. He also pressed for tax reform that would make corporate taxes and property taxes more equal (the latter were 35 percent higher) and provide added revenues for *expanded* services to needy groups—the postwar depression was still on. In what was probably the bitterest legislative battle in modern state history, aroused conservative forces made a strong appeal for public support in a devious, heavily financed campaign, but the governor's reorganization and tax measures carried by narrow margins.

The inevitable showdown between progressive and conservative forces came in the 1922 state election. In the Republican primaries, the conservative Friend Richardson, backed by a business coalition that included the Big Three Republican Press, beat out Stephens for the gubernatorial nomination, but lieutenant governor C. C. Young, a strong Progressive leader, won reelection. With Republicans in the ascendancy, these primary victories were tantamount to election.

The Richardson administration raised conservative hopes for a renovated government. Richardson was a newspaper publisher who rose from assemblyman to state printer and state treasurer by canny maneuvers during the Johnson administration. His inaugural speech calling for strict economies in state government set the tone for his administration. Attention focused on the newly adopted executive budget (1922) and on the governor's chief budgetmaker, Nellie Pierce, a Cal Tax official appointed to head the state board of control. The proposed budgets presented to the 1923 and 1925 legislatures made drastic across-the-board cuts that crippled state departments and institutions, notably those providing education, health, and welfare services and those performing regulatory functions. In the ensuing public outcry and stormy legislative battles, the penny-pinching governor generally held the line. He vetoed Progressive attempts in the assembly to restore cuts, and conservative forces sustained his vetoes. But his irrational management actually increased state expenditures. It also provoked the opposition into forming the Progressive Voters League (1924, modeled upon the earlier Lincoln–Roosevelt Republican League), which subsequently forced the governor to restore some budget cuts and blocked his attempts to weaken the civil service and other dubious schemes. Richardson proved to be a narrow-minded, petulant chief executive with a talent for faulty logic and little ability for managing state affairs or dealing with his chief supporters, notably banking and corporate groups. The budget was the stormy petrel of the Richardson administration; the governor's mismanagement of the budget contributed to his defeat for reelection.

The mid-decade national and state elections involved California in another round of progressive vs. reactionary contests for government control. The 1924 national elections reflected further party deterioration through bitter factionalism. In the state Republican primaries, Johnson lost his presidential bid to Coolidge. On the Democratic side, William McAdoo, Wilson's son-in-law and his Secretary of the Treasury, had moved from New York to Los Angeles in 1922 to build a political base, with Phelan's backing, for a presidential bid against New York's popular governor, Al Smith. The two liberals deadlocked in the famous 104-ballot count at the Democratic national convention, which finally settled on an incongruous candidate (John Davis, a corporation lawyer and a Morgan attorney). The Progressives fared better in the 1926 state elections. C. C. Young beat out Richardson and went on to win the governorship. He had the hard push of the PVL and financial backing from the banker Amadeo Giannini and movie magnate Joseph Schenk, but Johnson's active campaigning seems to have been decisive in his primary victory. When Young campaigned successfully with Senator Shortridge in a show of party unity for election victory, Hichborn expressed the foreboding of Johnson and others that the "Progressive fly had become enmeshed in the reactionary net."

The Young Administration (1927–1931) represents the high tide of postwar Progressivism. Young had a spotless Progressive record in his rise as an original Lincoln–Roosevelt Leaguer, assembly speaker, and lieutenant governor. He was also the most experienced and efficient governor up to that time. As chief executive he fashioned the executive budget and civil service into efficient tools, and effected major reorganizations bringing state government to its highest peak of performance.

Young's sincere attempts to unite warring party factions by distributing appointments and other gubernatorial favors with judicious impartiality only got him into political hot water. Disenchanted Progressive leaders privately criticized the governor's apparent naiveté and timidity. Some charged him with selling out to special interests and pointed to the influence of men like Giannini, Schenk, and an up-and-coming lobbyist, Arthur Samish. Reactionary forces were no less placated by the governor's olive branch, even though the chief executive made important and evidently damaging concessions on matters like tax equalization. They wanted complete implementation of their con-servative programs.

In the 1930 state elections, conservative forces made another all-out effort to replace the governor with their choice. In the Republican primaries, Young (with Samish as his manager) lost the gubernatorial nomination to James Rolph, Jr. The nattily dressed Rolph (boots and carnation were his trademarks) was San Francisco's long-time popular mayor and was backed by the Fleishhacker and other powerful business groups—he made history by campaigning the state by charter plane. The conservative Republican ticket, with its wet San Francisco governor and dry Los Angeles lieutenant governor (Frank Merriam), backed by the powerful Republican press trio, was too strong for the Democratic opposition.

The Crucial Decades

When the American nation confronted a devastating depression in the 1930's and a world war in the 1940's, it faced crucial tests for survival. The Great Depression plunged the nation into a severe economic decline marked by deteriorating industries, extensive unemployment, and widespread misery. The failure of President Hoover's halfway measures to stem the nation's growing paralysis paved the way for the dramatic administration of President Franklin D. Roosevelt (1933–1945). With inspiring confidence, Roosevelt launched his comprehensive New Deal program for relieving distressed groups and revitalizing the economy. Federal intervention through extensive regulation and huge subsidies brought immediate relief for millions of people, but produced only partial economic recovery and precipitated major political complications.

By 1938 the President had shifted the nation's direction, turning attention from the New Deal at home to the growing crisis abroad. As Germany, Italy, and Japan threatened world peace, Roosevelt took measures to prepare the nation's defenses and abandon its isolationist position in order to join the European allies in measures of collective security. When World War II descended, Roosevelt led the nation in mobilizing manpower and resources at home for the global conflict, and spearheaded the United Nations as a postwar vehicle for maintaining world peace.

The nation during these hectic, momentous years underwent far-reaching changes. Roosevelt dominated his administration like few other presidents since Washington, imposing the stamp of his leadership on domestic and foreign affairs. The New Deal he instigated brought about a major reordering of society well in accord with American tradition and experience. The federal government became a more active force in state and local affairs, paving the way for expanded inter-governmental cooperation. It also intervened more directly in economic affairs to remedy imbalances among business, farmer, labor, and other groups and to stabilize the economy. Federal programs also attended to the depressed lot of ethnic and other underprivileged groups. While rural agrarian groups had been receiving considerable federal attention, the New Deal extended the federal largess to urban industrial groups for the first time. The New Deal was not a new game with new rules, as historians Commager and Morrison point out, but a "reshuffle of the cards that too long had been stacked against the workingman and farmer and the small shopkeeper—and one might add, disadvantaged city people.

While the public limelight focused primarily on the federal government, major institutions were also undergoing change. The Depression did more than turn public confidence from local and state government to the national government for managing pressing problems. It undermined public faith in the basic business philosophy of a self-regulating economy based on natural economic laws. The nation's power center moved from the business capital of New York's Wall Street to the government capital of Washington, finance capitalists were replaced by high government officials.

California's distress from the sudden economic slowdown of the national depression was intensified by the flow of poverty-stricken people from other states seeking better opportunities. Promoters attracted large followings to unusual schemes—the engineer-managed society of Technocracy, Inc., Commonwealth's cooperative society, and the Utopians—that evoked ridicule and, later, fear among state leaders. Organized special-interest groups refined their strategies and tactics in applying pressure on public officials. Partisanship was revived with the Roosevelt wave and the resurgence of Democratic voters who, by mid-decade, outnumbered Republicans. Factionalism was rife as extreme groups from ultra-conservative to outright socialist organized and reorganized coalitions for capturing party and government control. The Progressive vs. reactionary alignments of the previous decade gave way to sharper conservative vs. liberal alignments in state politics oriented to fundamental bread-and-butter issues. The state government, handicapped by intense pressures from proliferated organized groups and lacking effective leaders and resources to cope with overwhelming depression problems, turned to the federal government. The Roosevelt administration was quite willing to extend aid and to intervene directly, so much so that federal programs profoundly shaped the course of state affairs. California in the 1930's, like every other state, operated in the shadow of New Deal politics.

The Rolph administration (1931–1934) bore the early brunt of the depression that hit California by 1931. The genial, debonair "Sunny Jim" Rolph exhibited a penchant for gubernatorial ceremony, for personal patronage appointments, and for spendthrift practices that ignored the growing crisis. Described as a Nero fiddling while the state was collapsing, Rolph on one occasion met unemployed "hunger marchers" at the state capitol and disarmed them with charming cordiality without doing much else to relieve their hardships. His political stance was uncertain. He signed the Progressive-backed Central Valley Water Project so bitterly opposed by PGE and other public utilities. He scuttled the carefully worked-out progressive-reactionary revenue compromise by vetoing the state's first personal income tax and signing the first sales tax, a move which favored big business elements at the expense of general taxpayers. The governor's impish pranks and warm sentiments were legendary and apparently provoked genuine public affection. Herb Phillips, the *Sacramento Bee's* astute political editor, observed that the governor's antics had a perverse entertainment value at a time when there was little to laugh about.

The 1932 election was a turning point for the nation as the Democrats ousted the Republicans from control of the federal government. William McAdoo, with Hearst's backing, led the California delegation to the Democratic national convention. At a critical juncture, he swung the delegation to insure the presidential nomination of Franklin Roosevelt over his erstwhile rival Al Smith. McAdoo won Shortridge's seat in the United States Senate and became an ardent New Deal supporter and dispenser of federal patronage for California. The Progressives being in disarray, conservative forces cinched their grip on Republican Party leadership. They retained party control for the next decade.

The 1934 state election marked a critical showdown for control of state government. With the depression in its darkest days, conservative, liberal, and extremist groups fought desperately for state control which each believed to be necessary for relief, if not survival. Rolph's sudden death just before the election campaign threw the gubernatorial race wide open: fifteen candidates entered the fray, including three Republicans, nine Democrats, a Progressive, a Socialist, and a Communist. The primaries gave the ultra-conservative Frank Merriam, Rolph's successor as lieutenant governor, the Republican nomination; Raymond Haight (descendant of a former governor) became the candidate of the Progressive-Commonwealth Party. The big surprise was the stunning victory of Upton Sinclair, the famous novelist and two-time Socialist gubernatorial candidate (1926 and 1930), who captured the Democratic nomination with a primary vote exceeding that of the top eight gubernatorial candidates.

The election campaign was easily the most savage and bitter in the state's modern history. The radical Sinclair heralded a drastic proposal for pulling the state out of the depression. His EPIC, or End-Poverty-In-California Plan, by which unemployed workers would produce for their own needs rather than for profit in state-sponsored land colonies and factories, won masses of people by its evangelical appeal. The fear-ridden business community, backed by other property interests, launched a heavily financed, vicious scare campaign that produced near public panic over Sinclair's utopian scheme. Under Louis B. Mayer, the movie mogul and Republican state chairman, the film colony alone raised at least $500,000 for the campaign and produced films with fake scenes linking EPIC with Russian communism. Governor Merriam enhanced his cause by wrapping himself in a "temporary cloak of progressivism" and by entering into a secret agreement with conservative Democrats (engineered by J. F. T. O'Connor, a Roosevelt appointee) not to obstruct the New Deal in California. Merriam won the three-way contest with a plurality vote; one observer commented that the choice had been between Sinclair's impractical scheme and Merriam, who was as modern as a dinosaur.

The Merriam administration (1934–1939) managed state affairs in a routine, undistinguished fashion during the main depression years. Merriam, a long-experienced legislator was as somber and dull as Rolph had been cheerful and colorful. Merriam was the last gubernatorial representative of nineteenth-century conservatism (at least until 1966), a man of shrewd caution and standpat views, who called conferences to study vexatious depression problems rather than to propose solutions. He followed Richardson's practice in freely using the veto to hold the line on an austere budget, cutting down government services to arrest the depletion of the treasury, but cooperated in carrying out the federal-state relief programs in accordance with his secret agreement. Fortunately for Merriam's record and the state's citizenry, the New Deal program did much to alleviate pressing problems in providing immediate relief, in supplying jobs, and in furnishing old age and unemployment benefits. These federal programs also undercut radical proposals like the old age pension plans which upset political applecarts in the state elections (Townsend's Plan of $200 monthly payments for elderly people in 1934, and the Ham'n Eggs Scheme of $30 every Thursday in 1938). Merriam's ultra-conservatism was neutralized by a liberal bloc (headed by Culbert Olson, the EPIC-endorsed senator from Los Angeles). Merriam's standpat position on controversial special-interest issues irked both conservatives and liberals enough to doom his chances for reelection.

The 1938 election brought another conservative-liberal show-down for state control, a replay of 1934 without the fire-and-brimstone extremism. Merriam won a bitter contest over his lieutenant governor in the Republican primary. The Democratic primary came up with a new liberal slate headed by Culbert Olson, the party chairman and gubernatorial candidate, and Sheridan Downey, Sinclair's former running mate and heir to the remnants of EPIC, who bested the Roosevelt-supported McAdoo for the United States Senate seat. Conservative forces attempted to launch another scare campaign along 1934 lines on Merriam's behalf, only to have it backfire—they had cried wolf once too often against Olson, a less vulnerable candidate than Sinclair had been. Olson's forces conducted a skillful, enthusiastic campaign, making effective use of the radio to compensate for little newspaper support. His appeal to bring the New Deal to California won Roosevelt's endorsement. Olson won handily as the first Democratic governor in the twentieth century, in the face of a national trend to Democratic setbacks.

The Olson administration (1939–1943) was a belated attempt to bring the New Deal to California. The governor openly endorsed Roosevelt's program, and proposed a series of reforms that included rehabilitating state regulatory and service agencies, introducing public health insurance, and expanding relief programs based on public works. But Olson's long experience as an astute legislator, first in Utah and then in California, was not matched by his sorry experiences as chief executive. Plagued by bad luck, as Merriam had been favored by good, he was hampered by his stubborn temperament and serious illnesses at critical times, and by determined legislative opposition to his program. Conservative forces in the legislature, backed by aroused special interests, weakened the governor's well-prepared budget (worked out by Stanford Professor Dewey Anderson, a tax expert), undercut the state relief administration, and blocked most of the governor's reform measures. They were able to do so by splitting the slim Democratic majority to organize a tight anti-administration "economy bloc." Olson's skill as legislator and politician thus failed to carry over into the governorship. In the 1942 state election showdown, Olson lost the governorship to Earl Warren, an attractive candidate who projected a nonpartisan image. Conservative joy over Olson's defeat was not to last long, for Warren was soon to carry forward Olson's liberal program. In Robert Burke's comment, Olson had departed from office without cleaning out his desk.

ANALYSIS

Political Organization

The Progressive Movement

The reform movement that began with the Grangers in the 1870's arose again with the Populists in the 1890's, evolved into a crusade under

President Roosevelt after 1900, and reached its climax in the Progressive Movement after 1910. The emerging Progressivism was a more broadly based movement than its predecessors. It embraced political, economic, and social reforms at the local, state, and national levels. It represented a middle-class revolt against the rising industrialism and urbanization that were transforming the old order of society and undermining traditional values. Its leadership came mostly from urban middle-class groups, especially professional men and independent businessmen, but it drew support from elements of all parties and from farmer and labor groups. The motives of these groups varied widely, but they shared the common protest against an old order dominated by the privileged few, which threatened their status and perverted American ideals of democratic rule. They sought to remedy their grievances by capturing the party and government apparatus from an unsavory alliance of machine bosses and business tycoons. Through this apparatus they would reshape society.

Though Progressives were lineal descendants of the Populists, they differed from their ancestors in important ways. The Populists are generally characterized as having an idealism rooted in an uncompromising Puritan morality, a cynical outlook, narrow views limited by their agrarian origins, and a tendency to try to curb exploitive elements in society. The Progressives embraced an idealism steeped in a warm Social Christianity, an optimistic outlook, a broad vision born of their urban cosmopolitanism, and a desire for the flexible rules and practical solutions applicable in a changing society. As historian George Mowry puts it, Populism arose from angry farmers striving for "belly reforms" in times of acute depression, whereas Progressivism came from indignant professionals and businessmen during relatively prosperous times seeking reforms rather of "the heart and the head than of the stomach." Where Populists entertained visions of mystical and utopian societies, Progressives envisioned the present society reformed by harmonious relationships and humanitarian impulses.

California Progressivism, so Mowry tells us, was a microcosm of the national movement. It contained the same basic elements to a more marked degree than any other state. Almost half of the state lived in urban areas populated by a large upper middle class, employer and labor groups engaged in bitter industrial disputes, widely divergent political groups (like the Southern Pacific machine and the Socialist Party), and conservative-liberal party factions battling for political control. It was strongly influenced by Progressive developments at the national level and in other states, notably in Wisconsin under Governor Robert La Follette

(1901–1908) and New York under Governor Charles Evans Hughes (1906–1910). That California was long overdue for reform—diverse discontented groups were chafing hard at the Southern Pacific reins—may account for the state's remarkable record in achieving comprehensive reforms in so short a time.

California Progressives were a variant of the national profile. Their leaders comprised a wide assortment of reform-minded people: conservatives and radicals, rich and poor, idealists and pragmatists, from all walks of life and from all parts of the country. They included antimachine politicians who had fought the Southern Pacific and local bosses for years; former machine bosses who became reformers out of conviction or opportunism; business, farmer, and labor leaders who decried machine influences that hurt their enterprises or jobs; leaders of civic, fraternal, and women's organizations who denounced machine corruption of society.(One also found similar types in the opposite camp for different reasons.) Progressive leadership, however, was dominated by a small, exclusive group of like-minded men who were in the saddle of state government and gave direction to the movement in California. Most of this inner group were comprised of young men of the upper middle class, college-educated, financially well-off, and by occupation editors, lawyers, independent merchants, and manufacturers. They were steeped in the idealism and morality of New England-based Protestant religions (most were Congregationalists) and saw society in terms of good and bad. They were rank individualists of the Jeffersonian school who feared concentrated power which jeopardized the democratic, competitive order of society and their economic stake in it. For this reason they hated business monopolies, and even more, labor unions. Predominantly of old American stock, they carried biases against alien immigrants and racial minorities, especially against Asians, whom they believed to be diluting their race and institutions. Driven by strong self-righteous, humanitarian, moralistic, and ethical instincts, they sought to remake California society in their image.

The Johnson Machine

The Progressives, in their attempt to become the custodian of the public interest, developed a political machine. Its leadership centered in a small, closely knit group comprising select members of the Lincoln–Roosevelt Republican League (like Chester Rowell) and other Progressive leaders. Head of the group was Hiram Johnson, who so dominated its affairs that it was called the Johnson machine. Johnson demanded complete loyalty and dealt ruthlessly with deviants and opponents, which antagonized many of the assorted reform groups in the loose Progressive coalition; each group had equally strong reform ideas and resented any efforts to subvert its projects.

The Johnson machine rivaled the old Southern Pacific machine in power and proficiency. Indeed, the Progressive organization bore striking similarities in leadership, organization, and operations to its railroad nemesis. Actually the Progressives behaved much in the manner of any efficient political machine, though with important differences. The Progressives were completely dedicated to the public interest—as they construed it—rather than to special interests, although their concept of the people they served was a narrrow one. Their firm commitment to honest, efficient democratic government was attested by their incorruptible if arbitrary ways. While their short-lived machine failed to find effective solutions to immediate problems, it made lasting contributions in refocusing government operations on the public interest and in achieving a more effective performance. Such attitudes became trademarks of California's political system.

Political Parties

Progressive leaders were determined to eliminate the remains of party organization by which machine bosses had ruled the state for so long. They sponsored measures that retained the party structure but re-allocated its functions and spelled out in detail party procedures. The state convention was still at the top of the party hierarchy, but was assigned two relatively unimportant functions: to adopt the state party platform, and to select electors to vote for the party presidential candidate every four years. The state central committee was expanded to a more representative body, but it was so bulky and unwieldy that its functions as a central governing body were carried out in practice by the executive committee. Nonpartisan elections were prescribed for city and county offices (1911) and for school and judicial offices (1913), to eliminate local and some state offices as valuable patronage for rewarding party workers.

The most significant measure was the cross-filing law (1913), which allowed candidates of one party to secure nomination in another party. It not only undermined boss control but also eroded the power of party leaders to manage party affairs. Incumbents with the prestige of being in office more often than not won their seats because voters, especially newcomers to the state, were not always familiar with a candidate or aware of his true party affiliation. Dean McHenry described party cross-filing as an invitation to the masquerade, declaring it to be "one of the greatest barriers to party responsibility ever devised." No other state used it more extensively than California.

Party weakness led to innovations in the 1930's to compensate for it. Professional campaign firms, pioneered by Whitaker and Baxter (1931), provided expertise in guiding candidates and ballot propositions for special-interest groups to election victories. Auxiliary party apparatus was devised to accomplish what the regular party machinery could not in the way of effective campaigning for candidates. Alarmed at steady election losses during the depression years, Republican leaders formed the California Republican Assembly (CRA) to select promising candidates and press their election campaigns. One of the first politicians to realize the potential of both developments was Earl Warren, who hired Whitaker and Baxter and enlisted the CRA, which he helped found, to conduct his successful election to the governorship in 1942.

Organized Special Interests

Special-interest groups did not always take kindly to high-handed Progressive benevolence. By the 1920's they were organizing along several fronts for political action. Among those unrivaled in size and influence in their areas were the Southern Pacific, Bank of America, California Fruit Growers Exchange, Pacific Gas and Electric, and Standard Oil. They improved the regional and statewide associations whose purpose it was to coordinate their numbers for united action, notably the California Manufacturers Association, California Federation of Labor, the Agricultural Council (1921), and the most powerful one of them all, the California State Chamber of Commerce (1922). Governmental, professional, and citizen groups also developed effective vehicles for carrying their programs, among them the League of California Cities, County Supervisors Association, California Teachers Association, League of Women Voters (1922), and the California Spiritualist Association. Collectively they represented just about all major segments of society, plus a host of smaller groups. They came to be referred to variously as the fourth branch of government or the third house of the legislature.

By the 1930's special-interest groups had greatly expanded in dimension and scope. Their lobbyists increased until they outnumbered legislators four to one. They refined techniques of pressure politics. Their trade associations played a conspicuous role in synchronizing client-group interests with desired federal-state policies and programs emanating from the New Deal years. New groups represented even more narrow interests and performed more specialized functions: the Associated Farmers pressed their anti-union campaign, and class groups like the Townsend Clubs Associated sought old-age pensions. The labor lobby came into its own under the New Deal; it developed effective coordination of trade union groups working through regional and statewide associations. Thus, special-interest groups matured into highly organized, articulate groups playing the complicated game of power politics in ways not always visible to the public.

The chief lobbyist or legislative representative of these organized special-interest groups became the key figure in the political process. He constituted a new breed, an experienced professional politician who replaced the old-time party boss or company officer–business agent who had previously handled political matters. He gained prominence through his intimate knowledge of his client's business, his ability to persuade public officials, and his talent in getting things done. He was an expert in party and governmental affairs, well versed in the intricacies of legislative and administrative procedures in government and of party practices and voter behavior in election campaigns. He replaced the party boss as the indispensable political broker in public affairs, and was undoubtedly a more effective agent than his predecessor would have been in representing the heterogeneous urban industrial order.

The Samish Machine

Kingpin of the California lobbyists was Arthur Samish, who reached the zenith of his power around 1940. Samish rose in the 1920's from legislative aide to lobbyist. By the 1930's he had built up a large clientele of diverse industry groups, including banking, billboard, liquor, mining, racetrack, and trucking interests. His power rested on his command of the virtually unlimited funds contributed by his clients (the State Brewer's Association assessed five cents on every beer barrel for Samish's slush fund), which he used primarily to elect legislators and public officials and to secure ballot propositions. With his legislative bloc, Samish traded and bargained with other lobbyists and legislators and sold his influence for fees to industry and other groups desiring legislation. That the liquor and oil industries in California paid the lowest taxes of any state attests to his powerful influence. Samish operated through a small staff of expert advisors, a vast network of agents for information (according to him, "the damndest Gestapo you ever saw"), control of key legislative committees like those on finance and public morals, and certain executive agencies like the state equalization board. His organization was the only one of its kind: it constituted an independent political machine which owed allegiance to no single party or group and operated according to his whim. He enjoyed virtual legal immunity for his covert and somewhat shady deals. In 1938 he freely described his activities before the Sacramento County grand jury, which forwarded its investigation (the Philbrick report) to the state senate. The document was mysteriously eliminated from the senate journal; and although Governor Olson arranged for its publication, there were no further results.

A colorful complex figure, Samish was a brash extrovert who combined a genial manner, mean dispostion, and ruthless tactics. Powerful as he was, the charge that he was *the* boss of California politics is somewhat exaggerated for a state that had many "bosses" (for example, the soft-spoken Monroe Butler, who represented independent oil interests), but he was acknowledged to be a leader of such political brokers. As Governor Warren declared, Samish had unquestionably more power than the governor in matters affecting his clients. Samish was representative of the new lobbyist who was noted for his professional skill but untypical in that he had an independent personal machine.

As a group, lobbyists were of all types. There were both principled and unscrupulous men of professional and amateur standing, conducting their operations with soft- or hard-line approaches in secretive or open fashion. Their new status did not remove the stigma traditionally attached to their time-honored but universally condemned profession. The general public still viewed them as sinister figures perverting the democratic processes by their unseen machinations—which was often true. Either the public did not understand, or it understood all too well.

Administration of Justice

The Progressive administration in the course of reforming state government altered the judicial system. It succeeded to some extent in making the judiciary over into a more popular and democratic system. Citizens could remove "bad judges" by recall, more a potential than real threat since the device was rarely used, even against controversial judges. It intended to remove the party label in the election of judges to make them nonpartisan, and also limited their tenure. Actually the reform measure encouraged long tenure and executive appointments, for people tended to reelect the same judge whether or not they were familiar with his performance. The result was that judges served until resignation or death, and the governor appointed their successors. Progressives also pushed for a public-defender system, established by Los Angeles in 1914 and adopted by the state in 1921, by which public-financed lawyers defended citizens unable to pay for their defense. In making provision for citizens to amend the constitution and enact statutes by direct legislation, the Progressives contributed to lengthening the constitution until it became a maze of substantive laws and trivia, detailed provisions more appropriately located in statutory code, and obsolete provisions like the prohibition against dueling.

Before long, public attention turned again to law reform. During the Young Administration, a blue-ribbon constitutional commission (1929), appointed by the governor, did a commendable job of removing obsolete and redundant provisions from the constitution. The legislature, however, failed to adopt its report. Better luck came with the law-revision committee (1929), which undertook the technical job of revising the existing five statutory codes; it eliminated defects and classified the laws into 25 codes which were hailed as a "body of living laws." During the Depression, discontented groups pressured the 1933 legislature into calling a constitutional convention, a measure adopted at the next election. The 1935 legislature, however, refused to carry out the popular mandate on the grounds that it would be too costly during such hard times. Paul Mason, a leading constitutional authority, suggests that the legislature feared the predominance of radical groups and widespread socio-economic distress—a situation reminiscent of the constitutional crisis in 1878.

While these efforts for law reform were going on, the judiciary and law enforcement agencies were undertaking important administrative reforms. A judicial council headed by the chief justice was set up (1926) to adopt rules and regulations for the court system, reassign judges to help relieve crowded conditions, and recommend improvements for legislative actions. A commission on judicial appointments, including the chief justice and attorney general, was formed (1934) to act with veto powers on gubernatorial appointments to the appellate courts to improve the quality of judicial appointments. Such high-court reforms did not prevent the lower courts from developing into a hodgepodge collection of county, city, and township courts with overlapping jurisdictions. Nevertheless, California was lauded nationwide for pioneering these judicial reforms.

Law enforcement agencies were expanded to cope with new conditions arising from the growing state and rising cities. At the state level, attempts to establish a state police with general functions, as in other states, were regularly defeated by local pressure groups. The California Highway Patrol had developed by 1929 into a well-organized agency with uniformed mobile units for enforcing highway laws. The state department of professional and vocational standards was formed at the same time to consolidate agencies with police powers and special officers to administer various state license and regulatory laws.

At the local level, where a strong home rule precluded state interference, law enforcement was increasingly burdened by proliferating agencies handicapped by jealously guarded prerogatives and overlapping jurisdictions. Local agencies coped in various ways with urban problems made more complex by the rapid growth of business and industries and the inflow of heterogeneous people, including settlers, tourists, and transient workers. Los Angeles was a pacesetter for larger cities and urban counties. The police department expanded into a large organization of specialized bureaus (for example, crime detection, patrol, technical services) headed by a chief who more resembled a top administrative officer than a traditional police chief. The county sheriff was elected head of a uniformed police force performing similar functions outside city limits; he was hardly the typical sheriff of pioneer times. Berkeley was the pacesetter for the middle-size cities, which had converted from the rural constable to a city police department. Under August Vollmer, its long-time, innovative police chief (1907–1932), Berkeley developed a professional police force through college recruits and in-service training (the so-called Ph.D. cops, or supercops). It also pioneered in modern police detection, including criminal fingerprint and photograph identification and the lie-detector test, which were adopted by the state agency and the FBI for systematizing criminal identification and investigation. The California Peace Officers Association pressured the legislature (1934) into authorizing cities to establish a professional police force based on a civil service system.

Reform went far toward improving court administration and law enforcement, but its application was often uneven. Cities still felt the corruptive influence of unscrupulous business, labor, and vice interests, which led to reform shakeups in San Francisco (1937) and Los Angeles (1938). Local courts and police agencies sometimes suffered from treacherous elements and unmanageable situations. Vigilantism occasionally reared its ugly head. One type was the self-appointed law enforcement mobs, which seized and executed jailed persons awaiting trial. California led all states outside the Deep South in lynchings (18 between 1910 and 1934). Such incidents in California mostly involved white men accused of murders. Another type of vigilante activity was the volunteer group, usually consisting of citizens and businessmen, sometimes abetted by local officials, who inflicted cruel beatings on, or ran out of town, undesirable radical elements and labor union agitators who were "disturbing the peace." Representatives of law and order sometimes wore odd masks.

Fiscal Administration

The Progressive Administration after 1910 inaugurated a new era in fiscal administration. The new board of control which replaced the ex-officio board of examiners devoted full attention to efficient management of state finances. It set up an informal budget process for planning state expenditures and revenues for the first time in state history, requiring state agencies to channel their requests for appropriations to the board instead of going directly to the legislature. The new dual-tax system, by which state and local governments separately taxed their own tax sources (the former on gross receipts or franchises of corporate groups, and the latter from the general property tax), was launched with high expectations of increased state revenues. It soon became apparent that the fiscal program was not working out well. The board of control had difficulty centralizing fiscal control because of uncooperative independent state agencies. Tax studies revealed that corporate groups paid increasingly less than their share of the tax burden, while general property taxpayers paid proportionally more taxes. During the prosperous decade, property owners annually paid higher taxes as their land values rose, but corporations enjoying greater profits managed to defeat regular state tax rate increases by the legislature. Corporate strategy also defeated measures expanding the functions, programs, and facilities of state agencies and institutions which would have required additional state taxes. The warning sounded earlier by suspicious reformers of the dual-tax system (see Chapter 11) had come to pass.

The showdown over tax inequities came in the 1921 legislature. Governor Stephens led the fight for the King tax bill which substantially raised state tax rates on gross receipts of corporations to equalize their tax burden with that of general property owners. Corporate groups brought out the big guns to fire away at the Progressive reform measure in one of the bitterest campaigns in modern legislative history. (Among the able spokesmen for corporate interests was Carl Plehn, author of the dual-tax system!) In the stormy session the measure passed by a single vote. The Progressives also won showdown battles over two corollary measures: governmental reorganization, which regrouped state agencies and expanded state functions; and public school finance, which fixed state and local contributions in the constitution (see Chapter 16). The corollary measures proved more important than the tax law in the long run, since they established trends that persist to this day.

The warfare over state finances continued throughout the decade. State fiscal administration was improved by the 1922 constitutional amendment that formalized the executive budget system pioneered in California—the legal basis of our present annual budget process by which the governor and the legislature plan expenditures and revenues. Despite prosperous conditions, state agencies and institutions suffered from underfinanced programs and overcrowded facilities resulting primarily from inadequate tax revenues. A blue-ribbon tax commission revealed that corporations, especially banks, still escaped fair taxes, and proposed a new bank and corporate franchise tax which Governor Young personally carried to the legislature for unanimous approval. The reform measure, which repealed the tax on bank stocks and revised the corporation franchise tax, not only failed to produce anticipated revenues but also compounded tax inequities that favored corporations over general property taxpayers and big corporations over small ones. Franklin Hichborn tells us that Bank of America's taxes went down from over $650,000 to $25,000 and Standard Oil's from $350,000 to $25, and that Pacific Gas and Electric paid a tax rate one-third less than typical, small utility companies. The new tax measure had long-term consequences: it helped undermine the dual-tax system, and it added to the state equalization board another state administrative agency (Franchise Tax Board) to set a trend toward multiple state taxing agencies.

The Depression of the 1930's created conditions that led to the revamping of the state fiscal system. The new Department of Finance, through experienced administrators in the Rolph administration, systematized the comprehensive budget system into the workable setup in use today. The governor's spendthrift policies and pro-corporation views, however, helped to compound the fiscal crisis accelerated by the oncoming Depression. Particularly hard hit were local governments, the counties, and school districts, which were so little able to handle the worsened tax burden that several approached bankruptcy. The 1933 legislature was the turning point. Under corporate pressure it defeated a measure that would have raised long-delayed state tax rates, thus eliminating the 22-year-old dual-tax system and bringing the fiscal crisis to a head. Public attention then focused on the Riley–Stewart plan initiated by the state controller and an equalization board member but modified by special-interest groups in the legislative session. The predominantly urban and liberal assembly favored a personal income tax that would hit high-income groups. The rural and conservative senate pressed for a sales tax ostensibly designed to spread the tax burden, but which hit low-income groups harder. The legislature adopted the Riley–Stewart Act, a compromise measure that established an ad valorem tax on the property of corporations and general taxpayers, to be tapped by state and local governments. The new Riley–Stewart scheme replaced the Plehn dual-tax system. It eliminated the state tax on gross receipts of corporations, retained the state tax on bank and corporation franchises, and enacted new personal and retail sales taxes. Governor Rolph signed the Riley–Stewart measure and the sales tax but vetoed the personal income tax.

The next two legislative sessions rounded off the tax picture. The 1935 legislature, heavily represented by newly elected Democratic liberals who buttressed the older Progressive elements, finished the uncompleted job of the previous session. It enacted the personal income tax, adjusted the retail sales tax, revised the inheritance tax (enacted 1895), and extended the bank and corporate franchise tax to include public utilities. The 1937 legislature plugged up some remaining loopholes. It adopted a use tax to tap goods bought out of state and sold in California, and a corporation income tax to supplement the bank and corporate franchise tax, and it revised motor vehicle registration taxes. Dewey Anderson, a prominent tax expert, summarized the long battle over taxes by saying that the California system represented fairly well the "enlightenment of the people respecting taxation." It embodied the compromises of entrenched groups who sought to evade as much of the tax load as possible. All conceded the necessity of government services and of providing for them. However, each wanted the other to pay the tax bill.

Meanwhile the state and local governments were developing funds from outside sources. The new sources included subventions by which the federal or state governments made grants to aid lower governmental units in carrying out certain programs, and shared revenues by which the state would collect and distribute revenues to counties, cities, and towns as their share of allocated revenues. After 1910 federal and state subventions and state–local government shared revenues became regular and systematic revenues, especially for expanding social welfare services and administering motor vehicles and highway programs. After several decades of intense political interplay between major group interests, during war and depression conditions, the state established the basis of the fiscal system which operates today.

Government Reorganization

Government reorganization, as we use the term, refers to rearranging the structure, functions, and procedures of government institutions, usually to achieve better performance. The Progressives popularized the notion that reformers could accomplish improvements best through government reorganization on a continuous basis rather than in piecemeal fashion, or by constitutional revision in a general convention, as had been tried and found wanting. Government reorganization became a trademark in California political behavior.

The Progressives and other reformers sought to reshape government institutions into more workable, representative, and responsive agencies for the people. They attempted to reorient government to serve the public interest instead of private or special interests. The elected leader, whether mayor, county supervisor, governor, or president, would be a strong public man with broad vision, objectivity, and impartiality, who would devise administrative and legislative programs beneficial for the whole society. Professionally trained public servants would carry out these programs in particular areas. Agencies would be created and their functions expanded to insure attention to and continuity of these programs. The scheme emphasized honest, efficient, and economical government. It anticipated an informed electorate selecting good men for public office, with sound laws drafted by experts and enacted by a direct legislative process as well as by a conscientious legislature. It called for a budget system to plan revenues, a civil service employed on the basis of merit rather than personal or party favors, and periodic government reorganization to regroup agencies and functions in a centralized bureaucracy. Such a scheme would insure effective government performance and produce a harmonious, equitable society.

Governor Johnson led the way in launching governmental reforms. He sought to convert the role of governor into that of an active voice for the "whole people" by assuming firm personal control and by exercising the full powers of his office. Where governors before him had used these powers in limited fashion, Johnson exercised the full measure of these powers in a forceful manner for his entire program (the party platform). He sponsored moves to set up the state's first budget (apparently the nation's first, as well) and a civil service system as the first steps in eliminating party graft and patronage. He persuaded the legislature to delegate its ordinance, or rulemaking, powers to the governor or to state agencies so that they might issue administration regulations to implement his program.

Progressive leaders like C. C. Young (Republican, Berkeley) made important innovations in the lawmaking process to better implement the popular will in public policy. Most important was the divided session, or "split session," by which legislators could, during a 30-day recess, refer measures to their constituents. Important also were direct legislation; the initiative enabling the electorate to initiate laws; and the referendum, by which legislative bills could be referred to a vote of the people. Legislators also abandoned the traditional party caucus as the chief procedure for selecting their leaders. Henceforth, prospective candidates campaigned directly for assembly speaker and senate president pro tempore, bargaining for legislators' votes by promise of committee chairmanships and other favors. They also appointed a legislative counsel to assist them in drafting laws, constituting their first staff agency for expert assistance.

The state bureaucracy which took systematic form at this time was perhaps the most startling development. State agencies and boards greatly increased in number and size. Johnson's appointees to top positions in these bodies enthusiastically altered or revamped operations. They hired competent bureau chiefs and trained staff experts, instituted budget and civil service procedures, and utilized newly acquired rulemaking powers to prescribe regulations for administering programs in more businesslike fashion. Trustees of boards, likening themselves to corporation boards of directors, adapted business procedures in running state institutions in a more efficient manner. Through Johnson's personal leadership, the activities of state agencies and boards were synchronized in informal fashion through the state board of control.

By the 1920's government expansion engendered major problems that led to further innovations. The governor's position was improved with adoption of the 1922 constitutional amendment which established the executive budget, formalizing the governor's fiscal control of state agencies. As the state bureaucracy became burdened with numerous, costly, overlapping independent agencies awkwardly managed by multi-head boards, a movement got under way to centralize state operations in departments under single heads responsible to the governor. Progressive governors of the decade implemented the movement toward government reorganization. Governor Stephens's 1921 reorganization consolidated numerous agencies (58 of 112) into five major departments. Governor Young's reorganization rounded out this centralized scheme with four additional departments headed by directors appointed by the governor. Administrative principle or factional politics left education under its elected board and superintendent, and some 35 other agencies outside the governor's supervision. This basic department setup under single directors prevails today.

The legislature experienced major transformations during the decade. Legislators faced a sectional crisis over reapportionment. After the 1920 census, in which Los Angeles had more people than San Francisco, Northern California stood to lose its long predominance in state affairs. After a decade-long battle between rural–urban, north–south, and special-interest groups, the legislative deadlock resulted in the electorate's adoption of a constitutional amendment that changed the basis of senate representation, then based on population, to area (one senator for each county; no more than three counties to a district). Adopted in 1926, this so-called Federal Plan, a popular but misleading analogy to the Congress, resulted in the assembly–population and senate–area representation system which prevailed for several decades. It in effect gave a dominant position in legislative affairs to conservative forces, through rural representatives in the upper chamber, over liberal forces with urban allies entrenched in the lower chamber. As it turned out, disadvantaged groups, notably farmers, laborers, and those on social welfare, found other ways to achieve their ends. By the end of the decade, the governmental process had become a sophisticated operation involving intricate manueverings between administration leaders, legislators, and varied special-interest groups.

The legislature found its situation increasingly untenable during the Depression years. It was beset by running battles with the governor, pressure from numerous special interests, the growing complexity of state problems, and its cumbersome procedures for dealing with them. It took action to set its houses in order, primarily by asserting its prerogatives and by revitalizing its committee system. It set up interim committees to investigate state problems between sessions—a device California used more extensively than any other state. Frustrated by its dependence on the governor in budget matters, the lawmakers created a legislative auditor (1941) to conduct independent analyses of the governor's budget, the first of its kind in the nation. Eager to control its own house, the senate in 1941 transferred from the lieutenant governor his traditional power of appointing senate committees to a five-man senate rules committee headed by the senate president pro tem, reducing the lieutenant governor to figurehead president of the upper chamber. Both houses revamped their awkward, overlapping committee systems, reducing their committees by half. The legislature by this time had valuable assistance from its staff agencies, from the state library's reference service, and from UC's Bureau of Public Administration, which since the mid-1930's had provided special studies on problem areas. The legislature's reputation suffered from the shenanigans of lobbyists like Samish, and the perverted practices of some lawmakers, such as introducing "skeleton bills" or hi-jacking and "chloroforming" opposition bills. Nevertheless, it won national laurels for innovations and quality legislation and in 1940 ranked first among the states in volume of legislation.

Government reorganization wrought a transformation in operations and a realignment of governmental relationships. The governor became the prime mover in setting the direction of state affairs, whether backward or forward. His personality and ideas set the style of gubernatorial leadership. The state bureaucracy by 1945 comprised 14 departments, with the finance department exercising budget and housekeeping controls. A state personnel board administered a merit system for recruiting government employees (formalized and expanded in 1934). Administrative procedures for systematizing rules and regulations were codified in 1945. The legislature had streamlined its organization and procedures and consolidated house controls. Public participation in the lawmaking process through direct legislation was extensive; the electorate adopted one-third or less of proposed initiatives and referendums, but these constitutional proposals included significant measures like the state budget (1922), legislative reapportionment (1926), the Central Valley Project (1933), and civil service reform (1934). It also defeated drastic proposals like single tax and Ham 'n Eggs, an indication of voter resistance to radical reforms.

15 The Regulated Economy

THE SETTING

The Entrepreneurs

California's polyglot entrepreneurial class swelled with the entry of different kinds of native sons and ambitious immigrants. Entrepreneurs with special talents, modest savings, or "venture capital" developed enterprises that fulfilled the special needs of the state's expanding economy. A greater number than previously were college-trained— growers, manufacturers, and distributors, as well as professionals and scientists—although the self-made men who characterized the earlier generation were still around. Such imaginative and trained men seemed better able to master the intricacies of specialized, diversified industries and markets.

The small entrepreneurs still played a significant role in the state's economic development. Inventor–entrepreneurs, like Douglas and Lockheed in aircraft, Friden and Marchant in computers, and Packard and Hewlett (both Stanford graduates) in electronics, launched new enterprises that developed into major industries. Marginal film producers, like Metro, Goldwyn, and Mayer, who were shut out by monopolistic pioneer producers in the East came to California where they built their small companies and helped launch the worldwide movie industry. Small operators also spearheaded new directions for older industries; for example, small ranchers bred calves for the big ranchers' cattle-feeding operations. The innovative Paul Davies (a California-born Harvard graduate) built FMC, a small company of ingenious food-processing machinery into the nation's largest corporation of its kind. Not all small entrepreneurs, of course, graduated into the big time. The great majority of them remained small operators, but they dominated many industries, especially garment and metalware manufacturing, professional services like public relations and tourism, and the retail trades.

The big entrepreneurs still played a commanding role in the state's economy. Their preeminence was due to their strategic position in certain key industries and in the market economy. They were a varied lot. Stephen Bechtel and his talented sons built a family construction firm, expanding from railroad projects in the 1920's, to huge bridges and dams in the 1930's, to Pacific naval bases during World War II. Henry Kaiser, a native New Yorker of modest circumstances, a self-taught engineer, and a sometimes partner of Bechtel, became obsessed with industrial development in his adopted state; he applied big-scale technology to construction (bridges, dams, and roads) and manufacturing (houses, ships, and steel). J. Paul Getty of California and Howard Hughes of Texas, talented sons of wealthy men, apparently focused on amassing wealth, one in oil and the other in aircraft and movies; their California enterprises place them among the world's richest men.

A. P. Giannini, son of an Italian shopkeeper, was a self-made merchant, who later built his local bank into the world's largest. Regarded as the greatest innovator in modern banking, Giannini defied banking conventions (in a field where convention was sacred) to introduce new ways of extending credit and loans primarily to "the little fella"—small homeowners, farmers, manufacturers, and businessmen—but also to giant entrepreneurs like Kaiser. He was the epitome of the "pragmatic idealist," dedicated to the well-being of his native state. Probably no other person contributed as much to California's overall development in this period.

Business Organization

Proprietorships and partnerships were still the most common form of business organization, and even dominated certain industries. However, they often operated in a subordinate or secondary capacity, in the shadow of dominant corporate and cooperative groups operating in their areas, except in certain areas like services and trade. Farmers and manufacturers found it advantageous to expand individual or family-owned enterprises into large-scale corporations, which gave impetus to the so-called rural "factories in the fields" and huge manufacturing plants in urban areas. The corporate form gained wide popularity for its adaptability and flexibility in diverse situations, particularly in achieving economy and efficiency in the mass production and wide distribution of goods.

The cooperative was still widely utilized in agriculture and in certain manufacturing areas. Cooperatives like the California Fruit Growers Exchange—still the nation's largest—expanded in size and increased in numbers, acquiring elaborate structures like corporations and for the same ends. California's unique experiment with the state market commission (1915–1930) resulted in a code of cooperative law copied by other states. State cooperative leaders became important national figures. Aaron Sapiro, a brilliant lawyer and "sparkplug of the state market commission," became the evangelist of the nationwide cooperative movement. C. C. Teague, long-time CFGE president and a powerful figure in industry and government circles, was called "Mr. California Agriculture." The cooperative was an important countervailing force in California's agriculture and to some extent in the nation's.

The rise of the nation's supercorporations—industrial trusts and holding companies—had its impact on California as elsewhere. These big corporations not only grew at a faster rate than small corporations but they also became increasingly larger in size and scope to become dominating entities. Pioneered by electrical and automobile companies, they developed elaborate structures as part of business strategy to achieve more efficient operations and attain a commanding position in the national market. They established laboratories for research and development for devising new and improved products (General Electric and Westinghouse began this "competition of the labs"). They developed mass-production systems with conveyor belt–assembly line–standardized products techniques (perfected by Ford in 1914) for increased production at reduced costs—the so-called economies of large-scale production. They established vast plant facilities and scattered branch plants (made possible by improved communications, electric power, and motor transportation) for producing and distributing goods on a nationwide basis. They spearheaded aggressive advertising campaigns not only to fulfill consumer demands but to "create" and fashion their wants, making extensive use of magazine, newspaper, and radio media. They undertook costly public-relations programs to improve their image with a public suspicious of gigantic enterprises.

The corporation's growth was accompanied by drastic organizational changes. Big financiers and industrialists, in building up their corporate empires, converted an unwieldy structure in which a few executive officers had loose control over subsidiary companies, into an elaborate administrative structure which consolidated operating units into a single system under centralized control. Typically the new corporation comprised an administrative hierarchy of operating divisions, departments, and bureaus headed by ranking professional managers who applied scientific management to business operations. At the top, a central office, aided by staff agencies of experts in finance, personnel, research, and planning, coordinated functional departments like engineering, manufacturing, purchases, and sales. The larger corporation which had extended its territories and diversified its products decentralized its operations by creating regional, semi-autonomous divisions coordinated through the central office—a scheme pioneered in the 1920's by DuPont, General Motors, Sears, Roebuck, and Standard Oil. The holding company reached its high point with the pyramid, whose apex served as parent to one or more holding companies. This device enabled leaders of supercorporations to manipulate stocks and securities. Giannini built his great banking institution in this way, while Samuel Insull used it dishonestly to build a Chicago-based public utility which yielded him a huge personal fortune before it fell apart. The pyramidal holding company became the ultimate expression of large corporate organization. Some business leaders and economists decried the concentrated control and fragmented structure of supercorporations as unhealthy and unsound, but the nation up to the Depression years was swept away by the glamour of these gigantic enterprises that had contributed so much to its improved standard of living.

The corporate revolution profoundly altered the organizational arrangement of the market economy. It led to the preponderance of large firms. The famous Berle–Means study (1932) revealed that 200 corporations accounted for 65 percent of the nation's production and 77 percent of its wealth. Furthermore, in major industries like the manufacturing of automobiles, chemicals, and electrical equipment, and in meat packing, three to six firms controlled two-thirds of the industry's business. Small firms, however, greatly outnumbered big corporations and dominated fields like agriculture (except in California), construction, professional services, and retail trade. These large corporations attempted to outdo rivals by combining production and distribution operations in various ways to cut costs and improve efficiency. They developed branch plants and chain outlets for dispersing their products in local, regional, and national markets, promoting the sales of their brand products by extensive advertising. The trust and holding companies were natural vehicles for these huge integrated firms, though many medium-size corporations and some small ones also integrated their operations.

The emergence of the supercorporations and their ability to dominate the market led to what economists call an oligopolistic market—a market controlled not by a single firm but by several. Conspicuous were the Big 3 automakers (General Motors, Ford, and Chrysler) and the Big 6 steel companies led by United States Steel. Market prices were often set by industry leaders, rather than being the result of open interplay between sellers and buyers as in a competitive market. The consumer still remained the ultimate factor in the market economy. Consumers—not corporation leaders—determined what goods and services they desired or wanted, and if corporations charged too much, consumers simply went to other producers. Nevertheless, the big corporations in an oligopolistic market, while not the only reality in the market economy, exerted enormous political and social as well as economic powers that were proving a mixed blessing in the maturing industrial society.

DEVELOPMENT

The 1910's

The federal government after 1910 became more deeply involved in regulating big business and assisting agriculture and other segments to achieve a more balanced and viable economy. The Progressive campaign to break up the great trusts reached its peak in the half-decade after 1910. The United States Supreme Court upheld federal prosecution of Standard Oil, enunciating its famous "rule of reason" which held that the Sherman Act did not forbid all trusts but only unreasonable combinations in restraint of trade. This judicial principle in effect made reasonable monopolies legal (they had "economic legitimacy" and "social acceptability"). The court intimated that federal prosecutions should be based not on the size or power of corporations but on the unfair and illegal use of that power as determined not by law but by the common sense of judges.

Aroused by this "judicial legislation" but recognizing the futility of breaking up large corporations into small companies, Progressive leaders moved to assert congressional prerogative in regulating business practices. Spurred by President Wilson, Congress in 1914 enacted two landmark antitrust measures. The Clayton Act forbade monopolistic practices that lessened competition, such as price discrimination and exclusive deals. The Federal Trade Commission (FTC) was created to administer antitrust laws. It was to prevent corporations from using unfair methods in interstate commerce by issuing "cease and desist" orders enforceable by the courts. The 1914 antitrust legislation shifted attention from the size to the practices of trusts and other supercorporations. It placed government emphasis on maintaining fair competition—a tacit recognition of the benefits accruing from the large-scale production of supercorporations and of growing public tolerance of "monopolistic competition."

The Progressives also pressed for reform measures regulating other big businesses and aiding disadvantaged groups. Congress under bipartisan Progressive push provided for banking and currency regulation (Federal Reserve System, 1913), recognition of labor rights (Clayton, 1914), technical and financial aid to farmers (Smith–Lever county agents, 1914; Federal Farm Loan, 1916). World War I halted Progressive reforms but not government regulation. During the wartime emergency, Congress set up federal agencies (the famous six war boards) with dictatorial powers to direct the nation's economy. This decade inaugurated government controls of industry which persist to this day.

California's development reflected state extension of these national trends. The Progressive administration in power during the decade revamped economic policy and instituted state regulation for supplementing and extending federal trends. It strengthened the railroad commission (1911) to prevent railroad malpractices. It created independent commissions for regulating public utilities (1911—the most comprehensive measure in any state), for conserving natural resources (1913), for supervising corporation securities (1913), and for improving the lot of immigrants, small farmers (by extending rural credits and promoting land settlements), and other underprivileged groups. Apparently the Johnson adminstration deferred to the national government in antitrust matters (the Cartwright Act was used sparingly by the state courts only). It was not disappointed, for the United States Supreme Court ordered the severance of Southern Pacific from Union Pacific (1913), forcing them to operate as separate companies.

The state experienced rapid growth. Economic development was paced by expanded hydroelectric facilities, new highway construction, and expanded trade routes, especially with the opening of the Panama Canal (1914). Agricultural expansion spurred the growth of large-scale cooperatives and consolidated corporations. Industrial expansion stimulated construction and manufacturing industries in major cities—where employer groups and labor unions involved the communities in their industrial warfare. World War I greatly stimulated manufacturing industries, notably accelerating established shipbuilding and fledgling aircraft enterprises in the San Francisco Bay Area. It was a decade of growth amidst adjustment and travail.

The 1920's

The Republican administrations which guided the nation's economy during the decade reversed the Progressive trend toward government regulation. The conservative-minded Republicans implemented government laissez faire in national economic policy, primarily by administering antitrust and other laws in favor of business corporations and farmers cooperatives at the expense of labor unions. The United States Supreme Court, in ruling on federal prosecution of United States Steel (1920), the biggest trust of all, upheld the supercorporation on grounds that it had not abused its monopolistic powers—prompting opponents to charge the court had substituted a "rule of expediency" for the "rule of reason" a decade earlier. The action ushered in a second great wave of corporation mergers which lasted the decade; a notable feature was the gigantic merger of holding companies in the public-utility field. Conservative pro-business attitudes were reflected in the lack of antitrust actions (one scholar declared that the FTC tried to commit hara-kiri). Regulatory agencies like ICC and FTC were immobilized by budget and personnel cuts and by the appointment of businessmen as commissioners who curiously enough thus supervised the agencies designed to regulate them!

Trade associations gained new importance at this time. These industrywide organizations of business firms, widely established by 1920 to promote cooperative ventures, were allowed to exchange price and other market information and establish industry codes of fair competition. These practices were encouraged by the influential Commerce Secretary Herbert Hoover (1921–1929) and legalized by the United States Supreme Court in mid-decade decisions. The trade associations became the chief vehicles for the new competition; instead of secrecy and deceit as under the old competition, they stressed frank exchange and open agreements to coordinate competitive forces for better control of market conditions to insure better profits. Thus, corporations were able to cooperate in imposing industry-administered prices and regulating markets, contributing in another form to the regulated economy.

The spectacular development of big industry, with its attendant mass production of capital and consumer goods, wrapped the nation in an optimistic aura that clouded serious malfunctions in the market economy. While most manufacturing industries grew and prospered, farm groups suffered from falling prices and rising surpluses, and labor suffered deteriorating working conditions, primarily because of displacements by factory machinery and other technological improvements. Compounding the situation was a speculative fever which led people to spend savings and loans on personal luxury goods and on investments in land, stocks, and other get-rich-quick schemes. Financial and other institutions contributed their part in overheating the market economy by their easy credit practices and unsound fiscal policies. They extended money to consumers, corporations, and other groups for risky ventures, especially in the stock market. Finally the bubble burst with the great stock market crash in 1929, followed by a chain reaction of business failures, mass unemployment, and widespread public distress.

California in the 1920's was caught up in this ebullient growth. Its growth was sometimes in substantial form, as in agriculture and some manufactures, and sometimes in virulent form, as in land and oil speculations. The state, flushed with one of its greatest immigration flows, experienced growing industries, expanding urban and rural markets, and extending highway and rail transportation links. Older industries expanded, notably foodstuffs, hydroelectric power, lumber, and petroleum, but newer manufacturing and service industries, like movies, tourism, and the retail trade surpassed them. The Southern Pacific, after winning an ICC decision allowing the company to retain the Central Pacific (1922), undertook extensive improvement and expansion of its operations. Giannini's bank paced other financial institutions in liberalizing loans and credits at all levels, to corporate, cooperative, homeowner, and consumer groups. Major groups clashed in showdown battles for larger stakes in the economic expansion, including traditional big vs. small and Californian vs. eastern interests in food-stuffs, movies, petroleum, and motor transportation. The most portentous of these battles was the decade-long struggle between private utilities led by PGE and Progressive-led public groups over the state's hydroelectric and water resources. The prosperous decade had its unhealthy features of extensive speculation and depressed conditions of labor and other groups, but the general economic expansion was overwhelming enough so that the state did not feel the heavy impact of the national depression before the decade was out.

The 1930's

The widespread Depression of the 1930's revived and expanded government intervention in the nation's economic affairs. President Franklin Roosevelt in 1933 undertook drastic relief and recovery measures to relieve the desperate plight of people and to revitalize the declining economy. He launched a comprehensive program (First New Deal), which focused on extending federal assistance to big business (National Industrial Recovery Act) and to big farmers (Agricultural Adjustment Administration). Under NIRA, each industry drafted official codes of fair competition—which in effect were government-sanctioned industry codes—and labor unions for the first time won official sanction of collective bargaining. When business leaders balked and the Supreme Court invalidated parts of his program, Roosevelt around 1935 shifted gears. His revised program (Second New Deal) centered on federal help to labor unions (National Labor Relations Board) and small farmers (Second Agricultural Adjustment Administration). Federal loans and credits were extended widely to private and public enterprises. State and local governments administered federal public works as part of the general effort to speed economic recovery.

The Roosevelt Administration took steps to remedy corporate abuses which had been partly blamed for the business fiasco. Congress created a federal agency to regulate stocks and securities (Securities and

Exchange Commission) and wrote restrictions for public-utility holding companies. It amended the Sherman and Clayton Acts to help small middleman retailers who were hurt by the price-cutting practices of supermarkets, chain stores, and discount houses in interstate commerce. Congress also strengthened ICC, FTC, and other regulatory agencies, prompting FTC to revive vigorous prosecution of antitrust laws.

California suffered badly during the depression decade, often in a distinctive way. The state economy, at its peak in autumn of 1929, eventually felt the full impact of the nationwide depression by winter of 1931 and hit bottom by spring of 1933. The great economic slowdown led to numerous business bankruptcies, widespread unemployment, and acute public distress. Complicating the situation was the steady stream of migrants, mostly from dust-bowl areas of the South—the so-called Arkies and Okies, lured by hopes of jobs and relief. Masses of people were seized by extreme pessimistic moods, from quiet despair to desperate acts, although sensible men held their own. The state government creaked its way through the crisis. Government leaders, almost overwhelmed by the magnitude of problems, managed to hammer out expedient solutions with strong assistance from federal leaders. Business leaders reacted in positive and negative ways. Enlightened bankers like Giannini, manufacturers like Douglas Aircraft, and distributors like Safeway Stores, made important breakthroughs. Others of narrow vision, like Associated Farmers and the Southern California Council (a business-oriented coalition), fought defensive battles to preserve privileged positions against change.

The state at mid-decade witnessed climaxes to several excruciating showdown battles, notably the shipowners vs. the San Francisco longshoremen, whose strike spread to a Bay Area general strike; growers vs. farm labor unions in the Central Valley; the majors vs. independent operators in construction, lumber, and petroleum; the old public vs. private hydroelectric-power groups; and independent retailers vs. chain retail stores. All involved violated rights; violent showdowns were as bad as any experienced in the state's history. Out of the turmoil came uneasy armistices and compromises which supplemented positive forces bringing about the state's rapid economic recovery. The accelerated federal expenditures, first for economic recovery and then for national defense, speeded the return of relatively prosperous times by the end of the decade.

The New Deal and World War II greatly enlarged federal regulation of the market economy. Many regulatory agencies (the so-called alphabetical agencies) set up to administer emergency programs became permanent fixtures in the growing federal bureaucracy. Most economic sectors experienced the establishment of industry or government regulations, not just to restrain abuses in production and distribution but to control prices in the market itself—a truly revolutionary development in the nation's so-called capitalistic market economy. These measures brought about the most extensive regulation of American society up to that time.

ANALYSIS

Land

The emerging industrialism brought about a changed attitude toward land. Land was still important, but no longer the only important source of wealth. Manufacturing, construction, service, and finance industries (especially corporate investments) had become primary sources of wealth. No longer was land readily available at attractive prices; thus, it was managed with greater care to insure maximum benefits. Government agencies and private enterprises became deeply involved with each other, competing to shape public policies and cooperating to work out programs for effectively utilizing land resources—soils, grasses, timber, minerals, related water resources, and the land itself.

Public Lands

As Congress debated over public-land policies, government agencies and special-interest groups battled to inject their views and programs. They included settlers seeking homesteads, entrepreneurs wanting to exploit land resources for commercial profit, conservationists of the John Muir camp attempting to preserve the natural setting, and conservationists of the Roosevelt–Pinchot camp seeking the widest use of land "to do the greatest good for the greatest number of people." Some public sentiment favored federal cession of public lands to the states for their disposition. Eventually Progressive forces prevailed in obtaining policies for federal reserve lands that provided for multiple use of land and scientific management of resources, recognizing that each resource was related to others and that they should be treated together in total land development.

Congress continued its generous land distribution policy, primarily to help small settlers acquire land on the remaining less attractive public domain. It enacted the Grazing Homestead Act (1916) which permitted settlers to acquire large tracts (640 acres with another 160 for homestead) ostensibly to develop livestock enterprises. The poorly drawn law proved to be a land bonanza for all types of settlers. Lands distributed under this act were acquired by large ranchers to increase their holdings; by real estate operators who resold them, often in shady deals, to gullible city dwellers and out-of-state residents for farming or speculation; and by others, seeking the prestige of owning land, for building up little land empires. Such lax land policies led to continued land abuse, this time by small settlers as well as by large landowners.

Public alarm grew with the revelation of rapid land disposal (914,000 acres were filed in 1920 alone) and rampant land abuses. Finally in 1935 President Roosevelt issued his historic executive order which temporarily withdrew the remaining public domain from private entry. Congress shortly afterward enabled settlers to buy or lease small tracts for home, cabin, health, recreational, or business sites (1938). This measure stimulated considerable real estate business in mountain areas and became the most popular way to acquire public lands in California. One authority described these actions by the President and Congress as a case of "locking up the barn after the horse was stolen." But there still remained 15 million acres of widely scattered, unappropriated public domain which henceforth was distributed in far more restricted fashion.

Congress pursued several courses of action on other public lands. It expanded and consolidated existing reserves for preserving resources, such as timber stands, watershed areas, and wildlife refuges. In this connection, a National Park Service was set up (1916) to administer national parks and monuments for scenic and other interests—not for commercial utilization like forest reserves. As it had set aside forest reserves for lumbermen and ranchers, it set up mineral reserves for oil, coal, and other operators (1921) and grazing reserves for ranchers (1934). With the advent of World War II, Congress established military reservations for troop training, weapon-testing grounds, and other military activities, thus creating nonresource reserve lands. California's five military bases (Camp Pendleton in San Diego, Fort Ord and Hunter Liggett Military Reservation in Monterey, Camp Roberts in San Miguel, and Beale Air Force Base in Marysville) alone accounted for nearly a half-million acres. The federal acquisitions more than offset federal dispositions; in 1945 the federal government retained ownership of 29 million acres, or less than one-third of the state's area. The federal government as custodial agent for the people of the national interest was far and away California's biggest landowner.

The state followed the federal example in setting up and managing its reserve lands, but with much less success. The legislature finally reversed its mineral land policy (1921) and provided for operators to lease state-owned oil lands for drilling operations. It established the basis of a state park system (1927), expanded the wildlife conservation program, but did little to develop state forest reserves (see below). However small these beginnings, the state planted the seeds of a system of forest, mineral, park, and wildlife reserves which was to flower in the postwar years.

Private Lands

The continuing pattern of large landholdings and high land prices revived public alarm and government concern after 1910. The Progressives, always sensitive to big entrepreneurs outdoing small ones, initiated state action to remedy this land maldistribution. A blue-ribbon legislative commission (1917) reported on the extent of land monopolization: 350 proprietors owned over four million acres, some devoted to large-scale production but much of it lying idle; one firm (Southern Pacific) controlled 2 million acres, and four firms (including Kern County Land Company) together owned over half the area of Kern County.

Under Progressive influence, the 1919 legislature authorized a state-sponsored land colony—one of the most remarkable experiments in state governmental enterprises. A land settlement board headed by the celebrated irrigation expert, Elwood Mead, enthusiastically launched its well-publicized projects. It purchased lands and set up colonies at Durham in Butte County and Dehli in Merced County. After years of disappointing efforts, the colonies in 1930 were deprived of state funds and thereafter struggled on their own.

Land development in rural areas revealed an amazing diversity. Land colonies established before 1910, even those that experienced initial difficulties, now bloomed into substantial communities. They included corporate enterprises, like Kern County Land Company, and cooperative enterprises of numerous farmer-owned associations. The

California Fruit Growers Exchange, in the course of marketing products for its farmer members, came to manage their lands and shape their development. The Irvines built on their vast corporate ranch waterworks for intensive, diverse agricultural production, sold tracts to promoters for different kinds of communities (residential, recreational, and industrial), leased lands for oil development and livestock and crop production, formed a cooperative for marketing some of their products, and later released land for military use (El Toro Marine Air Base at Santa Ana).

The "Little Lander" colony established at San Ysidro near San Diego (1910) developed into a self-supporting settlement of dirt farmers who worked small lots. Raymond Anchordoguy, a poor French Basque immigrant, began around 1910 as a hired sheepherder and became a wealthy sheep rancher with large holdings in the Sacramento Valley. Sherman Weaver, a midwestern immigrant of American colonial stock, settled in Turlock in the 1920's where he rose from farm laborer to prosperous proprietor of a poultry business on his two-acre lot. Whether collectively or individually, land developers managed to do well.

These entrepreneurs were of all types; rural and city-bred residents of the state; immigrants from other states and from Europe, Latin America, and Asia; big and small promoters; speculators and bona fide settlers. They encountered common problems of high land prices; uneven quality of soils, minerals, timber, and water resources; unpredictable market conditions; and fluctuating business cycles. They attempted varied solutions, including careful management of their lands, leasing, renting, or purchasing their lands under different arrangements, rotating use of their land in various ways (single and diverse products), and orienting their production to specific markets. They made increasing use of professional managers and other trained personnel for handling such complicated operations. Success or failure depended on the ability of each to find the appropriate solution to the particular problems he faced in developing his lands.

Agriculture

Agriculture continued to expand, but the impact of two world wars and the prolonged depression in between strongly affected agricultural enterprises and markets. Farmers and ranchers accelerated production to meet the sudden enormous demands of wartime, and altered operations again to cope with oversupplied markets in peacetime. They also had to deal with problems arising from dietary changes (people ate less starchy foods and more protein), technological developments in production and distribution, perennial ravages of crop and livestock diseases, shifting markets at home and abroad, and general economic conditions. The state university, and state and federal agencies greatly extended valuable services, including basic research, technical assistance, educational programs, and product controls to help troubled farmers and ranchers deal with their perplexing problems. The role of agricultural experts is illustrated by UC's food scientist William Cruess who contributed to the commercial development of canned applesauce and fruit cocktails, artificial dehydration for dried fruits, and techniques for frozen foods. Farm journals like *California Farmer,* and *Pacific Rural Press*, kept farmers and ranchers abreast of latest developments.

Farmers organized effectively for political action and secured important government aid. During the Progressive era, Congress extended direct assistance through the agricultural extension program by which federal-state sponsored county agents advised farmers (Smith—Lever, 1914), and through land banks, which gave farmers long-term credit (Federal Farm Loan, 1916). The legislature in a remarkable move established a state market commission—the first of its kind in the nation—to assist farmers in setting up cooperative associations for marketing their products (see above). Plagued by depression conditions in the 1920's, grower—packer—shipper groups, with help from the state agricultural department and UC experimented with plans for controlling production voluntarily (e.g., marketing agreements for pro-rating pro-duction quotas) to reduce surplus crops and stop falling prices. When the nation's agriculture became chaotic during the 1930's, California farm groups pressured the 1933 legislature to set up state crop controls and mandatory market agreements (based on the earlier volunteer arrange-ments), anticipating Roosevelt's basic New Deal measure for agricultural recovery. The Agricultural Adjustment Administration, the key federal measure, supervised crop production by giving certain types of farmers benefit payments to curtail crops and by buying and storing their surplus crops. These state and federal programs underwent considerable trial and adjustment amidst much controversy. For example, California peach growers in the mid-1930's destroyed over 500,000 trees in a concerted move with canners to reduce the crop supply in order to raise the price of canned peaches. It took the economic boom of World War II to bring back agricultural prosperity. Nevertheless, California agriculture owed much of its relative stability and prosperity to a close relationship of industry groups and government agencies unmatched by other states.

Crops

Crop production became an increasingly complex affair. Farmers worked on purchased, leased, and rented lands to produce staple and specialty crops for specific markets. Many planted improved seeds and plants researched by the state university and governmental agencies and made greater use of chemical fertilizers to stimulate production. They still utilized cheap labor gangs (see below) but relied increasingly on machinery for planting, cultivating, and harvesting crops. Field operations were greatly mechanized by the all-purpose gas tractor which appeared in the 1920's, the diesel tractor first produced in 1930 by Caterpillar Tractors (a 1925 merger of the California pioneer firms, Best and Holt). Specialized machines for particular crops were developed by the San Jose-based Food Machinery Corporation (formed 1928, hereafter FMC); it became the largest firm of its kind in the nation. Farmers made extensive use of irrigation and electric power—California had more electrified farms than any other state. In financing these costly operations—land, facilities, supplies, machinery, and labor—farmers were able to secure credit on relatively easy terms from banks, notably Giannini's Bank of America, and other investment groups, like packers and farm machinery manufacturers who were eager to insure crop supplies to sustain their own operations. Confronted with such high operating costs, farmers concentrated less on quantity production (as in earlier times) and more on selecting crops to secure maximum use of their land for highest profit yields.

Some farm operations were exceedingly complicated and diverse. After World War I, Roy Pike of San Francisco acquired five grain ranches near Modesto and set up El Solyo Company (Spanish, "the pike"). Dividing his 55,000-acre spread into five operating units, he produced and processed over 75 different crops and livestock (many were experimental) and marketed through eight cooperatives and his own outlets. In 1944 FMC acquired El Solyo and revamped operations to put the ranch on a profitable basis. Another was Joseph DiGiorgio, an Italian-born, eastern-based fruit merchant, who bought Earl Fruit Company from Armour (see Chapter 12) in 1910 to augment his transcontinential distribution system. He acquired a 5000-acre Delano tract in 1919 and, when he became a full-scale California grower after 1930, built it up into a 25,000-acre ranch to become the world's largest grower of grapes, pears, and plums. DiGiorgio was a supreme entrepreneur of agribusiness, for in addition to his farm operations in California and Florida (he was the biggest citrus grower there), he conducted processing, packing, and shipping operations for his nationwide system.

In marketing their products, growers, canner—packers, and shippers competed intensely for their share of the so-called California pack. Big and small groups formed combinations primarily to break the control of eastern leaders: Armour and Swift through their strategic shipping facilities and American Can through its can-making monopoly. In the decade after 1910 deciduous fruit and nut growers formed additional cooperative marketing associations in individual crop areas. The five larger California canners, packers, and shippers (including the Fontana and Armsby firms), formed California Packing Corporation (1916, hereafter Calpak). Calpak operated 78 canneries, packing plants, and warehouses—50 in California and the rest in other states, including Hawaii and Alaska—for processing and distributing under its Del Monte label fruits, vegetables, and fish through its own sales outlets in 27 cities nationwide. The Californians got help from another direction. The Big 4 meatpackers were forced to break up their monopoly as a result of FTC antitrust action (Packers Consent Decree) and Congress's landmark law for regulating the livestock industry (both in 1921). Armour and Swift eventually gave up food distribution operations and non-agricultural properties. By the mid-1920's the big California operators had broken the monopolistic hold of eastern leaders to pace industry not only in the California pack but also in national markets.

Citrus and grapes illustrate the varied pattern of California's crop production. CFGE, the powerful cooperative marketing the famous Sunkist oranges, controlled over 70 percent of the state's citrus production. It easily led competition by expanding and specializing operations, such as its highly successful advertising campaign ("Drink an Orange") to sell canned orange juice in the 1920's. Grapes suffered the worst ups and downs of any industry. From its peak in 1910 it was practically dismantled by national prohibition in 1919, though a few producers survived by legal loopholes and imaginative ways. Revived by prohibition repeal (1933), it again became the nation's leader. Each California producer found his niche in small and big, cooperative and corporate production of standard and quality wines. Many were swallowed up after 1935 by eastern distilleries who were seeking to diversify their operations by absorbing California wineries. (National got Italian Swiss Colony and Schenley bought DiGorgio during the war years). The success of these operating patterns—ambitious entrepreneurs applying imagination and innovation to enterprises—was evident in 1945 when California ranked first in producing 42 of the 80-odd crops grown in the nation.

Livestock

The cattle industry underwent a remarkable transformation. As farmers extended crop production to fertile valley lands, ranchers were forced to move their beef cattle to less favorable, nonirrigated dryland ranges, including marginal grasslands in valley border areas and mountain woodland meadows. They benefited from such congressional measures as the 1916 Grazing Homestead Act, which made grazing lands in federal forest reserves available on generous terms (see above). Before long, the smaller, well-established rancher—the type who raised up to 300 head of cattle or 3000 sheep to support his family—replaced the large-scale operator as the mainstay of the livestock range economy. Other ranchers, including big operators like Miller and Lux and Kern County Land Company, found it profitable to concentrate either on breeding or feeding cattle for the market. Cattle breeders produced calves (using artificial insemination after 1930) which were sold directly off the mother for veal slaughter or to cattle feeders who fattened the animals on high-energy feeds in feedlots (large fenced-in tracts) for beef slaughter later. In meatpacking, Swift sustained its lead over the Big Four packers and rising newcomers, but now it stressed cooperative profit-sharing schemes rather than undercutting competition in dealing with local ranchers and packers. Beef cattle, which declined from a peak in 1910 to a 1930 low, rose again to become a major state industry after 1940. It had become a regulated industry subject to federal-state standards and to voluntary agreements among local livestock associations.

Mineral Resources

Mineral resources underwent unprecedented extensive exploitation after 1910. The expanding and broadening economy created heavy demand for more and different mineral products—construction materials (gravels, sand, stone, and cement) for homes, buildings, roads, dams; gas and oil, fuels and lubricants for industrial machines, ships, trains, automobiles; and metal alloys and rare minerals for steel, chemical, and other manufacturing enterprises. Before long, mining enterprises were aggressively prospecting for and developing over 60 kinds of minerals that put California in the front rank of the mineral-producing states. One writer predicted only half-jokingly that this rush for industrial minerals would exceed the importance of the rush for precious metals a half-century before. Petroleum development so overshadowed the other minerals that it became a major factor in public policy and economic development.

Government regulation shaped industry development along several lines. The federal antitrust prosecution of Standard Oil (begun 1906) culminated in the Supreme Court's 1911 decision ordering the New Jersey-based parent company to dissolve its nationwide system, with the result that its California subsidiary was reorganized as an independent corporation, Standard Oil of California. President Taft, in 1912, set aside public lands in California as naval oil reserves (Elk Hills and Buena Vista) for United States Navy ships then converting from coal to oil fuel. After a bitter, decade-long battle between oil companies and conservationists, Congress enacted the landmark federal mineral act (1922) which provided for oil and other operators to lease public lands and pay royalties for minerals taken from them. The public soon faced scandals from shady deals of unscrupulous oilmen. Edward Doheny, a pioneer California oil millionaire, paid a $100,000 bribe to the Secretary of the Interior (Albert Fall) to secure a lease for tapping the extremely valuable federal oil reserve at Elk Hills. The Secretary was convicted (1924) but Doheny went free—prompting the cynical aphorism: you can't convict a million dollars.

California supplemented federal regulation with state action. It inaugurated a state leasing program (1921) for regulating minerals extracted from tidelands and other state lands. When overproduction led to chaotic market conditions in the 1920's, the Secretary of the Interior (California's Ray Wilbur) helped set up the federal–state plan for allocating oil quotas among the states, and each state imposed allocations among its producers. The California legislature authorized (1929) volunteer prorating plans among producers, supervised by a state umpire, for restricting oil output—not arbitrary regulation by a state agency as in other oil states. Government mineral regulation in California aimed at curbing ruinous competition and promoting development.

A conspicuous feature underlying the state's oil development was the rampant speculation that kept the industry in constant turmoil. Oil strikes spurred numerous newcomers into the industry: speculators gambling on stock transactions, promoters pressing ambitious and sometimes fraudulent schemes, and assorted professional and amateur operators eager to build oil empires. The most spectacular of these many oil adventurers was C. C. Julian, a Los Angeles promoter who in 1922 set up a company and within a few months raised $11 million from 40,000 stockholders through fraudulent advertising. By 1930 his caper had snowballed into an enormous stock swindle amounting to around $100 million which resulted in the conviction of the bribe-taking district attorney, but not of the 40-odd prominent business, banking, and government leaders implicated in the scheme. Overlooked in public pre-occupation with government regulation, oil stocks, and the few scandals was the industry's remarkable development in meeting enormous demands for petroleum, which figured so importantly in the state's—and the nation's—economic expansion.

Industry development in this hectic period passed through three transitional stages. In the decade after 1910, the three principal producers—Standard, Union, and Associated—were joined by two more big producers: General Petroleum, organized 1912 by a San Francisco group, and Shell, a subsidiary set up in 1913 by the world-wide Royal Dutch Shell. Standard, General Petroleum, and Shell constituted the majors that dominated the state's oil production. Union Oil led the smaller independent producers who held their own; they organized into

The Standard Oil refinery at Point Richmond as it appeared in the 1920's.

an association (1914) to market their oil. During the decade, production centered in the San Joaquin where the bonanza fields (Coalinga, Kern, McKittrick, and Sunset–Midway) were fully exploited for the heavy crude.

The industry went through a major shakeup in the 1920's. The center of production shifted to the Los Angeles basis, which exploded with fabulous oil booms (Dominguez, Huntington Beach, Inglewood, Long Beach–Signal Hill was then the world's largest gusher–and Torrance). The southern field yielded lighter crude oil in gasoline production which proved a boom for the rapidly growing automobile trade. Numerous producers drilled small town lots, and minor refiners processed proportionally more gasoline. Union beat off Shell's attempt to swallow it–a big power play which caused a national furor (1921). Four eastern firms entered the majors by extending their operations: Tidewater, which merged with Associated (1926); Standard Oil of New York, which absorbed General Petroleum (1926, later Socony–Vacuum); Richfield; Texas, which merged with General Petroleum (1928). Standard of California kept ahead by absorbing Pacific Oil (1926), thereby increasing its oil output 50 percent, and by building up its vast distinctive system of service stations. (Associated and Pacific were Southern Pacific subsidiaries.) The industry market shifted in two directions during the decade: from oil to gasoline fuel, and from regional isolation to national interrelationships. It met overproduction in the California fields by expanding into the eastern markets; later, when Texas and Oklahoma gained ascendancy, it again concentrated on the western regional market.

The Depression set the stage for the third transition. Faced with surplus oil and low prices, producers resorted to the volunteer prorating marketing agreements described above. These self-imposed regulations affected about 60 percent of the producers and were effective through most of the decade. Texas surpassed California in the eastern fields to become the nation's ranking producer, but California still sustained a high level of production even with its curtailed oil programs. Of the seven majors that still dominated the California industry, all were eastern subsidiaries except two (Standard and Union). Together they controlled half the crude-oil production and four-fifths of refining and distribution operations. Standard Oil of California discovered oil in the distant Mideast fields, and with Texaco formed Arabian American Oil (1936) for marketing it. The majors also made important breakthroughs in petroleum technology. Their heavy research investments paid off in revolutionary catalytic cracking processes to break down crudes into refined fuels for automobiles and aircraft (thermal cracking, 1914–1928 and alkylation cracking 1928–1936). The majors, by incorporating expensive technology and by integrating production and distribution, were able to extend market domination. Government antitrust prosecution was practically nil; aside from the 1911 Standard Oil split was General Petroleum's penalty assessment for price fixing (1939).

The independents comprised large numbers (1,200 producers and 45 refiners). Among the independents who became bigger were Lyman Stewart's Union Oil; Harry Sinclair, the Oklahoma oilman involved in the Teapot Dome scandal (1923), who acquired Richfield to enter the California market (1932); and J. Paul Getty, the California oilman who made his first million when he was 23 (1916) and later fought Standard Oil of New Jersey for eventual control of Tidewater (1932-1952). The independents remained a substantial, highly organized group in maintaining their profitable share of the California market.

Timber Resources

The lumber industry entered a new era after 1910. Lumber companies still cut timber on former public domain but were restricted to national forests supervised by the U.S. Forest Service (USFS). They cut most of their timber from privately owned forest lands, which often contained the best timber stands. Numerous companies, especially smaller ones, engaged in marginal logging or milling operations, continued to "timber mine" (indiscriminately cut) such private lands, systematically depleting valuable forest areas. A few companies, especially large mill operators who owned substantial forest lands, employed trained foresters to develop scientific timber management practices for sustained production. Technology by the 1930's renovated traditional lumber practices. Loggers used power saws in cutting timber, electric-powered donkey engines, and tractors and trucks for hauling logs. Millowners developed large plants with specialized machinery and elaborate log pond and lumberyard facilities. Forest fires and tree diseases continued to plague lumbermen (the pine beetle in 1923 destroyed half the timber area in Modoc County). The state university and state and federal forest agencies were important allies of the industry: they supplied trained foresters, basic research, insect eradication, firefighting, and other services for improved preservation and utilization of timber stands on private as well as public forest lands.

State forestry programs lagged in the shadow of federal programs, despite widespread public interest. The state foresters (all Pinchot men down to 1930) introduced professional standards in state services but were stymied by the concerted opposition of conflicting groups, including the USFS, certain conservationist leaders, and lumbermen. Deeply concerned local groups did not remain idle. Many counties instituted volunteer fire warden systems. Los Angeles paced several counties in establishing professional county foresters and firefighting services to protect forest areas especially important for preserving local watershed areas. Among notable citizen group efforts were the Save-the-Redwoods League in Northern California which campaigned for the state park system to save valuable redwood timberland. The statutory California Conservation Commission (1911–1915) helped to spur public and private programs for reforesting depleted timberlands and for forest protection against fire, disease, and abusive lumbermen practices. Fortunately for Californians, federal programs and local measures did what state programs failed to do in conserving forest resources.

The industry continued to develop along earlier regional lines. The regions shared common features: A small number of large, integrated companies which combined logging, milling, and sometimes marketing operations and accounted for most of the lumber production, and numerous small companies which engaged in limited logging and milling operations. Each region had distinctive traits shaped by the type of timber stands and market conditions. In the pine and fir belt of the Northern Sierras, the large integrated companies pursued independent courses. Diamond Match, the nation's biggest matchmaker, followed enlightened and constructive long-range policies: it practiced careful timber management practices, it maintained its company mill town (Sterling) as a model community, it diversified operations and products on a sound businesslike basis. Red River Lumber was noted for its exceptionally short-sighted policies, destructive "cut-out-and-get-out" timber-cutting practices, and repressive labor policy. The tightly controlled company town of Westwood, developed after 1913 as a "capitalistic fief" of the T. B. Walker family, erupted in violent labor–management showdowns in the 1930's. A sharp contrast was nearby Susanville, a prosperous lumber town in the national forest area, which benefited from USFS cooperation with local box manufacturers (including a CFGE subsidiary) in maintaining a long-range "sustained yield" timber production program. Lumbermen of the region suffered continuously from chaotic conditions resulting from chronic overproduction and unstable markets.

Lumber companies operating in the northwest redwood belt were a sharp contrast. Industry leaders were a varied group, comprising Dolbeer and Carson, the pioneer family enterprise; Hammond, the Michigan-based corporation; Pacific Lumber at Scotia, Union Lumber at Fort Bragg, and the Redwood Manufacturing Company, a processing—shipping agency for small operators. These industry leaders formed the California Redwood Association (1916). It became a powerful vehicle for coordinating production and marketing policies for the redwood industry. In 1941 six company members of the association were convicted for using their lunch club, a subsidiary company of the association, to illegally fix lumber prices (reminiscent of the Gary Dinners in the steel industry)—the first time the federal government brought antitrust action against a lunch club! These six integrated companies survived industry ups-and-downs by close cooperation and careful management. They accounted for 98 percent of the region's production.

Lumber companies working the pine and redwood timber of the southern Sierra reached the peak of their operations in the 1920's, then declined abruptly in the 1930's. Madera Sugar Pine under astute management survived ruinous overproduction which bankrupted rival companies in the 1920's, but finally dismantled operations in the mid-1930's after systematically logging out its timber lands. Hume–Bennett, the Michigan-based corporation operating the great Sanger flume-mill operation, continued to be so plagued by financial troubles and fire destruction that the company eventually sold its lands to the USFS (which incorporated them into Sequoia National Forest) and its railroad and other iron scrap, much of which went to Japan in the years before Pearl Harbor. The heritage they left behind were memories of a colorful tradition of bustling lumber-mill towns and hard-working lumberjacks—and vast, clear-cut areas between Yosemite and Sequoia National Forests.

Water Resources

The accelerated flow of people and industries spurred intensive development of water resources. Californians worked out a variety of arrangements for developing water resources to acquire adequate supply for irrigation, manufacturing, and domestic purposes, and to construct flood control projects for preventing the damaging effects of excessive water runoffs. They made increasing use of new technology, especially costly improved gas and elecric pumps and turbines for digging deeper wells and for carrying surface water uphill and over great distances. They received help from the University of California, and from local, state, and federal agencies in working out construction, legal, and other technical problems impeding their advance. Conflicting groups fought heated battles over old issues like riparian vs. appropriation rights, and disparate new issues like federal vs. state water allocations (160-acre issue), north vs. south over state water distribution, single vs. multi-purpose projects, and private vs. public interests over water-power control. The bitterly contested and long drawn-out battles among government agencies and organized special-interest groups reflect the high stakes involved in water control and development.

Water Rights

Public clamor after 1910 led to a broader governmental framework for supplying urgently needed additional water and power, over which there was intense competition. Federal, state, and local governments were called upon to perform two tasks: regulate the water rights and assist the efforts of affected special interests seeking water, and develop regional and out-of-state sources to supplement dwindling water sources. Local ground and surface water supplies were steadily being used up by expanding domestic, agricultural, and industrial needs.

The legislature under Progressive aegis established extensive state apparatus for regulating and promoting water and power development. After a decade-long battle it set up a state water commission (1913) which approved the appropriation rights of those tapping rivers and other surface waters for different projects. It set up the state reclamation board (1911–1913) to develop coordinated projects for improved irrigation, flood control, and river navigation on the Sacramento and San Joaquin. It authorized cities (1911), counties (1913), and unincorporated areas (1921) to organize special districts for setting up their own water systems, including capturing and managing water for domestic and irrigation purposes.

Water rights and regulation were rounded out in the 1920's. The uneasy coexistence of the riparian and appropriation doctrines flared up when riparian owners of the lower San Joaquin River area sued Southern

California Edison, then constructing power projects on the upper San Joaquin tributaries, for interfering with the river flow. When the court favored the riparian owners (Herminghaus Case, 1927), aroused public opposition led to adoption of the 1928 constitutional amendment which stipulated that riparian owners be limited to "reasonable use" of their water rights, thus establishing a basic doctrine in resolving conflicts still operating today. Consolidation of water agencies into a single state department (public works, 1921; water resources, 1929) improved state administration, construction projects, irrigation, and other water programs. Local governmental units were authorized (1929–1931) to form water conservation districts, chiefly to construct dams and distribution systems. All these measures, amended and revised periodically, refined state and local responsibilities and provided the basis of the elaborate but efficient present-day setup.

Irrigation

Agricultural expansion, accelerated greatly during both world wars, spurred farmers to irrigate more lands for intensive crop production. They made increasingly effective use of prevailing irrigation organizations, shifting from one type to another and adding services to meet particular needs. Private canal companies faced growing business difficulties: many, including Miller and Lux, sold out to irrigation companies, but others, like Kern County Land Company, did better than before. Mutual water companies were confined to smaller projects (10,000 acres or less), mostly in Southern California. Irrigation districts increased so rapidly that by 1945 they accounted for one-third of the state's irrigated area. The U.S. Bureau of Reclamation (USBR) continued to supply irrigation water to farmers on federally sponsored projects at Orland and Yuma.

The Imperial Irrigation District, formed in 1911, was the world's largest (600,000 acres); it eventually bought out the Southern Pacific and other water projects (see Chapter 12), and built varied projects that drained intruding crop-destroying saline water, produced hydroelectric power, and brought in outside water (the All American Canal, which bypassed the earlier Mexican canal).

Reclamation

Flood control graduated from simple local projects to elaborate intergovernmental programs for curbing ravages of river overflows in the north and heavy winter rainfalls in the south. Local reclamation projects continued to build river levees, primarily on the Sacramento River. The state reclamation board coordinated these projects and supervised the great bypass system which conveys flood waters around Sacramento (California Debris Commission plan, see Chapter 12). After the destructive 1914 flood, Los Angeles organized a large flood control district (it embraced 2,700 square miles) and built a master network combining urban underground water—debris drainage, mountain water storage dams, and forest watershed protection with the help of federal agencies like the Corps of Engineers and USFS. It was the largest of its kind and a model for other local areas. The entry of the federal government into flood control began with the Sacramento project of 1916 (one of the first approved by Congress) and culminated in their intricate federal—state—local multiple water programs in different parts of the state managed by several governmental agencies. Such projects did much to minimize rainfall and overflow damage but did not entirely resolve the problem of ravaging flood water—the 1938 Southern California flood drowned 87 persons (some were swept down the huge storm drains) and caused over $75 million damage.

Municipal Water Supply

Municipal water supply systems, unlike those in other states, focused on conveying pure water from distant sources and maintaining the delicate balance between local ground and surface water supplies. Many cities (Sacramento, Fresno, and San Diego among them) bought out private water companies to set up municipally owned water systems for water supply, sewerage, and other uses. The San Diego city council hired the erstwhile water magician Charles Hatfield to fill the drying reservoir (1914); rainstorms not only filled the reservoir but also broke the dam, causing the city's worst flood—a remarkable coincidence of man's and nature's efforts.

The major urban centers continued their long drawn-out political and engineering battles over control of local water systems. San Francisco acquired rights of way to Hetch Hetchy in Yosemite from Congress (1913 Raker Act), bought out Spring Valley Water Company properties by 1930, and completed an aqueduct in 1934 for its combined local and Sierra water supply system. Oakland and eight other nearby East Bay cities had better luck; they organized into a municipal utility district in 1923, bought out the local water company in 1928, and

Opening of the Los Angeles Aqueduct. Sierra water carried from Owens Valley over a 230-mile canal-pipe system is just arriving at its Los Angeles reservoir terminus in this 1913 photo.

constructed their water supply system the next year (Mokelumne River–Pardee Dam system). Los Angeles, in its uninterrupted quest for water, expanded its Sierra aqueduct (the bitter feuding with Owens Valley settlers led to dynamite destruction of the aqueduct in the 1920's). By the mid-1920's it turned attention to the Colorado as a second source; it formed with 11 other Southern California cities the Metropolitan Water District, a public corporation which in 1939 completed a tremendous engineering feat, the intricate 240-mile aqueduct to Parker Dam. Each community had resolved its peculiar water problems by different solutions in the face of intense competition among affected groups. The measure of their success was their continued urban and rural growth which depended so greatly on adequate water supplies.

Public attention focused on grandiose multipurpose projects to supply the needs of two principal areas, the Central Valley and Southern California. These comprehensive projects were designed to make water available primarily for irrigation, flood control, hydroelectric power, and municipal services (domestic, firefighting, sewerage).

Central Valley development focused on legislative consideration of a state water plan in the 1920's. The plan, drafted by R. B. Marshall of the United States Geological Survey, centered on transferring Sacramento River water to the San Joaquin Valley. Progressive leaders carried the measure against bitter opposition of the private utilities, which felt the state plan jeopardized their large regional systems and attempted to scuttle it. The latter drew fire for their deceptive campaign and dubious practices. They set up dummy organizations (PGE's Greater California League in Northern California, and Southern California Edison's People's Economy League in Southern California), pressured banks holding company funds, and vilified the state plan as a socialist scheme. As historian Walton Bean points out, PGE, which denounced the state plan as socialism undermining free enterprise was, ironically, itself a private monopoly. The Central Valley Project, the state's first water plan, was finally adopted by the 1933 legislature, chiefly with organized farmer backing, and approved by statewide referendum.

The state water plan as finally implemented was a unique scheme for the comprehensive development of multiple water and power projects in the state's vast heartland. The Central Valley Project comprises the huge Shasta Dam at the Sacramento headwater for water supply (including domestic, agricultural, and industrial uses), flood control, river navigation, ocean water intrusion, and hydroelectric power for the north; canal systems for transferring water to the San Joaquin (Delta Cross Channel) and distributing them (Contra Costa and Delta–Mendota Canals); and Friant Dam for distributing Sierra water throughout San Joaquin east side, northerly through the Madera canal, and southerly through the Friant-Kern canal.

Several elements figure in this plan—the result of compromises. Northern California secured water rights protection (as provided in the 1931 Counties of Origin Act). State authorization was established for public power production and distribution (a Progressive maneuver in the

1933 Act). A federal 160-acre limitation was imposed on water users drawing from CVP for irrigation (as administered by the USBR). Private utility companies distributed Shasta Dam Power (as implemented in the United States Interior Department–PGE 1944 Agreement). By 1944 the project was nearly completed; it remains the basis of the state's great water and power system.

Southern California development focused on the federal Boulder Dam Project. The Boulder Project, conceived by Arthur Davis (John Powell's nephew), of the United States Reclamation Bureau, was carried into law by California's Congressman Phil Swing from Imperial and Senator Hiram Johnson, and signed by another Californian, President Hoover. The plan called for a dam near Boulder Canyon on the Colorado not far from Las Vegas, for flood control and hydroelectric power. The Boulder fight was complicated, long, and hard. It featured the 1922 Colorado River Compact by which six states having riparian rights to the river's water reached agreement for water allocation. It aroused bitter opposition from Southern California Edison, other private utility companies, and the powerful *Los Angeles Times* (the Otis–Chandler group felt their lands on the Mexican side of the Colorado threatened). Even Hoover entertained reservations about such government participation in private enterprise. The project when completed in 1936 was the world's biggest dam, at Boulder near Las Vegas. It created the world's largest reservoir, Lake Mead (named after Elwood Mead), and two prominent downriver dams: Parker, to feed a 240-mile aqueduct carrying water to Southern California coastal cities, and Imperial, to feed canals irrigating the Imperial and Yuma areas. By the advent of World War II, California was emerging with a complicated but comprehensive system of federal–state–local projects for water and power development that was remarkably well adapted to the needs of the ever-growing state. The state's wartime economic expansion would not have been possible without the additional water and power supply.

Fuel and Power

The state's ever-increasing power and fuel demands led to a tremendous expansion of gas and electric facilities after 1910. Private companies continued to be the chief power agencies. In Northern California, PGE under the Drum–Crocker group vied with Great Western under the Earl–Fleishhacker group for regional leadership. Great Western in 1924 absorbed San Joaquin Light and Power, but in 1930 the two giants merged their interests (James Black of Great Western became PGE president in 1935). PGE business acumen, engineering talent, and expanding programs made it the nation's second largest utility. In the south, Southern California Edison and Los Angeles City Water and Power Department paced the electric field, while Southern California Gas and Southern Counties Gas led the gas field. The San Francisco-based Pacific Lighting maintained its strategic position in the southern field.

The market entry of natural gas proved a boon to the power-fuel industry. It outdid manufactured gas as a cheaper, cleaner fuel for home heating and cooking, and for industry use. Shortly after big wells were opened in Central California (Buena Vista and Santa Maria), natural gas was piped to Los Angeles in 1913. San Francisco received its gas in 1929 when it was piped 230 miles from Kettleman Hills in the San Joaquin.

Many communities produced and distributed their own power through various arrangements. Of 20 cities owning distributing systems, five generated their own power, and the rest either purchased wholesale from private companies like PGE or from federal agencies like the USBR and distributed it locally (Glendale, Palo Alto, and Pasadena). San Francisco, the East Bay Municipal Utility District, and others sold power to PGE, which retailed it locally. Irrigation districts also produced and distributed power (notably Imperial, Modesto, and Turlock) and one district (Nevada) sold its stored water to PGE for its power plants en route to irrigated areas. These locally owned public utilities gained a proportionally greater share of the state's power production (around 2 percent in 1910 to about 25 percent in 1945). Federally owned power was distributed after the USBR began operating government power plants (see above). In these ways water and power kept pace with the state's rapid economic growth.

Manufacturing

Manufacturing enterprises emerged after 1910 as a major segment of the state's economy. Hitherto, California manufacturing had been chiefly a handmaiden processing raw materials for agriculture, mining, and lumbering. Aside from this, production had consisted of heavy goods like industrial machinery, locomotives, and ships. Now it embraced more varied consumer goods like fashionable clothes, home furnishings, and radios. The manufacturing base was broadened with the addition of new industries producing such goods as aircraft, automobiles, and heavy steel. All were of strategic importance for local, regional, and nationwide markets.

Manufacturing was stimulated by steady growth and greatly accelerated by both world wars. It increased every year (except for three) at an even greater rate than the nation's; the state rose from fifth to third rank during World War II alone. The increase owed much to large capital investments from eastern financiers, talented local managers, adequate industrial supplies, and cheap hydroelectric power, petroleum fuel, and water supply. The decisive factors were raw materials supplied by western mines, semifinished materials and heavy factory machinery provided by the eastern firms, abundant labor from the new immigration, expanded local markets from heavy population demands, and ready-made trade opportunities in the western region and foreign markets. These elements gave substance and added stability to the state's manufacturing development, not evident to such a marked degree elsewhere in the nation.

California carved out a distinctive manufacturing structure. Creative entrepreneurs, often talented teams of inventors, engineers, and businessmen, developed substantial enterprises from modest beginnings. They suffered from the normal growing pains of their adolescent enterprises and from the dominant position and discriminating practices of older established eastern industries. San Francisco was the chief manufacturing center to the mid-1920's when Los Angeles gained prominence; Oakland and Long Beach developed as important supplementary manufacturing areas to them. Los Angeles played up the advantages of moderate climate, open terrain, and abundant labor, which atttracted industries like aircraft and motion pictures; these, in turn, produced a chain reaction of many related subsidiary manufacturing companies. Another notable feature was the corporation branch plant, California branches in the East and eastern plants in California—so many so that the state was described as having a branch plant empire. Public regulation was not yet extensive, a notable exception being federal prosecution of abnormally large companies for antitrust violations.

The state's iron and steel industry did not achieve maturity until the advent of World War II. Steel production increased fivefold during World War I and enjoyed modest growth thereafter. The few small and scattered independent companies were gradually absorbed by the eastern giants. They included the two leading California independents that had

San Francisco and Los Angeles plants: by 1930 United States Steel acquired Columbia (an earlier merger of Utah and California plants), and Bethlehem acquired Pacific Coast Steel. The state's iron and steel production, oriented to the demands of local manufacturing enterprises, had limited capacity and lacked blast furnaces for producing heavy steel. The eastern giants still ruled the scene with a heavy hand; they imposed an arbitrary 10 percent higher cost rate that was greatly resented by California purchasers. A dramatic turn came in World War II. In response to the war emergency Kaiser overcame enormous obstacles to build the state's first completely integrated iron and steel mill at Fontana. For the first time California had an independent local supply of strategic pig iron and steel ingots that broke the hold of the eastern giants and their price discriminations. The Kaiser mills assured greater economic independence and maturity.

Angelenos made a spectacular break in California's garment industry which had traditionally been dominated by eastern textile manufacturers. Numerous garment makers made a conspicuous appearance in Los Angeles in Los Angeles during the 1920's. Several factors conspired to accelerate them to prominence in the 1930's. One was the motion picture industry, which attracted talented designers (Irene at MGM, Edith Head at Paramount) who clothed film stars in fashions that caught the public fancy and precipitated fashion trends. Another factor was astute businessmen and willing financiers (generous Ben Meyer of Union Trust Bank was regarded as the industry's godfather), which enabled numerous entrepreneurs to parlay imaginative ideas from shoestring operations to substantial apparel enterprises in what was considered a high-risk industry. Outstanding designer-entrepreneurs paved the way for California's entry into the world of fashion, notably in leisure clothes like women's playsuits and men's sportshirts (Joe Zukin). These leaders not only defied New York and French fashion leaders (a sacrilegious act in the industry) but established casual clotheswear under California trademarks throughout the world. By 1945 Los Angeles had 422 established garment makers (of which only 23 had survived from the 1920's) to rank third behind New York and Chicago; it outranked them both in sportswear.

Even more remarkable than these major manufacturers was the diverse lot of inventive specialty manufacturers in other fields. Attention has already been called to Caterpillar Tractors and FMC in farm machinery, and there were other such entrepreneurs in mining, lumbering, and other industries. Alfred and Rodney Marchant invented the first electric calculating machine. Their Oakland company (formed 1913) competed with Isaac Friden's San Leandro firm (1934)—together they accounted for almost half of national market sales in 1945. Walter Schlage designed the unique button-cylindrical doorlock that made his name a household word. His San Francisco company (formed 1921) produced 150 types of locks to rank behind Yale Locks, the old-time national industry leader. Byron Jackson shifted from producing water pumps to bazooka-type contraptions which he invented for freeing trapped underground oil pools. His Los Angeles company (Perfo-Jet, 1921) became a world leader in oil-drilling equipment. Edmund Price, described as a "Bostonian and Wall Street refugee," persuaded his aircraft company (Strato-Jet, 1929) to concentrate on exhaust-manifold assemblies for airplanes; it became the leader in heat-resistant metal products. These creative enterprises were usually headed by teams of inventive engineers and astute businessmen with keen insights into market opportunities.

Labor

California's labor situation after 1910 developed into an exceedingly complex pattern that differed in important respects from the national pattern. The labor force increased phenomenally; it exceeded the population growth rate and grew at a far faster rate than the nation's. It featured large marginal groups like women and children, and tourists and transients who constituted important seasonal labor and contributed to labor mobility. It also featured a higher proportion of workers in trades and services than in agriculture and manufacturing, just the reverse of the situation in other urban states. This fluid environment and hetero-geneous working force account for the remarkably resilient, uneven, and expansive character of the state's labor market in this period. Labor–management relations were highly organized, with a diversity of methods and techniques not found elsewhere in the nation. California became a laboratory for national labor–management developments: it included all major aspects of the labor–management struggle in carrying industrial warfare to extremes, and in spearheading new directions for employer–worker relationships.

Government played a key role in shaping labor developments. The Progressive victory in 1910 with a waving banner proclaiming social justice for the workingman was the signal for revitalizing state labor policy. The legislature between 1911 and 1913 enacted 30 of 41 proposed measures, most of them protective laws dealing with hour, wage, and safety standards. The legislature also created agencies for carrying out these programs, notably for helping workers find jobs (state employment bureaus), for administering workmens compensation for workers injured on the job (Industrial Accident Commission), and for improving facilities for new immigrants (Immigration and Housing Commission). The legislature never equaled this record before or after this time, and no state ever matched it for the bulk of labor legislation in so short a time.

Governor Johnson made the difference on many of these measures which sharply divided Progressive conservatives and liberals. When confronted with the union-backed measure for restricting court injunctions (so often used to break strikes), Johnson backed off, deciding as George Mowry puts it, that "discretion was the better part of politics." While listening on the long-distance telephone to Theodore Roosevelt's views *against* the eight-hour-day limit for working women, the governor signed the measure for it.

Industrial Labor

Industrial conflicts assumed a broader dimension after 1910. The recurring cycle of prosperity and depression caused shifts in the labor market which upset working conditions and intensified labor–management disputes. Generally, employer groups were better organized and had the powerful support of established community leaders. Labor unions continued to divide sharply over goals, strategy, and tactics, ranging from the conservative AFL, which sought employer accommodations within the capitalistic system, to the radical IWW, which attempted through violence to replace capitalism with a worker-based syndicalist society. Employer groups and labor unions fought each other ruthlessly. They carried their disputes from industry to citywide and regional areas, seeking allies and extending the battle in hopes of winning the war. Labor–management disputes broke out in the cities, towns, and other places throughout the state. They centered in San Francisco and Los Angeles where employer and union groups battled to implement the open or the closed shop for their metropolis.

The earlier skirmishes developed into full-scale industrial warfare after 1910. In the south, the 1910 bombing of the *Los Angeles Times* (see Chapter 12) set the stage for a major showdown. The famous trial that led to the conviction of the McNamara brothers, radical leaders in the labor movement, was a bitter affair which resulted in jury-tampering charges, surprise confessions (on attorney's advice), high-level backstage agreements, inflamed public reactions, and nationwide attention. In the aftermath, employer groups united forces behind Otis's long anti-union campaign. The Los Angeles Merchants and Manufacturers Association (LAMM) became the chief vehicle not so much to open shops to nonunion men as to drive out labor unions altogether. A blue-ribbon commission set up by Congress in 1914 to investigate the situation observed that the Los Angeles open-shop campaign actually called for a closed shop with the lock on the other side of the door.

San Francisco enjoyed relative quietude until World War I broke the calm. To offset the citywide union drive for higher wages, business leaders organized a "patriotic" public parade demonstration for United States intervention in the European war, which many suspected was a thinly disguised effort to smear labor unions opposing the war as disloyal. The affair resulted in the famous Preparedness Day bombing in which 10 persons were killed and 40 injured. Thomas Mooney and another radical labor agitator (Warren Billings), convicted as the perpetrators, became martyrs of the labor movement and attracted worldwide sympathy. The San Francisco Chamber of Commerce, which hitherto had stood aloof from industrial disputes though it had sponsored the parade, now launched an aggressive open-shop campaign. It set up the Industrial Association (1921), featuring for the first time a united front of employer groups. Under the National Association of Manufacturers' (NAM) American Plan banner, San Francisco was proclaimed an open-shop town, a worthy colleague of Los Angeles. The bombing of the *Los Angeles Times* (1910) and the Preparedness Day bombing, both instigated by radical elements, brought major setbacks to the labor movement. Over the next decade-and-a-half, repressive employer groups ruled the roost in both metropolitan communities in dictating working conditions and labor–management relations.

Labor–management relations were drastically shaken up during the Great Depression. New Deal measures aimed at uniting all groups for economic recovery provided for "fair labor" practices, granting for the first time federal sanction of labor's right to collective bargaining (1933) and uniform wages and hours (Fair Labor Standards, 1939). Congress set up the National Labor Relations Board (NLRB, 1935) for enforcing these measures. The labor movement was revitalized by the sympathetic treatment accorded by the Roosevelt Administration, but it became so badly divided that the industrial workers (auto, coal, steel) broke away in 1934 to form the Congress of Industrial Organization (CIO) while the AFL continued along traditional craft lines.

California's response to these New Deal measures was violent. The two metropolises developed into armed camps between employer and union groups. When NLRB sought to implement the federal-guaranteed collective bargaining rights for labor unions, in Los Angeles, the LAMM continued its obstreperous campaign of outright defiance, prompting a United States Senate investigating committee (La Follette Committee) to remark that its intransigence had no equal in the nation. In San Francisco, the longshoremen went on strike when shipowners refused to recognize their union despite federal sanction for collective bargaining. The unprecedented three-month waterfront strike, under Harry Bridges's maritime federation, at last united longshoremen with seamen. A devastating four-day general strike, which drew in teamsters and other unions, brought about a massive economic paralysis and running battles involving local police and national guard that resulted in several killings and extensive property damage. The NLRB mediated a compromise settlement that turned out to be a strategic victory for the unions—the unions gained control of the hiring hall, thereby controlling working conditions. The maritime federation soon came to grief. After a bitter leadership struggle, Bridges led his longshoremen into CIO ranks, and Harry Lundberg's seamen joined the AFL. Labor unrest continued along other fronts and areas throughout the decade.

A significant development came out of the decade which would have future ramifications. In a remarkable move, Bridges's longshoremen negotiated with the Employers Waterfront Association, a coalition group, a single contract covering job control and work production. The San Francisco Employers Association and the Labor Council the next year worked out a comprehensive group contract which replaced individual contracts for three-fourths of the employees working in the Bay region—with the result that the city had fewer strikes than Los Angeles and the nation. This master contract agreement in employer–union relations became a California trademark and a national model for areawide collective bargaining agreements in other industries.

Agricultural Labor

Agricultural labor was a sharp contrast to industrial labor. It comprised for the most part unskilled workers employed for seasonal or casual jobs on farms, constituting a vital element as labor gangs for large-scale agricultural enterprises which appeared in great numbers after 1910. At that time farm laborers comprised residents in towns, quasi-gypsy groups from the Sierra foothills, and wandering vagrants, ranging from professional tramps to drifting workers (the so-called bindle stiffs). The lot of farm laborers was worse than that of industrial workers. Their plight was publicly dramatized for the first time by the famous 1913 Wheatland strike on the Durst ranch near Marysville, the state's largest employer of farm labor. Some 2,800 workers, including men, women, and children, were lured by deceptive advertising to the 1,500 available jobs in the harvest. Oppressive conditions and woefully inadequate facilities (only eight outdoor toilets for them all) led to violence between workers and local law enforcement officials that resulted in several killings and the calling up of the national guard to restore order. Two "labor agitators" (Richard Ford and Herman Suhr), both IWW members, were convicted for second-degree murder, while Durst, who was as much to blame for the tragedy as anyone, escaped punishment.

The farm labor situation was altered by several developments after 1920. As the dominant Japanese workers were phased out by World War I, the farm labor market was augmented by other large groups. In the 1920's Filipinos and Hindus were imported from East Asia, and Mexican workers, pioneering the migrant family caravans—bus and auto—entered California. Growers recruited workers through improved advertising campaigns and a contract system by which the labor contractor supplied the workers and assumed liabilities. The set-up brought peace to the fields, but the workers suffered from deplorable working conditions from growers' negligence and from wage deductions by labor contractors (workers paid employment and transportation charges). The violent outbreak and brutal suppression of the 1928 Imperial Valley strike was the result of oppressed Filipino workers attempting to replace the abhorrent contract system with their union. Farm employers hardly ever lacked abundant workers so vital for harvesting their perishable crops.

Farm labor conditions were worse during the 1930's. Depression-ridden farmers from the southern states, the famous Arkies and Oakies, arrived to reintroduce white domestic labor in the California fields. A rash of strikes and violence broke throughout the state. A communist-led union launched drives to organize lettuce workers (Salinas, 1934) and cannery workers (Modesto, 1935). Growers, struck by genuine fear, organized the militant Associated Farmers, which conducted a vigilante-type community campaign, using terror tactics and repressive police action. The AFL was conspicuous in its sideline role,

Arrival of the Oakies during the Depression. Poverty-stricken Oklahoma families pause on the roadside near Blythe on the California border in this 1935 photo. The cars often carried all their wordly possessions, including beds.

except in the 1934 cannery strike where it conspired with employers to defeat its radical rival. Farm employer groups, joined by the State Chamber of Commerce and urban employer groups, pressured Congress in 1938 to exempt farm laborers from provisions of the Fair Labor Standards Act, Social Security, and other New Deal measures designed to protect workers. The public was hardly aware of the real situation until the LaFollette Committee revealed the nature of the violence and extensive violation of civil liberties. It reported that California, between 1933 and 1939, had 180 agricultural strikes involving 90,000 workers in 34 counties, noting that only 2 percent of the farms employed the bulk of the 200,000 migratory workers.

Transportation

Railroads

Railroad regulation was firmly established after 1910. Under Progressive aegis, the railroad commission was recreated as a strong body with

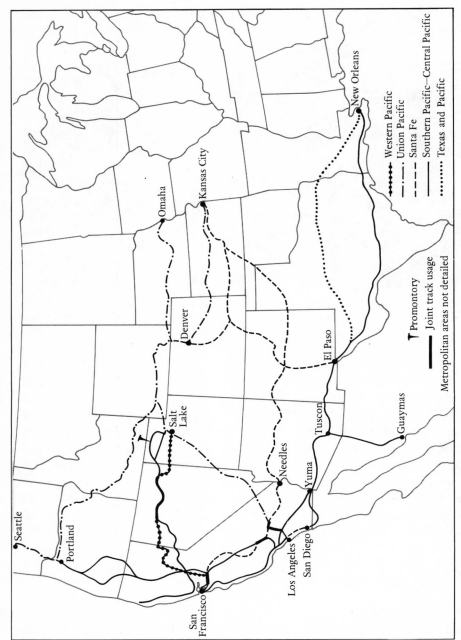

FIGURE 9 Major transcontinental railroad routes.

Legend:
Western Pacific
Union Pacific
Santa Fe
Southern Pacific—Central Pacific
Texas and Pacific

T Promontory
Joint track usage
Metropolitan areas not detailed

powers to regulate rates, safety facilities, service standards, finances, and securities, not only of railroads but of other transportation and of telegraph-telephone communication as well. The revitalized commission during the Johnson-Stephens administration undertook its task with zeal against the Southern Pacific and others. When it found Wells Fargo received from its rate charges up to 136 percent profit returns and gave 300 percent dividends, it reduced the company's rates to a 10 percent level. Congress enacted the 1920 Transportation Act which gave ICC primary jurisdiction in the nation's railroads. Thereafter ICC preempted antitrust railroad prosecutions and much of state regulation. The Southern Pacific got off the hook of a 1918 antitrust action aimed at separating it from the Central Pacific railroad when the ICC ruled (1923) that it was in the public interest for the parent to retain the subsidiary. This move was strongly supported by farmers and shippers who benefited from the Southern Pacific efficient service. The Southern Pacific was no longer the ogre of old.

Railroads, as the chief carrier of people and freight after 1910, felt the challenge of autos and ships (Panama Canal). The Southern Pacific, still the state's dominant railroad, was hampered after 1910 by federal antitrust prosecutions which virtually halted its growth. Then after 1920 it revived its expansion program; it constructed additional local feeder and interstate lines, leading the nation's railroads in construction. It built modern facilities in Los Angeles for freight (Union Terminal, 1920) and passengers (Union Station, 1939), the latter with Santa Fe and Union Pacific. It acquired interest in other transportation lines, notably Pacific Greyhound Bus and Pacific Motor Transport (both 1930) for coordinated truck-rail deliveries. When hit by automobile competition, the Southern Pacific developed the San Francisco-Los Angeles Daylights, popular passenger express trains introduced in 1922 and rejuvenated with fast streamliners in 1937. By 1940, the Southern Pacific, with headquarters shifted from New York to San Francisco, was still an enormous holding company with 52 subsidiaries, operating one of the nation's longest railroads and ranking among the nation's largest corporations. The railroads—the Southern Pacific with Santa Fe, Union Pacific, and Western Pacific—still held their own in long haul passenger and freight, but were losing ground to motor transportation in short haul transportation.

Motor Vehicles

Motor transportation accomplished the remarkable transition from infancy to maturity within two decades after 1910. The automobile, truck, and bus sectors each went through the familiar pattern of industry development, from experiments of entrepreneurs, to intense competition among numerous companies, to consolidation of many into a few dominant corporations—the Big Three of the industry: Ford, General Motors, and American Motors. In California as elsewhere, Ford's inexpensive, efficient Model T's (1911, the famous tin lizzies) and Model A's (1929) were immensely popular, along with General Motors' varied lines of family sedans and sports cars (especially the open-back, rumble-seat models). Trucks and buses were used for freight and passenger hauls. Detroit paced the nation's auto—truck—bus manufacturers, but Los Angeles, which got Big Three branch assembly plants in the 1920's, emerged in second place.

Automobiles spread rapidly as the chief means of personal transportation for work and recreation. The rapid development of auto travel in the 1920's was spurred by attractive, low-priced cars for the general public, neighborhood repair garages and service stations, extensive state highway and local road construction, and motor inns for overnight accommodations. (It is said that a San Luis Obispo operator in 1925 coined the word *motel* for his place by combining the words *motor* and *hotel*.) The auto industry spawned related industries like travel services, auto supplies, second-hand cars (the source of "jalopies" for many youths) and racing cars (flamboyant professional drivers, like Barney Oldfield, had large public followings). Conspicuous in promoting road tourism, driver aids, and highway safety were the state's leading motor associations, among the most highly developed in the nation, the California State Automobile Association (1921) and the Southern California Automobile Association (1922). California led all states in the number of automobile users; in 1940 one of every four persons owned a car.

It took two decades to develop government programs for regulating motor vehicles and for constructing highways. Milestones in this evolutionary development were the establishment of the state highway commission (1911) for supervising construction, the state highway department (1920) as its operating arm, the state highway patrol (1929) as an expanded uniformed statewide patrol force, and the motor vehicle department (1931) from agency to department status. To finance these costly highway programs, the legislature first relied on extensive bond financing (enacted 1911, 1915, and 1919), then switched to gasoline taxes after 1923 as a less painful and more convenient way to distribute costs among highway users. Federal aid after 1916 became an

An impetus for the state highway system. A familiar country scene was a car struggling through a muddy road in winter; the road became rutty and dusty in summer. The scene above is a Cadillac sedan on El Camino Real (today's Highway 101) below Ventura in 1912.

increasingly important supplemental source of funds for state highway construction. No state matched California's prodigious program for highway development—perhaps no state had such compelling economic need and such formidable problems in knitting together its far-flung geographic areas.

Aircraft

The aircraft industry experienced a prolonged infancy and adolescence. Pioneer inventor–entrepreneurs established the small, single-owner, plane manufacturing plants which characterized the fledgling industry in the first three decades. Among the early aircraft builders were Californians like the Lockheeds (1916), John Northrop (1922, Lockheed's chief designer), and Donald Douglas (1924, Martin's chief designer). After a long struggle over costly experiments and for business survival, aircraft builders enjoyed an industry revival during the 1930's. Public interest in aviation was sparked by Charles Lindbergh's daring 1927 New York–Paris flight over the Atlantic (Ryan built his plane in San Diego) and other noted flyers like Amelia Earhart and Howard Hughes. In the mid-1930's European governments, then the United States government, stepped up orders for military aircraft for their national defense programs. Major manufacturers soon located in Southern California to capitalize on such favorable factors as open terrain, moderate climate, trained labor force, and low building costs. Los Angeles became the center for Douglas, Hughes, Lockheed, Northrop, and Vultee, and San Diego for Consolidated and Ryan.

World War II brought the industry to maturity. President Roosevelt's call for 50,000 planes a year for the war effort galvanized the industry. By war's end Southern California's aircraft producers were the state's leading manufacturers and the nation's leading aircraft producers. The few dominant companies operated huge, complex production plants. Yet the industry faced an uncertain future in converting from wartime military to peacetime commercial aircraft production.

Communications

Telephone and Telegraph

The communications industry underwent major reorganization and expansion. Federal Telegraph was set up (1911) by California's Cy Elswell around a talented research team headed by Lee De Forest. It pioneered the nation's wireless system, which threatened Western Union's (WU) wire setup and developed intercontinental wireless to share leadership with Marconi's company. Under threat of antitrust prosecution, Morgan's monopolistic American Telephone and Telegraph (ATT) ceased acquiring independent telephone companies and relinquished its control of WU (Kingsbury Commitment, 1913), thus ending its ambition to unify the nation's wire communications into a single system. Thereafter ATT concentrated on its research patents (mostly developed by its famous Bell Lab), long distance system, and subsidiary companies to become the nation's largest corporation. Pacific Telephone and Telegraph, its 5-state affiliate, easily led rivals in California. The Morgan-backed International Telephone and Telegraph (1920) emerged to rival ATT and WU. It reached agreement with ATT to keep within their respective fields of foreign and domestic telephone operations, and absorbed Federal Telegraph and Mackay's Postal Telegraph (1928) to better complete with WU. Government regulation was implemented at the federal level through ICC and, after 1934, through the Federal

Communications Commission, and in California by the State Public Utilities Commission (1923). Land and ocean telephone and telegraph, which had been wracked so long by intense competition, achieved maturity and stability through technical advances, cooperative operations, and government control much to the customers' benefit and the public interest.

Electronics and Radio

The remarkable development of radio technology led to the creation of a new industry in wireless communications. California's inventor-entrepreneurs helped establish the foundations for electronics. Federal Telegraph's laboratory trained scientist inventors and spawned major inventions. Fred Terman switched from Federal Telegraph to Stanford where he built the university's famous electronics research laboratory. Youthful inventors trained in these two labs branched out with their own enterprises. Pridhem and Jensen with a businessman-partner launched Magnovox (1918) to produce the first loudspeakers, which replaced earphones on radios. Philo Farnsworth put out the electronic camera (1923) and developed the television transmission (1925, officially credited to RCA's Vladimir Zworykin). Farnsworth's operation was later absorbed by Philco (1931). Charles Litton (1931) manufactured precision vacuum tubes to become the nation's leader. Charles Packard and William Hewlett (1938) developed electronic measuring instruments to become the world leader. Among self-taught pioneers who did well was Ralph Heintz whose firm (1921) designed short-wave sets for ships and aircraft and for Admiral Richard Byrd's famous South Pole Expedition (1929). Lee De Forest, father of electronics, spanned the 3 decades between Palo Alto, the East and Pasadena, pioneering radio and television devices, which he produced or sold as patents to Bell and RCA. The San Francisco and Los Angeles areas developed from pioneer centers for electronic research into chief production centers for electronic products during World War II.

The radio industry took shape during the first two decades. Radio broadcasting developed with Charles Herrold's first broadcast of the human voice (KQW-KCBS, San Jose, 1909), WEAF station for the first commercial broadcast (New York, 1922), and NBC's first coast-to-coast radio broadcast (1928, National Broadcasting Company). Home radios improved as vacuum tubes replaced crystal sets and loudspeakers replaced earphones, and by mass production techniques—by 1929 4.5 million Americans owned radios. RCA (1919, Radio Corporation of America) emerged after a decade of intense competition as the industry leader controlling strategic licenses and patents. Manufacturing was dominated by the Big 5 (led by RCA, GE, Westinghouse) radio parts, while Philco, Magnavox, and Zenith were leaders in radio assembly and distribution. National broadcasting grew with NBC, CBS (Columbia Broadcasting System), Mutual (1936), and ABC (1945, American Broadcasting System); by the mid-1930's they relocated western headquarters from San Francisco to Hollywood. The nation's film capital became a logical center for choice as a radio capital.

Motion Pictures

The motion picture industry after 1910 evolved into a highly sophisticated industry. It was shaped by technical innovations in cameras, film, and projectors, and by organizational innovations in production, distribution, and exhibition. The highly volatile entertainment industry exuded a glamor which had wide public appeal and profoundly affected social mores. It also entailed big power plays among rival corporations; ruthless competition on the one hand, and abusive monopolistic practices on the other, that provoked endless antitrust litigation.

The basic structure of the industry was established in the first three decades when silent pictures flashed on theater screens. The movie trust (see Chapter 12), comprising the ten leading film producers who controlled the motion picture patents to dominate the industry, was finally dissolved in 1917 by the United States Supreme Court for antitrust violation. Independent operators were already making headway through innovations. William Fox, a film distributor, integrated producing, distributing, and exhibiting into a large-scale operation beginning in 1910. Jesse Lasky and his director Cecil De Mille produced the first long feature film (a 1912 five-reeler). Carl Laemmle, another producer, introduced the star system (1914) for popularizing leading actors as public personalities. All were to be industry patterns.

Then came a series of incorporations and mergers among expanding rival groups. Paramount (1914) was organized by the five biggest distributors who absorbed (1916) Lasky and Laemmle. United Artists (1919) was formed to distribute films for a talented group of actors and directors including Charles Chaplin, the renowned comedian, Douglas Fairbanks, the swashbuckling hero, Mary Pickford, America's Sweetheart, and the pioneer director, D. W. Griffith. The company under Joseph Schenk's management became a leading independent. Marcus Loew organized West Coast Theatres (1921) to operate his vast theater chain. Metro-Goldwyn-Mayer (1923) was formed to combine three producer–distributor companies. Fox bought Loew's theaters on his death in 1927. By 1930 the industry was dominated by five integrated majors (Fox, Loew, Paramount, RKO, and Warners) and three partially integrated minors: Columbia and Universal (which produced and distributed Grade B films) and United Artists (which distributed films for such independent producers as Howard Hughes). The independents, who earlier had fought industry monopolists, had themselves become a virtual monopoly.

The industry, despite its public popularity and powerful organization, suffered badly from the Depression. Fox, hit by government antitrust and company bankruptcy, was taken over by the New York-based Rockefeller's Chase Manhattan bank, and reemerged in 1935 as 20th-Century Fox. Paramount, RKO, and Universal also went into receivership but were revived by other eastern banks. Some did well: Walt Disney formed his company (1932) to produce the highly popular animated cartoons, notably Mickey Mouse and his gang. However, after three turbulent decades, Hollywood still had not overcome problems of size and competition despite its brilliant record of technical achievements.

Banking

Public policy after 1910 provided for increasing government regulation of the state banking system. The California legislature, which had established the present-day setup for state regulation of banks (1909, see Chapter 11), adopted a 1912 measure which strengthened the state bank superintendent, brought foreign banks under state control, and broadened the basis of banking activities. Congress in 1913 overhauled the nation's banking system, reducing the complex decentralized setup with a simplified central banking system. It created a Federal Reserve System comprising 12 regional districts—San Francisco became headquarters for the 12th district—whose activities were coordinated by a national governing board comprising banker members. Two decades of experience revealed serious deficiencies, punctuated by FRS failure in preventing the unprecedented bank failures during the Depression years. Congress responded by creating the Reconstruction Finance Corporation (RFC, 1932), which extended loans to troubled banks and other needy institutions and strengthened the FRS (Bank Acts, 1933 and 1935), which put the governing boards under federal officials and extended federal credit to insure bank solvency and individual deposits in financial crisis. These and other measures contributed to bank stability and a flexible currency, but did not entirely resolve fiscal problems.

California enjoyed unprecedented expansion of banking activities hardly paralleled by other states. A major factor was A. P. Giannini, the aggressive San Francisco banker, who developed bank branches to extend loans and other services to entrepreneurs and other people as conventional banks were unable or unwilling to do. Giannini built his Bank of Italy with branch banks (the first in 1909) to become the state's largest bank by 1920. He launched a nationwide system, purchasing the old New York-based Bank of America and establishing Transamerica (1927) as the holding company for his banks, emerging in time as the world's largest bank. Giannini fought long intense battles along the way with local bankers, like Fleishhacker in San Francisco and Sartori in Los Angeles, with powerful national bankers like J. P. Morgan, with state and federal officials passing on branch banks, and with organized opposition in the legislature and Congress. He also had strong allies, notably bankers like William Crocker, politicians like Hiram Johnson and William McAdoo, and numerous bank clients and stockholders who benefited from his liberal banking policies. When Elisha Walker (the New York banker he put in charge of Transamerica on his retirement in 1928) began dismantling his great banking empire in the stock market, Giannini emerged from his sick-bed in an Austrian sanitorium to recapture Transamerica. After a bitter year-long nationwide campaign in which Giannini personally canvassed the numerous stockholders in the state for votes, Giannini won the stockholders' election to regain control; he took the helm and rebuilt the corporation. Giannini revolutionized banking practices with important innovations, notably the lease-rental plan for farmers to continue working on foreclosed lands and the famous Time-Plan for consumers to buy automobiles and other products on installment. His liberal loan policies for small and big enterprises, which ranged from fledgling enterprises like movies and aircraft to huge public projects like the Golden Gate Bridge (he backed it when no one else would), contributed greatly to the state's economic development. The measure of his success lies in the other California bankers and investors who took his cue and did likewise in the expanding state.

The state's financial institutions expanded along other lines. Major banks continued mergers and branch systems. Bank of California merged with Hellman's Union Trust (1923), and Crocker merged with San Francisco National to form Crocker National (1927). Sartori's Los Angeles Security and First National built up a branch system that was second only to Bank of Italy. Independent banks fought hard against branch bank incursions, but the tide against them was evident by 1945 when figures revealed that the state's ten largest banks controlled 80 percent of total deposits. Important in the state's growth were the expanding activities of the insurance companies, building and loan societies, savings and loan associations—each was a story of dramatic growth and business-technical innovations. Also important were eastern financiers, like Wall Street bankers, who played a conspicuous role in extending credit and making loans to various California enterprises. California not only developed enormous resources for capital investments but conceived complicated financial schemes for its ever-continuing growth.

Trade

Domestic Trade

California's domestic commerce was greatly enhanced by its growing preeminence in the trade of the West. San Francisco and Los Angeles outpaced Portland and Seattle as the chief distribution points in the Pacific trade. Los Angeles passed San Francisco as the state's leading distribution center; the completion of modern highways through the Tehachapis in 1928 was a significant factor in swinging the rich San Joaquin Valley trade from its San Francisco orbit to Los Angeles, which by 1945 was rapidly overtaking Chicago as the chief producing and distributing center for the states west of the Mississippi. California's trade lines by this time had become inextricably interlaced with the nation's complex domestic and foreign trade patterns.

In California, marketing patterns, affected by the state's expanded population, industrial growth, and ever-growing list of consumer goods, underwent major change. In the wholesale trade, the general wholesaler (full line, full service) lost his commanding position—but not his importance—to the speciality wholesaler, manufacturer, and large retailer, who each developed ways to circumvent him. In the retail trade, large retailing organizations—mail-order houses, chain stores and supermarkets—soon overshadowed the general store in rural towns and department stores in cities. All grew because of advantageous features, then had to alter their operations to survive intense competition and changing economic conditions.

The mail-order houses reached their peak in the decade after 1910. Montgomery Ward and Sears, the two leading houses, continued to captivate customers with their encyclopedic order catalogues and mail deliveries. They met their crises in the 1920's by setting up numerous retail stores in different communities; Sears was apparently first in California with its Los Angeles store in 1927.

Chain-store systems swamped the nation in the 1920's. California was saturated with them, including national grocery chains like Atlantic and Pacific (A & P), department-store chains like J. C. Penney's, variety chains like Woolworth's five-and-dime stores, drug chains like Walgreen's. It also had flourishing local chains like Safeway Stores and Owl Drugs in Northern California, and Ralph's grocery stores and Thrifty drug stores in Southern California. Safeway was the most spectacular. The Oakland-based company, formed in 1926, expanded into a vast integrated chain that by 1945 had 2,100 stores to rank second after Atlantic and Pacific, the nation's oldest and largest chain. When the Depression came, most chains cut back on branch stores while some broadened their lines, like grocery chains which added apparel and hardwares, and variety chains which added higher-priced and better quality merchandise.

Supermarkets, originating in the East (1931), entered California by the mid-1930's. First established by independent grocers, they were quickly taken up by chains and by independents in other product lines, who established big single stores. These economy-minded stores, featuring diverse products at low prices, customer self-service, and cash and carry, were well adapted to Depression-ridden operators and customers.

The traditional independents suffered badly in the competition with these large retailers. The central downtown department stores, however, did not fade out as generally believed. They held their own by building branch stores or merging with rivals. San Francisco's Emporium and Oakland's Capwell's merged in 1927. Bullock's of Los Angeles set up branch stores (Wilshire, 1929; Palm Springs, 1930; Westwood, 1932); it merged with I. Magnin's of San Francisco in 1945. Specialty stores (apparel, furniture, hardware) survived by limiting operations and personalizing services. The general store in rural towns became practically extinct by 1930 except in remote communities.

The manufacturers, wholesalers, and retailers fought long running battles for control of the state's market areas. Foodstuffs offer a clear illustration of the organized competition. Independent retail grocers operated through areawide corporate or cooperative groups; United Grocers in the Bay Area was a pacesetter for expanded operations and efficient services. They had effective regional associations like the northern-based California Retail Grocers Association and the Southern California Grocers Association. The chain grocers effectively countered efforts of the independents to eliminate them. Safeway cultivated strong alliances with statewide farmer cooperatives and other organizations through generous business deals and special services which paid unexpected dividends. During the Depression, when grower–processors faced ruin because of surpluses (lambs in 1932, peaches in 1934), Safeway conducted intensive sales campaigns and disposed of them, winning the deep gratitude of the producer groups. When independent grocers pressured the 1935 legislature to enact a retail-store license tax (based on gross sales of individual stores) designed to drive chain stores out of business, the chain stores launched an intensive and successful referendum campaign to repeal the act. The outcome was apparently affected by the farmers who had not forgotten the Safeway venture, and supported the chains.

The emergence of chain stores with their mass distribution and price-cutting activities brought the fair trade movement to a climax in the 1930's. The legislature enacted the 1931 law which authorized voluntary price maintenance contracts between manufacturers and retailers. Two years later it made such contracts mandatory by stipulating that a contract signed by one distributor was binding on all distributors! These pioneer fair trade laws swept the nation. By 1937 a total of 42 states had modeled similar legislation after the California laws. The California legislature also enacted the 1935 and 1937 Unfair Practices Act which greatly expanded upon the 1913 measure prohibiting price discriminations. Congress followed suit by passing two notable measures—both anti-chain store measures—prohibiting price discriminations (1936, Robinson–Patman) and upholding resale price maintenance (1937, Millard–Tydings) in interstate commerce. With government entry into the marketplace, the nation took a big step toward a regulated economy.

Foreign Trade

California's foreign trade patterns were shaped by the tariff and other trade developments. The Panama Canal, completed by the United States in 1914, improved the state's market outlets and increased the trade volume in California ports. California producers formed cooperative export associations in dried fruits (1919), redwood lumber (1923), and wine (1941) to stabilize earlier export arrangements. While the nation's staple producers (e.g., wheat and corn) suffered from foreign tariff barriers in the 1920's, California producers fared well through aggressive promotions of their specialty products in the external trade. Foreign trade was significant to the state's expanding economy in two notable respects: it provided an alternative outlet for certain industries suffering or countering trade discriminations of Eastern producers, and it absorbed the surpluses of troubled industries.

16 The Plebeian Society

A. SOCIETY

THE SETTING

California acquired an ever more heterogeneous population in the period 1910-1945. The state still lured immigrants from home and abroad with its well-advertised advantages for business investments, work opportunities, recreation, and retirement. And the two world wars and the Great Depression brought people who altered the population pattern. The accelerated migratory flow of new residents, transient workers, and tourists into and within the state contributed to greater mobility, accentuating California's image of people on the move. The population became more evenly distributed in age, race, and sex, a characteristic feature of a maturing society. More people lived in urban areas than rural areas, and California took on the character of an urban state.

California's accelerating urbanization and industrialism after 1910 brought a change in its social base. People from scattered places, but predominantly the Midwest, poured into the cities and big towns, which offered opportunities for a better life. Industries, especially manufacturing, were located primarily in and around the metropolitan ports of San Francisco, Los Angeles, and later San Diego. They provided better-paying jobs and not only increased the number of managers, white-collar office workers, and blue-collar factory workers, but raised their standard of living and enhanced their aspirations, especially for cultural and recreational activities.

Improved communications and transportation encouraged these trends. The movies, newspapers, and radio advertised the urban way of life. The automobile enabled people to reach scattered cultural and recreational centers, whether the concert, theater, and dance hall downtown, or boating, hiking, and swimming at the seashore or in the mountains. The automobile and the movies helped draw the towns closer to the attractions of the cities—so much so that before long town life took on many characteristics of city life. Where urban cultural activities had been largely oriented around the city's upper and to some extent middle classes, they were now accessible to all classes and to rural people as well. The leveling effects of urban and industrial forces led to the rising prominence of a plebeian or middle-class society.

DEVELOPMENT

Nationally, the flow from rural to urban life produced major social changes after 1910. Progressive reformers attempted to stem the tide of socio-economic imbalances and maladjustments arising from the rural-urban transition. They represented a two-fold effort: One was to perpetuate the Protestant ethic values that were deeply rooted in rural communities and to some extent in the cities, as manifested in antivice laws (gambling, liquor, and prostitution) which climaxed in national liquor prohibition (1919). The other was to democratize the American system, as in the case of revised family laws and women suffrage (1919). World War I brought drastic changes in people's lives as men and women moved from city to city and region to region (notably the Negroes' migration from the South to the North) for wartime service in the military and defense industries. The traumatic experiences engendered by wartime dislocations and postwar maladjustments resulted in widespread insecurity and disillusionment among people who had been uprooted from the secure moorings of home and community life. The Progressive era which had imbued people with exalted ideas of a democratic world resulted in alienated people with shattered ideals struggling to make out in a topsy-turvy world. The decade set the stage for the revolutionary social changes of the 1920's.

The Twenties

By the 1920's the social currents surfaced and swelled to produce major socio-economic changes. The accelerated movement of people from rural communities led to profound changes in life styles and social attitudes as they adapted to the diverse ways of urban life. The urban life styles widened opportunities for work and play; young people had greater freedom to partake in the exciting adventures of city living. Industry in partnership with technology mass-produced automobiles, radios, home appliances, and other consumer goods that improved living standards for countless people.

The impact of these changes was especially pronounced on urban families. Typically, families lived in single or duplex city houses with modest-size lawns. The households had labor saving appliances, like ranges with automatic ovens, refrigerators, and vacuum cleaners; the kitchens were stocked with canned and packaged foods. Family entertainment centered on favorite radio programs, and families played store-purchased games like croquet, checkers, and monopoly (a game particularly befitting the business ethic of the day). Parents and children argued over using the family car, each wanting to escape from the house for his fun. Community ties were looser in the city; parents rarely knew their neighbors well and were more selective about going to church or participating in civic activities. Urban families were strong on personal privacy and on doing their own thing; they were less beholden to social conformity, which was conspicuous among families in rural communities.

This changing society, which was upsetting traditional ideas and values, aroused concern among established middle-class groups. President Harding called for a return to normalcy, a reiteration of those traditional values intimately identified with nineteenth-century rural America. His message caught the troubled mood of people living in "Middle America" who held to the superiority of WASP ideas (White Anglo Saxon Protestant) and felt cherished American ways threatened by rising cities with their large ethnic minorities and by the unconventional ways of the modern young generation. The conservative-minded Republican administrations of the decade did their part to strengthen such nativist, puritanical, and superpatriotic sentiments. In the course of dismantling Progressive socio-economic reforms, the national administration sponsored the Red Scare campaign against "radical agitators" preaching "revolutionary changes," often violating their civil liberties, and the nation's first general law restricting foreign immigration (1924). The reactionary mood of insecure middle-class elements condoned and even supported extremist right wing groups. The revived KKK, whose activities were formerly against Negroes in southern rural communities, now struck at Catholics and Jews as well as Negroes in northern and western cities, including those in California.

The public reactionary mood and repressive activities of the 1920's alienated many groups. Generally they were disenchanted by the emerging industrial order with its worship of machines and money. Many were disillusioned by Progressive failure to achieve reforms that would preserve democratic values at home and abroad. Their ire focused on the conservative-minded administrations in national and state governments, which served as fountainheads of authority for perpetuating big business interests and pressing reactionary programs which subverted libertarian activities. These groups particularly resented public obsession with materialistic values and social conformity at the expense of humanistic values and individual freedom. They found recourse in different ways. Some joined extremist left-wing groups, like the Socialists and Communists, to press radical causes. Others withdrew to secluded colonies and communes of various cults and sects which offered spiritual solace. Though small in number, these two groups evoked either public repression or ridicule, while the alienation of these groups with prevailing society was total.

The startling development of the 1920's, however, was the rise of rebellious youth. They were generally independent-minded young people from prosperous urban white middle-class families engaged in doing their own thing, taking jobs and living adventurously as befitted personal life-styles. They were enamoured of the Bohemian artists, musicians, and writers, whose free forms of individual expression voiced much of the same discontent with the prevailing society. Freud's ideas of sex and psychoanalysis and Omar Khayam's hedonistic poems had great appeal. They were also addicted to fancy dress, cars, jazz, dancing the fox-trot, and indulging in sexual experimentation ("necking" and "petting" were coined during the decade). Hollywood films set styles of behavior and conduct for the youth; many emulated favorite idols among glamorous movie stars. They found a hero in F. Scott Fitzgerald's *This Side of Paradise* (1920)—a world weary college youth who finds solace in several love affairs from a society of "dead gods and shaken faiths." Mark

Sullivan comments that adults were alarmed with Fitzgerald because they felt he knew what he was writing about. Young people caught up with the new excitement and variety of city life usually gravitated toward Bohemian colonies in metropolitan centers like New York (Greenwich Village), San Francisco, and Los Angeles. "Flaming youth" went out with the flamboyant Twenties, but the new freedom in social mores carried over into the somber Thirties.

Women in particular benefited greatly from the laxity of social conventions. Unprecedented numbers of them obtained college educations and self-supporting jobs. Emboldened by a greater sense of independence, they demanded social equality with men, openly indulging in smoking, drinking, and sexual relations in ways that upset traditional male prerogatives. Symbolic of the era were the flappers, independent-minded young women wearing knee-length skirts and facial makeup; they were portrayed in unflattering caricatures as giddy sex-conscious girls with only boys on their mind. The flapper of the 1920's gave way to the sirens of the 1930's, self-confident women who wore "clothes molded to their bodies" and were intent on being independent. Women won wide public acceptance of their new status in society.

The Southern California Style

California came to epitomize much of the "Art Nouveau" or "new art" way of life that swept the nation after World War I. The urban and industrial forces then transforming American society were particularly pronounced in California, where the accelerated flow of people produced varied consumer goods and services tailored to their needs. Restless people, usually middle-class sorts with money in their pockets, found in the relatively open environment a social tolerance that gave them a wider freedom of choice in cutting their niche. Southern California, with its attractive scenery, moderate climate, and unlimited opportunities, was bait for ambitious people on the make. It contributed to a style that emphasized casual living at work and play in an atmosphere marked by a new morality of widespread hedonism.

The distinctive type of living in the Los Angeles metropolis came to be known as the Southern California style. The metropolitan setting provided the basis for its social disparity—a pronounced population dispersion and an industrial decentralization from downtown Los Angeles to widely scattered communities extending from the mountains to the sea. It was less citified than any of the nation's metropolitan areas. Its people were primarily WASP, seeking to establish suburban communities that would combine rural living—single homes within a homogenous community—with city pleasures. The suburban communities varied widely in their socio-cultural makeup. In secluded communities were countless communes and retreats of various cults and sects, which offered their converts a tranquil existence away from the "mad world." R. M. Fogelson describes the dilemma of Angelenos unable to reconcile their ambitions for a great metropolis with their visions of community, handicapped as they were by a "chronic nostalgia for a bygone world." As an Angeleno confided in his diary (1928), "Once a rustic, always a rustic—the simple life for me—but living the simple life in these days is a very complicated proposition."

ANALYSIS

The People

Population rose from 2.4 million in 1910 to 6.9 million in 1940. World War II helped bring the population total to 9.3 million by 1945. The California-born remained in about the same proportion (37 percent), but immigrants born in other states increased substantially at the expense of foreign-born. Most of the statewide immigrants came more from the Midwest, the northern tier of midwestern states, rather than from the nation's population center in the East. The foreign-born population was more multinational, with a greater proportion from southern and eastern Europe than before. The complexion of the population underwent startling changes. By 1920 more people lived in urban areas than in rural areas, and by 1940 urban centers contained almost three-fourths of the population, most of them in the metropolises of San Francisco, Los Angeles, and San Diego. San Francisco led Los Angeles in population until 1920; by 1940 four other communities had joined the big-city ranks (over 100,000 population): Oakland, Long Beach, Sacramento, and San Diego. Agewise, young adults still constituted the bulk of the population, but older people (the highest number of any state) gained at the expense of youth. Sexwise, women had just about caught up with men in population numbers by 1940. Racially, whites constituted about the same overwhelming proportion as before. Negroes (the term used at the time) exceeded Japanese, but Mexican-Americans were the leading racial minority. The young and middle-aged urban white dominated the population scene.

Communities

The Counties

The county was greatly affected by the impact of urbanization and industrialization. New towns and growing cities rapidly occupied rural areas and created new problems for county governments. People and industries moving into open areas demanded municipal services like sewer lines and street lighting, and their requirements for additional water supplies and paved roads compounded county problems. Land developers pressured the counties as well as the cities to extend municipal service to their subdivisions, where neighboring cities were unable or unwilling to do so.

The counties were also affected by the increasing involvement of state and federal governments in local affairs. The pressure for state and federal aid came primarily from local government officials and special interest groups when it became apparent that county and city agencies were unable to cope with certain types of community problems. Under Progressive aegis after 1910, state government extended funds and services in such areas as health, highways, water, and welfare, and imposed state fiscal and administrative controls to insure adequate performance. When the Roosevelt Administration launched the comprehensive New Deal programs to cope with the Depression, federal aid supplemented a variety of local programs in education, health, welfare, and public works. These state and federal programs altered the county's traditional role as a prime mover in local affairs. The county was relieved of certain functions but assigned new responsibilities in carrying out state-federal programs, enhancing its role as administrator of the state government. County home rule had developed into an expanded concept.

The counties, affected in different ways by these changes, became more varied than ever. Los Angeles emerged by 1945 as the nation's biggest agricultural and manufacturing county. In sharp contrast were the small-sized counties—heavily populated and industrialized San Francisco and sparsely settled agrarian Alpine in the Sierra. An airplane pilot flying over a typical county might observe bustling cities with suburban clusters, numerous towns, and huge checkerboard tracts of cultivated fields and manufacturing plants. All were connected by paved highways, railroads, elevated hydroelectric powerlines, wormlike oil pipelines, and concrete-lined water aqueducts.

Cities and Towns

Cities and towns continued to grow as before with important differences. Promoters had less land and less incentive for planning, advertising, and selling whole towns, so there were far fewer town booms. People and industries concentrated in established communities and settled areas. They were lured by energetic promoters of farm and manufacturing investments and employment, oil bonanzas, movie fame, recreational activities, as well as the traditional real estate speculation and tourist attractions. Civic and business leaders, confronting the severe community problems imposed by the rapid influx of people and industries, initiated movements for planned growth to insure orderly development. The League of California Cities (1921) offered a forum for representatives of the cities to compare notes and work together in resolving local problems.

The local communities changed in other ways. Cities continued to incorporate and annex adjoining areas, sometimes growing into large cities. Rural towns experienced the impact of urban influences, notably expanding banks, manufacturing and transportation enterprises, and the mass media, which were breaking down traditional village norms and rural ways. In remote areas, lumbering and mining corporations still operated company towns. Utopian colonies flourished briefly (five new ones during the 1910's) but only two survived beyond 1940. Town promoters developed recreational communities along scenic Southern California beaches and in Sierra mountain areas in more systematic fashion than before. The big impetus for these developments came from the fabulous boom of the 1920's and wartime expansion.

The Boom of the 1920's

California's boom of the 1920's was historically the state's biggest boom and the nation's largest internal migration. In the decade after 1920 over one million people poured into the state in the first great migration of the automobile age. People came seeking well-advertised employment in farming and manufacturing, quick riches in real estate and other business ventures, fun and pleasure in touring and vacationing in scenic and playground areas. Most of the people flowed into Southern California (72 percent), dazzled by the lure of oil bonanzas, the glamorous motion picture industry, and exciting real estate speculation. Oil promoters enticed gullible investors with bizarre and sometimes fraudulent schemes, like the celebrated Julian Swindle (see Chapter 15). Hollywood agents pressured and were pressured by starry-eyed youths and ambitious parents with talented children hungering for movie fame. Booster organizations, public and private, had a field day with excursions and cultural and recreational events enshrouded in legend and ballyhoo.

Promoters and boosters appealed particularly to middle-income groups with money to invest in business and entertainment, but in the process drew people from all classes and walks of life. So intense was the spirit of high adventure in Southern California that one writer described the decade as "a big debauch, a protracted orgy." Like the earlier argonauts, many people who came looking for quick riches lost their shirts instead; too broke to go back home, they joined the natives as permanent residents. The decade produced a spate of new towns and unincorporated communities; Los Angeles County alone had eight new towns. Where the earlier booms had focused primarily on town lot speculation and agricultural and commercial enterprises, the 1920's boom consisted primarily of city subdivision speculation and industrial enterprises. The wild land schemes of yesteryear had given way to the rational plans of college-trained, state-licensed agents for real estate and land development companies.

Community Development

Towns and cities were transformed by urban influences that altered traditional community patterns. Towns were affected in varying degrees by urban incursions, like the branch banks, stores, and plants of city-based firms, and municipal facilities like paved roads and sidewalks and well-developed public utilities. Families of farmers, ranchers, lumbermen, and miners in outlying hamlets and towns made regular trips to these bigger towns to shop for groceries, home items, and personal services, or to go to the movies or other commercial entertainment. Their daily routine and personal values reflected facets of city life, and their familiarity with the outside world was greatly enhanced by their increased involvement with it. These towns remained essentially small communities but their character changed with the advent of nonrural people, manufacturing industries, commercial entertainment, and municipalized public services. Except in remote hamlets and small towns, the village tradition of independence and individuality was giving way to the municipal tradition and mass uniformity of the cities.

The cities, especially those in the San Francisco Bay Area and the Los Angeles basin, were drastically altered by the impact of urban forces. They experienced rapid population growth and increased manufacturing activity which converted them from essentially trading centers to complex commercial–industrial urban entities. The city pattern changed with the regrouping of people, business, and factories. The central region became a downtown business district marked by big department stores, professional buildings, commercial establishments, and an enlarged civic center, as most people and industries took flight to outlying suburbs. The city occasionally annexed neighboring rural areas, which were converted into residential and industrial tracts. People were dispersed throughout the city area. Generally, wealthy and middle-income people moved to attractive suburbs fostered by real estate developers using property deed restrictions to impose financial limits and bar non-whites—a practice which confined the poor and racial minorities to the crowded central region. People who came to the cities for good jobs and an exciting life became disenchanted with the accelerated pace, impersonal relations, and congested conditions of urban life. In moving to the suburbs, they apparently sought to recapture the pleasant leisure and open space associated with rural life. So pronounced was the suburban movement in Los Angeles by the 1930's that its communities were described as a "collection of suburbs looking for a city."

A Tale of Two Cities

San Francisco experienced a more upward and concentrated expansion than did Los Angeles. The prosperity of the 1920's engendered another wave of building construction: in the central business district, department stores and other commercial buildings reached massive proportions, high-rise office buildings reached 15 to 25 stories, and near the bayside waterfront a cluster of tall buildings graced the city skyline. The streets radiating from downtown were lined with numerous apartment buildings of all sizes for rich and poor families, sandwiching occasional neighborhood shopping centers. Further out, the streets with rows of single-family and duplex homes extended to the city limits. The downtown area was so congested that after 1920 shipping, manufacturing, and other industries relocated to East Bay ports, thus completing the city's transition to a governmental, financial, and commercial center for the metropolitan area. San Francisco emerged as a compact business metropolis located in a picturesque peninsula setting and peopled by multinational and ethnic groups whose variegated cultural ways lent a rich cosmopolitan flavor to community life.

The city as a maturing metropolis did not fare well. Community leadership reflected more often the narrow conservatism of civic leaders and powerful business elements (as represented by de Young's *Chronicle*) than the imaginative schemes of businessmen (like James Phelan), when dealing with vital city problems. Contributing to San Francisco's difficulties were the city's apathetic voters (less than 25 percent turned out for bond elections) and aggressive leadership in Oakland and other Bay cities. The imposing civic center (completed by 1916) set a trend for large-scale administrative centers in the nation's cities, but it only partially fulfilled Daniel Burnham's far-sighted plan for the city's modern development. In dealing with local transportation problems, the city had built scenic parkways and wide boulevards by 1920 but spent so much on strategic tunnels and rail extensions that little was left for the much-needed rapid transit program. In resolving its water problem, the city won its battle for Hetch Hetchy reservoir in 1913, but did not buy out the Spring Valley Water Company until a decade later (success came in 1928 with the fifth bond election) and the water project was not complete until 1934—a lengthy time and high cost for securing municipal control of its water supply. As for power supply, the city signed away its strategic distributing rights to Pacific Gas and Electric (the 1913 Hetch Hetchy Act expressly forbade the city to give its rights to a private utility), losing the advantages of municipal power ownership that its southern rival enjoyed.

Los Angeles underwent a phenomenal outward growth and development witnessed nowhere else in the nation. Boosters and promoters refined techniques for luring out-of-state people and industries, emphasizing Los Angeles's pleasant environment of open space and diverse resources as a place to live, play, and retire, as well as work. The expanding business district became increasingly congested with heavy traffic and big structures—three- to twelve-story office buildings, department stores, apartment houses, and manufacturing plants. Real estate developers aggressively promoted suburban industrial and residential tracts, encouraging trends of population dispersion and industrial decentralization to the outlying areas. They laid out attractive subdivisions with tree-lined, paved streets and landscaped lots for single-family dwellings carefully tailored to the desires of native American whites of upper and middle incomes. Fogelson tells us that the flight to the suburbs—by retired magnates, former farmers, ambitious laborers, and those with education and skills—was an attempt to recapture the rustic and homogeneous life of rural communities. It produced a fragmented residential metropolis sprawled out in the panoramic open plain where the native white majority had fashioned their version of provincial community life. The Los Angeles metropolis was to be a forerunner of California's fragmented society.

Los Angeles achieved a remarkable balance of interacting forces involved with city development. In the struggle for community leadership, progressive-minded businessmen and government officials (like J. R. Haynes and William Mulholland), who believed in an active municipal government, exerted strong influence in the early decades, while reactionary forces (led by the Chandler interests), who advocated government laissez faire, had the upper hand in the later years. Progressives were particularly imbued with the idea of municipal ownership of public utilities, which would provide cheap communications, fuel, power, transportation, and water for attracting people and industries and spurring economic development. In their eyes, this was a pragmatic approach for stimulating capitalistic enterprises, though reactionary colleagues branded them as socialists.

The public–private power struggle in city development was a long but decisive one. The city secured municipal control of water and hydroelectric power by the time the Los Angeles aqueduct from Owens Valley was complete (1913). In the 1920's it pressed the federal Boulder Dam project and sponsored the Metropolitan Water District as a cooperative venture of Southern California cities for tapping the Colorado to secure additional power and water (1938). The city took possession from the Southern Pacific of the Wilmington tidelands (1911). It set up a municipal agency to coordinate rival railroads into a unified system (1928) and acquired federal funds for harbor dredging (1932) that helped convert Los Angeles into one of the world's largest ports. The city cooperated closely with private developers in building subdivision streets and with county and state agencies in building an arterial network of streets, roads, and highways that enabled motor vehicles to move about the metropolis. The city also modernized its government organization. It set up a planning agency (1920) to pioneer zoning classification for orderly land use, revised its charter (1924) to streamline municipal government operations, and provided for a new civic center and a much expanded park and recreational system. Private interests had their victories; they successfully resisted municipalization of electric railways and gas and telephone utilities.

The struggle between public and private interests had salutary effects. It spurred each to develop its resources and services more effectively, and eventually it encouraged them to accommodate their differences for greater gains. Their ambitious programs often fell short of their aims and resolved older problems only to create new ones. Nevertheless, they achieved a spirit of mutual accommodation that seemed singularly lacking in the rival northern city.

Metropolitan Development

A metropolis (from the Greek, "mother city") is a central city with satellite communities within its orbit. The modern metropolitan area, as we know it, comprises assorted communities revolving around nucleus cities tied together by complicated governmental arrangements, a complex commercial–industrial base, and a proliferated social setup. The 1910 Census for the first time provided a specific definition for the new phenomenon; it defined a standard metropolitan area as comprising a core city of 50,000 population within a related area having 100,000 people. In California the metropolis took its modern form after 1910.

The San Francisco metropolitan area emerged as an entity of the nine counties bordering the Bay (see above). The urbanization of the East Bay altered the historic relation between San Francisco and its transbay neighbors. Oakland developed as a nucleus city for the East Bay, standing out as a residential area populated by people of varied income and ethnic groups and an industrial center enhanced by an improved deep harbor, water supply, and strategic location. The city's conservative leadership (represented by Knowland's *Tribune*) reflected preoccupation with downtown development and certain East Bay developments at the expense of regional projects. Berkeley with its ranking university emerged as a bedroom community and manufacturing area. Its municipal government won national laurels, notably its council-manager plan (1923), pioneer city planning, scientific police administration, and quality public school system. Richmond became a highly concentrated diversified industrial area (over 60 plants of 20 major industries). It beat out rivals like South San Francisco which took

Urbanization and industrialization in the East Bay. Homes and factories extend continuously from Oakland's downtown business center (14th and Broadway) to Berkeley with the University of California in the extreme background. The downtown scene (circa 1912), with its triangular building for effective space utilization and its rail transit, stand in sharp contrast to present-day high-rise buildings, automobiles, and parking facilities.

hold as an industrial community after manufacturing industries moved into the area in greater numbers around World War I. With improved transportation links in the 1920's and 1930's, Marin County and the Peninsula enjoyed rapid development as big estates and farmlands were subdivided into bedroom communities. San Jose, chief trading center at the Bay's south end, emerged as the nation's most productive area (highest crop yield per acre).

The regional facilities that developed were a blend of private and public enterprises. The water barrier of the Bay and Delta, which made San Francisco the nation's most bottled-up city and restricted areawide development, was partly overcome by bridge projects. Private enterprises built the railroad bridges over the Dumbarton (1910) and Carquinez Straits (1930), and for motor vehicles the Antioch Bridge (1926) and

Carquinez Bridge (1927, the world's highest and an engineering marvel). In response to public sentiment, the 1929 legislature created a unique state agency (California Toll Bridge Authority) for sponsoring new projects and eventually taking over private toll bridges for a state system. After a decade of bitter controversy and protracted delays, the two great Bay landmarks were complete: the huge San Francisco–Oakland Bridge (1936), the world's largest, and the picturesque Golden Gate Bridge (1937), the world's longest single span. Bridge development overcame the major physical obstacle to metropolitan unity.

Metropolitan Los Angeles encompassed for the most part a single huge county. After 1910 the Los Angeles basin experienced a faster and greater flow of people and industries moving in and about Los Angeles and surrounding communities in continuous swirling motion, accelerated by the boom of the 1920's and wartime expansion in the 1940's. The central region was filled out and the downtown area became congested, while the eastern, western, and coastal plains became completely covered with cities and small communities. So extensive was population dispersion into outlying areas that Los Angeles had the nation's lowest population ratio between city and suburbs (3 to 1 compared to New York's 23 to 1 and San Francisco's 30 to 1)—a radical difference between it and the nation's other metropolitan areas.

Los Angeles's environment provided opportunities for special-interest groups to develop their type of community, continuing the earlier pattern of communities that acquired distinctive characters or specialities. Beverly Hills developed as an exclusive enclave for its new-rich citizens, notably movie celebrities and long-time mayor Will Rogers, the lovable cowboy philosopher–humorist. Westwood was built as an elegant residential community and homesite for the University of California at Los Angeles (UCLA). El Segundo (Spanish, "the second one") took form when Standard Oil established its second refinery. Torrance was designed as a model industrial–residential community by utility magnate Jared Torrance. Watts, known earlier as Mudtown, was subdivided for low-income Negroes (25-foot lots purchased at $1 down and $1 a week). Palos Verdes in the hilly southeastern corner of the county was planned as the "metropolis's finest," an exclusive garden suburb with winding parkways. These newer communities often reflected close cooperation between civic officials, big developers, and prominent landscape architects; F. L. Olmsted, Jr. (like his father a noted architect and planner) had a hand in planning Torrance, Palos Verdes, and several other communities.

The older established cities were reshaped by newcomers and took on a different character. Burbank expanded from a ranch to a residential–industrial community when Lockheed Aircraft and Warner Brothers movie studio moved there. Glendale was reawakened with the Pacific Electric line from downtown Los Angeles and evolved into a middle lower-class community. Hollywood evolved from a dusty, staid village to a cosmopolitan urban community, a natural center for the arts and entertainment, and movie capital of the world. Long Beach was shaped by a heavy midwestern and predominantly middle lower-class immigration to become the "Iowa of California." It evolved into a conglomerate of communities for factory workers, retired elderly, a carnival playland, a naval base, a major port, and an industrial center (manufactures, oil, and shipping). Santa Monica expanded from a seaside residential resort into an industrial center after Douglas Aircraft relocated there. Pasadena, a showcase community in the Southland, lost its original midwestern and eastern traits and acquired a distinctive character marked by a blend of its celebrated millionaire's row, a large number of churches, its extensive cultural–educational-intellectual activities, and annual tourist attractions. Perhaps nowhere else could people so easily find the community of their choice, especially one oriented to their income level, racial stock, or social taste.

Metropolitan area developments focused on the expansive efforts of Los Angeles City and County. Los Angeles City continued its aggressive campaign of absorbing outlying areas to provide additional space for community expansion. It merged eight incorporated cities by consolidation, including Hollywood (1910), Venice (1926), and Watts (1927), and over 75 unincorporated areas by annexation, ranging from the enormous San Fernando (1915) to minuscule splinters to straighten boundary lines. The city area became four times larger (over 100 square miles in 1910 to 450 square miles in 1930) to be the nation's largest city. In most instances, Los Angeles desired to secure additional communities to help utilize and pay for its surplus water, and the communities in return wanted to benefit from the city's cheaper water and other municipal services.

Los Angeles's aggressive approach was also exemplified in dealing with transportation services. Between 1910 and 1930 the monopolistic electric railroads of Huntington's local Los Angeles Railway and Harriman's interurban Pacific Electric, under sound management and with updated equipment, provided efficient low-cost services. Prominent developers laid out long, wide boulevards for facilitating motor traffic. The most famous was Wilshire Boulevard built up after 1928 by a local developer (A. W. Ross) with cooperative property owners from downtown Los Angeles to the sea at Santa Monica. It featured the world-renown Miracle Mile, a carefully planned section with imposing office buildings, massive department stores, and large apartment houses built in modern style in an attractive setting. A trend for the future began in 1941 with the opening of the freeway between Los Angeles and Pasadena, one of the nation's first.

Social Classes

The American class system underwent major transformation after 1910. The continuous process of industrialism and urbanization, accelerated by two world wars, had leveling effects. It reshuffled major groups, blurred class lines, and changed social mores. The upper strata of society reflected these changes. New-rich elements, like high-salaried business executives, government officials, and movie stars, entered the upper class gaining social recognition by assimilating into high society or forming new social elites. Professional men like business managers, government administrators, and physicians rose into the upper-middle class, acquiring sufficient wealth and emulating high society with fashionable homes and country clubs. The decline of the plutocrats was followed by new elements in the nation's leadership elite: patrician reformers (like the two Roosevelts and Wilson) in politics and the professional executive in the business world.

California's class system accentuated national trends. Perhaps more than in any other state it assumed irregular forms and mutations, conditioned by the state's rapid development and dramatic changes. From a heterogeneous population rose varied new rich elites, notably oilmen and movie stars, but also business executives, government leaders, financiers, and industrialists. The growing informality and new freedom in social mores, especially after the 1920's, separated the staid genteel set from the modern-thinking "smart set" and the globe-trotting international set. They varied widely in their social and personal life styles.

The life of high society in San Francisco and Los Angeles reveals the wide diversity of the social elite. San Francisco was still the center of high society, even though it had lost some of its former sway. Established families, like the Crockers and Floods, Hales and Spreckels, were joined by new-rich families, like the Armsbys, the Fleishhackers, utility manager Charles Black, and hotelman Louis Lurie. Phoebe Hearst, in her Moorish hacienda in Pleasanton, and James Phelan on his Saratoga estate carried on the older tradition of lavish entertainment. William Crocker helped build the exclusive Burlingame Country Club (1923) for his set, and Louis Lurie threw colorful parties. The Palace Hotel and the Fairmont Hotel, built by James Fair's daughter, were favorite social centers of the Bay Area elite.

High society in Los Angeles, in sharp contrast to the Bay City, had less visibility. Established families and new-rich elements sometimes intermingled but usually associated with their kind. Pacing the social leadership were the Chandlers, Lettses, Otises, and Sartorises. New-rich elite, especially oilmen and movie celebrities, won wider attention for their showplace homes, social extravaganzas, and personal escapades. These social elites lived in exclusive enclaves located in scattered places like Beverly Hills, Holmby Hills (Westwood), Malibu, Pasadena, and the San Fernando Valley. The Los Angeles Country Club was the symbolic center for the social elite of the metropolis.

Public extravaganzas were more common to Los Angeles than San Francisco. Among the biggest were the exotic, world-famous film premieres at Grauman's Chinese Theater, a showplace for new-rich movie celebrities; the showy cultural events at the large, open-air Hollywood Bowl auditorium; and the gaudy, well-publicized spectacles conducted by Aimee McPherson at the huge Angelus Temple. Nowhere else in the world could the elite and plebeians rub shoulders and gape at each other so freely.

Middle- and lower-class society had its upper, middle, and lower subclasses with different group organization and social mores. Communitywide organizations, like service clubs, church groups, and nondenominational organizations (the Boy Scouts, Girl Scouts, YMCA, and YWCA) played significant roles as social centers. They brought newcomers together with old-timers and to some degree blended lower with middle-class elements. The lower class seemed stratified as before, its hobo class and its sharply divided poor whites and racial minorities pursuing different life styles. Unlike the elite, whose activities were regularly reported in society columns of local newspapers, middle- and lower-class groups had few vehicles publicizing social activities, hence the dearth of their public record.

Extremist Groups

Extremism took on new dimensions with the advent of major crises and great social upheavals at home and abroad. Industrial and urban trends, punctuated by two world wars and an unprecedented depression, transformed people's lives, defeating as well as enhancing their aspirations and their images of society. The revolutionary upheavals which led to totalitarian regimes in Russia, Germany, Italy, and Japan aroused Americans over the spread of communism and fascism and the decline of worldwide democracy and capitalism. The expanded role of government in implementing Progressive and New Deal reforms and the generally isolationist posture of United States foreign policy enhanced the feelings of insecure reactionaries and the frustration of idealistic radicals.

The Left Wing

The growing left wing reached a peak and went into decline after 1910. Riding on the nationwide reform wave carried by Progressives, the Socialist Party peaked in the 1912 presidential election when Eugene Debs, the party standard-bearer, captured 6 percent of the vote. In California, the state Socialist Party peaked in the 1910 elections when Job Harriman, the gubernatorial candidate, polled 13 percent of the vote, and socialist candidates captured several legislative seats and municipal offices, including Berkeley's mayorship. These socialist office-holders showed a propensity for moderation and compromise, cooperating with Progressives in carrying out reform programs rather than pursuing revolutionary dogmas. The charismatic Harriman campaigned vigorously for the Los Angeles mayorship in 1912 and 1914, only to be thwarted by the city's bitter showdown between business and labor (see Chapter 15). Thereafter Debs, the gentle "John the Baptist of American socialism," concentrated on establishing the Llano colony near Los Angeles as a model socialist community.

Meanwhile, the anarchistic Industrial Workers of the World (IWW or Wobblies—an Otis label) dedicated to the "historic mission of the working class to do away with capitalism" was active in organizing California farm laborers and other workers, which involved them in freedom-of-speech fights with local authorities. In Fresno (1910), IWW members were arrested for street assemblies prohibited by municipal ordinance; when thrown into jail en masse, they continued disruptive tactics by loudly singing radical songs, provoking guards into drenching them with fire hoses. In San Diego (1912), businessmen formed vigilante groups that brutally beat up IWW members in a similar freedom-of-speech incident without interference from onlooking police. Governor Johnson's investigator (the respected Harris Weinstock) wondered in his report who, vigilantes or Wobblies, were the *real* anarchists.

The Socialist fate was sealed by internal dissensions over party priorities at home and abroad. The party split into moderate and radical positions over the IWW's campaign in the labor movement and over American intervention in World War II, particularly the priority to be given to the workers' class war against capitalism. The communist takeover of Russia (1917) under Vladimir Lenin gave Marxian socialism new vitality through its emphasis on a dedicated party elite. Lenin's call for a worldwide communist revolution split the American socialists further into bitter factions. Communists formed into minuscule groups: the Communist Party of the United States and the Communist Labor Party (CP and CLP, both 1919). The Socialists deteriorated into a shadow organization; party leadership after Debs's death (1928) passed to Norman Thomas, an articulate former minister, who stressed Christian socialism and practical reforms.

The Right Wing

The right wing rode high during the 1920's, which sociologist Seymour Lipset calls a "backlash decade" marked by widespread bigotry and repression. Conservative forces spurred by reactionary elements launched a vigorous campaign to eliminate the liberal reforms of Progressives and the national threat of "wild-eyed Communists" and other radicals in an effort to restore the "normalcy" of American nativism and Protestant morality. They operated as pressure groups in the Republican Party to eliminate government regulation and to restrict foreign immigration, and in industry associations like NAM to repress labor unions and radical elements. Reactionary elements activated nativist associations to strike at alien groups, patriotic societies to reinforce conservative values in public institutions, and Protestant evangelical sects to crusade for religious fundamentalism. The second Ku Klux Klan (revived 1914) had by mid-decade of the 1920's over three million members; it drew recruits throughout the South and West in its campaign against Catholics, Jews, and Communists, as well as against Negroes. It attempted to reverse trends of sexual freedom and the religious liberalism said to be undermining white American and Protestant values.

In California, extremism was accentuated by the rapid changes wrought by the population and industry boom of the decade. Many natives and newcomers unable to cope with the changing environment developed into what writer Carey McWilliams calls "alien patrimonies," maladjusted people unhappy with their lot and filled with nostalgia for better times. Nativist groups found ready recruits among the heavy immigration into the state; Los Angeles alone had over 200,000 annual transients. The California Joint Immigration Commitee widened its statewide anti-Japanese campaign into a national campaign against Orientals; it helped shape the nation's first general law (1924) for restricting foreign immigration. The KKK was especially strong; it had pocket strongholds in Los Angeles and San Francisco's East Bay regions. Reactionary elements, operating in the guise of patriotic civic groups in several communities, sometimes succeeded in removing alleged radicals from government and school posts.

Reactionary elements also carried out a vociferous campaign against labor unions. The aggressive U.S. Attorney General A. Mitchell Palmer provided the spark when he launched a nationwide "Red Scare" campaign (1919–1921) to round up and arbitrarily deport alien Communists, but which indiscriminately included undesirable labor leaders and other radical agitators. California, like many other states, adopted a criminal syndicalism law (1919) which prohibited forceful and violent acts aimed at changing industry ownership or political control. While the measure ostensibly aimed at Communists, it was used as the basis for government prosecution of union organizers, Socialists, and other radical agitators, resulting in numerous arrests and convictions. (Of 524 persons arrested over a five-year period, 264 went to trial and 128 were sent to prison.) In the San Pedro waterfront strike (1921), police arrested Upton Sinclair for reading the Constitution in a platform speech on private property, despite the mayor's assurance of noninterference. (The incident led to formation of the local chapter of the American Civil Liberties Union.) The Los Angeles police maintained a "Red Squad" which conducted a systematic repression, marked by professional informers and the use of tear gas and clubs. The state supreme court in an only-one-of-its-kind decision upheld an injunction against an IWW organizer, overriding his constitutional rights on the grounds that government was protecting the people against a public nuisance!

A celebrated case was that of Charlotte Anita Whitney, a niece of Stephen Field and an Oakland socialite active in social work, who was convicted under the 1919 law for her CLP membership. (The U.S. Supreme Court in its landmark decision on this case officially replaced the common law doctrine of "dangerous tendencies" with the "clear and present danger" doctrine in deciding freedom-of-speech cases.) She remained out of prison during appeal and was eventually pardoned by Governor Young (1927). Sinclair remarked caustically of the governor's action that the law worked differently for the rich and poor, alluding to the many IWW and other radicals still in jail. McWilliams claims that the "radicalism that flourished under the lash of persecution" contributed recruits to the mass political movements of the 1930's.

The 1930's

The 1930's were an "eccentric decade" for extremist movements. The Depression with its widespread unemployment and socio-economic upheaval intensified class conflicts. Extremist groups evolved into mass movements, usually under demagogic leadership, sponsoring drastic remedies for society's ills. Left-wing extremists benefited from the Roosevelt Administration's emphasis on liberal reforms. The Socialist and Communist parties gained membership and exerted influence on liberal forces. The small Moscow-directed Communist Party had members and fellow travelers who formed underground cells and front organizations and infiltrated several federal agencies, CIO labor unions, university campuses, and the mass media, especially publishing houses and the movie industry. The Share-Our-Wealth organization (1933–1935) was headed by Governor Huey P. Long who ruled Louisiana like a police state and operated his national movement in a fascistic manner in promoting a populist-type program before his assassination.

Reactionaries flourished, too. The liberally oriented House Un-American Activities Committee (HUAC) listed over 200 right-wing extremist groups. The Silver Shirts (1934), recruited mainly from former KKK members, were a hybrid of nativist tradition and revolutionary fascism; they called on industrialists to help suppress labor unions through violent means. The National Union for Social Justice (1934) was organized by Father Charles Coughlin, a Catholic priest, who broadcast from his Detroit-based radio station a call for a genuine fascist revolutionary movement, lauding Hitler and Mussolini as heroes against Communism and big-business enemies.

California had the full array of these movements. Communists operated through underground cells and youth movements on college and university campuses, notably UC-Berkeley. They infiltrated the movie industry and the labor union movement, playing active roles in the San Francisco labor–management showdowns, notably in the waterfront strike and the Central Valley cannery workers strike. The Socialists under Upton Sinclair's leadership cloaked their socialist programs under a palatable name (EPIC)—a tactic copied from the successful Non-Partisan League in North Dakota during the 1920's. In 1934 they captured the Democratic Party leadership in the primary election and gave the Republicans a run for their money in the bitter general election campaign. The Silver Shirts won numerous recruits, especially in Southern California, but Father Coughlin's movement apparently had little appeal. The anti-democratic extremist movements reached their peak at the height of the Depression; most declined with the advent of World War II.

Ethnic Groups

California's ethnic pattern was intensified by urbanization. Racial immigrants from different nations and various parts of the country poured into California, often leaving oppressive conditions in their native areas for well-advertised economic opportunities and better living conditions. The Japanese, Mexicans, and Negroes gravitated in large numbers mostly to Los Angeles but also to San Francisco and other communities, settling, like their Chinatown predecessors, in enclaves or ghetto areas—the Little Tokyos, Mexican barrios (neighborhoods), and Niggertowns. Indians generally remained out of public view, isolated in rancherias in remote rural areas. White nativists who had earlier made the Chinese their target now turned their ire on ambitious Japanese, the numerous Mexicans, and other minorities like Filipinos and Hindus.

Asians

The Japanese were the chief focus of public intolerance after 1910. The Progressive administration moved to sharpen the color lines. As Hiram Johnson complained to Lincoln Steffens, their "superiority, their ascetic efficiency, and their maturer mentality made them effective in competition with us." Anti-Japanese sentiment surfaced again when the United States was negotiating with Japan a treaty for restricting immigration. The governor reached agreement with President Taft to hold off on anti-Japanese action. By terms of the 1911 treaty, Japan agreed not to issue passports to laborers (with no mention of women) and the United States agreed to respect the civil rights of Japanese. With the pressure off, the 1913 legislature adopted the Alien Land Act, which prohibited Japanese as aliens ineligible for citizenship from purchasing farmlands or leasing them longer than three years (an attempt to phase out long-term rental arrangements). The Japanese capitalized on legal loopholes by acquiring wives from Japan (the so-called picture brides) and transferring land titles to their American-born children.

Nativist groups around 1920 revived the anti-Japanese movement. It was spearheaded by V. O. McClatchy of the *Sacramento Bee* with wide support from organizations like the American Legion, AFL, State Chamber of Commerce, State Grange, and the Hearst papers. James Phelan in his forays into politics (see Chapter 14), made bait of the Japanese, accusing them of illegal entry, moral turpitude, murderous treachery, promiscuous breeding, and other "crimes." In the heat of the inflammatory campaign, the legislature initiated and the voters approved the 1920 constitutional amendment prohibiting Japanese land purchases, leases, and transfers; the measure proved to be an empty gesture because of earlier loopholes. The anti-Japanese movement reached its climax when the California-based League for Oriental Exclusion joined eastern nativist groups in persuading Congress to enact the 1924 Immigration Act to prohibit the entry of Asians. The anti-Japanese movement abated until World War II, though the League, primarily as a lone McClatchy operation, continued its blatant propaganda.

The Japanese accommodated to local discriminations in varied ways. They exploited gaps in the economy, running small businesses and family enterprises. They were still able to acquire land by leasing and even purchasing lands from sympathetic landlords. Working as a self-regulated group they endured low wages and long hours to produce high quality crops and distribute them through cooperative family schemes. George Shima developed innovative managerial techniques for managing his corporate enterprise. In 1920 these Japanese entrepreneurs owned 1 percent of the land but accounted for 10 percent of the state's crop value. Their children, having been indoctrinated in public schools, disdained the family farm and caste and made their mark in business, professional, and skilled occupations in the city. Like the Chinese, they masked hurt feelings with stoic or disdainful attitudes which provoked American charges of their implacable reserve as "covert treachery."

Then came the shock of Pearl Harbor in December 1941. Many Americans were gripped by a rabid nativism induced by war hysteria and fanned by newspaper sensationalism. Anti-Japanese elements in California took advantage of the situation, whipping up fears of invasion, sabotage, and espionage by Japanese agents and Japanese American cohorts (charges unproven after the war). This led to the removal from the Pacific Coast of the Japanese and confiscation of their property. The Army's Western Defense Command supervised the forced relocation of 112,000 Japanese, of which 70,000 were American born, from the three Pacific Coast states to ten distant concentration or relocation camps (two in California). This unprecedented confinement of American citizens, which led to gross violation of constitutional rights, was sanctioned by the courts as a military necessity in wartime. Hindsight shows that it was unjustified. In time, the Army in its official war history suggests that the federal government and the military had bowed to local civilian pressure for Japanese-American removal. The Army pursued the opposite course in Hawaii, where the Japanese could have been potentially more dangerous at the time. In this sorry episode, the nation lacked effective leadership to head off this relocation movement and prevent this travesty of justice.

The Latins

California's small Hispanic population was altered after 1910 with the arrival of Mexican nationals. There were two waves of immigrants from Mexico: after 1910 came middle-class elements and workers fleeing the turmoil of the proletarian revolution in Mexico, and after 1920 came transient laborers to harvest field crops, primarily in the Southern California area. The latter were either *braceros* (or day laborers) organized by private labor contractors, or unorganized caravans of migrant farm families traveling from farm to farm for work. By 1930 California's Latin population (Spanish-speaking citizens and noncitizens) swelled to an estimated 300,000, of which over half were in Los Angeles and San Bernardino counties. The Los Angeles Latin ghettos (East Los Angeles and Chavez Ravine) acquired the character of a Mexican barrio, an urban village where indigent people had a sense of community and a feeling of rural independence.

The increasing number of Mexican immigrants provoked alarm and intensified the hostility of nativist groups. By the 1920's the state AFL leaders voiced labor sentiments against Mexican competition and launched drives in Congress to restrict Mexican labor, only to be defeated by big farmer and allied groups. When the Depression came, the Secretary of Labor spearheaded a campaign to relieve unemployment by deporting alien Mexicans. Los Angeles cooperated zealously in the arbitrary roundup and shipment of aliens to Mexico at public expense; the voluntary and forced exodus numbered over 50,000 in 1931 alone. One newspaper commented on the Secretary's "gladiatorial spectacle" which compounded gross injustices, including the deporting of some California-born Latins.

The war years intensified the paradoxes of Anglo behavior toward the Latin minority. As Mexican-Americans went into the military service and war industries, the Los Angeles barrios became the ugly scene of racial violence, fanned by bigoted groups, newspaper sensationalism, and public reaction. A 1941 street fight between two Chicano youth gangs over a girl led to a harsh police crackdown; of 24 arrested, 9 were convicted and later all were released. This was followed by a series of violent incidents. The climax came in 1943 with the indiscriminate attacks on youthful zoot-suit gangs (so-called for their fancy-cut suits and colorful shirts) by restless sailors awaiting war assignments, followed by police dragnets and citizen raids on the terrorized barrios—a revival of the dreaded vigilantism. On another front, the United States and Mexico set up a government-regulated bracero program, by which Mexican labor gangs filled the depleted ranks of farm workers who had gone into military service and war industries in harvesting the California crops. The wartime situation intensified the social problems of the Latins, even though they figured importantly in the national defense effort.

Negroes

The Negro's lot improved after 1910. The immigration of Negroes from traditional rural strongholds in the South to cities in the North and West gained momentum. Strong leaders and organizations paved different paths. They had help from sympathetic whites, including Progressives, who thought education was the path for Negroes to rise to middle-class status. Booker T. Washington's emphasis on self-help and self-reliance still called for tacit acceptance of segregation. William Du Bois's militant crusade against racial discrimination led to the formation of the National

Association for the Advancement of Colored People (NAACP, 1910), to remove legal barriers against Negroes. The National Urban League, also formed the same year, provided social services for helping Negroes adjust from agrarian to city life. In the 1920's the Negro movement made headway with Marcus Garvey, whose mass appeal inspired racial pride and black nationalism (Negro businesses and immigration to Africa). It led to renewed expression in the arts (the so-called Negro Renaissance) and gains in politics, business, and the professions. Negro extremists formed small racist cults, like Elijah Muhammed's Black Muslims (1930) which preached a blend of black separatism and Islamic religion in fending off the "white devils." White racism reared its head periodically but seemed to be abating in the face of growing public recognition of Negro rights in the 1930's and 1940's.

California reflected national ramifications of the Negro movement and white racism. Negroes migrating in larger numbers from Southern rural communities and Northern urban ghettos concentrated mostly in cities of the Los Angeles and San Francisco areas. In Los Angeles, Negroes moving to the suburbs met mixed reactions: Booker Washington had difficulty acquiring his home in white middle-class San Gabriel, Jackie Robinson's family had none settling in attractive Pasadena, and all were *unwelcome* in KKK strongholds like Compton and Manhattan Beach. Negroes developed their own business, fraternal, social, and other organizations, creating a black subculture. They formed state and local chapters of the NAACP and the National Urban League under leaders like E. B. Ceruti and Charles Darden for improving their situation in politics, education, and the professions. Their battles for equal rights and against injustices were long and difficult. In Berkeley, for instance, a school-board president advised a Negro group (1936) that their request for a black teacher in the public schools was held in abeyance because of protesting citizens who had as much right to their views (a black teacher was eventually hired in 1944). Talented Negroes, like Ralph Bunche in the federal government and Kenny Washington in football (UCLA), made their own way. Blacks suffered discriminatory practices but were spared violent incidents which visited other racial minorities.

Indians

Indians in California continued to suffer public ambivalence. They experienced more liabilities than benefits from federal and state programs. The Bureau of Indian Affairs' (BIA) expanded medical services (1910) were hardly adequate for dealing with the deplorable Indian health problem resulting from widespread disease (rampant tuberculosis and trachoma) and malnutrition—one doctor served 600 Indians for two months of the year. Under Progressive aegis, the BIA and state groups campaigned successfully to lure Indians into public schools, but school officials responding to community pressure relegated Indian children to inferior separate classes. State court decisions confirmed Indian citizenship but denied them rights to equal education and, on technical grounds, workmen's compensation for job injuries.

Occasionally, efforts were made to redress land injustices. A coalition of Indian organizations and sympathetic allies like the powerful Commonwealth Club initiated a move to compensate Indians whose ancestors had been unjustly deprived of their lands under the 1851 treaty. The Indians had relinquished 75 million acres of land for some 7.5 million valuable acres promised by the treaty, but received only 624,000 acres in rancheria and reservation lands—figures which a scholar likened graphically to a basketball, a golf ball, and a BB shot. After 15 years of complicated political negotiation and legal maneuver, the federal government awarded the California Indians five million dollars, a figure based on the "curious but unhappy" formula of deducting federal expenditures since 1850 ($12 million) from promised treaty benefits ($17 million). Little had changed since Franklin Lane's trenchant observation (1915) that the Indians had been "spun around like a blindfolded child in a game of blind man's bluff . . . (he) has been confused in his thought because we have been confused in ours."

The Indian response seemed to be much as it had been in the earlier period: Indians adapted to the exigencies of their situation. The most dramatic instance was the appearance in 1911 of Ishi, the last surviving Yahi, who gave up his lifelong woodland seclusion (see Chapter 13) in 1910 to spend his remaining years under the protection of UC anthropologists. Indians lived in the relative seclusion of distant reservations and rancherias. At intervillage festivals, Mission Indians fought contests with hypnotic powers, which could kill rivals. Indian assimilation into American society increased as young Indians migrated into cities for better jobs and living conditions often losing native traits through intermarriage and improved status. Sherbourne Cook estimated that over a tenth had become migrants, overcoming a "fundamental inertia during generations of strict localization" to move out of primitive habitats into urban centers. Most Indians, however, remained on rancherias and reservations, still suffering in poverty from substandard housing and public neglect.

The Family

The family institution underwent a revolution from the urban-industrial impact after 1900. Family ties were breaking down from the effects of the move into cities, expanded job opportunities, automobile and other improved transportation, recreational and social diversions outside the home, scientific and technological developments. The psychological theories pioneered by Freud and Jung gained wide popularity; they gave family members new freedoms—and other problems of individual adjustment. Divorces were high and the birth rate declined. Companionate marriages were regarded less as "living in sin" than finding out about each other before going into formal matrimony—reminiscent of the trial marriages among New England Puritans in colonial times. Voluntary or planned parenthood gained popularity after 1920 when crusaders like Margaret Sanger successfully campaigned for legal dissemination of birth control information.

In California the forces reshaping the family institution seemed particularly pronounced. The urban family outnumbered the rural family. Both felt the impact of maturing urban-industrial forces that were reshaping the nation's society. The family institution was less oriented to male sovereignty and economic survival of the family unit than in earlier times; it focused more on the rights and well-being of each family member. Under Progressive aegis, family laws were rewritten to give attention to property rights of family members and their individual rights, such as providing for easier divorces and child rights. The family became marked by individualism and separatism, though some families retained traditional traits of interdependency and unity. It carried out fewer religious, educational, and welfare functions than formerly. Responsibility for these was assumed by church, school, governmental agencies, and private organizations. Family members, singly or together, were absorbed in a wide variety of activities outside the home. The automobile became an indispensable vehicle. The attractive California environment, especially in the Southland, featured diverse recreation in city (for example mini-golf), beach, and mountain communities for families as well as tourists.

The middle-class urban family came to be the majority. It centered on the nuclear family (husband, wife, and children), revolving around the private affairs of each and their personal interrelationships. Typically, family life was more flexible and self-serving for its members than before. Husband and wife often took off from home, going separate ways to work and play, and taking off together for an evening with friends or in town. The husband worked farther from home and changed jobs frequently. The wife stayed home to raise the children but sometimes took a job to produce the family income that would meet higher costs of living and desired personal luxuries. She enjoyed greater freedom from time-consuming homemaking chores because of the availability of ready-made clothes, canned and packaged food, and mechanical appliances like gas and electric ranges and refrigerators. Children took off for school or joined friends; they enjoyed greater independence as parental restraints loosened and youth activities opened up, notably the YMCA and YWCA, Boy and Girl Scouts, and in rural areas, the farmer-oriented 4-H clubs. Family members pursued varied civic, recreational, and social activities, whether with volunteer groups like service clubs and the Parent–Teacher Association (PTA), or in commercial entertainment like dancing, movies, or sports. They might take off together for holidays, and vacation trips to the beach, mountains, or other distant places. The urban family had less cohesion and greater mobility, giving parents and children wider opportunity for personal development—though at the cost of family solidarity and security so conspicuous in the previous period.

Civic, church, school, and other community leaders never ceased efforts to strengthen family ties. By the 1940's they were rewarded by a growing movement in that direction. Food-related and house appliance industries encouraged home cooking and selling household products, as glamorized by General Mills's Betty Crocker. The mass media did their part; magazines, movies, and radio increasingly extolled family virtues; the San Francisco radio serial "One Man's Family" gained wide popularity. The outbreak of war and breakup of families for military service and defense work, however, stalled the movement.

Women

After 1910 the women's movement in California, as elsewhere in the nation, manifested fundamental changes. The maturing industrial–urban forces that were breaking down the family were adding new dimensions to women's lives. The long battle for woman suffrage gained new momentum and reached its climax when California in 1911 and the nation in 1920 (19th Amendment) provided voting rights to women. Constituting a forceful element in the Progressive Party, feminist leaders spearheaded legislative measures for improving woman's rights, notably by revising family laws. California's persistent Katherine Edson won her long battle when the 1923 legislature adopted a maximum-hour law for women and children.

Sex discrimination prevailed widely. Women earned less pay than men for the same work and rarely broke male barriers to strategic positions at the supervisorial level, much less in top management of government and business. World War II was a turning point as women proved their ability at men's jobs, unskilled, skilled, and professional, in factories and offices in major industries. The shift from work at home to work outside the home, and to a role in the nation's business world and labor force amounted to a revolution.

The changing status of women was accompanied by a drastic alteration in their social relationships. The capable homemaker was no longer the cherished ideal. Women sought fulfillment as wives and mothers in the home and as active members of the community. The way was paved by what Page Smith calls the "new prophets." Havelock Ellis who preached the delights of sex in marriage, Sigmund Freud and Carl Jung whose psychological studies gave insight into women's psyches, and Karl Marx whose dogmas gave women full equality—such ideas gained popularity in the 1920's. Charlotte Perkins (see Chapter 13) was the link between the early woman's rights reformers and modern woman's personal freedom and self-attainment; her ideas won wide acceptance by the 1930's. Female freedom was manifested in a variety of ways. Women seemed more obsessed with personal appearance, particularly in face makeup, improved body figures, dress fashions, and fads. They organized for political activity, reform causes, community services, and social affairs. Girls were more bold in social relations with boys, paying their way ("Dutch treat") and having casual sex relations. Southern California became a pacesetter for modern women's mores: the film industry provided fashions and fads for imitation, with glamorous movie idols as examples, and bathing beauty contests for best-figure awards.

The new freedom did not always augur well for women. Many were uncertain and dissatisfied with their new-found possibilities.

Anthropologist Margaret Mead suggested that they reassess their roles in the family institution and in the community. However, the public felt—though many decried the new feminism—that the woman's movement was coming of age.

Public Entertainment and Recreation

Public entertainment as organized affairs for mass audiences became a conspicuous development in California after 1910. As cities grew, civic-minded groups formed into associations to promote artistic, cultural, and intellectual activities for the community, expanding public libraries and museums, and building facilities for art galleries, music halls, theaters, and public auditoriums. They raised funds through public subscription, sometimes supplemented with municipal and county allocations. Occasionally wealthy citizens contributed funds to favorite projects or donated their estates and collections to the community. Colleges and universities, following UC-Berkeley's example, became important cultural and intellectual centers in their communities, offering concerts, exhibitions, debates, and lectures. In many communities local choral groups, bands, and symphony orchestras were mainstays of cultural activities. By the 1920's the organized tours sponsored by national syndicates made regular appearances; they included celebrated artists, prominent lecturers, and music and drama groups who toured the cities, bringing new vistas of cultural entertainment to mass audiences. In the 1930's the federal government was another catalyst. The WPA-sponsored Federal Arts Projects gave impetus to building facilities and providing employment for jobless actors, musicians, painters, and writers who performed and produced works for the public under federal auspices.

Recreation also developed into mass activity. Climate, scenery, and natural resources coupled with available leisure provided impetus for expanded facilities and extensive activities for play and sport. Municipal and county governments expanded parks and playgrounds to accommodate growing local needs. In the metropolises, the principal parks evolved into cultural-recreational complexes, with amphitheaters, arboretums, zoos, and stadiums for diverse events. San Francisco's Golden Gate Park featured the Japanese Tea Garden, de Young Museum, Steinhart Aquarium, and Kezar Stadium. In Los Angeles, Griffith Park acquired its famous Greek theater, plantarium, and zoo while Exposition Park (converted from the old agricultural park, 1910) developed its County Museum of History, Science, and Art (1913) and Coliseum (site of the 1932 Olympics). Entrepreneurs developed commercial facilities for professional sports; by the 1920's large crowds packed auditoriums and stadiums to see boxing and wrestling bouts, auto and bike races, baseball and football games. Colleges and universities developed auditoriums and stadiums for varsity sports like basketball, baseball, and football, which also drew large crowds. The federal government did its part, especially in the 1930's when the CCC developed numerous sites and extensive trails in the Sierra for public camping and hiking.

Public entertainment became increasingly oriented to the metropolitan orbit rather than to the city or town. People traveled by auto, bus, or streetcar to distant cultural and recreational events, whether painting exhibitions or music concerts in other cities or college football games in outlying areas. San Francisco was still the chief center of state cultural activities, the drawing card for Northern California communities. It drew people to its symphony orchestra (1911, the nation's first municipally financed one), the de Young Museum (expanded 1917), the California Palace of the Legion of Honor (1924), the Opera House (1932), and the Museum of Art (1935, for modern painting). The university towns of Berkeley and Palo Alto developed into important cultural and intellectual centers.

The Los Angeles metropolis acquired a distinctive character that earned its reputation as the nation's leading playground. Several forces conspired to shape its cultural and recreational complexion, notably imaginative entrepreneurs, aggressive civic groups, annual waves of tourists and vacationers, and a congenial environment. Los Angeles acquired its Southwest Museum (1914), Philharmonic orchestra (1919), Chouinard Art School (1921), Otis Art Institute (1924), and several theater groups. Perhaps symptomatic of its schizoid culture were the popular long-running productions of the Pilgrimage Amphitheatre (1920) featuring the life of Christ and the Theatre Mart running a revived old-time melodrama *The Drunkard*—the latter setting a world record for continuous performances. Other public attractions were the Pasadena Playhouse (1916), which pioneered the community theater movement and launched many movie stars on their careers; the Hollywood Bowl (1922) designed by Frank Lloyd Wright, which was the world's largest amphitheatre; the Huntington Library (1928) with its public art gallery and museum; and the Long Beach Pike with its flamboyant amusement park. Old landmarks were converted to new attractions: Riverside's Mission Inn inaugurated its sentimental mission play productions (1923), and Venice was converted from a cultural conglomerate to a children's playground paradise. Entrepreneurs developed popular special attractions, notably the alligator farm, the ostrich farm, and the famous Knott's Berry Farm. This rich diversity of activities scattered throughout the wide Los Angeles basin produced what Carey McWilliams terms "a slight case of cultural confusion." Probably none of the nation's metropolises epitomize as well as Los Angeles the idea of mass entertainment and recreation in a plebeian society.

B. CULTURE

THE SETTING

The impact of industrial and urban forces accelerated the growth and preeminence of a consumer culture oriented to middle-class tastes and values. Industry in alliance with technology developed the movies and radio as the chief media for mass entertainment. They were also major instruments in propagating urban values. Their programs originally played on rural themes (farm stories, hick jokes, and country music) but by the mid-1920's shifted increasingly to urban themes (city dramas, crime, sophisticated comedy, jazz), though sentimental music and western dramas continued as staple fare. Families clustered around the home radio to listen to favorite programs with commercial breaks for business firms to advertise their products. They stocked their home libraries with assorted books, including "best sellers" popularized by book clubs (for example, Book of the Month, 1926). Mark Sullivan claims that books reached more Americans in the 1920's than at any previous time. The unprecedented mass production of paperback books, phonograph records, and art reproductions made classical and popular works available to middle- and low-income groups which previously were confined to elite and prosperous elements. The consumer culture went hand in hand with mass society—both were well-fed products of business and industry. Their impact shaped the direction of developments in education, literature, religion, and other cultural areas.

The emerging new order brought strong reaction from dissidents who protested in the 1920's. Many who had been enraptured earlier with Progressive idealism became thoroughly disillusioned with the postwar world. They were unhappy with Americans abandoning reform and internationalism and embracing the business ideology of material success. Sinclair Lewis exposed this obsession of Middle America with business ways in biting satire. His *Babbitt* (1922) was a small town real estate broker who, tired of the business treadmill, went to the city for a fling in bohemian and radical circles, then returned to the smug contentment of middle-class respectability (hence babbitry). Disenchanted artists and writers gravitated to New York's Greenwich Village or left "uncivilized America" for bohemian and cosmopolitan ways. Styled the Lost Generation by Gertrude Stein, a Californian whose Paris salon attracted many American expatriates, they expressed extreme disillusionment. One of them, Ernest Hemingway, caught their mood in *The Sun Also Rises* (1926), which tells of such a group in Paris who drown themselves in liquor to forget the complicated world, sober up and get drunk again when they realize the world is as complicated as ever. Scholars also took their swipe at the business-oriented society. John Dewey was a representative of the unreconstructed liberals. In *Individualism Old and New* (1930) he castigated the perverted individualism of business-minded leaders and called for a planned society under public control as an alternative to the "collectivism of business."

ANALYSIS

Education

Progressive education was the pervading spirit of the school system in California as elsewhere in the nation. As a historian of the movement, Lawrence Cremin tells us, progressive education was "American Progressivism writ large . . . a many-sided effort to use the schools to improve the lives of individuals" in a puzzling urban–industrial society. It carried earlier reforms to their logical conclusion: professionally trained teachers tailoring instruction to different types of children for developing their capacities and abilities in a classroom environment. The school would be the model of society (a Dewey concept) and the curriculum would emphasize vocational training with courses focusing on health, family, and community life. The result was a wide application of experimental ideas, many mild but some extreme. Progressive education not only brought about a drastic transformation of the school system but also affected all levels of education and evoked political–social repercussions. Crusaders for progressive education fought each other and defenders of the conventional school system in countless battles in school districts, the legislature, and Congress. The complex movement was caricatured as a "Bohemian school where children run wild in orgies of naturalistic feeling," doing injustice to many tough-minded scholars and administrators who sought realistic solutions to the perplexing problems of society. Progressive educators and their allies attempted to use the schools in remaking society. They saw in the schools the key to social progress.

Primary and Secondary Schools

The Johnson Administration laid foundations with such measures as providing for the nonpartisan election of local school boards furnishing free state-printed textbooks to local school districts (both 1911), and also converting the state board of education from an elective to an appointive body (1913). The 1920's were a "golden age" for the public school system. School finances were revamped (1921) by replacing corporation and special school taxes with a broader setup in which school funds were raised from the local property tax and state funds (allocated to school districts on the basis of student attendance). The state educational hierarchy underwent reorganization twice (1921 and 1927) to take on its modern form: a ten-member board of education as the governing body for the state department of education, and the state superintendent of public instruction as the board's executive officer. The newly created state department expanded greatly with generous budgets and increased personnel. Under the dynamic Will Wood, a progressive educator who rose through the ranks to be state superintendent (1919–1927), public education advanced on all fronts with the big push of a powerful education coalition comprising teacher groups like California Teacher Association and California Federation of Teachers (an AFL affiliate formed in 1919), the state PTA (incorporated 1923), university groups like UC and Stanford, and diverse allies. In the mid-1920's Governor Richardson, with the backing of business groups like the conservative California Taxpayers Association, denounced education as "extravagance . . . gone riot," and slashed the education budget. State Superintendent Wood rallied education forces in a hard-hitting counterattack that not only forced the governor to retreat but also carried through education reforms. Progressive education in the 1920's was in its heyday.

During the Depression years of the 1930's, counties and school districts faced a serious financial crisis that forced severe school retrenchments. The state bailed them out in the Riley Tax Plan (1933) which abolished county taxes and increased state support. Local school superintendents and boards resolved their problems with ingenious solutions. For example, Pasadena's superintendent John Sexson introduced the 6–4–4 plan (six years of elementary school, four years of junior high, and four years of junior college), which sustained the city's quality education. The war years compounded Depression difficulties with additional burdens on the state's educational system. California's three decades of advances in education placed the state clearly in the vanguard of the nation's best public school systems.

Colleges and Universities

The University of California after 1910 expanded in new directions. Wheeler's regime was marked by a "golden age" for undergraduate students, rapid development of research programs under prominent scholars and scientists, and broadening educational and professional services for the public. The president had built too well (so UC chronicler Verne Stadtman tells us), for the university soon outgrew his paternalistic, autocratic style and its original campus. The board of regents was reorganized into a more effective governing body by a constitutional amendment (1918) which enhanced its political independence and provided the university with greater flexibility for future growth. The faculty had gained stature in size and prestige from its research contributions and public services, which became integral rather than auxiliary university functions, and exerted greater influence in university affairs after its academic senate reorganization (1916). Southern California's rapid growth prompted local leaders to press for a branch or duplicate of the university in the Southland. After the 1919 legislature approved the conversion of Los Angeles Normal as a southern branch, it took a decade to overcome various difficulties before UC developed its southern branch at Westwood, to become UCLA.

Student life took on a new dimension. Students went through the familiar academic cycle of class lectures, laboratory experiments, library study, and examinations in wide-ranging curricula. They became more preoccupied, however, with extracurricular activities like student government, varsity sports (some became national or Olympic champions), fraternity–sorority socials, club affairs, and collegiate fads (Cal students vied for the national goldfish-swallowing record). The charge that the new student breed was less studious and more frivolous belied the record of outstanding graduates like author Irving Stone, efficiency expert Lillian Gilbreth (immortalized by her children in *Cheaper by the Dozen*), chemist Glenn Seaborg, economist John Galbraith, public administrator John Gardner, oil tycoon J. Paul Getty, corporation executive Paul Davies, government leader Earl Warren, and university president Robert Sproul.

When Robert Sproul came to the post in 1930, UC acquired its most effective modern president. Sproul was a business manager rather than an academic man like his predecessors. He was a UC alumnus (the first to be president), UC's top fiscal administrator, and a popular figure. Sproul took over a complex university, performing different functions on far-flung campuses, and built it into a more cohesive unit with a well-defined purpose, thereby updating Gilman's comprehensive university idea. In place of Wheeler's outworn concept of the university as a close-knit family, Sproul advocated the concept of "One Great University" under centralized administration extended over widely scattered affiliates and branches. Where critics hit university trends toward dispersion, professionalism, and specialization, Sproul made a virtue of the university's size and diversity. With a heterogeneous faculty, student body, and board of regents, Sproul became the personification and living reality of university unity. Throughout the trying Depression and war years, he provided leadership that enabled the university to surmount formidable problems while sustaining its status as the world's largest university of national prominence. The university had become a viable force in California life. It was indeed a mirror of its society in modern setting.

Journalism

Personal journalism gave way to business journalism as powerful egocentric publishers were superseded by business-minded publishers. The passing of the old order was marked by publishers who made heavy investments for expanded operations and faced ruinous competition, mounting costs, and unsteady revenues. This situation accelerated the consolidation movement by which newspaper chains purchased, merged, and eliminated papers for improved operations and business profits.

Frank Munsey, a self-made financier who set out to build an all-powerful chain monopoly, shook up the New York scene by purchasing and juggling major papers. Among the survivors were the Reids, who merged their *Herald* (1925) into their *Tribune*, and the Sulzberger family, who kept intact their prestigious, prosperous *Times*. E. W. Scripps's great national chain passed (1922) to his son and his editor–manager, Roy Howard, who expanded it as the Scripps–Howard chain, absorbing important papers like Pulitzer's *World* (1931) into the nation's strongest chain. W. R. Hearst, Scripps's chief rival, built his chain by wholesale newspaper acquisition to become the world's largest chain by the early 1930's, but business setbacks forced him to relinquish control to a management group at the end of the decade. The patterns accentuated a trend toward a smaller number of papers controlled by a few wealthy owners; exceptions aside, their conservatism became more pronounced with prosperity.

Hearst was an anachronism of personal and business journalism, an outdated version of the old-style powerful, eccentric publisher. He used his newspaper empire to influence local politics in California and New York (see Chapter 14) and to promote his ambitions for the United States presidency, wielding powerful political influence in Democratic party politics. Where Pulitzer and Scripps personified dignified liberalism, and Robert McCormick (Medill's grandson) identified with personal crusades, Hearst crusaded with fanatical zeal for varied causes that eventually found him on both sides of major issues. He fought rivals with ruthless stubborness, as in the bitter Chicago showdown fight with McCormick's *Tribune* where both men used gangsters for newspaper truck deliveries, with the inevitable street warfare. From his famous San Simeon castle in California he personally directed his newspaper empire along with other far-flung business enterprises—as so memorably portrayed by Orson Welles in the movie *Citizen Kane*. For a half-century he was a powerful figure in public affairs, an intriguing and complex personality who was loved and hated for his causes, often by the same people.

California journalism was shaped by the nationwide consolidation and chain movements. Hearst and Scripps continued their battles with each other and with local publishers in the state's metropolitan areas and rural communities. The Scripps empire, in the wake of family quarrels and the founder's death (1926), was partially dismembered as West Coast papers eventually evolved into a separate Scripps League headed by E. W.'s grandson John. In San Francisco, Michael de Young absorbed Spreckels's *Call* (1913); his son-in-law and heir, George Cameron, hired outstanding editors, like old-time Chester Rowell in the 1920's and young, brilliant Paul Smith in the 1930's, who attempted to build the *Chronicle* into a West Coast version of the *New York Times*. The *Chronicle* managed to sustain its leadership against Scripps's *News* and Hearst's homegrown *Examiner* and the latter's *Call-Bulletin* (brought and merged in 1931). In Oakland, Joseph Knowland after rounding out his congressional career acquired the *Tribune*, which led the Hearst and Scripps papers there. In Los Angeles, Otis's *Times* passed on to his son-in-law and heir, editor Harry Chandler, and Earl's *Express* came under its editor–manager, Edward Dickson. The *Times* built up its lead against the *Express* and forays by Scripps's *Record*, Hearst's local *Examiner* and Cornelius Vanderbilt, Jr's *News*, a local unit of the latter's conservative national tabloid chain. In later realignments, Hearst combined purchased papers into the *Herald* (1922) and the *Express* (1934), while Manchester Boddy, a creative, youthful publisher, acquired the *News* and its rival *Record* to cut an important niche in local journalism. In the Central Valley, the McClatchys began building their *Sacramento Bee* into a regional chain with *Bee* papers in Fresno and Modesto to head off Scripps and Hearst papers there.

Newspaper publishers exerted powerful influence in local and state public affairs. The *San Francisco Chronicle*, *Los Angeles Times*, and *Oakland Tribune* by the 1920's constituted the Big Three of the Republican press, which together could reputedly swing election contests in the then virtually one-party state. The younger generation of talented publishers was exemplified by Smith in San Francisco and Boddy in Los Angeles; they reflected a strong sense of newspaper professionalism and civic responsibility. Despite monopolistic tendencies of urban newspapers, California seemed to have a fairly flexible newspaper setup which allowed for wide dissemination of conservative and liberal views on public issues of the day.

Literature

In the wake of changing America, writers experimented with forms and techniques to find a literary expression compatible with the maturing industrial society. The realist movement divided into what scholar

Robert Richards calls different tempers: realism which represented actual society, naturalism which analyzed the evils of society, impressionism which emphasized moods and sensations to reveal the reality of experience, and expressionism which used symbolism, psychology, and different narrative techniques to show reality. Writers showed a tendency to hop-skip-and-jump among these categories. Some blended in, or even resorted entirely to, romanticism.

California literature became immersed in the national and international mainstream. Local writers who became involved in national and international literary movements include Gertrude Stein, who expatriated herself to Paris where she maintained a famous literary salon, and Robert Frost, who moved to New England to become its representative poet. Others who made their mark and then moved east include playwrights Sherwood Anderson and Sidney Howard, and writers like John Steinbeck and William Saroyan. Some established writers, like Theodore Dreiser, F. Scott Fitzgerald, and Margaret Mitchell, came and stayed briefly to have a fling at movie scenarios, while others, like Henry Miller and Upton Sinclair, settled permanently, and Dreiser returned late in life. Among the many foreign writers who left their mark were Aldous Huxley and Thomas Mann, who made their homes in Southern California, and visiting Britons like J. B. Priestley and Evelyn Waugh. All had an impact on California writers.

San Francisco and Los Angeles suffered diminished stature as regional centers of outstanding local-color schools—urbanization evidently sapped their vitality. In San Francisco, Ina Coolbrith, belatedly honored as California's poet laureate (1915), spent her last years as matriarch of a local group which attempted to keep alive the memory of famous pioneer writers. With Coolbrith's passing in 1928, newcomers with a cosmopolitan outlook, like critic and poet Kenneth Rexroth, took over the local literary scene. Creative writers drifted to Carmel where Mary Austin and Jack London (around 1903) had paved the way for a congenial colony for their kind. UC—Berkeley had in its faculty outstanding writers like Mark Schorer and George Stewart. In Los Angeles, the passing of the Lummis group coincided with the arrival of the movie colony. Movie producers and directors exploited talented writers with high salaries for film plots and scenarios, engulfing creative writing in a devastating commercialism. Many creative writers fled the Hollywood circuit for Laguna Beach and other lesser sanctuaries in Southern California. Between the northern and southern retreats were

Big Sur and Salinas, where Robinson Jeffers and John Steinbeck broke ground.

Jeffers was a poet known for his originality and independence. After attending schools in Pennsylvania and abroad, he completed his education at Occidental College and the University of Southern California, and spent the remainder of his life around Carmel and Big Sur. A man of cultivated tastes, he developed a lyrical love of scenery and intense feelings against merciless nature, violent people, and a cruel society. He wrote feelingly: "The seafog was coming up the ravine, fingering through the pines, the air smells of the sea . . . my girl and my dog were with me." *Give Your Heart to the Hawks* (1933) is a tragedy of a ranch family on the Sur coast destroyed by sex and violence, a parody of the Biblical Cain and Abel story. In his *Shine, Perishing Republic* he begins with:

> While this America settles in the mould of its vulgarity,
>> heavily thickening to empire,
> And protest, only a bubble in the molten mass, pops and sighs out,
>> and the mass hardens,

and ends by saying:

> And boys, be in nothing so moderate as in love of man, a clever
>> servant, insufferable master.
> There is the trap that catches noblest spirits, that caught
>> —they say—God, when he walked on earth.

Although Jeffers suffered harsh criticism of his style and themes, Lawrence Powell says he caught the "power and glory, the strength and tenderness and a prophetic vision"—one might add, especially for us today.

Steinbeck was a novelist famed for his socio-economic themes. Born in the Salinas Valley and educated at Stanford, he devoted his life to writing, often working at laboring jobs for background material. In his delightful stories *Tortilla Flat* (1935) and *Cannery Row* (1944), he portrays Mexican-Americans in a life of robust living, getting bread and wine without degrading themselves by working at a job—whimsically satirizing middle-class mores. In the tradition of Jackson's *Ramona* and Norris's *Octopus*, he wrote *Grapes of Wrath* (1939), as an anthologist team puts it, "a classic statement of California's hazy conscience over the maldistribution of wealth." *Grapes of Wrath*, for which Steinbeck received the Pulitzer Prize, is an epic chronicle detailing the plight of destitute farmers during the Depression who fled from Oklahoma's "Dust Bowl" to California's promised land, only to find organized hostility, exploitation, and tragedy. While he won acclaim for later stories on such diverse subjects as casual laborers (*Of Mice and Men*, (1937) and Norwegian resistance to the Nazi occupation (*The Moon is Down*, 1942), many critics feel he never matched the literary peak of *Grapes of Wrath*, after leaving California for the East. Like Bret Harte he was played out after he had worked his "golden vein."

Jeffers and Steinbeck are generally regarded as California's most prominent writers of the period. Appropriately reflecting upon the diversity of the state's population, one was an immigrant who remained and the other a native who left. One wrote introspectively of strong passions of nature and its impact on the life of man, the other was an extrovert who wrote with deep understanding of society and the impact of its forces on men's lives. Both shared common traits: they found their genius in the Monterey area on California's central coast; they exploited rural and agrarian workingman themes; they expressed a warm humanism and a love of humanity in their works without being overwhelmed by their skepticism and their sometimes pessimistic mood. They seemed to be reaching for universality in their writings in contrast with the regionalism of the earlier local-color schools. Both men are genuine products of California's many-sided society.

California became a haven for leaders of those distinctive American genres, the western and detective stories. Cowboy or western stories reached their high point with Harold Bell Wright, whose immensely popular classic, *The Winning of Barbara Worth* (1911), fictionalized the Imperial reclamation story. Stewart Edward White and Zane Grey told of frail easterners toughened by cowboy experiences and the hard desert environment. The detective story, which gained popularity after 1920, updated the Poe tradition by creating sleuths who solved "whodunit" mysteries in fast-paced suspense stories. Dashiell Hammett, a former private investigator, created the urbane Nick Charles and tough-guy Sam Spade (made famous in the movies by Humphrey Bogart). Erle Stanley Gardner quit law practice to write best-selling stories of Perry Mason, a clever Los Angeles defense attorney (popularized by Raymond Burr on television), whose trial cases were sometimes required reading for law school students. Western and detective story writers attained wide popularity for their books, and some of their fictional characters became stars in the movies.

Critics decried the declining quality of literary works caused by the callous exploitation of writers and the rabid commercialization of the mass reader market for entertainment thrills. Others pointed to the democratization of literature and its reorientation to the needs of a maturing urbanized society, well exemplified in California's literary trends.

Religion

Religion felt deteriorating effects from the impact of the maturing urban–industrial order. Protestantism reached its peak around 1910. Crowded churches, strong missionary activity, and religious–social reforms reflected the high tide of moral idealism and religious devotion to "win the world for Christ in this generation." The moral and religious enthusiasm of the Social Gospel movement which gave Progressive reform its crusading fervor was played out by World War I. Disaffected Protestants hastened the decline, notably Negro groups which broke away to form their own churches, and Holiness-type churches like the Seventh-Day Adventists, Church of God, and Assemblies of God (1914), which surged forward with new vitality. Los Angeles continued to be the "radiating center" for black Pentecostalism (Seymour's mission, see Chapter 13), which extended across the nation. Most conspicuous of such Holiness churches were Jehovah's Witnesses, a revitalized group which preached immediate salvation or fiery damnation; they won notoriety for refusing to salute the American flag.

Even more significant than these shifts in church organization, according to religious historian Winthrop Hudson, were the major religious camps oriented to theological and sociological issues of the times. They included liberal or progressive denominations affiliated with the National Council of Churches (organized 1908) which stressed "cooperative. Protestantism" in adjusting their faith to the changing conditions, the Adventist–Holiness coalition which emphasized fundamental doctrine and practices, and assorted independents like the Lutherans. In the Protestant realignment the Baptists passed the Methodists, with the Lutherans a surprising third, in the long list of proliferated denominations. The Catholics, Jews, and Eastern Orthodox gained many converts from the new immigrants, but they too had serious, painful conservative–liberal conflicts, especially over use of the native tongue and customs in worship services.

In the disillusionment and insecurity that beset the American people in the 1920's and 1930's, Protestantism went into decline. Out of the reactionary mood that emerged after World War I came a rejection of the social gospel and reaffirmation of religious orthodoxy. It fitted well with the temper of patriotic sentiment and political conservatism of the 1920's, as expressed in the slogan "Back to Christ, the Bible, and the Constitution." The sign of the times was seen in the dismal failure of the highly touted Interchurch World Movement (1920–1921), the "Americanization" of the Catholic, Jewish, and Eastern Orthodox churches, and the dramatic rise of the Fundamentalist Movement. The Fundamentalists (a term coined in 1920) were primarily religious conservatives who were alarmed by the moral laxity and religious deemphasis, and battled to restore Biblical authority and orthodox doctrine in their churches, often with fanatic belligerency. The Fundamentalist–Liberal showdown in the famous 1925 "Monkey Trial" involving a Tennessee biology teacher acted out a "national comedy" over the primacy of the Bible over Darwinian evolution. The trial discredited the Fundamentalists and demoralized even liberal forces, despite their token victory.

In the religious recession that occurred after 1925 the churches struggled valiantly to stem membership losses and public apathy. Churches with sedate and prosperous members constructed Gothic edifices to maintain a dignified, prestigious appearance. Less secure churches resorted to huckstering methods to sell religion. Ministers were told "Early to bed and early arise, preach the gospel and advertise," which they did with snappy slogans like "Be a Sport—Come to Church" and "Worship Increases Your Efficiency." Churches that employed specialists to recruit members, raise funds, and expand social services acquired a professional, bureaucratic character which improved their efficiency but undercut the volunteer work and grassroots sentiment that had been the traditional strength of church organization. By the end of the 1930's, the seminaries, then the churches, experienced a reawakening of public interest in religion which was accelerated during World War II.

California manifested local variations of these national developments, usually in more intensive form because of its accelerated urban–industrial forces and heavy immigration flow. Southern California was the focus of religious ferment which gave rise to so many different religious cults and sects that it emerged as a world center for them. Forerunners were the theosophists in the person of New Yorker Katherine Tingley, who set up international headquarters near San Diego (see Chapter 13), and the New Thought movement, the "Boston craze," which reached Los Angeles via San Francisco. They ranged from Krotona, another theosophist group in Hollywood (1911), then Ojai (1920); the Rosicrucians, a secret order of European medieval origin, with branches in San José (1912, a world center) and Oceanside; Abdul Baha's Baha'i, a Persian cult (1912); Paramananda's Vedanta retreat at La Crescenta (1923); to Yogananda's Self-Realization Fellowship in Los Angeles (1925). The latter two Hindu swamis in America had their counterparts in American Christian missionaries in India.

Such movements got wide attention. By the 1920's Los Angeles was a "breeding place and rendezvouz of freak religions." There were imported and native cults (new organizations) and sects (offsprings of parent organizations) which centered on colorful leaders preaching esoteric doctrines and practicing bizarre rites in what Carey McWilliams calls "exaggerated religiosity." Their dogmas were metaphysical excursions into mystical, psychic, and occult realms. Their worship services featured ancient deities and exotic incantations in Oriental settings. They attracted people from all walks of life, particularly the elderly and indigent, with creeds ranging from love of humanity to fear of damnation and with fads like health foods, vegetarianism, and yoga. These pseudo-religious movements usually consisted of a small group of dedicated followers who attracted crowds of curious and interested spectators which sometimes developed into enormous audiences. Among the largest and most colorful in the 1920's was the Los Angeles-based Four Square Gospel founded by Aimee Semple McPherson, a magnetic personality who capitalized on sensational stunts to promote her streamlined version of faith healing and Christ's imminent return. The most conspicuous in the 1930's was I AM, a personality cult which McWilliams describes as "a witch cauldron of the inconceivable, the incredible and the fantastic . . . a hideous phantasm." *Life* magazine reported (1935) of Los Angeles: "This lovely place, cuckoo land, is corrupted with an odd community giddiness . . . nowhere else do eccentrics flourish in such close abundance. Nowhere do spirtual and economic panaceas grow so lushly." The phenomenon of such movements is perhaps best explained by historian W. W. Sweet, who reminds us of religious corruption among migrating people deriving from loosened ties with traditional faiths. Cult movements generally moved westward and Los Angeles was the last stop.

Meanwhile, orthodox churches were active in less dramatic efforts to revitalize church activities. Larger churches built huge edifices in variegated styles, like Gothic-style Grace Cathedral in San Francisco and Los Angeles's St. John's in Romanesque and B'nai B'rith in Byzantine. Pasadena paced Southern California cities whose churches vied with one another in building imposing edifices on downtown streets and extending social activities to different adult and youth groups. When confronted with the controversial race issue during World War II, Pasadena Presbyterian's enlightened minister (Eugene Carson Blake) publicly welcomed Japanese and other racial groups to worship services. Southern California churches won some notoriety with bizarre slogans, extensive billboard advertising, and other brazen huckstering methods for recruiting members and funds, which only reflected their determination to survive the difficult times.

Science and Technology

American science and technology, in step with urban industrialism, reached maturity after 1910. They acquired something of a godlike posture from the public belief that they were the master keys for unlocking life's mysteries and for remedying problems of society. Science became an independent well-defined profession built upon substantial foundations. It developed a broad base of operations, well financed and strongly supported by industry and government. Scientists not only increased greatly in number (from about 5000 in 1910 to 25,000 in 1940) but were better trained and enjoyed enormous prestige. In campaigning for funds for expanded research, they emphasized utilitarian aspects that appealed to foundation, industry, and government contributors, thus closing the gap between basic and applied science. Their discoveries were dramatically changing people's lives like aerodynamics in aircraft, electrodynamics in electronics, and virology research in medical science. Technology emerged as a profession comprising college or university-trained technicians in chemistry, engineering, physics, and other sciences. The new technology, so writer Peter Drucker tells us, was much more than applied science merely to produce improved products and processes for industry. It produced innovations that altered people's lives, notably mass production and automation as major precursors of social change.

The government role in science and technology, like the rapidly rising foundation, industry, and university programs, continued to be conspicuous. The Progressives, strong proponents of utilizing government science to resolve problems in society, complemented the federal scientific establishment. Scientist administrators in the role of bureau chiefs received generous funds from Congress, recruited technicians through the civil service system, and launched programs that served industrial needs. The representative figure was Gifford Pinchot of the United States Forest Service, a talented scientist, administrator, and politician, who established a scientific forestry program oriented to the productive uses of land and resources for the public good rather than merely for industry needs. After the outbreak of World War I, California's astronomer–scientist, George Hale, headed the move that set up the National Research Council for coordinating the activities of scientists at home and abroad for the Allied war effort. During the 1920's the NRC under Hale became the chief dispenser of Carnegie and Rockefeller grants for peacetime projects. While the Smithsonian Institution suffered from lagging public support, federal agencies pioneered social science research in fields like agricultural economics (1921) and the federal bureaucracy (1923, Brookings Institute). Herbert Hoover, an engineer by profession, spurred government encouragement of industry research while serving as secretary of commerce and later as president. It remained for the Roosevelt Administration to bring government science to its peak. Spearheaded by Agriculture Secretary Henry Wallace, a talented scientist–administrator–politician figure like Pinchot, spurred the application of science and technology to New Deal programs for resolving socio-economic problems of the Depression. During World War II, scientists occupied strategic positions in United States defense and military programs for the Allied effort.

California became closely involved with national and international science. The universities and colleges expanded their science departments and institutes with combined federal, state, foundation, and industry funds to attain preeminence in the varied fields of life, social, and physical sciences. They lured world-renowned scientists like Einstein, who served in temporary positions, and Robert Millikan, who came from Chicago (1921) to head the California Institute of Technology, where he won awards for electronics and cosmic ray discoveries. They provided the atmosphere which enabled talented scientists to make diverse contributions to international science, notably UC's physicist Ernest Lawrence, physiochemist Glenn Seaborg, and biochemist Joel Hildebrand; along with Cal Tech's physicist Lee Dubridge. In astronomy, George Hale, long-time director of the Carnegie-backed Mt. Wilson observatory with its 100-inch telescope, spearheaded construction of Mt. Palomar's 200-inch telescope, the world's largest (completed 1948). Under Cal Tech's administration, both observatories made significant solar and stellar discoveries for international science. Landmark developments in the social sciences were marked by UC's Samuel May in public administration, Stewart Daggett in transportation, Ewald Grether in business administration; Stanford's Ellwood Cubberly in education, and Lewis Terman in educational psychology; and UCLA's Roscoe Pound in jurisprudence. The state government's scientific establishment, broadened from agricultural to industrial research after 1910, followed the federal pattern but did not achieve the preeminence of university, industry, and foundation scientific endeavors.

California's technology presents a similar story of innovation and progress. We have already seen the valuable role of inventors and innovators in advancing technology in agriculture, forestry, mining, manufacturing, public utilities, transportation, and trade. Electronics was a dramatic example of this many-sided development. Federal Telegraph, the nation's pioneer electronics firm and for many years the largest. continued to spawn many outstanding inventors from its laboratory, Stanford's Frederick Terman (Lewis's son) trained electrical engineers who formed their innovative firms in the Bay Area, thus sustaining the cooperative university—industry relations. With World War II came the flood of federal funds and urgency of military demands expanded its scientific endeavors to produce radar, sonar, and supersonic technology which helped revolutionize military warfare and establish electronics as a major state industry. Technology, like science, had become vital for the survival of national society.

Philosophical Views

American philosophy after 1910 traveled a difficult path made by a changing society. It came into its own as an independent field with its own organization and methods. It gained a new freedom in speculative thought and a greater concern for man in real society. Philosophers were switching their allegiance from religion to science, relying more on secular reason than theocratic beliefs, though some continued to work within religious concepts. Like the new scientists, their outlook was more humanistic and utilitarian. They were more concerned with ethical values than with religious or strictly scientific values, focusing attention on man's behavior in the world rather than on his relations with God or on his strictly laboratory discoveries.

Consequently, philosphers differed widely in their diagnosis of man and society. This led to varied reinterpretations and new directions. Their springboards in the main were Royce's idealism and James's pragmatism. Idealism as a dominant force waned with the Progressive decline (Royce came to his end in 1916) but it continued to find expression in different schools, like the subjective or mental idealism (for example, the Berkeleyans) and objective or speculative idealism. Pragmatism with its emphasis on nature and human experience found broader expression and wide application among the new philosophers who took root after 1910 and flowered by the 1930's. They shared a pragmatic humanistic outlook and emphasized an attitude, an approach, and a program rather than a static philosophical system or doctrine as their predecessors had done, focusing attention on the dynamic character of a changing society. They spearheaded movements of realism and naturalism with their several schools, laying the foundation for the social philosophy which included a theory of social change. By so doing they left traditional philosophy, which explained the way men and society *ought* to be, for a philosophy that was oriented to the way men and society are.

The foremost philosopher of the period was John Dewey, who left the education field at the University of Chicago in 1904 for philosophy at Columbia University in New York. Dewey, in reaction to idealism, had drifted into naturalism to become a leading exponent of experimental naturalism. Dewey was James's disciple but differed from his mentor on important points. Where James focused on the individual as the guiding voice of society. Dewey stressed social control and action; to him individuals were products of changes in society. Dewey spoke of faith in human nature and progress in society, stressing man's capacity to adjust to changes in society.

Dewey's ideas have special relevance to social theory and the real world of the American political economy. Democracy was more than a form of government, it was a mode of living based on fundamental ideas like individual freedom and the order of society. Where Marx emphasized class conflicts, Dewey stressed the interaction of pressure groups based on the vested interests of associated individuals—the special-interest groups in our story of California history. Liberty and equality are not natural rights, as Locke and Jefferson proclaimed, but the "fruits in the life of the individual derived from fraternal cooperation in a democratic society." Men live together in voluntary association and work out their programs through democratic processes. Government acts as the servant of various volunteer groups with diversified interests and regulates them only to prevent one from frustrating the others. Individual freedom in society thrives on fraternal cooperation.

Dewey's concept has broad application to the American experience. Progressivism and the New Deal arose in response to the inadequacy of the laissez faire idea of individual freedom without government regulation. Both sought to reconstruct institutions of the political economy to remedy the situation. Where the Progressives focused on improving the democratic processes, the New Dealers concentrated on action programs. The New Dealers, more than the Progressives, recognized that individual freedom and social security go together; hence their government reforms which expanded programs for economic security and social welfare to raise and sustain the citizen's standard of living. The Roosevelt Administration applied experimental reforms to reconstruct institutions for a more effective functioning of the political economy. Dewey's philosophy was applied extensively in education, law, public administration, sociology, and other fields. His ideas are reflected in California's historical experience—so much so that one is tempted to regard California as a social laboratory for Dewey's ideas and practices.

SUMMARY

California became immersed in the national mainstream after the turn of the century. California's political economy was directly shaped by actions of the federal government: presidential politics and policies, congressional programs, and court decisions. All of these aided in the development of California's mixed agricultural-manufacturing economy. Federal regulatory and remedial programs during the two world wars and the Depression profoundly affected socio-economic developments in the several ways. The impetus provided by eastern-based firms helped broaden California's manufacturing base and develop the state as a regional unit integrated in the nation's market economy. Eastern financiers and industrialists played conspicuous roles in the state's economic development. Californians competed and collaborated with them in developing regional and national markets. By 1945 California was inextricably involved in the national political economy.

California became increasingly oriented to new business and manufacturing trends which contributed to a maturing agrarian–industrial economy. Innovative entrepreneurs, professional managers, engineers, and scientists were key figures in paving the way for the state's expanded industrial development. In each industry area, dominant groups battled each other and smaller contenders for their share of the market. They obtained government aid and imposed industry restraints, like franchises and licenses, not only to promote enterprises but also to regulate markets for sustaining continued expansion. Eventually the state, then the federal government, regulated market activities to insure fair competition among contending groups, especially in business, farming, labor, and transportation. California emerged as a regulated society governed by rules imposed by government and industry.

In the course of four and a half decades, Californians developed the apparatus for managing the increasingly complex political economy. Government reorganization was undertaken periodically to adjust political institutions to the changing conditions wrought by the expanding agrarian and manufacturing industries. As the political party apparatus was dismantled by reform forces, corporate groups, followed by labor, farmer, and other organized special interests, developed the legislative lobby as an effective device, directly soliciting public support for candidates and laws (initiatives and referendums) in election campaigns, and applied pressure to the legislature for desired measures. Organized special interests emerged as the prime movers in governmental affairs and industry operations. Powerful corporate groups having inherent advantages of size and money were able to sustain their dominant position, and other organized special-interest groups found effective ways to counter them and improve their position. Independent farmer, business, and manufacturing groups, and later labor unions, developed cooperative and corporate devices for achieving voluntary action usually through industry associations or government agencies. They enlisted state and federal agencies to support them. Organized citizen groups in communities, especially in Southern California, succeeded in persuading government agencies to undertake public projects, like electric power and water supply, taking away from corporate enterprises whatever interest they may have had in that area.

The interplay of these various groups, then, resulted in the development of elaborate public and private apparatus, voluntary and mandatory arrangements, for organized special interest to cooperate and compete in the state's political economy. Unorganized groups, like farm labor and racial minorities, still suffered from discriminatory and exploitive practices of organized groups. Significantly, the state government, and later the federal government, emerged as referees in sustaining a certain balance among all these groups. They also provided public services and facilities to fill in gaps for achieving a better functioning political economy.

The conspicuous feature of this period is California's emergence as an industrial society. The period set the framework for California's modern life style. It developed an updated version of representative government, which stressed organized special interests and periodic governmental reorganization, and a capitalistic economy regulated by voluntary and mandatory arrangements of government and industry. It produced a social order marked by a multigroup elite, a stratified middle class, and ever-widening cultural diversity of its heterogeneous people. Government replaced business as the chief custodian of the public interest. The period also witnessed institutional growth which led to large organizations with hierarchical bureaucracies operated by professional managers, and an urban culture centered on growing cities which was rapidly replacing the rural order. California became symbolic of the young, growing adult already applying restraints of self-discipline.

Overleaf: Minuteman II over the Pacific. A sunset launching of the ICBM missile in a 1967 trial operation at Vandenberg Air Force Base.

VIII   The Challenges of Growth

1945-1975

With the end of World War II, California embarked on a period of unprecedented growth and development. The glittering prospects of business investments, employment opportunities, and good living conditions continued to attract a high influx of people and industries. Towns became cities, and cities expanded into metropolitan areas. Local industries became increasingly interlinked with regional and national industries to serve widely dispersed and expanding markets at home and abroad. Industrial expansion accelerated as small and large enterprises, manned by specialized professionals, technicians, and skilled and unskilled workers, developed ways for cooperating and competing with each other for a profitable share of the growing markets. Government programs became a vital force as local, state, and federal agencies worked in partnership to produce public facilities and services for aiding enterprises and helping people to adjust to new conditions in every major sector of society. The combination of a growing population, expanding industries, and an effective government sustained a dynamic market economy and produced a complex society of enormous vitality. California emerged as the nation's most populous and affluent state. Its spectacular growth provoked major problems resulting from drastic adjustments to changing conditions in the political, economic, and social spheres, adjustments which continually taxed the imagination of leaders and the resources of the state. A turning point came in the 1960's when the state and national leaders had to deal with the serious imbalances of the growing society. The challenges of growth, which had previously focused on expansion during prosperity, were now concerned with contracting forces in the approaching hard times.

---

17 Egalitarian Politics
18 The Managed Economy
19 The Fragmented Society
20 California Prospectus

17 Egalitarian Politics

THE SETTING

The nation in the postwar era experienced rapid and drastic changes brought on by technological forces and a population growth which led to social revolution. While the nation was converting from wartime to peacetime and adjusting to its new role as world leader, major business, farmer, and labor groups established new positions in the postwar society. Before long, dominant groups confronted handicapped industry groups and disadvantaged ethnic, poor, and female elements, who also demanded their rightful place in the affluent society. In California, these varied minority interests acquired talented leaders and developed effective devices for applying group pressure to achieve their aims. They joined forces with sympathetic politicians (usually Democrats), who overcame discriminatory barriers to capture party and government leadership. Government leaders were generally referees in these show-downs between entrenched groups and their contenders, but leaders of public and private institutions also were forced to deal with demands of handicapped and disadvantaged elements. These contending groups were less interested in remaking society to conform to the traditional

Progressive model. They strove primarily to secure the same rights and privileges as dominant groups entrenched in the political economy and a fair share of the power and wealth. The egalitarian spirit and aggressive drive of these minority groups acted as catalysts in postwar politics. To be sure, there were other forces at work, but in California the interplay of dominant and contending groups was so conspicuous and visible that egalitarian politics proved to be a leading trend.

The Party System

Governor Earl Warren developed a brand of politics which was called nonpartisan but was actually bipartisan. His rule profoundly affected the course of party development in the postwar period. The governor relied on his personal organization rather than on the cumbersome regular party machinery to manage his election campaigns, making direct appeals for campaign funds and for public support of his "nonpartisan" programs. By virtue of the personal popularity and prestige resulting from his effective leadership, he was able to retain control of the Republican party machinery. By dissociating himself from the campaigns of party candidates to legislative and other state offices and refusing to align with liberal or conservative factions, he was able to sustain his independence as chief executive and his moderate approach to state affairs. With California's peculiar cross-filing system, Warren was able to follow this course. His independent and bipartisan approach did much to contain factional disputes within his party and to confound Democratic party chieftains in primary and election campaigns.

Warren's departure from the state opened the way for partisan and factional conflicts which led to the elimination of cross-filing and the revival of the two-party system, along with a proliferation of party machinery. In the 1950's the Democrats emerged from their long eclipse as a rejuvenated opposition to the dominant Republicans. Both parties felt the impact of Young Turks—bright, youthful party politicians who outmaneuvered sluggish Old Guard leaders to revitalize the party organization. In the 1960's factionalism badly split both parties and caused further proliferation of party organization. The administration of Edmund Brown, with its frank emphasis on Democratic liberal programs, not only accelerated Republican partisanship but also intensified the conservative–liberal conflicts in both parties. The conservatives and liberals each had confrontations with extremist elements who splintered off to form their own organizations, and each of these spawned still other splinter groups (see below). These factional groups, ranging from reactionaries on the right to radicals on the left, fought dominant conservative–liberal moderates for party and government control. Their battles carried over into the 1970's.

Government System

Warren's administration updated the Progressive concepts of government and reshaped state government in the postwar period. Because he was a long-time, strong, and popular governor, his beliefs became embedded in the governmental process. That the government should serve all the people rather than any particular special-interest group was an article of faith with him. Government should be an active and positive force in serving the needs of the people, and all branches of government should cooperate in administering the public interest. Warren believed in social progress rather than the status quo, recognizing that a growing state with a dynamic political economy needed to keep up with changing conditions. He saw government as a cooperative endeavor of politician and citizen and attempted to develop in his administration a united front of government leaders and open communications with the public to achieve that relationship. He sought the participation of affected groups in formulating government policies and programs and made bipartisan appeals for public support, giving a new dimension to the concept of nonpartisanship. He regarded fiscal control and meritorious appointments as the keys to effective administration of governmental activities, becoming a supporter of scientific management and the professional bureaucracy when both elements were in ascendancy in public affairs. Guided by a pragmatic outlook, he focused on workable solutions of immediate problems, realistic planning for long-range social goals, and piecemeal approaches in making administrative changes and reorganizing government. By his leadership and example, he inspired government leaders and administrators at the state and local level and won wide public confidence.

Governmental activities grew enormously until they permeated the daily lives of people and just about every sector of society as never before. State government was a chief focus of politics, for it shaped basic programs for local governments and served as a principal intermediary for federal domestic programs. The governor was firmly established in his position as chief spokesman of the people and was a leading decision-maker in governmental affairs. His position as chief executive was strengthened by an expanding personal staff for close liaison with public groups, centralized managerial agencies for effective budget, personnel, and program control, and an enlarged state bureaucracy of professionalized agencies for carrying out his programs. He also proved effective as chief legislator, relying primarily on personal appeal and allied legislators to secure his program. The legislature emerged as a remarkably efficient and independent second branch. It further streamlined its organization and procedures and increased staff agencies and other professional services, which enabled legislators to be more the master and less the servant of dominant special interests. The judiciary was likewise strengthened by internal reforms. It emerged as a powerful third body marked by increased prestige and greater proficiency. State government, through administrative reforms and professional services, had vastly improved its ability to manage the complex problems of a growing state. Its performance, however, relied heavily on quality leadership, on cooperative relations among the three branches, and on the public climate.

Governmental affairs at the local level told a similiar story. Local governments grew enormously as counties, cities, and towns expanded government functions and activities and special districts increased in number. These governmental units improved their services through an experienced staff, budget and personnel control, and cooperative relations with neighbor governments. They were able to perpetuate the strong tradition of local home rule through administrative reforms and professional services.

Meanwhile California became thoroughly immersed in the national mainstream. Federal primacy in governmental affairs, established earlier by New Deal and wartime programs, was extended by successive postwar administration domestic programs, from Truman's Fair Deal to Johnson's Great Society. These programs reflected expanded activities at the state level under Warren, Knight, and Brown, and at the local level in pacesetting urban counties and cities like Los Angeles. These governmental programs, aimed primarily at resolving pressing problems of the growing society, ran the gamut from military defense through economic development and social services to urban redevelopment. They accelerated important trends in intergovernmental relations and regionalism—for example, the federal, state, and local governments developed in specific areas arrangements for coordinating their efforts in jointly administering welfare programs. California pioneered in these intergovernmental programs which were popularized as the government partnership. The state emerged as the focus of a regional complex: it comprised distinctive regional units well integrated into the statewide political economy and was itself part of the Far West region, which was integrated into the nation's political economy. This synchronization of the nation's political economy through the government partnership and regional development helped to sustain the postwar prosperity.

California in the course of the postwar period completed its transition from the old-style to new-style politics. It was a difficult and painful passage. People changed from one reference group to another (like school, job, church, clubs) as their status and values changed in the fluid society. Groups proliferated into subgroups and sub-subgroups, producing a maze of conflicting or harmonious group relationships. Group confrontations were as intense as ever and sometimes irreconcilable, and compromise solutions were not always peacefully accepted. The independent voter became significant in state elections. It took

State government and how it grew! Four generations of symbolic buildings: Governor Leland Stanford's home (1862), the state capitol (1874), state office building (between the first two, 1923), and the Resources Building (foreground, 1970).

time and experience to develop workable solutions and relationships—that traditional process of conditioning opposition groups and educating the public to accept reasonable arrangements. State politics became a dynamic process as varied groups competed or cooperated in pursuing programs to preserve their status and integrity in a changing society. Here, then, was a contemporary version of Madison's concept of group conflicts as it operated in modern-day society.

DEVELOPMENT

The Affluent Decades

The United States after 1945 entered a remarkable period of revolutionary developments compounded by the affluence and anxiety of its people. The nation confronted a complicated situation at home and abroad. State and national, foreign and domestic affairs were so intertwined that each could no longer be considered without the other. The wartime alliance of the Allied Powers degenerated into a Cold War (Walter Lippmann's term for hostilities short of military warfare) between the United States and the Soviet Union for supremacy in world affairs. The national economy made a painful but surprisingly successful conversion from wartime to peacetime conditions, chiefly as a result of expanded federal expenditures for foreign-aid programs, military adventures in Korea and Vietnam, national defense facilities, explorations in space, and domestic programs in public works and social reform. The nation experienced an unprecedented prosperity nurtured in wartime and sustained in peacetime, abetted by federal regulatory mechanisms (expanded New Deal agencies) to prevent economic downswings reminiscent of the Great Depression. These developments foreshadowed profound changes and deep conflicts.

The public spotlight in the postwar years focused on the president and his programs. By 1947 the Truman administration had set the nation on its course. It enacted the landmark Employment Act and created a National Economic Council for implementing federal commitment to full employment and a stable economy. It set up a National Security Council to coordinate diplomatic and military policies for fulfilling the nation's foreign commitments. National defense was bolstered by unifying the Armed Services and reorganizing the Army and Navy under a new defense secretary, and by creating an unprecedentedly large peacetime army based on universal military training. The Atomic

Energy Commission (AEC) implemented federal control of nucle-research and development. Congress generally gave bipartisan support to these foreign, defense, and scientific programs.

The president's postwar leadership in domestic programs took on new significance with his increased responsibilities for sustaining economic prosperity and social equilibrium. His programs reoriented older issues to new concepts: the tariff evolved into trade expansion; government regulation of business (antitrust policies) extended to labor, farmer, and other groups; and tax reform became an antiinflation device. President Truman set the pace for social reforms when he launched a broad program to remedy injustices among underprivileged groups in American society. His Fair Deal was a revival of the New Deal in that it extended federal aid for education, health, and welfare (social security), but it put a new stress on federal promotion of civil rights (fair employment practices) and urban renewal (low-cost housing). Successive presidents presented their own versions of these programs. Eisenhower's Moderate Republicanism called for reducing federal centralization and business regulation. Kennedy's New Frontier emphasized civil rights, tax reform, and a "war on poverty." Johnson's Great Society brought to fruition major features of the Kennedy and Truman programs. Congress was sharply divided on these domestic programs, subject as it was to well-organized pressures of business, labor, farmer, and other special-interest groups. The Supreme Court under Earl Warren played a significant role, constituting a powerful positive force in deciding conflicts and emphasizing national direction.

Public policy provided the framework for startling changes in economic and social life. The nation experienced the greatest and longest (1945–1965) period of prosperity in its history. The American people enjoyed the highest per capita income and level of consumption of any people at any time in world history. Yet their anxieties over their affluence and the imbalances and maladjustments in their society prompted historian William Leuchtenburg to characterize the postwar years as "a troubled feast."

Politics of Nonpartisanship

California emerged from the upheaval of World War II with a drastically different and rapidly changing society. The war brought about a greatly expanded government bureaucracy, a broadened industrial economy, and large population dislocations. The state faced a formidable task in converting from wartime to peacetime conditions, dismantling federal–

state war agencies, reorienting industries from defense and military production to civilian production, and meeting the needs of people adjusting to new ways. It was confronted by a huge backlog of unfinished business, long-delayed public works like buildings, dams, and roads, overcrowded public institutions such as hospitals and prisons, and much-needed social services for the aged, handicapped, and unemployed—all had been deferred because of the pressing needs of the Great Depression and World War II. There was a serious employment problem: the labor force was expanded by 750,000 California servicemen and women returning to find jobs, and some 250,000 newcomers, like defense workers and military personnel, who had come as temporary residents during the war and chose to remain. The University of California's government expert, Samuel May, predicted that the state faced the prospect of a postwar depression and unemployment for a million people—however, this prediction did not materialize.

Warren launched a broadly-based comprehensive program of state action for dealing with the multitude of postwar problems resulting from the unprecedented population growth and industrial expansion of wartime. He sponsored a broad, representative state commission (1943) for stabilizing the state's economy, stimulating industrial development, expanding employment, and correcting social maladjustments by improved state services for less fortunate people. The commission within five years made major contributions in promoting and coordinating public and private efforts that helped California avoid the anticipated postwar depression and serious unemployment problem.

Warren also pressed for extensive socio-economic programs and governmental reforms for carrying them out. His programs included wide-ranging measures for tax reduction, expanded public works, extended unemployment insurance, increased social services, better crime enforcement, and improved management of state institutions. However, his programs for compulsory health insurance, minority problems, and conservation fell victim to the pressure politics of opposing special interest groups. Steering wide of comprehensive government reorganization, he concentrated on piecemeal administrative reforms which greatly improved state services. A surplus of revenues arising from wartime savings (the rainy-day fund—see below), coupled with postwar prosperity, presented Warren with a golden opportunity to expand the programs he felt California needed.

Earl Warren's gubernatorial record helped perpetuate the Republican dominance in state politics. He spearheaded the Republican landslide in 1946. He won reelection by capturing the nominations of both parties in the primary elections, being the only governor in the state's history to do so. Among other winners were Goodwin Knight for lieutenant governor, Thomas Kuchel for state controller, William Knowland (whom Warren appointed to the deceased Hiram Johnson's seat in the United State Senate in 1945) for senatorial reelection, and Richard Nixon for a congressional seat. Nixon unseated Jerry Voorhis, the respected liberal Democratic incumbent whom Washington correspondents had voted the best congressman from the West, in a vituperative campaign on the communist issue. In 1948 Warren made his foray into national politics to become Thomas Dewey's running mate in the ill-fated campaign against Truman, who won reelection to the presidency in a surprising upset victory. Warren's favorable exposure in national politics more than offset the stigma of Dewey's defeat.

The Republican tide rolled in again in the 1950 election. Warren won an unprecedented third term by defeating Democratic challenger James Roosevelt, a California congressman and son of Franklin Roosevelt. The Republicans made a sweep of all but one state office and won majorities in both houses of the legislature. Other notable winners included Knight, who rode on Warren's coattails to reelection, Edmund "Pat" Brown, San Francisco Democratic district attorney who won the post of state attorney general, and Nixon, who won the United State Senate race against Helen Gahagan Douglas, liberal congresswoman, with near accusations of communist affiliation. Such "communist smear" tactics, at a time when the nation was in the throes of Wisconsin Senator Joseph McCarthy's reckless anti-communist crusade, earned for Nixon the undying enmity of Democrats. This later helped undermine the bipartisan harmony built up by Warren.

The 1952 election represented a high point for California Republicanism. In the presidential campaign, Warren was the dark-horse candidate in the event of a liberal–conservative deadlock between Dwight Eisenhower, the popular wartime European commander, and Robert Taft, son of the former president and leader of the postwar conservative bloc in Congress. Eisenhower emerged as victor, with Nixon as his running mate, in the intra-party contest and went on to win the national election. Warren appointed Thomas Kuchel, the state controller, to Nixon's vacant seat in the United States Senate and, in time, Kuchel became a strong liberal power in the Senate. Warren reached the summit of his career when Eisenhower selected him to be Chief Justice of the

United States Supreme Court, thereby giving Californians top positions in national leadership.

Nonpartisan politics continued under Warren's successor, Goodwin Knight. As lieutenant governor, Knight had projected a conservative image with his attacks on Warren's fair employment practices and social welfare programs, prompting predictions that he would break clean with Warren's nonpartisanship. As governor, however, Knight hewed to Warren's bipartisan approach; his moderate–liberal stance perpetuated Warren's coalition, renewing the reign of nonpartisan politics in state affairs. He retained most of Warren's appointments, continued Warren's policy of respecting legislative prerogatives, and followed the main line of his predecessor's program without adding to or detracting from it. He cinched his position by securing AFL–CIO support with his prolabor position. In the 1954 election Knight handily defeated Richard Graves, respected executive director of the League of California Cities and Democratic gubernatorial nominee. The Republicans that year made a near sweep of state offices, the reelected Brown being the only Democratic winner. Despite Republican apprehensions concerning his free-wheeling political approaches, Knight proved to be a competent governor and pragmatic politician who likened his philosophy to the ancient saying, "Moderation is best—avoid all extremes."

Meanwhile the Democratic party was experiencing a rejuvenation. Young Turks disenchanted with the party's failure to win elections with their voting majority (Democrats exceeded Republicans in voter registration) set out to circumvent Old Guard leaders and revitalize the party organization. Taking their cue from CRA experience (see below), they built up voluntary local clubs utilized in the 1952 presidential campaign as a formidable grassroots foundation for a statewide federation, and organized formally in 1953 as the California Democratic Council (CDC) headed by Alan Cranston. The CDC spearheaded the cross-filing reform by securing the 1954 law that restored party labels on election ballots. Democratic local and state victories soon closed the gap between Democratic and Republican forces.

The 1958 election was a turning point for both parties and for state politics. William Knowland, who was up for reelection in the senate, chose to run for governor, presumably as a steppingstone to the presidency. Knight angrily resisted the move and campaigned hard for renomination. Party leaders, including Nixon, steered party money away from Knight, finally pressuring him into seeking the senate seat so that Knowland could run for governor. The Democrats by this time had put together a well-oiled organization under united leadership with an attractive slate which included Brown as the gubernatorial standard bearer, Alan Cranston for state controller, and Clair Engle, prominent liberal congressman, for the United States Senate. The election campaign was an extraordinary spectacle of Republican demoralization and Democratic resurgence. Knowland abandoned the successful Warren nonpartisan formula, campaigning hard for a conservative program. His endorsement of antilabor "right to work" legislation alienated party moderates and liberals and sent labor "roaring into the fight" for the Democrats. Brown played the Warren formula, expounding a "responsible liberalism" with favorable reference to the Johnson–Warren tradition in a wide appeal for bipartisan support from those disenchanted with the Republican extremist program and the power politics involved in the "Big Switcheroo" pulled off by Republican leaders. In the election the Democrats made a near sweep of state offices and won a majority in both houses of the legislature. Brown defeated Knowland by more than a million votes, and Engle roundly beat Knight. The postwar era of "Republican nonpartisanship" inaugurated by Warren came to an end. For the second time since the turn of the century, the Democrats were at the helm of state government.

The Return to Partisan Politics

The Brown administration began auspiciously. The governor in his inaugural set the course for "responsible liberalism," which he defined as a liberal government meeting the concerns of the people without catering to special interests, pampering citizens, or threatening state solvency. He declared, "We walk in the giant footsteps" of such memorable governors as Johnson and Warren, setting "our sights to match their achievements." He provided able and energetic leadership, appointing talented men to key positions and relying on Democratic teamwork. He appealed for bipartisan support, selected a Republican businessman (Bert Levit) to be his finance director, retained several Warren–Knight appointees, and emphasized the bipartisan character of his program.

The Democratic administration, exultant after 60 years in the desert, set out to implement the governor's ambitious program. (The Olson administration, which preceded Warren's, had been too brief and controversial to be the real test of Democratic rule as Brown's forthcoming administration would be.) The 1959 legislature enacted 35 of 40 measures recommended by him to set a record of accomplishment comparable to that of the 1911 legislature. Notable were: the abolition of cross-filing to end "legalized nonpartisanship" and restore party responsibility; a Fair Employment Practices Commission to eliminate discrimination in public places; an economic development agency to implement long-range planning for attracting new industries and employment; increases in unemployment insurance and welfare benefits; a consumer council to prevent deceptive advertising practices; a huge bond issue to finance the long-delayed state water project; a master plan for higher education, fair housing, and urban redevelopment; and increased taxes to wipe out the state treasury deficit, balance the budget, and pay for the new programs. Among the defeated measures were a minimum wage law and fair labor standards act, and the abolition of capital punishment—all highly controversial measures. Despite the broad advance of state government on several fronts, the administration programs evoked considerable intra- and inter-party conflict and public controversy, particularly during Brown's second term. Nevertheless, Brown's record places him among the leading governors in administrative and legislative accomplishments—one of the ablest in state history.

Brown had uneven success as a party politician. He was a seasoned politician strong on personal appeal and good intentions but he lacked finesse and skill in political maneuver so that he appeared a bumbler. In the 1960 election he was unable to prevent party leaders from splitting over several national contenders. Democratic disunity helped Nixon carry the state and deprived the Democrats of any party credit for Kennedy's final victory over Nixon. In the 1962 state election Nixon challenged Brown for the governorship. It was to be Nixon's springboard for another chance at the presidency. During the bitter campaign, Nixon talked loftily of national and international issues while Brown hit hard on bread-and-butter state issues and his gubernatorial accomplishments. Brown's upset victory marked him as a "political giant killer."

The year 1964 witnessed a conservative upswing in national and state affairs which focused on the Johnson–Goldwater battle for the presidency. In California the conservative–liberal imbroglio ripped apart both parties, especially in the matter of the senate seat of ailing Clair Engle, soon to die of cancer. The Democratic camp became bitterly divided when Pierre Salinger, a San Francisco journalist and President Kennedy's popular press secretary, flew into the state to beat out Cranston. The Republican camp was swept by aggressive conservative forces which captured party leadership and pushed for George Murphy, a former movie star, who went on to beat Salinger for the senate seat.

The 1966 election brought a major shift in state politics; it resembled the 1958 election with opposite results. The political tide this time ran against the Democratic administration as resurgent Republican conservative forces led by Ronald Reagan attacked Brown's "tired liberalism." Reagan, like Murphy, had been an active amateur in Republican politics during his career as a movie star; he parlayed his lack of government experience into an attractive campaign as a citizen–candidate for governor who would restore sanity in public affairs. The Republicans were able to contain bitter factionalism when the state party chairman issued the 11th commandment ("Thou shalt speak no evil of other Republicans") to candidates in the primaries. Democratic factionalism broke into the open when several gubernatorial candidates launched campaigns of accusation against Brown. Brown nevertheless won his primary, as Reagan did his, but two million votes which had gone to nine other candidates were up for redistribution in the general election.

In the bitter election campaign, Brown and Reagan hit hard at each other's extremist views, but both downplayed their respective liberal and conservative stance to convey middle-of-the-road positions on most state issues. The campaign was complicated by several controversial conservative–liberal ballot propositions, notably fair housing and obscenity. During the "long hot summer" of the campaign, violence erupted over civil rights and urban ghetto incidents. Brown's replay of citing facts and listing his accomplishments was no match for Reagan's glamorous showmanship and attractive rhetoric which promised to end high government spending, cut back excessive welfare benefits, and restore local government and private initiative. Reagan beat Brown by a million votes and the Republicans captured nearly all state offices, while the Democrats retained a bare margin in the legislature. The state's political pendulum, under the force of partisan politics, had swung abruptly from left of center to the far right.

Reagan's administration signaled the return of conservative rule after a 30-year hiatus since Merriam's governorship. Right-wing forces were rejuvenated, for conservatism under a glamorous governor had suddenly become attractive and respectable. The governor, in carefully staged public appearances, projected the image of an aggressive chief executive wasting no time in reconstructing society in the conservative mold. His Creative Society would reduce government expenditures and taxes, cut back social welfare, and downgrade state government in an effort to restore initiative to business, the people, and local government. He made wholesale replacements in state appointments, putting Republican businessmen and other party faithful in top administrative positions and on numerous boards and commissions. He proposed in his budget a 10 percent cut in state expenses, revamping the finance department so that it could better implement reduced costs and operations of state agencies and programs. Within two months of making this proposal, however, he brought in supplemental budget requests which substantially reduced the proposed cuts; in the following year many of his initial budget cuts were restored. Nevertheless he spearheaded cutbacks in mental health, public education, social welfare, and other state programs, shifting such burdens to local governments. Thus the governor proved to be a man of his word in carrying out his campaign pledges.

Reagan's apparently simplistic approaches to complex state problems complicated management of the state's political economy. His manner, coupled with his political inexperience, contrasted sharply with his postwar predecessors who managed public affairs through tempered approaches, judicious compromises, and pragmatic solutions. His appointment of businessmen with little or no government experience to key administrative positions disrupted the equilibrium of many agencies and departments. Able and experienced men did much to improve the governor's program, but often they came into the administration late and left early for higher positions. A notable example was Caspar Weinberger, who served effectively but briefly as Reagan's second finance director. He went on to serve in high positions in the Nixon administration in the Federal Trade Commission, in the Budget Bureau, and as Secretary of Health, Education, and Welfare. Democratic lawmakers with their Republican allies were able to give the governor a "run for his money" on administration measures and to curtail extreme proposals, but otherwise the governor had his way in achieving major features of his program. Reagan was without peer as spokesman for his party and for the people—as he viewed them—right-thinking, Middle American conservatives. He made effective use of the mass media, notably in frequent television appearances, so that despite administration setbacks he sustained his personal popularity. Reagan's conservative emphasis temporarily subdued Republican factionalism but helped entrenched liberal forces in Democratic party leadership.

The Anxious Years

By the mid-1960's the nation was in the throes of perplexing crises. Disenchantment with the unpopular war in Southeast Asia, the persistent inequities suffered by disadvantaged minorities, and costly, overextended government programs led to violent showdowns involving peace activists, racial groups, tax revolters, university students, and other dissatisfied elements. The prosperity cycle wavered toward an economic downswing.

The 1968 election was a turning point in national and state politics. It was punctuated by the showdown of conservative and liberal forces across the nation over the volatile issues of the Vietnam war, violence in the cities, and radical confrontations on college campuses. The presidential campaign, one of the stormiest in American history, was marked by the decision of President Johnson not to run for reelection, the assassination of Robert Kennedy in Los Angeles on the eve of the primary election, the violent disruption at the national Democratic convention which nominated moderate Hubert Humphrey over radical-supported Eugene McCarthy, and the Californian-dominated national Republican convention in which Nixon easily beat Reagan's bid to control conservative forces. In the bitterly fought election, Nixon won over Humphrey by less than 1 percent of the popular vote, about the same margin by which he had lost the Presidency to John Kennedy 8 years earlier. In the state midterm election, Republican forces were badly divided when Max Rafferty, the archconservative state school superintendent, edged out popular Senator Thomas Kuchel in the primary election. This prompted angered liberal Republicans to help elect Democrat Alan Cranston to the United States Senate in the general election. The Republicans recaptured the state legislature after a decade of Democratic domination.

The 1970 state election was crucial to both parties. The campaign focused on the gubernatorial contest between Reagan and Unruh; each was his party's ranking leader in fact as well as in title (unlike most previous contests). It also focused on control of the legislature, for the victorious party would carry out legislative reapportionment after the decennial census. The Democrats undertook an aggressive party registration drive that summer, while Republicans confidently believed that their decade-long project (Cal Plan) to capture this particular legislature would be climaxed by their candidates riding to final victory on the popular governor's coattails. The electorate ran true to form in voting the split-ticket, perpetuating the Progressive tradition of voting for the man. Reagan won his battle for reelection, but his party lost the war to capture the legislature, which went to the Democrats by a narrow margin. The Republicans retained most state offices, losing the secretaryship of state to Edmund Brown, Jr. (son of the former governor) and the "nonpartisan" state school superintendency to Wilson Riles, a moderate Black, who dislodged Max Rafferty. Democrat John Tunney, an attractive young congressman identified with the Kennedy circle, defeated Republican incumbent George Murphy for the United

States Senate seat. Republican disappointment over losing control of the legislature was matched by Democratic jubilation as expressed by Unruh, who, having lost his gubernatorial bid, remarked that they had "cut Ronald Reagan's coattails off at the lapels."

Reagan's second administration brought about a realignment of party leadership and programs. Reagan, who had already tempered his conservative position, now adopted a more moderate stance on administration programs to follow more closely the pragmatic ways of previous governors—as one observer put it, once he was convinced that the public had disassociated his program from his Democratic predecessor. When Unruh retired from state politics (at least temporarily), Democratic leadership became an open contest among top leaders like Edmund Brown, Jr., and Robert Moretti, an Unruh protégé and his successor to the assembly speakership. Democratic moves to reapportion the legislature in accordance with constitutional requirements were frustrated by the united Republican front spurred by Reagan, with the result that the state supreme court undertook the task. As the state headed into hard times, the governor and the legislature continued to wrestle with each other over appropriate remedies reflecting their conservative and liberal approaches, coming up with expedient compromises to deal with pressing problems.

A turning of the tide came with the 1974 state election when the Democrats made a near sweep of executive offices. In the primary election for governorship, Brown beat Moretti and other rivals for Democratic nomination, while Houston Flournoy, the state controller, won Republican nomination. (Reagan chose not to run again.) In the general election, Brown edged out Flournoy to become the state's youngest governor since the 1850's. Other Democratic winners were Mervyn Dymally, the Los Angeles senator who became the first black lieutenant governor; March Fong, the Oakland assemblywoman who was the first of her race and sex to win high office as secretary of state; Ken Cory for state controller; and Jesse Unruh for state treasurer. Evelle Younger, the incumbent attorney general, was the lone Republican victor. The election marked the end of an era, one opened and closed by Republican governors of different stripe (Warren and Reagan). The new era augurs changes with the return of the Democrats to the helm of state government with the presence of youth, women, and racial minorities in the leadership. As the nation plunged deeper into hard times, Governor Brown gave a low-key inaugural characterized as "no grand promises, no rhetoric, just plain talk," which reflected his campaign promise for a "New Spirit" and a no-nonsense budget. He called for restoring public confidence in government and putting California back to work.

Meanwhile, public attention turned to the national administration, which asserted its prerogatives in handling growing crises. After narrowly winning in 1968, President Nixon sought to counter the political excesses and urban violence of the mid-1960's by fostering moderation and a return to centrist politics in his bid for the support of "Middle America," the so-called silent majority who best represented middle-class American mores. Typically he followed conservative approaches on civil rights and crime, and liberal approaches on welfare programs, but was brought back in these and other areas to the middle-of-the-road. In coping with the ugly war in Vietnam and runaway inflation, Nixon followed his "game plan" of keeping government interference to a minimum consistent with the conservative philosophy of emphasizing local government rule and private initiative, especially by big business. The Nixon program coincided with Reagan's program whenever they followed conservative lines, but Nixon's startlingly liberal welfare program prompted Reagan to force the federal administration to a palatable compromise. In administration strategy, so historian William Leuchtenburg tells us, Nixon played the role of the Great Unifier to promote a statesmanship image, while Vice President Spiro Agnew played the rowdy role of the Great Polarizer to nettle Democrats and other liberals and to strengthen support among conservative Middle Americans—a role which Vice President Nixon had played earlier to President Eisenhower.

Nixon's dream of a strong unified America under his leadership came to grief in his second administration. In the 1972 presidential election, he beat George McGovern, the "Prairie Populist" and controversial candidate of the badly divided Democratic Party, in a landslide popular vote that was the biggest in Republican history and exceeded only by Lyndon Johnson. Convinced that he had a popular mandate for conservatism, Nixon abandoned his centrist policies for hard-line conservative policies, though he was forced to back down on such issues as student violence (Kent State) and accelerating inflation. Nixon's ambitious scheme, however, was undone by the Watergate Affair, the worst scandal in the nation's history. In the long unraveling exposés of corruption in the administration, Agnew was forced to resign from the vice-presidency on a felony charge and in less than a year Nixon gave up the presidency after admitting complicity in the Watergate scandal. Gerald Ford, Republican minority leader of the House, who had been appointed as vice-president, moved into the presidency to bring an end to the constitutional crisis. A short time before Nixon's departure from the presidency, Earl Warren had stepped down from the chief justiceship, bringing to an end California's unique position in the nation's leadership.

A Profile of Two Men

Earl Warren and Richard Nixon were products of the California mainstream. They represent two types of politicians in public life, each a facet of American tradition. Both men were Californians born of humble circumstances, raised and educated in the state. Each made a long career in politics, rising from local office to high national office. One rose through the state executive branch to be governor and later chief justice of the national judiciary. The other graduated through both houses of Congress to the vice-presidency and presidency. It was Chief Justice Warren who administered the oath of office to President Nixon. The similiarity of the two men ends there.

Warren and Nixon in many ways were opposites in personality and style. In the course of their political careers they developed distinctive traits, which became part of their public personalities. Where Warren was dignified, expansive, and friendly, Nixon was known to be devious, secretive, and reserved. Warren was a man of principle known for his integrity and sincerity—his career was unblemished by corruption or scandal. Nixon was an elusive figure, whose integrity and sincerity were suspect from the beginning of his career—his involvement in shady deals earned him the epithet of "Tricky Dick." In politics the two differed greatly in aim and methods. Warren demonstrated a consistent adherence to the public interest and to the Constitution. On the campaign trail and in public office he focused attention on governmental programs to remedy pressing problems in society. He spoke to the issues and obtained bipartisan support. Nixon operated through partisanship and personal politics, resorting to tactics that critics decried as unfair and unscrupulous. In campaigning for congressional office he concentrated on attacking personalities: his ploy was to condemn his opponent's alleged communist affiliation, though he rarely discussed communism as an issue. When he did speak to the issues, as in his unsuccessful campaigns for governor and president, he came off poorly against issue-oriented opponents (Edmund Brown and John Kennedy). When he succeeded to the presidency, he substituted rhetoric for realistic treatment of the issues. It was a measure of the two men that Warren publicly acknowledged regret for a major political mistake (his support of the wartime Japanese-American evacuation) and Nixon avoided acknowledging his involvement in the Watergate scandal until he was forced to do so. At the end of their political careers, Warren gracefully retired from high office, while Nixon reluctantly resigned rather than face an impeachment trial for malfeasance in the presidency. The relationship between these two Californians became clear on Warren's death. In Warren's files, it was reported that the folder on Nixon was found empty.

ANALYSIS

Political Organization

The Warren Machine

Earl Warren carried his independent style into state politics. He viewed himself as a Progressive in the Hiram Johnson tradition; actually his Progressivism was less parochial, more flexible, and better adapted to the realities of his time. He parlayed his nonpartisan approach and moderate stance into an effective formula for winning wide support from both parties and from the general public. He avoided the personal and ideological clashes that had plagued former governors, keeping free of intra-party factionalism and inter-party struggles. He spoke on issues and cited his accomplishments in the context of public support and the people's interest, without referring to his party's position—thus arousing the ire of Republican Party leaders.

Warren's personal organization was set up to win public support for carrying out his ideas and programs. His base of operations was the governor's office, which he had expanded into an effective mechanism for that purpose. He utilized the political apparatus that would best carry out a particular objective. In party politics he relied heavily on the CRA, which he had helped found (see below), to carry out his gubernatorial election campaigns. In governmental affairs he worked through the administrative machinery, particularly the finance department, but occasionally set up an independent agency, like the crime commission (see below), to achieve a specific end not otherwise obtainable. His personal organization comprised party workers and public officials who carried out a particular phase of his program and operations. He had valuable assistance in the beginning from Whitaker and Baxter, a public relations firm specializing in electioneering, which reportedly taught him how to smile and show off his photogenic qualities. He also benefited from powerful allies in the ranks of business, farmers, labor, the professions, and government, who contributed in their own way to his remarkably successful gubernatorial career. Nevertheless, Warren was complete master of his own house, making decisions and taking actions according to his own principles. So effective was his mode of operation that politicians and yeomen around the state capitol referred to the Warren Machine.

Organized Special Interests

The organized special interests grew enormously in power and influence. They increased in number until over 650 had registered as lobbyists at the state capitol (1974). Earlier they represented mostly major business, professional, governmental, and community groups, but today they include a wide variety of big and small interest groups in every major sector of society. They are organized either as individual groups or as associations, and may operate singly or through coalitions, for one occasion or alternately on a continuing basis. They may be active in the public or private arena of the political economy, and are most visible when involved in government programs or when competing in the marketplace, as in the 1973–1974 energy crisis. They may be represented by a single person or by a group and may have a large well-financed staff or no staff at all. They may work through a faction, a party, or the government, at the state or local level, or they may work the whole system. Their influence is so great that no special-interest group can well afford not to be so organized if it wishes to influence public policy—or even survive the competition with other groups. Two groups have gained increased stature. With the acceleration of governmental activity in the postwar years, lobbyists of state agencies and departments increased in such numbers that their activities were channeled through the governor's office for better coordination (Brown's brainchild continued by Reagan). Out of the social revolution in the 1960's lobbyists for the effectively organized so-called public-interest groups advocating civil rights, consumer interests, environmental protection, and an end to poverty gained new prominence. The entry of these groups into the ranks has "democratized" the system of organized special interests which has lost much of the political exclusiveness of former years. Organized groups, then, have evolved from an elitism of dominant groups to a pluralism of diverse groups, each seeking in its own way to promote and protect its interests through government.

Lobbyists have acquired a mantle of respectability since winning wider public recognition of their valuable services. State laws have given them official recognition, notably the 1949 law which required them to register and report expenditures and the 1962 constitutional amendment which eliminated lobbying as a felony and redefined its status. The news media in publicizing lobby activities subjected them to public scrutiny. Lobbyists still perform the valuable function of supplying party leaders and public officials, especially legislators and administrators, with basic and technical information for formulating public policies and implementing government programs. They have attempted to improve their image by using the title legislative advocate, counsel, or representative; the traditional term remains, however, though the function has taken on broader scope. They have refined lobbying techniques but still lobby the legislature with "facts, friendships, favors, and flimflam." Powerful lobbyists have generally abandoned the shady methods of the Samish era, relying more on professional expertise than personal favors, on systematic staff work rather than individual freewheeling, and on public support rather than private deals. They wield enormous influence with the financial clout they use for political campaigns and public relations, and through slanted technical information which they present to governmental officials and the public. They may appear before legislative committees, in administrative offices, or "work the halls" in the traditional lobbyist way of getting votes or support at the right time and in the right place. However, they generally do their most effective work behind the scenes and out of public sight. Lobbyists compete and cooperate for legislative support for measures affecting their clients but they also serve as an indispensable aid to legislators in lining up votes behind measures. They exert enormous influence with their financial contributions in election campaigns, when candidates require substantial sums to pay for costly campaigns to public office. Jesse Unruh, who won a reputation for skillfully manipulating campaign funds from lobbyists for legislative elections remarked it was a legislator's trick of the trade to accept needed lobbyist funds and not be corrupted by them. It was he who called campaign funds the "mother's milk of politics."

Public mistrust of the lobby system took a turn toward political reform, especially after exposure of the Watergate scandal. When the legislature rebuffed reform efforts in 1972, reform groups headed by Common Cause, a nonprofit public service corporation set up by John Gardner, and People's Lobby campaigned for a state initiative. The measure was adopted by an overwhelming vote in the 1974 primary election despite strong opposition from an array of special interest groups, including the AFL-CIO and the State Chamber of Commerce. The landmark political reform measure imposes limitations on expenditures in election campaigns, requires financial disclosure by givers and takers, and assigns strong enforcement powers to a Fair Political Practices Commission. Time will tell its fate.

Political Parties

The state-wide party system as it now exists is an amorphous structure of vaguely related units. Since 1945 regular or formal party organizations have changed little in basic form, although they have become even larger and more cumbersome vehicles for drafting party platforms and conducting candidate campaigns for state and local public offices.

The state central committee, which met after the convention to elect party leaders, was hamstrung by its large membership (over 800), discord, and required procedures (for example, that the chairmanship alternates between north and south). However, it performed the important function of selecting party officers, including the state party chairman, who managed the party organization and campaigns and served as the party's chief spokesman between elections. The central committee was so stacked with nominees and holdover incumbents to public office that the party projected an elitist rather than a popular image. Compared to the Democratic organization, the Republicans had a much better financed, organized, and staffed setup.

The unwieldy and unrepresentative party structure paved the way for political accommodation and innovation. Candidates for elective local, state, and federal offices established personal organizations for raising funds and conducting their campaigns. Special-interest groups also set up independent organizations to mobilize funds and support for their candidates and ballot propositions. Partisan groups formed extra-legal or unofficial party organizations (so-called because the election code makes no reference to them) to revitalize the party structure, whether they were Young Turks replacing Old Guard leaders (CRA and CDC) or conservatives and liberals implanting their ideological positions on the party image (UROC and DVC). These candidates and groups usually had their showdowns in primary elections, the winners of which could then rely on regular party backing in their general election campaigns. In the absence of strong grassroots organization, the candidates, factions, and parties relied heavily on the mass media (billboards, newspapers, radio, and television) to appeal directly to the voters in primary and general elections. Facing a volatile and unpredictable electorate and the high stakes of election victory, they also relied on professional firms to manage their campaigns. These political management firms—notably the pioneers Whitaker and Baxter, Baus and Ross, and Spencer and Roberts—were so successful with their expertise in party relations that they have become permanent fixtures in election campaigns.

Voter behavior and election results reveal the character of the California electorate in the postwar period. Democrats have consistently held the edge over Republicans in voter registration by three to two, but have been more apathetic in voting at the polls and more apt to cross party lines, even since the abolition of cross-filing. Republicans generally display better party loyalty and unity; they have had higher election turnouts which have compensated for their minority registration. Voters have had opportunities to indicate ideological choices on public policies and programs: the Democratic Party has projected moderate to liberal positions, and the Republican Party moderate to conservative positions. The voters, however, show a tendency to vote for the personality of the man rather than his personal principles or his party's position, hence the emphasis on using the mass media to project a favorable personal image tailored to voter preference. Voters have generally selected candidates with moderate views and have taken middle-of-the-road positions on ballot propositions, steering shy of extremist candidates and radical proposals. A survey shows that almost a third of the voters have made up their minds on candidates and issues before the primary election, and 90 percent have decided to vote the party label in the general election, leaving a critical margin to the remaining 10 percent of voters in close elections. It is this freewheeling, uncertain small pivotal vote that accounts for the erratic and unpredictable election results and the independent, even fickle, behavior of the electorate in California. The electorate has been subjected to deceptive practices and the "dirty tricks" of unscrupulous politicians, as in the 1964 election, and has shown considerable apathy in voting at the polls (but probably no more nor less than in other states despite the wide publicity given to California incidents).

Apparently, the revived two-party system had a significant impact in reshaping the political scene. In the struggle between Republicans and Democrats to secure state command, each took advantage of legislative power to realign election districts (as required after each federal census) in order to strengthen party control, the Republicans in 1951 and the Democrats in 1961. Out of this development, so Eugene Lee tells us, have emerged two elective arenas, each totally different from the other. The first is the competitive statewide arena where the two-party battles are fought for the offices of governor, United States senator, and president. The second is in the frequently noncompetitive districts where one-party contests take place for legislative and congressional seats, focusing on candidates of the same party in primaries where victory is tantamount to election. The "deck was effectively stacked against effective two-party competition" in such a way that a majority of legislators have not faced competition from their own party in primary elections and have seldom faced strong competition in the general election.

Superimposed upon these two elective arenas are regional and socio-economic divisions which condition voting behavior, namely the generally liberal trend of the north and the conservative trend of the south in voting on ballot propositions and statewide candidates. The Republican–Democratic contest for state control has also extended to the legislature, where the party caucuses have been revived and developed as active forces in the legislative processes. These developments were still in a transitional stage as California entered the 1970's.

Administration of Justice

In order to cope with postwar problems, California's judiciary and law enforcement agencies pressed reform efforts to improve its legal and administrative apparatus. The constitutional, statutory, and administrative laws continued to be scrutinized by government bodies. A constitutional amendment (1962) removed a handicap by establishing a constitutional revision commission with a permanent staff. The commission within five years completed major revisions of key articles. Its subsequent failure to secure electorate approval (1968) of key articles, though it got important amendments, was attributed to faulty political strategy rather than to a lack of public awareness—yet another aspect of the difficulties confronting constitutional reform. The separate law revision committee continued its work in extracting antiquated provisions from the statutory code; by 1965 it completed the evidence code and began study of the penal code, winning national applause for its achievement. The expansion and proliferation of legal codes into more refined systems is exemplified by the codified rules and systematic procedures provided for state agencies (Administrative Procedures Act, 1945). The heart of that system was the pool of judicial officers or administrative judges who were available to adjudicate cases arising from the licensing and disciplining of businesses and professions by some 50-odd state regulatory agencies. Law administration was becoming a highly complicated process indeed.

The state supreme court took the initiative in pressing for improvement of the court system. Judiciary reform was personified by Chief Justice Phil Gibson, the practical administrator, and his successor Roger Traynor, the philosophical scholar. Gibson, who had been Governor Olson's finance director before coming to the high bench, was regarded by one of his critics as short on law but "one hell of an administrator." He set up the system for reassigning judges to overloaded courts—the so-called flying squadron—to relieve heavy caseloads and speed up justice. Traynor, a former University of California law professor with a brilliant analytical mind, inspired the high quality of postwar court decisions (which are said to be required reading for justices of the United States Supreme Court, the only state supreme court decisions to enjoy that distinction). The court was noted for its outstanding justices, a remarkable balance of legal viewpoints, and its belief in "judicial activism." Its work complemented the judicial activism of the United States Supreme Court under Chief Justice Earl Warren, and broke new paths by its decisions on administrative operations, criminal procedures, and senate reapportionment.

The broadly based judicial council, developed into an active body under Gibson, spearheaded major reforms. It remedied the "bewildering maze" of lower courts by securing voter approval (1950 constitutional amendment) for organizing the lower courts into seven categories, which vastly reduced their numbers from 768 to 400 and eliminated over-lapping jurisdictions. It tackled the problem of incompetent judges who at the time could be removed only by the difficult and embarrassing processes of electorate nonreelection, recall, or legislative impeachment. The council's efforts (finalized by 1966 constitutional amendments) resulted in a judicial appointments commission for passing on guber-natorial nominations to the high bench and a judicial qualifications commission for censoring or removing judges for misconduct. The judicial council also inaugurated a unique series of statewide conferences of selected judges, lawyers, public officials, and citizens to recommend court reforms. It received valuable help from an administrative staff headed by Ralph Kleps, a distinguished former legislative counsel, thus relieving judges of administrative and research chores. Despite its aggressive imaginative efforts, however, the judicial council in the 1970's was still dealing with the perplexing court overloads and other persistent problems which seem to defy solution.

Law enforcement experienced a dramatic transformation. The state in general and the cities in particular confronted increasing social disorganization which led to increased criminal activity, traffic conges-tion, and other serious law enforcement problems. The attorney general, as the state's chief law officer, was head of an expanding department (Department of Justice, created 1944) which evolved into an active law-enforcing body working closely with the judiciary and local police agencies. The character of the office reflected the personality of its chief. Attorney General Frederick Houser (1947–1951) brought discredit by his egocentric behavior (he was nicknamed "Napoleon") and by a lax attitude toward organized crime which landed two top aides in jail for extortion. Frustrated by his inaction, Governor Warren set up an independent crime commission as a "publicity whip" to go over the attorney general's head in alerting local police agencies and the public to the activities of the Mafia, which had entered the state after the war. The commission exposed mob leaders linked to the national crime syndicate and to organized rackets like gambling, prostitution, and business extortion. Later attorney generals greatly expanded the criminal and civil law functions of the office. Edmund Brown (1951–1959), Stanley Mosk (1959–1967), and Thomas Lynch (1967–1971) developed the effective system of bureaus headed by expert deputy attorney generals. Evelle Younger (1971–) reoriented the department's attention to consumer fraud, environmental protection, and court reform. The attorney general's office evolved from a traditionally perfunctory body to a dynamic state law enforcement agency.

Local police agencies, particularly in metropolitan areas, bore the brunt of growing crime and lawlessness which taxed their capacity to maintain community law and order. The county sheriff and city police chief were handicapped by the "home rule" tradition which stressed local primacy in law enforcement and resulted in community independence. They also encountered difficulties over overlapping police jurisdictions and uneven law enforcement activities in metropolitan and even rural areas. They instituted numerous reforms to cope better with such situations, including expanded departments with bureaus for crime, traffic, technical services, and other specialized activities, modern facilities like mobile patrol units, electronic communication, and data processing. They developed cooperative relations, notably mutual-aid pacts, among local and state (California Highway Patrol) law enforcement agencies. They benefited greatly from the improved recruitment and training of police officers provided under the Peace Officers Standards and Training (POST). Despite their professional efficiency and systematic operations, law enforcement agencies suffered from an undermanned police force and inadequate public support. Their problems were compounded by the violent community showdowns in the mid-1960's over racial incidents, peace demonstrations, and student unrest.

Los Angeles and Berkeley were both pacesetters in law enforcement and the focus of early community violence. Los Angeles, under its autocratic police chief William Parker, developed its police department into the nation's largest, with a reputation for professional elitism.

Parker claimed that it was the police who best handle social problems from growing urban disorganization. When the black community of Watts erupted (1964) in racial violence, resulting in several deaths and extensive property damage, the police came under fire for their racist attitudes and hard crackdown on minority groups; actually they had strong support from like-minded public officials and citizen groups. Berkeley, under police chiefs carrying on the Vollmer tradition (see Chapter 14), built an enviable reputation for police professionalism and community relations. It pioneered in-service training, a neighborhood police service plan suited for middle-size cities, and a code of ethics adopted by the international police association. When student unrest at the University of California erupted into campus and street violence, Berkeley's police found their effectiveness undercut both by the interplay of radical agitators provoking confrontation and by the combined forces of the hard-line sheriff's department and the national guard units called by Governor Reagan, who was intent on "cracking down with a vengeance." Both cities experienced several years of smoldering discontent. In the surprising aftermath, Los Angeles elected a black mayor who worked well with Parker's moderate-minded successor, while Berkeley's city council under radical–liberal leadership assumed an anti-police stance which had undermined its world-famous police department. Community leadership, experts contended, was the hope in resolving excruciating law enforcement problems arising from the accelerated social disorganization in urban areas.

Fiscal Administration

The Warren–Knight administrations were able to manage state finances without experiencing serious problems. The tax structure remained essentially the same; income and sales taxes led in supplying state revenues, while the property tax continued to be the chief source of local revenues. The state administration benefited from the cooperative endeavor of the finance department and the legislative analyst office in budgeting expenditures to match revenues. It was aided by the so-called rainy-day fund—surplus tax revenues accumulated in wartime for financing public works to be built after the war—which was used up by 1950. It also benefited from postwar prosperity conditions. Important adjustments were made in special areas. Highway finances were revised (Collier–Burns Act, 1947) by increasing gas and diesel fuel taxes and motor vehicle fees and redistributing these to pay for the greatly accelerated state highway program. The local sales and use tax measure (Bradley–Burns Act, 1955) authorized counties, as well as cities, who already had such authority, to levy such taxes to supply needed revenues to pay for expanded local government functions and services. The measure provided that the state collect and distribute these taxes, thus establishing the pattern of state–local shared revenues. These pioneering schemes are conspicuous features of the present fiscal setup.

The Brown and Reagan administrations, on the other hand, encountered increasing difficulty in handling growing fiscal problems that led to the most serious fiscal crisis since the Great Depression. Both faced rising costs of government from increasing inflation, expenditures steadily outstripping revenues, and growing disenchantment of the taxpayers. The Brown administration launched a broad tax program; it instituted cigarette taxes, increased taxes on personal income and corporation franchises, raised bank and insurance rates, and expanded state–local shared revenue programs. These measures did nothing more than tinker with the existing system. They alleviated the situation only temporarily in the face of runaway inflation and incipient tax revolts. The Reagan administration met the situation with across-the-board budget cuts and resistance to practical remedies like the withholding tax, which Brown had already tried unsuccessfully to introduce. The Republican governor and the Democratic-controlled legislature became so enmeshed in compromising their conservative–liberal positions that they virtually deadlocked over tax reform. Exasperated with the legislature's refusal to adopt his tax reform proposal, Governor Reagan, in an unprecedented move, called a special election in the autumn of 1973 on a constitutional amendment embodying his proposal. The scheme called for imposing a limit on local property taxes while transferring state functions to local governments and shifting the burden from property owners' taxes to personal income taxes subject to local control. It was apparently considered by the voters as too drastic a solution or too simplistic an approach for resolving the complicated tax problem, and they defeated it by a large majority.

Nevertheless tax experts point out that California has developed a well-working, broadly based fiscal system hardly matched by other states. A legislative committee (1965) reported that the diversified tax pattern conforms closely to the revenue structures for all states combined—"a scaled-down version of the overall tax pattern." It also pointed to a remarkable balance in the tax burden distribution not evident in other states; for instance, personal income taxes match corporation taxes (12 percent) in total revenues. The citizenry has gotten what it asked for. It demanded government services which private enterprises could not adequately perform and expanded state functions when local government functions were inadequate. It has enjoyed a high level of government services which has contributed to improved living standards. Yet Californians still confront serious difficulties. The legislative analyst has pointed out the persistent problems of elasticity under fluctuating economic conditions in balancing revenues with expenditures and in distributing the tax burden equitably. The economic downswing in the early 1970's has compounded the worsening fiscal crisis with intensified public disenchantment and governmental confusion over how to deal with the vagaries of the economy.

Government Reorganization

Government reorganization has had the practical aim of making the state government more effective by reordering the agencies of the executive, legislative, and judicial branches. It has moved along different lines in the course of adapting to changing conditions. Governor Warren during his administration carried forward Progressive concepts which emphasized centralization, professionalization, and uniformity for efficient and economical operations. The prevailing model was the departmental organization operating under a single chief through a hierarchy of divisions, bureaus, and sections manned by professional administrators as well as technical and clerical personnel. As the government's functions expanded and proliferated, and as government activities extended from Sacramento throughout the state, experts of government organization called for revised concepts. They urged grouping related departments in fewer units to improve liaison between leaders at the top and regionally decentralized divisions and bureaus under semiautonomous administrators who could better cope with regional problems and alternative procedures. Government reorganization was subject to the struggles of professional experts over opposing principles like centralization and decentralization, and of rival politicians over politically expedient or professionally sound solutions. The way to reorganization was paved, nevertheless, by leaders in each of the three branches, such as Governor Warren, Assembly Speaker Unruh, and Chief Justice Traynor.

Earl Warren extended Progressive concepts to the governorship. Confronted with formidable problems resulting from rapid population growth and industrial expansion, and an unwieldy governmental structure to deal with them, he emphasized his role as a strong chief executive providing effective administration—much as industry requires strong executives. His personal traits were well suited to the task: abiliity and experience, an orderly mind, broad perspective, and mastery of detail. He expanded the governor's office with additional staff, selecting specialists for their expertise and liaison with government, industry, and other public leaders. He revived the governor's council (Young's cabinet idea) for communicating more effectively with autonomous state executives like the attorney general, and for coordinating programs of the governmental departments. He promoted the finance department and state personnel board as the chief managerial agencies for improving operations in the executive branch. By appointing talented men to key administrative posts (often after a nationwide search), he helped fashion agencies and departments into effective organizations. In dealing with the broader and more complicated problems, he set up general conferences and special commissions, drawing on representative public officials, professional experts, affected special interests, and leading citizens. They exchanged ideas and recommended solutions for complex problems of aging, crime, mental health, and economic development. He used the radio and the newspaper to educate the public to the issues and enlist their support for his programs—his personal appearance and impressive manner made him "look every inch a strong and popular governor." He once expressed his approach as "get the facts, know what you're going to do, and if you have public support, grab the ball and run like hell."

Warren's successors differed in style of gubernatorial leadership but brought little change in the governor's office. The Republican Knight and the Democrat Brown were frank Warren admirers and sought to emulate his role as chief administrator. Knight continued Warren's nonpartisan approach and liberally oriented program and retained many of his key administrators. Brown attempted to assert party leadership in carrying out his Democratic program in a way reminiscent of Johnson's Progressive program, but after his honeymoon with the legislature he reverted to bipartisan ways. Reagan sought to create his own image of the governor, a "citizen governor" who would implement a conservative program to reverse the trend to big government. He departed from his predecessors by his uncompromising ways, his appointment of businessmen with little or no government experience to key administrative posts, and his reliance on popular rhetoric for emotional appeal and public support. Made wiser and more experienced through the trials of his first administration, he revised his stance by his second administration and became more moderate, rational, and practical, like his predecessors, in managing state affairs.

The rapid growth of the state bureaucracy resulted in administrative problems which led to periodic reforms. During the Warren regime, departmental reorganization continued along earlier lines: grouping agencies of similar functions under major departments, transforming boards and commissions from administrative and policy-making bodies into advisory and appeals agencies, and centralizing authority under the governor and the department chiefs responsible to him. In the 1950's four new departments were created (alcoholic beverages, banking, military, and water resources) and three others were division graduations (highway patrol, fish and game, and youth authority). During Brown's administration, attention shifted to executive reorganization: grouping related departments together into fewer units to achieve better top-level coordination of administration programs for more effective gubernatorial direction. In the 1960's agencies and departments were regrouped under top-level agencies (the eight set up by Brown were reduced to four under Reagan) headed by administrators appointed by the governor. This arrangement enabled the governor to concentrate on the key administrators in making policy and coordinating programs, leaving department and agency chiefs to manage routine operations, thus achieving a more rational basis of government organization. A permanent commission (Commission on State Government and Economy, 1961) was set up as a body of prestigious citizens to make ongoing recommendations for improved governmental operations. This "Little Hoover Commission" appears to have been a less ambitious but more practical version of the celebrated federal model for governmental reorganization. The state bureaucracy had grown to enormous size but through periodic reforms it retained the strength to exert a powerful influence on local government and to affect federal programs in California.

The legislature underwent a political revolution which resulted in major reforms. The ruling bipartisan cliques, which had developed in wartime, guided legislative affairs in the postwar decade. The assembly was managed by an inner circle headed by Speaker Charles Lyons and his successor, Sam Collins, in alliance with the Samish machine and the oil lobby. The senate was ruled by a cabal of wealthy senior members who by virtue of their strategic position were able to block legislation and exert a dominant influence over the lower house. In 1949 the legislature received a black eye when *Colliers* magazine (1949) exposed Samish's shady activities and included the famous picture of the impish superlobbyist dangling a puppet whom he addressed as Mr. Legislature. Following public outcry and gubernatorial pressure, the legislature adopted a lobby regulation law (1949) requiring lobbyists to register and report salaries and expenses. The lobbyist–legislator clique fell into further disrepute when Samish went to jail for income tax evasion, and the two former speakers were indicted on legislative bribery charges.

The legislature's complexion began to change in the 1950's. In the assembly, insurgent forces evolved into a broad coalition of economic, regional, sectional, and partisan elements (conservative–liberal, north–south, rural–urban, Republican–Democratic). They constituted the anti-clique elements who took over assembly control after 1951. A new breed of younger, aggressive, party-minded freshman assemblymen, like Caspar Weinberger (Republican, San Francisco) and Jesse Unruh (Democrat, Los Angeles), added vitality to insurgent forces. In the senate, the ruling cabal was reduced by death and retirement until by 1956 leadership had passed to a broader bipartisan and multifaction coalition headed by the president pro tem, Hugh Burns (Democrat, Fresno). With the revival of party labels in state elections (1954), legislative party caucuses were organized effectively for the first time since the Progressive era, and Democratic legislators pressed hard for party measures. Staff agencies were built into effective organizations for assisting members, notably the legislative analyst (the 1941 auditor renamed) under Alan Post and the legislative counsel under Ralph Kleps—both men epitomized the professional expert in government. Among the new staff agencies were a legislative auditor (1955) to review state agency accounts and a legislative reference service (1959) to supply quick information.

Legislative reforms in the 1960's completed the metamorphosis of both houses. Under Speaker Unruh's aggressive tactics, assemblymen demanded and received equal treatment from senators who traditionally had dealt with lower house colleagues in a condescending manner. Following the state supreme court decision (1964) affirming the high court's one man–one vote doctrine, the senate was forced to reapportion the upper chamber. Senate districts, which had been based on counties since 1928, were realigned according to population, thus giving a vote preponderance to urban over rural, and south over north. (Los Angeles, which had had one senatorship, now had 14½.) After a painful transition the senate emerged as a more representative body to closely resemble the assembly setup. Both houses built staffs of administrative assistants for members and professional consultants for committees and even aides for party caucuses—totaling over 1500 in the 1970's. A national commission continued to give the California legislature top rank for achievement and performance.

18 The Managed Economy

THE SETTING

Entrepreneurs

As the nation's economy expanded in the postwar years, business enterprises of all types flourished. Entrepreneurs, in acquiring a college education as well as practical experience, were better trained for business management. Many who had served in administrative and technical positions in wartime defense industries and the military service acquired managerial and other specialized skills applicable to peacetime enterprises. After the war, they were able to finance small and large ventures with personal and company savings accumulated from wartime profits, and with liberal loans from banks and other financial institutions. They also received generous government loans and subsidies like those provided by the G.I. Bill for returning veterans and the RFC (Reconstruction Finance Corporation) for big-thinking entrepreneurs like Kaiser.

In California, entrepreneurs found the expanding state economy particularly favorable for starting up and extending enterprises. Some entrepreneurs sustained comparatively small-scale operations in their specialty, like Charles Litton and David Packard in electronics. Some developed small enterprises into large nationwide firms, like Howard Ahmanson who built up Home Savings and Loan into the nation's largest. Successful big entrepreneurs branched out into other areas, like Henry Kaiser who established huge corporations in several fields. Talented men from other states and abroad, lured by California's attractive environment and favorable opportunities for business investments, poured into the state to exploit promising prospects. Businessman Ray Kroc bought out McDonald's and developed the small Pasadena-based hamburger drive-in chain into an international system. Scientists Simon Ramo and Dean Woolridge left Hughes Aircraft and with businessman William Thompson formed a company which managed a missile production program for the U.S. Air Force (the ICBM for which Ramo had been chief scientist); Thompson-Ramo-Wooldridge soon developed into a multinational conglomerate. Poor men could still make the big time: Jesus Monroy, a penniless Mexican immigrant and former dishwasher at a Fosters cafeteria, bought the Fosters chain in a $2 million deal (1974). The pioneer family firms were still around and doing well, notably Levi Strauss whose great-grandnephews (Peter and Walter Haas, Jr.) presided over the company's postwar growth into the nation's leading clothier featuring assorted Levis.

Entrepreneurs found the California market arena a formidable challenge to survival. California consistently led the other states in both number of new enterprises and number of bankruptcies, although the former generally exceeded the latter. Dynamic and imaginative entrepreneurs helped spearhead the state's spectacular economic development.

Business Organization

The change in business organization in the postwar years was more one of degree than of form. Small, medium-size, and large firms grew in numbers, increasing in about the same proportion to each other. Small enterprises remained about the same in size; they were the proprietors and partners of unincorporated businesses who constituted the bulk of entrepreneurs (3½ million of the nation's 4 million in 1950). They dominated the services and trades (barber shops, gas stations, insurance brokers, real estate firms) and retail stores (druggists, grocers). They were also conspicuous in certain segments of construction and manufacturing. Medium-size firms, those employing 100 to 1000 employees, were especially prominent in professional areas like accounting, architecture, engineering, and law, but were found in just about every area. Sandwiched between the large number of small firms and small number of large firms, they constituted a powerful group which greatly influenced business ideas.

Big firms grew to enormous size. They had met wartime demands for accelerated production and sophisticated military weaponry by developing large-scale operations, scientific research, and technological innovations, and carried forward these trends in the postwar period. Representative of these huge enterprises were General Motors, the nation's largest corporation, which expanded operations in California; and California-based Lockheed in aircraft and Litton in electronics, which extended their operations nationwide and abroad. Litton was taken over in the mid-1950's by Charles "Tex" Thornton who (with financial expert Roy Ash) within a decade built the Beverly Hills firm into a gigantic conglomerate comprising 50 companies operating 145 plants in several states and foreign countries to produce over 500 items, including some for national defense.

These supercorporations were organized as holding companies serving as parent to numerous subsidiary companies. They comprised a complex hierarchy of divisions, departments, and bureaus headed by professional managers and manned by numerous professional, technical, clerical, and trade workers. Many firms decentralized their operations for more effective production and distribution of their products. Some became multinational corporations by developing facilities abroad in order to capitalize on cheaper labor, tax benefits, and foreign markets. Few as they were in number, they were dominant in some financial, manufacturing, and transportation fields. In manufacturing, where concentration was greatest, the nation's top 500 corporations in 1960 employed about 13 percent of the labor force, accounting for 57 percent of sales and 72 percent of the profits. Such enterprises found the corporate device particularly flexible and adaptable in amassing huge capital to finance the mass production and distribution of standardized products for the expanding consumer and industrial markets.

The class of professional managers grew in number and status. They generally flowed from colleges and universities trained in business administration and a broad educational outlook. As masters of the intricacies of small or large enterprises in complex markets, they increasingly acquired the control that had previously rested with owners.

As lower-echelon administrators, they constituted a formidable corps of business bureaucrats who showed (like their government counterparts) a tendency to attain job status and security through cooperation with and loyalty to their superiors. As the management group operating large corporate enterprises, they gained greater control than entrepreneur and stockholder owners by their ability in business administration and executive leadership. The professional manager was personified by California's Robert McNamara who was one of the team that developed the Army Air Force's celebrated world-wide statistical account system during World War II and Ford Motor Company's reorganization after the war; he went on to a brilliant career as president of Ford, Secretary of Defense in the Kennedy–Johnson administrations, and president of the World Bank.

Entrepreneurs and managers made wider and more sophisticated uses of corporate and cooperative devices. Both types had special advantages of adaptability and flexibility for business owners and managers seeking legal protection, tax benefits, competitive advantages, and profit margins. Entrepreneurs converted their family-owned farms and manufacturing and retail enterprises into corporations to develop their small-scale enterprises. Small producers and distributors, especially in agriculture and retail trade, formed cooperative organizations as a way to bypass middlemen and to check corporate chains like supermarkets. Big-business promoters utilized corporate forms to build large, medium, and even some small firms into gigantic enterprises. They maintained company subsidiaries, branch offices, and plant operations throughout the nation and the world. Industry leaders made wider use of trade associations and national organizations (Committee for Economic Development) to promote business research, influence government actions, and cultivate public support.

Other groups also utilized cooperative and corporate devices. In agriculture, the corporate Calpak and cooperative CFGE behaved alike in many ways. Labor unions developed into businesslike organizations operated by professional managers who even performed entrepreneurial functions like investing union funds in corporation stocks. They formed effective interunion associations to negotiate contracts with industry leaders for better working conditions, to organize strikes against target companies, and to build pressure for government action and promote public relations. Even consumer groups utilized corporate and cooperative devices. Berkeley Coop, which carefully tailored grocery and merchandise sales to customer desires, has become so institutionalized as a way of life for its members that its governing board elections resemble city council elections in their conservative–liberal–radical split. Such elaborate uses of cooperative and corporative devices by small and big enterprises complicated the government's efforts to regulate them, making it almost impossible for the citizen to comprehend the setup.

DEVELOPMENT

California's economy experienced another round of dramatic growth and development during the war and postwar years. Environmental conditions like temperate climate and available resources were major drawing cards for luring into the state industries and people, including entrepreneurs, job-hunters, and defense workers. The steady population growth perpetuated by natives and immigrants increased demands for consumer goods like home appliances and personal luxuries and for industrial goods required for buildings, factories, and public facilities (hospitals, schools, roads, and utilities). Business firms of all types inside and outside of the state were attracted by prospects of lucrative profits. California's markets became complex components of the nation's; its subregions were interwoven in various ways with the western region and the national economy. The state became the "metropolis of the western region"; Los Angeles superseded Chicago as the chief market center for the west.

The most significant factors in shaping California's postwar economy were the expanded roles of technology and government. Technological development established earlier in several fields was greatly accelerated during wartime to meet defense and military requirements, and extended in the postwar years to other areas. Subsequently business firms and government agencies refined their techniques for streamlining management and operations along scientific lines, notably in aerospace, communications, electronics, national defense, and outer-space exploration. Some firms developed professional management teams for systems engineering, by which a staff of experts undertook a huge complex project like a factory plant or a military weapons system. Bechtel made a speciality of systems engineering in construction projects, ranging from industrial parks, military bases, petrochemical refineries, and nuclear power plants to residential communities and water development. So important was the role of technology in the market economy that economic developments in the postwar years were designated as the Technological Economy.

Government activity expanded from prewar regulation in strategic areas to postwar regulation in large areas of the market economy. Federal, state, and local regulation, confined earlier to general rules and standards for business, farmers, labor, and other major groups, developed into elaborate procedures. Federal and state regulation in the previous period had been generally restricted to preserving natural resources like oil, timber, and water, and mobilizing manpower and industries during such crises as a war or depression. Now, in the postwar period, government regulation also focused on allocating natural resources for military and other strategic programs and on broad guidance to coordinate manpower, industries, and resources to perpetuate present growth for future development. Governmental activities rationalized in the name of security and economic growth were powerful forces operating on the market economy. They contributed more than ever before toward a managed economy.

1940's

California experienced phenomenal growth and development during World War II. National military and defense programs shook up the market economy and reoriented it to the emergency needs of wartime. Federal agencies armed with dictatorial powers brought about drastic changes in a short time. They built up factories and plants for war production, allocated natural resources to needed industries, reordered the lives of people for military service or defense production, and imposed controls to insure implementation of the nation's wartime programs. California occupied a strategic position in wartime operations. Facing the Pacific Ocean, it was the chief funnel for military troops and supplies into the Pacific theater of conflict. Having prewar facilities for aircraft, electronics, and shipbuilding, its defense industries received a giant share of federal contracts. It was apparent by war's end that the state's market economy would never be the same again.

Uncertain postwar prospects aroused the apprehensions of government officials, industry leaders, and thoughtful citizens. Governor Warren persuaded the legislature to establish the state reconstruction and reemployment commission to undertake a broad program to prevent industry breakdowns and unemployment. The commission in its 1945 report confirmed anticipated concerns. It reported that employment, which had reached a wartime peak of 3.5 million and dropped to 3.2 million in 1945, was still well above the 2.5 million of 1940. While manufacturing suffered a great decline at war's end, federal civilian employees had doubled during the war from (237,000 to over 500,000). The broadly representative body undertook comprehensive programs for providing reemployment of discharged servicemen and displaced war workers, promoting industry conversion from wartime to peacetime production, and developing new industries, markets, and the state's human and physical resources for the "economic and social improvement of the general public." Before disbanding in 1947, it performed a valuable role in coordinating private efforts and federal–state programs for postwar growth.

When the war ended in 1945, the nation went through a painful conversion from a wartime to a peacetime economy, including industry dislocations and high unemployment caused by the dismantling of military and defense operations, and severe shortages accompanied by runaway inflation in the civilian sector. Congress set the nation's course when it adopted the 1946 Employment Act which set up a Committee (later Council) of Economic Advisers (CEA) to advise the President on lessening unemployment during recessions and curbing inflation during prosperity. This landmark measure marked formal acknowledgment that the federal government assumed responsibility for maximum employment and high annual income. As President Truman declared, it stressed public–private coordination to make the economy what we want it to be within limits. Thereafter, federal regulation of the economy was implemented through several authorities. The 1950 Celler–Kefauver anti-merger measure, which tightened the 1914 Clayton Act (Section 7), was becoming a powerful instrument in regulating corporate growth by acquisitions and mergers. More and more agencies regulated activities within their particular jurisdiction. Modern government planning and regulation had become institutionalized.

California struggled through postwar troubles but came out with a flourishing market economy. It managed to prevent the anticipated depression through aggressive expansion with help from government aid programs. Manufacturing industries converted rapidly from military to consumer–industrial production. Manufacturing, along with construction, trades, and service industries, was greatly stimulated by pent-up demands accumulated from wartime. Federal aid came through Atomic Energy Commission (AEC), which expanded nuclear research and development at UC-Berkeley, through RFC, which helped finance corporate ventures of entrepreneurs like Henry Kaiser (see below), and through the Department of Defense (DOD), which continued to award military and defense contracts to aircraft, communications, and electronic firms. Another stimulus was the state building program undertaken by the Warren administration to construct long-delayed public facilities, notably in education, transportation, and water projects (see Chapter 17). Farmers after suffering temporary setbacks benefited greatly from revived agricultural subsidies. Labor unions suffered public backlash from strikes but managed to prevent legislative enactment of a Little Taft–Hartley Act adopted by many other states. Business and industry acquired generous bank loans for financing expanded enterprises. These elements formed the basic pattern which persists to this day.

1950's

The nation enjoyed a prosperity boom but experienced major shifts in its development. When the Korean War broke out in 1950, federal military–defense programs were greatly expanded and expenditures skyrocketed to become henceforth the chief items in the federal budget. Social security benefits were increased (1954, 1958) until practically all job categories were covered by either government (including state and local) or private programs. Congress established the Small Business Administration (1953) to make loans available to needy small enterprises, while terminating RFC (1954) to end its long, successful career underwriting loans for big business and government enterprises. Badgered by the conservative-minded Eisenhower administration, Congress weakened the agricultural subsidy program (1954) and tightened labor union regulation (Landrum–Griffin, 1959). When the Soviet Union launched Sputnik into outer space in 1957, Congress launched a crash program, authorizing huge federal funds for education and industry to accelerate the United States missile and space program. A general mood of smug satisfaction ignored disturbing signs of socio-economic imbalance which contributed to temporary recessions (1954 and 1957) during the decade.

California's economy was spurred by a big shot of federal defense expenditures. DOD expenditures went up 246 percent during the decade, compared to business expenditures, up only 76 percent. California passed New York (1953) to become the nation's leading prime contractor, garnering around one-fourth of all federal defense contracts. Over 70 percent of the state's allocation went to the Los Angeles metropolis. The state's favored position was attributed to its capacity to handle DOD's demanding requirements. It had the edge over rival states because its businessmen had concentrated heavily on research and development—a key element in defense contracts—for long-range profits, while others had gone for conventional weapons for immediate profits. Its educational institutions, notably UC, Stanford, and Cal Tech ranked among the best in the nation—provided the necessary scientists and technicians. Its diversified and well-developed industries, particularly aerospace and electronics, had large-scale plants and other facilities capable of building complex communications, missile, and weapon systems. Defense expenditures vastly accelerated expanding industries and the population explosion.

1960's

The exhilaration and tribulations of the eventful decade were reflected in the nation's economy. The Kennedy–Johnson administration moved to remedy chronic socio-economic problems and a persistently sluggish economy by comprehensive reforms. It accelerated federal public works programs (especially highways) and trade expansion to stimulate industry and employment. It undertook regional development to rehabilitate depressed areas (Appalachia). It launched a "war on poverty" (Economic Opportunity Act, 1964) which sponsored federal projects providing to impoverished youth and adults basic education and work experience for better jobs. The increased tempo of the Vietnam war accelerated federal defense expenditures to higher levels. In a drastic shift from orthodox economics to Keynesian economics, Congress approved a tax cut of over $10 billion (1964) to stimulate business investment and consumer purchases. This remarkable "feat of social engineering" helped sustain prosperity. Before the decade was over, consumer and industrial spending had risen dramatically. Ten million new jobs had been created, over 14 million people had passed over the "poverty line," and the federal government took in more tax money than ever before. Public applause over prosperity, however, was offset by the "creeping inflation" of high incomes and costs, and by growing civil disorders which from mid-decade developed into more violent showdowns over peace demonstrations and racial incidents. The decade ended with the Nixon administration attempting to apply different solutions to the perplexing problems of an erratic economy and widespread social discontent.

California moved in step with national developments, but took independent action to resolve its own problems. The Brown administration kept pace with the Kennedy–Johnson administration in promoting programs to alleviate socio-economic problems. It supplemented federal programs and extended state programs for expanding education, transportation, and water supplies. It focused attention on serious imbalances in the state economy, especially its heavy dependence on federal defense programs, the continued presence of the poor and other neglected groups, and the fiscal difficulties of local governments in handling their problems. Borrowing from federal experience, Governor Brown spearheaded state planning for economic development, inaugurating the Governor's annual economic report (1964) and a state development plan, the nation's first. The finance department, with its planning agency, collected information on population growth and economic activity, distributing it to local, state, and federal agencies, as well as to special-interest groups and industry, and using it to formulate or revise state policies and programs. As the aerospace industry suffered setbacks from shifting federal defense programs, Brown encouraged aerospace firms to apply their research and development skills in state government, especially in developing sophisticated social planning for orderly state growth.

The state planning program made some headway in coordinating public and private efforts for long-range economic development plans. However, it encountered administrative difficulties and philosophical differences over extending the state's role in economic planning. The Reagan administration felt the state's role, as Caspar Weinberger pointed out, should be limited to furnishing broad guidelines and general principles to local or regional agencies at their request. Critics charged that by relocating the agency (renamed state office of planning and research) in his office, the unsympathetic governor had effectively buried the state planning function.

The Reagan administration bore the brunt of economic problems worsened by uncontrollable inflation, dislocated defense industries, rising unemployment, and a spreading tax revolt, compounded by violent showdowns on city streets and university campuses. Governor Reagan's conservative philosophy and expedient measures for state economic programs did little to remedy pressing problems which worsened with the nation's economic downswing in the 1970's.

ANALYSIS

Land

The growing concentration of population and industry in metropolitan areas led to intensive development of the urban areas and their spread into rural regions. In two decades after World War II an estimated three million acres of the state's agricultural land, much of it prime growing area, was withdrawn for nonagricultural uses. Assorted federal, state, and local agencies competed with each other and with varied private enterprises for use of strategic lands and their resources throughout the state. This scramble for available land and resources spread from metropolitan areas to remote regions of the state, the Sierra, the northern mountains, and the southeast desert. These developments not only resulted in rapid depletion of valuable resources but produced widespread air and water pollution, forest despoliation, oil spillovers, and soil displacement. By the mid-1960's public outcry against deterioration of the environment shifted attention from land development to environmental protection. The public was confronted with a crisis over the territorial imperative.

Public Land

For two decades after World War II federal land policies continued without basic change. Congress annually made adjustments of existing policies at the behest of governmental agencies, industry associations, and other special interests, which led to further proliferation of federal programs. It approved the President's Reorganization Plans (1946) which housed public land agencies in the United States Interior Department. The Bureau of Land Management (BLM), which combined the General Land Office and Grazing Service, became the chief agency for handling public lands, including urban real estate for federal buildings. Its title reflected the changing emphasis from land disposal to management of land and its resources. Assorted agencies expanded landholdings for different purposes, including the United States Forest Service (USFS) for timberland and water programs, the National Park Service (NPS) for park expansion, the Corps of Engineers for dams, reservoirs, and storage, and the DOD for military facilities. These agencies worked out complex arrangements with each other and with state and local governments and private enterprises for purchasing, leasing, and swapping lands. Federal landholdings came to constitute almost one-half of the state's lands (48.7 percent).

State agencies continued to develop established public land programs. The State Lands Division still disposed and leased state school lands (500,000 acres remained of the original 5.5 million grant). Critics cited California's shortsighted historic policy compared to other states, which continued to collect substantial revenues from original school land grants. The State Beaches and Parks Division greatly expanded land-holdings for extensive public recreation facilities in coastal, mountain, and desert areas. The Legislative Analyst periodically took it to task for excessive preoccupation with costly land acquisitions and specialized facilities at the expense of basic camp and picnic sites for general visitors. This state agency captured national attention under the Brown Administration with its pioneer "California Outdoor Recreation Plan" but lost it when the Reagan Administration reduced required funds and gave it low priority. Activities of the State Forestry Division are discussed below.

Private Land

The earlier pattern of private land ownership was much the same in the postwar period. California was among the top ranking states with the largest number of individual landowners, including homeowners and property investors. A few owners having huge landholdings were still a conspicuous feature. The Nader Report (*Land and Power in California*, 1971) revealed little had changed: 25 owners held 13 percent of all private lands, 45 firms held 61 percent of corporate farmlands, and 20 proprietors owned 43 percent of timberlands. The Southern Pacific with its 2.4 million acres led the list of the biggest landowners, including Kern County Land Company, PGE, Standard Oil of California, Tejon Ranch, and Boise Cascade.

The big landowners reflected the changing socio-economic attitudes manifested in postwar land development. They adopted sophisticated techniques for careful land and resource management for long-range conservation and profit. The Southern Pacific after 1945 undertook active development of its lands and in 1970 consolidated land operations under two new subsidiaries: a land company for managing its farm, grazing, mineral, timberlands, industrial properties, and other urban real estate; and a development company for operating ventures like its 22,000-acre Fresno farm for growing grapes and its $81 million San Francisco commercial-office complex (1 Market Plaza). Tenneco, a conglomerate created from Tennessee Gas Transmission comprising aircraft, chemical, petroleum, and ship-building companies, exemplified the industrial corporations invading agribusiness; it acquired Kern County Land Company (1967) and other companies (farm machinery and food container manufacturers, and the nation's largest fresh fruit-vegetable marketer) for controlling food production "from seedling to supermarket." The Irvine Company underwent a complicated transition that eventually resulted in a master plan for long-range development which balanced tenancy with joint and individual operations, agricultural tracts with residential subdivisions and industrial parks, the military reservation for El Toro Marine Base, and the university campus at UC-Irvine.

In the 1960's a land rush, reminiscent of the land booms in the nineteenth and early twentieth centuries, was under way throughout California. It was spurred primarily by urban dwellers seeking second homes in coastal, desert, and mountain areas for family retreats and recreation. Big and small land developers built up subdivisions of all types and sizes, including attractive cabins, standard houses, mobile homes, apartment buildings and huge multistory condominiums for vacationers, transient workers, and retired people. Unscrupulous developers engaged in rampant exploitation through substandard construction, deceptive advertisements, and reneged promises of community services. Boise Cascade, which for a while was the nation's biggest lot seller, paid a $60 million court settlement to compensate defrauded lot buyers in the Central Sierra area (1973). The land boom was accompanied by inflated land values and overdeveloped or incomplete subdivisions which imposed serious burdens on rural counties which often had to extend costly public services to remote areas to accommodate resident newcomers. The situation was worsened with the onset of economic recession in the 1970's.

Environmental Protection

Eventually, intensive use of land and resources led to a public reckoning. The problem surfaced soon after the war in the Los Angeles metropolis where the heavy concentration of people and industries accelerated pollution of the atmosphere. Emissions from automobile and truck fuels and wastes of home incinerators and manufacturing plants combined with sunlight and warm–cold air currents to produce widespread smog (smoke combined with fog) which enveloped the downtown area with suffocating air. With the spread of urban sprawl, layers of smog moved with the air currents into neighboring cities and soon afterwards into adjoining rural areas, where the contaminated air damaged orchard and field crops. Before long, smog from the Los Angeles area extended to distant cities like Bakersfield and even caused damage to timberlands in the far-off San Bernardino forests. The San Francisco area also developed smog but a more serious pollution problem resulted from the dumping by cities of home and industry sewage into the Bay. Extensive filling of the tidelands reduced the area of the Bay and resulted in the building up of waterfront lands for future development. Irregular land use contributed another kind of air and water pollution: the wastes of lumber mills and oil-drilling operations in mountain and coastal areas, and salt-water penetration from the Bay into the Delta area.

Public response to the steady deterioration of the urban and rural environment was irregular. Governmental action usually came when problems became serious enough to arouse widespread public concern. Congress and the state legislature gave token attention to the growing air and water pollution after the war, but it remained for local governments to spur state and federal action, which in turn spurred other counties and cities. When smog conditions became acute in Los Angeles, the county pioneered the nation's first air pollution district with a regional agency endowed with mandatory powers (1946). Effective state and federal anti-smog action was forthcoming a decade later. In Santa Clara county, public alarm at widespread conversion of highly productive farmlands into residential and industrial tracts prompted the county to implement a plan (1953) for preventing non-agricultural use of farmlands. The legislature followed through with a state greenbelt measure (1955) which provided tax relief for affected growers to preserve farmlands from the urban sprawl of nearby cities.

By the 1960's public reaction was aroused by the problem of environmental decay. The conservationist movement made headway as assorted groups launched frontal attacks on despoliation of lands, depletion of resources, and contamination of the atmosphere. Imaginative conservationist leaders effectively dramatized the problems. Among these were Alfred Heller and Samuel Wood, who in 1961 organized California Tomorrow, Inc., to carry on their crusade for environmental planning. They exerted enormous influence in spurring public interest and in presenting imaginative schemes for preserving the state's precious environment. The legislature under conservationist pressure authorized regional agencies to carry out plans for environmental protection, notably the San Francisco Bay Conservation and Development Commission (1967). The legislature also formed the State Water Resources Control Board for implementing stronger controls on water pollution and improved programs for water quality. When it failed to act on other measures, conservationist groups sponsored state initiatives to secure voters' approval to the California Environmental Quality Act (CEQA, 1970) and the California Coastal Zone Conservation Commission (1972). The CEQA, which required "environmental impact reports" before projects were undertaken for land development, proved to be a landmark measure. Special-interest groups are still grappling with the complicated problems arising from these measures for preserving the state's environment.

Meanwhile, the federal government became more involved in the California environmental picture. Congress was spurred by a powerful coalition of conservationist and consumer groups into enacting environmental measures like coastline improvements, highway beautification (anti-billboard), and clean air and water. It enacted the Federal Clean Air Act with specific guidelines for quality air standards to be enforced by the Environmental Protection Agency. Critics argue that the Reagan Administration "dragged its feet" in drafting required state and local guidelines, so California has not benefited much from the important program.

Agriculture

The state's ever-expanding agriculture continued for the most part along earlier lines after the war. Farmers and ranchers became fewer in number but operated on a larger scale on more lands. Agricultural lands increased up to 41 million acres, of which 10 percent were in crops and the remainder for grazing. Growers compensated for farmlands lost to urban sprawl, primarily by more intensive crop production. Farms declined sharply in number, from 225,000 to 60,000, but their average size went up from 250 acres to 470 acres. Of the 60,000 farms in 1970 over 70 percent were commercial, the rest were owned by institutions or part-time residents like hobby-farmers or self-subsistence farmers. The measure of their success is reflected in the fact that Californian farmers, who constituted 6 percent of the nation's farmers and worked 2 percent of the nation's cultivated land, earned 9 percent of the total agricultural income.

Corporations and cooperatives maintained their relative prominence in the state setup. Corporate farms were of all types, operating under individual, partnership, and corporate ownership with small and large landholdings. Family farms incorporated in large numbers, especially after a 1958 federal law extended corporate tax advantages to family-owned enterprises. The big corporate farms loomed large in the state production; four or so of them dominated in each crop area and 45 of them accounted for over half of crop production. Del Monte corporation (formerly Calpak) and the cooperative California Fruit Growers Exchange were not only state leaders but also the world's largest of their type.

California growers benefited from updated federal and state agricultural programs. The California Marketing Act (1949) extended pre-war state marketing agreements to include processors as well as producers in a move to correct supply–demand maladjustments and to eliminate unnecessary economic waste. California growers were in a unique position of having several state and federal programs (including marketing agreements of the 1930's) to choose from in developing cooperative arrangements for research, promotion, and marketing. California ranchers received similar benefits when a 1957 state law set up marketing agreements for the livestock industry. California's agricultural pattern has become so complex that generalizations must allow for the many exceptions.

Crops

California growers carried forward improvements in farming operations to keep up with postwar agricultural expansion. They refined devices and techniques in purchasing or renting lands, in selecting crop varieties for each year's production, and in working out contract arrangements for marketing their crops with an eye to advantages to be gained from government subsidies, cooperative programs, and tax benefits. They sought expert services from business, professional, and government specialists in making critical decisions. Growers still faced perplexing problems resulting from sudden disasters and technological breakthroughs that altered farm operations. When pear trees began dying off for unknown reasons (100,000 by 1960), UC launched a cooperative investigation extending to several states and countries to find the guilty insect and cultivate a disease-resistant pear stock to save the state crop. A UC-Davis scientist–engineer team (G. C. Hanna and Coby Lorenzen) teamed to "undo the impossible" by developing a tough-skinned tomato and a mechanical picker for harvesting the crop. Some machines are ingenious. A lettuce harvester equipped with an electronic brain "feels" each head of lettuce then "tells" the following cutter bar whether or not to take the plant. A grape harvester hits the trellis wire supporting the vines then catches the grapes as they fall off. Southern California had at least 30 greenhouses that were using hydroponic techniques to raise plants without soil through nutrient solutions. These innumerable miracle-a-day improvements by university and government scientists in field stations and laboratories usually took years to discover and develop for commercial use. Growers still had to deal with persistent unresolved problems like farm labor (see below), unpredictable weather, and fluctuating markets. Farming was still a tough business.

Earlier trends persisted in the state's agriculture. Among the major crops were alfalfa (for cattle feed), citrus, grapes, and cotton (the most valuable); lettuce and tomatoes became big newcomers, grains and potatoes enjoyed a revival, and the nut crops (almonds, walnuts) did well. The big outfits were still around and doing well. FMC (renamed Food Machinery and Chemical, 1947) became a multinational corporation engaging in diverse manufactures; it moved to Chicago headquarters (1974). The supercorporations also outdid small outfits in garnering government benefits: Tenneco's KCLC in 1969 collected $1.5 million in subsidies and $13 million tax credit despite its $464 million profit, and one grower (J. G. Boswell) received $4.4 million in subsidy payments. (Congress soon after established a $55,000 limit on such subsidies.) California ranked first in 50 of the nation's 80-odd crops, accounting for over 30 percent of the fruit production and 60 percent of the vegetable crop.

Livestock

The livestock industry, still prominent in the state's agricultural picture, underwent major changes. Cattle breeders improved the meat content of beef cattle by using imported semen (especially from French and German purebred bulls) for artificial insemination in crossbreeding superior stock. A UC-Davis veterinary scientist (Delbert McKercher) discovered the disease responsible for sporadic abortions in cows (as high as 75 percent in some herds) and developed a treatment that helped reduce costly losses. Ranchers benefited from favorable grazing policies on government lands, which drew sharp criticism from conservationist groups. Most cattle were still bred in foothill regions, shipped to feedlots, and processed in nearby slaughterhouses. Urban pressures and truck transportation advantages induced packers to sell city stockyards for factory sites and relocate their slaughterhouses near rural feedlots. Packers also diversified marketing arrangements by selling "beef on the hoof" or partly processed meat for consumers with food lockers and home freezers. California ranchers and packers confined their operations to state markets, with some trade to Latin America and Southeast Asia, leaving national markets to neighboring states and Texas.

Mineral Production

The mineral industry expanded along the same basic lines after the war. Mineral production fluctuated with national developments. It went up to meet postwar demands in the building and manufacturing industries, spurred by the population boom and national defense programs, and leveled off in the 1960's with defense reductions and growing shortages of some minerals. California was still one of the chief mineral producers, ranking first in 16 categories of 60 commercially produced minerals. Its ranking metals, gold and mercury, along with its iron, were supplemented by rare metals for superalloys developed after the war for tools and machines, aircraft, and spaceships. Industrial minerals became as important as the more glamorous metals. California led the nation in concrete materials (cement, gravel, sand, and stone) used so heavily in the construction industry, and boron with its diversified uses from soaps to rocket fuels. (The boron open mine pit in Kern is so deep it can hide a 30-story building!) Mineral fuels—natural gas and petroleum—on which 90 percent of the west is dependent for fuel, accounted for two-thirds of the state's mineral production. California ranks third to Texas and Louisiana in the nation's petroleum production.

Petroleum

The petroleum industry experienced tremendous growth and major changes. California still retained the basic structure of a predominantly industry-regulated setup. It remained the only major oil-producing state where the petroleum industry was not regulated by state agency. Oil continued to be produced by big and small independents and majors, operating mostly in the Los Angeles area (1/5) and the San Joaquin (3/5). They drilled deeper with improved rigs, tools, and machinery: in 1974 a Kern County operator reached a record depth of 22,000 feet. The big corporations invested heavily in research and development for discovery of new wells and for improving existing fields. Individual operators had 40 percent of the wells but often worked over "stripper wells" and were plagued by dry wells so that they accounted for only 25 percent of oil production. The California Oil Producers Association, comprising majors and independents, provided a basis for industry self-regulation (its conservation committee recommended production rates voluntarily followed by operators to insure maximum efficiency and yield). Producers encountered new versions of older problems like fluctuating markets, wildcat producers, and uneven supply.

Petroleum refining and distribution underwent important changes. Oil was still conveyed from the wells to nearby trunk pipelines (about 75 percent) and tanker ships for delivery to refineries, mostly in the Los Angeles and San Francisco areas. Los Angeles, which acquired eight of the ten new wartime plants, outdistanced its northern rival. The large refineries developed into huge complexes of automated operation. They added catalytic cracking units to thermal cracking processes for breaking crude and refined oils into fuel oil, gasoline, lubricants, and by-products required for transportation and other industries. Union Oil set the pace when it built the largest catalytic cracking plant on the Pacific (1952) to convert crudes into marketable chemical by-products, and built its famous "unifining" cracking plant (1964) which achieved the "industry ultimate" in utilizing all residue. Through catalytic processes, they produced refined fuels required for jetcraft and space-craft. With the help of petrochemical research, they put out specialized products used by growers for fertilizers and by manufacturing firms for producing plastics, synthetic fibers, and synthetic rubber products. Independent refineries lacking resources to engage in costly cracking processes and volume production either concentrated on simpler operations, like refining crudes for basic products, or went out of business, as over half of them did. The majors by controlling the pipelines, big refineries, and distribution outlets, cinched their grip on the industry, though they still had to contend with powerful indepen-dents and an unpredictable public.

Market developments at home and abroad affected the character of California's petroleum industry. Nationally, petroleum and natural gas replaced coal as a major fuel, especially in the East, a long-time user. (As an industry spokesman put it, "they pack a bigger punch per pound and per cubic foot.") The crudes lost popularity to refined oils from which more gasoline could be extracted. Gasoline bypassed fuel oil in importance (1948) with the upsurge of motor vehicle transporation and the conversion of many industries to natural gas. Intense competition for petroleum, spurred by refined oil demands, prompted American companies to work over existing fields for secondary recoveries, to extend drilling into the coastal tidelands of the Gulf and on the Pacific, and to search out and develop new fields in Alaska, Canada, Latin America, and the Middle East. The majors retained their leadership position in the industry by their integrated production-refining-transporting-distributing operations and by heavy investments in petrochemical research to produce numerous by-products for their markets.

California emerged as the nation's chief petroleum user but ranked third (after Texas and Louisiana) in petroleum production. Unable to supply its heavy postwar demand, California moved from its historical position as an oil exporter to become an oil importer. With the rise of Texas and Oklahoma producers and midwestern operators, California lost its big share of the eastern market, turning more to its own market and the Pacific markets (Hawaii, Alaska, Southeast Asia). In the course of postwar competition, outside producers breached the state barrier, including major producers like Tidewater (1942) and independents like Douglas (1953). Texaco acquired a pipeline in the San Joaquin (1942). In the shift of industry leadership, Union Oil graduated to the majors to join Standard Oil, Mobil, Tidewater, and Shell as the largest integrated oil corporations operating in the state while Signal emerged as the leading independent.

The petroleum industry had several contests with the public over government policy. Oil companies tapping the tideland oil off the California coast were involved in disputes with federal and state agencies claiming jurisdiction in the three-mile offshore area. Eventually, the majors won strategic public bids for local offshore drilling at Long Beach, Santa Barbara, and other areas. In the 1956 state initiative sponsored by several majors as an "oil conservation measure," the majors proposed a plan replacing voluntary with mandatory regulation of oil production. They claimed the plan would promote oil conservation, but rivals charged it was a bald attempt to control if not eliminate the independents. After a bitterly fought campaign, the measure went down to resounding defeat in the 1956 general elections. In 1969 the tidelands issue appeared again at Santa Barbara when the Union Oil facility broke and released an enormous amount of oil seepage which polluted the sea and coastline. After a massive clean-up effort, a temporary moratorium was imposed on oil drilling. In 1972 the nation became enmeshed in a world-wide energy crisis provoked by serious fuel shortages at home and abroad. The American petroleum industry's effort to meet accelerated demands for gasoline and oil products and limited available supplies created an untenable market situation, compounded by industry competition, government regulation, and the Arab oil embargo. The fuel crisis created an unprecedented public reaction that was still running its course at mid-decade.

Timber Resources

In postwar developments, timber demands for the building boom and the restricted lumber production in Oregon and Washington (the nation's chief lumber-producing areas) greatly stimulated California production. Nationwide companies extended operations into California, often absorbing local firms. The large corporations with forest holdings conducted huge, integrated logging–lumbering operations, improving techniques for fuller utilization of forests ("weed species" like white fir) and diversifying their operations. Smaller operators–millowners or independent loggers selling to them–contracted with local farmers, ranchers, and other residents, who were happy to profit from timber cut on their lands. Lumbermen operated mostly on privately owned timber lands (80 percent) or on federal forest reserves, mostly in the northwest area, but also in the Sierra. Loggers used chain saws, diesel tractors, and trucks to cut and move out timber in rapid and systematic fashion. The big mills handled two-thirds of the total volume, but the small and medium-size mills handled three-fourths of the lumber marketed as dressed or finished lumber. California produced most of the lumber used in the state (close to 60 percent) but it was also a big exporter in some species, especially its redwood for eastern markets. California was first in lumber consumption and second to Oregon in timber production.

Government programs still figured importantly in industry operations. Congress extended federal–private cooperative programs for implementing the "sustained yield" principle on public and private forest lands (1944). Sustained yield involved planned timber cutting, tree replanting, and forest protection for insuring continued growth. The state legislature did its part with the Forest Practices Act (1945) which established state standards and regional districts for administering state standards on private forest lands, depending on voluntary compliance rather than enforcement with penalties for violations. Under such a setup, forest management was carefully followed on federal and state forest reserves and often by big lumber companies with large forest holdings. Large proportions of private forest lands owned by small landowners rarely reflected evidence of careful forest management. Under mounting conservationist pressure, the legislature enacted the landmark 1973 measure, which supplanted the 1945 act with tighter timber cutting regulations and forestry conservation practices on private lands.

Colleges and universities rendered important assistance. They trained the professional foresters hired by government agencies and lumber companies, and did yeoman work in applying scientific principles to forest operations. They continued to make valuable research contributions, as in the case of the bark beetle, especially the western pine beetle, which was far more responsible than fire for vast destruction of California pine forests. A UC-Berkeley forestry scientist (appropriately named David Wood) made the breakthrough in discovering the sex life of the bark beetle, the key to controlling the problem. Research of UC and other scientists demolished the long-held idea that brushland was essential for maintaining healthy forests and watershed areas, thus reducing the bitter controversy over the brush-burning issue among state leaders.

Industry patterns, still oriented along regional lines, were altered by postwar developments. The Northwest, the nation's last stronghold of lumber barons, acquired a new face. The Big Six who had ruled most of the redwood industry for so long (see Chapter 15) gradually faded into the background. Local control was reduced by the entry of outsiders, notably big-timers like Georgia Pacific and Weyerhaeuser. Old practices of selective tree cutting, which allowed for regeneration and left redwood forests reasonably stable, gave way to new methods of clear-cutting for seedling plantings, resulting in the contrasting scenery of open areas and redwood forests. The Douglas fir forests, hitherto inaccessible geographically for profitable exploitation, underwent large-scale timber cutting reminiscent of the old timber-mining days. The fir boom ended in the mid-1950's with depleted forests, a ruined landscape, and a depressed regional economy. Devastating floods (1954–55 and 1964) compounded the destruction; they washed logging debris down torrential rivers and left in their wake destroyed buildings and bridges, damaged freeways, and diminished communities.

Despite rapid timber depletion of the area, forestry officials point out that 750,000 acres of old-growth trees of the original two million acres of redwood forests still remain. The famous redwood forests showed a remarkable capacity for replenishing themselves with second-growth timber. Meanwhile, the growing number of tourists and vacationers spurred state and federal agencies to expand facilities for recreation and sports in public park and forest areas of the region. The National Park Service undertook development of a large, national redwood park which would adjoin state parks and absorb a major lumber company (Arcata), encountering strong opposition from lumber companies, local business interests, and many local public officials. The old redwood empire is still undergoing transition.

In the Central Sierra, the lumber industry in this predominantly pine forest area was characterized by small and medium-size firms engaging in specialized but profitable operations in uncontrollable competition. Critics pointed to the widespread forest depletion and ruined timber resulting from logging malpractices and overdeveloped mill operations. Another trend was outsiders like American Forest and Boise Cascade, who moved into the Central Sierra during the 1950's to build up large timber holdings for lumber operations. Struck by declining lumber markets in the 1960's, they diversified operations by converting forest lands into residential subdivisions of second homes for year-round skiing and boating and other recreational activities for urban dwellers. Boise Cascade was held to account for its real estate shenanigans, as previously mentioned. Sierra lumbering, like the Northwest, is still coping with an uncertain future.

Water Resources

Water resources were greatly expanded to meet the enormous requirements of the growing population and expanding economy. Water requirements were heavy in every category: in the home, a toilet flushing used 3 gallons and the washing machine 20–30 gallons; in industry, the canning of a crate of lima beans consumed 250 gallons and the refining of a barrel of petroleum 18 water barrels. Agricultural use far outstripped home and industry uses: irrigation consumed about 90 percent of the state's annual water supply (eight of nine trillion gallons of water). Californians refined techniques and expanded facilities of established systems in collecting and distributing water for varied needs. In postwar development of water resources, the new emphasis was on state control over public and private water projects, overall water planning and development on the basis of statewide use and long-range needs, applied technology in water conservation (for example, seawater conversion into fresh water), and recreational uses of water facilities (boating on water reservoirs). The State Water Resources Department (SWRD, reorganized 1956) emerged as the prime mover in synchronizing federal–state–local water programs, but local agencies and private enterprises were still major vehicles for undertaking water development.

Water Rights

Competition for water rights was as intense but more intricate than before. The SWRD's Water Rights Board was still the chief agency for resolving complex problems over water titles; it applied the doctrine of the most reasonable beneficial use (see chapter 15) in disposing riparian, appropriative, and correlative (underground water) rights of water users. Controversial cases still filled the court dockets. Orange, Riverside, and San Bernardino counties fought a long, costly court case over their respective shares of the Santa Ana River flow. Los Angeles water users spent $5 million in legal fees during 16 years of litigation over pumping water from the west coastal underground basin; they finally accepted reduced pumping water quotas that would safeguard against saltwater intrusion. The United States government attempted to revoke the 1902 Reclamation Act (see Chapter 15) which exempted from the 160-acre limitation Imperial Valley farmers who had been irrigating vast acreages with federal water. California's long legal battle with Arizona over Colorado River water rights (revived 1952) culminated in a United States Supreme Court decision (1961) that reduced California's allotment for Arizona's benefit. The 1961 legislature tightened up state regulation of the underground water basins. Critics thought California had an equitable and stable system for resolving perplexing problems of water rights.

Irrigation

Irrigation continued to be of strategic importance to agriculture. California's irrigated land (8.5 million acres), which represented one-fourth of the nation's total, was concentrated in the Central Valley (70 percent) and Southern California (17 percent). The growers drew from surface water and underground water for forage, orchards, and field crops. In supplying irrigation water, mutual water companies and public irrigation districts gained at the expense of private water companies. Growers encountered serious problems of quality as well as quantity of water. For example, the Imperial Irrigation District, still the world's largest public water district, developed costly special facilities to remove sediment from Colorado River water delivered in the All American Canal and to leach salt minerals from fields.

Reclamation

Reclamation, conceived primarily for flood control, was still vital to state water development. The state reclamation board served as an effective watchdog in approving waterworks that might affect the Sacramento Drainage Canal system (see Chapter 15). The federal Corps of Engineers expanded its dam–reservoir facilities (35) for flood control throughout the state, notably dams like Coyote on the Russian River, Folsom on the American, Isabella on the Kern, Pine Flats on the King, and Dos Palos on the Trinity. Los Angeles and other metropolitan areas improved their dam–reservoir systems for regional flood control, often with federal assistance. Rampaging floods which periodically hit the state (1955 and 1964) proved the effectiveness of most flood control facilities in minimizing destruction.

Municipal Supply

The urban counties and cities built up established systems to secure additional water for expanding community needs. San Francisco developed cooperative schemes with several irrigation districts and the federal agencies for new aqueducts and new reservoirs using the Tuolumne watershed. The East Bay Municipal Utility District built a new reservoir (Comanche) and expanded pipe and canal lines from the Mokelumne which would double its water supply. Los Angeles increased its reservoirs to over 100 in the metropolis and up to 6 in Owens Valley; it also drew bigger allotments from the Metropolitan Water District (MWD). San Diego expanded local facilities and built an aqueduct (1952) into the Colorado River Aqueduct. County water agencies became popular vehicles for developing local multiple-purpose water projects (421 between 1945 and 1965) for collecting, storing, and distributing water on an areawide basis. State aid was forthcoming in loans and grants made to local public agencies undertaking such costly projects (Davis–Grunsky, 1957). The southern metropolises paced other communities in developing ways to improve local water supply. Los Angeles recycled waste water through chemical treatment in sewerage plants and San Diego converted seawater through distillation in a nuclear power plant. PGE and Southern California Edison periodically contracted with cloud-seeding firms for improving precipitation. Water development was a never-ending process.

Multiple-Purpose Projects

Public attention focused on multiple-purpose projects for water development of the entire state. Despite the last-ditch efforts of opponents, the Central Valley Project was completed (CVP, 1951) with the operation of Shasta Dam for stabilizing the Sacramento River flow, the Delta Cross-Channel for the north–south water transfer, and Friant Dam for distributing Sierra water on the San Joaquin east side (see Chapter 15). Realizing CVP would be obsolete before completion, the 1947 legislature authorized future planning by SWRD, which came up with the comprehensive California Water Plan (1951). The plan provoked bitter controversy among public and private interests; it also revived sectional animosities between the water-laden, sparsely settled north and the thirsty, populous south. Such differences were eventually resolved by astute compromises pushed by Governor Brown, who persuaded all parties to "start shoving dirt and stop slinging mud," and by public approval of the huge construction bonds (Proposition 1, 1960). Where CVP was federally financed and constructed, the California Water Plan projects were state enterprises, and thus not subject to the federal 160-acre limitation. Big and small growers with their allies still fought excruciating political-legal battles over rights to draw irrigation water from these government projects as affected by the federal limitation law.

The California Water Plan dwarfed the CVP which it supplemented. Hub of the plan was the Delta area where the Sacramento and San Joaquin rivers join; its system of levees and channels were developed into a giant waterhole to comprise the Delta Pool for conveying northern waters throughout the central and southern regions of the state. Other components of the plan were Oroville Dam (the nation's highest) on the Feather River for supplying the Delta with additional water, the North Bay aqueduct (Novato Reservoir), and South Bay aqueduct (Airline Reservoir) for carrying Delta water to the San Francisco Bay

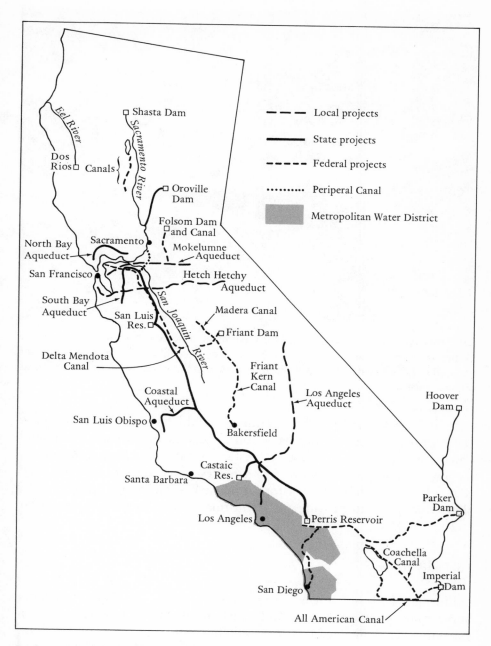

Legend:
- – – – Local projects
- ——— State projects
- - - - - Federal projects
- ·········· Periperal Canal
- ▨ Metropolitan Water District

Map labels:
Shasta Dam, Eel River, Sacramento River, Dos Rios, Canals, Oroville Dam, Folsom Dam and Canal, North Bay Aqueduct, Sacramento, Mokelumne Aqueduct, San Francisco, Hetch Hetchy Aqueduct, South Bay Aqueduct, San Luis Res., San Joaquin River, Madera Canal, Friant Dam, Delta Mendota Canal, Friant Kern Canal, Los Angeles Aqueduct, Hoover Dam, Coastal Aqueduct, San Luis Obispo, Bakersfield, Castaic Res., Santa Barbara, Los Angeles, Perris Reservoir, Parker Dam, Coachella Canal, San Diego, Imperial Dam, All American Canal

FIGURE 10 Major California Water Projects.

California Aqueduct. After projected diversions of 6 percent for northern areas and 37 percent for the San Joaquin from the total of 4.3 million acre-feet of water, the remaining 57 percent is lifted over the Tehachapi mountains to Los Angeles, as shown above.

area, and the 444-mile California Aqueduct which carried water from the Delta into Southern California. Future plans include a Delta Peripheral Canal for a north–south water transfer on the Delta east side and the northwest component with its dam–reservoir system on the Eel, Klamath, and Trinity Rivers for additional water supply. The present plan is designed to provide for California's water needs up to the year 2020.

Fuel and Power

California's fuel and power resources were greatly expanded to supply burgeoning population and industrial needs. Attention focused on expanding existing facilities and building interregional systems. PGE, which emerged as the nation's largest private utility company, and Pacific Lighting, the nation's largest gas distributor, extended gas transmission and distribution lines for home heating and industrial heating and power in their respective northern and southern bailiwicks. The wider use of gas, arising from its low cost and anti-smog rules, led to increased gas demands, which both companies met by importing gas from Texas through El Paso Natural Gas (1947) and from Canada through Pacific Gas Transmission, a joint enterprise of private companies spearheaded by PGE. In 1960 Tennessee Gas Transmission (company re-named Tenneco 1966), the nation's largest pipeline company which delivered Texas gas to eastern states, challenged El Paso Natural Gas's grip on southwest gas transmission, precipitating a long complicated inter-industry battle involving giant corporations like Standard Oil of New Jersey, the nation's largest gas producer, the major California gas and electric companies and the Los Angeles Water and Power Department. Following a Federal Power Commission ruling, El Paso Natural Gas shared the California market with Transwestern Pipeline (allied with Tennessee Gas Transmission). California, which in 1945 supplied its own gas, was by 1970 acquiring three-quarters of its gas from several western states and Canada.

Hydroelectric power expansion continued along earlier lines of private and public development. Congress authorized the U.S. Bureau of Reclamation (USBR) to expand hydroelectric plants for producing electricity and extending distribution lines. However, opposition from PGE and private utility allies against such government competition in electricity distribution (the revenue producing part) resulted in extending the earlier practice of divided territories and customers. USBR produced and distributed most of its own power in the Central Valley through its dams on the Sacramento (Shasta and Keswick), on the American (Folsom and Nimbus), and on the Trinity. Hydroelectric power limitations due to postwar competition for water resources caused PGE and other private utilities to develop steam plant facilities and interregional systems. Southern California Edison (still a leading utility innovator) won laurels for building the nation's most efficient plant (Oxnard) and the first fully automated plant (Huntington Beach). Both companies paced national development of nuclear power plants for generating electricity: PGE at Eureka and Southern California Edison at San Onofre near San Diego. PGE also paved the way for geothermal power: its plant at The Geysers near St. Helena taps underground heat for generating electricity. Postwar developments were capped by the Pacific Intertie System and the California Power Pool (1960–1961) by which California's public agencies and private utilities acquired hydroelectric power from Bonneville Dam on the Columbia River through a complicated setup of power transmission and distribution for diverse needs ranging from customer services to pumping plants moving water from Northern California to the Southland. This landmark event inaugurated a new era in cooperative relationships between public agencies and private companies who for so long fought for dominance of California's power supply.

Manufacturing

Manufacturing activities after the war were still concentrated in the Los Angeles, San Diego, and San Francisco metropolises, but they also developed in other metropolitan areas of the Central Valley, notably Sacramento and Stockton, Fresno and Bakersfield. In the metropolitan areas, some manufacturing firms filled up established industrial areas in older cities, but many moved into industrial parks and subdivisions of outlying cities and suburban areas, showing a propensity for large, modern plants with uncrowded one-story buildings and ample parking. Manufacturing firms were of all types and sizes, ranging from small companies producing standard or specialized goods to supercorporations which manufactured diverse products.

The defense industry, comprising the manufacturers of aircraft, electronics, guided missiles, military ordnance, ships and tanks, became in the 1950's California's—and the nation's—biggest industry. These firms represented the state's fastest-growing industries and accounted for almost one-fourth of manufacturing employment (400,000 of the six million labor force). They were concentrated in Los Angeles, where most of them maintained major office and plant facilities. Each of these manufacturers was profoundly affected by defense programs. For example, aircraft manufacturers broadened operations to produce jets and later spacecraft, taking on the character of aerospace firms working for the government—for a while 90 percent of their business was with the Pentagon. Lockheed and North American developed into multinational conglomerates under top-flight professional management teams. The defense industries also stimulated other industries, especially nonelectrical machinery and transportation. When California was hit by defense cutbacks in the 1960's, these manufacturing firms adapted operations to consumer and industrial markets, faring far better in adjusting to changing conditions than similar companies in other states. By 1970

California had 18 major categories of manufacturing. It became the nation's second-ranking manufacturing state after New York, accounting for 10 percent of total production.

California's iron and steel industry enjoyed steady growth. After phenomenal wartime expansion which tripled the state's steel output, the iron and steel makers expanded facilities and operations to supply California's booming economy. The iron and steel plants were located mostly in the Los Angeles and San Francisco metropolitan areas. Two of the Big Six of the steel industry centered operations there: U.S. Steel in Pittsburg and Torrance, and Bethlehem, which concentrated on structural steel for the building industry, in South San Francisco, Vernon, and after 1962, Richmond. Kaiser, which bought the Fontana plant it built for the federal government during the war, undertook periodic expansion for modernizing facilities and diversifying production (1949, 1964). It was the only integrated steel plant on the Pacific Coast, including blast furnaces for producing iron directly from ore, and electrolytic tinning and hot strip mill-finishing facilities.

Electronics

The electronics industry experienced spectacular postwar development. From prewar development of the movie projector, radio, television, automatic machine controls, measuring instruments, and photoelectric systems, it evolved into a wide array of microwave, radar, and sonar devices perfected during wartime. The vacuum tube, the heart of these devices, was superseded by the transistor (developed in 1947 by a Bell lab team and Stanford's William Shockley), which was cheaper, smaller, and more reliable. Where the vacuum tube controlled the flow of electrons by gas or vacuum, the transistor or semi-conductor comprised solid materials, like silicon crystals, hence solid state. Miniature printed circuit boards soon replaced conventional wire circuits to round out transistor development. Thereafter, electronic research and development occurred in many areas, including color television, mobile two-way radio, microwave relay for long-distance short-wave communication, and computers for processing information (EDP or electronic data processing), for making complex calculations at lightning speeds, and for operating all types of automatic machinery. Electronic devices were used in such diverse operations as business accounts, industrial production, professional calculations, medical surgery, and entertainment. They included microscopes that measured to one-billionth of an inch to orbiting satellites that transmitted photos of distant planets. The field of electronics represents a revolutionary development in modern technology that touched just about every area of people's lives.

California became a national center for electronics and related fields. Its prewar foundations were broadened by wartime and postwar expansion, chiefly in the Los Angeles and San Francisco Bay areas. Stanford's Frederick Terman was a moving spirit in building up the famous industrial park which attracted important electronics firms and helped make Santa Clara county a national center of the industry (over 800 firms in 1974). The industry pattern took form during and after the war when electrical firms, including majors like General Electric and Westinghouse, and leading radio manufacturers, like Philco and Zenith, established branch plants or absorbed California firms to broaden their base for producing and distributing electronic products. Before long, giant corporations from other industries moved into the electronics field, as in the case of aerospace firms like General Dynamics, Lockheed, and North American, which acquired defense contracts for building electronic components for jetcraft, missiles, and spacecraft projects. Other California firms emerged as industry leaders in specialized areas, including Ampex for magnetic tape recorders, Eimac for power tubes used in computers building automatic machinery and missiles, Hewlett-Packard for some 1,500 kinds of scientific instruments, and Varian for klystron tubes used for microwave and radar devices.

Scientist–inventors left company and university labs to form their own companies, usually taking on businessmen partners, for producing and marketing products in electronics and related fields. A notable example is the Varian group, which formed Specta-Physics (1960) to develop the laser device that one of them invented; it became the world's leading producer of gas lasers and inspired other companies to produce other kinds of lasers. (Laser devices generate powerful light beams which are used for such diverse purposes as aligning underground pipe in construction and conducting delicate brain surgery.) When IBM (International Business Machines), the giant leader of the computer industry, moved into the Bay Area to expand operations after the war, several California firms cut niches with specialized products, notably miniature computers, prompting *Fortune* magazine to observe such companies did well "zig-zagging in peripheral market areas." No other state matched California's unique role in national development of the electronics field.

Labor

Industrial Labor

California's complex labor pattern, established by 1940, evolved into an even more complicated setup in the postwar years. The labor force grew enormously with the wartime boost given to aircraft, electronics, and shipping production and the postwar expansion of other manufacturing industries producing consumer and industrial goods. Labor unions moved quickly after the war to organize workers in the new and expanding industries. Their successful membership drives and favorable collective bargaining contracts in many industries placed California among the leading states having the most highly organized workers.

A conspicuous development in postwar labor–management relations was the multiemployer collective bargaining agreement with labor unions. Pioneered by Harry Bridges's Longshoremen's Union in the 1930's (see Chapter 15), it became a characteristic feature of labor–management relations on the Pacific Coast. In most of the major industries, areawide labor unions negotiated with multiemployer groups master contracts establishing working conditions on an industrywide basis. Employer associations were organized on the basis of a particular industry, such as aircraft, maritime shipping, shipbuilding, and motor transportation. By 1947 three-fourths of San Francisco's employees were covered by such master agreements, and within a decade a high proportion of union workers in Southern California were covered by such arrangements.

Meanwhile, national developments were shaping union developments and labor–management relations in California. In the painful postwar transition to peacetime economic production, the nation experienced several years of industrial warfare. Landmark events were the 1947 Taft–Hartley Act which prohibited unions from engaging in unfair labor practices (including the closed shop); the giant union rivals consolidating their organizations into the AFL–CIO (1954) and forming a Political Action Committee (PAC, 1955) to apply pressure politics at the state and national levels; and the 1959 Landrum–Griffin Act which tightened up union accountability for its actions. Union troubles were compounded by United States Senate investigations (McCarthy and McClellan committees) exposing Communist affiliation and corruption in some unions, which prompted the AFL–CIO to expel guilty unions, including the Teamsters, whose leaders, Dave Beck and James Hoffa, eventually served jail sentences for fraudulent activities. The AFL–CIO had attained the status of Big Labor to vie with Big Business and Big Farmer as major forces in shaping national economic policy.

California labor fared relatively well through the course of national events. The United States Justice Department failed in its long campaign to deport Australian-born Harry Bridges, ostensibly for perjury in immigration proceedings, but widely believed to be inspired by AFL and business elements to remove the powerful, radical-minded longshoreman union leader from the California waterfront scene. The state avoided the course of many states in enacting Little Taft–Hartley laws and overwhelmingly defeated the anti-union "right to work" initiative in the 1958 state election (see Chapter 17). The governors from Warren to Brown displayed sympathetic labor positions; Governor Knight exchanged political support with the AFL. The state legislature steadily improved workmen's compensation and other labor benefits; by the mid-1960's it opened the way for public employees, including teachers, to enter collective bargaining with government employers. During the Reagan administration, the AFL–CIO managed to preserve its gains with help from the Democratic legislature, despite the governor's unsympathetic union views.

California's labor unions had a mixed record of achievement. The state's AFL–CIO merged into the California Labor Federation (1958), but it did not include Bridges's longshoremen and warehousemen or the teamsters unions. Union membership had grown steadily (from 1.4 million in 1950 to 2.2 million in 1974), but industry-by-industry membership varied widely. Automation, which resulted in wholesale replacement of workers by machines, took on a new dimension as computers replaced men in guiding and manipulating machines. Some industrial plants had achieved partial automation, notably in the petroleum and utility fields. A landmark agreement was worked out between Bridges's longshoremen-warehousemen union and the Pacific Maritime Association (1961), which allowed shippers to institute labor-saving machines in return for guaranteed economic protection for union members. Labor-management relations had become an incredibly complicated affair.

Agricultural Labor

The agricultural labor picture contrasts sharply with industrial labor. After the war, farm labor was about the only major group of unorganized workers. They were specifically excluded from federal labor laws, like fair labor standards, minimum wages and social security, and did not benefit from state laws like disability insurance and minimum wages extended to other workers. These migratory, seasonal workers still "rode the circuit" to work the harvest of orchard and field crops in labor gangs. Their ranks were swollen with Mexican workers imported under the *bracero* program ("the strong-armed ones") or "wetbacks" who crossed the border illegally to work in the California fields. The bracero program, which had been introduced as a wartime measure (1942 for World War II, renewed 1952 for the Korean War) had developed into a long-range, cheap labor supply for the California growers until 1964, when Congress finally terminated the program. Under the terms of the U.S.–Mexico agreement, the federal government supervised the Mexican workers employed by labor representatives of the growers, a unique instance where the government supplied employers with their labor.

Farm laborers generally worked at stoop labor for low wages under poor working and living conditions. A governor's investigating committee in the 1960's pointed out that only 25 percent lived in decent housing and over 30 percent of the housing had open "pit privies" for toilets and inadequate water facilities. They generally worked for giant corporate farms, which comprised 7 percent of the farms and employed over 70 percent of the farm labor, of which 80 percent were braceros (1960). The growers' tendency to use the Mexican workers prompted a writer to comment that the growers, to keep wages low, pitted alien workers against American workers, who were often forced to subsist on local welfare rolls.

By the 1960's public attention was drawn to the farm labor situation. Two groups moved into the San Joaquin fields to organize workers into a union and secure collective bargaining rights. They included the Agricultural Workers Organizing Committee (AWOC, 1959) sponsored by the AFL–CIO, and the National Farm Workers Union (NFWU, 1961), organized by Cesar Chavez, who went from farm laborer to community service worker to union organizer to help his people in the fields. In 1965 AWOC, comprising mostly Filipino workers, joined shortly afterwards by Chavez's NFWU, struck the big growers in the Delano area. When the growers resorted to strikebreakers, AWOC and NFWU combined forces to form the United Farm Workers and called a nationwide boycott, which applied to grapes and other products of the growers, like DiGiorgio's canned goods (sold under the S&W label) and

Schenley's liquors. The farm labor coalition soon evolved when Bridges's Longshoremen's Union honored the boycott by refusing to move grapes out of the Pacific Coast ports, and civil rights workers, notably churchmen and students, joined the Delano picket lines. The longest farm labor strike in American history terminated in 1966 when Schenley and then DeGiorgio signed contracts with the NFWU. In 1970 when Chavez moved into the Salinas lettuce fields, local growers quickly signed contracts with the Teamsters Union, which reneged on its promise to NFWU not to organize fieldworkers, thus complicating the labor–management struggle in the fields.

Meanwhile, Congress under pressure of Kennedy and Johnson forces (Chavez converted Robert Kennedy to his cause) terminated the bracero program (1963) and extended federal funds (1964 Economic Opportunity Act) to help migrant workers, including better housing. The move to extend federal labor laws to farmworkers was defeated by Chavez, who would have had to give up his strategic weapon of secondary boycott, which was illegal under federal law. By the mid-1970's the farm labor situation in California still remained complex and uncertain.

Transportation

Motor Vehicles

Motor vehicles after 1945 were more than ever a dominant force in society. The automobile became practically indispensable to family life, particularly in suburban areas. Trucks, with their inherent advantage of store-to-door deliveries, far outdistanced the railroad in intercity transportation. California still led the nation in motor vehicles. By 1970, it registered over 10 million cars (10 percent) and 1.5 million buses and trucks (12 percent). Los Angeles county, which had the world's heaviest concentration of cars, was exceeded by only three states (New York, Pennsylvania, and Texas). Southern California boasted a car for every two people. The state also recorded the highest figures for accidents, congestion, and pollution, but these figures, when considered on a per capita basis or by detailed record accounting (often not kept elsewhere) or by remedial measures (usually pioneered by Californians), reveal that California fared well compared to other states in dealing with such problems.

The federal and state government accelerated highway and road development to meet burgeoning postwar demands. The Federal Highway Act (1944) allocated $1.5 billion for the newly inaugurated Interstate Highway System, for local primary and secondary roads (farm-to-market and feeder roads), and for roads in national forests, national parks, and other public lands. The State Highway Act (Collier–Burns, 1946) established the postwar basis of California's system. The landmark act strengthened control of the state highway commission and its corollary State Highway Division (SHD) in planning, constructing and maintaining the state highway system, including highways through cities. It also increased highway users taxes by 50 percent for financing the costly expansion; and it revised the formula for allocating state funds between Northern and Southern California (45-55 ratio) with a guaranteed share for all counties after the north-south allocation (Mayo Amendment).

Federal and state policies were revised a decade later. The Federal Interstate and Defense Act (1957) enlarged federal responsibilities in highway development. The measure financed 90 percent of highways built for the interstate system connecting the nation's principal cities. The legislature approved the state freeway system (1957)—the nation's first—which, coupled to federal aid, proved to be a boon to the state's transportation system. The legislature also pioneered in remedial measures dealing with growing problems, notably pedestrian malls in city downtown areas (1960), state motor vehicle pollution board (1960), mandatory anti-smog devices (1963), and a state scenic highway program (1965). No other state matches California in the extent of such programs.

By the 1970's public disenchantment with the automobile culture and freeway system was manifested in various ways. Local communities for some time fought running battles over the SHD's preoccupation with the engineering aspects of highway construction and its disregard for esthetic and human values. Conservationist and environmentalist groups joined local communities in imposing strictures, though the SHD with powerful allies like the "freeway lobby" seem to be retaining the upper hand. More and more people were using public transportation for getting to work, the motorcycle and bicycle for personal transportation. Berkeley and other communities charted bike routes through city streets with penalties for cars encroaching on them. No one seemed sure which direction the declining motor vehicle industry and local revolts against autos and freeways would take, but it was clear that transportation was undergoing a major change.

Railroads

The nation's railroads went into steady decline after the war. After impressive wartime achievements without government management (unlike World War I), they failed to keep up with national growth, steadily losing rail mileage and passenger service but not freight. Automobiles, buses, and trucks took over the bulk of passenger and freight traffic; oil pipelines and freight barges emerged as effective rivals with land and water transport; and the airlines finally exceeded the railroads in passenger service (1957). The railroads made valiant efforts to keep up with competition: they modernized operations by phasing out steam engines for more flexible diesel engines and introduced innovative passenger car features like the Vistadome (1945) for unobstructed views of passing scenery. Shippers used pneumatic machinery for loading and unloading freight cars. Congress lent belated assistance with the 1958 Transportation Act which gave railroads greater freedom from government regulations. It relieved the railroads of declining passenger business by setting up the National Railroad Passenger Corporation (Amtrak, 1970), a quasi-public corporation which operated a basic intercity railroad passenger service.

In California, the railroad business was still an important factor of state economic life, though rail mileage declined (7,950 in 1940 to 7,750 in 1960). The railroads improved equipment and facilities for better service, especially in moving freight, the moneymaker. The Southern Pacific was still first in railroad operations, but important positions were held by Western Pacific in the north and by Santa Fe and Union Pacific in the south. The SP reorganized and modernized its railroad operations. It moved its corporate home from Kentucky to Delaware (1947) when Kentucky began collecting personal property taxes, raising SP's tax bill from $100,000 a year to $4 million though the railroad did not operate in that state. It reequipped its famous trains for postwar passenger service, notably the new Sunset Limited streamliner between Los Angeles and San Francisco, the Cascade overnight and Shasta daylights from the Bay Area to Portland (new), and the Golden State for the Los Angeles-to-Chicago run. It specialized in synchronizing train–truck operations for store-to-door deliveries through its subsidiary truck companies, still retaining its monopoly in moving perishable foodstuffs in the Imperial and Salinas valleys. It specialized in sophisticated piggyback truck–trailer and ship container freight services (moving 250,000 units annually), hardly matched by its rivals. It extended its pipeline into six other states (2,750 miles) for moving refined petroleum product and coal slurry for other industries. The Southern Pacific encountered public resistance as it downgraded passenger services (after 1955) for profitable freight operations. The Southern Pacific's 12-state empire, which included over half of the railroads in California, was the nation's largest railroad until the Burlington–Northern 1971 merger.

Aircraft

The aircraft industry experienced phenomenal expansion with the upsurge of postwar airport construction and air travel. Defense expansion during wartime resulted in the building of new airports and enlarging of old ones (2,500 to 3,000 between 1941 and 1945) for military service. After the war Congress enacted the Federal Airport Act (1946) which inaugurated a national airport plan with federal funds available for constructing and extending local airports—as high as 70 percent for municipal airports. The 1958 Federal Aviation Act with the Federal Aviation Administration (formerly Civil Aeronautics Administration) assigned national defense and commercial aviation requirements. State and local governments also contributed to airport development. The state established rigid safety standards for local and private airports and matched county and municipal funds for local airports. By 1970 California had over 1,800 airports, 90 heliports, and 41 military air bases. Los Angeles and San Francisco International airports, the focal points for California air travel, underwent periodic expansion to keep up with the heavy traffic in passenger and freight service. They ranked second and fifth respectively among the nation's airports in size and scope of operations.

Airport expansion reflected the enormous popularity of air travel in California. By 1950 California led the nation in airline passenger travel, and by 1970 over three million persons traveled the airlines annually. Californians far outdistanced other states in interstate and foreign travel (12 million in 1963). Businessmen and public officials commuted regularly on the Los Angeles–San Francisco run and among other California cities. Los Angeles and San Francisco airports annually moved ten and seven million passengers respectively—the air corridor between the two metropolises was the world's busiest. Private flights matched commercial flights; the state registered over 110,000 licensed pilots and 17,000 private aircraft, most of which were used for business and recreation. Californians were deeply immersed in the air age.

California's aircraft companies experienced sharp fluctuations of good and bad times. After the war, the big producers—Douglas, Lockheed, North American, Northrop and Vultee—made the painful transition from military to commercial plane production, closing down branch plants, consolidating facilities, and designing and producing aircraft to capture markets. The Korean War and defense expenditures dramatically revived the sluggish industry. Douglas which had an early edge with its talented plan designers, was overwhelmed with defense orders it was unable to handle. Mismanagement by the founder and his son—successor led to costly mistakes, and financial woes of the 1960's prompted Douglas's bankers to force a merger with the Kansas-based McDonnell Aircraft, whose owner had been quietly buying up Douglas stock. Lockheed, North American, and General Dynamics, along with Washington-based Boeing, emerged as the leaders in the nation's burgeoning aerospace industry, which expanded from jetcraft and missiles in the 1950's to spacecraft in the 1960's. All developed into huge conglomerates comprising diversified companies producing and distributing varied products in plants scattered in other states and countries for regional, national, and world markets. They owed much of their success to effective lobbying for defense contracts and generous federal underwriting of production costs. Even these supercorporations had their troubles, however, especially with defense cutbacks during the Vietnam slowdown in the 1960's, and in some cases of corporate mismanagement. Lockheed, which had grown under top leadership, suffered mismanagement in the supersonic transport (SST) program during the 1960's, and Congress had to bail it out with additional financing. The aerospace industry, like other industries, had its share of troubles with the economic downswing of the 1970's.

Communications

Motion Pictures, Radio, and Television

These three segments of the communications industry were involved in a complex inter-industry setup, evolving from separate developments after World War II. The motion picture sector emerged from the war under oligopolistic control of the Big 5—MGM, Paramount, RKO, 20th Century Fox, and Warner—which had integrated film production and distribution with theater circuits. (They produced over 40 percent of the films and owned one-eighth of all theaters to control the great majority of first-run films—the big money makers.) The setup was drastically altered when the federal government revived its antitrust suit against Paramount (1946), which culminated in the Supreme Court Decision ordering the Big 5 to divest their theater circuit and halve the number of their theaters to restore competition in the field. In the shakeup that followed, independents like Columbia, Universal, and United Artists gained in film production and distribution.

The motion picture companies were shaken up by other developments. Technology made its impact with larger screens, color films, 3-dimensional films, and stereophonic sound (Cinerama) in movie theaters. Important producers, directors, and film stars became independent; they secured percentage cuts of film profits and sometimes rented company facilities to produce their own films. More and more companies filmed productions in European locations to escape high taxes and labor costs. Foreign companies invaded the American market with quality films produced by outstanding directors, like France's Truffaut, Italy's Antonioni, Sweden's Bergman, Japan's Kurosawa. Independent companies operating out of New York, San Francisco, and other cities also made inroads on the Hollywood film market with the experimental films, and later, pornographic and underground films.

Hollywood took on a new look as outsiders took over movie corporations from film-oriented management. Pioneering the new look were Arthur Krim and Robert Benjamin, a lawyer-management team who took over United Artists (by 1955); they curtailed film production, rented and sold the company's film library and studio properties, and diversified company operations other ways. Walt Disney, who played Pied Piper to the nation's children for years, formed companies to produce films for movies and television and to sponsor spectacular recreational resorts (Disneyland and Disney World). Another trend began when Paramount was taken over by ABC radio-television (1953) and Warner by International Latex (1954) in a process of corporation mergers and demergers still going on today. When television hit its stride in the 1960's, television company producers made increasing use of movie libraries and studios in producing filmed entertainment in this business marriage of convenience.

A similar inter-industry battle developed when David Sarnoff's RCA encountered rivals out to break its long-time domination of the nation's entertainment, especially from CBS under William Paley's leadership. In phonographs, CBS's Columbia 33-rpm records won over RCA Victor's 45 rpm records (1949), when the LP's replaced the conventional 78 rpms. In radio, RCA was hit on two fronts. CBS ended RCA's NBC leadership in radio broadcasting, which Paley achieved by luring enemy talent like Jack Benny and Red Skelton with better deals. Zenith led a successful revolt against RCA's monopolistic licenses for which radio manufacturers paid substantial royalty fees; by 1974 Zenith passed RCA in radio manufactures with California's Magnavox gaining ground. In television the long complicated industry warfare over RCA's electronic color and CBS's mechanical color television systems ended with RCA losing the battles but winning the war, in that its system was adopted nationwide. By 1960 television hit its stride; four out of five families had a television set.

By 1970 the entertainment media had developed into a complex setup of which California was an integral part. Californians were generally on the periphery of the eastern-based inter-industry struggles concerning phonographs, radio, and television, but they were leaders in technological developments. They also contributed innovations in radio and television programming, including educational programs, listener-sponsored stations (pioneered by Berkeley's KPFA radio station in 1949), public service broadcasts, and underground stations (led by Los Angeles's KTTV). Hollywood had lost its prewar prominence as the world's film capital, but it was still the nation's leader in radio and television show productions.

Telephone and Telegraph

Wireless communication underwent remarkable development with the application of electronics technology. Western Union completed a 7500-mile transcontinental microwave system between the key cities of Boston, New York, Los Angeles, and San Francisco for handling every form of electronic communication in huge volume at high speeds. Despite telephone competition which forced reduced field operations, Western Union still dominates the state telegraph. Mckay, its chief rival, and five other companies concentrate on cable and radio service to foreign countries. Pacific Telephone and Telegraph and General Telephone (which operates in Southern California) dominated the state's telephone field, which has over 40 small companies. Technology made possible special telephone service for mobile units (auto or truck to home or office), for giant companies (PBX switchboards), for transmitting radio and television programs, for data transmission, teletypwriter, telemeter, and telephone transmissions.

The monopolistic industry continued to be dominated by American Telephone and Telegraph at home and International Telephone and Telegraph (ITT) abroad. They enjoyed public acceptance of their benign power and wealth until the Watergate investigation exposed ITT's business deals involving the Nixon administration. ITT also captured public attention when it grew into a huge conglomerate (it acquired 150 companies between 1960 and 1970) and invaded the American market, which ATT had by common agreement. In 1974 ATT was hit with a U.S. Justice Department antitrust prosecution, the Justice Department's biggest on record.

Trade

Domestic Trade

Marketing activities underwent major changes that were particularly pronounced in California. The catalyst was the consuming public, which not only grew in proportion to the rapid population, but acquired wartime savings and higher incomes to purchase long-coveted consumer goods like fashionable clothes, household appliances, and children's toys. Wholesalers and retailers focused on these consumer buyers, encouraging credit and installment payments, discount buying and trade-ins, bringing to a postwar peak marketing trends underway since the turn of the century. Consumer purchasing power soared ($23 billion in 1951 to $56 billion in 1960) and greatly accelerated the trend toward discriminatory or selective buying. After 1960 wholesalers and retailers gave increasing attention to youthful buyers who became conspicuous consumers of stylish clothes and specialized merchandise. The proliferated consumer market helped set the stage for postwar developments in marketing activities.

The expanding retail trade, especially in the growing suburban areas, shook up conventional marketing ways. Manufacturers along with wholesalers and retailers concentrated on products of different colors, styles, and types, which resulted in an unprecedented diversity of consumer goods. As suburban communities grew, neighborhood and regional shopping centers sprouted up to meet customer preferences for quick convenient shopping trips. These shopping centers ranged from a few acres to over 100 acres and included various combinations of general, specialty, and variety stores. The supermarkets set a trend by selling nonfood products, especially household merchandise, which hurt variety stores. Discount houses set another trend; they originated as buyer clubs whose members paid lower prices when patronizing certain stores and blossomed out by the 1950's. These large stores, located in low-rent areas, bought in bulk or job lots from manufacturers rather than wholesalers, and they oriented store operations to presold customers by limited advertising and sales promotion and reduced personal service to undersell rivals. Other suburban stores were forced to adopt or improve upon such techniques to survive the competition. These developments, in turn, forced other stores to adopt or improve to survive the competition, which resulted in immensely complicated marketing operations.

In the city, downtown stores and chain stores were hard hit by these developments. The downtown stores, committed to the conventional setup of strategic location in high-rent areas, heavy advertising and sales promotion, and customer services, struggled to survive by expanding operations or simply went out of business. The big department stores set the pace for branch store operations. In the Southland, Broadway Stores, following Bullock's prewar examples, established branch stores in Palm Springs (1950), Beverly Hills (1952), and Pasadena (1958), while in the north the Emporium established stores in Stonestown (1950), Palo Alto (1956), and San Jose (1957). Bullock's and I. Magnin (1956), followed by Broadway and Hale (1970), merged their respective Los Angeles and San Francisco regional store chains. The chain stores underwent a wave of mergers with conglomerate corporations sometimes taking over. In the grocery field, Safeway, under aggressive management, extended its chain operations into other states and countries (Europe after 1952 and Australia by 1957); it toppled Atlantic and Pacific from its historic leadership position to lead the nation's grocery chains. National and regional chains fought each other and local independent stores to sustain their share of the expanding market, as exemplified by United Grocers, which retained its position in the Bay Area.

Foreign Trade

Meanwhile California's foreign trade received new inpetus from several developments. The transport system was greatly expanded with extended highway and railroad facilities, big truck trailer vehicles, gigantic ocean tankers, and jumbo cargo aircraft after 1970. San Francisco Bay had the largest number of ports (22), but Los Angeles emerged as the nation's second biggest port after New York. Sacramento acquired a ship channel to compete with Stockton's earlier example (1933) for moving Central Valley products on ocean vessels. Ports developed for specialized uses like oil shipments (Huntington Beach, El Segundo, Ventura, and San Luis) and lumber (Eureka and Fort Bragg). Technology made its impact with mechanized facilities for handling cargo (fork lift, loading cranes, and container shipments) and automatic operations. California's strategic position built up by Pacific operations during World War II was enhanced by accelerated postwar trade with Latin America and the Mideast in the 1950's and with the Orient after 1970.

19 The Fragmented Society

A. SOCIETY

THE SETTING

California after 1945 experienced a population explosion that, within two decades, made it the nation's most populous state. People continued to pour into the state. For over two decades after 1945, an estimated 1500 people arrived daily to take up residence in the state. Their numbers were swelled by a spectacular baby boom. The overwhelming proportion of people (over 90 percent) lived in urban areas, most of them in the metropolitan areas of Los Angeles, San Diego, and San Francisco.

As elsewhere in the nation, California's continuing industrialization and urbanization resulted in further transformation of the physical environment and of people's lives. As the central areas of cities became congested, people moved into less dense suburban areas and sparsely settled farmlands on the urban fringe. These were mostly middle-class white families escaping business and traffic congestion, deteriorating schools and public services, and the ghettos of racial minorities and poor whites, who remained in the city centers. Suburban areas, growing with gas stations and shopping centers, later augmented by industries occupying remaining tracts, extended the urban continuum into rural areas. Vast transportation networks carried streams of people between the residential, commercial, and industrial subdivisions of the metropolitan orbit. The trend of "megalopolis in motion," which had occurred in the three largest metropolitan areas before the war, now took place in a half-dozen new metropolises and numerous smaller cities along the coast and in the central valley. The dispersion of heterogeneous people among the different types of communities contributed to the making of a fragmented society.

DEVELOPMENT

The immediate postwar years provided the setting for the consumer society. Returning servicemen and defense workers, loaded with government benefits (for example, GI loans) and war savings, found jobs and searched out homes, usually in new subdivisions in outlying city areas. Their steady incomes and profitable investments enabled them to build a life of abundance and pleasure that had been denied them during the Depression and World War II.

Suburbia came to represent the social norm in California and other urbanized states. It comprised mostly white, middle-class people who lived in custom-built or tract houses with spacious lawns in planned subdivisions complete with churches, schools, shopping centers, and other public facilities. Home reflected variegated family styles. Family meals might be store-bought, pre-cooked dinners, or home cooked from packaged or fresh foods. Households featured electrical appliances for cooking, cleaning, and yard work, as well as radios, phonographs, and television sets for entertainment. Home recreation and sports, spurred by mass production of inexpensive equipment, widened opportunities for family entertainment. In Southern California, home swimming pools became a status symbol. A Los Angeles county survey revealed that one in ten families owned a pool, and most of them lived in suburbia. For many people, the home rather than the community became the social center.

The emerging consumer society produced strong but mixed emotions. Some pointed to fragmented family relations: the commuting father often absent from home, the harried mother beset with endless family chores, and the permissively raised, freely roving children. Some declared people's lives enriched by the abundance of consumer goods; others retorted that their lives were "anesthetized" and "homogenized" by a bland uniformity. (The supermarket that featured 1,500 items in 1945 and over 5,600 items a decade later showed a sharp rise in sales of medicinal drugs like aspirin and tranquilizers for tension.) Critics declared people to be so preoccupied with personal status that they had become passive about public affairs, obsessed with material wants and insensitive of human concerns, especially of less fortunate people. Furthermore, said critics, people had become so devoted to the pleasure principle that they were subverting the Protestant ethic, the cohesive moral force holding American society together. Thoughtful men became increasingly aware that the apparently healthy society had cancerous sores.

The year 1960 was a turning point in postwar society. President Kennedy inaugurated a reawakening for Americans with an inspiring call to ask not what their country could do for them, but what they could do for their country. The Peace Corps, which attracted mostly idealistic youth to socio-economic programs for helping needy people in under-developed nations, drew most of its recruits from California; UC-Berkeley led the nation's colleges and universities. President Johnson implemented landmark measures for civil rights, and economic and educational opportunities for racial minorities and other underprivileged groups at home. Michael Harrington's *The Other America* (1963), which spotlighted the hard-core poverty group as a social problem in that they lacked the education and job skills to be employable, shocked the Johnson Administration into launching the War on Poverty program. In California, the Brown administration enthusiastically carried out these federal programs. By mid-decade, however, the liberal government programs for domestic reform bogged down under the financial needs of the accelerating war in Vietnam, and under the impatience of the grassroots movements for civil rights and peace.

Social Revolution

Meanwhile, protest movements in reaction to the consumer society grew into a full-scale social revolution by the mid-1960's. The civil rights movement for black equality extended to equal rights for Chicanos,

Indians, the poor, and women, each moving in different directions and occasionally overlapping. The peace movement evolved from small pacifist groups protesting nuclear warfare to a large coalition acting to end the Vietnam war. Interspersed with these movements were disenchanted youth of two types who sometimes came together for a common cause. One type were alienated youth, initially, "rebels without a cause," who sought personal meaning in life through countercultural experiences. They were the "beat generation" of the late 1950's and the "hippies" of the 1960's. The other type were student activists who, having swung from liberal to radical leaders, by the mid-1960's had abandoned the ineffectual Old Left ideological stance (communism and socialism) for more pragmatic New Left techniques of direct action for immediate results. All these movements culminated in a series of violent incidents and major showdowns between 1964 and 1968, ranging from local confrontations in scattered communities and on college campuses to mass marches on the national capitol in demonstrations for civil rights (1963, 1964), peace (1967, 1969), and the poor (1968).

Extremist groups of the right and left, notably the John Birch Society and Students for a Democratic Society (which came under radical control after 1966), wrought havoc with the traditional politics of conservative and liberal groups seeking remedies by compromise. Examples were the role of reactionaries at the 1964 Republican National Convention (Goldwater campaign) and the radical disruption at the 1968 Democratic National Convention. Toward the end of the decade, adamant conservative forces routed confused liberals, captured public support, and took over governmental leadership: in 1966 Ronald Reagan won the governorship from Brown in California, and in 1968 Nixon won the presidency. The active phase of social revolution had passed its high point, but its repercussions were felt well into the decade of the 1970's.

ANALYSIS

The People

Population jumped from 9.3 million in 1945 to about 21 million by 1975. California's population increased around 50 percent each decade, far exceeding the nation's average, which was more or less 15 percent. It passed New York as the most populous state in 1962 and by the 1970's constituted 10 percent of the nation's population. The native-born, spurred by the postwar baby boom, rose in proportion to the state's population but were still outnumbered by immigrants by approximately a 44 to 56 percent ratio. Immigrants came mostly from the Midwest (28 percent), more from the northern tier than from the southern tier of midwestern states, though a greater proportion than before came from the Pacific, Mountain, and Northeastern states. More immigrants came from Texas than any other state; in some years Texas received more Californians than California received Texans. The foreign immigrant (about 8 percent) was numerically less significant than in previous decades. Still California had the greatest number of any state in every category of national group, which attested to the heterogeneous character of its people.

The postwar population picture showed significant changes. Southern California increased its lead substantially over Northern California, though all areas showed appreciable population gains. The Southern California counties more than doubled in people, from 5.6 million in 1950 to 10.8 million in 1960, with Orange County registering the greatest increase (215,000 to over one million). The city of Los Angeles grew by leaps and bounds to over 2.4 million people; it not only outdistanced San Francisco (740,000) but overtook Chicago to become the nation's second largest city. Military personnel were an important segment of the state's population; members of the Armed Forces stationed in California constituted 10 to 12 percent of the state's total. Racially, Blacks outnumbered Latinos, Asians, and Indians; these comprised around 25 percent of the state's total. Young adults were in the majority, with the state's median age at 30. The great number of youths who were born after the war gave them population predominance when they reached maturity in the 1960's. The preponderance of racial minorities and youth would have important bearing on historical developments in the 1960's and 1970's.

Urbanization was the most conspicuous feature of the state population picture. California developed a population density in settled areas exceeded by only two states (New Jersey and Rhode Island). The state's three metropolitan areas in 1945 increased by the mid-1970's to a dozen metropolises scattered along the central coastal and Central Valley areas. Over 90 percent of the people lived in these urban areas, 75 percent of them in the metropolises of Los Angeles, San Diego, and San Francisco, with 50 percent in the Los Angeles metropolis alone. Surprisingly, Los Angeles city population concentration was far less than that of New York City (1,500 to 16,000 people per square mile), reflecting the former's outward expansion and the latter's upward expansion. The urbanization trend owed much to the flow of immigrants from other states to California urban centers.

Communities

The Counties

County areas were greatly transformed by accelerated industrialism and urbanization which now affected rural as well as urban counties. The urban sprawl created by expanding city areas cut deep into surrounding agricultural lands and other free-belt areas, drastically altering the landscape. A jet pilot flying over an urban county would see congested nucleus or core cities surrounded by a conglomerate mass of residential, commercial, and industrial subdivisions extending to green farmlands and brown mountain areas beyond. Ribbonlike freeways and highways interweaving among rural and urban areas of the county carried flowing streams of auto, bus, and truck traffic. The countryside was also marked by occasional thoroughfare railroad tracks, spindlelike hydroelectric transmission lines, and concrete aqueducts carrying water from distant dams and reservoirs. The panaromic landscape might present a dazzling sight bathed in sunlight or a depressing view clouded with yellow-gray smog.

  The postwar picture was symptomatic of the county governmental situation. The counties were constantly preoccupied with perplexing problems of the amorphous urban sprawl which overlapped city, county, and special district boundaries. County officials were besieged by varied needs of diverse special-interest groups, especially residents, businessmen, and industrialists in outlying subdivision areas seeking municipal facilities and services. Local politicians working with county officials and administrators, sometimes with help from state and federal officials, developed complex cooperative arrangements for carrying out diverse government programs serving the needs of different groups. Los Angeles continued to pace the counties, conceiving sophisticated uses of local powers, special district organizations, and contractual agreements among intra- and intergovernmental agencies, though several progressive-minded urban and rural counties made imaginative contributions. Some larger counties were performing over 900 different types of activities emanating from 22 basic functions. The

California counties, so widely disparate in form and style, were regarded as the nation's strongest county governments and won national laurels for innovative programs and professional performance.

Cities and Towns

The postwar population and industry explosion left indelible marks on city and town development. People in general as well as manufacturing firms exhibited wider choices than previously in selecting communities; most of them concentrated in growing metropolises, but many located in distant valley and mountain areas easily served by freeways. Community builders made bold and often risky concessions, public and private institutions making generous loans for home and plant construction, and county and city officials extending costly municipal services to newly developed areas. Big contractors used monster machines to raze downtown building blocks, uproot valley tree groves, and level rugged hills in laying out vast tracts for community projects like civic centers, business and commercial centers, and residential and industrial sub-divisions. Private land developers built up in suburban and rural areas subdivisions of crowded tract homes or spacious custom homes, and of regional shopping centers and industrial parks with long, low buildings and large parking lots. Even remote Sierra regions and the forbidding Colorado desert areas were transformed by budding new communities. While some marveled at these modernized communities and diverse adaptations to changing conditions, others decried bewildering local governmental problems and the appalling environmental deterioration accompanying uncontrollable development.

The most conspicuous manifestation of this uncontrollable growth was the urban sprawl that appeared in the state's metropolitan areas. The urban sprawl profoundly altered the character of the cities. It gave rise to the so-called phantom cities, a phenomenon described by conservationists Alfred Heller and Samuel Woods, who also coined the term "slurb" for urban sprawl—"sloppy, sleazy, slovenly, slipshod semi-cities." The new phantom cities share with traditional cities an urban character but differ in that they are not self-contained communities operating on their own resources as before. The unincorporated city, where some 50 percent of the people live, is served and governed by the county or a special district. There are over 2000 special districts providing over 100 types of services, the largest being the Metropolitan Water District which distributes Colorado River water throughout the five Southern California counties. The special-interest city exists to serve a particular socio-economic interest, usually initiated by an industry group or land developer. Conspicuous examples are Industry, which is 18 miles long and at some points 200 feet wide; Dairyland, which is advertised as having 5000 cows and 500 people; and Rolling Hills, a lovely residential area overlooking the Pacific—all located in Los Angeles county. The contract city is exemplified by Lakewood (1954), the first one, a community built up by private developers and which purchases municipal services from Los Angeles county. The seasonal city is primarily a recreational community in a mountain, seacoast, or desert area, where people maintain second homes for escape from urban living. The legitimate city, which includes established communities like Berkeley and Pasadena, has lost much of its self-reliance and independence to outside pressures and governing bodies. Despite their disparate backgrounds, Berkeley and Pasadena had acquired similar community traits that prompted municipal officials to develop close ties in working out common problems—in the manner of sister cities. The regional city, comprising the state's metropolises, is treated below.

Another postwar phenomenon is the "instant city" created by private developers as a self-contained community. It is best typified by Foster City on San Francisco Bay and Valencia in Los Angeles's San Fernando Valley. Foster City, named after the Oklahoma land developer behind it, is a land-filled, bayside community featuring diked canals and lagoons, designed to accommodate 35,000 people. Valencia, planned by a land development firm for Newhall Land Company's largest ranch property, envisages a community for over 250,000 people, the nation's largest (along with the Irvine's development). Both cities feature planned neighborhood clusters of family homes and apartment buildings with a civic center, buried power lines, and spacious recreation parks and shopping malls. By the mid-1970's, these advertised "garden cities" were experiencing serious financial and governmental problems.

Each city and town developed its version of handling community problems arising from local growth. City councils encountered and dealt with crisscrossing interests of such diverse groups as downtown merchants, neighborhood improvement associations, and real estate and subdivision developers in establishing priorities for government programs in community development—each group advocating its idea of community. The city fathers responded to such community pressures by annexing neighboring areas, changing building codes and zoning lines to control subdivision development, and adjusting budgets to secure revenues for financing greatly expanded municipal services. They sought county and state aid; when this proved inadequate some went to Washington to secure federal assistance, especially for community redevelopment projects. Some cities, like San Leandro, even turned down federal offers for such urban redevelopment schemes, preferring "to go it alone" to preserve home rule integrity—and being financially able to do so. In Petaluma, the city council, plagued by growth problems, attempted to restrict population growth by municipal ordinance; the issue, which involves interference with a person's freedom of movement, is still pending court decision (1974). In Berkeley, radical elements launched an intense campaign to decentralize municipal functions on a neighborhood basis—implementing a version of participatory democracy—which badly split the once congenial community. However, it still retains its highly touted city-manager system and was singled out in a 1974 national survey as foremost in community services.

Metropolitan Developments

The metropolis became an enlarged theater of urban and industrial forces which were transforming the cities and towns within it. People and industries, whether locally established or newly arrived, dispersed about the metropolitan area, locating in favorable or strategic communities, so that the metropolis became a conglomeration of specialized areas of residential tracts, business and shopping centers, and industrial parks inside or outside of established cities and towns. The central city assumed greater importance as an administrative center for business, industry, and government of the widening metropolitan orbit. Larger satellite cities evolved into central cities with dependent neighboring communities. Smaller cities and towns emerged as specialized areas, whether bedroom, business, governmental (military facility), manufacturing, recreational, or shopping communities. The steady process whereby growing communities incorporated into cities, and cities annexed adjoining areas, soon urbanized the entire region. The metropolitan area became a regional city, a metropolis converted into a megalopolis.

The pacesetters for California metropolitanism were still Los Angeles and the San Francisco Bay Area. The Los Angeles metropolis became a focal point for the Southern California megalopolis. The conversion took place with the continuous outward expansion from six urban centers (Los Angeles, San Diego, San Bernardino, Santa Barbara, Santa Ana, and Ventura) until by 1960 the entire southern plain and adjoining valleys were urbanized (50 persons per square mile by census definition). The area comprised six urbanized areas with 12 central cities and a number of secondary city centers. Los Angeles, the primary city, experienced a unique development of centralization and decentralization which made it into a complex functioning city. Its central business district, with corridor avenues like Wilshire Boulevard, contained business, commercial, financial, industrial, and governmental office buildings and facilities, interspersed with apartment buildings and park areas. Its peripheral areas comprised assorted residential, shopping, and industrial subdivisions. With removal of the building ceiling (1956) high-rise buildings appeared in the downtown and suburban areas. Los Angeles paced other central cities like Alhambra, Beverly Hills, Burbank, Hawthorne, Inglewood, Long Beach, and Santa Monica. The historic community decentralization of the Southern California metropolis was attributed to a combination of factors: single-family homes, auto-freeway complex, high personal income, cheap land, easy construction loans, decentralized employment, skilled labor, and expanding market areas.

The San Francisco Bay Area also emerged as a regional city, differing from its southern neighbor in important respects. San Francisco lost considerable status as primary city for the metropolis. It suffered industry relocations and a slowdown in population growth, though it retained its position as administrative and fiscal center for the region and as the core for satellite cities on the Marin and San Mateo peninsulas. The city's downtown rejuvenation with attractive high-rise buildings after the mid-1960's did not alter this trend. Oakland and San Jose emerged as central cities to assume relative independence from the former metropolitan parent city, San Francisco. Generally speaking, Oakland is a nucleus for East Bay communities as San Francisco is for the peninsula communities; both cities are intertwined. As geographer James Vance points out, the Bay Area emerges as a metropolis of urban realms, each realm a functional equal to all others who share a common urban culture, an idea of equality and concert to constitute "sympolis." The metropolis has such a high degree of localized home–job–recreation arrangement, encouraged by its periphery or outer-belt freeway system, that people and industry can and do disregard San Francisco. San Franciscans may believe their cosmopolitan city to be the center of the universe; it is hardly the basic core of the metropolis.

In governmental matters the northern and southern metropolises continued to differ in general setup and basic approaches. A key element

Los Angeles. Expansion from pueblo to metropolis—experimental determination of the limits of growth.

is the character of the primary city. Tightly knit San Francisco, with its consolidated city–county government, still operated in many respects in its tradition of nineteenth-century politics. The city fathers tended to favor downtown business and labor union interests at the expense of the residents, especially minority groups. Amorphous Los Angeles, with its separate city and county governments and strong tradition of progressive rule and area development, exhibited expansive innovative and professional tendencies befitting a mid-twentieth-century setup. (However, professionals occasionally exhibited a "blind eye," as in the case of governmental neglect of the Watts area, which later exploded in violence.) In the workings of local politics, each councilman ruled his bailiwick through a coalition of assorted interests in a way that precluded the dominance of downtown business interests or any single group, a fact recognized by the *Los Angeles Times*, which broadened its downtown stance to a suburban perspective. Postwar development of the northern and southern metropolises exemplified the strong persistence of local historical tradition.

Community Development

Local and state governments confronted serious community problems intensified by industrialism and urbanism. The sudden growth during wartime and postwar years spurred another wave of new communities incorporating into cities and cities annexing adjoining unincorporated county areas. A Community Services Act (1951) enabled people in unincorporated areas to set up special tax districts to obtain desired municipal services of different sorts. A County Services Act (1953) enabled the counties to sell municipal services to special districts requesting them. The intense competition among the counties and their cities for state revenues to help pay for increasing local governmental costs prompted the legislature to issue an ultimatum for them to get together and resolve their differences. The result was the landmark Uniform Sales and Use Tax Act (1953) whereby each county and city received a share of such taxes collected by the state. A startling development resulting from the act occurred when Lakewood, a new community built by private developers, purchased practically all of its municipal services from Los Angeles county with its share of local sales and use taxes, spurring a trend among cities and special districts to do likewise. Such trends improved the ability of local governments to meet community demands for municipal services so important to the life style of its inhabitants, thereby enhancing home rule.

By the 1960's city and county officials were dealing with increasingly complicated governmental problems accompanying continuous growth. They cooperated at the local level and through their statewide associations in developing workable solutions. They relied increasingly on the city manager and the county administrative officer for professional expertise in managing diverse governmental functions. Growing cities exercised restraint in annexing areas, less inclined to expand city territory than in earlier years, particularly in merging unincorporated neighbors eager to benefit from established, low-cost municipal services. Pasadena led the way in ending this freeloading practice by devising a formula for equalizing costs between the city and newly merged areas. A 1963 state law provided for the creation of county-sponsored local formation agencies which had authority to approve or disapprove annexations and incorporations, a move enabling counties to bring some order out of uncontrollable growth.

County and city officials also worked out cooperative schemes for regional approaches to areawide problems affecting their jurisdiction, particularly in the metropolises. Areawide special districts, which had been used earlier in resolving regional park, planning, and water-related problems, were utilized in dealing with postwar problems in particular areas—notably Los Angeles for air pollution (1946) and San Francisco Bay Area for rapid transit (1960) and conservation (1968). The multipurpose district was a vehicle for county and city officials for facing metropolitan-wide problems; it was pioneered by the Association of Bay Area Governments (ABAG, 1960) and followed by the Southern California Association of Governments (SCAG, 1964). Federal and state agencies also became involved in areawide approaches to socio-economic problems like conservation, health, and water. The metropolises emerged with many forms of localized and regional governments, with fragmented structures and engaging in overlapping activities. Political scientist Eugene Lee says the "crazy patchwork of fluid intergovernmental relationships" has resulted in so overfragmented a local government structure as to frustrate meaningful self-government for sound socio-economic development. Community home rule has emerged in the postwar period as a vital and complicated concept.

Colonies, Communes, and Retreats

Utopian communities flourished as before in varied fashion and with uneven success. California was a fertile area for experimental forms of living: it contained the greatest number and widest variety of these postwar communities. These communities developed along several broad lines. Older colonies after the war either dwindled out (Holy City, theosophistic Point Loma) or lingered on (cooperative Tuolumne Farms, organized 1946). Monastic communities did well, though some disappeared or struggled on (Paramananda's La Crescenta). Several older and newly formed monastic communities, like Krotona and Meher Baba in Ojai and the Zen retreat at Tassajara, gained recruits in the 1960's from hippies and other dropouts from society who were attracted to the religious ideas of Asian cults.

Disenchanted leaders and groups fashioned specialized communities for particular members' purposes. In 1958 Charles Dederich, an unemployed refugee from alcoholism, founded Synanon (said to be a mispronunciation of "symposium") to rehabilitate drug addicts through rigid self-help techniques, role-playing games, and highly structured communal living. Synanon grew into a multimillion dollar institution with large facilities in Santa Monica, San Diego, and the Bay Area, attracting drug addicts and professional workers throughout the nation. Mike Murphy converted his family's hot springs resort near Big Sur after 1963 into a highly sophisticated pleasure retreat operating as Esalen Institute with facilities in Los Angeles, San Francisco, and other places. Esalen (the name was taken from Indians native to the Big Sur area) took shape with contributions from its residents and visitors, notably psychiatrists Frederick Perls (Gestalt therapy) and William Schutz (author of the best seller *Joy*) and mystic Alan Watts. Its scenic panorama of mountains and ocean and its permissive environment provided the setting for many forms of individual behavior and group experience. The authoritarian Synanon commune and the libertarian Esalen retreat inspired numerous and varied offshoots, most of which are in California.

The commune idea took on expanded form with the coming of the hippies. These hippie communes had antecedents in early nineteenth-century utopian colonies, including communes with anarchistic structure (sponsored by Josiah Warren) and unorthodox sexual arrangements (Oneida). Forerunners of the postwar movement were experimental refuges in the Bay Area: Ken Kesey's La Honda (1961), a retreat for his friends which included buildings for particular activities (The Shack, appropriately, was for shacking up), and Freedom Farm (1963), set up by a young landowner for several families to live in communal fashion. The hippie commune took form in San Francisco when hippies moved from North Beach to the Haight–Ashbury area, where they built up their own community, establishing the basis of the urban commune. When the Haight–Ashbury degenerated after 1966, hippies moved out and settled on the lands of friendly owners (notably Lou Gottlieb's Morningstar Ranch and William Wheeler's ranch), then invaded other areas, including Freedom Farm, to implement their version of the rural commune. California reportedly has two-thirds of the nation's hippie communes scattered in secluded buildings and homes in cities and isolated rural lands throughout the state.

The communes and retreats are significant developments in postwar society. Like the earlier colonies, they are composed of groups of disenchanted people withdrawing from society to live in their version of the ideal community, only now they are far more numerous and varied and have attracted a greater proportion of young people. They have evolved into distinct social movements which have affected public attitudes and group behavior in modern society.

Social Classes

The American class system continued to be shaped by earlier trends of class leveling wrought by industrialization and urbanization. An urban class structure, with the family still the basic unit, had evolved into a five-tier structure. The upper class, comprising an elite closely knit by personal and business ties, exerted considerable influence in public affairs. The middle class, making up the bulk of people (79 percent), was stratified into upper, middle, and lower levels. It is a "variable kaleidoscope" including business proprietors, professional managers, white- and blue-collar workers, each with distinctive values and all imbued with some degree of upward mobility to improve their status. The majority of middle-class families, according to sociologist Joseph Kahl, generally have a stable family-centered life marked by moderate education and occupational achievement. The lower class comprises unskilled workers who are employed erratically or chronically unemployed. They are generally trapped in a rigid way of life marked by inadequate homes, education, and jobs, and stunted ambitions.

Startling developments were transforming the class system. Statistics for the two decades after 1945 revealed the gross national product increased four times and disposable personal income 2½ times. With the declining numbers of the superrich and of poverty groups (people earning less than $3000 went down 10 percent), some scholars predicted the eventual realization of the near complete middle-class society, hailing middle-class suburbia as the social norm. However, a breakdown of personal income showed that the top and bottom one-tenth had declined but the top second one-tenth had gained considerably, while the middle ranges remained more or less stable and the lower ranges showed only modest gains. Figures for 1960 showed the top 10 percent owned two-thirds of the nation's liquid assets, while over half the nation's population had no assets, relying entirely on personal income for subsistence. The observation that the rich were getting richer and the poor poorer was not facetious. Furthermore, sociologist E. D.

Baltzell asserted, the nation has a "crisis in moral authority" chiefly because the upper class imbued with WASP (White Anglo Saxon Protestant) values has failed to share upper-class traditions by absorbing distinguished members of racial minorities into the elite caste of leadership. The California scene, as revealed by meager available evidence, seemed to mirror the national norm, with emphasis on class flexibility and fluidity of class lines.

Extremist Groups

Disenchanted people protesting seesaw trends in society sought redress in organized action which led to a revival of extremist movements. The postwar emergence of the United States as the most prosperous nation, accompanied by expanded New Deal programs and greater American involvement in world affairs, set the stage for left- and right-wing extremism. Public sentiment, reacting to labor–management showdowns at home and American setbacks abroad (A-bomb secrets, Berlin blockade, the China debacle), soon swung to the right. Henry Wallace's Progressive Party rallied a united left front, but after Wallace's overwhelming defeat in the 1948 presidential election, the communists and socialists sank to near oblivion. Sociologist Daniel Bell pronounced their dénouement in *The End of Ideology* (1960), though radical elements had campaigned for equality for Blacks and for pacifist causes (Peacemakers, 1948).

Meanwhile, reactionary elements gained ground. They comprised new-rich businessmen, better-off workers, and farmers centered in the agrarian Midwest, who suffered anxieties over personal status and national security affected by postwar developments. They lent support to aggressive conservative leaders in Congress, especially in the House Committee on Un-American Activities (HUAC), attempting to reverse the Fair Deal tide. Out of this situation, Joseph McCarthy, senator from Wisconsin, welded disaffected right-wing elements into an anti-Communist crusade that spawned in the early 1950's a reign of fear and hysteria in public affairs. Congress, state legislatures, and other institutions gripped in the Communist-scare campaign imposed loyalty oaths and other devices to weed out suspected Communists in government, business, labor unions, and other places. McCarthy's excessive actions eventually led to his downfall (1954), but the Communist-scare campaign drifted on to the end of the decade.

California was a focal point of the anti-Communist campaign of the 1950's. The reactionary HUAC, in annual "fishing expeditions" to their favorite target state after 1951, hunted for Communists; they succeeded in black-listing a number of suspected writers, directors, and producers in Hollywood's movie industry. The legislature's Un-American Activities Committee degenerated into persecutions and was quietly phased out after removal of its erratic, discredited chairman (Assemblyman Jack Tenney). The University of California's Board of Regents, spurred by reactionary members, took unprecedented action in forcing the dismissal of administrators and faculty members who refused to take a special loyalty oath (1952) because they felt it was in violation of academic freedom. The courts later ruled the oath unconstitutional.

In the 1960's extremism enjoyed a heyday in California and the nation. Right-wing groups grew out of several reactionary constituencies but all were united in attacking liberal administration on the welfare state and the Communist menace. The John Birch Society (JBS, 1958), the most conspicuous of these groups, was organized by Robert Welch, a Massachusetts candy manufacturer disillusioned with the Eisenhower Administration for not implementing "true conservatism" and not halting Communism. The JBS operated secretly through front organizations in carrying out such campaigns as impeaching Earl Warren, eliminating the income tax, and getting the United States out of the United Nations. Its covert activities were exposed when Thomas Storke, the Santa Barbara editor, revealed a JBS student front organization on the UC-Santa Barbara campus, a journalistic feat which won him the Pulitzer Prize. The JBS reached its peak in the 1964 Republican convention in a showdown between the Goldwater and Rockefeller forces, which contributed to the Republican debacle that year. Its stronghold was California, especially in the Southland, which contributed the most members and several important leaders. Another conspicuous right-wing group was the Minutemen, an offshoot of the KKK (revived 1954 in Southern California), which campaigned against Blacks and Jews. Right-wing groups also operated through conservative education and religious organizations, notably the Christian Anti-Communist Crusade, and backed public-office candidates carrying their message.

Left-wing groups in the 1960's were predominantly alienated youth who foresook traditional ways to cut their own niche in society. They comprised mostly idealistic, well-off, white middle-class youth who had been educated to American ideals of freedom and equality only to learn society was rife with social conformity, racial discrimination, and other perverted ideals. They arose like a "phoenix from the ashes" and moved in two directions. The person-oriented, nonpolitical beat-hippie youth dropped out from society to live their chosen life style among their kind. The society-oriented, political-minded student activists sought radical reforms of institutions which they believed had been perverted by the "Liberal Establishment."

The political-minded students took on the label of New Left to show disdain for the Old Left, such as the Socialists, whom they accused of betraying the radical cause by cooperating with liberals and also blamed for their failure to achieve reform. They listened to sympathetic elders (Herbert Marcuse, C. Wright Mills, Paul Goodman), but they developed their own organization and methods through trial and error. In 1960 student activists organized independently on several university campuses (Michigan, Wisconsin, UC-Berkeley) and soon after came together to set up Students for a Democratic Society (SDS, 1962), a youth affiliate of a socialist group (League for Industrial Democracy, headed by Michael Harrington). A larger number of students became involved in socio-political movements, joining Blacks for civil rights in the South, students in campus revolts, draft protesters in anti-Vietnam demonstrations, and farm laborers in California's Delano strike. Militant white student radical leaders (like Tom Hayden, an SDS founder) had strained relations with liberal white and black leaders, and even radical black leaders, because of differences over strategy and tactics.

A turning point was the campus revolt at UC-Berkeley where Mario Savio and other student leaders demonstrated that radical tactics like direct confrontation, flaming rhetoric, and hard-line demands could win political battles against the administration and other authorities. By 1966 the SDS broke into two factions, one reorganized as a military revolutionary group under Tom Hayden. For the remainder of the decade, student activists under the banners of SDS and several local groups engaged in confrontations with authorities backed by police, state militia, and National Guard forces on university campuses, in city streets, and in the nation's capital. The violent showdowns resulted in numerous injuries, a few fatalities, and extensive property damage. A climax came with the showdown at the 1968 Democratic National Convention when public hostility turned into a general backlash against students.

After 1968 the radical left movement subsided. UC-Berkeley experienced a brief flare-up in a local demonstration for converting a vacant university lot into a People's Park (1970). Militants like the

Weathermen went underground and occasionally surface in capturing headlines with terrorist violence (Marin County Courthouse breakout, 1971; Symbionese Liberation Army shootout, 1974). The presence of scattered miniscule groups armed and committed to revolutionary dogma leaves an unfinished page to the movement.

Ethnic Groups

California's postwar ethnic population became increasingly larger and urbanized. All races grew in substantial numbers; by 1970 Chicanos and other Latinos (1.4 million) still led over Blacks (850,000), Asians (350,000), and Indians or Native Americans (90,000). Most were concentrated in the metropolitan areas, manifesting a rural–urban shift, but unlike Caucasians, gravitating to the city downtown and metropolitan central city areas. The growing concentration of minorities in the central city enlarged the ghettos, as in Los Angeles where the central area comprising segregated and integrated neighborhoods resembled a mosaic of different colors, bordered by white surburbia. Los Angeles had the greater number of racial minorities, but San Francisco had the most Chinese. The two metropolises had well over half the state's minority groups, although all metropolitan areas had conspicuous numbers.

Several postwar developments altered the ethnic picture. The ethnic population became more dispersed and stratified into distinct groups. Large numbers of each minority group, benefiting from better education and improved jobs, moved up the social scale from lower to middle class, though a greater proportion of them still held factory and other blue-collar jobs. The higher-income minorities generally moved into middle- and sometimes upper-class neighborhoods, which were segregated or integrated depending on local circumstances. The pattern of nativist sentiment underwent change. Racial discrimination continued after the war in less obvious ways; later it developed into more open forms. It was manifested through segregation in public schools, racial covenants in home purchases, racial bars in labor unions, and selective employment in administrative and management jobs of government and industry. Racial discrimination seemed to lessen toward the Chinese and Japanese, who assimilated into middle-class neighborhoods and occasionally intermarried with Caucasians. It focused more sharply on Blacks, whose presence was made more visible by their color and whose large migrations, especially from the South, often spilled over from ghetto areas into neighboring communities. The generation gap among minorities was particularly pronounced between rebellious youth and their traditional-minded parents who were inclined to accommodation with white majority ways. These various forms of racial discrimination aggravated race conflicts, weighing heaviest on the poverty-stricken class. The situation provided the setting for the urban revolts of the 1960's.

The Racial Uprising

California became deeply involved in the national movement for minority rights. The movement evolved in two stages. The first stage came with the war when Blacks began their campaign for civil rights, which focused primarily on the South. It was spearheaded by the NAACP which pressed for legislation and litigation for implementing constitutional rights, the National Urban League which provided community services, especially for Southern Blacks who migrated to Northern cities, and the Congress on Racial Equality (CORE, organized 1941) which developed nonviolent techniques like "freedom" bus rides and restaurant sit-ins for black resistance to discrimination.

The second stage came in the 1960's with the drive of minority groups for their rights which spread throughout the nation. This drive moved in two directions: middle-class moderates desiring integration into white society pressed for political and legal rights and equal economic opportunities; and radical middle- and lower-class youth, student activists, and ghetto militants, advocated race separation to emphasize racial pride and ethnic traditions. The decade was highlighted by the mass march on Washington which featured Martin Luther King's stirring "I have a dream" speech before the Lincoln Memorial (1963), the Kennedy–Johnson antipoverty and equal economic opportunities and voting rights programs (1964), and the urban ghetto revolts (Harlem, 1964; Watts, 1965). Black Power groups, inspired by Malcolm X (1965) and crystallized in the Black Panthers (1967), combined racial pride and economic deprivation with direct action to set a mode and style. Other minority groups attempted their version (Brown Power, Red Power) with less successful results. Eventually each group went its own way. Compared to other states, California's distinctive multiracial setup and its social mobility produced varied forms of interracial relationships that require separate treatment of each group.

Asians

The Asians continued their separate group patterns after the war. The Orientals showed substantial gains in socio-economic positions; a higher proportion of them were better educated and held more professional and technical jobs than whites. A change in public attitude became evident when Congress altered the immigration laws, abolishing Chinese exclusion (1943) and incorporating Japanese into the national quota system (McCarren—Walter Act, 1952). The Filipinos, however, were among the most deprived and depressed minority groups; unlike the urban-oriented Orientals, they were mostly unskilled workers evenly distributed among rural and urban areas.

Sore spots still remained. San Francisco's Chinatown, the oldest of the nation's continuous ghettos, was second only to New York's Manhattan in population density. It became more crowded with the postwar influx of anti-Communist non-English-speaking immigrants from China. Its thriving restaurants and shops contrasted sharply with its cheap garment industry operating in backstreet "sweatshops." The poverty-stricken families who remained after enterprising families left to merge into white society, had an appallingly high incidence of crime and suicide. Chinatown had changed little in basic structure; it still operated through the Chinese family and district associations under the leadership of the Six Districts without the strong control of earlier times.

The Japanese fared better. Caucasians referred to them as the model minority. Known for their conservative ways and compliant attitudes, the Japanese occasionally demonstrated a capacity for fighting blatant discrimination. In Los Angeles, the Japanese community, in a remarkable display of aggressiveness, successfully defeated the county administration attempt to remove from office the chief medical examiner—coroner, Dr. Thomas Noguchi (1969). By the 1970's Chinese and Japanese youth were pressing for Asian Studies on college campuses to learn more of their ancestral heritage.

Indians

Federal policies greatly altered the traditional treatment of California Indians. The Indian Claims Commission was set up by Congress (1946) to provide federal compensation for Indian land losses and treaty violations. The California Indians after 16 years of litigation received $29 million for clear federal title to over a million acres of land, a situation that was described as a "government forced sale." The termination policy was invoked by Congress (1953) under anti-Indian pressure for relocating Indians from government reservations to urban centers in a scheme to shift Indian responsibilities from the federal to state government. Under the auspices of the Bureau of Indian Affairs (BIA) western Indians were resettled in California cities in such large numbers that by 1960 over half the Indians in California lived in urban areas. The BIA quickly ended special services for Indian education, health, and law enforcement but retained control over rancheria and reservation lands (all but 5000 of 500,000 acres), contrary to termination policy. Federal termination brought mixed reactions from the California Indians; some regretted the loss of federal aid while others resented unfulfilled federal responsibilities for land improvements (housing, roads, sanitation, and water resources). Most shared hostile feelings toward the BIA for its cavalier paternalism and gross mismanagement of Indian affairs in California.

The California Indians remain an anomaly as a minority group. Even today, they lie essentially outside the mass of minority people who are encouraged to assimilate into the American system. They have been practically shut out of the governmental system, having no vehicle for representation in state and local government. They are the lowest group in every socio-economic category, including education, health, housing, and employment, and receive the least attention of federal-state aid programs for minority groups. Their problems have been obscured by the more aggressive urban Indians of organized tribes who migrated from other parts of the nation and have successfully drawn public attention to their problems, as dramatized by the urban Indian takeover of Alcatraz Island (1969). The California Indians are victims of a prejudice not experienced by other minorities or so pronouncedly by other Indians—a discrimination compounded by neglect and rejection.

Latinos

Mexicanos (American and Mexican-born) and other Latinos (Spanish-speaking people) revealed wide disparities in status and group discriminations. In urban areas many with better jobs and higher incomes moved into outlying middle-class neighborhoods, intensifying the predominantly lower-class character of the downtown barrios. In Los Angeles, which had the nation's largest concentration of Mexicanos, the barrios were crowded with assorted middle and lower class, natives and nationals, legal and illegal residents (Mexican nationals without official permits), whose life styles blended Mexican village and American city traditions. The urban Latinos were active in organizing local associations for asserting their rights. In Orange County, the League of United Latin

American Citizens secured a federal injunction (1946) prohibiting several school districts from operating segregated schools—nine years before the famous 1954 Supreme Court school desegregation decision. In Los Angeles, the Community Service Organization (CSO) registered voters who helped elect Edward Roybal as the first Latino city councilman since the 1880's. The Latinos, however, still felt varied forms of discrimination in public schools, in the Catholic Church, in labor unions, and in government and industry employment.

During the 1950's the Latinos suffered from types of government discrimination not experienced by other minorities. The McCarthy Anti-Communist Crusade manifested racist overtones when government investigators focused on Latino activities in community organizations and labor unions. Even the CSO found it necessary to conduct Red-baiting activities to survive such attacks. Federal intervention in California's farm labor problem resulted in the federal "revolving door" policy whereby border restrictions were relaxed to allow legal and illegal Mexican workers to fill labor shortages until after the harvest, when border restrictions were tightened up and the "illegals" were suddenly rounded up for deportation. In Los Angeles, federal and local officials (under provisions of the McCarran–Walter Acts, 1952-1954) systematically raided the barrios and made house searches, and in the process also deported legal residents who happened to be labor "agitators" attempting to organize farm laborers.

A Latino awakening came in the mid-1960's. As Latinos, particularly Chicanos, became increasingly aware of their subservient status in such areas as education, employment, and welfare, they moved to assert their rights. Middle-class Latinos rallied to organizations like the Mexican American Political Association (MAPA), a community service group for helping Mexican nationals and disadvantaged natives. Militant youth in the barrios formed the Brown Berets, based on the Black Panthers. Student activists on high school and college campuses formed campus organizations which became associated with MECHA, a militant Chicano student movement. Los Angeles was the scene of several incidents in the national Chicano movement, notably the mass student walkout in East Los Angeles high school (1968) in protest against inferior educational facilities, and the national Chicano moratorium against the Vietnam war in Laguna Park (1970). Both began as peaceful demonstrations and ended in harsh police crackdowns and mass violence. During the 1970's the movement evolved into a multifront campaign of

Latino groups attempting to find their own place in a more tolerable Anglo society.

Blacks

California's heavy influx of black migration from the South was concentrated in the state's two largest metropolises. Where the white population had tripled in the two postwar decades, the black population increased five times in San Francisco and ten times in Los Angeles. In the Bay Area, Blacks at first concentrated in war industry centers like San Francisco's Hunter's Point, Richmond, and West Oakland, then spilled over into adjoining neighborhoods and communities. Community responses were reflected in Berkeley, which absorbed the Richmond spillover that soon altered the city's racial composition, and San Leandro, where local interests erected a racial barrier to keep out the West Oakland black overflow and preserve the city's white complexion. In Los Angeles central area, the steady black inflow and upward class movement of prospering Blacks transformed the multi-ethnic ghettos into a large area of ethnic enclaves of all classes, whose boundaries were marked by freeway and railroad lines and an encircling tier of white communities.

Government agencies reported from time to time on the deterioration of urban ghettos, but local and state officials chose to ignore the worsening situation. The California Real Estate Association (CREA) and its local affiliates actively worked to preserve white segregated areas. Local ACLU and NAACP chapters worked closely with allied white groups to promote community interracial harmony and to secure court actions nullifying discriminatory practices. The U.S. Supreme Court in a landmark decision (1948) ruled that racial covenants were constitutional but unenforceable, rationalized by the 6th Amendment which protects property and the 14th Amendment which prohibits racial discrimination. The Brown Administration, which won election with strong minority group support, launched a campaign to end racial discrimination. The 1959 Civil Rights Act (sponsored by Los Angeles Democrat Jesse Unruh) prohibited discrimination in private employment and authorized discriminated persons to seek compensation. The 1963 Fair Housing Act, sponsored by Berkeley's black assemblyman Byron Rumford, forbade discrimination in the sale and rental of residential property. The aroused CREA immediately campaigned for a state ballot measure (Proposition 14) to repeal the Rumford Act. After a bitter campaign over the measure, the electorate in a 2-1 vote in the 1964 election passed the open-housing measure, declared unconstitutional by the state supreme court two years later.

The black situation in the urban ghettos was close to the boiling point. Federal, state, and local antipoverty and expanded welfare programs had improved the status of many Blacks but urban redevelopment and other community programs fell far short in alleviating oppressive ghetto conditions. Compounding the problem was black unemployment—almost double that of Whites. Watts, the Palm Tree Ghetto, came into public focus as a troubled community which had developed into a powder keg. The predominantly black community contained both attractive upper- and middle-class homes and shabby, crowded lower-class dwellings and run-down business sections where merchants charged more for food and merchandise than in white communities. Community relations were marked by class and racial tensions and mutual hostility between residents and city police. In August 1965, Watts exploded into violence, resulting in six days of arson and looting, and leaving 34 dead (practically all Blacks) and $40 million in property damage. A year after Watts, violence erupted in San Francisco's Hunter's Point and other California cities. In the aftermath, government agencies and business firms expanded aid programs for ghetto areas. Aerojet corporation established an all-black subsidiary (Watts Manufacturing Company) which benefited from defense contracts.

By the mid-1960's California was thoroughly involved in the national movements for civil rights and black liberation. The campaign for black equality won wide support. Black and white leaders worked closely through civic organizations like NAACP chapters and League of Women Voters to promote black rights in government, industry, schools, and other institutions. The campaign for black liberation widened as more Blacks developed self-help enterprises and programs—notably, business firms set up with liberal government-backed loans, black studies and other experimental education programs on college and school campuses, and recreational and other community facilities. The black power movement found an aggressive exponent in the Oakland-based Black Panthers, formed in 1966 by the articulate, young militants Huey Newton and Bobby Seale. A variety of other groups throughout the state developed programs for promoting the black cause.

The 1970's witnessed remarkable changes in the status of Blacks and in public attitudes. The "white backlash" from the violence of the 1960's gave way in the 1970's to widespread white cooperation and toleration, marked by "uneasy truces" in many communities. State and federal agencies pressed diverse programs designed to help Blacks, and cities showed greater sensitivity to racial groups. Black politicians made impressive gains in public office. Unlike black predecessors, they won important offices with substantial white votes (Tom Bradley as Los Angeles mayor, Wilson Riles as state school superintendent), and assumed legislative leadership positions (Mervyn Dymally in the senate and Willie Brown in the assembly). Most significant of all was the growth of racial pride, independence, resourcefulness. California provided a fluid environment for Blacks and white allies to develop varied responses in lessening overt forms of prejudice and discrimination, not withstanding occasional setbacks.

The Family

Spurred by continuing urban and industrial forces and by socio-economic developments after the war, the family institution underwent important changes. Family relations became more open and varied as a result of postwar economic prosperity and extended freedom for women and youth. The Kinsey reports (1948 and 1953) revealed that premarital sex and "deviant" behavior like adultery and masturbation were fairly common practices despite rigid sex laws and codes. The number of divorces and of unmarried people living together reached all-time high figures. Sexual freedom was enhanced by the widespread use of birth-control measures. Family organization and practices occasionally took experimental forms like spouse swapping and the group family relationships of hippie communes. There was a growing public tolerance toward diverse family ways and sexual behavior, including interracial marriages, homosexual associations, and experimental family forms.

The emerging pattern of the majority family reflected a continuation of earlier trends toward a relocation of family functions and roles. Family relations were more person-oriented; they rested heavily on individual needs and the personal happiness of each member. Father and mother constituted a leadership coalition dividing family and household responsibilities by common agreement, hardly the patriarchal setup of earlier times. Many parents raised children "according to the book"—Dr. Benjamin Spock's popular *Common Sense Book of Baby and Child Care* (1946). Criticized as overly permissive, Dr. Spock insisted on treating the child as an individual in his own right. Companionship among father, mother, and children in recreational activities (rather than in the work area as before) was an important bond enhancing family unity—the theme of "togetherness" publicized by public leaders and the mass media in the 1950's. The family, as sociologist Floyd Martinson puts it, catered to the needs and desires of its members and did not require members to subjugate their needs and desires to those of the family.

California provided an open environment for diversities in family experience. Family types ranged from the nuclear family to extended kinship organizations, including variations among minority groups. Family styles were immensely varied, a fact attributed to class differences, multi-ethnic diversities, regional varieties, and changing socio-economic conditions. Families were more prone to individual styles than to social conformity, at least in urban communities. There was a high regard for family privacy and a wide tolerance for individual deviations. Whether one believed the family was in the process of disorganization or reorganization, California's experience demonstrated the family institution had enormous vitality.

Women

The status of women was profoundly altered by postwar developments. Everywhere women appeared to be gaining stature, but a closer examination revealed a different picture. In family affairs, many women still followed their husband's dictates. Women were increasingly active in community affairs, political parties, professional associations, labor unions, and in rising social movements, but their efforts toward higher status or leadership met either meaningless concessions or outright hostility from men. For example, Stokely Carmichael, a radical black leader, declared that the position of women should be prone. In education, a greater number of women attended college but proportionally fewer women were college graduates in the 1950's than in the 1920's. In the employment market during the two postwar decades, women workers increased to constitute over 35 percent of the labor force but they were relegated mostly to semiprofessional and clerical jobs and were paid less than men on the same job. The woman's rights movement was at low ebb. Older organizations, like the General Federation of Women and the National Woman Suffrage Association, were described as merely ceremonial affairs.

The 1960's witnessed a rejuvenation of the woman's rights movement. A national movement sprang from President Kennedy's commission on the status of women, headed by Eleanor Roosevelt, which reported (1963) widespread practices of discrimination against women. Other events spurred the national movement. Betty Friedan's best seller *The Feminine Mystique* (1963) popularized ideas of self-fulfillment enunciated a half-century earlier by California's Charlotte Perkins. The landmark 1964 Civil Rights Act, which prohibited racial discrimination in employment, also forbade sex discrimination, a "joke" provision inserted by a frustrated racist Southern senator, which women's groups took deadly seriously. The National Organization for Women (NOW, 1966) organized by Betty Friedan and others, emerged as a powerful lobby group pressing for women's legal and political rights. Presidential executive orders were issued to enforce anti-discrimination measures in federal employment (1962) and federal contract jobs (1967). The movement was carried forward in the 1970's with the Equal Rights Amendment to the federal Constitution (1970, still pending ratification by the states) and by the Women Education Act (1972) for extending equal rights and opportunities to women in remaining areas of discrimination. California women were deeply involved with NOW since its inception (Aileen Hernandez was president, 1969-1970), and several local movements promoted particular aspects of women's rights.

Public Entertainment and Recreation

Public entertainment in California received new impetus with the growing concentration of people in metropolitan areas. It assumed new dimensions as a by-product of the consumer society—people having acquired time and money from better jobs sought fun and leisure in assorted cultural and recreational activities. Corporate enterprises expanded local facilities and developed large playgrounds in strategic coastal, desert, and mountain areas. Representative were Disneyland (1959), built by Walt Disney as a children's paradise, and Squaw Valley (1961), developed under joint state-private auspices as a ski resort complex after the 1960 Olympic Winter Games were held there. State and local governmental agencies expanded public camping, picnic, and playground areas in unprecedented fashion, notably in specialized recreational activities like marinas for boating. By the 1960's, just about every accessible coastal, lake, desert, and mountain attraction had been committed for commercial and public recreation and sports, including boating, swimming, and skiing, though mountain climbers and hikers could still find refuge for their quiet pastimes in remote areas like the High Sierra.

The metropolitan centers spearheaded the cultural boom which swept the state. San Francisco looked to its established galleries, museums, theaters, and opera house, enhanced by a few outstanding additions, notably the de Young Museum acquisition of the famous Brundage Oriental Collection (1960) and its celebrated resident drama group, American Conservatory Theatre. Richmond Art Center, a community institution evolved from a prewar WPA project, and Oakland's modernistic museum complex (1966) including the state's largest collection of California art, were impressive testimonies of industrial cities developing outstanding cultural centers. Los Angeles emerged as the state's cultural leader following a burst of expanded, innovative facilities built by generous municipal and county support second to none in the state and by numerous philanthropies organized by the resolute Dorothy Chandler (Norman's wife). Highlights were the Chandler Pavilion (1964) with its Mark Taper Forum and Ahmanson Theatre for the performing arts and the refurbished Los Angeles County Art Museum (1965), the largest since the National Gallery in Washington. With older institutions like the Hollywood Bowl and Pasadena Playhouse in decline, Los Angeles provided a regional focus for revitalizing high arts in the metropolis.

Other developments added new dimensions to the state's cultural scene. A California Arts Commission (authored by Jesse Unruh in the 1965 legislature) was set up to encourage the formation of local arts councils and tours of exhibitions and performers to small communities. Colleges and universities, paced by UC-Berkeley, Stanford, San Francisco State, and UCLA, expanded facilities to become important centers for training performers and presenting exhibitions and productions in diverse arts. The counterculture of the 1960's and 1970's spawned numerous small makeshift galleries and theaters for experimental art and dramas of the subculture, and the spectacularly successful rock-music festivals for mass audiences in large auditoriums and open parks. California's cultural boom, in both the high arts and popular arts, was an extension of a worldwide cultural explosion. Observers commented that California was unmatched in the amount and diversity of its cultural and recreational offerings and opportunities.

B. CULTURE

THE SETTING

The booming postwar economy, which produced an expanded consumer society, also contributed to a wider spread of consumer or mass culture. Technology combined with mass production contributed FM radios with more channels for specialized programs and high fidelity and later stereophonic sound. The mass merchandising of long-playing records and paperback books made available an incredible variety of classical and popular works. The home stocked with books and records became a cultural center tailored to the individual tastes of family members. Television quickly supplanted radio and motion pictures as the chief medium of mass entertainment. About 65 percent of families in the mid-1950's and over 90 percent a decade later owned TV sets.

DEVELOPMENT

The postwar cultural boom was manifested in community develop-ments. Los Angeles and San Francisco were still the chief centers but other cities and towns throughout the state also developed important cultural centers. Public facilities for the arts and spectator sports (baseball, basketball, football) were expanded to meet the cultural and recreational demands of the burgeoning population. Judging from attendance records and program fares in public entertainment, more people enjoyed a wider variety of cultural offerings than ever before. High culture enjoyed a vogue; statistics revealed that Californians spent more money on tickets to symphony concerts than on baseball games and were among the top-ranking state populations in the purchase of classic literary works and art reproductions. Popular culture with its mass youth appeal swept the scene. Teenagers were dazzled in the mid-1950's by new trends in comic books (the satiric *Mad Comics*), rock music played on electric instruments, and a new dance called "the twist." Television presented programs that combined elements of mass-oriented

Hollywood films and sophisticated Broadway plays, contributing to further standardization of public taste by producing "better entertainment but worse art." Mass consumption, said the critics, was debasing creativity and quality standards in both high and popular culture.

Counterculture

A cultural protest grew in the mid-1950's and early 1960's in which rebellious youth and allied adults fought against conventional mores and traditional values. The essence of their protest was a reaction to the social conformity, materialistic values, community disorientation, and vast institutional organizations engendered by the consumer society with its attendant mass culture. They sought personal meaning for their existence through life experience. In their quest for experience they indulged in drugs, sexual freedom, esoteric cults, and communal living, sometimes in extreme and bizarre ways. Their long hair and their individual and group life styles were badges of social protest and personal identity. Their antisocial ideas and behavior contributed to profound changes in cultural norms. The counterculture was the cultural phase of the social revolution.

The counterculture was a product of several movements which converged and flowered into a broad rebellion. The "beat" movement, an updated version of American bohemianism, was launched by writers and musicians who developed personalized styles in spontaneous literature and improvisatory jazz. Allen Ginsberg's *Howl* (1959), a founding document of the counterculture, punctuated random statements with obscene idiom to expose hypocrisies and perversions in conventional society. The beatniks popularized marijuana, communal living, and Zen Buddhism. The flower children, who appeared briefly, were school dropouts who "radiated innocent love." The hippies, their successors, turned to hallucinogenic and hard drugs like LSD ("acid") and heroin, group sex, family or tribal communes, and mystical or occult sects. They foresook beat centers for their own communities, moving from North Beach to the Haight–Ashbury district in San Francisco, from Greenwich Village to the East Village in New York, and to their own section in Los Angeles's Venice East district. San Francisco's Haight–Ashbury became the nation's leading "hip" community in the mid-1960's. An invasion of teenage runaways seeking thrills, and of criminal elements exploiting the drug traffic, resulted in sporadic crime and

Secessionists of the Sixties.

violence that contributed to the community's rapid deterioration. Thereafter, hippie youth gravitated to small communes in urban homes and on farms or assimilated into society, often retaining hip ways.

Pioneering individuals and experimental groups lent a popular expression to the counterculture. They developed folk songs to express protest (Joan Baez's gentle and Bob Dylan's hard-hitting indictments), twist-style dances with their bump-and-grind gyrations. The Beatles, a popular English quartet who burst on the American scene, revolutionized commercial folk and rock by their musical invention and showmanship. They bridged the gap between Elvis Presley's country rock and Chuck Berry's rhythm-and-blues and began a new era in worldwide pop music. San Francisco's Grateful Dead, a pioneer hippie band, carried Beatle music forward, adding acid to rock. An ominous innovation was made by Timothy Leary, a UC graduate and Harvard scientist turned drug prophet, who popularized hallucinogenic drugs like LSD and attempted to establish a drug-oriented cult. These pioneers gave to the counter-culture forms and a style for delivering the "message."

By the mid-1960's the counterculture movement with its heroes and public gatherings had arrived. Ken Kesey, author and an early hippie folk hero in California, embraced a psychedelic life style marked by madcap adventures recorded by his Boswell, Tom Wolfe, in *The Electric Kool-Aid Acid Test* (1966). The "acid test" which Kesey inspired was a public gathering featuring stage shows with rock bands, flashing colored and strobe lights, film-slide picture projection, and other gimmickry, rounded off with audience participation in "acid dropping" to produce a "happening" for all concerned. The pioneer San Francisco show (1966) led Bill Graham, a local entrepreneur, to stage similar shows in his Fillmore West ballroom in San Francisco and the Fillmore East in New York City. Another type of public gathering was the festive celebration of life featuring music, dancing, and drug use in open-air arenas. First launched in San Francisco's Golden Gate Park (1967), these public happenings reached climactic proportions with New York's joyous Woodstock Festival (1969) for over 300,000 paying and free-loading participants and with California's free concert at Altamont (1971), a farewell present of an English rock group (Rolling Stones) which ended in chaos and violence.

The counterculture with its radical innovations was a catalyst for reshaping institutions and people's lives. It was manifested in experimental educational programs and the free university idea, the underground press in journalism, folk religion and radical theology (Death of God movement). It gave new expression to literature, music, and art of both high and popular culture. It opened new possibilities in life styles for straights or squares as well as for hippies. Even more startling was the blending of consumer culture with the counterculture as corporations capitalized on hippie styles, and hippie entrepreneurs turned captialist to peddle their wares and services. The consumer culture paid the counterculture the compliment of imitating it.

Interspersed in the counterculture were two other important movements: encounter groups and participatory democracy. Encounter groups focused on group and individual development for improving human potentiality, and were a reaction to the stultifying effects of authoritarian leadership and social conformity. It grew out of wartime behavioral research (command decisions) by the U.S. Navy and postwar research of the National Education Association which led to techniques changing group behavior (Training-Groups). A UCLA group went further to develop techniques altering individual behavior (Sensitivity Training). By 1960 the movement had taken basic form in group therapy sessions in which its participants hoped to achieve self-discovery through personal confrontation in group encounters.

Participatory democracy, or PD, was an alternative to representative democracy. It was a protest against the centralized authority and impersonal rule of large institutions operated by professional managers through vast hierarchical bureaucracies. It sought direct action by grassroots members in making decisions affecting their interests. The idea underlying participatory democracy—decentralized power to prevent tyrannical authority—was also basic to representative democracy as conceived by Jefferson and Madison. Participatory democracy surfaced by the mid-1960's in the writings of New Left leaders Paul Goodman and Tom Hayden, and was applied by radical groups attempting to democratize institutional processes. The participatory democracy and encounter groups movements represented people developing alternative solutions to an oppressive technocratic society, the one through institutional changes and the other by personal adjustment.

The consumer culture and the counterculture were catalysts of a profound revolution in society that was still underway in the mid-1970's. The Yankelovich study (1974) reveals that countercultural values are rapidly penetrating the rest of society to the extent that major changes in the American workplace are forthcoming over the next few years. Sydney Ahlstrom, writing in the perspective of world history, suggests that with the passing of WASP in the United States and the decline of the Protestant Establishment in the West during the 1960's, the Great Puritan Epoch which began in the sixteenth century appears to be ending. We seem to be experiencing a transition from the Puritan ethic to a different social ethic, marking a watershed in American and world history.

ANALYSIS

Education

Primary and Secondary Schools

California experienced unprecedented public school expansion as a result of the postwar baby boom. The state made a heavy commitment for updating facilities and programs, with the state budget devoting 40 percent for education and local school districts making record expenditures. The school districts bore the burden of financing and developing expanded school facilities. Disparities widened among the districts—the rich and poor, the big and small—resulting in uneven facilities which ranged from one-room schoolhouses to Los Angeles's extensive unified school system (elementary, junior high, and high schools).

Conservative citizen groups, in sporadic and often nationally publicized incidents, attempted to arrest current trends in progressive education. In Pasadena, they forced the resignation of a prominent school superintendent (Willard Goslin, 1950) after a prolonged and bitter community showdown. In Paradise, they spurred the school board into firing a popular, liberal teacher (Virginia Franklin) who had won national awards as an outstanding instructor. Actually, California in the course of sustaining its commitment to quality education had absorbed into the state school system tenets of progressive education, which had ceased to be an identifiable movement by the mid-1950's.

By the 1960's public education underwent a drastic transformation. Gross deficiencies in the nation's educational setup prompted Congress to enact landmark federal aid programs. When the Russians launched the first spacecraft (Sputnik, 1957), Congress provided funds for expanding math and science courses in school curricula (National Defense Education Act, 1959). Under pressure from civil rights groups, it financed Headstart and other programs in a move to equalize educational opportunities for black and other disadvantaged children (Elementary and Secondary School Act, 1966). The Brown administration not only matched federal funds but extended state efforts in revamping the public school system in tune with changing conditions. The legislature enacted a series of reform measures, ranging from school consolidations for improved efficiency, special projects for disadvantaged students, revised requirements for teacher certification, and alternate choices for classroom textbooks. These measures did much to help sustain California's highly touted system of public education. It also imposed heavier tax burden on property owners which later contributed to local tax revolts (see Chapter 17).

The state continued to suffer nagging problems of uneven educational standards and racial discrimination. The state school board was immersed in running feuds over issues of fundamental versus progressive education, notably revising school textbooks to give "God equal treatment with Darwin" in explaining man's creation (1971). Some communities launched innovative programs to achieve racial balance, paced by Berkeley's school bus program and Sacramento's school reorganization scheme. Most communities procrastinated on the matter. A 1967 report revealed that 85 percent of the state's black students still attended segregated schools. In Los Angeles, a local court took the unprecedented step of going beyond the 1954 U.S. Supreme Court desegregation decision by declaring de facto segregation to be illegal (1964). Public attitude was reflected in the 1970 election for state school superintendent when the reactionary Max Rafferty was replaced by moderate Wilson Riles, the nation's first black state school superintendent. Progress reports were conflicting on student improvement in academic performance as a result of steady school integration. Despite trials and tribulations, California's school system still rated high in national reputation.

Colleges and Universities

The state's institutions of higher learning underwent phenomenal expansion. After the war, returning veterans supported by federal education grants (G.I. Bill), defense workers, and other youth crowded public and private colleges and universities. These institutions developed greatly expanded undergraduate and graduate programs that turned out the professionals and technicians needed in the booming postwar industries. They did the job so systematically that they earned the reputation of being academic mills and learning factories.

The public institutions reflected the startling changes in conspicuous ways. The junior colleges increased to over one hundred, with some colleges operating two or more campuses. These institutions had grown into full-fledged two-year colleges showing little trace of their former post-high school status. Sponsored by local districts, the junior colleges showed great adaptability to changing conditions, especially in expanding academic and vocational programs to meet community needs. The four-year state colleges increased by 10 for a total of 21. They broadened their curricula in the physical and social sciences and expanded graduate programs to the point where they competed seriously with the universities in offering master's degrees. UC's multi-campus system greatly expanded in size and scope, sustaining its reputation as the world's largest and one of the top-ranking among the nation's universities for quality education. To cope with increasing difficulties in managing the burgeoning growth of higher institutions, the 1959 legislature set up a Coordinating Council of Higher Education to administer a master plan that would integrate the financing and development of campus facilities and programs. The public institutions had a salutary effect on private institutions, like Cal Tech, Stanford and USC, which also expanded in size and scope to share in the state's growth. California's stature in higher learning was reflected in the fact that its institutions contained 20 percent of the members of the prestigious National Academy of Sciences and 36 Nobel Prize winners, most of them located at UC-Berkeley.

The Campus Revolt

Postwar growth had so changed the complexion of the university system that it evoked public reaction in the 1960's. The harbinger of change was UC-Berkeley, the bright jewel in the state's educational system. Clark Kerr, who succeeded Robert Sproul as UC's president (1958), in his famous Harvard lecture (1963) declared that the university had become a "multiversity, a vast bureaucratic organization operated by professional administrators in carrying out disparate functions"; it constituted a knowledge industry for government and business and as a central conduit for society in general, serving as the chief entry into the professions and occupations. Kerr also pointed out that the university faced serious problems resulting from administrators excessively preoccupied with organizational matters, a faculty overly absorbed in research and services, and neglected students affected by reduced emphasis on undergraduate instruction.

Student attitudes by the 1960's were changing from preoccupation with campus fads (for example, men's panty raids on women's dormitories), sports, and job training to involvement in civil rights and peace demonstrations. The revolt was sparked (1964) when UC officials curtailed political activity that had been conducted for some time on an adjoining off-campus site, provoking student leaders to launch the Free Speech Movement and earning Berkeley's reputation as the "cradle of student revolt in America." The FSM, which involved student–faculty support for the time-honored issue of academic freedom, evolved into campus demonstrations (1965) of radical student leaders, particularly against the Vietnam War. Over the next few years the beleaguered administration was embroiled in sporadic confrontations with student groups, which sometimes culminated in violent incidents on campus and on Berkeley streets. By the mid-1970's, with the end of the war in Vietnam, the university experienced relative quiet. The administration faced other problems, like faculty demands for collective bargaining, and students were inclined to pursue their interests in more private ways.

The events at Berkeley had major repercussions throughout the state. Student revolts for different causes and objectives erupted on college campuses, notably at San Francisco State, Stanford, and UC campuses at Los Angeles and Santa Barbara. The state colleges and junior colleges, learning from such experiences, instituted administration and educational reforms. Their troubles were compounded by "Third World" groups seeking costly educational programs oriented to their interests and the inflationary pressures of the receding economy. However, college campuses were reflecting a different climate in the 1970's. Students, according to a 1974 Yankelovich study, seemed less radical and more conciliatory toward society in general. The generation gap between these young people and their parents was not nearly as great as the gap within the generation, college and noncollege students, the latter becoming alienated and taking on the radical views of earlier students.

Journalism

Journalism in the United States continued to be dominated by the chain newspapers, although there were a number of independent metropolitan papers. The Hearst chain was greatly reduced in size (from 26 dailies in 1935 to 11 in 1962) but it still led the field in newspaper circulation, followed by old-timer Scripps–Howard, newcomer S. E. Newhouse, and several small chains (Cowles, Gannett, Knight, Ridder)—all being dwarfed by a rising Canadian and international press lord, Roy Thompson. Leading the nation's prestigious metropolitan dailies were the *New York Times* under Arthur Sulzberger's son-in-law, then grandson (after 1964), the *St. Louis Post Dispatch* under second- and third-generation Joseph Pulitzers, and the *Washington Post* under Philip Graham and later his widow Katherine (after 1968). Journalists in rating newspapers for comprehensive and honest news coverage and social responsibility listed the *New York Times* as front runner and the *Los Angeles Times* among the top 15 of the nation's 1,700-odd dailies.

In California, the metropolitan papers, which still dominated journalism in the state, changed family hands and moved in new directions. With the deaths of egocentric founders or their business-minded sons and sons-in-laws, ownership passed to family heirs, but management was headed by independent offspring who cut a different style. The *Los Angeles Times* passed from Harry Chandler to his son Norman (1944) and then to Norman's son, Otis (1960). Otis Chandler replaced the paper's narrow Republican partisanship with an enlightened editorial policy marked by fair news coverage of Democratic Party politics and labor union activities. The Hearst empire, after the death of its lordly and eccentric founder William Randolph Hearst (1951), passed on to his five sons, with W. R. Hearst, Jr., taking over the editorship of the *San Francisco Examiner* and Randolph Hearst presiding over the Hearst publications. Hearst, Jr., tempered his father's policies, granting local editors some autonomy and stressing news objectivity. (He won a Pulitzer Prize in 1956 for news reporting). The *San Francisco Chronicle* after George Cameron's death (1955) was taken over by conservative Charles de Young Thieriot, grandson of Michael de Young. The *Chronicle* compensated its compromising editorial policies with a home-based stable of local columnists unmatched in the country, topped by witty ubiquitous Herb Caen. The *Oakland Tribune* management passed from founder Joseph Knowland to his son William (1955), who ran it after political retirement until his death (1974), and then to his son, Joseph. The *Sacramento Bee* passed from C. K. McClatchy to his daughter Eleanor (1958), who sustained the paper's Democratic tradition, its leadership in the Central Valley, and its position as chief reporter on state politics.

Other developments altered the character of journalism in the state. The newspaper giants developed into supercorporations with diversified operations. In meeting damaging competition from other mass media, Hearst eventually acquired 14 magazines and several television and radio stations. The Chandlers acquired a magazine, radio and television stations, a paper production company, and unrelated subsidiaries. Community papers in scattered towns, hit hard by financial woes and uneven circulation, resorted to group ownership schemes to achieve economy and efficiency. The long-time trend toward group ownership developed into "galloping consolidation" during the 1960's to include over half of the town dailies. Such consolidations raised the spectre of federal anti trust actions until Congress enacted the 1971 Newspaper Conservation Act which insured legality of such schemes.

Another development was the emergence of the New Journalism in the underground press of the 1960's. Originally a reaction to the bland conformity and pro-establishment orientation of the regular press, it evolved into an important anti-establishment vehicle of the hippie generation. The alternative press was pioneered by two New York social protest papers (*Village Voice,* 1954; *Realist,* 1958), which served mature readers of *Mad Comics*. Both attacked sacred cows and used obscene language to prove papers could be different and survive. The hippie underground version of the alternative press was represented by Art Kunkind's pioneering *Los Angeles Free Press* (1964), the short-lived *Open City* (1964) in San Francisco, and Max Scheer's celebrated *Berkeley Barb* (1965). The impact of the underground press was enormous. The *Chronicle's* Scott Newhall declared that the regular press, which was in danger of dissolving into a gray mass of non-ideas, would be replenished by the underground press "to keep it alive."

The press gained in public stature with better news coverage, though suffering from chronic habits of slanted news and viewpoints. It did outstanding yeoman work battling goverment censorship and exposing corruption, notably the Watergate scandal. Newspaper historian John Tebbel reminds us of journalism's strategic role in a free society: it is the only institution specifically protected by the Constitution (First Amendment).

Literature

Literature, like the changing society it mirrored, experienced an upheaval marked by sharp breaks with past traditions and values. Writers utilized or blended literary genres like naturalism, realism, and romanticism to voice humanitarian protests over conformity, corruption, and material-ism in the affluent society.

The flaming 40's, punctuated by the hot and cold wars, produced a spate of popular but generally undistinguished literary works, accord-ing to critics. Norman Mailer, Harvard graduate and World War II veteran, wrote an immensely popular novel, *The Naked and the Dead* (1948), which portrayed the demoralization of an army platoon in Pacific jungle warfare. Literature of the 1950's, according to critic Warren French, was emotionally arid and tacky, lacking in style and good taste. J. D. Salinger, who more than any other writer caught the new spirit of the decade, won wide popularity for his *Catcher in the Rye* (1951), a provocative novel of adolescent youth struggling in a bewildering adult society. The decade witnessed the emergence of promising black writers (James Baldwin) and bohemian "beat" writers, who projected an unconventional life style into free literary form to register their supreme disillusionment with society.

The eventful decade of the expansive 1960's, stirred by youthful rebels and social revolution, led literary development in new directions. The federal court permitted American publication of the long-suppressed novels of D. H. Lawrence (*Lady Chatterley's Lover*, 1928) in 1960 and of Henry Miller (*Tropic of Cancer,* 1934) in 1962. The court in effect gave writers open license to sexual expression in literature. Self-styled hippie writers wrote personal testimonies in shapeless, experimental forms, but other youthful rebels followed conventional literary forms to put across their message. California's Ken Kesey's *One Flew Over the Cuckoo's Nest* (1962) was a parable of an individual being suppressed for the group's good in a mental ward. In Saul Bellow's *Herzog* (1964), a middle-aged Jewish intellectual survives excruciating life experiences, contented in the end "to be just as it is willed." Some thought Bellow's book was the best postwar novel. The youthful temper in the literature of the decade reflected a determination of the young to make peace with society on their own terms. Many were deeply involved in movements for civil rights, peace, and the poor.

California's literary scene sustained its variegated character. California was among the top-ranking states in annual book sales. The poet Kenneth Rexroth and his friends spearheaded a postwar literary revival in San Francisco. Literary centers for creative writing increased and expanded, notably in Bay Area and Los Angeles colleges and universities, sometimes under distinguished writers, like UC's Mark Schorer (*The State of Mind,* 1947), George Stewart (*Fire,* 1948), and Stanford's Wallace Stegner (*Angle of Repose,* 1971). The academicians were more outstanding for scholarly writing in specialized fields than creative writing, although a few, like UC's political scientist Eugene Burdick (*The Ugly American*, 1958), won national acclaim. The older prominent writers continued to mine their familiar literary lodes seemingly untouched by the impact of swirling momentous events. Most passed from the scene in the 1960's (Huxley, Jeffers, Sinclair, Steinbeck, Saroyan). A few who made their mark were Budd Schulberg for movie scenarios (*On the Waterfront,* 1954) and Allen Drury, a California journalist before he went east, for his Pulitzer Prize-winning novel *Advise and Consent* (1959). California, it has been said, was representative of democratic rather than elitist tradition in American literature.

The most conspicuous postwar literary development was the beat movement. It evolved in San Francisco from the literary renaissance or reawakening sponsored by Kenneth Rexroth and other established writers. It took form with the arrival of Lawrence Ferlinghetti (1953), who became owner of City Lights bookstore and pioneer publisher of beat writings, and of radical writers led by Allen Ginsberg (1954) and Jack Kerouac (1949), who found the city a congenial haven for their "scratchings." In his pioneering poem *Howl* (1955), Ginsberg castigates the corrupted society by ruthlessly exposing its hypocrisies. *Howl* marked a new direction for protest literature; local prosecution of Ginsberg and his publisher, Ferlinghetti, on obscenity charges resulted in their acquittal and gave beat writers their green light. Kerouac's pacesetting novel *The Dharma Bums* (1958) tells in the loose style and structure of his spontaneous prose the story of his beat friends in search of dharma (truth) through Zen Buddhism. Henry Miller said of Kerouac, "he's not cool, he's red hot; if he's far out, he's also near and dear, a blood brother, an alter ego." The beat writers were an ambitious group of well-educated literary craftsmen, free-wheeling anarchists, anti-authoritarian and anti-establishment. They owed much to Walt Whitman and Miller, and they in turn influenced contemporaries like Mailer. Many went back to New York after 1960, leaving San Francisco to the local writers. Beat repercussions are still being felt in the 1970's, notably hippies and others imbued with the anarchist tradition and experimental literary forms.

Religion

Religious developments were profoundly affected by the great changes in postwar society. Churchmen expressed concern about the urban and industrial forces shaped by science and technology, which contributed to further secularization in religious affairs. They were heartened, however, by the strong religious impulse that came out of wartime experiences.

By 1950 religious revivalism was sweeping the nation. Billy Graham, an itinerant evangelist carrying the rural Fundamentalist tradition to urban masses, catapulted to national prominence after a 1949 Los Angeles mass rally in which he converted a number of prominent people, including a notorious racketeer (Mickey Cohen). He combined business organization, adroit publicity, and entertaining rallies to popularize "old-time religion," blending interdenominational, anti-Communist, and ultra-conservative sentiments. Theology loomed large with Reinhold Niebuhr, apostle of neo-orthodox theology. Niebuhr decried the liberal's belief in human reason and social reform and urged return to orthodox theology to recapture faith in God, still favoring social change and respect for science (unlike the Fundamentalists). Churches gained membership and accelerated building construction ($26 million in 1945, over $1 billion in 1960). Earlier interchurch cooperation culminated in the World Council of Churches (WCC, 1948) and the National Council of Churches (NCC, 1950). Church denominations undertook mergers to bring together long-divided factions, notably Congregationalists with the Evangelical Reformed (1957, thereafter United Church of Christ), Presbyterians (1958), and Lutherans (1960). Interchurch union, a joint effort proposed by two California prelates, Presbyterian Eugene Carson Blake and Episcopalian James Pike, made plans for consolidation (1962). Interfaith harmony among Catholics, Jews, and Protestants made historic progress when the beloved Pope John XXIII paved the way with his memorable call for Christian unity (Vatican II, 1962). The postwar religious revival signaled another Great Awakening in American history, with significant differences from earlier revivals (1760, 1800, 1840, 1880, 1929) of Protestant evangelism.

By the 1960's, religious developments reached a turning point. Evangelism and neo-orthodox theology had become vogues. Billy Graham's highly touted 1959 New York mass rally was described as a case of David meeting Goliath, who yawned. Reinhold Niebuhr gave way to his brother, Richard, whose *Radical Monotheism* (1960), says Sydney Ahlstrom, marked a requiem for neo-orthodoxy and an opening for secular theology. A radical theology emerged with the "Death of God" movement whose exponents argued that the traditional "mythological God" was dead in that people no longer fully embraced it, and presented different versions of a meaningful "living God."

The churches were also hard hit by the social revolution. Organized churches suffered a decline in membership and building construction. Their large bureaucracies manned by professional staffs were considered aloof from grassroots membership. Clergy and lay groups had excruciating showdowns over the church's role in mass movements for civil rights, peace, and the poor. They were divided among the religious orthodox who believed the church should stay out of such movements and concentrate on God, the "churchgoing bourbons" who supported church involvement as long as it upheld traditional American values like property rights and business ethics, and the new breed who urged church involvement in reform movements to carry out

Christ's campaign for social and economic justice. A hero of the new breed was Blake, a former Pasadena minister who presided over the national Presbyterians, the NCC (1955), and later the WCC (1965-1972); he was among the first high churchmen to oppose McCarthyism and to be jailed for civil rights demonstrations in the 1950's, and was an articulate church spokesman for social reform in the 1960's.

California, the epitome of religious pluralism, accentuated national developments. During the 1950's established churches and various cults flourished as before. The Pacific School of Religion, the West's largest interdenominational seminary, was a stronghold of neo-orthodoxy. The Full Gospel Businessmen Fellowship (1951) carried the pentecostal experience to numerous communities, while the Christian Anti-Communist Crusade sponsored local seminars throughout the state. Zen Buddhism, stressing self-discipline and spiritual meditation, was spurred by newcomers to the Bay Area, former Anglican minister Alan Watts (1951) and Japanese priest Shunryu Suzuki (1958), whose American converts included beat writers and their followers.

In the religious upheaval which accompanied the social revolution of the 1960's, established churches were shaken out of traditional ways by deviant clergy and members. James Pike, San Francisco's controversial Episcopalian bishop, underwent church trial for unorthodox views and later made a surprising conversion to spiritualism. Many churches made valiant efforts to tune in with people's needs. Berkeley's First Unitarian Church suffered a serious split when dissident members formed a separate fellowship; the revived church shifted from its intellectual stance to diversified social programs oriented to multigroup interests. The California Unitarian Conference at one of its annual meetings featured hippie leader Ken Kesey, who reportedly "blew the mind" of his audience. Clergymen of all faiths played significant roles in varied social action programs in rural and urban areas, notably the 1964 landmark Delano strike of farm laborers. Some church leaders fought to hold the line for orthodoxy. The conservative Cardinal McIntyre ignored liberalizing reforms adopted by Vatican II, provoking rebellious sentiment among his Los Angeles constituency. Catholic nuns and priests there and in other places discarded traditional dress, modes, and rituals for more modern and relevant ways.

A startling development was the growing popularity and wide proliferation of cults and sects representing the religious side of the counterculture movement. Where earlier "protest religion" had been generated by adult revivalist groups within the church, the postwar versions were spawned mostly by youth groups outside established churches. Jesus cults stressing Protestant fundamentalism took diverse courses. The Jesus people or Jesus Freaks were a spinoff of a Hollywood Presbyterian church youth group which went independent; they "dressed straight and acted square" in delivering their message at mass music rallies. The Christian World Liberation Front, a countermove to the radical left Third World Liberation Front, consisted of a midwestern student group which invaded the UC-Berkeley campus to launch their crusade in hippie dress and jargon. Eastern religions enjoyed a popular revival, especially among hippie youth. Zen Buddhism spread rapidly with the establishment of Zen centers in major metropolitan areas and of a large retreat at Tassahara (1967) in the remote Los Padres National Forest. Hindu gurus (teachers) attracted large followings, notably Yogananda's Self Realization Fellowship, Mahareshi's Transcendental Meditation (1958), and Prabhupada's Krishna Consciousness (1965), whose shaven-headed youthful disciples in their yellow robes appeared in city streets chanting "Hare (lord) Krishna." While theosophical sects withered away, occult groups gained in popularity; they indulged variously in astrology, mysticism, witchcraft, and the psychic, sometimes using consciousness-expanding psychedelic drugs. While many Californians belonged to established churches, large numbers belonged to these complex, sophisticated cults and sects, seeking the religious experience or spiritual feeling that would give meaning to existence and a sense of ultimate reality. Indeed, Californians were unrivaled in their expression of the American concept of religious liberty.

The nation's religious development during the early 1970's reflected both church disarray and spiritual renewal. Interchurch unity was weakened by dissident groups seeking structural changes in the Protestant Union Plan, the NCC, and the WCC. Protestant churches, except for the conservative Lutherans, Mormons, and Holiness-type churches, continued to lose membership. Pope Paul IV postponed Vatican II reforms for church modernization (1969), which confused and alienated some Catholics. Judaism experienced mixed developments of declining synagogue membership and growing interest in Jewish mysticism (Hasidism). Catholic and Protestant churches underwent various forms of religious renewal, ranging from pentecostal experiences, participatory democracy of women and other groups seeking active leadership roles previously denied them, and psychotherapeutic encounter groups seeking to heighten religious experience. Religious cults and sects drew adults as well as youth seeking instant salvation or inner peace in a troubled world. The spiritual result of such developments was, to use Ahlstrom's phrase, dissensus was more visible than consensus. Evidence for God's love of the world was hard to find.

Science and Technology

American science and technology came of age during World War II and in the postwar period. During the war, the federal government mobilized the nation's scientists on an unprecedented scale. The Office for Scientific Research and Development (OSRD, 1941), along with the Navy and War Departments, recruited scientists for numerous military projects. Emigré scientists who fled dictatorship and war in Europe, like Germany's Albert Einstein and Italy's Enrico Fermi, played important roles in the war effort and became valuable members of the American scientific establishment.

The intimate relationship between government and science, fostered in wartime, continued after the war. Successors to the OSRD emerged in the Atomic Energy Commission (AEC, 1946), the National Science Foundation (NSF, 1950), and the National Aeronautics and Space Administration (NASA, 1958), which parlayed huge funds to universities, industry, and research institutes for diverse military and peacetime purposes. The Defense Department led the way for other departments like Agriculture, the Interior, and Health, Education, and Welfare to expand government staff and facilities and to extend the contractual services of industries and universities and other institutions for scientific research and development in their specialized areas. The federal scientific establishment assumed enormous proportions. The impulse for this postwar development came from varied sources: American–Soviet rivalry for supremacy in military weaponry and in outer space, industry competition for federal contracts, and public demand for consumer goods.

California gained strategic prominence in the nation's expanding science and technology. During the war, it played a conspicuous role in the nation's military and defense programs with its established scientific research and manufacturing facilities in the Los Angeles and San Francisco areas, which became aerospace and electronic centers. Its scientists made significant contributions, notably E. O. Lawrence and Robert Oppenheimer in nuclear physics, Stanford's Frederick Terman in radar, and Cal Tech's Theodor von Kármán in rocketry. In the postwar period, government and industry were lured by the state's congenial environment, its favorable climate, its available open space for factory sites and field laboratories, its expanding colleges and universities providing professional experts for consultation and trained personnel for staff, and its intimate manufacturing and market orientation for science industries. The Los Angeles and San Francisco areas expanded from nucleus centers to huge regional complexes of government–industry–university enterprises engaged in defense and civilian research and manufacturing in the public and private sectors of the political economy. The alliance of science with government and industry was a major factor contributing to California's remarkable prosperity.

The enormous strides of science and technology were manifested in far-reaching ways that amounted to a revolution. Major institutions— business, industry, government, education—employed research teams of assorted experts to work out feasible solutions to perplexing problems of the everyday or futuristic variety. Their activities ranged far and deep, developing nuclear, solar, and thermal energy power sources, converting salt water into fresh water, conceiving chemicals and machines for particular uses in agriculture and manufacturing, delving into eugenics to understand the riddles of human and plant life, exploring psychiatry to influence individual and group behavior. They relied heavily on electronic computers which processed mass information for particular uses, including office operations for business firms, production and distribution calculations for industrial corporations, and administrative procedures for governmental agencies. The home, too, became filled with such varied products of science and technology as vitamin pills, color television, microwave ranges, and assorted mechanized household items. Science and technology had not only opened new vistas of knowledge and invention—they had become big business.

Research and Development

A major postwar development was the blending of scientific research and technological development into single units, popularized as R & D. California's pioneering experiences led to several modes for the nation's cooperative government–industry–university R & D endeavors. Rand, which originated as an Army Air Force venture with three Southern

California aircraft companies (Douglas, North American, and Northrop), evolved into an independent prestigious nonprofit corporation serving government and industry. UC-Berkeley under government and industry auspices expanded with far flung activities for basic and applied research for military and civilian purposes. Stanford with businessmen-alumni support launched Stanford Research Institute (1947) as a nonprofit institution tackling industry problems; it expanded into diverse military and civilian projects to accommodate government and industry needs. The Los Angeles-based North American Corporation set up two divisions for nuclear research and rocket development (Atomics International and Rocketdyne) complete with a science center and field laboratory for defense and civilian production. Cal Tech operated its pioneer Jet Propulsion Laboratory for NASA, becoming chief agent for missiles (ICBM or Intercontinental ballistic missiles) and outer space programs (Ranger—Surveyor moon probes, Mariner—Voyager Mars and Venus explorations). It still operated for Carnegie Institute the observatories at Mt. Wilson and Mt. Palomar (the latter completed in 1948). By the 1960's the nation had 450 of these "think tanks" and over 1000 nonprofit R & D institutions and industries.

New directions were set for nonprofit research in the social sciences. The Center for the Study of Democratic Institutions was established at Santa Barbara (1959) for scholars and experts to come together and apply their intelligence to restoring vitality to democratic ideals in society. The Center for the Study of Behavioral Sciences was set up by Stanford at Palo Alto (1964) for scientific studies of man's behavior. The Center for the Study of the Person established at La Jolla (1967) concentrated on psychotherapy experiments (encounter groups) for individuals searching for meaning in life.

The public romance with science resulted in a changed status for the scientist in society. The scientist figure was no longer a solitary individual working on a chosen problem in a remote laboratory; he was usually a member of a research team working on an assigned group problem. He seemed more versatile and tuned in to the ways of the world than his predecessors. Scientists, saddled with awesome responsibilities in the nation's defense and economic prosperity, came through with brilliant achievements which raised their prestige to an all-time high. They broke new ground in human knowledge and achievements—landing a man on the moon, cracking the genetic code to solve the riddle of life itself. Eventually, however, public disenchantment set in because of the havoc reaped by science, particularly germ warfare, plant defoliation, and saturation bombing in Vietnam, and because of congressional investigation of certain scientific industries for excessive profits, government favoritism, and conflict of interest (Aerojet, 1963, Thompson-Ramo-Wooldridge, 1965). Many scientists began to question the morality of some aspects of their research. A significant step was taken (1974) when a National Academy of Sciences committee headed by Stanford's Paul Berg called for an international moratorium on research creating hybrid organisms (pioneered by Berg himself) which might have hazardous consequences for the human race.

SUMMARY

California emerged in the postwar period as a strategic regional entity in the nation's political economy. As one of the nation's most affluent and populous states, it loomed large in public affairs. The state had developed a well-working sophisticated governmental apparatus, a highly productive complex market economy, and viable social and cultural institutions—all played vital roles in the state's dynamic society as well as that of the nation. Federal officials had to reckon seriously with California, as state officials had to consider the federal role in planning and implementing public programs.

During the two-and-one-half decades of the postwar period, California demonstrated a remarkable capacity to meet the challenges of burgeoning growth brought on by population explosion and industrial expansion. Under the enlightened, pragmatic leadership of the Warren administration, followed by the Knight and Brown administrations, the state played a strategic role in coordinating diverse public programs designed to meet growth problems—notably, updating state institutions to achieve better performance, and supplying funds and services to help industrial enterprises and local governments and to achieve a more effective functioning of the whole society. State and local governmental agencies and business firms aggressively pressed for federal funds and services to stimulate their operations, often acquiring more than the state's share of the national largess.

Industry was no less energetic and innovative. Large and small enterprises acted vigorously to meet the huge and varied demands of consumers and industries. They not only came to dominate the western regional market (Los Angeles soon displaced Chicago) but also acquired an increasingly larger share of nationwide and world markets. California outdid other states in the market economy by capitalizing on strategic advantages, particularly its emphasis on long-range planning, research and development, and professional management. These methods were conspicuous in the well-publicized aerospace and electronics industries but were actually employed in just about every area, including agriculture, the state's top-ranking industry. The resilience of California's market economy was demonstrated by industry adjustments to severe dislocations resulting from defense cutbacks after World War II and in the late 1960's. The successful workings of California's postwar political economy may be measured by its gross product and the living standard of its people, which are exceeded by only five nations in the world.

By the 1960's the state, like the nation, was experiencing an adverse tide in public affairs. The booming political economy, as it turned out, perpetuated sore spots in the socio-economic picture, especially that of persistent poverty amidst widespread prosperity. State and federal officials since World War II had liberalized programs to help disadvantaged people, but such measures too often raised expectations while falling short of their goals, thereby giving rise to frustration and anger. The situation was compounded after 1960 when the Kennedy–Johnson administrations shifted national priority from domestic programs to military operations with acceleration of the war in Vietnam. By mid-decade a widespread protest movement emerged when discontented elements stepped up campaigns for public attention to their problems, including farm workers for union representation, racial groups, and women for political and economic rights. The violent showdowns between established authority and rebelling groups by the middle 1960's intensified public hostility and soon produced a general backlash against protesting groups. The Johnson administration, like the Brown administration in California, attempted liberal compromises; however, approaches based on expediency only provoked further showdowns and violence. The Nixon administration, and the Reagan administration in California, followed up with hard-line approaches, conservative programs designed to disengage the federal and state government and restore local rule and private initiative. Both retreated from untenable positions to expedient approaches. Eventually Nixon's programs were reduced to shambles by Watergate and other scandals.

By mid-decade of the 1970's, California—like the nation—was beset by a series of crises. Political leadership was in transition, and the onset of hard times, compounded by the energy crisis, worsened the nation's economic health. The social revolution had simmered down, but the counterculture which it helped perpetuate was being absorbed into the mainstream. All reflected powerful underlying forces which were transforming the character of society itself.

California has been steadily evolving into a technocratic society. Its political economy reflects extensive application of science and technology for the mass production and distribution of goods for the consumer society, a version of the people's capitalism in regulated form. In the course of postwar transition, California elaborated and refined the institutional apparatus developed during the previous industrial era. Government is the prime mover of the political economy but it operates in a more complicated setup: federal–state–local intergovernmental relationships shaped by the pressure politics of numerous organized special interests. Industries have expanded their horizons with the development of conglomerate and multinational corporations operating in nationwide and worldwide markets, and they have narrowed market operations with big and small enterprises producing consumer goods tailored to customer desires. The complex system of cooperative and corporate devices, voluntary and mandatory arrangements among industries and between government and industry have become more complicated than ever before. The technocratic society contributed much to raising living standards for more people. It also encouraged trends to social conformity among people, professional impersonalism among leaders and workers, and vast institutional hierarchies in government and industry, which contributed to social revolution and the counterculture.

20 California Prospectus

California stands out today as the epitome of a balanced society. It is a microcosm of the nation's society with its system of representative government reflecting organized special interests, a capitalistic economy characterized by mixed private–public enterprises and a regulated market economy, and a pluralistic social order comprised of heterogeneous people and immense cultural diversity. Nowhere does a society offer such a congenial environment for people to live the personal life style of their choice. The crises of our times are producing profound changes in present-day society which are indicative of a coming new era. The challenge before us is sustaining an order of society that will insure human fulfillment amid social diversity. Judging from historical experience, Californians with their penchant for adaptation and innovation can be optimistic about the future.

Sources of California History

A favorite pastime of Californians—whether layman or student, amateur or professional—is exploring California's past. We may study the development of our town or city, visit the Spanish missions and the Gold Rush towns, conjure mental pictures of our past by exploring local and state exhibitions and landmarks. Such sites can be found by consulting in a local library the American Museum Association's *Official Museum Directory* with its list of over 100 California museums or by writing the California State Parks and Recreation Department in Sacramento for its list of some 800 registered landmarks. These museums and landmarks include restored Spanish missions and Mexican rancho casas from San Diego to Sonoma; the reconstructed gold mining towns of Coloma and Columbia; preserved American homesteads of different eras; industry exhibits like the Maritime Museum, Standard Oil, and Wells Fargo in San Francisco; and local exhibitions like the Los Angeles County and Oakland museums.

One can develop a hobby or vocation in historical research and writing by perusing the collected materials of historical societies or public and university libraries. Notable are the comprehensive collections of the incomparable Bancroft Library at UC–Berkeley, the California State Archives and California State Library in Sacramento; and the special collections of the California Historical Society in San Francisco, Huntington Library in San Marino, Stanford University, UCLA, and the Los Angeles, Oakland, and San Francisco public libraries. The Conference of Historical Societies, a statewide organization of over 150 local and state societies (headquartered at University of the Pacific in Stockton), is an avenue for joining other California history buffs.

A word about accurate information. Even source documents like the 1849 Constitutional Convention roster require critical scrutiny; it was carefully drawn up by the secretary (J. Ross Browne) from the delegates themselves, but it contains errors and misinformation. I depended heavily on Bancroft's history with its biographical appendices and extensive page footnotes (especially volume 7), government documents like the *California Blue Book* (early editions are best) for political information, and the U.S. Census (though constantly revised) for socio-economic data. Diligence and patience with such documents bring rewarding dividends.

Bibliography

Below is a basic list of selected materials for additional information. The list includes major works in each area, oriented to the particular approach of this book; as such, it is not complete and necessarily excludes many important articles and fine books. The list is designed to fill a gap in California bibliography, a suggested list for the average reader—a sort of Everyman's Library in California History—which can be tailored to individual desires by contracting or expanding this list. One can acquire less accessible books, periodicals, documents, and theses through interlibrary loans, and utilize microfilm or photocopy services to reproduce desired materials for a library collection. (The materials used in the 5-year research for this book, including numerous UC graduate theses and secondary works in related fields not generally used by Californian historians, are found in my manuscript, *The Dynamics of California Society, 1847–1975*.) Books are listed in abbreviated form; asterisks (*) indicate books available in paperback.

General Works

Bancroft, H. H., *History of California*, 7 vols.(1888). Reprinted 1966-1970.
Bean, Walton, *California* (1973).
* *California Information Almanac*. Published periodically.
Caughey, John W., *California* (1970).
* Caughey, John and LaRee, *California Heritage* (1962). A literary anthology.
* Durrenberger, Robert W., *Patterns on the Land* (1972). A chart and map book.
Federal Writers' Project, *California* (1939). A basic guide book, revised 1967.
* Gilmore, N. Ray, and Gilmore, Gladys, *Readings in California History* (1966).
Gudde, Erwin G., *California Place Names* (1949). A geographical dictionary.
* Hartman, David N., *California and Man* (1968). A geography textbook.
* Hutchinson, W. H., *California* (1969). A short survey with literary style.
* Oakeshott, Gordon B., *California's Changing Landscapes* (1971). A geology textbook.
* Pitt, Leonard, *California Controversies* (1968). Major issues in state history.
Watkins, T. H., *California* (1973). An illustrated history.

Regional Works

* Farquhar, Francis P., *History of the Sierra Nevada* (1969).
Fogelson, Robert M., *Fragmented Metropolis* (1967). Los Angeles area.
McGowan, Joseph A., *History of the Sacramento Valley*, 2 vols.(1961).
* McWilliams, Carey, *Southern California Country* (1946).
Scott, Mel, *San Francisco Bay Area* (1959).
Smith, Wallace, *Garden of the Sun* (1930). San Joaquin Valley.

Indian and Hispanic California

Beilharz, Edwin A., *Felipe de Neve* (1971).
Bobb, Bernard E., *Viceregency of Antonio Maria Bucareli in New Spain* (1962).
Bolton, Herbert E., *Outpost of Empire* (1931). Anza expedition.
Chapman, Charles E., *History of California: Spanish Period* (1921).
* Chapman, Charles E., *History of Spain* (1918). For Spanish background.

Francis, Jessie D., *Economic and Social History of Mexican California* (PhD thesis, UC, 1935).

Geiger, Maynard J., *Life of Junipero Serra*, 2 vols.(1959).

Hansen, Woodrow J., *Search for Authority in California* (1960). 1821–1849 period.

Heizer, R. F., and Whipple, M. A., *California Indians* (1965). A source book.

Hutchinson, C. Alan, *Frontier Settlement in Mexican California* (1969). Hijar-Padres Colony.

* Simpson, Leslie B., *Many Mexicos* (1964). For Mexican background.
* Stewart, George R., *California Trail* (1962).

American California—Political

* Bean, Walton, *Boss Ruef's San Francisco* (1952).
* Buchanan, William, *Legislative Partisanship* (1963). 1935–1960 period.
  Burke, Robert E., *Olson's New Deal for California* (1953).
* DeVoto, Bernard, *Year of Decision, 1846* (1942). For background to Interregnum.
  Grivas, Theodore, *Military Governments in California, 1946–1850* (1963).
  Hichborn, Franklin, *California Politics, 1890–1939*. Typescript in California State Library.
  Melendy, H. Brett, and Gilbert, Benjamin F., *Governors of California* (1965).
* Mowry, George E., *California Progressives* (1951).
  Philips, Herbert L., *Big Wayward Girl* (1968). Politics, mostly 1940–1967.
  Pitchell, Robert J., *20th Century California Voting Behavior* (PhD thesis, UC, 1955).
* Royce, Josiah, *California, 1846–1856* (1886). See 1948 reprint.
* Swisher, Carl B., *Constitutional Convention, 1878–1879* (1930).

American California—Economic

Brubaker, Sterling L., *Impact of Federal Government Activities on California's Economic Growth, 1930–1956* (PhD thesis, UC, 1959).

Clar, C. Raymond, *California Government and Forestry* (1959).

Clelland, Robert G., *Cattle on a Thousand Hills, 1850–1880* (1951).

Coleman, Charles M., *P.G. and E. of California* (1952).

Cross, Ira B., *History of the Labor Movement in California* (1935).

Daggett, Stuart, *Chapters in the History of the Southern Pacific* (1922).

* Galbraith, John K., *New Industrial State* (1971). Background to present economy.
  Gates, Paul W., *California Ranchos and Farms* (1967). 1846–1962 period.
  Harding, S. T., *Water in California* (1960).
* Heilbroner, Robert L., *Making of Economic Society* (1962). Background to economics.
  Hutchinson, Claude B., editor, *California Agriculture* (1946).
* Jacobs, Lewis, *Rise of the American Film* (1939).
  James, Marquis, and James, Bessie R., *Biography of a Bank* (1954). Bank of America.
  Kelley, Robert L., *Gold vs Grain* (1959). Miner-farmer debris conflict, 1850–1890.
* Kerr, Clark, and Adler, Curtis, editors, *West Coast Collective Bargaining Systems* (1955–1957). Ten industry monographs.
  Lavender, David, *Great Persuader* (1970). C. P. Huntington and the railroads.
  Nadeau, Remi, *Water Seekers* (1950).
  Nash, Gerald D., *State Government and Economic Development* (1964).

* Paul, Rodman W., *California Gold* (1947).
  Robinson, W. W., *Land in California* (1948).
  Stimson, Grace H., *Rise of the Labor Movement in Los Angeles* (1955).
  White, Gerald T., *Standard Oil Company of California* (1962).

American California—Social

* Ahlstrom, Sydney E., *Religious History of the American People* (1972).
* Baltzell, Earl D., *Protestant Establishment* (1966).
* Burnham, John C., *Science in America* (1971). See period introductions.
  Cloud, Roy W., *Education in California* (1952).
* Daniels, Roger, and Olin, Spencer C. Jr., editors, *Racism in California* (1972).
* Frakes, George E., and Solberg, Curtis B., editors, *Minorities in California History* (1971).
* Gladfelder, Jane, *California's Emergent Counties* (1969).
* Hale, Dennis, and Eisen, Jonathan, editors, *California Dream* (1968).
* Hine, Robert V., *California's Utopian Colonies* (1953).
  Leuchtenberg, William E., *A Troubled Feast* (1973). American society since 1945.
  Lillard, Richard G., *Eden in Jeopardy* (1966). Southern California focus.
* Lipset, S. M., and Raab, Earl, *Politics of Unreason* (1970). Right-wing movements.
  Pearsall, Robert, and Erickson, Ursula S., editors, *Californians*, 2 vols.(1960).
* Pitt, Leonard, *Decline of the Californios* (1966).
  Shaffer, Ralph E., *Radicalism in California* (PhD thesis, UC, 1962). 1869–1929 period.
* Smith, Page, *Daughters of the Promised Land* (1970).
  Stadtman, Verne A., *University of California* (1970).
  Starr, Kevin, *Americans and the California Dream.* (1973). 1850–1915 period.
  Tebbel, John W., *Compact History of the American Newspaper* (1969).
  Walker, Franklin, *Literary History of Southern California* (1950).
* Walker, Franklin, *San Francisco's Literary Frontier* (1939).
  Wecter, Dixon, *Saga of American Society* (1937). Background to social classes.
* Wollenberg, Charles, compiler, *Ethnic Conflict in California History* (1970).
* Wood, Samuel C., and Heller, Aldred E., *Phantom Cities of California* (1963).

Bancroft's history is unsurpassed and is basic to any collection. Nash is a pioneer work on California's political economy; factual errors should not detract from its intrinsic value. One should have a U. S. history textbook; the multi-volume *New American Nation Series* (Harper & Row, available in paperback) was used for this book. Articles in the journals of historical societies (available through membership or in local libraries) are valuable sources, notably *California Historical Society Quarterly, Southern California Quarterly,* and *Pacific Historical Review.* Government reports issued periodically by state and local agencies and the legislature are also valuable sources, particularly the governor's annual budget and the legislative analyst's report on it. For updating past trends, see the *California Journal, Sacramento Bee,* and a college reader (Dvorin-Misner and Lee-Hawley are good) on state politics; *California Management Review, Fortune,* and *Moody's Manual* on economic developments and corporate histories; *Atlantic, Harper's,* and *Commentary* for socio-cultural developments.

Index